DAVID NICOLLE

MEDIEVAL WARFARE SOURCE BOOK

Christian Europe and its Neighbours

Overleaf: 'Jael slaying Sisera', from a Georgian manuscript, late 14th–early 15th centuries. Although sometimes thought to be from the 13th century, the arms and armour illustrated in this manuscript indicate a later date. They are largely Iranian Islamic in style, though also having some similarities with late medieval Byzantine military equipment. (Psalter, MS. A. 1665, f.205, Manuscript Institute of the Georgian Academy of Sciences, Tiblisi, Georgia)

DAVID NICOLLE

MEDIEVAL WARFARE SOURCE BOOK

Christian Europe and its Neighbours

BROCKHAMPTON PRESS
LONDON

In Memory of a friend and mentor, Dr. Ada Bruhn de Hoffmeyer, and my late father, Patrick Nicolle. Also thanks to the History Department of Nottingham University for providing such excellent facilities.

Even if I'd a lion for foe I'd dare,
Were he seen or unseen, my sword to bare.
Those destined alone in a tomb to lie,
Cannot laze at home in another's care.

Why, when your enemy's destroyed by fate,
Exulting shout so loud and great?
When others die how can you rejoice?
Since death will claim you too – early or late.

(Two quatrains by Ibn Iskandar, Prince of Gurgān, *c.*1082)

Arms and Armour Press
An Imprint of the Cassell Group
Wellington House, 125 Strand,
London WC2R 0BB

This edition published 1998 by Brockhampton Press, a member of Hodder Headline PLC Group

ISBN 1 86019 8619

British Library Cataloguing-in-Publication Data: a catalogue record for this book is available from the British Library

Designed and edited by DAG Publications Ltd. Designed by David Gibbons; layout by Anthony A. Evans; edited by Michael Boxall; Printed at Oriental Press, Dubai, U.A.E.

Jacket illustrations:
Front: 'Battle between the Banu Shayba and the Banu Zabba tribes' in the *Warqa wa Gulshah*, Persian 12th–14th century. (MS.HAZ.841, p.10/12a, Topkapi Library, Istanbul). Back, top: Yilanlikale, a largely 13th-century Armenian castle which stood close to the frontier between the Crusader Principality of Antioch and the Kingdom of Cilician Armenia. Back, bottom: Joshua dressed as a Byzantine soldier on a 10th-century wall painting in the monastery church of Osios Loukos in Greece.

Medieval Warfare Source Book
Volume 1: Warfare in Western Christendom
follows the same pattern as this second volume, including Biographies, Sources, Miscellanea, Glossary and Index. The main chapter headings are:

'Barbarian' Invasions and the 'Barbarian' States (400–650)
Early Medieval Europe (650–1100)
The High Middle Ages (1100–1275)
Late Medieval Europe (1275–1400)

CONTENTS

INTRODUCTION **8**

I. BYZANTINES, PERSIANS AND MUSLIMS (400–750) **9**
Major Campaigns 11
ARMY RECRUITMENT 11
Romano-Byzantine Armies 11
Sassanian Armies 13
Semitic and African Forces 15
The First Muslim Armies 16
Armies of the Umayyad Caliphate 16
MILITARY ORGANISATION 17
Romano-Byzantine Armies 18
Sassanian Armies 21
Semitic and African Forces 23
The First Muslim Armies 24
Armies of the Umayyad Caliphate 24
STRATEGY AND TACTICS 25
Broad Strategy 26
Troop Types 29
Battle Tactics 29
Combat Styles 34
Field and Camp Fortifications 35
WEAPONRY AND HARNESS 35
Archery 36
Swords and Daggers 37
Spears and Javelins 37
Other Weapons 37
Shields 37
Helmets 37
Body Armour 37
Limb Defences 38
Horse Harness 38
Horse Armour 38
FORTIFICATIONS 39
Romano-Byzantine Armies 41
Sassanian Armies 42
Semitic and African Forces 43
The First Muslim and Umayyad Armies 44
SIEGE WARFARE 44
Romano-Byzantine Armies 45
Sassanian Armies 46
The First Muslim Armies 46
Armies of the Umayyad Caliphate 47
NAVAL WARFARE 47
The Mediterranean and Atlantic 47
The Indian Ocean 47
Riverine Warfare 48

II. CHRISTIAN–MUSLIM CONFRONTATION (750–1050) **49**
Major Campaigns 51
ARMY RECRUITMENT 51
Christendom: The Byzantine Empire 51
Christendom: The Iberian Peninsula 54
Islam: The early ᶜAbbāsid Caliphate 54
Islam: The Successor States 56
Islam: The Fāṭimids (to 1171) 58
Islam: The Far Maghrib and al-Andalus 58
MILITARY ORGANISATION 59
Christendom: The Byzantine Empire and the Caucasus 59
Christendom: The Iberian Peninsula 60
Islam: The early ᶜAbbāsid Caliphate 61
Islam: The Successor States 63
Islam: The Fāṭimids (to 1171) 65
Islam: The Maghrib and al-Andalus 65
STRATEGY AND TACTICS 66
Broad Strategy 66
Troop Types 68
Battle Tactics 70
Combat Styles 73
Field and Camp Fortifications 73
WEAPONRY AND HARNESS 73
Archery and Slings 73
Swords and Daggers 74
Spears and Javelins 75
Other Weapons 75
Shields 76
Helmets 76
Body Armour 76
Limb Defences 78
Horse Harness 79
Horse Armour 79
FORTIFICATION 80
Christendom: The Byzantine Empire 80
Christendom: The Iberian Peninsula 80
Islam: The Early ᶜAbbāsid Caliphate 80
Islam: The Successor States 81
Islam: The Fāṭimids (to 1171) 81
Islam: The Far Maghrib and al-Andalus 82
SIEGE WARFARE 83
Christendom: The Byzantine Empire 83
Islam: The early ᶜAbbāsid Caliphate 85
Islam: The Successor States 85
NAVAL WARFARE 87
The Mediterranean and Atlantic 87
The Indian Ocean and Riverine Warfare 88

III. TURKS, MONGOLS AND THE RISE OF RUSSIA (600–1400) **89**
Major Campaigns 94

Army Recruitment 94
Turkish Central Asia 94
Non-Turkish Peoples 95
Russia 95
The Mongols 97
The Rise of Tīmūr-i Lank 98
Organisation 98
Turkish Central Asia 99
Non-Turkish Peoples 99
Russia 100
The Mongols 101
The Rise of Tīmūr-i Lank 103
Strategy and Tactics 103
Broad Strategy 103
Troop Types 104
Battle Tactics 105
Combat Styles 108
Field and Camp Fortifications 108
Weaponry and Harness 108
Archery and Slings 109
Swords and Daggers 109
Spears and Javelins 109
Other Weapons 109
Shields 112
Helmets 112
Body Armour 114
Limb Defences 116
Horse Harness 116
Horse Armour 117
Fortification 118
Turkish Central Asia 118
Non-Turkish Central Asian Peoples 118
Russia 118
The Mongols 120
The Rise of Tīmūr-i Lank 120
Siege Warfare 120
Naval Warfare 122

IV. CRUSADER, RECONQUISTA AND COUNTER-CRUSADE (1050–1400) 123
Major Campaigns 125
Army Recruitment 129
Christendom: The Byzantine Empire 129
Christendom: Armenian and Georgia 131
Christendom: The Crusades and Crusader States 131
Christendom: The Iberian Peninsula 133
Islam: The Eastern Lands 134
Islam: The Middle East 135
Islam: North Africa and al-Andalus 140
Islam: Sub-Saharan Africa 140
Military Organisation 141
Christendom: The Byzantine Empire 141
Christendom: Armenia, Georgia and Christian Africa 142
Christendom: The Crusader States 143
Christendom: The Iberian Peninsula 145
Islam: The Eastern Lands 145
Islam: The Middle East and Egypt 146
Islam: North Africa and al-Andalus 149
Islam: Sub-Saharan Africa 149
Strategy and Tactics 150
Broad Strategy 150
Troop Types 153
Battle Tactics 154
Combat Styles 158
Field and Camp Fortifications 159
Weaponry and Harness 159
Archery and Slings 159
Swords and Daggers 161
Spears and Javelins 163
Other Weapons 163
Shields 163
Helmets 163
Body Armour 165
Limb Defences 167
Horse Harness 167
Horse Armour 167
Fortification 167
Christendom: The Byzantine Empire 167
Christendom: Armenia and Christian Africa 168
Christendom: The Crusader States 168
Christendom: The Iberian Peninsula 170
Islam: The Eastern Lands 171
Islam: The Middle East and Egypt 171
Islam: North Africa and al-Andalus 172
Siege Warfare 173
Naval Warfare 178
The Mediterranean 178
The Atlantic 182
The Indian Ocean and Red Sea 182
Riverine Warfare 182

V. CHINA, THE FAR EAST AND INDIA (400–1400) 183
Major Campaigns 187
Army Recruitment 189
China 189
Korea 189
South-East Asia 189
India 190
Military Organisation 191
China 191
Korea and Japan 194
South-East Asia 194
India 194
Strategy and Tactics 195
Broad Strategy 195
Troop Types 195
Battle Tactics 196
Combat Styles 198
Field and Camp Fortifications 198
Weaponry and Harness 198
Archery 199
Swords and Daggers 200
Spears and Javelins 200
Other Weapons 201
Shields 201
Helmets 201
Body Armour 201
Limb Defences 202
Horse Harness 204
Horse Armour 204
Fortification 204
Siege Warfare 205
Naval Warfare 208

VI. BIOGRAPHIES 211
Abu'l-Ṭayyib al-Ju'fī al-Mutannabī 213
Alexander Nevski 213

Amde-Siyon I 213
Bahrām 213
Chingiz Khān 213
David IV Aghmashenebeli 215
Dhū Nuwās 215
El Cid 215
Evrenos Beg 215
Heraclius 215
Ibn Abī 'Āmir al-Manṣūr 215
James I 217
John Cantacuzenus 217
Khālid Ibn al-Walīd 217
Khaydār al-Afshīn ᶜAbbāsid 217
Khusrū I 217
Li Shih-min 217
Mansa Mūsā 218
Nicephoros II Phocas 218
Rājarāja I The Great 218
Samuel Ha-Nagid 219
Tancred 219
Usāma Ibn Munqidh 219
Yūsuf Ibn Tāshufīn 220

VII. SOURCES **221**
General Works 223
Byzantines, Persians and Muslims 223
Christian–Muslim Confrontation 223
Turks, Mongols and the Rise of Russia 224
Crusade, Reconquista and Counter-Crusade 225
China, South-East Asia and India 227
Fortification and Siege Warfare 227
Laws of War and Prisoners 228
Military Theory and Training 228
Morale and Motivation 229
Communications 230
Horses, Harness and Land Transport 230
Naval Warfare, Water Transport and Combined Operations 230
Flags and Heraldry 231
Arms, Armour and the Weapons Trade 231
Firearms 232
Miscellaneous 232

VIII. MISCELLANEA **233**
LAWS OF WAR 235
Byzantium, Reconquista and Crusade 235
The Muslim World 236
Other Religions 237
VICTORS AND VANQUISHED 239
Distribution of Booty 239
Prisoners, Enslavement and the Treatment of Non-combatants 241
INTELLIGENCE AND ESPIONAGE 244
TRAINING 246
THE SINEWS OF WAR 251
Taxation and Pay 251
Feeding an Army 255
MEDICAL SERVICES 257
MORALE 258
Religion 258
Literature and Literacy 263
Music 265
Drugs and Alcohol 267
LONG-DISTANCE COMMUNICATIONS 267
TRANSPORT 268
Land Transport 268
River Transport 273
COMBINED OPERATIONS 273
Raiding 273
Horse Transports 274
Coastal Landings 275
FLAGS AND HERALDRY 277
The Orthodox World 277
Iberia and the Crusader States 278
The Muslim World 278
Non-Islamic Asia 283
UNIFORMS: DECLINE AND RISE 284
THE MEDIEVAL ARMS INDUSTRY 288
Mining, Materials and Techniques 288
Arms Manufacture 290
The Arms Trade 291
FIREARMS: ORIGINS AND DEVELOPMENT 294
Fire Weapons 294
Gunpowder 294
Grenades and Rockets 296
Cannon 296
Handguns 296

IX. GLOSSARY **297**

INDEX **311**

INTRODUCTION

The Medieval World has sometimes been described as a World of Divided Regions, suggesting that the main civilisations from the fall of the western Roman Empire to the discovery of the Americas were ignorant of each other, developed independently and were somehow stunted by their supposed isolation. This is a complete misrepresentation, particularly in terms of military history. As one cultural historian has commented, from the 7th to the 12th centuries 'there was neither East nor West'. Not until modern times, with the increasing dominance of Western civilisation, has there been such a widespread interplay of ideas, technological developments and political forces as were seen between the 5th and 14th centuries.

On the other hand western Europe was for many years an economically and politically unimportant corner of the great Eurasian land-mass. Only in the 11th and 12th centuries did the West re-emerge; its increasing confidence, wealth and power resulting in extraordinary campaigns of aggression. In addition there was remarkable trading exploration, often backed up by force, deep into the sub-Arctic and Atlantic. It is, for example, often forgotten that the Americas were discovered by Europeans who were still in many ways medieval. The Modern World may already have been born in the 15th century, but was still being suckled by its medieval mother. For the first time Africa also opened up to the outside world during the Middle Ages - not to Europe but to the rival and less domineering civilisation of Islam. A similar process had taken place in south-east Asia where three great cultures competed for influence: namely India, China and Islam.

During these tumultuous yet fruitful centuries warfare was often characterised by long-distance campaigns. Religious and political ideas, artistic motifs, new food plants and animal breeds, technological developments, new weapons and tactics, all followed in the footsteps of armies, merchant caravans and trading ships. Generally speaking these new ideas spread from East to West. Despite occasional examples of extraordinary devastation, the destruction wrought by medieval warfare tended to be localised; paradoxically it also often served as a vehicle for cultural interchange.

This second volume of the *Medieval Warfare Source Book* covers a very large area, ranging from Christian Europe's struggles with neighbouring non-Christian peoples through the sweeping conquests which characterised Central Asian history, the fast-changing cultural and military situation in Africa and the comparatively unchanging civilisations of the Far East. One way or another events in these regions were connected, however distantly, because the Medieval world was anything but a place of isolated or insulated cultures.

D. Nicolle; Woodhouse Eaves, 1996

I
BYZANTINES, PERSIANS AND MUSLIMS
(400–750)

BYZANTINES, PERSIANS AND MUSLIMS (400–750)

Major Campaigns 11
ARMY RECRUITMENT 11
Romano-Byzantine Armies 11
Sassanian Armies 13
Semitic and African Forces 15
The First Muslim Armies 16
Armies of the Umayyad Caliphate 16
MILITARY ORGANISATION 17
Romano-Byzantine Armies 18
Sassanian Armies 21
Semitic and African Forces 23
The First Muslim Armies 24
Armies of the Umayyad Caliphate 24
STRATEGY AND TACTICS 25
Broad Strategy 26
Troop Types 29
Battle Tactics 29
Combat Styles 34
Field and Camp Fortifications 35
WEAPONRY AND HARNESS 35
Archery 36
Swords and Daggers 37
Spears and Javelins 37
Other Weapons 37
Shields 37
Helmets 37
Body Armour 37
Limb Defences 38
Horse Harness 38
Horse Armour 38
FORTIFICATIONS 39
Romano-Byzantine Armies 41
Sassanian Armies 42
Semitic and African Forces 43
The First Muslim and Umayyad Armies 44
SIEGE WARFARE 44
Romano-Byzantine Armies 45
Sassanian Armies 46
The First Muslim Armies 46
Armies of the Umayyad Caliphate 47
NAVAL WARFARE 47
The Mediterranean and Atlantic 47
The Indian Ocean 47
Riverine Warfare 48

The massive migrations which characterised the early Middle Ages affected the entire ancient world from the Roman Mediterranean through Sassanian Iran to China, with practically every people from near barbaric tribes to sophisticated civilisations being involved in wars that reshaped the world. Many of the barbarian conquerors who survived this time of turmoil set up new states modelled on those they had defeated. Meanwhile some earlier civilisations survived in modified form, defended by armies that had been influenced by those of the so-called barbarians.

One large region stood apart from the first barbarian eruptions. This was Arabia, whose time of expansion came two centuries later. In the intervening years several northern Arabian leaders attempted to dominate the entire peninsula while to the south the ancient civilisation of Yemen entered its own Dark Age before the coming of Islam in the 7th century. The first century of Arab-Islamic expansion was itself a relatively straightforward though amazing piece of military history. It also had a greater impact on world history than any other event of the Middle Ages. Yet the Arabs were far from being a militarily homogeneous group. Northern Arabs from the Syrian to Iraqi frontiers differed from those of Central Arabia and had little, except a new-found Muslim faith, in common with the settled peoples of southern Arabia. Urban merchants and farming peasants from the oases differed socially and militarily from nomadic bedouin, while the latter were also divided into groups according to the terrain they inhabited and their possession of differing proportions of camels, sheep or horses. In fact the main thrust of the Prophet Muḥammad's social teaching emphasised settled and urban values as opposed to those of the bedouin.

Peoples caught up in the early Arab conquests varied even more. They ranged from the sophisticated armies of the Byzantine and Sassanian Empires to the primitive Berbers of North Africa; from Nubians of the Sudan to Central Asian Turks who were themselves as varied as the Arabs, from the warlike Buddhist Turco-Iranian states of Transoxiana and Afghanistan or the almost Romanised Visigoths of Spain to the highly civilised but militarily backward states of Hindu India. Furthermore the early Muslim Arabs, aware of their limited military manpower, eagerly enlisted the skills of their foes, soon recruiting defeated enemy troops and tribes or converting them to allies. Having conquered a large part of the known world, the Muslim Arabs settled as garrisons. In some areas they Arabised the conquered region, in others they were themselves absorbed by overwhelmingly numerous subjects.

Major Campaigns

c.400: Autonomous La<u>kh</u>mid Arab state established on desert frontier of Sassanian Empire.

Early 5th century: Large-scale Arab raiding into Roman Syria.

480–4: White Huns (Hephthalites) invade Sassanian Iran.

522: Axum (Christian Ethiopian ally of Byzantine Empire) conquers Yemen.

531–79: Rule of <u>Kh</u>usrau I, Sassanian Empire of Iran reaches greatest extent; imposes superficial control over Arabia via La<u>kh</u>mid Arab surrogates.

533–4: Byzantine reconquest of North Africa.

570–1: Ethiopian army in Yemen attempts to conquer western and central Arabia.

571: Blue Turks and Sassanians destroy Hephthalite White Huns; Sassanians take eastern Iran.

c.574: Sassanian Empire conquers Yemen from Ethiopians.

Late 6th century: Tribal upheavals in Arabia undermine Sassanian control.

c.600: Emergence of Ghana, first recorded state in West Africa.

602–28: Sassanian invasions of Byzantine Empire; occupation of Syria, Egypt, eastern Anatolia.

624–7: War between Muslim Arabs in Medina and pagan Arabs of Mecca.

626–7: Avar and Sassanian alliance besieges Byzantine capital of Constantinople; Byzantine defeat of Sassanians.

627: Byzantine Empire defeats Sassanian Empire.

629–30: Muslim-Byzantine clash in southern Jordan.

630: Muslims take Mecca.

632: Death of the Prophet Muḥammad.

632–3: Ridda Wars; consolidation of Muslim power throughout Arabia.

633--51: Muslim-Arab conquest of Palestine, Syria, Iraq, Egypt and Iran.

643–c.707: Muslim-Arab conquest of North Africa.

670–8: Unsuccessful Muslim-Arab attack on Constantinople.

674–715: Muslim-Arab conquest of Transoxiana.

694: Reputed Berber-Jewish attempt to invade Visigothic Spain from Morocco.

710–13: Muslim-Arab conquest of lower Indus valley (modern southern Pakistan).

711–13: Muslim-Arab conquest of Iberian peninsula; temporary occupation of south-western France.

717–18: Second unsuccessful Muslim-Arab attack on Constantinople.

732: Muslim raid into France defeated at Poitiers.

739: Possible Muslim expedition across Sahara from Morocco.

744–8: Fundamentalist *<u>kh</u>araji* Muslim uprisings in Middle East.

747–50: Rebellion in *<u>Kh</u>urāsān* spreads westward; Umayyad Caliphate overthrown and replaced by *ᶜAbbāsid* Caliphate.

ARMY RECRUITMENT

Rome and Sassanian Iran, the two great empires of the late classical Middle East, developed similar systems whereby frontier peoples were often recruited as auxiliaries or allies. But whether this was a result of mutual influence or was a common response to a common problem remains unclear.

Romano-Byzantine Armies

The domestic and élite forces of the Romano-Byzantine Army have been covered in Volume I. In some respects, however, auxiliaries of Middle Eastern origin were of greater significance since they could be described as 'the wave of the future'.

While the western Roman Empire withered away, the eastern half survived. Here troops of Germanic origin continued to

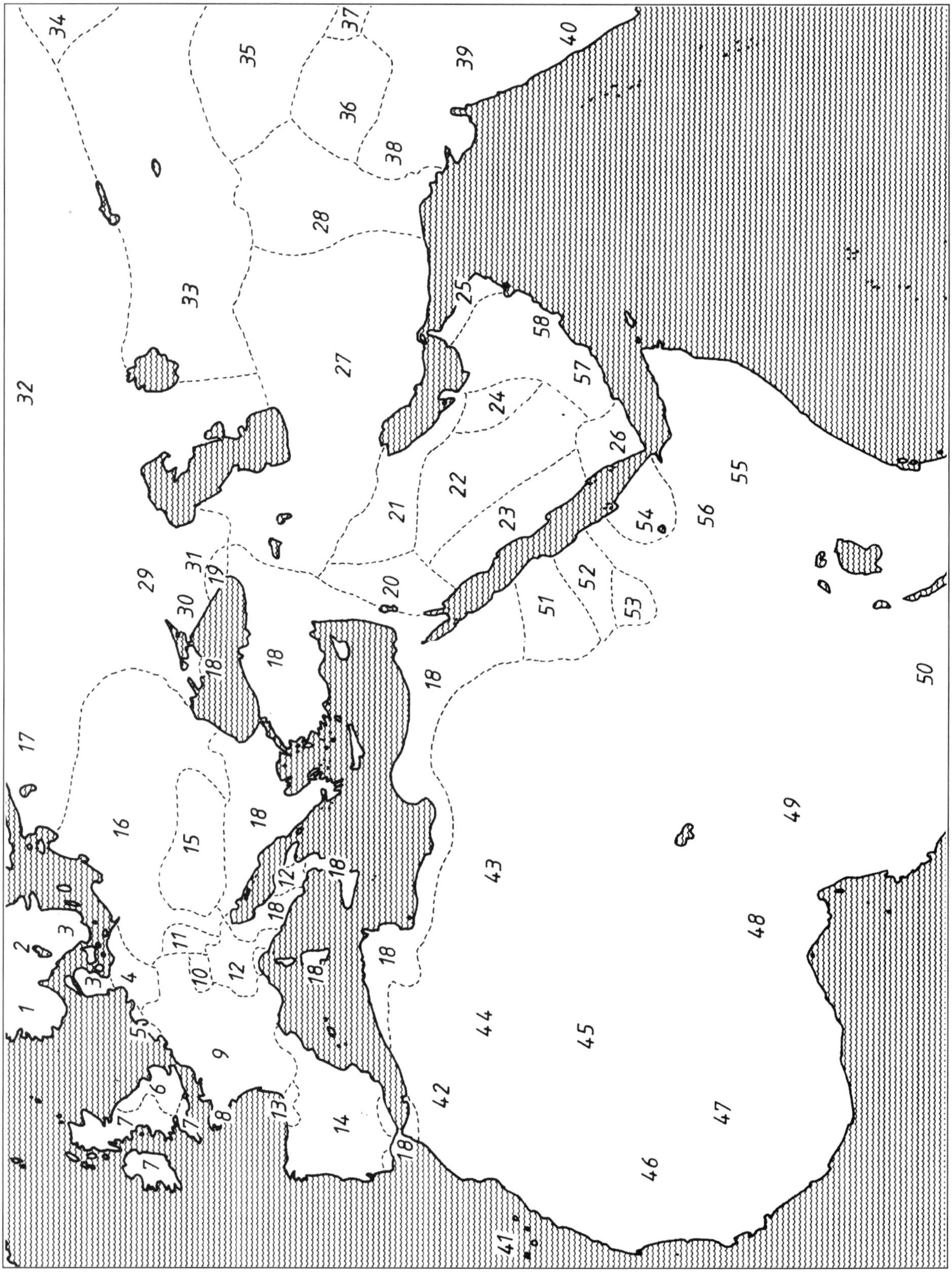
1
2
3
4
5
6
7
8
9
10
11
12
13
14
15
16
17
18
19
20
21
22
23
24
25
26
27
28
29
30
31
32
33
34
35
36
37
38
39
40
41
42
43
44
45
46
47
48
49
50
51
52
53
54
55
56
57
58

Left: Europe, northern Africa and western Asia, c.600

1. *Norwegians*
2. *Swedes*
3. *Danes*
4. *Saxons*
5. *Frisians*
6. *Anglo-Saxon kingdoms*
7. *Celtic kingdoms*
8. *Brittany*
9. *Frankish Kingdom*
10. *Allemani*
11. *Bavarians*
12. *Lombards*
13. *Cantabrians and Basques*
14. *Visigothic Kingdom*
15. *Avars*
16. *Slavs and Balts, possibly under Avar suzerainty*
17. *Finno-Ugrians*
18. *Byzantine Empire*
19. *Lazica*
20. *Ghassānids*
21. *Lakhmids, under Sassanian suzerainty*
22. *Kinda*
23. *Hijaz*
24. *Yamāmah*
25. *Oman, under Sassanian suzerainty*
26. *Yemen, under Sassanian suzerainty*
27. *Sassanian Empire*
28. *Hephthalites, etc., under Sassanian suzerainty*
29. *Khazars*
30. *Western Uigurs*
31. *Alans*
32. *Sabirs*
33. *Western Turkish Khānate*
34. *Eastern Turkish Khānate*
35. *Tibet*
36. *Sthaneswara*
37. *Nepalese*
38. *Gurjaras*
39. *Chalukyas*
40. *Small Indian states*
41. *Guanches*
42. *Western Berbers*
43. *Garamantes*
44. *Tuareg*
45. *Zanata Berbers*
46. *Fulani*
47. *Ghana*
48. *Nok*
49. *Bantu (origins)*
50. *Bantu (area of settlement)*
51. *Nobatia*
52. *Makuria*
53. *Alwa*
54. *Axumite Ethiopia*
55. *Somali (origins)*
56. *Galla*
57. *Ḥadhramawt*
58. *Dhufar*

play a prominent role. A feature of early 5th-century eastern Roman armies, however, was an increasing emphasis on internal recruitment though this did not guarantee loyalty because the ranks included Manichaeans, Jews and assorted pagans who were distrusted by the majority of Roman Christians.

Internal recruitment may have provided the bulk of infantry, but the cavalry continued to include a great many non-Romans; for example Huns following the collapse of the Hun Empire, Alans who were originally Iranian nomads from the steppes, plus Germanic Goths and Herules. During the 6th century cavalry were also being raised in traditionally 'warlike' regions of what was left of the Empire such as Thrace and Illyria in Europe, Isauria in Asia.

The sudden revival of east Roman military fortunes under Justinian was carried out by an army that may have had an increased 'barbarian' element; Justinian even establishing an élite mobile force of captured Ostrogoth cavalry in Egypt. Under his immediate successors other groups of Germanic warriors were transferred from Italy to the Balkans, and in fact Goths who followed the heretical Christian Arian sect soon formed the Romano-Byzantine army's heavy cavalry élite known as *optimates.*

Other 'outsiders' recruited in the late 6th century included Germanic Lombard mercenaries from Italy, and Monophysite Christian Armenians who, though officially regarded as heretics, were considered excellent warriors. Within Armenia itself military service was a privilege largely reserved for the land-holding *azatani* minor aristocracy and sépouh free men. Elements of the Armenian military élite were settled or at least served in Thrace, Pergamum (modern Bergama), the Danubian frontier and Cyprus.

Meanwhile the military situation evolved differently in Byzantine Syria where *indigenae* or 'local' troops had included Arabs as well as Aramaens since the 4th century. By the mid-6th century the few Romano-Byzantine forces in northern Syria included urban militias which, in Antioch at least, seem to have been associated with the turbulent Green and Blue Circus factions. A few *limitanei* (frontier troops) still existed, but were unlikely to have still been recruited from Romano-Byzantine veterans. By the 6th century other forces had risen to prominence on the desert frontier; these being *foederati* allies or auxiliaries from nomadic tribes. By 542 Berber warriors from North Africa were also mentioned in the Byzantine east.

Late Roman recruiting systems clearly continued well into the 7th century but then a variety of military groups migrated into Anatolia following the Muslim Arab conquest of the remainder of the Middle East. These included Goths, refugees from Syria, Macedonian Slavs and Central Asian Turks. At the same time the Byzantine authorities moved whole populations from the threatened eastern frontiers to Europe. Military obligations were probably increased in most areas, including the capital Constantinople whose militias were responsible for manning the city walls.

Following Byzantium's massive losses of territory to the Muslims, later 7th and 8th century armies included far fewer foreigners than before. Nevertheless internal recruitment remained expensive, slow, disruptive, and as a result warlike border peoples were still enlisted wherever possible, the most important being the Armenians, several of whom achieved positions of high command. Much of the Christian Arab *Ghassānid* tribe served Byzantium against their Muslim fellow Arabs, while others remained in Syria, gradually converted to Islam and rose to prominence as civilian administrators and later also as soldiers.

Sassanian Armies

A Roman description of Sassanian armies as consisting of cavalry recruited from freemen and infantry enlisted from serfs is grossly over-simplified. In fact pre-Islamic Iranian society had features in common with Hindu India. The population was virtually divided into castes based upon supposed 'conquering Aryan' or 'conquered Semitic or Dravidian' ancestry. Theoretically warfare only involved the upper 'military castes'. Of course this did not work in practice and the majority of *pāighān* (infantry) were probably peasants. Nevertheless the free *āzātān* (minor aristocracy) did form the bulk of Sassanian

'The Siege of the Citadel of Faith', Byzantine-Coptic wood carving from Ashmunaim, 5th–6th centuries. Only the leaders in this scene wear 'classical' Roman armour, ordinary soldiers having plain mail hauberks, though one of the attacking horsemen does appear to be wearing scale armour. (Staatliche-Museum Dahlem, I. 4782, Berlin)

cavalry, and some Sassanian magnates had guards of highly trained military slaves.

In reality the Sassanian army included mercenaries, particularly in frontier forces, plus huge numbers of allied or tributary tribal auxiliaries. The bulk of such troops came from the mountains and coastal plain of northern Iran, Sijistān, whose warriors were reputedly of Saka origin (the Kushans and Chionites of northern Afghanistan). Others were recruited from the Caucasus mountains, Armenia and Khūzistān. The plains of Iraq were inhabited by peaceful Aramaeans among whom Christianity was spreading fast, and more warlike Arab tribes. There was also the largest Jewish community in the ancient world which had earlier provided soldiers for the Herodian kings in Palestine.

In the 6th century Khusrau I's military reforms attempted to convert the Sassanian *dihqān* from a class of minor military gentry to paid professional troops while also downgrading indigenous Iranian troops in favour of mercenaries, allies and tributary frontier peoples. Hence late Sassanian armies came to include large numbers of Alan Iranian nomads, Khazar Turkic nomads, Abkhazians from the Caucasus, Daylamites from the Caspian mountains, Turks from Khurāsān and Sughdians from Transoxiana. The Sassanian policy of large-scale deportations of defeated enemies also led to unexpected communities appearing far from their original homes.

The question of Sassanian-Arab relations in the 5th and 6th centuries remains unclear, though Arabs were certainly playing a major military role while Sassanian imperial influence was widespread across most of the Arabian peninsula. Ironically the powerful Lakhmid dynasty of Arab frontier kings was removed by the Sassanians only a few years before the Muslim Arabs erupted across the same frontier. By then the Sassanian system of 'client' Arabian tribes was also in disarray, probably destroyed during the Ridda wars during which Muslims extended their control throughout Arabia.

Semitic and African Forces

While Germanic peoples were laying the foundations of medieval European states in the west of what had been the Roman Empire, an equally important new force was evolving in Arabia. The supposed nomadisation of Arabia during the Roman era appears to be a myth, an essentially nomadic way of life having dominated for millennia. On the other hand there were considerable differences between supposedly nomadic tribes; distinctions reflecting the ecology of various areas. Basically the *badū* or bedouin were camel herders of the deep desert, the *swāyiḥ* of the semi-desert or steppe raising camels, sheep and goats, while the *ra^{c}w* semi-nomads lived on the edge of the cultivated areas and raised only sheep. The most powerful tribes tended to be *swāyiḥ* capable of dominating the less mobile *ra^{c}w* and of obliging the less wealthy *badū* to retreat deeper into the desert when threatened. Meanwhile the term *sarakēnoi* (Saracens) was used by Romano-Byzantines for tribal Arab peoples rather than settled Arabic speakers within imperial territory.

Arabia had a much smaller pool of military manpower than the neighbouring Romano-Byzantine and Sassanian empires, yet this was partially balanced by the high military skills of the Arab tribes. As a result the neighbouring empires put great effort into controlling this small but potent military source of light cavalry raiders and camel-riding mounted infantry archers.

The Roman-Byzantine Empire also found it effective and cheap to pay frontier tribes to extend the Empire's influence deeper into Arabia. This evolved into the *phylarch* system in which the chief of a specified tribe was paid to defend the imperial frontier and eventually being made responsible for order within some parts of Syria and Palestine. In Sinai, meanwhile, a special group of slave recruited soldiers known as *condomae* protected the ancient St. Catherine's Monastery from nomad raiding.

In contrast, the Sassanian Empire preferred to support settled dynasties of Arab origin; the most potent being the autonomous Lakhmid state with its capital at al-Ḥīra on the edge of the Iraqi desert. In turn the Lakhmids tried to model their army on that of the Sassanians, with an élite of professional mercenaries backed up by a Lakhmid tribal militia, outlaws given protection in return for military service and hostages from subordinate tribes. The Sassanian Emperor also lent the Lakhmid king a unit of élite Sassanian *asvaran* armoured cavalry.

Within Arabia itself there were a variety of military systems in addition to tribal forces. In Yemen troops knows as *aḥābīsh*, may have included mercenaries descended from the Ethiopians who occupied the country in the 6th century, while the *aḥābīsh* of Mecca appear to have been a confederacy of small clans with no apparent Ethiopian connection. The term *mawāli* was also applied to some troops in pre-Islamic Mecca. This has sometimes been interpreted as soldiers of slave origin but is more likely to have indicated men who had been given honorary membership of a particular tribe in return for military service.

In Yemen itself the ancient state fragmented after the 1st century, each small region now being dominated by a tribal *qayl* or 'duke'. They could summon military support from local tribes as well as their own troops recruited from a high status but non-noble south Arabian warrior class referred to in surviving inscriptions as *Q-S-D**

On the other side of the Red Sea the Roman-Byzantine Emperor Justinian reportedly recruited a force of Nile Valley Nubians and Blemye (modern Beja) eastern Sudanese nomads to support this Ethiopian invasion of Yemen, but very little is known about Ethiopian, Nubian or Blemye forces at this time. The Ethiopian kingdom of Axum and the emerging Christian Nubian kingdoms of northern Sudan were certainly structured states, and even the nomadic Blemye had some sort of military organisation, both Nubians and Blemyes also serving as mercenaries in Byzantine Egypt.

Meanwhile there were major military changes in North Africa from the Germanic Vandal conquest, through the Romano-Byzantine reconquest to the arrival of the Muslim Arabs. By the 5th century military leadership of the Roman provinces fell to the partly Berber partly Latin élite. Existing *gentiles* or local forces were intended to deal with tribal raiding from beyond the frontier. The frontier *limitanei* of Roman North Africa also came largely from the local population. But the Vandals who established their kingdom in North Africa in 429 never appear to have enlisted Berber support. On the other hand Berbers who had been demilitarised under Roman rule rediscovered their military heritage during this period, being recruited as *foederati* following the Byzantine reconquest. A decline of Byzantine authority by the 7th century in turn led to a further revival of tribal leaderships. Much of Morocco and parts of Algeria were, in fact, dominated by nom-

*The vowels are not shown on pre-Islamic south Arabian inscriptions and so are mostly unknown. The vowels of this word are unknown, as is the case with most such inscriptions, but the similarity with the K-SH-T vowels of the kshatriya warrior caste of Hindu India is unmistakable. Although many warriors were also recruited from nomadic Arab tribes, surviving inscriptions suggest that there was usually only one camel-mounted soldier for every three infantrymen. In the early 6th century a powerful Yemeni ruler, the Jewish king Dhu Nuwās, again emerged, but his persecution of the Christian minority prompted a Christian Ethiopian conquest of Yemen.

inally Jewish tribes and there are even hazy records of a Jewish Berber attempt to raid Visigothic Spain where their co-religionists were suffering persecution.

The First Muslim Armies

With the coming of Islam the Arab peoples changed from being clients to rivals of the Byzantine Empire. Most troops were infantry drawn from settled tribes while the few available cavalry were mostly drawn from bedouin tribes. They, however, remained unreliable, undisciplined and only superficially Muslim. At first these forces were recruited in the Hijaz, the birthplace of Islam, but as more troops were needed other tribes that had accepted Islam at a later date were permitted to take part, including Yemenis. Only when the problem of numbers became acute were tribes that had fought against Islam during the Ridda Wars allowed to join increasingly successful campaigns against the Byzantine and Sassanian Empires. Yemenis in particular proved to be highly effective infantry archers and by the mid-7th century a large part of the Muslim army based in fertile Syria claimed Yemeni origin. In contrast the unreliable bedouin were encouraged to settle in largely abandoned frontier regions north of the Euphrates. The first Rāshidūn Caliphs also won over most of the powerful tribes of the Syrian desert frontier, the same troops who had been so effective under the Byzantine *phylarch* system. The same was true of the frontier tribes of Iraq where, however, the Muslims found it necessary to incorporate several Christian and perhaps even pagan Arab tribes which had already been raiding the crumbling Sassanian Empire.

A further response to the Arabs' acute shortage of manpower was the use of *mawālī* or 'clients', men accepted as honorary members of a tribe though not born into it. At first they appear as non-combatants but within a few decades they were clearly fully fledged fighting troops. The only clear reference to African soldiers is in Egypt where one of the last Byzantine governors had an élite guard of black troops. The ruler of Christian Nubia also agreed to continue sending fighting men to serve in Egypt after the Muslim conquest. Most of Islam's first naval troops were coastal Yemenis, such men being settled along the Egyptian coast and forming the fighting backbone of the first Umayyad fleets.

Of particular significance for the future of Muslim military recruitment was the eagerness with which the Arab conquerors enlisted their defeated Sassanian foes, often under preferential conditions compared to the Arabs themselves. The Prophet himself had accepted the ex-Sassanian *abnā* (garrisons) of Yemen into Muslim ranks. Elsewhere ex-Sassanian troops were known by various names: cavalry *asāwira*, from the original Persian *asvārān;* infantry *al-ḥamra*, 'the red ones', probably referring to the paler skins of Daylamis from northern Iran. Then there were the more obscure *zuṭ*, *sayābijah* and *andaghān* from southern Iraq, descended from Indians transported there by various Sassanian rulers.

Armies of the Umayyad Caliphate

By the time Muᶜāwiya, governor of Syria, took over as the first Umayyad Caliph in 661, the Muslim army was a professional force of largely Arab troops, a large proportion of whom had settled in conquered territories. The élite of the Umayyad

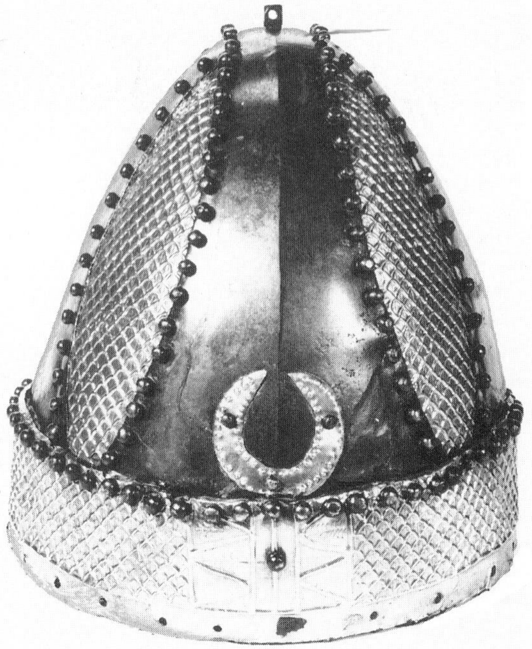

Left: *Sassanian-Iranian helmet with a 'heraldic' crescent on the front and a talismanic bird's feathers pattern over much of its surface; from the Amlash region 5th-6th centuries. This, one of the best preserved and most decorated Sassanian helmets, is a fine example of the 'Parthian Cap' form of construction. (Römisch-Germanisches Zentralmuseum, inv. O.38823, Mainz)*

Below: *Sassanian sword and scabbard, probably from Transoxiana, 6th–7th centuries. Again, the feathered decoration is seen, here on the scabbard, and was probably for talismanic protective reasons. (Author's photograph; Metropolitan Museum of Art, no. 1965.65.28, New York)*

The silver 'Isola Rizza Dish' found in northern Italy was probably made by a Byzantine craftsman for an Italo-Germanic ruler, 6th–7th centuries. The horseman wears a lamellar cuirass copied by Byzantine cavalry from those of their steppe nomadic foes. (Author's photograph; Castelvecchio Museum, Verona)

army now consisted of the *ahl al-shām* ('people of Syria') who included the descendants of previously pro-Byzantine tribes as well as Muslim conquerors. In addition to this largely urban-based élite there were tribes from the Syrian Desert and an ill-defined northern frontier zone facing Byzantium. Separate from this Muslim military élite were troops from the still Christian Arab tribes of northern Syria, known in the written records as Nabataeans and *musta^{c}a'riba* ('those who became Arab'). The later Umayyads also employed *ja^{c}ā'il* (mercenaries) who were not listed in the *dīwān al-jaysh* (ministry of war). In other parts of the Caliphate Arab provincial troops gradually declined into a *muqātila* (local militia).

By the mid-8th century largely non-Arab *mawālī* had become an important element in eastern armies. They came from many areas; some as volunteers, some as levies from conquered Persian and Turkish peoples. Persian *asāwira* had been stationed in Palestine and Syria since the mid-7th century. Others troops were recruited in the mountains of Afghanistan, and captured warriors from Sijistān were similarly sent back to Iraq as an élite bodyguard for the man who had conquered them. The same happened to Sughdian troops from Būkhārā, and fully equipped cavalry were supplied to the Caliph's army as tribute by at least one Turkish ruler.

Other non-Arab troops included Armenian mercenaries, Christian auxiliaries from the Syrian coastal mountains, and Coptic Egyptians. Of greater military significance were large numbers of warlike Berbers, some superficially converted to Islam, some Jewish and some still pagan, enlisted by the Umayyad governors of North Africa. The conquerors of the Iberian peninsula were soon joined by ex-Visigothic forces who helped Muslim forces retain control of part of southern France for almost half a century.

MILITARY ORGANISATION

There were several similarities between Romano-Byzantine and Sassanian armies, and these two imperial powers were also influenced by, and had military influence upon, their smaller neighbours. The Sassanian army had been regarded as a model by several others, and the extensive reforms carried out by Byzantine emperors in the late 6th and early 7th century were remarkably similar to those undertaken a few decades earlier by the Sassanians. Similarly the early Arabs

Although probably made in Coptic Egypt, this embroidered textile shows a ruler seated in the manner of a Sassanian or early Islamic ruler. He, like two dismounted horsemen above, wears a mail hauberk; the enemy on foot seem to include long-haired tribesmen and an African. This textile remains a mystery, but might have been made during the brief Iranian occupation of Egypt in the early 7th century, or for the first Muslim Arab rulers a few decades later. (Musée Historique des Tissus, inv. 243, Lyon)

regarded the Sassanian army as being skilled and well equipped though lacking in stamina. In fact it was the structure of Arabian society that led the Umayyads to maintain a tribally organised rather than Sassanian-style army, and once they were overthrown by the ᶜAbbāsids Iranian military traditions soon reappeared.

Romano-Byzantine Armies

The late Roman command and administrative structures were severely damaged by barbarian invasions during the late 4th century. In the eastern provinces these were gradually rebuilt, but service conditions for ordinary soldiers became desperate.

Elite guard regiments were raised in the meantime, but most of them then gradually declined into parade units. These included the *scholae*, the *candidati* élite group within the *scholae*, and the *excubitores* whose commanding officer remained an influential figure close to the Emperor's person. Such formations also served as a staff college from which senior commanders could be selected. Along the eastern frontiers the *limitanei* were replaced by new defensive structures. Until the 6th century much of this area remained under dual civil and military governors, though occasionally these were combined under a *Dux*. By the late 5th century the old frontier forts had been abandoned, at least by soldiers, and there was no longer a clear frontier across the desert – and may never have been. Instead the semi-desert steppes of what are now eastern Syria and Jordan remained an area where pro-Roman and pro-Sassanian nomadic tribes competed for grazing land while their sponsors struggled to extend their own influence.

This did not mean that there were no disciplined and trained troops in the area. Sources such as the Notitia Dignitatum show that late Roman regiments recruited from the Arab population included horse-archers, fully armoured *clibanarii* (close-combat cavalry) as well as infantry *cohorts*. Yet responsibility for protecting this vulnerable frontier increasingly fell to the *phylarchs* and their troops. The *phylarch* system developed during the 5th century, almost certainly in response to the effectiveness of the comparable pro-Sassanian La<u>kh</u>mid Arab kingdom on the other side of the desert. Early in the 6th century the Emperor Justinian raised this system into a tribal monarchy while at the same time downgrading the importance of the Romano-Byzantine *Duces* or frontier governors. The Ghassānid tribe was eventually made responsible for the entire frontier from the Euphrates to the Gulf of Aqaba. From then on they were an 'inner shield' for Byzantine Syria, protecting merchant caravans, policing the tribes, guarding the frontier and providing auxiliaries even on distant campaigns. An 'outer shield' under less direct Imperial control policed more distant tribes and helped spread Byzantine influence through conversion to Christianity. Other lower ranking and temporary *phylarchs* often existed deeper inside the Arabian peninsula (see below for further information).

The ancient kingdom of Armenia straddled the northern part of the frontier between the Romano-Byzantine and Sassanian Empires. After Armenia lost its independence in 428 the Armenian military aristocracy of higher *ishkhans* and lesser *nakharars* continued to play a key role under a foreign ruler, each senior nobleman having his own small following. Under Byzantine domination, Armenia's defences depended upon Byzantine garrisons in the main fortresses, but the authorities also ensured that the Armenian nobility and their troops were available when needed.

The central armies of the Romano-Byzantine Empire revived during the reign of the Emperor Justinian; the most prestigious elements being the *Palatine* Palace guard regiments stationed around Constantinople. Cavalry had now become a dominant élite, though still a minority. Compared with the great days of the Roman Empire, Justinian's armies were small but were well-equipped and trained. At the same time the Emperors were reluctant to allow potentially ambitious generals large forces loyal to themselves. Such a personal following, of which the Emperor had his own, was called a *comitatus*. Nevertheless the concept of the *comitatus* gradually spread beyond the ruler's control so that even powerful provincial nobles acquired them. Sometimes this led to a confusing overlap of the military responsibilities of regional field armies and *comitatenses* (provincial garrisons).

Other terms introduced for military units were now mostly Greek rather than Latin. During the 6th century the *tagma*, for example, was a tactical and administrative unit of about 300 men. Ten *tagmata* theoretically formed a *meros* or regiment, with a *moera* as an intermediate formation. Ideally three *meroi* regiments formed an army.

By the 6th century the *foederati* had evolved into regular regiments largely recruited from non-Romano-Byzantines and stationed in many provinces. Their senior officers, the *archontes foideraton*, were senior to the ordinary *tribunes* of *tagmata* units, the *foederati* now being regarded as front-line élite. These *foederati* were then grouped into larger corps during the reforms of the 6th century. While *foederati* were a front-line élite, *optimates* were the heavy cavalry élite of the centrally based reserve of the 6th-century army. The *bucellarii* first emerge as the private military attendants of various important people, but during the 6th century *tagmata* of *bucellarii* were listed within the regular field army. *Bucellarii* also formed the guards of leading generals though semi-private *bucellarii* remained in the provinces.

During the 6th century the Romano-Byzantine Empire often had to abandon the old ideal of keeping civil and military administrations separate. There was at the same time a clear militarisation of local administration. Everywhere it seemed that the army increased its influence as soldiers bought local land with which to support themselves at a time when payment from the central government was haphazard. The 6th

Carved relief of warriors fighting lions, from Zafār near Yarīm, Yemen, 3rd century. The costumes, shields and sword are more like those of the Byzantine Mediterranean than those of the nomadic peoples of Central Arabia. (Professor P. Costa photograph; present whereabouts unknown)

century also saw a type of virtually territorial soldier who would come to dominate later Byzantine military history. These were the *stradioti* who first appeared in Egypt as local garrison troops, primarily to support frontier forces within their own province. The military structure of Byzantine Egypt was different from that of most other areas, perhaps because it faced relatively minor military threats. Within Egypt proper there were three separate *Duces*, plus the two *Duces* of what is now Libya, each with his own corps of mercenary *bucellarii*. The bulk of forces in Egypt remained, however, a locally recruited Coptic levy.

The western parts of North Africa were reconquered from the Vandals by Justinian's army and had a more formidable military establishment. Here the governor or *exarch* commanded the armies, led military expeditions and had considerable freedom of action. Beneath him were various military leaders, the most senior being the *domestic* or *hypostrategus*, while the arsenal at Carthage was under a *sacellarius*, a administrative or financial rather than operational officer. Although the Byzantine army in North Africa was small compared to its Roman predecessors, its units may have been larger than was normal elsewhere. As in Egypt, the regional military governors of Byzantine North Africa and the small Byzantine parts of southern Spain had the rank of *Dux*. There were many *foederati* of Berber origin in North Africa, sometimes under direct Byzantine command, sometimes remaining under the leadership of their own tribal chiefs, the most senior of whom might be given the title of *praefectus*.

The 7th century saw huge changes in the Byzantine Empire. The Emperor Heraclius not only broke with tradition by leading his army in person, but he initiated an era of military reorganisation which continued as his successors struggled in the face of huge losses of territory. During this period the Byzantine army also came to look upon another of its enemies, the Avars, as their military pattern. The organisational and command structure had to be rebuilt during the disastrous Sassanian wars and during the subsequent struggle against the Muslim Caliphate. Fragmented imperial guards units were brought together into a smaller number of regiments known collectively as the *obsequium*. Further reforms during the 8th century reflected the declining prestige of some units and establishment of new ones. Basically, however, the Palace or Imperial regiments based around Constantinople formed the *tagmata* which operated as an élite reserve in support of provincial forces which bore the initial brunt of any invasion. The *tagmata* also formed the nucleus of any larger field army recruited for a specific campaign.

During the early 7th century Byzantium was confronted by an awesome array of foes, and Byzantine provincial forces were scattered over a vast area. Efficient, mobile, autonomous field forces seemed the only answer. One of the earliest and most effective was the *opsikion* which emerged in Bithynia by 626 to defend the capital from Muslim attack. Initially it probably consisted of Imperial guards but it also included troops known as *gothograeci*, perhaps the descendants of Germanic Goth soldiers who had formed the élite of a late 6th century field army in the same area. The *opsikion's* operational area

Above: *Soldier or huntsman on a 6th-century mosaic from the Byzantine Great Palace in Constantinople. This appears to be light infantry equipment, with leather or quilted armour, a sword in a baldric rather than belt, and a large shield. (Author's photograph; Mosaics Museum, Istanbul)*

was at first very large and, with the subsequent development of *themes*, it was split into three. At this stage there were no territorial *themes* as such, only regional field armies which came to be known as themes. In reality the famous Byzantine *theme* system of military provinces with associated garrisons evolved over a considerable time though it existed in a rudimentary form by the end of the 7th century, and the term still referred to a provincial army rather than the province itself. By the second half of the 8th century, however, the dispersal and territorialisation of all Byzantine forces except those based around the capital was complete.

Sassanian Armies

The élite of the Sassanian army was traditionally regarded as being tougher and better disciplined than late Roman troops. It consisted of *asvārān* (armoured cavalry) who, though not strictly forming part of the nobility, were given land in return for military service. Such troops were registered by the Sassanian government in a document known as the *nipīk* which also included sons who expected to take over their father's role.

Before the military reforms of Khusrau I the Sassanian army was under the *Irān-spādbadh* (Minister of War). A regional commander (*spādbadh*) directed lesser military officials (*kanārangs* or *marzbāns*) according to area. Until the early 6th century there was also a separate war-leader known as the *Artīshtāransālār*. Elite guard units included the *Varhranīghān-khvadhāy* ('immortals'), and the *Jān-avspār* ('self-sacrificers'), under the commander of a *pushtīghbānsālār*. Ordinary infantry units were led by a *pāyghānsālār*, small units of infantry archers under *tīrbadhs* being stationed in many villages. The largest formation in a Sassanian army was a *gund* or corps under a *gundsālār*. Next came a *drafsh* and a *vasht*, perhaps comparable to a regiment and a battalion. Regular troops lived in *ambāragh* (barracks), often with a *ganz* (arsenal) attached, these being administered by the eldest of the senior officers called the *Irān-ambāragh-badh*.

The importance of the reforms carried out in the mid-6th century by the Sassanian *Shāhanshāh* ('King of Kings'), Khusrau I, is hard to exaggerate since they probably influenced reforms within the Romano-Byzantine Empire and, more significantly, were seen as a military ideal throughout much of the Muslim world for centuries. Most obviously Khusrau I divided the Empire into four large defensive regions, each under a senior *marzban:* Khurāsān in the north-east, Fārs-Susiana in the south-east, Iraq in the south-west and Azerbaijan in the north-west. These were sub-divided into smaller regions under a lesser *marzban* who had civil as well as military responsibilities; in Khurāsān such an official was known as a *kanārang*. The interior of the Empire was also under lesser *marzbans*. Smaller still was a *shahr* which was a district around a town governed by a *shahrīgh* chosen from the local *dihqan* gentry. These in turn were subdivided into *kuras* and again into village *rustaqs* or *tasugs* headed by *dhīs* (village chiefs).

Khusrau I's reforms also changed the command structure of the Sassanian army. The Chief Minister or *Vuzurg-framādhār* remained deeply involved in military affairs, but the role of Commander-in-Chief was replaced by a *spāhbadh* appointed for a specific offensive campaign. If the Empire were invaded,

Right: *Mid-6th-century church floor mosaic, depicting an Arab bedouin leading a camel. Since this was made in an area close to the desert frontier of the Byzantine Empire, its portrayal of a pre-Islamic Arab tribal warrior is very realistic, above all in the size of the man's infantry bow which he carries around his neck. (Fr. M. Piccirillo photograph; in situ, Monastery Church of Kayanos, Valley of Mount Nebo, Jordan)*

Left: *Romano-Byzantine two-piece iron helmet from Hadithah, 4th–early 7th centuries. It is likely to date from shortly before the Muslim-Arab conquest of Syria, and is a clear example of the simple mass-produced helmets used by late Roman and early Byzantine troops. (Author's photograph; Castle Museum, Karak, Jordan)*

Left: *Byzantine-Goth gilded iron shield boss from the Crimea, c.400. (Author's photograph; State Hermitage Museum, St. Petersburg)*

Two knives or short-swords from Hadithah, 4th–early 7th centuries. One still has part of its bronze guard or quillons and is virtually identical with a weapon found on a victim of an early 8th-century earthquake farther up the Jordan Valley. (Author's photograph; Castle Museum, Karak, Jordan)

the *marzban* of the frontier region involved assumed command. An army commander might also be known as a *pādhghūspān*, though the latter was originally a lesser military leader under a *spāhbadh*. The *Artīshtārānsālār* ('chief of the soldiers') was technically senior to a *spāhbadh*, but perhaps only in an administrative role. The commander of cavalry was now known as the *Asvārān-sardār*.

Several new élite guard units were also created, these normally being named after the ruler who established them, this idea also continuing throughout the subsequent Islamic centuries. Khusrau I was similarly credited with improving the system of military reviews which were now carried out by a senior military secretary. Altogether Khusrau's reforms gave the *Shāhanshāh's* government great power but also contained the seeds of fragmentation under a weak ruler. The old landed aristocracy was gradually replaced by a military 'nobility of service' and soldiers were recognised as a distinct class within an Empire that was becoming increasingly militarised under regional warrior-governors.

In some areas the frontiers of the Sassanian Empire were even more blurred than those of the Romano-Byzantine state. This was particularly so in the east and north-east where many Iranian-speaking regions lay beyond effective Sassanian control, several being under local rulers descended from Hun invaders. Sassanian domination of much of the Arabian peninsula had generally been nominal, with the Sassanians supporting semi-settled rather than nomadic tribes. The most obvious were the Lakhmids of Al-Ḥīra, but the Sassanian Empire also gave political, military and financial assistance to the Banū Ḥanīfah of Yamāmah in central Arabia and the Julanda of Oman in return for local recognition of Sassanian suzerainty. The first unit of Sassanian *asvārān* (cavalry) to drive the Ethiopians out of Yemen did not stay, though the descendants of a second force were still there at the time of the Muslim conquest.

The last Sassanian armies which failed so catastrophically against the Muslim Arabs had been organised on essentially the same lines. The one disastrous change had been the abolition of the autonomous Lakhmid principality, perhaps because these Arabs had been about to convert to Christianity. The Sassanians, however, lacked suitable troops and the strength to defend this desert frontier effectively. The Sassanian Emperor's hold over the *marzbān* (marcher-lords) also seems to have been failing. Defeat by the Byzantine Empire, internal quarrels within the imperial family, plummeting prestige in Arabia and a series of floods in Iraq also contributed to a weakening of the Sassanian army.

Semitic and African Forces

The military structure of pre-Islamic Arabia was strongly influenced by the neighbouring Romano-Byzantine and Sassanian Empires. Nevertheless its military potential remained unrecognised until a sudden explosion of Arab-Islamic power in the 7th century.

The ancient priest-kingdoms of southern Arabia had evolved into secular monarchies centuries earlier, these in turn fragmenting to leave Yemen dominated by a tribal aristocracy known as the *ashrāf* which still owed military and administrative duties to monarchs who had little authority. In fact Southern Arabia, Yemen, the Hadhramawt and Oman were now a collection of minor states under some degree of Sassanian control though often dominated by bedouin tribes. Local kings seem to have varied in power, rather like those of early Anglo-Saxon England. Horses were rare, yet these little armies were quite sophisticated and handed on a vital tradition of discipline to their Muslim successors.

Southern tribes were not really kinship groups, while towns formed communes dominated by *qayls* owing allegiance to a local king. Armies consisted of three parts: the ruler's own *khamīs* (indigenous élite) which was a communal levy or professional force, local levies raised and led by their *qayls*, and a very small cavalry élite which never acted independently. A fourth element could be provided by bedouin auxiliaries or allies, those known as *t-m-h-r-t* or 'trained' perhaps being professional mercenaries of bedouin origin. Other south Arabian military terms included: *m-ṣ-r* (army on campaign); *g-y-s* (small force assembled for a specific task); *m-q-d-m-t* (vanguard); *g-z-w-y* (raiding column); *q-r-n* (garrison troops); *s-r-h-t* or *n-s-r* (support column); *ᶜn-t* (relief column); *ḥ-y-f* (possibly flanking force); *'ys* (junior leader or officer); *q-d-m* (commanding officer); and *m-ḥ-r-m* (agricultural land set aside to feed the *khamīs* élite). A clear distinction was also made between horse-riding cavalry and other 'mounted' troops who were camel-riding infantry. A further distinction was drawn between riding camels, baggage camels and those carrying the army's water supply.

The Ghassānid Arab *phylarchs* controlled territory and subordinate tribes beyond the frontiers of the Romano-Byzantine Empire where they were considered independent rulers. Militarily their power was based upon tribal encampments known as *ḥīra*, or in Greek, *parembole*, a tribal leader thus being called a *strategos parembolon nomadon* by his imperial suzerain. The main Ghassānid *ḥīra* was on the Golan plateau within Romano-Byzantine territory, though the bulk of Ghassānid troops were probably based on the edge of the desert. Though his men were still nomads, the *phylarch* tried to copy Romano-Byzantine military systems and it seems that such troops formed a *jaysh*, the normal later Arabic term for a properly structured army, their leaders including a *jarrār* (commander of one thousand), a word also used in Yemen.

On the other side of the Red Sea the ruling élite of the Axumite kingdom in Ethiopia had converted to Christianity in the 4th century while Axum rose to become a considerable military power. A relatively sophisticated command structure soon developed for an army which consisted of *sarāwīt* (regular troops) and a larger number of *ēḥzāb* (irregulars). A Greek description of an Axumite royal procession in 530 shows that the kingdom was rich and used similar ceremonials to the Arab *phylarchs* of Syria. But other evidence suggests that the Ethiopian occupation army in Yemen suffered deep social divisions between the rich and the very poor common soldiers. Other than this almost nothing is known of Axumite military organisational structure except that an army was known as a *m-ṣ-r*, as in southern Arabia, or a *ḥezb*.

Three kingdoms of Nubia in northern Sudan converted to Christianity late in the 6th century. The northernmost, Nobatia, included a stretch of the Nile valley evacuated by the Romans which provided defence in depth for centuries to come. But virtually nothing is known of the early armies of the southern Nubian kingdoms, Makuria and Alwa. Fragmentary evidence concerning the nomad Blemye-Beja state between the Nile and the Red Sea suggests that, in the 6th century, its rulers used a Romano-Byzantine model for their army, including the Greek term *phylarch*, and reflected that of the ancient Meroitic kingdom of Sudan, itself modelled on Pharaonic Egypt.

The First Muslim Armies

In many ways the first Muslim armies were modelled on those of pre-Islamic south Arabia. Since all Muslim men had a military obligation, the *jaysh* or army was virtually synonymous with the people. At first the only distinctions were those between infantry and cavalry though at an early stage troops were divided into *ᶜirāfa* (pay units of ten to fifteen men). A large proportion were set up soon allocated to a *ribāṭ* which at this stage meant garrison duty, initially in areas facing external threats or internal rebellion. *Amṣār* (cantonments) for soldiers and their families were set up in conquered cities or newly established towns, those close to the Arabian desert perhaps serving as assembly points for tribal troops. In general the Muslim conquerors continued to use the military structures they had found, though in some areas these were simplified. The Muslim Arab conquest of Iran took decades during which the Muslims had to organise virtually static front lines. As a result the first *thughūr* or military frontier-provinces appeared in northern Iraq and western Iran. Behind them the new Iraqi city of Kūfa served as a base-area and main *amṣār* (garrison).

Armies of the Umayyad Caliphate

The *jund* or regional organisation of Islamic armies is traditionally attributed to ᶜUmar, the second Caliph. In reality it should probably be credited to the first two Umayyad Caliphs Muᶜāwiya and Yazīd. These *junds*, like the later Byzantine *theme* armies, were based upon fortified provincial cities. All soldiers were registered with the government *dīwān* or ministry so that they could draw regular pay. Muᶜāwiya also turned the old *bayt al-māl* communal treasury and weapons' store into a government *dīwān* dealing with military salaries and pensions. Over the next decades small provincial *dīwāns* were also established.

The earliest Syrian *junds* of Damascus and Hims were those most closely associated with the Caliph and probably served as élite units comparable to the subsequent *Palatine* regiments and *tagmata* of the Byzantine Empire. Others soon followed elsewhere, the most important consisting of loyal *ahl al-shām* Syrian Arabs though the bulk of *jund* troops remained potentially disloyal non-Syrians. *Ahl al-shām* based in the east were rotated back to the Arab heartlands with each change of governor. There was also a clear distinction between internal forces including *shurṭa* (security troops), whose role was essentially static, and field or frontier forces.

Late 7th-century gold coin of the Umayyad Caliph ᶜAbd al-Malik. The first Muslim rulers or Caliphs, carrying a straight sword on a baldric were depicted on coins until pictorial images were replaced by solely written inscriptions. But the image itself continued to be used in carving and on wall-painting well into the 8th century. (British Museum, London)

Provincial *wālī* (governors) normally relied on *jund* troops from the same tribe as themselves. Meanwhile the entire tribal system was restructured during the Umayyad period, the old tribal ᶜ*ashīra* having proved too small to be an effective army unit. So the tribes were brought together into a smaller number of large tribal divisions, several artificial tribes called *qabīla* being created to accommodate those who fell outside the existing system. These perhaps camouflaged the existence of large numbers of non-Arab *mawālī* troops. Some Umayyad governors actively attempted to suppress tribal ᶜ*aṣabīah* (solidarity) which, though it strengthened morale, could act as a focus of discontent.

By the end of the Umayyad period the old Arab tribal system was, in fact, withering fast. Regimental units, whether tribal or otherwise, were commanded by *quwwād* officers while senior command positions went to members of the Umayyad ruling family. In several cases *jund* armies had a dual leadership, with one commander leading those on campaign while another either headed those remaining on garrison duty, or the *naẓīr* reserves, or a second column when the army marched on two fronts. An ᶜ*aṣā* (baton) was used as a symbol of command, much as it would later be in so many European armies.

While Muslim armies swept east and west, a relatively static situation developed along the Byzantine frontier. Here Muslim defences were at first improvised but the second Umayyad Caliph strengthened this front, both to defend his capital Damascus and as a launching pad for further invasions of Byzantium. These *junds* had much in common with the old Roman Syrian *limes*, though facing in the opposite direction. By the late Umayyad period proper *thughūr* (military marches) faced Byzantium; their structure reflecting the two or three strategic passes through the Taurus and Anti-Taurus mountains. As opposition to the Umayyads increased, six Syrian and Egyptian *jund* divisions went to al-Andalus, the Muslim parts of what are now Spain and Portugal, in 742. The fact that many of these loyal forces were still there may have prompted a surviving member of the Umayyad family to flee westward following the ᶜAbbāsids' revolution of 750.

STRATEGY AND TACTICS

The idea that medieval armies lacked discipline, even in western Europe, is incorrect; the discipline of professional Romano-Byzantine, Sassanian and Islamic Middle Eastern forces was in many ways comparable to that of modern armies. Nevertheless tactics tended to be simple and conservative.

The 'Citadel of Khusrau' stands in the centre of the much later castle at Rustaq in Oman. It is a simple but massive triangular fortification built around a natural outcrop of rock and may date from the Sassanian occupation of the eastern Arabian peninsula in pre-Islamic times. (Author's photograph)

Broad Strategy

Late Roman and early Byzantine strategy preserved the Eastern Empire for centuries. Until the 6th century fixed garrisons were backed up by field armies. In rich but vulnerable Syria, for example, bedouin raids were normally met by a gathering of the closest *limitanei* frontier troops while defence against a major Sassanian invasion would rely on the garrisons of fortified cities plus a field army. But during the 6th century garrisons were greatly reduced while the *limitanei* virtually disappeared. Active frontier defence fell to Arab *phylarchs* who, like their opposite numbers on the Sassanian side of the desert, protected the cultivated zone and in turn raided enemy territory. In the mountainous terrain of Anatolia Romano-Byzantine forces developed a sophisticated system of defensive guerrilla warfare, a strategy that would later prove its worth against Muslim-Arab incursions. A similarly defensive strategy was used in North Africa.

Caution remained the hallmark of Byzantine warfare, major battles being avoided in favour of prolonged campaigns of attrition. The enemy was rarely met on the frontiers but would instead be harassed while the local population took refuge in fortified towns. This strategy failed against the Muslim Arabs because they, unlike earlier raiders, did not retreat to the desert but instead defeated local Byzantine forces almost every time they met. Once Muslim strength was seen to be growing rather than decreasing, the Byzantine Emperor gathered a large army in Anatolia and met the Muslims at the full-scale battle of Yarmuk – whose outcome ensured that Byzantium's loss of Syria was complete, though resistance was continued by bands of irregulars and took the Caliphs' armies many years to root out. At the same time a large swathe of territory was abandoned and its fortifications destroyed to create a no-man's-land between Byzantine and Muslim territory. Behind this barrier Cappadocia became the Byzantines' main military base area against increasingly Muslim incursions; the main *opsikion* army in Anatolia defended the capital and other lesser Byzantine field forces undertook increasingly independent action. Many decades would pass before this fragmented Byzantine system could muster sufficient troops to meet enemy raiders in force or undertake effective counter raiding.

Less detail is known about Sassanian armies of this period, but they are unlikely to have learned much from Roman or Romano-Byzantine tactics. Similarly little is known or can even

Rock-relief carving showing the Sassanian Shāhanshāh or perhaps an Imperial Prince hunting antelope. Two other large horsemen carry bows around their necks, as was also seen in Arabia. An orchestra is seated in a raised pavilion in the top left-hand corner. (Iranian Cultural Heritage Organisation; in situ Ṭāq-i Bustān, Iran)

be deduced concerning Sassanian strategy during the Empire's collapse. One tradition has it that the regional commander of Iraq advised engaging the Arabs in many small encounters, but was overruled by the Shāhinshāh who demanded a single great victory. The result was catastrophic defeat at the battle of Qādisīyah. Thereafter Sassanian forces within Iran adopted a more defensive approach but were defeated none the less.

Warfare in the Middle East often saw a clash of different military mentalities, the most striking being that between the imperial Romano-Byzantine and Sassanian armies on one side and the northern Arabian tribes on the other. Here it is important to note that bedouin forces were not free to roam the desert at will but were constrained by available water sources. As a result they, like merchant caravans, normally stuck to known routes. While the imperial forces attempted to take territory and fortified places, the pre-Islamic Arabs had virtually no interest in fixed positions. Their concerns were access to water, adequate grazing areas, and domination of tribal rivals. When faced by the might of Rome or Iran they had the advantage of being able to withdraw into the desert; not into areas devoid of life but to those where their own local knowledge enabled them to survive. They were most effective when making rapid raids deep into enemy territory, usually by light cavalry since the northern tribes' control of the grazing steppes enabled them to maintain moderate horse herds.

Within the tribal context most warfare involved rival bedouin tribes who might also threaten merchant caravans in order to extort protection money. This *razzīa* or *ghazw* warfare rested upon economic pressure to weaken an enemy's ability to survive in harsh ecological conditions. Campaigns tended to be prolonged but resulted in few casualties and were governed by customary rules based upon mutual self interest. When nomadic bedouin tribes clashed with settled Arab tribes the former tended to threaten the latter's life-supporting groves of palm trees, again with minimal loss of life.

South Arabian strategy focused on two or more allied forces meeting at a sometimes distant location, often after long night marches, then seizing control of enemy towns, regaining or defending their own. One legend recalls how a Yemeni army attacked the distant town of Yamāma after three days of gradual approach behind a screen of branches, each held by one man. The similarity with the story in Shakespeare's *Macbeth* a thousand years later is remarkable.

The best-documented southern Arabian campaign took place in what Muslims remember as 'The Year of the Elephant' during which the Ethiopian governor of Yemen sent a column against the still pagan town of Mecca as part of a larger effort to crush resistance to Ethiopian domination. A second column, in which the Ethiopians were supported by the Arab Kinda confederation, had greater success and crushed the rebels at Ḥulubān.

The little that is known of warfare on the other side of the Red Sea shows that the introduction of the camel during the early centuries had a military impact comparable to that of the horse among the Plains Indians of North America. The Sahara could suddenly be crossed with relative ease, those tribes who possessed camels now being able to raid and trade far afield while Nilotic Nubia, which had been the easiest link between north and south, lost its monopoly. In North Africa the Berbers continued to rely on a simple and apparently limited form of raiding warfare, similar to the Arab *razzīa*, consisting of small-scale raiding, surprise attacks and ambushes, making use of hilly or forested terrain and avoiding major confrontations with powerful Romano-Byzantine forces.

The first Muslim campaigns against their Byzantine and Sassanian neighbours were similarly preceded by extensive raids avoiding major garrisons or fortified places. At the same time the Caliphs consolidated their control over the semi-desert steppes along the Byzantine and Sassanian frontiers, this in turn enabling small forces of Arab cavalry to be transferred rapidly between the Iraqi and the Syrian fronts to tip the balance in more than one battle. Overall strategy remained cautious; invasions only involving as many troops as were thought necessary, additional reinforcements being sent when needed. On the other hand early Muslim and Umayyad armies were exceptionally resourceful, the Arabs also eagerly adopting new weapons and techniques.

During these early conquests the Muslim Arabs were strategically much more mobile with excellent long-distance communications which enabled them to assemble forces with

Wall-painting showing an archer shooting at a castle, from Khirbat al-Mafjar, Palestine 743–4. This archer's arms and armour are essentially Byzantine though the painting was made for an Umayyad Muslim Caliph. It also includes a very early representation of the technique of 'shooting under a shield' which remained part of a Middle Eastern archer's training throughout the Middle Ages. (Israel Antiquities Authority photograph; Rockefeller Museum, East Jerusalem)

remarkable speed, this compensating for their numerical inferiority. Early Muslim forces were less manoeuvrable in mountainous areas where their small cavalry forces often ranged far ahead of the infantry, apparently because the single-humped dromedaries used by Arab mounted infantry were much less suitable.

Cilicia in the west and Maraş in the east soon became the main springboards for summer campaigns into Byzantine Anatolia. A large raiding force might also winter within Byzantine territory, having seized a castle and planted crops to harvest in spring. The most ambitious campaigns against the Byzantine capital of Constantinople were decisively defeated. Meanwhile Muslim advances on the far west and east, in France and Transoxiana, halted for several reasons: they were no longer economically viable, Muslim manpower was stretched to its limit, and the Arabs had reached climatic zones where they had no wish to settle.

Troop Types

Whereas previous Parthian rulers of Iran had led armies which included great numbers of horse-archers, the importance of these declined during the early Sassanian period though cavalry itself remained the decisive arm. The great majority of Sassanian horsemen were now spear-armed close-combat cavalry, many on armoured horses. Like the Romans the Sassanians learned from the Hun invasions and as a result there was a revival of horse-archery during the late 4th and early 5th centuries. Nevertheless Sassanian archery remained a largely infantry affair, such infantrymen being trained to shoot fast and accurately from behind the protection of large wattle mantlets. Other Sassanian infantry armed with swords and spears seem to have been capable of meeting Romano-Byzantine foot soldiers face to face. A Sassanian use of war elephants, though never on a large scale, was probably learned from their Kushan neighbours in Afghanistan. Such beasts were still in use in the late 6th century and there is some evidence that they might have been armoured.

One technological development which had a profound impact on Arabia, and later in the Sahara, was a new form of rigid wood-framed camel saddle. Unlike the old unframed saddle which was strapped behind the camel's hump, this new saddle was mounted on top and not only enabled the animal to carry heavier loads but meant that a man could now fight from camel-back. In fact it altered the whole balance of power within the desert world, the neighbouring Mediterranean and Iranian Empires finding it increasingly difficult to dominate their Arab neighbours in the way they had done for a thousand years. From Parthian times onwards Arab horsemen were noted as spear-armed cavalry, Arab foot soldiers as infantry archers. The two clearly operated in close conjunction, a horseman often riding to war on camel-back with an infantryman as a passenger while his valuable warhorse followed behind. The main exception to this pattern was in Yemen where there were few warhorses until the early 7th century. Neither camels nor horses were mentioned in 4th-century Ethiopia while those in the army which occupied Yemen in the 6th century only appear to have belonged to officers, the rest of the Ethiopian army consisting of javelin-armed infantry. A century or so later, however, the governor of the northern Nubian military frontier distinct of Nobatia was called 'Lord of Horses' while the area around what is now Khartoum would soon develop into an important horse-raising centre.

The now-extinct 'forest elephant' of northern Africa had been used in war by the ancient Carthaginians. Ethiopian rulers had also used war elephants since ancient times and these were still found in the Horn of Africa until the 6th century. By now, however, the Ethiopians were using them for parade purposes and to pull the king's chariot. The famous animal which accompanied the Ethiopian army during its attempted attack on Mecca in 'The Year of the Elephant' was probably a parade or morale-boosting beast, perhaps serving as a rallying point for Ethiopian troops. On the other hand the Nubians may have used true war elephants for a further century.

Evidence suggests that infantry archers dominated both Ethiopia and Nubia, many unusual archers' stone thumb-rings being found in early medieval graves in the Nile valley. Greek and Roman sources also described the huge bows used by *Aethiopians*, by whom they meant the inhabitants of what are now the Sudan, Eritrea, Ethiopia and Somalia. Such weapons were of simple rather than composite construction, being far larger than 6th-century Sassanian bows, and were used at least until the 7th century.

Battle Tactics

Whereas Roman armies of the early 5th century left most manoeuvre to their 'barbarian' allies or auxiliaries, the early 6th-century Romano-Byzantine armies used sophisticated tactics involving several different kinds of troops. Most had been learned through experience of fighting Central Asian foes. A new 'ideal' cavalry formation was developed, consisting of two lines of cavalry about 400 metres apart, the rear consisting of one-third of the total and acting as a reserve, though both lines were also trained to change front. The centre of the front would be eight men deep, its flanks four deep while the commander and his guard unit remained between these two blocks of cavalry. There were more armoured men at the front, flanks and rear, those at the front also having armoured horses against harassment by horse-archers. Each division consisted of offensive *cursores* armed with bows, protected by *defensores* who followed up their repeated attacks closely. The continued use of similar tactics in the medieval Middle East and Spain for the next thousand years is proof of their effectiveness.

The written sources of this period suggest that there were also minor changes in Romano-Byzantine infantry formations. Sixth-century formations were described as square or rectangular, each file commanded by an officer with the *ilarch* or squad leader in the front rank. If enemy cavalry attacked from the front these formations would be preceded by unarmoured skirmishers armed with slings. The two front ranks of the main formation would shoot their arrows horizontally against the enemy's horses, those to the rear shooting high to drop arrows on the enemy, in an endeavour to force them to raise their shields and expose their horses. Men would only pick up their spears if the enemy came close. Other information concerning Romano-Byzantine infantry indicates great attention being paid to the danger of surprise attack, changing front, wheeling and changing the shape of infantry formation. Romano-Byzantine armies also used the traditionally nomadic tactic of feigned flight, even dropping non-essential items of kit to make the flight seem real.

Like their age-old Roman foes, the Sassanian armies suffered serious defeats at the hands of Huns. But the Sassanians, unlike the experimental Romano-Byzantines, do not appear to have developed any new tactics. Roman sources indicate that the typical Sassanian battle array divided an army into a centre, ideally on a hill, with two wings; herds of spare horses being kept at the rear. Other literary sources suggest that cavalry could be ahead of the infantry with infantry archers concentrated on the defensive left flank. Other evidence places elephants behind the horsemen but ahead of infantry or forming a living 'wall' behind the foot soldiers. Medieval Islamic writers offered several descriptions of the Sassanian battle-array which may be based on lost earlier records. For example, a late 10th-century Persian source states that the Sassanian ruler placed his cavalry on the wings, infantry in the centre with elephants behind them, plus an élite force of reserves to the rear. A 13th-century Perso-Indian writer offered a plan of the Sassanian array, with a large curved formation at the centre with large cavalry forces on the left to protect the herds, a large formation of 'guards' on the right, with baggage, infantry and a hospital to the rear protected by a rearguard. In general Sassanian cavalry were used for skirmishing or scouting and to support élite heavy cavalry. Infantry archers shot volleys to order, advancing in ranks with other foot soldiers who could make ferocious infantry charges. Yet the Sassanians made little use of flanking movement or feigned retreat, though they did take effective advantage of broken ground in the face of a stronger enemy.

Early Arabic poetry makes much of individual combat by champions of the opposing armies, as was traditional in Sassanian Iran, but battles themselves were largely fought by infantry archers. A small number of mailed cavalry often preceded foot soldiers into battle, again in Sassanian style. The larger number of northern Arabian armoured spear-carrying *foederati* in the late Roman army were described as charging in a wedge-shaped *cuneus* which was capable of routing a comparable formation of Goths. Compared to such tactics the traditional battle array of south Arabian kings, as preserved in a 13th-century Persian military manual, consisted of three divisions with flanks thrown forward but no cavalry. Two additional divisions were drawn back on each flank, each supported by small mounted units. Further supporting elements stood behind the centre and to the rear, covered by a small rearguard, again without cavalry.

In complete contrast early medieval Berber battlefield tactics relied on one massive charge. Berber forces did, however, enjoy great tactical mobility because of their light equipment and abundance of horses, but were strategically slow because they tended to take their families and flocks with them.

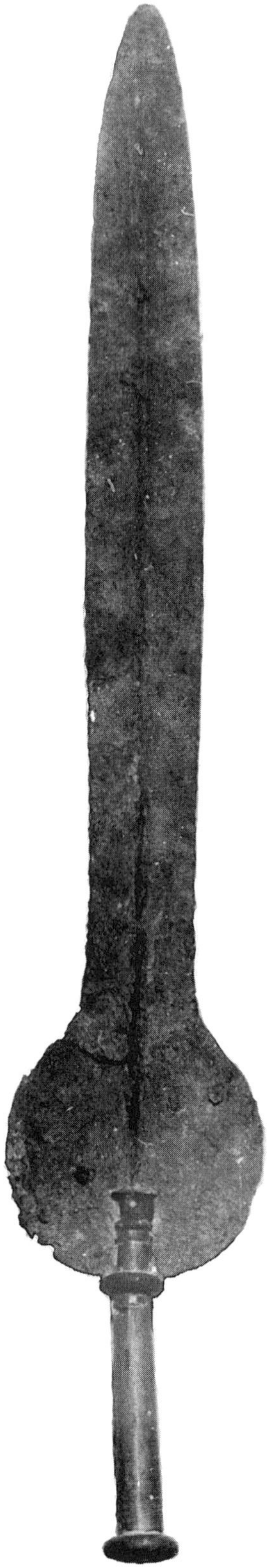

Far left: *Iron spearhead with silvered socket from Ballana; Nubian, 4th–5th centuries. This was clearly a decorative ceremonial weapon, but similarly shaped spears appeared in art from Egypt and Nubia for many more centuries. (Archaeological Museum, Cairo)*
Near left: *Short sword in a decorated silver scabbard from Ballana; Nubian, 4th–5th centuries. Various Middle Eastern desert peoples were renowned for their short infantry swords, including the pre- and early Muslim Arabs. (Archaeological Museum, Cairo)*
Right: *Decorated leather shield from Ballana; Nubian, 4th–5th centuries. Virtually identical shields were still being used by the Bāja nomads of northern Sudan in the 19th century, a remarkable example of stylistic and technological continuity. (Archaeological Museum, Cairo)*

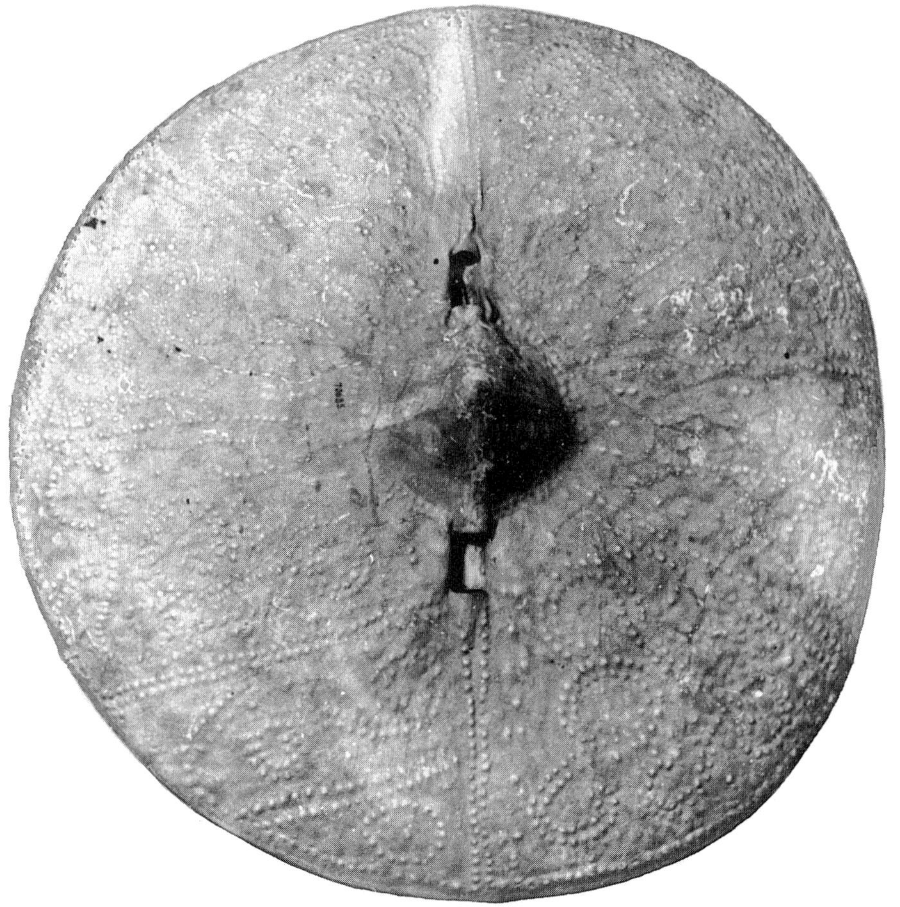

The tactical use of elephants in the Ethiopian army differed from that in India or Sassanian Iran. In Africa these creatures were placed with the infantry in the front rank or even thrust ahead as a vanguard, and are said to have had leather-covered towers on their backs, each carrying six men though this number is certainly an exaggeration. The role of camels was entirely passive. By the 6th century great numbers were clearly available to the Ethiopians and the Sudanese Beja as beasts of burden. Camels could also be hobbled in a large circular formation as a living field fortification, known in Arabic as an *ᶜawd* and to the Romano-Byzantines as a *kuklos*. Women and children would remain within this circle while men defended its perimeter with shield and javelin. The North African Berbers used the same living fortification to protect archers, slingers and men with spears thrust into the earth as pikes. In a perhaps distinctive variation some Berber armies might station their cavalry on a nearby hill, ready to charge any enemy who attacked the circle of camels.

The Arab conquests were carried out by infantry, a large proportion of whom were archers. These victories were also won in an area where cavalry had dominated for centuries, but this did not change the basic cavalry orientation of Middle Eastern warfare. Instead the Muslims recruited horsemen as soon as they were able to do so. On the other hand the next centuries saw an important change in the character of Middle Eastern warfare; a Central Asian tradition of horse-archery becoming dominant as the essentially static Levantine archery tradition declined.

The Byzantines and the Sassanians regarded cavalry as their élite, the early 7th-century Byzantines training their best men to use bows from horseback while the rest used spear and shield. Similarly the Sassanian élite consisted of highly disciplined armoured horse-archers famed for their speed rather than the power of their shooting. The best were capable of shooting a volley or *panjgān* ('handful') of five arrows and then snatching a further five from their quiver. The subsequent domination and prestige of Turkish horse-archers has obscured the fact that many Arab warriors had been noted infantry archers. There is evidence that, like the Byzantines, they were disciplined enough to shoot volleys at command. While these early Muslim-Arab archers were often less effective than their Byzantine foes, they were clearly very effective against Sassanian cavalry.

Descriptions of battlefield wounds indicate that, though arrows in the face caused many losses, the most common injuries were to legs and feet, the least common to shoulder, hand or torso. This strongly reinforces other evidence of close infantry combat with sword and shield most dramatically illustrated in stories about the *mubārizūn* ('champions') who duelled between the ranks of opposing armies. Cavalry played their part with the long spears that would remain traditional bedouin Arab weapons well into the 19th century. At first such horsemen were lightly armoured, but by the late Umayyad period Muslim-Arab cavalry had acquired much more equipment so that they proved superior to Central Asian Turks in close combat.

In contrast the Muslims' African foes had fewer cavalry. Among the Nubians only the king rode a full-sized horse, others having ponies while the bulk of Nubian troops remained infantry archers. A large proportion of Berber warriors in North Africa were still armed with slings, though these were effective enough against enemy cavalry to remain in use for several more centuries.

One feature stands out as an almost universal characteristic of battle from the mid-7th to mid-8th centuries. This was the attempt by both sides to storm the enemy's encampment at a greater or lesser distance behind his battle-lines. Before this could be done, of course, the enemy's front had to be broken. Byzantine military manuals, such as the *Strategikon* attributed to the Emperor Maurice, describe the Byzantine theoretical or ideal battle-plan in detail. The army should be in two lines, the second forming a reserve to guard against flank attacks. Where possible there should also be a mobile reserve or *droungos*. Spear-armed cavalry stood in the centre of the first line with infantry archers on their flanks, the wings consisting of companies of defensive troops on the left and a smaller number of offensive companies on the right. Throughout the entire medieval period, in all parts of the known world, the right was used offensively, the left defensively, perhaps for the simple reason that men carried their shields on their left shoulders, their weapons in their right hands.

The tactics described in the *Strategikon* were used in reality, though not always with success. The feigned flight was known as the 'Scythian ambush'; the 'Scythian drill' was an encircling movement. The 'Alan drill' consisted of a single line of attackers and defenders making repeated attacks and withdrawals. The 'African drill' had a single line of defenders with attackers on both flanks, the 'Italian drill' consisted of two lines of mixed attackers and defenders and was regarded as best.

In contrast the Sassanians were said to draw up their forces in three large divisions with infantry in the centre, cavalry on the wings. According to the Strategikon they did not make use of feigned retreat. On the other hand Sassanian armies sometimes had stone-throwing engines mounted in wagons spaced along their front. Sassanian 'shower shooting' techniques gave covering fire to units as they attacked but were not particularly effective at long range or against prepared positions. Here the Sassanian use of elephants with archers and javelin-throwers on their backs, and supported by infantry, seems to have been designed to terrify and intimidate an undisciplined foe. The failure of such creatures against the Muslims in Iraq suggests that the Sassanians under-estimated the discipline of these new enemies. In later battles the Sassanians fought cautiously, for example adopting a defensive position on the slope of a hill with spiked *calthrops* scattered ahead of their line.

For their part the early Muslim-Arabs fought tactically defensive battles within an offensive strategy, siting themselves in naturally strong positions. Once this had been done their main tactic was one of repeated attack and withdrawal, the *karr wa farr* so similar to the Roman-Byzantine *cursores* and *defensores.* Battles tended to begin with archery skirmishing though the bulk of infantry archers were normally placed on the flanks. During these early years the first Muslim armies always relied on the long-established five-fold division of forces known as the *khamīs* consisting of a *muqaddamah* (advance guard), *qalb* (centre), *maymanah* (right wing), *maysarah* (left wing) and *sāqah* (rearguard). Such tactics continued well into the Umayyad period, and when a force of Muslim Arab rebels allied with the Turks in Central Asia, the largely cavalry Turks were placed on the traditionally offensive right flank while the Muslims took the traditionally defensive left. The limited evidence suggests that the few Muslim cavalry tended to be placed on the right wing but in the early days were too few to be used in direct charges against the enemy. Instead they attempted to outflank and harass an enemy or to pursue him once defeated.

Such tactics continued to be used until late Umayyad times, though with an increasing reliance on offensive cavalry. These were soon divided into *katība* operational units of about 100 men subdivided into smaller *miqnab.* Infantry still fought in close ordered ranks or *ṣaff* though the horsemen could also be grouped into a small closely packed formation called a *ta^{c}biya,*

Left: *Romano-Byzantine clay lamp with seven burners from Alexandria, perhaps 5th century. It is decorated with the story of David and Goliath. Goliath has a helmet similar to the sallet which reappeared in Italian art many centuries later. He also has long mail or lamellar armour and a sword which appears to hang from a baldric. Such features suggest that the lamp may be as late as 6th century. (Gift of Rebecca Darkington Stoddard, 1913, Yale University Art Gallery, New Haven)*
Right: *Two stucco heads of soldiers from Khirbat al-Mafjar, Palestine, 743–4. Both men are wearing qalansūwahs (quilted caps) probably over helmets. The remains of painted mail hauberks can just be seen on their chests, and both have mirror-image baldrics slung from their shoulders. (Israel Antiquities Authority photograph; Rockefeller Museum, East Jerusalem)*

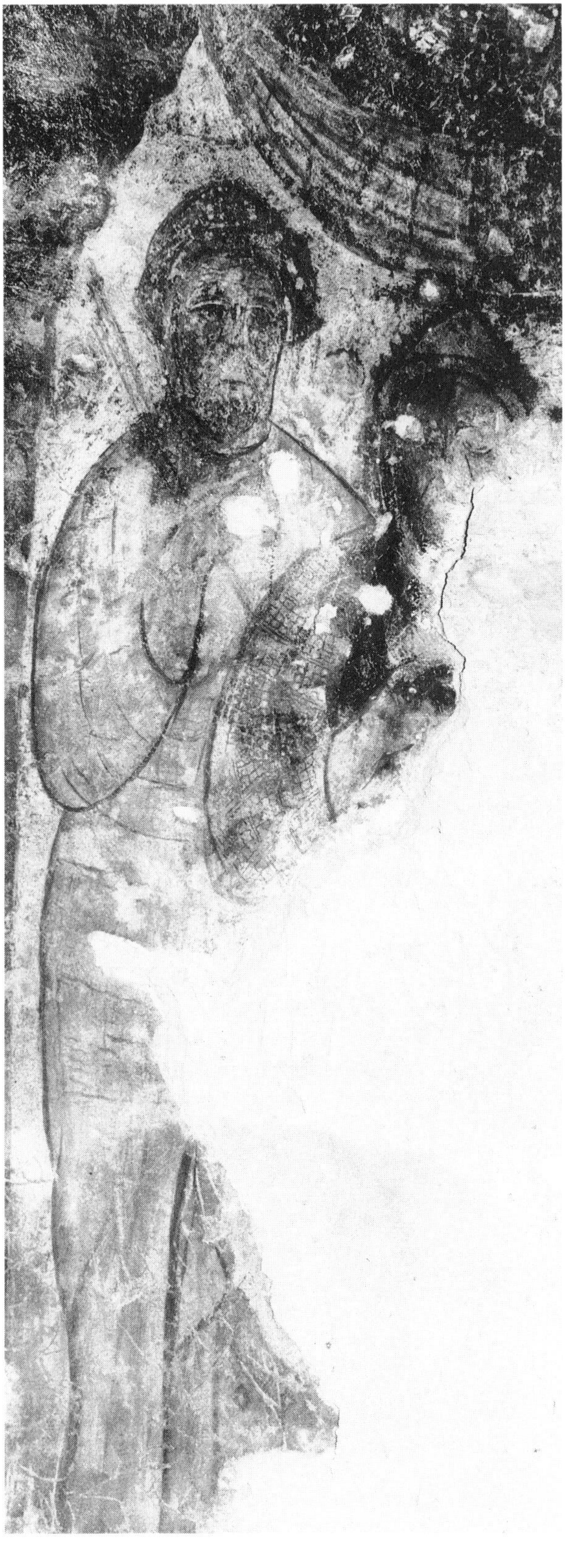

A wall-painting showing two infantry guardsmen. The man on the left has a mail coif around his neck and chin, the man on the right appears to be wearing a helmet with prominent rivets, as used by Sassanian soldiers a century earlier. (Author's photograph; in situ, Qusayr Amra reception hall, Jordan)

which was similar to the later western European *cuneos* cavalry formation.

The last Umayyad Caliph, Marwān II, made determined efforts to introduce fundamentally new tactics and is credited with abandoning the *khamīs* in favour of smaller *karadis* (cavalry squadrons) which manoeuvred in a single rank. Other newly introduced military terms indicated a use of special reconnaissance patrols, raiding formations of various sizes and squadrons of armoured cavalry, while the lack of new terms for infantry reflected their unchanging defensive role.

Knowledge of the enemy's tactics also lay behind efforts to overthrow the drum-master in a Turkish army, thus destroying his communications. On the other hand the long-established reluctance of Arab troops to fight at night seems to have applied well into the ᶜAbbāsid period. Other evidence from the early ᶜAbbāsid period describes cavalry dismounting to meet an enemy charge with their spears thrust into the ground like pikes. Other sources suggest that the ᶜAbbāsid army from eastern Iran included a higher proportion of cavalry which gave them greater flexibility.

Combat Styles

It may have been the case that the Romano-Byzantines, having learned so much from their Hun and Avar foes, were the leading force in Middle Eastern archery by the 7th century. By now the Arabs were using Byzantine rather than Sassanian archery techniques. Unlike the Sassanians, Romano-Byzantine archers emphasised the power rather than speed of shooting. Both Romano-Byzantine and Sassanian horse-archery was largely performed while the animal was standing still, a tactic continued by professional if not nomadic horse-archers of the later medieval Middle East. Meanwhile all Romano-Byzantine archers were advised to vary their 'draw' or technique of pulling back a bowstring by using various finger draws as well as the more powerful Central Asiatic thumb-draw. They were also trained to shoot at an angle to the enemies' ranks in the hope of getting around the opposition's shields.

The Sassanian habit of sending forward champions to duel *mard-u-mard* ('man-to-man') before battle was joined may have been exaggerated in idealised later tales. Nevertheless the Sassanians appear to have been responsible for transmitting, though not necessarily inventing, a new style of fencing which later became known in Europe as the 'Italian grip.' Here the forefinger was curled over one *quillon* of the sword guard, adding power to a forward lunge compared to the old 'Classical grip' in which all the fingers were wrapped around the hilt. Placing a finger over the *quillon* was not, however, a balancing device but increased the power of the blow by shifting the centre of balance closer to the tip of the blade.

This oversized Sassanian-style cavalry sword of the late 6th–early 7th centuries was found in the ruins of Byzantine Aphrodisias, by the Aegean sea. It was probably symbolic, though swords almost as large as this do appear in Sassanian art. (K. Erim photograph; Site Museum, Aphrodisias, Turkey)

Field and Camp Fortifications

Written evidence dealing with the Romano-Byzantine armies of this period indicates precise training in setting up and defending field fortifications. In the 6th century this went so far as to ensure that men in their tents kept spears upright at their feet with shield resting on the spearshaft and holding-straps towards the man while the rest of his kit was on his left as he slept. Beyond the camp's perimeter, spiked *calthrops* were scattered to lame an enemy's horse and perhaps cause the animal or its rider to cry out and thus alert a sentry.

Less is known about Sassanian encampments and field-fortifications except that these included a ditch and palisade, not to protect the baggage train but as a refuge in case of defeat. The Sassanians also built temporary defences with sandbags, a remarkably modern concept that might have originated in the eastern province of Khurāsān which was renowned for sappers and siege engineers throughout the Middle Ages.

During this period all armies used some kind of field fortifications or obstructions. Many armies, including the Byzantine, often travelled with their families plus substantial supply and siege trains, thus needing large base-camps. Once again the Strategikon supplies interesting details, including reference to numerous *paraportia* ('gates') in such field fortifications, probably for cavalry sorties. Another new departure for the Byzantines was the use of carts as defences; in other words an early form of *wagenburg* almost certainly learned from steppe peoples. The carts formed an outer defence guarded by infantry archers with a wide *intervallum* between it and heavy infantry plus cavalry stationed at the centre. Sassanian field fortifications sometimes also included wagons a bowshot to the rear of the infantry's main position.

The traditional view that early Muslim Arabs made no field fortifications could be misleading since it is clear that they used lines of hobbled camels and perhaps even the guy-ropes of their tents as effective barriers, these proving particularly effective against Byzantine cavalry who then became easy targets for infantry archers and javelin infantry. Within a few decades, however, Muslim Arab forces were using entrenched field fortifications even in minor inter-tribal quarrels.

WEAPONRY AND HARNESS

Central Asian weaponry had an influence on both late Roman and Sassanian military equipment, but most importantly upon Middle Eastern arms and armour from the 5th to 15th centuries. There were, however, few changes in Byzantine equipment during the 7th and 8th centuries, except for a tendency to use less armour as armies became fragmented and territorialised.

This carved relief of the story of 'Daniel in the Lions' Den' from Alcaudete near Jaén in southern Spain is usually thought to date from the late 5th–early 6th centuries, but the costume and head-cloths of the soldiers look unlike anything Byzantine or Visigothic. The carving may in fact date from about the time of the Muslim-Arab conquest, in which case these soldiers are probably based on the invaders. (Museo Arqueológico Nacional, Madrid, Spain)

Mail was the most important form of armour though there was a gradual increase in the use of small lamellar cuirasses. The last Sassanian armies may also have used more lamellar as part of a general spread of Central Asian fashions. According to the Byzantine *Strategikon* most infantry used bow and sword rather than spear and shield. This same source states that Central Asian cavalry were particularly adept in switching from sword or spear to bow with ease, many of them wearing mail armour while their élite had horse armour of iron or felt.

The situation of the first Muslim armies was different, though they were not as poor in weaponry as is sometimes believed. Most armour was clearly of mail, though a few champions may have had lamellar cuirasses. Helmets were worn by the élite and often included face-covering mail aventails as a defence against arrows. As the Muslim conquests expanded, so the Muslims captured more material. Nevertheless very few Umayyad cavalry used horse-armour, lamellar cuirasses or the more advanced form of helmet and arm-defences.

Archery

Simple bows lose their strength if kept strung, whereas it was thought better to keep fully composite bows strung. Whether this accounted for the use of two distinct types of bowcase, one for strung and another for unstrung bows, remains unclear. Both were used in many parts of Asia and eastern Europe by both settled and nomadic peoples.

The box-like quiver with a lid, as used by 6th-century Romano-Byzantine archers, was not suitable for rapid shooting whereas Sassanian archers, who did not adopt the powerful Avar-style bow, continued to rely on high-speed shower-shooting tactics. In this they relied on a Sassanian version of the finger draw in which an archer protected his right-hand fingers with a flap of leather.

Bows of simple or 'self' construction continued to be used in many regions, particularly large forms being found in Nubia. Whereas little is known about Byzantine bows during the 7th and 8th centuries, they were of the same composite construction as earlier, and the same is true of Sassanian bows. Once again more is known of Arab-Muslim archery despite the fact that the Arabs never achieved a great reputation as archers. The typical Arab bow was an infantry weapon made almost entirely of wood, since suitable horn for a fully composite construction was unavailable in Arabia. Yet this was not a simple longbow as seen centuries later in England. Some were simple bows, though of a more scientific shape than the plain longbow; others were constructed from several pieces of glued wood. Wood was often imported from Sassanian territory, Africa or India and included species related to the lime tree and dogwood. Some were probably similar to the massive 2m-long weapons used by Somali and Sudanese big-game hunters early in the 20th century. Other references indicate that partially composite and imported fully composite bows were also known. These, with a quiver for their arrows, were slung from the shoulder in infantry fashion. Although direct evidence is lacking, it seems likely that the 7th-century infantry archers of both Byzantium and the Sassanian Empire were similarly equipped.

Another distinctive weapon made its appearance at about this time. This was the arrow-guide which enabled an archer to shoot small, flat-trajectory dart-like arrows using an ordinary bow. Its precise origin remains a mystery, though it is first mentioned in the Middle East by Byzantine sources, where it was known as the *solenarion*. Such weapons were also used by infantry far to the east in Korea. Muslims soon learned of it from the Byzantines and, like their foes, found it useful against Central Asian harassment cavalry. They also adopted the pellet-bow, though this was used in hunting rather than war. A continued use of slings on the flanks of early Islamic armies is possible, though such primitive weapons would soon have been abandoned.

Swords and Daggers

Whether the short Arab *sayf* had any connection with the Romano-Byzantine *semispatha* or earlier *gladius* remains unclear, though its name stems from the Greek word for a sword, *xyphos*. Another form of cutting, but clearly not thrusting, short sword has been found in Nubian graves, with blades averaging 45cm. The Berber horsemen of North Africa were similarly described as wielding short swords, a surviving earlier example being virtually identical with a Roman *gladius*.

A 4th-century Armenian description of a Sassanian cavalryman stated that he wore a short sword on the right, a long sword on the left, and had a dagger partially hidden in the folds of his clothes. Romano-Byzantine sources from the 6th century also make a clear distinction between long and short swords. Several very large weapons have been found in Iran and neighbouring regions, the most extraordinary example having been excavated at Aphrodisias in western Anatolia and probably dating from the late 6th–early 7th century Sassanian invasions. The weapon was as tall as a man and may indeed have been more symbolic than for real use.

During the early Islamic conquests two distinct traditions of sword design existed in the Middle East: the long-bladed cavalry weapon preferred by Byzantines and Sassanians, and the short infantry sword for which early Muslim-Arabs were noted. In the steppes to the north the Khazars reportedly despised double-edged swords and preferred those with a single edge – clear indication that the sabre or its straight single-edged predecessor was already ousting earlier forms.

Spears and Javelins

Spears remained the most common weapon in almost all areas, but included several specialised forms. Those of 6th-century Romano-Byzantine cavalry had wrist-straps at the centre of the shaft, an idea copied from the Avars, early Arab spears being particularly long with reed shafts, the best coming from the Gulf coast or India.

Many peoples used javelins, particularly late Roman and early Byzantine troops. They were also characteristic of Ethiopian infantry, Berber and perhaps Nubian horsemen. In Arabia, however, javelins remained uncommon though one form of possible javelin or perhaps staff weapon was carried as a mark of command. More typical of this area was the very long and heavy *qanāh* spear with its large blade and pointed foot. It came in a variety of sizes, each with a specific name; those of cavalry averaging about 6½ metres in length, those of the infantry as little as 3 metres. The typical Persian and Turkish *miṭrād* spear was lighter and was also hollow, probably being made from two pieces of wood glued together like the later medieval western European lance.

Other Weapons

Various types of war-axe were used in early medieval Europe, but a completely different form was used by late Sassanian cavalry; this being confirmed in an early 7th-century Chinese description of 'the West'. Armenian cavalry, who were virtually identical with those of Iran, are similarly said to have used axes. A pre-Islamic carving from Ẓafār in Yemen illustrates a kind of axe which is also shown in undated rock-drawings from other parts of the Arabian peninsula, though in the hands of infantry. Another less reliable later source suggests that Sassanian cavalry used maces.

Tradition states that early Muslim-Arabs knew nothing of oil-based fire weapons; but they must have learned fast for they used incendiary grenades against Indian war elephants in 712.

Shields

Most 6th–7th-century shields were of traditional wooden construction, except in Arabia where hardened leather shields appear to have been the norm and in Tibet which was soon to become noted for the export of leather shields. In fact leather shields were more characteristic of Africa and the Middle East. Berber cavalry carried a small one, and a grave in Nubia yielded a large round leather shield remarkably similar to those of 19th-century Beja nomads from the same area.

Helmets

No archaeological evidence survives to support written evidence that low-grade Romano-Byzantine auxiliary troops used a leather helmet, but two early medieval crocodile-skin helmets have been found in Nubia. The fact that several early medieval helmets from the steppe regions of eastern Europe consist of metal segments sewn together with leather thongs or metal wire also suggests a nomad tradition of sewn leather helmets.

Whether the Iranian mail aventail attached to the rim of a helmet was the same as the 6th-century Sassanian neck and shoulder protection (*grīvpān*) is unclear. By then, however, the Romano-Byzantines had also adopted a padded neck and shoulder protection from the Avars. Called a *stroggulion*, it was only worn by cavalry.

Abundant pictorial and more limited archaeological evidence show that the majority of 6th–7th-century helmets were of segmented construction. Those of Byzantium and many in the Sassanian armies still consisted of two parts joined along a central comb, while a *spangenhelm* construction using four or more vertical segments was normal in Turkish or Central Asian areas. Quite which people produced the first one-piece iron helmet is unknown, though China seems an obvious candidate. Previous one-piece helmets had been of bronze, but a low-domed one-piece iron helmet was recently excavated in Transoxiana and dated from the late 7th or early 8th century. An Arabic description of a battle in 704 stated that some of the Tibetans and Turks wore what sounds like this same sort of protection. These also appear in Umayyad art at about the same time.

Body Armour

The Chinese regarded mail as a 'Western' form of protection, which meant the civilisations of Iran and the Middle East. Mail was the most common form of armour in the early Byzantine army, in Sassanian Iran and among pre-Islamic Arabs whose name for a mail hauberk, *dir*ᶜ, may again have originally come from the Persian *zirh*. The fact that this was cleaned in a mixture of oil, camel-dung and sand shows that it was indeed made of mail.

Within Iran the lamellar armour characteristic of the previous Parthian Empire declined in favour of the mail *zirh* hauberk, at least until the 6th century when Central Asian influence led to a revival of lamellar in the form of a *jawshan* cuirass. Whether the *tanūrigh* ('baking oven') armour attributed to the heaviest late Sassanian cavalry was a specific form of lamellar cuirass is not known. Meanwhile the use of lamellar persisted in neighbouring Transoxiana, Afghanistan and north-western India. A fragment of 6th- or 7th-century lamellar armour from south-western Iran confirms the use of alternating rows of iron and polished bronze lamellae as shown in the art of this and subsequent centuries. Only a few years later a T'ang Chinese source called such a mix 'lion armour'. Perhaps this lay behind the poetic 'panther', 'leopard' and 'lion' armours worn by heroes in several Persian, Georgian and Armenian medieval epics. Bronze lamellar armour had been used by eastern Mediterranean troops in the Roman army, but probably widened in popularity in the 6th century when there are references to gilded *thorax* cuirasses being worn by senior Romano-Byzantine officers.

According to the Byzantine *Strategikon* the last Sassanian armies wore lamellar as well as mail, but some doubt may be cast on the accepted translation by a Greek reference, dating from about 615, which states that a heavy *louriken* 'cuirass' consisted of three layers of *zaba* (mail). Lamellar armour was, in fact, much more characteristic of Transoxiana and Central Asia where a sophisticated variety of differently shaped and sized lamellae were laced together to provide more or less flexible sheet protection for different parts of the body.

Limb Defences

Romano-Byzantine limb defences, such as *gonuklaria* (greaves or chausses for infantry), *periknemides* (vambraces for infantry), and *keiromanika* (gauntlets) were probably made in both laminated and splinted forms. Fragments of splinted limb defences, probably dating from the 8th century, have been found in Byzantine-influenced regions of the Caucasus. The *bazabanag* – later called *bāzūband* – (arm protection) and *sirinapa* (leg defence) of Sassanian Iran would seem to have been of sophisticated construction, probably in the laminated style shown in great detail on 6th- to early 9th-century Transoxianan wall paintings. A remarkable pair of plated gauntlets is also said to have been unearthed in a late Sassanian context, though this dating remains dubious. Splinted and laminated limb defences, particularly for the arms but sometimes also the legs, remained more typical of Transoxiana than Iran and the Middle East. Arm-defences appear in Romano-Byzantine as well as Sassanian art and literature, and were occasionally mentioned in early Arab-Islamic sources, but they seem to have declined in popularity during the 7th and 8th centuries.

Horse Harness

A wood-framed saddle placed a rider's weight on each side of the animal's spine which was protected by a hollow chamber from front to rear of the saddle. But not all peoples adopted this new device which is seen as one of the most significant technological developments of the early Middle Ages. Arab and Berber nomads, for example, continued to ride on padded saddles or even reputedly bareback. Berbers are also said to have ridden without using a bit though this may have meant that they used all-leather or rope *bozal* bridles lacking metal elements. Such a *bozal* may also have lain behind the otherwise unique horse-harness found in Nubian graves, where the bit consists of a ring around the horse's mouth, almost like a metal *bozal*.

Stirrups, which enabled a horseman to use various weapons more effectively, were in use throughout the Eurasian steppes by the beginning of the 7th century. The earliest documentary reference to them in the Middle East or Europe is in the *Strategikon,* and the Byzantines may in fact have adopted them by the end of the 6th century. Sassanians, Armenians and Georgians do not appear to have done so before the Muslim-Arab invasions of the 7th century. Meanwhile stirrups feature in almost all the art depicting horsemen in neighbouring pre-Islamic Transoxiana. Greeks, Romans and Arabs were described as leaping into their saddles before the advent of stirrups, but the Iranians' larger war-horses meant that they were helped to mount in what became seen as a typical Persian manner. For many decades early Muslim Arabs regarded the use of stirrups as a Persian habit and a sign of weakness. They also rode on padded leather rather than the wood-framed saddles used by their northern neighbours and may even have controlled their horses by using an all-leather or rope *bozal* form of bit-less bridle, all of which suggests that early Muslim-Arab cavalry were not merely few in number but used primitive harness. When they did adopt metallic stirrups during the closing years of the 7th century, they copied the Turks rather than the Byzantines.

Horse Armour

Generally speaking the élite cavalry of steppe cultures made greater use of horse-armour than did their settled rivals, though styles varied considerably. For example the pre-Hunnic Bosphoran Kingdom of the Black Sea was under strong Sarmatian and Iranian influence in its styles of limited horse-protection, whereas the Turks of Mongolia and eastern Turkestan used much more substantial hardened leather lamellar horse-armour which covered the entire animal. Horse-armour used by the notably metal-rich Armenians was probably iron, while the Sassanians generally used lighter and more extensive felt or quilted horse-armour similar in shape to a later medieval European caparison. By the early 7th century both Byzantines and Sassanians used considerable amounts of horse-armour,

Right: *Rock carving, probably of Khusrau II, as a Sassanian heavy cavalryman, early 7th century. His horse wears armour on the front only; the rider has a full mail hauberk plus a mail coif or aventail. His quiver hangs from a belt, but his bowcase appears to be attached to the far side of his saddle. (Iranian Cultural Heritage Organisation; in situ, Ṭāq-i Bustān, Iran)* the Sassanians perhaps even putting armour on their war elephants. According to the Romano-Byzantine *Strategikon,* Avar-style horse-armour was useful for officers as it protected the animal's head, bridle and front, though not its rear. Despite the famous carving of a very late fully armoured Sassanian ruler riding a horse with such Avar-style lamellar armour protecting only the front of his horse, it was the Sassanian tradition of large sheets of felt or quilted material that influenced horse-armour in the early Islamic Middle East. A pre-Islamic carved relief from Ẓafār in Yemen may depict horse armour, though this is unclear and would in any case reflect the influence of occupying Sassanian forces. Clearly, however, the Arabs adopted such equipment within a few years, the first reference apparently dating from a Muslim invasion of Nubia in 651-2.

FORTIFICATIONS

Fortifications played a major role in resisting the 'barbarian' invasions in the Mediterranean and Middle East, but all settled peoples relied on fortification to some extent, even if the structures they erected were not so imposing and therefore

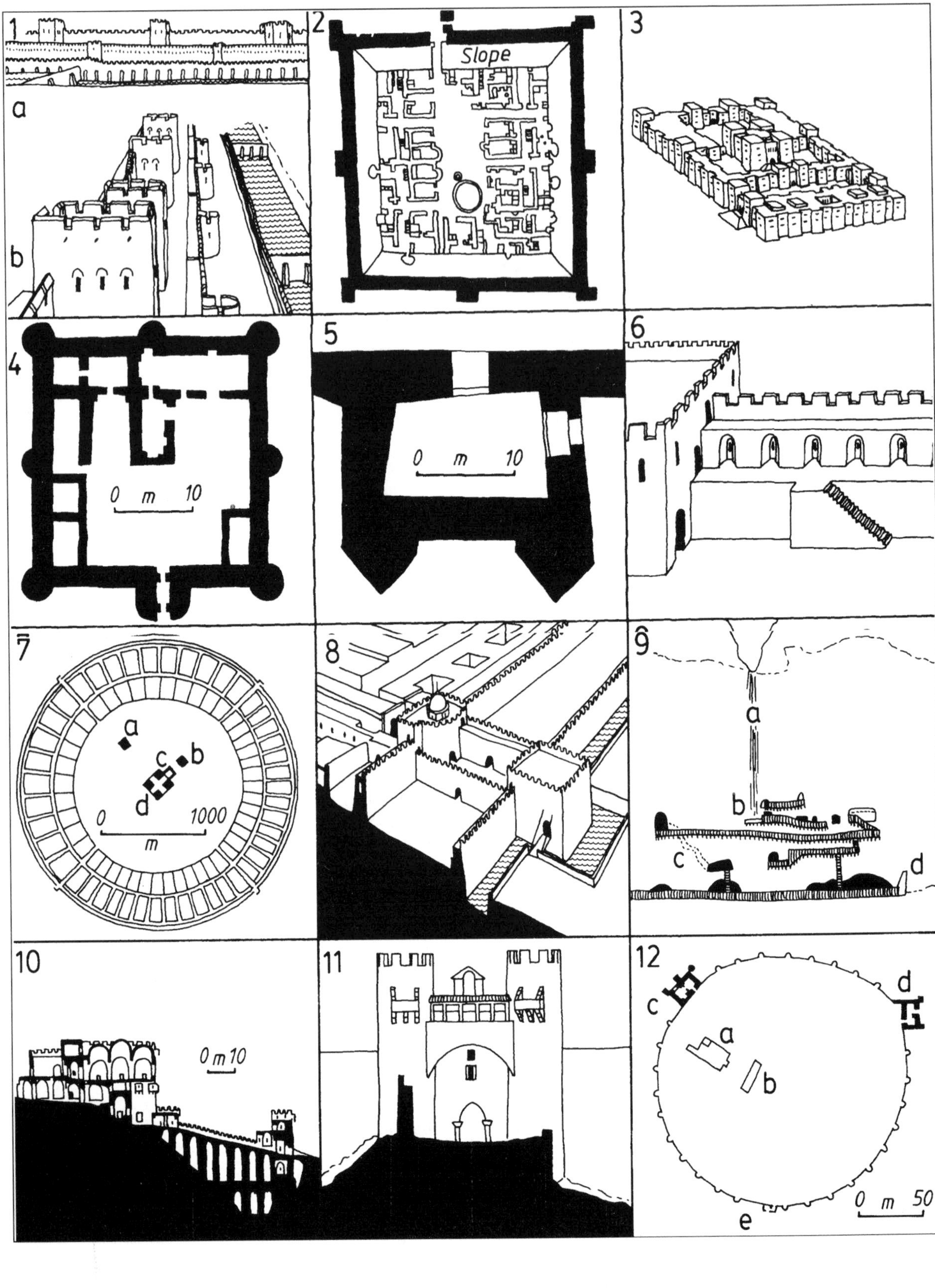
1
a
b
2
Slope
3
4
0 m 10
5
0 m 10
6
7
a
b
c
d
0 1000
m
8
9
a
b
c
d
10
0 m 10
11
12
c
d
a
b
e
0 m 50

not so carefully studied by archaeologists as those of the Romano-Byzantine and Sassanian Empires.

Romano-Byzantine Armies

The most dramatic example of late Roman military engineering is the triple land wall of the Byzantine capital Constantinople, now Istanbul, but the towers and gates of Thessaloniki and Antioch also witness the importance of military architecture during this period. A particularly ambitious programme of restoration and new fortification followed the reconquest of North Africa. Whereas the Romans had concentrated on protecting the main cities and roads, the Romano-Byzantines defended cities with separate citadels and erected isolated citadels within their territory plus numerous smaller *castellae* along the frontier. They converted some massive earlier religious and non-military structures to castles, a short-cut also seen in other parts of the Empire, but their techniques and designs were oddly old-fashioned. The 'bent entrance', for example, was already known in Asia but was not used here.

Along the eastern desert frontier monasteries and *lavra* (monastic retreats) were also fortified or had small *castron* (outposts) built nearby against the threat of bedouin raids. Fortification of the Syrian desert frontier followed a rather special pattern as a result of the delegation of defence to *phylarch* forces. The idea that there was ever a fixed Roman desert frontier is probably mistaken, but even as late as the 5th century fortifications were erected in an apparent effort to ensure that the tribes were not won over by the rival Sassanians.

Many small outposts were built in what is now Albania during the 6th century; and a narrow strip of Imperial territory along the Mediterranean coast from Alexandria to Cyrenaica consisted of a chain of small forts linking larger fortresses and towns. Libya and the provinces to the west were also characterised by fortified granaries, again designed to stop nomad raiders not invading armies. A chain of small forts watched over the vulnerable but vital road linking Egypt and Palestine, and others guarded desert road-junctions in southern Palestine. Within the more fertile province of Syria local magnates and bishops seem to have taken the initiative in constructing local refuges, though crude defences around many villages were probably erected by the inhabitants themselves.

This was a time of experimentation, several medieval features of defensive architecture evolving and spreading in rudimentary form before the coming of Islam. The *machicolation* which enabled defenders to shoot on attackers who had reached the foot of a wall was, for example, seen in <u>Gh</u>assānid-Byzantine Syria. Although the bent entrance was not used, Romano-Byzantine military architects sometimes achieved the same result by adding an extra wall ahead of existing 'straight through' gates. Nevertheless Byzantine military architecture of

Left: Fortification; Southern Europe and Western Asia

1. Reconstructed views of the triple land-walls of the Byzantine capital, Constantinople:
a from outside the city
b above the walls looking south. (after Meyer-Plath and Schneider)

2. The fortified market area at Qaryāt al-Faw, capital of the Kinda tribal confederation in central Arabia, 1st–5th centuries. (after al-Ansary)

3. The vast fortified palace of Ta'akha Maryan at Axum in Ethiopia. The overall complex was 80 x 120 metres. (after Krencker)

4. The fortified palace or reception hall at Atshān in Iraq, late Umayyad or early ᶜAbbāsid, mid-8th century. The fortifications appear more businesslike than in the similar Umayyad 'desert palaces' in Jordan and Syria.

5. Southern gate of the Byzantine acropolis at Ankara in Turkey, mid-7th century, showing the bent entrance and the characteristic 'keel-shaped' towers. (after de Jerphanion)

6. Restored view of a typical Byzantine gallery wall showing defence at two levels. (after Foss and Winfield)

7. The ᶜAbbāsid Round City of Baghdad, 754–75. This essentially a fortified palace enclosure including a 'wheel' of barracks and administrative offices. The residential and commercial city consisted of several suburbs outside this circular complex.
a Caliph's guards
b police
c palace and mosque. (after Cresswell)

8. Reconstruction of one of the four inner and outer gates of the Round City of Baghdad, mid-8th century. (after Herzfeld)

9. Reconstruction of the cave-fortress of ᶜAin Ḥabīs in northern Jordan. This was used by both Crusaders and Muslims in the 12th century, being based on an earlier Byzantine lavra or monastic retreat. The four levels of man-made cave must have been linked by external wooden walkways, as shown here.
a seasonal waterfall from the top of the cliff
b catchment system channelling water into a cistern in a second-level cave
c near-vertical tunnel excavated by Muslim engineers during their siege of 1182
d stone gateway across the entrance-path to the lower level of caves. (after Nicolle)

10. Section through the main entrance complex to the citadel of Aleppo, 1211, showing the gatehouse, a fortified bridge over the moat and the massive barbican which includes a reception hall. (after Michell)

11. The gate of Siguenza castle in north-eastern Spain, 1124. Although it was built after Siguenza was conquered by the Christians, its design is very similar to the Islamic military architecture of the Middle East, though on a smaller scale.

12. The fortified port of Qsar al-Saghīr on the shores of the Straits of Gibraltar in northern Morocco, 12th–14th centuries. It lies less than 150 metres from the existing beach, which might have been closer when these fortifications were built, and the interior would have been almost entirely filled with residential and commercial structures. The naval orientation of Qsar al-Saghīr is shown by the fact that its 'sea Gate', the Bāb al-Bahr, was also the largest.
a main mosque
b hammam public baths
c Bāb al-Bahr
d Bāb al-Sabta (Ceuta)
e Bāb al-Fas (Fez). (after Redman)

the 7th and 8th centuries seems to have been characterised by a hurried strengthening of fortifications, the conversion of massive existing structures such as theatres and a generally conservative style of defence.

Sassanian Armies

The Sassanians founded many new cities during the early centuries of their empire, but these were administrative or military headquarters rather than fortified centres. Later Sassanian walled cities were found around the frontiers rather than at the heart of the empire. At the same time many of the regularly planned fortifications of the war-torn Mesopotamian frontier, which earlier archaeologists have tended to take as Roman, may have been Sassanian. The Qaṣr al-Khusrau at the Sassanian military headquarters of Rustaq in Oman may be an interesting example of a simpler eastern frontier fortress. It is triangular in plan, built around a rocky outcrop, with no towers and a single sloping entrance dug through the rock from the base of the wall to its interior.

The most distinctive form of Sassanian frontier defence consisted of immensely long walls, dikes and ditches. This method of deterring nomad incursion had been known in Iraq for a very long time, but they began to re-appear during the reign of Yazdajird II in the mid-5th century. Different designs and methods of construction were used in different areas. For example the so-called Shāpūr's moat and similar 'ditches' in southern Iraq seem to have consisted of a ditch with widely spaced watch-towers plus one or more *anbār* (fortified barracks) to the rear. A wall that ran from the foot of the Caucasus mountains to the Caspian Sea at Darband was unique because the cost of its garrison was supposedly shared by the Sassanian and Roman-Byzantine Empires. It was impressive enough to be remembered in later centuries as *Bab al-Abwāb*, 'The Gates of Gates'. Another series of walls and ditches ran

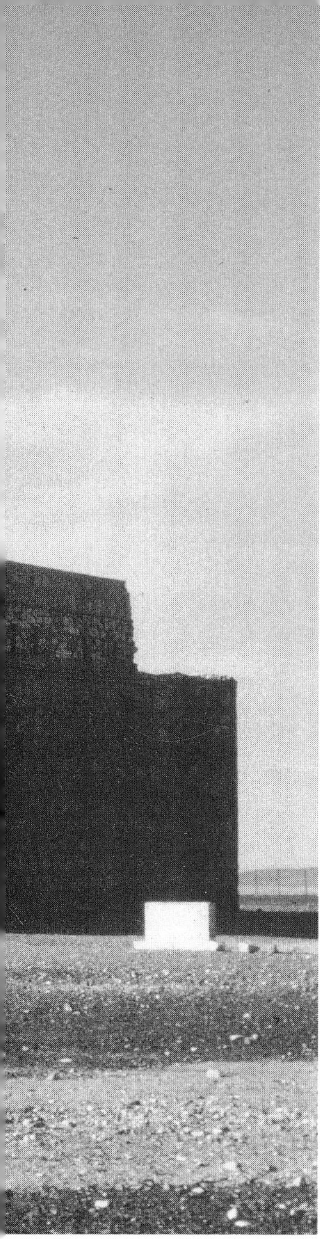

The fortified 'desert palace' at Qasr al-Kharānah on the edge of the Jordanian desert is one of the earliest surviving Islamic structures and was built in Sassanian rather than Romano-Syrian style. It has very little decoration, but included stables for camels and horses and probably served as a military staging post where Umayyad tribal armies could gather. (Author's photograph)

south of the Elburz mountains to keep out Daylami raiders, but the most ambitious of all was intended to defend fertile Gurgān. This was known as 'Alexander's Wall', though Alexander the Great had nothing to do with it; the Turks gave it the highly descriptive name of 'The Red Snake' because it meandered for at least 170 kilometres from the south-eastern corner of the Caspian, perhaps even having a later extension as far as the vital oasis garrison town of Marw. Behind these remarkable defences the late Sassanians may have developed a defensive Maginot-Line mentality, and the western walls were simply swept aside by the Muslim Arabs in the 7th century.

Pre-Islamic Transoxiana was a land of castles. Here the typical town was called a *shahristān,* having a citadel inside or next door, plus suburbs outside the main town walls. The local *dihqan* élite mostly lived in *kūshk* (villas), some fortified against nomad raids, in the fertile oases and river valleys. Many of these fortifications were allowed to crumble during the subsequent peaceful centuries of Muslim rule, but their advanced designs included a circular concentric plan, rectangular courtyards with large arched and shaded recesses at the sides, the fully developed bent entrance and colourful stucco decoration, all of which would influence Muslim defensive and civilian architecture.

Semitic and African forces

It is often assumed that peoples beyond the Romano-Byzantine Empire's desert frontier had no knowledge of fortification or siege warfare, but this is a great over-simplification. Even the primitive North African Berbers had a tradition of building simple fortified towers that dated back before the Roman occupation. In Syria and Jordan Roman frontier forts were largely abandoned during the 6th century, being handed over to Ghassānid Arab *phylarchs*. Several were then used for religious purposes. But the semi-nomadic and settled Arabs of these regions also erected many large fortified clan or tribal houses within some of the bigger fortresses, occasionally incorporating tall towers like those of medieval Italy. Meanwhile Ghassānid rulers built several fortifications within Byzantine territory and in the steppes. Beyond the Via Nova Traiana, which marked the limit of Romano-Byzantine rule, some 5th and 6th century settlements seem to have had simple fortifications while several unusual fortifications within the frontier zone may be Ghassānid *maṣāni*ᶜ (military bases) rather than Romano-Byzantine foundations.

On the other side of the desert Lakhmid rulers had two large fortresses or palaces within an outer wall of baked brick at their capital of al-Ḥīra. Deep inside the Arabian peninsula the powerful Arab Kinda tribal confederation had its capital at Qaryāt al-Faw set on a naturally defensible escarpment with an additional wall one kilometre from the town. In the middle of the town stood a fortified rectangular market with separate buttressed walls with a gate. The towers were of mud-brick on a base of carefully cut stones, the same system seen in Sassanian Iran and used in the Islamic Middle East for many centuries.

All but the smallest Arabian oasis communities had their own *uṭum* (tower forts) as refuges, some belonging to specific clans or tribes. These could not only house garrisons of several hundred men, but contained large arsenals and even had stone-throwing machines upon their roofs. The provisions for these tribal tower-houses apparently came from tribally owned gardens and date-groves in the surrounding oasis. None survive, though they sound similar to the tower-houses of Yemen, many of which are hundreds of years old.

A rarer form of Arabian fortification was a large open walled space such as existed at 6th-century Tāif in the southern Hijaz and perhaps at Jurash in the neighbouring ᶜAsir region. Tāif consisted of a rectangle of walls enclosing separate small and probably tribally organised hamlets. There were also plenty of more normal forts and castles in Yemen, some ruins near Yemen's Red Sea coast traditionally being attributed to a prince who led a rising against Ethiopian occupation. In reality the pre-Islamic Arabs, or at least those from towns and settled agricultural zones, were far from ignorant of military architecture or siege warfare.

The First Muslim and Umayyad Armies

During the first decades of Islamic expansion the Caliphs had little interest in building large defensive structures. Nevertheless written sources indicate that fortifications were erected in several places, those within Arabia almost certainly using the existing mud-brick technology and including one palace-castle in the Wādī al-Qurā built by an exiled Christian Arab leader. This part of the northern Hijaz continued to be noted for fortified and irrigated 'pleasure palaces' well into the ᶜAbbāsid period.

In contrast the Umayyad century saw many ostensibly fortified, so-called 'desert palaces' dotted around Syria and Jordan. Their fortifications were often more apparent than real, since it seems that the Umayyad ruling family took the appearance of Romano-Byzantine and Ghassānid or Lakhmid fortified residences as their model. Other 'desert palaces' were redecorated Roman frontier forts. On the other hand several Umayyad 'desert palaces' are located in strategic positions in relation to grazing areas and tribal migration routes, so perhaps their fortified appearance and rich decoration emphasised the existence of a new political order.

In general the closer Umayyad fortifications were to the Byzantine frontier, the more businesslike were their defences. Some must have served as fortified bases for the élite āhl al-Sham as well as being princely residences. Nevertheless the only Umayyad urban defences yet identified are those of the Citadel of Amman in Jordan though other cities are known to have been given defensive walls at about this time including Medina and Mosul. In Amman, however, a simple buttressed wall with small square towers is similar to the earliest known ᶜAbbāsid castles in Cilicia. Far to the east the Muslims also maintained some of the long walls erected by their Sassanian predecessors to keep Turkish nomads out of cultivated areas.

SIEGE WARFARE

Although a great deal is known about Romano-Byzantine siege warfare, little is known about Sassanian methods in this field and even less concerning the other peoples of western Asia and North Africa. The techniques of siege warfare saw the introduction of several significant new weapons. Torsion powered stone-throwing machines remained in widespread use, but the beamsling *mangonel* reached the Middle East from China via various Central Asian peoples in the 7th century.

A stretch of the southern end of the Land Walls of Constantinople (Istanbul) showing the outer ditch, the first main wall and the higher inner wall with its great towers. Although restored many times during the Middle Ages, the bulk of these walls date from the 5th century. (Author's photograph)

Aerial photograph of the Ghassānid phylarchs' fortified palace at Khirbat al-Baidah in southern Syria. (Fr. Poidebard photograph)

This was the man-powered type, not the counterweight *trebuchet* invented some five centuries later. Equally dramatic was a new form of petroleum-based incendiary weapon generally known as *'Greek Fire'* which is said to have been invented by an Egyptian scientist who fled to Constantinople following the Muslim conquest. Simpler petroleum- or bitumen-based incendiary devices had, of course, been known for centuries, but this new form was almost impossible to extinguish, would burn on water and could soon be propelled through a siphon.

Romano-Byzantine Armies

A mid-6th century military treatise, probably written by an engineering officer in Justinian's army, lists various methods of attacking fortified places, including mining and fire beneath the walls, the entrance to such a mine being protected by a wheeled 'tortoise' or wooden shed with additional screens against enemy archers. The author maintained that the 'modern' way to deal with such a 'tortoise' was to pinpoint the mine itself, then presumably attack it via a countermine. Efforts could also be made to bar the 'tortoise's approach with an earthen bank and then hurl bundles of burning hay, reeds or wood. As yet the mixture of oil and sulphur later known as *Greek Fire* was apparently more terrifying than destructive. Most interestingly, this source describes a wheeled wooden sling or gantry which could be moved along the top of a wall to drop a heavy stone on any enemy 'tortoise' that managed to reach the wall. This is virtually identical with a machine used in China, by Muslim defenders against Crusaders early in the 12th century, and which also appears in a mid-13th-century French manuscript. Most 7th-century Byzantine siege engines were the same as those used in previous centuries, including smaller anti-personnel stone-

One of the earliest surviving machicolations is over the door of a tower built in about 412, attached to a house popularly known as 'the barracks' in Umm al-Jamal, on the edge of the desert in Jordan. The inhabitants were Christian Arabs owing allegiance to the Ghassānid phylarchs and, more distantly, to the Byzantine Emperor. (Author's photograph)

throwing devices. When attacking enemy fortifications the Byzantines were adaptable and inventive, for example diverting the course of a river with sacks full of stones to erode a wall's foundations.

Sassanian Armies

Almost all that seems to be known about late Sassanian siege warfare is that the Sassanian army continued to be effective and used similar methods to their Romano-Byzantine foes. The Sassanians may, however, have used beamsling *mangonels* against Byzantine Jerusalem at the start of the 7th century and against the Muslims a few years later, though the precise chronology of the spread of the *mangonel* remains unclear. Although the Sassanians also used wooden siege-towers, mining remained the normal method of breaching a wall.

Pictorial and documentary evidence both indicate that the man-powered *mangonel* was known in pre-Islamic Transoxiana, the Muslims adopting it as the *manjanīq*. The Armenians also appear to have had considerable skill in siege and counter-siege, particularly in mountainous terrain. In southern Arabia, meanwhile, siege warfare largely consisted of taking control of surrounding locations then blockading a town into submission.

The First Muslim Armies

It is generally believed that nomadic peoples such as the northern Arabs and North African Berbers had neither capability in, nor enthusiasm for, siege warfare. Yet the fact that the Sassanians suddenly abandoned all save one of their fortified places in Iraq following their defeat in battle suggests that the invading Muslim-Arabs were not as ignorant of siege engineering as is often thought. Early forms of torsion-powered stone-throwing engines and the defensive use of incendiary devices were certainly known in early 7th-century western Arabia, though the Prophet Muḥammad's use of sections of moat to close the gaps between the outermost houses of Medina to make a defensive line manned by archers was regarded as a Persian idea. Nevertheless siege techniques remained simple, the attackers generally relying on the gradual destruction of gardens and palm groves to induce surrender. During the first phase of the Muslim conquests a small fort was sometimes built to block the anticipated approach route of a relief army. Nevertheless it is clear that the Byzantines and Sassanians under-estimated the Muslims' knowledge of siege warfare and the speed with which they learned. Within a very few years the newcomers were using *burj* (mobile wooden towers), *dubbāba* (movable wooden shed-like structures), *naqb* (mining techniques), the *manjanīq* (beamsling machine) and the *ᶜarrāda*, a term which seems to have covered most existing torsion-powered stone-throwing machines.

Armies of the Umayyad Caliphate

During the Umayyad period Caliphal armies not surprisingly became expert in siege warfare, having learned from many conquered foes. Nevertheless it was still quite normal for the defeat of a relieving force outside a besieged place to precipitate surrender without the need of a direct assault. This would remain characteristic of medieval siege warfare for centuries. On other occasions the prolonged blockade of a great city like Constantinople necessitated building barracks for the besieging troops and even digging frost-proof shelters for the winter. Like many soldiers, Umayyad troops probably used sexual imagery when naming pieces of military equipment. For example there was the 'splay-legged' mangonel and the *ᶜarūs* ('bridegroom') stone-throwing machine, the latter probably being a single-armed torsion-powered device.

NAVAL WARFARE

There was no real Romano-Byzantine navy until the later 7th century when a war fleet re-appeared in response to the threat posed by new Muslim-Arab fleets based in Syria, Egypt and North Africa. Meanwhile the Indian Ocean remained what it had almost always been; an arena for trade rather than for confrontation.

The Mediterranean and Atlantic

The technological revolution which was to have such a profound impact on medieval European shipping had the same impact throughout the Mediterranean, the greatest changes being a shift from hull-first to frame-first construction and the adoption of large triangular lateen sails (see Volume I). They would, however, take longer to spread beyond the Mediterranean out into the Atlantic.

At the end of the 6th century the Byzantine Empire dominated the Mediterranean and Black Seas from naval bases at Carthage, Alexandria, Acre and Constantinople. Yet there were few warships because the Empire faced no serious foes. This began to change when the Sassanians occupied Egypt and Syria then, more significantly, with the permanent Muslim conquests of these areas plus North Africa and the Iberian peninsula. Thereafter Mediterranean fighting galleys almost certainly had two banks of oars, tactics being based on small squadrons of ships using loose or compact formations plus ruses such as feigned flight. If there was any real difference between Byzantine and early Islamic warships it could have been in the taller forecastle of the latter; this being used for stone-throwing machines and to give a height advantage when boarding enemy vessels.

The first big Mediterranean sea battle for several centuries took place near Cape Chelidonia off the Lycian coast in 655. Here the Byzantines were defeated at sea and a skirmish on shore in a clash known as the Battle of the Masts because the Muslims had landed to cut tall trees for the masts and yards of their new fleets. This was a portent for the future, since lack of large timber hindered Muslim naval development throughout the medieval period. During the battle itself Byzantine ships were either moored in close formation or were tied together, the Muslims winning because of superior boarding tactics.

The important role of the Sassanian Persians in Middle Eastern naval developments has only recently been considered. During their brief occupation of the eastern Mediterranean they occupied the Greek island of Rhodes, almost certainly using captured Syrian, Cilician or Egyptian ships. The subsequent Muslim conquest of the same regions brought the Arabs to the shores of the Mediterranean, not for the first time but now as a great military power. Arabia had a far more important naval heritage than their initially cautious attitude to the Mediterranean might suggest. Pre-Islamic south Arabians had been raiding Sassanian coasts since the 4th century, and various other tribes from the Gulf and Red Sea regions also had a maritime tradition, the same peoples being selected as garrison troops for strategic coastal bases such as Alexandria following the Muslim conquest.

Byzantine naval attempts to retake Egypt convinced Muᶜāwiya, the governor of Syria and subsequently first Umayyad Caliph, of the need for a Muslim Mediterranean fleet. The first was built in Egypt, where all qualified sailors were registered for naval service, despite the fact that the overwhelming majority were still Christian, and used Acre and Tyre as forward bases. The bulk of the first marines were of Yemeni origin while Persian and Iraqi shipwrights were also brought from the Gulf to construct and man shipyards in Palestine and Lebanon. In fact it seems likely that Persian as well as Arab influence lay behind the spread of the triangular lateen sail from eastern seas to the Mediterranean.

Other naval bases and fleets were established in newly conquered Tunisia and Libya; the resources of wood, iron and tar essential to medieval naval warfare being available in North Africa. From the early 8th century onwards these new Muslim navies regularly raided the Byzantine-held islands of the western Mediterranean, mirroring the annual raids undertaken on land in the east. The main fighting ship was a galley called a *shīnī* which, like Byzantine galleys, had from 140 to 180 oarsmen. With very few exceptions the oarsmen in medieval galleys, Christian or Muslim, were paid volunteers – not slaves.

The Indian Ocean

During the 4th and 5th centuries the western Indian Ocean was dominated by merchants and seamen from the Sassanian Empire. Arabs also took part but Romano-Byzantines played a very minor role. The little that is known about Sassanian maritime organisation suggests that the empire's sailors – if not its merchants and naval commanders – came from the largely Arab coastal communities of the Gulf and of Oman. The Sassanian garrisons in Oman also guarded communications between Iran and isolated Sassanian outposts in Yemen. It is also interesting to note that an Arab chief who seized the island of Jazīrat al-Fara'ūn in the Gulf of Aqaba, using it as his lair from which to prey on Roman-Egyptian shipping, came from Sassanian territory. The same island was seized by another adventurer in the 6th century, this time a Jewish Arab from the Hijaz or Yemen.

Generally speaking, however, the pre-Islamic Arabs were more active as merchants than 'pirates', despite the fact that the incense trade of southern Arabia had collapsed following the Roman Empire's conversion to Christianity. Arab ships appear to have been more suited to deep-sea Indian Ocean voyaging than the confined waters of the Red Sea. Here large rafts carried goods between Africa and the Arabian peninsula. South Arabian inscriptions mention *ᶜ-s-d-q* (small ships) like the later Arab *sunbūk*), and *ᶜ-f-l-k* (larger vessels) like the subsequent Arab *fulk* or Byzantine *eflokion*, all of these operating from the Indian Ocean rather than Red Sea coasts. Sudanese Blemmye raiders who attacked Roman-Byzantine Sinai probably commandeered an Egyptian ship and crew for this operation, and the Ethiopian army which invaded Yemen in the early 6th century seems to have been carried in ships supplied by the Romano-Byzantine Empire. These vessels were, however, capable of adopting a dense formation close enough inshore to support the Ethiopians during their final battle with Dhu Nuwās, the famous Jewish-Arab king of Yemen. The Ethiopians' influence in the Red Sea area declined after they were forced out of Yemen by the Sassanians.

The first Muslim fleets in the Indian Ocean were built under Persian guidance. Here the Red Sea was the first area of naval concern to the new Muslim state and it was the disastrous Muslim naval expedition against Abyssinia in 641 which prompted the Caliph to ban maritime adventures, a prohibition which lasted several years. Egyptian grain which had previously fed the Byzantine capital of Constantinople now went to Medina in Arabia, the first capital of the Muslim Caliphate. A Roman canal linking the Nile to the Red Sea at Qulzum near modern Suez was also restored before 644. By 723, however, following the shifting of the Caliphal capital to Damascus, this canal silted up again. Meanwhile the Ethiopians' loss of control over Eritrea to various non-Arab Muslim tribes in the 8th and 9th centuries turned the Red Sea into a Muslim lake, consequently removing the need of warships in this area.

Riverine Warfare

In Egypt the Byzantines had a specialised riverine warfare base at Aswan to deal with the persistent threat of Nubian and nomad Beja raiding. Sassanian armies were also credited with good river-crossing capability, particularly in 7th-century Iraq, and this may have been inherited by Muslim Arabs who were to show the same ability in Transoxiana a century later.

The Citadel of Amman photographed by the Ottoman Turkish Air Force in 1918, showing the location as it was before the huge expansion of modern Amman. This was an important place in Umayyad times and the hill-top had a fortified wall around the top. The remains of the Umayyad palace at the northern end of the hill and the massive covered market-place in the centre can still be seen. (Royal Jordanian Geographical Society)

II
CHRISTIAN–MUSLIM CONFRONTATION
(750–1050)

CHRISTIAN–MUSLIM CONFRONTATION (750–1050)

Major Campaigns 51
ARMY RECRUITMENT 51
Christendom: The Byzantine Empire 51
Christendom: The Iberian Peninsula 54
Islam: The early ᶜAbbāsid Caliphate 54
Islam: The Successor States 56
Islam: The Fāṭimids (to 1171) 58
Islam: The Far Maghrib and al-Andalus 58
MILITARY ORGANISATION 59
Christendom: The Byzantine Empire and the Caucasus 59
Christendom: The Iberian Peninsula 60
Islam: The early ᶜAbbāsid Caliphate 61
Islam: The Successor States 63
Islam: The Fāṭimids (to 1171) 65
Islam: The Maghrib and al-Andalus 65
STRATEGY AND TACTICS 66
Broad Strategy 66
Troop Types 68
Battle Tactics 70
Combat Styles 73
Field and Camp Fortifications 73
WEAPONRY AND HARNESS 73
Archery and Slings 73
Swords and Daggers 74
Spears and Javelins 75
Other Weapons 75
Shields 76
Helmets 76
Body Armour 76
Limb Defences 78
Horse Harness 79
Horse Armour 79
FORTIFICATION 80
Christendom: The Byzantine Empire 80
Christendom: The Iberian Peninsula 80
Islam: The Early ᶜAbbāsid Caliphate 80
Islam: The Successor States 81
Islam: The Fāṭimids (to 1171) 81
Islam: The Far Maghrib and al-Andalus 82
SIEGE WARFARE 83
Christendom: The Byzantine Empire 83
Islam: The early ᶜAbbāsid Caliphate 85
Islam: The Successor States 85
NAVAL WARFARE 87
The Mediterranean and Atlantic 87
The Indian Ocean and Riverine Warfare 88

The establishment of the ^{c}Abbāsid Caliphate in 750 was followed by the gradual fragmentation of the Muslim world. As a result the confrontation between Islam and Christendom became a struggle between many armies using different military systems while a naval front also developed in the Mediterranean. Arabs declined in military importance, being supplemented by newly converted Iranians, Turks, Berbers and others. Many peoples were also drawn into the struggle on the Christian side, ranging from Nubians and Ethiopians to Italians, Armenians and Georgians. In some places the religious frontier was very blurred; for example a half-Armenian half-Arab dynasty arose in eastern Anatolia, claimed by neither side and an enemy to all. Minor religions or heresies similarly found a refuge in this area.

Muslim Arabs were the first conquerors of Central Asia to come from the west since Alexander the Great, but this first wave of expansion largely ended in the 8th century. Thereafter the Muslim world, like Christendom, was wracked by internal conflicts as the central authority of the Caliphs crumbled. Most regional successor dynasties had military origins, while these new rulers also modelled their smaller armies on that of the ^{c}Abbāsid Caliphate in its age of greatness. In Central Asia some Turkish peoples had already adopted Buddhism or Nestorian Christianity. Others gradually converted to Islam while those farther afield generally remained shamanist-pagan. One powerful group, the Khazars, adopted Judaism and blocked the further spread of Islam northwards for decades. Far to the west in Morocco most, though not all, of the Jewish Berber tribes gradually converted to Islam, the heretical Judeo-Muslim Barghāwata of the Atlantic coast remaining a powerful force into the 10th century.

Major Campaigns

751: Muslim-Arabs defeat T'ang army at Talas.
755–6: Surviving Umayyad prince seizes control of al-Andalus (Muslim Iberia).
755–72: Berber rebellion in North Africa.
778: Carolingian campaign south of the Pyrenees defeated at Roncesvalles.
801: Carolingians seize Barcelona from Muslims.
803–6: Annual raids by ^{c}Abbāsid army into Byzantium reach Black Sea.
811–19: ^{c}Abbāsid civil war; religious and provincial uprisings.
827: Muslim invasion of Sicily.
830–8: ^{c}Abbāsid-Byzantine war.
838–41: Muslims occupy part of southern Italy.
850: Muslims sack Rome.
852: Byzantine naval raid on Egypt.
861–73: War between Ṣaffārids and Ṭāhirids in eastern Iran.
869–83: Zanj rebellion in Iraq.
870: Muslims conquer Malta.
900: Sāmānids defeat Ṣaffārids.
901: Muslims complete conquest of Sicily.
901–6: Qarāmita fundamentalist uprising; seize Damascus, Basra.
905: ^{c}Abbāsids regain Syria and Egypt.
913–34: Abortive Fāṭimid invasions of Egypt.
920: Andalusians defeat León and Navarre at Val de Junqueras.
939: Andalusians defeated at Alhandega.
966–8: Byzantine invasions of Syria.
969: Fāṭimid conquest of Egypt.
974–5: Byzantine invasions of Syria.
981: Andalusians defeat Spanish Christian alliance at Rueda.
983–1055: Buwayhid civil war in Iraq and western Iran.
985: Andalusians sack Barcelona.
995–9: Byzantine invasions of Syria.
997: Andalusians sack Santiago de Compostela.
999: Qarākhānids seize Transoxiana.
Late 10th century: Christian kingdom of Axum in Ethiopia overthrown by Agau people from south-western Ethiopia; establishment of Zagwe dynasty.
1000–59: Byzantium conquers Armenia.
1008: Ghaznavids defeat Qarākhānids in northern Afghanistan.
1029: Ghuzz-Saljūq Turks invade eastern Iran.
1031: Abolition of Umayyad Caliphate of al-Andalus; fragmentation of Muslim Iberia.
1038: Saljūqs defeat Ghaznavids.
1042: Saljūqs defeated by Arabs at Tal Afar.

ARMY RECRUITMENT

Christendom: The Byzantine Empire

A constant feature of Byzantine military history was the empire's shortage of military manpower, particularly on the eastern frontier. This resulted in transfers of population to counterbalance losses caused by war, first against the Sassanians, then against the Muslims. Recruitment from outside the empire was another solution, yet the proportion of foreigners was higher when Byzantium was on the offensive, fewer in periods of defence.

By the early 9th century the *optimates* had been subdivided, the Germanic *gothograeci* declining in status and absorbed by the *opsikion* army which was itself a provincial force. Apart from palace guards, the *tagma* was the élite of 9th-century Byzantine forces, its recruits being eighteen or over and serving until middle age. The majority of Byzantine soldiers were probably obliged to serve in return for land or other privileges, eventually evolving into the famous *theme* provincial armies which first appeared in eastern regions. *Theme* soldiers would not have farmed their own land but might have lived off its rents, since the Byzantine authorities still tried to keep military and agricultural functions separate. *Theme* armies normally included four times as many infantry as cavalry, some foot soldiers forming a heavily armed élite by the 10th century, the cavalry by then also including *trapezitai* 'called *chosarion* by westerners' according to one Byzantine source – in other words hussars. Meanwhile poorly equipped regional javelin troops and infantry archers were not considered regulars.

Armenians continued to play a prominent role in all ranks, large numbers having migrated from those areas conquered

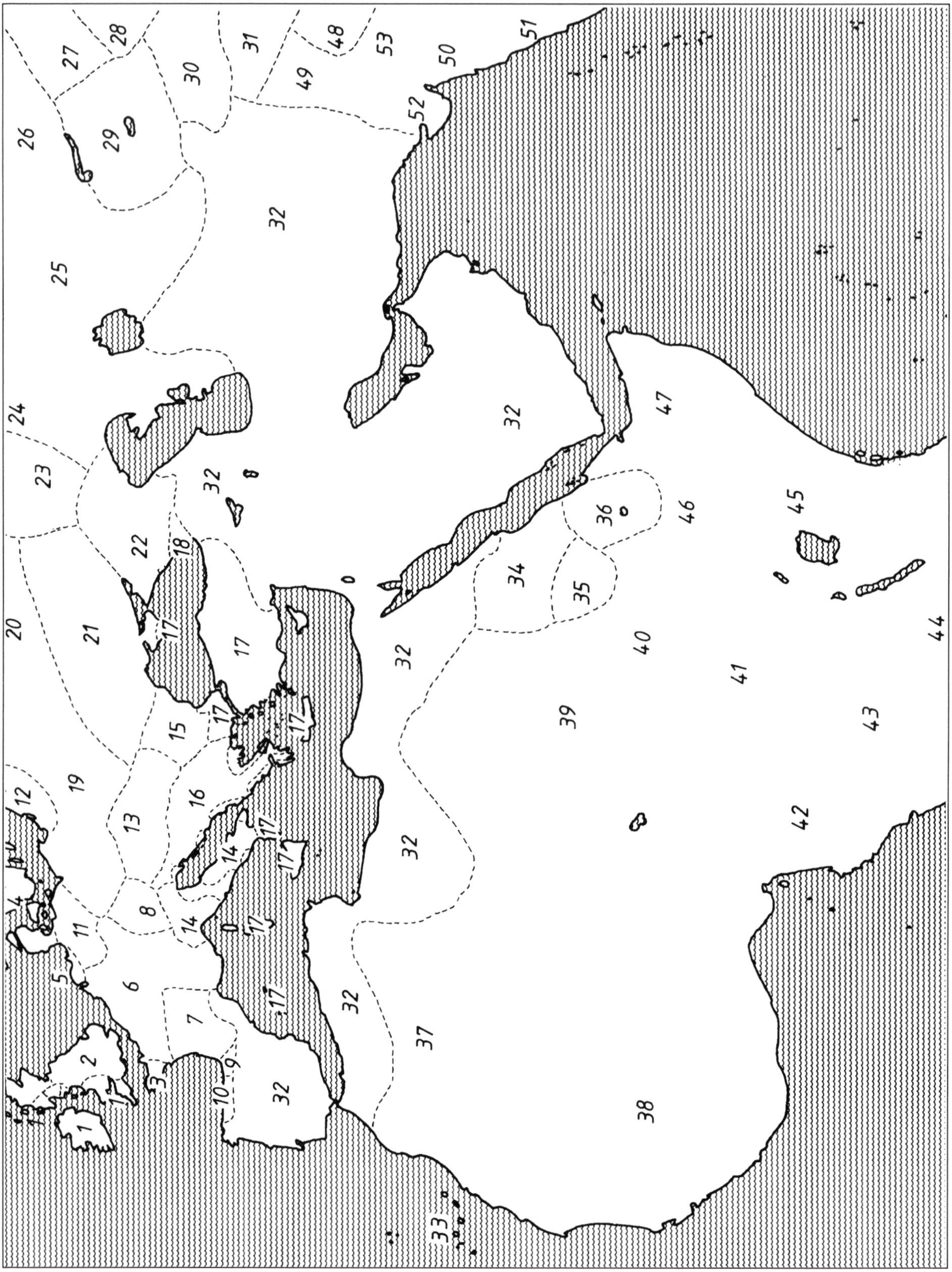
1
2
3
4
5
6
7
8
9
10
11
12
13
14
15
16
17
18
19
20
21
22
23
24
25
26
27
28
29
30
31
32
33
34
35
36
37
38
39
40
41
42
43
44
45
46
47
48
49
50
51
52
53

Left: Europe, northern Africa and western Asia, c.750

1. *Celtic kingdoms*
2. *Anglo-Saxon kingdoms*
3. *Brittany*
4. *Danes*
5. *Frisians*
6. *Frankish Kingdom*
7. *Aquitaine*
8. *Bavaria*
9. *Basques*
10. *Asturias*
11. *Saxons and Thuringians*
12. *Balts*
13. *Avars*
14. *Lombards*
15. *Bulgaria*
16. *Southern Slavs, Vlachs*
17. *Byzantine Empire*
18. *Lazica*
19. *Slavs*
20. *Finns*
21. *Magyars*
22. *Khazars*
23. *Volga Bulgars*
24. *Bashjirts*
25. *Western Turks*
26. *Kimāks*
27. *Kirghiz*
28. *Uighurs*
29. *Karluks, under Chinese suzerainty*
30. *Chinese Empire*
31. *Tibet*
32. *Muslim Caliphate*
33. *Guanches*
34. *Makuria*
35. *Alwa*
36. *Ethiopia*
37. *Berbers*
38. *Ghana*
39. *Darfur*
40. *Kordofan*
41. *Azande*
42. *Fang*
43. *Bakuba*
44. *Balunda*
45. *Kitara Ganda*
46. *Galla*
47. *Somalis*
48. *Pala Kingdom*
49. *Kashmir*
50. *Rashtrakutas*
51. *Kulam-male*
52. *Valabhi*
53. *Malwa*

by the Muslims. Most served in *theme* frontier armies and were recorded in Cyprus by the 9th century. The majority were infantry, being highly regarded as siege troops though they were said to be 'careless sentries'. Armenians were also suspect as religious heretics or, worse still, non-Christian Paulicians. This dualist faith believed in equal powers of good and evil, and later re-appeared as the Bogomil heresy in the Balkans and the Albigensian heresy of southern France. The brutality with which the Byzantines crushed the Paulicians led many to migrate into more tolerant Muslim territory where they fought for the frontier *amir* of Malatya. Their descendants, described as 'sun worshippers', were still to be found in 12th-century Syrian armies.

Other warriors crossed the frontier in the opposite direction, including some Arabs and Kurds. A small number of Persian Muslim troops also fled into Byzantine territory following an unsuccessful rebellion and settled in Byzantine Paphlagonia. Turks in the 9th- and 10th-century Byzantine army came from pagan, Buddhist and Zoroastrian regions and included the *Pharganoi* palace archer-guard from Farghāna, almost 3,000 kilometres east of the Byzantine frontier. In the mid-11th century the Byzantines also enlisted Pecheneg Turks from the Balkans.

At first Slavs played a minor role in Byzantine forces, though Bulgarians were recruited after Byzantium's reconquest of the southern Balkans. *Rhos* or Russians enlisted in the 10th century would have included men of Scandinavian origin since they played a significant role in the foundation of the first Russian state. But by the 11th century Slavs were sec-

A silver-gilt repoussé plate found in Siberia, but made in eastern Iran or Transoxiana in the 8th–9th centuries. The owner's name Pūr-i Vahman was probably a Persianised early Muslim Arab name, while the rider has late Sassanian east Iranian style costume and weaponry and uses stirrups not seen in earlier art. (State Hermitage Museum, St. Petersburg)

A wall-painting showing the Forty Martyrs, Byzantine 963–9. Their armour varies considerably, and includes a probably hardened leather cuirass worn by the warrior centre-left. Two of the soldiers are carrying single-edged straight swords. (Author's photograph; in situ 'Dovecote Church', Çavuşin, Turkey)

ond only to Armenians among non-Greek troops. Other western recruits included Albanian mountaineers from the Balkan *themes*, Romanian-speaking Vlach nomads from Thessaly and, in the mid-11th century, Norman heavily armoured cavalry from southern Italy attracted by Byzantium's ability to pay hard cash. Meanwhile the Emperor Constantine IX disbanded 50,000 Armenians, many of whom took service in Muslim Egypt.

Christendom: The Iberian Peninsula

From the 8th to 10th centuries the kingdom of Asturias maintained several aspects of Visigothic military tradition while at the same time reflecting Muslim influence from the south of the peninsula. The king had an entourage of élite *milites*, probably mounted, while infantry, probably recruited from free peasant communes, played the major role. But a different army developed as the Christians pushed southward, towns as well as noblemen now having a significant military function. In León and Castile free men were apparently equipped by the king to whom some townsmen and villagers perhaps owed direct service. Urban cavalry and infantry certainly existed by the 10th century. In 11th-century Castile powerful magnates or *ricos hombres* served as regional governors and in the ruler's retinue, some of them also having their own *masnada* (military retinue). The famous El Cid was from a lesser aristocracy of *infanzones*. The urban militias were divided into *caballería* (cavalry including non-noble *caballeros villanos* or 'peasant cavalry'), and *peonía* (infantry). In Portugal comparable *cavaleiros vilãos* came from richer non-noble families while the *peões* came from poorer land-holding families.

Islam: The Early ᶜAbbāsid Caliphate

The Umayyads were overthrown by an Arab, not Persian rebel army. This first ᶜAbbāsid force was, however, largely recruited from Arab troops long resident in Khūrāsān; to a large degree Persianised, they were often referred to as *Khūrāsānis*. Unlike the Umayyad army, this *Khūrāsāni*-Arab force was recruited on a territorial rather than tribal basis. Meanwhile the defeated Umayyad Syrian-Arab *Ahl al-Shām* remained in existence though with less prestige. The early cAbbāsid army also included a remarkable variety of other geographical units, sections of Baghdad being allocated to men from almost every eastern province. Although the first half-century of the cAbbāsid Caliphate saw Persian *Khūrāsāni* troops absorbed into the Arab military élite of that area, it was not until the death of the great Caliph Hārūn al-Rashīd that these Persian *Khūrāsānis* marched west and became a dominant military force in Baghdad.

The slave-recruited soldier known as a *ghūlām* or *mamlūk* first made a significant impact on Muslim military recruitment during the cAbbāsid period. Slavery in the Islamic world was, of course, based upon an entirely different principle from slavery in the Roman Empire. Slaves played virtually no role in agriculture or industry but became increasingly important as servants, administrative functionaries and above all as soldiers. The slave could also reach the highest level in Islamic society. Turks were considered the best soldiers, Greeks predominating in science and Chinese in art. Military slaves were normally freed when training was complete or when their first owner died. Some were prisoners of war, but the majority resulted from Central Asian chiefs selling their own people or oversized families their own children, the main sources being the Turkish Kimāk, Biīa, Ja'rīa, Khazlay and Ghuzz tribes, Samarkand being the main distribution centre. Those who entered the Caliph's service were generally given Turkish wives of slave origin, and were forbidden to intermarry with other ethnic groups in the belief that this would ensure the continuation of their fighting capabilities. One 10th-century general stated that 'a soldier must be able to take with him everything he possesses, wherever he may go, and nothing must hold him back'. Nevertheless the loyalty of such troops was not taken for granted so they were well treated and highly paid.

Turkish *ghūlāms* were never a majority of the cAbbāsid army and at first the *Khūrāsānī* Iranianised Arabs formed the military élite, their descendants in Baghdad becoming the infantry *abnā'* of later years; many Arab-*Khūrāsānīs* also migrated to the frontiers as volunteers. Subsequent recruitment of *Khūrāsānīs* largely consisted of Persian-speaking Iranians, many from the old Sassanian local élite of *dihqāns*. Meanwhile existing Arab units remained on the military lists, particularly in Syria and Egypt. Arab soldiers from settled

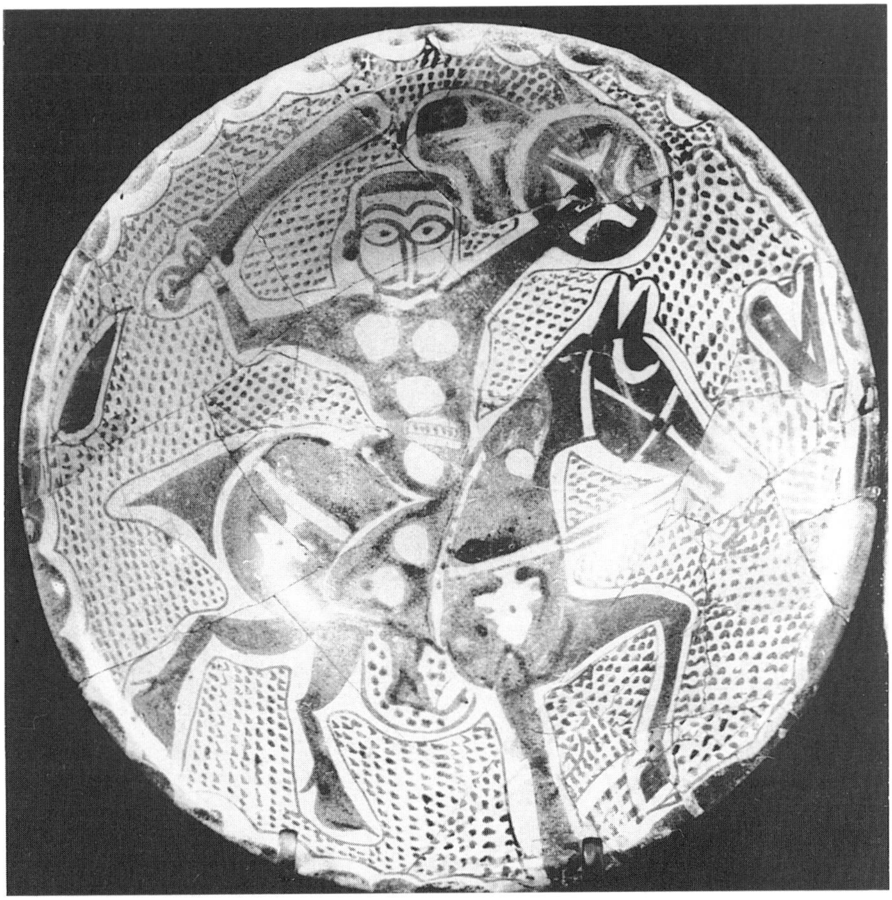

Lustre-ware dish from Iraq, 10th century. The cavalryman has a broad straight sword and a small shield. The pommel of his sword appears to be of the hollow ring type seen in various parts of early medieval Asia, from Japan and Korea to eastern Europe, and may reflect the extraordinary long-distance trade in weapons which took place at this time. (Keir Collection, London)

rather than nomadic communities also played a significant role along the Byzantine frontier, those of the Diyabakr region being notable in siege warfare. They also included the *Ṣaᶜālīk* ('ruffians') or adventurers grouped around local military leaders. In 833-4, however, Arab troops were finally removed from the military registers which meant that they lost their regular pay though they still served as volunteers.

There were some Turks in later Umayyad armies, but such warriors were first recruited in large numbers in the early 9th century following the Caliph al-Ma'mūn's offer of equal military status to Transoxianans who converted to Islam. This was part of an effort to Islamise Transoxiana and gain access to the vast pool of military manpower in the steppes beyond. The first Transoxianans included freeborn Turco-Iranian *Būkhārīs*, *Khwārazmians* and those known simply as 'Turks'. The first reference to Turkish *mamlūk* or *ghūlām* slave soldiers was in the bodyguard of the Caliph's brother in about 815. The bulk of the Caliph al-Muᶜtaṣim's Turkish troops in the mid-9th century were probably prisoners of war. These troops, free and slave, included established military leaders from beyond the Muslim frontier as well as ordinary fighting men who arrived with their entire families, many settling in the Caliph's new capital of Samarra in Iraq. Within three generations they were fully Arabised however. The old ᶜAbbāsid army was disbanded in 936, some years before the Buwayids of Iran seized control and reduced the Caliph to a figurehead. It was also in the 10th century, as the ᶜAbbāsid Empire fragmented, that the fully developed *mamlūk* or *ghūlām* military system was finally introduced, large numbers bolstering the defences of Tarsus in the face of revived Byzantine aggression in the mid-10th century.

Although slave-recruited *mamlūks* came to dominate the military establishments of the Muslim Middle East, other troops served in the Caliphs' armies during the heyday of ᶜAbbāsid power. These ranged from specialist elephant-mounted fire-troops from Sind to a rabble of urban poor called the *ᶜurāt* who fought with desperate courage but minimal weaponry. The importance of these sources of recruitment may be reflected in the number of known senior generals from each group during the reign of the Caliph al-Muᶜtaṣim: 24 *Khūrāsānīs*, 19 Transoxianans, 17 Arabs, 12 Turks and 2 *abnā*.

Islam: The Successor States

Following the fragmentation of ᶜAbbāsid authority, political power largely fell to soldiers of Turkish *mamlūk* origin. This slave-based élite perpetuated itself by purchasing its own military slaves. It was characterised by a system of *sinf* or loyalty in which *mamlūks* were devoted to those who had purchased, trained and paid them, a loyalty which could rarely be inherited by the sons of their first military patron. In fact the freeborn sons of *mamlūks* were regarded as much inferior military material.

Similar *sinf* loyalty was found among other military groups, often based on ethnic origin or regimental identity. Arabs, for example, re-appeared in a leading military role in the 10th century, as did tribal Kurds from the Zagros mountains, more recently converted Daylamis of northern Iran and the still backward Berbers of North Africa. As the Caliphate fragmented, its smaller successor states recruited from limited areas.

__Below:__ A 10th-century plate from Nīshāpūr in eastern Iran. Cavalrymen in mail and lamellar armour, as seen here, appear on many pieces of ceramic from this source. But this plate is unusual in also illustrating a foot soldier carrying a large oval shield and two javelins as were used by the famous Daylami infantry of the period. (Author's photograph; Museo Nazionale d'Arte Orientale, inv. 2629/3258, Rome)

Nevertheless many rulers believed that recruiting from several different sources promoted competition, hindered military coups and provided a balance of forces. The Sāmānids, for example, used Turkish *mamlūks* to balance the indigenous Iranian *dihqān* aristocracy while also enlisting Tajiq eastern Iranians, Turkish tribal horse-archers from Central Asia, Arab and Kurdish cavalry, Daylami and Hindu Indian infantry. The *dihqāns* may subsequently have been absorbed within the assorted *muṭṭawi'a* (religious volunteers). These tended to be orthodox Sunni Muslims and included *ghāzīs* or men who dedicated their lives to defending Islam's frontiers, retired old soldiers, runaway peasants and *āzādayān* (short-term volunteers from prosperous families). Fiercely fundamentalist *khawārijis* were also operating in the eastern provinces though they were more prominent in the Middle East. In western Iran Daylamis and troops from neighbouring Ṭabaristān balanced the ubiquitous Turks. In fact poor and mountainous Daylam became a major exporter of infantry, forming the original power base of the Shia Muslim Buwayid dynasty. The Shia Daylamis' traditional rivals, the Sunni Gilānis of the south Caspian coast, were similarly infantry.

Farther west the Arab Banu Kilāb of northern Syria and the Banu ᶜUqayl of northern Mesopotamia established their own dynasties and armies while the Kurdish Marwānid dynasty in Armenia was founded by the leader of the local *ṣaᶜālīk* and *ghāzī* (adventurers and volunteers). The 10th century saw some of the most varied armies in Muslim history. The Ḥamdānids of Syria, for example, enlisted ex-Byzantine converts as well as Armenians who retained their Christian faith. One army of the subsequent Mirdāsid dynasty was commanded by a Christian vizier while the walls of Aleppo were defended by the city's Christian, Jewish and Muslim inhabitants.

The population of Syria had defended its own cities since the 8th century. By the 9th century Damascus had a *maᶜūna* (unit of auxiliaries), in the 10th Aleppo's resident garrison seems to have incorporated the old *shurta* (local defence force), while the 11th century saw the rise of *ahdath* (militias) owing primary allegiance to their own cities. The *ahdath* did not, however, take root in Iraq though a volunteer force raised in Baghdad to face a threatened Byzantine invasion in 971-2 included ordinary citizens armed with bows.

The successor states of Egypt and North Africa developed in a different way, drawing upon different sources of recruits. Slaves of black African origin played a significant military role

Right: *Early 10th-century 'Goliath' carved on the outside of the Armenian 'Church of Gagik', on the little island of Aght'amar in Lake Van, Turkey. The Philistine giant has a scale or lamellar cuirass, laminated arm defences, a mail coif or tippet and apparently a hood like that found at Moshchevaya Balka on the other side of the Caucasus mountains. The hilt of his straight sword is also remarkably similar to that found in the Sirçe Liman shipwreck off western Anatolia. (Author's photograph)*

in Ṭūlūnid Egypt, serving as infantry alongside Turkish and *rūmi* cavalry who were probably ex-Byzantine prisoners of war. Armenian troops were already important enough to have their own suburb in the Egyptian capital, while the rest of the Ṭūlūnid army consisted of Daylamis, local Egyptian Arab tribes and *mawāli* (Arabised clients of various Arab tribes).

The first independent Aghlabid rulers of what is now Tunisia felt threatened by *jund* territorial troops and so created a slave-recruited black African army mirroring the Turkish *mamlūks* of eastern Islam. The Aghlabid force which conquered Sicily was led by an Arab élite but largely consisted of Berbers from the Huwwārah tribe, plus smaller numbers of Khūrāsānis and African slave soldiers. As the invasion progressed, many Greek-speaking Sicilians also converted to Islam and fought alongside the invaders.

Islam: The Fāṭimids (to 1171)

The army of the Shia Muslim Fāṭimid Caliphate had a long history and its recruitment changed considerably from the early days in North Africa, through the conquest of Egypt to the final period when the state was essentially a military dictatorship with a puppet Caliph. Berbers of the Kutāma tribe, for example, formed the backbone of the first armies and remained important until the mid-11th century, together with the Berber Ṣanhāja tribal confederation, though Barqīya from Libya and Bāṭilis cavalry from Morocco were fewer in number. However, virtually all the Berber units were disbanded by the Armenian *vizier* Badr al-Jamāli in 1073.

Many Fāṭimid sailors came from Sicily and Libya while naval troops included Berbers and Arab bedouin. An élite of 'black' marines was particularly feared, but whether these were of African origin or were from Zawīla in the Sahara remains unknown. Africans certainly played a major role. In the early 11th century Maṣmūda Saharan Berbers formed the bulk of Fāṭimid infantry. Other 'blacks', as they were called in the Arabic sources, included Zanj and other mercenaries from Eritrea, Ethiopia and Somalia as well as slaves purchased via Nubia. Nubians themselves also served in Fatimid armies.

Although fewer in number, bedouin Arab troops were highly influential, particularly after the capital moved from North Africa to Cairo. Whole tribes migrated into Egypt from Palestine, Syria and northern Arabia, some as auxiliaries, others as professionals. Meanwhile Arab soldiers served the Fāṭimids in Syria and Palestine; where the port of Asqalan was to hold out against the invading Crusaders for several decades.

Arabic-speaking but non-tribal people had a limited military role, normally in urban *ahdath* militias and as untrained rural volunteers at times of crisis. The substantial Jewish population of Jerusalem had close connections with the Fāṭimid garrison at the time of the First Crusade, though largely on the supply and support side.

The Fāṭimids' first Turkish *mamlūks* were inherited from the previous Ikhshīdid dynasty. Experience of fighting Turkish *mamlūks* in Syria then rapidly convinced the Caliph al-ᶜAzīz to build a new army on the same pattern. Not surprisingly the Fāṭimids' eastern foes did not want élite recruits to reach Egypt and so the Fāṭimids could not recruit very many. As a result the eastern-style élite of the later Fāṭimid army was an extraordinary mix of prisoners of war and freebooting mercenaries.

Daylamis also reached Egypt where they were particularly welcome because, like the Fāṭimid Caliphate itself, they were Shia Muslims. They then seem to have formed the élite corps of *naffāṭun* (fire-troops). The first Armenian soldiers were probably ex-Byzantine troops captured in Sicily, but larger numbers arrived after Armenian frontier units in the Byzantine army were disbanded in the 11th century. Thereafter Armenians became so important that several Fāṭimid *viziers* were selected from among their commanding officers.

Among other assorted nationalities recorded in Fāṭimid ranks were Kurdish archers in the *shurta* of Damascus, Russian prisoners from the Byzantine army, Christian Sicilians, western European and Greek mercenaries, both known as *rūmis,* and slaves of supposed Slav origin known as *ṣaqāliba* consisting of European slaves purchased via Venice and Spain.

Islam: The Far Maghrib and al-Andalus

The military history of Morocco from the decline of the ᶜAbbāsid Caliphate to the rise of the Murābiṭin (Almoravids) in the 11th century is little known. The most powerful group was the Ṣanhāja confederation whose military élite were described as spear-armed horsemen. On the Atlantic coast the Barghawāta sub-tribe of the Maṣmūda Berbers had diverged so far from Muslim orthodoxy that they were declared 'infidel', their numerous and effective cavalry finally being crushed by the Murābiṭin in the 11th century.

The Murābiṭin themselves carved out one of the largest empires in medieval history, covering half the Iberian peninsula and reaching right across the Sahara. Its first army was recruited from several Berber tribes including the Jāzūla, Lamṭa, Zanāta and Maṣmūda. As the army grew it recruited large numbers of African slave-troops of whom the *ḥasham* formed a cavalry guard alongside a small force of Christian Spanish captives and mercenaries. By the time the Murābiṭin invaded Spain their army included a small number of Arabs and perhaps a few Turkish horse-archers.

Al-Andalus, Muslim Spain and Portugal, had a distinctive military structure following the overthrow of the Umayyad Caliphate in 750. A surviving member of the Umayyad family then escaped to establish a new Umayyad state in Iberia which became the most advanced civilisation in western Europe. Its armies were as mixed as those of the east, though drawn from very different sources. In the early days non-Turkish *mamlūks* formed an élite based in Cordoba around which free Andalusian fief-holding soldiers assembled, plus mercenaries, religious volunteers and urban militias. The freeborn local elements were, however, severely downgraded in the late 10th century to be replaced by enlarged *mamlūk* and mercenary units.

The first Berber conquerors either returned to North Africa or were absorbed into the new Arabic-speaking Andalusian military élite. However, a new wave of Berber cavalry recruits was enlisted by the *vizier* al-Manṣūr at the end of the 10th century, retaining a separate identity after Umayyad rule in al-Andalus collapsed some decades later.

'Acclamation of an Emperor', in a Byzantine manuscript of c.860. New Byzantine rulers are believed to have been raised on a shield by their troops as part of the ceremony whereby the army showed its loyalty to a new ruler. Here the soldiers have long straight swords in scabbards attached to their belts, in the manner copied from the Persian Sassanians or Turks. (Chludov Psalter, Historical Museum, Moscow)

The earliest military élite of al-Andalus was Arab, however, and its descendants formed Andalusian *jund* provincial armies based upon older tribal identities. Andalusian Muslims as a whole were very mixed, including families descended from converted Iberian Christians and Jews, mercenaries and military slaves from many lands, and the original Muslim conquerors. An aristocracy of *Mozarab* or 'Arabised' Christians also played a military role, usually in inaccessible frontier regions where the authority of Cordoba was weak. In the 9th and 10th centuries *mamlūks* were recruited from Christian prisoners of war and slaves, these forming an élite corps of heavy cavalry. At the same time Christian and Muslim, European and African mercenaries were enlisted; those based around the palace in Cordoba being called *ḥashām*.

During the first half of the 11th century al-Andalus fragmented into an astonishing array of tiny states known as *taifa* kingdoms. Most were too small to maintain a large army, their recruitment patterns reflecting the ethnic or tribal origins of their feuding dynasties: Arab, Berber, *ṣaqāliba* Slav or Andalusian. Some enlisted Christian mercenaries while a few relied on indigenous urban militias. The army of Granada, though dominated by Berbers, included some *ᶜabīd* ('white slaves') and *wūsfana* ('black slaves'); one commander of this polyglot army being the Jewish poet Samuel Ha-Nagid.

MILITARY ORGANISATION

Christendom: The Byzantine Empire and the Caucasus

The Byzantine Empire was divided into military zones in the mid-8th century, and the following century saw increasing emphasis on the varying of recruitment of military units to inhibit coups. By the 10th century the Byzantine state was highly militarised, the bulk of effective troops being on the frontiers rather than around Constantinople. Metropolitan forces such as the *tagmata* and guard regiments served as strategic reserves to be sent where needed. These palace units included the *hetaireia,* mace-armed *manglavitai* security police and *pantheotai* who may have been guards officers. When such guards regiments declined in effectiveness, their men could garrison provincial centres, their officers remaining in the palace for parade purposes while new guards such as the *athanatoi* ('immortals') of the Emperor John Tzimiskes were raised. The most famous of these were the 11th-century *Varangians* recruited from Scandinavian, Russians and eventually Anglo-Saxons.

Ordinary *tagmata* soldiers lived on their pay while some *theme* troops were also paid in cash, though the majority probably lived off the rents and produce of estates which they could not sell without government permission. To check the kit and competence of provincial units the Byzantine government held occasional *adnoumia* musters or reviews. If a man had become too poor to maintain himself as a soldier he might become a batman, be transferred to the irregulars or be sent to garrison a fort.

The structure of the Byzantine army was complex by the 10th century, with the *domestic* as the most senior officer, assisted by the *topoteretes* who commanded provincial detachments of the élite *scholae* in peacetime or half the *scholae* on campaign while the *chartoularios* commanded the other half. The rest of the army was theoretically divided into *turma* brigades of three to five *droungoi* battalions each consisting of five *banda* companies. There were normally three *turma* in each *theme*, commanded by a *turmach* who was junior to a general and had the status of a *protospatharios*, though in the Byzantine Empire such honorific titles did not necessarily indicate a specific military function. The *bandon* (pl. *banda*) was the smallest tactical cavalry unit, traditionally consisting of about thirty cavalrymen, whereas the normal operational formation was a *parataxis* of 300 men. The ideal 10th-century Byzantine infantry formation consisted of 500 armoured *oplitai* regulars with 200 javelin and 300 archer auxiliaries.

The structure of *theme* armies differed from that of metropolitan forces, the *theme* system also being extended to the European coastal provinces in the 9th century. Eastern *theme* were commanded by a *strategus*, except for the *Opsikion theme* near the capital which was under a *Count*. Meanwhile a *Count of the Walls* was responsible for the defence of Constantinople itself.

With the fragmentation of Muslim territory, the organisation of Byzantine frontier defences was divided into smaller units to face more numerous enemy concentrations. Military commands known as *kleisourai* ('mountain passes') now appeared, each with its own small force, these *kleisourai* still being backed up by *theme* armies. By the late 9th century, however, the initiative had passed to Byzantium and the frontier was reorganised yet again with the addition of offensive forces under the command of a *dux* or *turmach*. Small infantry formations were similarly recorded in the mountainous east, under officers with the Armenian title of *zorovar* or general.

Anatolia, whether Greek-, Armenian- or Kurdish-speaking, had in fact provided the best troops in the Byzantine army. The eastern frontier was home to the heroic *akrites* frontier warrior whose exploits filled the pages of medieval Greek tales. Elsewhere the less epic but equally important provincial militia came to be known as *stradioti*. Shortly before the Saljūq Turkish storm erupted from the east, the Byzantines occupied Armenia, replacing its military obligations with taxes. As a result much of the Armenian military élite emigrated to find employment in Christian Georgia or in Muslim Egypt. As the Armenians declined, their place was partially filled by Norman, *Varangian* and other western mercenaries. These did not form fixed garrisons but acted as an élite field force operating from the main Byzantine strongholds. When faced by relatively small numbers of Saljūq and other Turkish nomad invaders, however, they and the remaining indigenous Byzantine forces collapsed.

Some western *themes* supported navies rather than land forces while areas such as Albania were still largely defended by tribally organised indigenous peoples. In contrast the local armies of Byzantine southern Italy, and of Sicily until this fell to the Muslims, remained highly professional. Nevertheless the Italian *theme* armies were disbanded in about 1040, to be replaced by local part-time militias supported by units sent from Constantinople.

Virtually nothing seems to be known about the military organisation of the Christian kingdom of Georgia, but Christian Armenia regained its ancient independence under Muslim suzerainty in the 9th century. It also had a notably well-equipped army capable of fending off both Byzantine and Muslim interference, at least until the Byzantines took over in 1044. Here the countryside was dominated by a military aristocracy of *nachararks* most of whom had their own *azatk'* forces maintained by an agricultural class of non-military serfs.

Christendom: The Iberian Peninsula

The military situation south of the Pyrenean mountains differed considerably from that to the north. In Christian Iberia urban militias were an early development, defending their own territory and supplying troops for one of several Christian states in what became Spain and Portugal. This did not reflect earlier Visigothic influence, but other aspects of military organisation probably did to varying degrees. Asturias and Galicia retained a strong Visigothic heritage. León and Castile were superficially influenced by France while Aragon and Catalonia had much in common with southern France. Here military duties were normally linked to land-holding such as the freehold *alodial* estates of Catalonia. More typically western European *benefice* (feudal *fiefs*) could also be found. In Navarre, León and Castile the nobility were largely independent of royal interference while their military tenants again normally held land freehold. In León and Castile the citizens of important towns were also almost free of outside interference.

Of course the military organisation of these Christian states changed over the centuries, Visigothic influence being strongest in Asturias where, by the 9th century, the king had an entourage of *milites* or professional cavalry maintained by *prestamo* (*fiefs*). They were led by a *comes* or *count* assisted by a *majordomi* or *majorini*. While it has been suggested that the continued importance of cavalry again reflected Visigothic tradition, infantry predominated in the earliest years when the Christians only held the mountainous northern fringe of the peninsula. Cavalry came to the fore after the expanding states reached the rivers Douro and Ebro in the 9th and 10th centuries. Navarre was now squeezed out of a southward push known as the Reconquista, and its armies remained largely infantry.

Newly important cavalry forces were recruited from the aristocracy and from towns. It was, however, difficult to impose a traditional European aristocratic military organisation in areas which had become very urbanised under Muslim rule such as the Ebro valley. Meanwhile in the sparsely populated central plains noble *caballeros hidalgos* served as élite cavalry in return for *fiefs* or pay, non-noble *caballeros villanos* or *caballerías* (lighter cavalry) being raised in towns and villages, serving, like the *pedones* or *peonías* (urban infantry), in return for tax and other privileges.

On the island of Sardinia, and to a perhaps lesser extent Corsica, the normal western European feudal system simply did not develop. Instead the local military and administrative structure reflected Roman origins, Sardinia remaining divided among rural chieftains and organised in several *judicatures* dominated by local dynasties.

Islam: The Early ʿAbbāsid Caliphate

The ʿAbbāsid army or *ahl al-khūrāsān* which overthrew the Umayyads in the mid-8th century was built upon a new military register in which troops were listed by family and place of origin, all having theoretically equal status be they Arabs, Persians or of mixed origin. All these men were supposedly full-time professionals, their loyalty to the ʿAbbāsid dynasty verging on the fanatical. But this loyalty focused upon a family rather than an individual or upon Islam as a whole, leading to problems when future ʿAbbāsid claimants plunged the Caliphate into civil war.

This huge military machine was provided with a suitably large military base – the remarkable Round City of Baghdad. It was intended to be a vast garrison at the centre of an empire which was now the biggest state in the world. Guard units, other regiments and paramilitary militias all had their cantonments; the vital *ḥaras* (security forces) and *shurṭah* (police) lived within the outer circle of the Round City, the Caliph's palace occupying its centre. Other troops lived in suburbs of a sprawling metropolis far outstripping Byzantine Constantinople or the tiny towns of medieval western Europe in size.

Other well-supplied garrisons served as mobile provincial armies against rebels or invaders. The Anatolian frontier was also reorganised in the late 8th century, with a new region known as the *awasim* being established behind the existing Umayyad *thughūr* as a support or base area. But while this was happening the ʿAbbāsids lost control of much of the Arabian peninsula, becoming, like their pre-Islamic predecessors, rulers of the agricultural and urban but rarely the nomadic parts of the Middle East.

Early ʿAbbāsid armies consisted of twice as many infantry as cavalry while even the latter often acted as mounted infantry. During the 9th century, however, true cavalry armies emerged, by which time the army as a whole had divided into more functional units with a clear distinction between garrison and expeditionary forces. The former maintained internal security, the latter defended the frontiers. These forces consisted of *murtāziqah* (regulars) and *mutaṭawiʿah* (volunteers); the professional heavy infantry being called *ḥarbīah*, archers *rāmīah*, while there were also *naffāṭun* (a corps of fire troops). Regiments were more like private armies recruited by the *qā'id* (general) who commanded them. Otherwise military units were organised on an ad hoc basis. The new title of *amīr al umarā'* (leader of leaders) was adopted for the ʿAbbāsid army's overall commander. Theoretically an ordinary *amīr* led 10,000 men, a *qā'id* 1,000, a *naqīb* 100, and an *ʿarīf* 10 men.

Senior officers were largely selected on the basis of hereditary privilege or political reliability rather than proven military ability and there was no promotion structure. The 10th-centu-

Fragment of painted paper showing a Turkish cavalryman on the left and a Berber or Arab infantryman on the right, from Fustāt in southern Cairo; 11th–12th centuries. This painting probably represented the two main parts of the Fāṭimid army in a display of unity which was not always evident in reality. (Museum of Islamic Art, inv. 13703, Cairo)

'St. Phiobammon' in a wall-painting from the Church of ᶜAbd Allāh Nirqi; Nubian, early 11th century. The horseman is in the typical pose of an eastern warrior saint, but he is wearing a belt with the decorative pendants adopted in Egypt and much of the Muslim world as a result of Turkish influence. He also has a short-sleeved mail hauberk. (Author's photograph; Museum of Coptic Art, Cairo)

ry Arab observer al-Jāḥiz of Basra made some remarkably modern comments on senior military command. In his opinion it had nothing to do with physical courage but required mental courage, strength of character, calmness and the ability to face the possibility of disaster, as well as a willingness to accept responsibility.

The dominant military class lived in towns and, like their Umayyad predecessors, officers owned estates which they rented out to the peasantry. In addition to its loyalty to the ᶜAbbāsid family, the army was characterised by strong bonds of loyalty between officers of the same generation, and between officers and *tabᶜīyya* (ordinary soldiers), the resulting mutual loyalty being known as *iṣṭināᶜ*. Muslim troops also tended to be better paid than their Byzantine or western European contemporaries. But an increasing use of extremely expensive *mamlūk* troops meant that governments needed ever greater amounts of hard cash. By the mid-9th century revenues were insufficient, so the military were permitted to collect taxes directly, this 'tax farming' eventually leading to a widespread militarisation of the state. Eventually it also led to the *iqṭāᶜ* system of non-inheritable revenue-providing estates. The *iqṭāᶜ* was not, however, a feudal system of military obligation in return for land as seen in western Europe but was merely a method of supporting troops, often as an additional layer on top of existing *jund* provincial forces. *Iqṭāᶜs* also varied enormously, ranging from provinces for senior commanders to a single house for a low-grade frontier soldier.

The role of *istirᶜrāḍ* or *ᶜarḍ* (military reviews) was very important during the ᶜAbbāsid period, since it was here that a soldier's kit, competence and pay were assessed. Here too the *Dīwān al-Jaysh* ('war office') selected best, moderate and inferior troops then allocated their duties; the best going to the ruler's palace units, the moderates to senior commanders and the inferior to distant provinces. The competence of mercenaries was also assessed. Another highly structured element of the ᶜAbbāsid army was the *iṣṭabl* (stables) responsible for maintaining the numbers and quality of cavalry mounts, having its own rank and pay structure. Similar though smaller organisations soon appeared in provincial capitals and quite small fortresses.

Early ᶜAbbāsid Baghdad has been described as a military presence of staggering variety and dimensions, but, perhaps because of its power as well as its turbulent reputation, the Caliph al-Muᶜtaṣim built a new capital at Samarra to accommodate his new Turkish *mamlūk* army, only a few Arab and North African guards units accompanying him from Baghdad. In Samarra each military group had its own quarter where they were kept strictly separate from the civil population. Even so the Caliph's élite *jund al-ḥadra* and *rajul al-musāfiyah* guards remained a minority, only half of these being *mamlūk* Turkish horse-archers.

The bulk of the army was always stationed in the provinces, professional troops garrisoning tense areas while quieter regions had local forces or part-time militias. Since the Caliph's capital in Iraq and strategically vital Syria were both close to the Byzantine frontier, the governors of these regions put a high priority on military affairs, including the *shurṭa* garrisons which were still more than mere police forces, auxiliary *maᶜūna* and conscripted *ajnād (jund)* who were now more of a local militia. Closer to the frontier were the *awasim* and the *thughūr* which to some extent overlapped. Basically the *thughūr* consisted of military provinces along the frontier while the *awasim* formed a staging area behind it. The *thughūr* developed from the previous Umayyad left and right frontier flanks, each facing one of the main mountain passes into Byzantine territory. In the *awasim* all resources were supposedly dedicated to defence and, unlike the situation on the Byzantine side of the frontier where the Emperors gradually lost control, the Caliphs' constantly re-asserted their authority. Nor did the *thughūr* become a home to a semi-independent warrior élite like the Byzantine *akritoi*. Instead the urge to *jihād*, or fighting in defence of Islam, was so strong that professional soldiers and short-term volunteers constantly arrived in the area, but under the strict control of military governors who maintained Caliphal authority.

The eastern provinces of the Caliphate meanwhile developed their own distinctive character, even before the fragmentation of ᶜAbbāsid authority. In parts of Transoxiana, for example, the first small but highly mobile Muslim Arab garrisons tended to live in villages around the main cities, living on the rents of newly won estates. Local converts and non-military settlers also gathered into *futūwa* groups, their members being known as *fityān*, who were essentially religious but marched alongside military forces as volunteers. They were never under effective government control and sometimes developed heretical views. By the 9th century some had their own fortified *ribāṭs* where the *fityān* both prayed and helped maintain security. In later decades some *futūwa* groups accepted Jews and Christians as provisional though not full members. The influence of militarised Buddhist monasteries upon these organisations was probably quite strong.

The fragmentation of the vast ᶜAbbāsid Caliphate resulted from financial collapse, not military defeat. The later Caliphs simply could not pay their troops and had to ask powerful local governors to take over this responsibility, even eventually in Baghdad itself to which the government had returned following the unsuccessful experiment of Samarra.

Islam: The Successor States

The military structures of the successor states reflected local circumstances though they did attempt to imitate the great days of ᶜAbbāsid power. The 10th century saw the full introduction of the *mamlūk* or *ghulām* system pioneered by the ᶜAbbāsids themselves – at least in areas able to enlist such expensive slave-recruited élites. Retaining the loyalty of such *mamlūks* was even more difficult and all too often they become wandering bands of highly effective mercenaries,

Right and below: Panels on an ivory box, depicting various warriors; Byzantine, 11th–12th centuries. Although classical in spirit, the military equipment shown in this detailed carving reflects that of Byzantine light infantry of these centuries. (Author's photograph; State Hermitage Museum, St. Petersburg)

though there were examples of regiments lasting for up to three generations through continued recruitment.

In 10th-century Armenia, despite its close proximity to the centre of the Caliphate, several minor Muslim and Christian principalities emerged, relying on their own military resources, receiving minimal assistance from the centre and rarely helping one another in the face of Byzantine aggression. The way in which Muslim frontier regions defended themselves is illustrated in detailed information concerning the fortified city of Tarsus. Here counter-raids were normally summoned during the main Friday religious service. Much of the city's population was still dedicated to *jihād*, the *ghāzis* or 'fighters for Islam' including permanently resident *muta'ahhilīn* and temporary *ʿazzāb* (bachelors) some of whom remained in Tarsus until old age. When these *ghāzis* were called to arms they assembled at specified city gates, younger men acting as messengers to summon older troops. Banners were given to cavalry units while infantry were attached to such cavalry formations. The younger *ghulām* soldiers were commanded by older men who also acted as their religious guides or *shaykhs*. The numerous towers of Tarsus seem to have been owned by citizens rather than by the government and served as barracks for both temporary and permanent warriors. Other houses inside the town were designated as *ribāṭ*, *dār*, *zāwiya* or *khānqāh* for volunteers, some of them being large enough for 150 troops. One *dār* was described as

Panels on an Andalusian-Islamic carved ivory box, made at Cuenca in 1026, from the Treasury of the Monastery of Santo Domingo do Silos. Both the infantry archer and the cavalryman are wearing mail hauberks and, with the exception of the infantryman's large Arab-style composite bow, are equipped in the same manner as their northern Christian foes. (Museo Arqueologico, Madrid)

having living-rooms upstairs, while shops on the ground floor were rented out to raise money for horses and weapons.

To the south-east, *ahdath* urban militias reached the peak of their military effectiveness in the early 11th century, having absorbed earlier militia structures and in several cases being capable of raiding Byzantine territory and fighting in open battle against Byzantine invaders while their members were often paid regular annual salaries. Farther south in Egypt the bedouin remained a state within a state, playing a minimal military role. During this period Egyptian armies were very similar to those under direct ᶜAbbāsid rule, though the Ṭūlūnids were credited with introducing elephants to the country for parade rather than operational purposes.

In Iran the Ṣaffārid dynasty also attempted to ape ᶜAbbāsid military structures, but this period was more notable for a revival of pre-Islamic Persian military traditions beneath a Muslim veneer. The annual review of Ṣaffārid troops was, for example, carried out at the festival of *Nawrūz,* the old Zoroastrian Persian New Year. Here, in the presence of the ruler, two drums signalled the assembly, whereupon the men and their kit were inspected before being paid. The specifically Persian military rank of *sarhang,* a junior officer between an ordinary cavalryman and an *amīr,* was also used by the Ṣaffārid army.

More is known about the Sāmānid dynasty of Transoxiana and eastern Iran. For example it included a *dīwān al-jaysh* (war office), a *dīwān al-barid* (communications or postal service) and a *dīwān al-mushrif* (intelligence-gathering service). In the 10th century several minor *dīwān* departments were also set up, one specifically for urban police and another mobile department for the army while on campaign.

The forces of the Shia Muslim Buwayhid dynasty of western Iran were organised in a manner halfway between the old mixed armies of the ᶜAbbāsids and the new *mamlūk* forces. It was also characterised by a system of public oath-taking ceremonies, and of elaborate chains of such oaths intended to cement loyalty between the ruler and his officers, between officers themselves, and between officers and men. It was not particularly effective and Buwayhid rulers chose to hold separate military reviews for their Shia Muslim Daylami infantry and for their Sunni Muslim largely Turkish cavalry.

Far away on the easternmost frontier of the Muslim world the little-known Qarākhānid state ruled the steppe frontier of Central Asia, straddling the Tien Shan mountains into what is now Chinese Turkestan. Here an Iranian minor aristocracy of *dihqāns* saw a brief military revival though the Qarākhānid state was essentially Turkish and clung to nomadic military traditions. By the 11th century it was divided into tribal fiefs whose loyalty to the ruler depended solely on his military success.

Islam: The Fāṭimids (to 1171)

The Fāṭimid conquest of North Africa and Egypt led to considerable reversion to older forms of organisation, largely because the Fāṭimids were unable to build a new-style slave-recruited Turkish army. In North Africa, in the early days, Fāṭimid forces were essentially tribal, though subdivided only into *ᶜirāfa* (tactical or pay units) like the Umayyad army of two centuries earlier.

Once in Egypt, however, the Fāṭimids attempted to copy classic ᶜAbbāsid military organisation. Although there was a substantial garrison in the new capital of al-Qāhira (Cairo), the bulk of troops were stationed in Syria with a secondary headquarters in Damascus or Aleppo. Southern Egypt was defended by a smaller garrison at Aswan, though in general the Fāṭimids maintained friendly relations with the Christian states of Nubia.

The Fāṭimid army consisted of regiments identified either by the ruler who raised them, their commanding officer or their technical function. One distinctive formation was the *hujarīya,* a training structure arranged in age groups. Regiments were subdivided into smaller units down to groups of ten men. Ranks included three grades of *amīr,* three grades of lower ranking *khāṣṣa* or ruler's attendant, and *qā'id* much as in the ᶜAbbāsid army. The highest rank was held by the commander of Syrian garrisons who was usually known as the *amīr al-juyūsh* (commander of armies) or *amīr al umarā'* (commander of commanders).

Officer loyalty was encouraged by the system of patronage known as *iṣṭināᶜ* as in the Buwayhid army, whereas the ordinary soldiers' loyalty tended to reflect ethnic origin and be focused on their own senior officers. The Fāṭimids did not, however, adopt the Buwayhids' system of *iqṭāᶜ* (fiefs) for some time. Instead officers took over the task of tax farming in the 11th century, handing the revenues over to the government which then returned a certain proportion as a supplement to normal pay. By this time some senior *amīrs* were also involved in financing long-distance maritime trade. A special army secretariat listed the names of all soldiers, where they were stationed, and organised reviews. Troops themselves fell into four financial categories depending on whether they were assigned to a castle and assimilated into the local population, subject to rotation between regions, attached to a mobile field army, or were mercenaries paid via their commanding officers, most of this complex military administration being carried out by Christian scribes.

Detailed information survives concerning Fāṭimid parades. For example regiments took part in Muslim religious festivals as well as secular events such as the opening of the canals to start Egypt's annual irrigation. On such occasions each man was given a paper which explained where he was to go and what he was to do, suggesting widespread literacy, this often involving displays such as forming two 'fortresses' of cavalry and infantry based upon battlefield formations. Soldiers riding elephants also took part.

Islam: The Maghrib and al-Andalus

Little is known about the military organisation of North Africa following the decline of the ᶜAbbāsid Caliphate. The *iqṭāᶜ* system was introduced to Muslim Sicily, the western part of the island also being divided into *iqlīm* districts each with a *jund* territorial army. In Morocco small states comparable to the better-documented *taifa* states of the Iberian peninsula dominated the north before the whole country fell to the Murābiṭin in the late 11th century.

In al-Andalus the Arabs and Berbers took over existing territorial estates while some of the previous Germanic Visigothic élite also survived, converting to Islam and being absorbed within a new military structure. In fact a link between military obligation and land-holding did characterise al-Andalus to a greater degree than elsewhere in Islam. Nevertheless fortresses and fortified towns formed the basic framework of military organisation.

The Umayyad rulers of Cordoba largely adopted ᶜAbbāsid military systems and at first the Andalusian army consisted of *junds*, each based in a *kūra mujannada* (military province), these being backed up by élite units in the capital. One *jund* was that led by the *wālī* (governor) of Seville who had about 500 regular cavalry based at Carmona. Descendants of mercenaries and *mamlūks* in the capital formed a similar *jund* around Cordoba. By the 10th century the military *dīwān* ministry was itself divided into three sections dealing with professional mercenaries, provincial contingents and short-term volunteers.

The command structure was much like that of the ᶜAbbāsid army, except that in 10th-century al-Andalus a *qā'id* commanded the army and there were the additional ranks of *Ṣāḥib al-shurṭa* (head of police) and *Ṣāḥib al-madānah* (city governor). The government stables near Cordoba were a huge organisation with squads of one hundred riders each commanded by an ᶜ*arīf* (an officer under the overall authority of the cavalry commander and looking after 2,000 war horses). Andalusian *jund* cavalry, many maintained by *iqṭāᶜ* (*fiefs*), were organised into squadrons and operated alongside a less disciplined army of infantry volunteers. ᶜ*Arḍ* reviews were as important as elsewhere, these being organised by a specially commissioned officer who also arranged large-scale *burūz* (parades) before major military expeditions.

The Andalusian frontier was structured along much the same lines as the ᶜAbbāsid frontier facing Byzantium. Highly militarised *thughūr* (provinces) opposed the Christian states; Saragossa facing Catalonia, Aragon and Navarre; Medinacelli facing León and Castile, though the situation facing Portugal is less clear. In the 10th century each was governed by a *Ṣāḥib al-thughūr* whose function was different from those governing central provinces. He was senior to other military commanders, had the rank of *qā'id* and led his own forces. In some cases he also had a fleet under his command since naval raids by Fāṭimids in the Mediterranean and Vikings in the Atlantic had led to a thorough re-organisation of Andalusian maritime defences.

Urban *futūwa* or *ahdath* military organisations developed much later in al-Andalus than in the Middle East, emerging as a belated response to the Christian invasions in the late 11th century. Only in the capital, Cordoba, did a militia play a significant role in the emergence of a small *taifa* state when the Umayyads finally collapsed in 1031. Basically there were two types of *taifa* state in 11th-century al-Andalus; relatively large ones in sparsely populated regions close to the Christian frontier, and much smaller statelets in the very urbanised south, largely reflecting the old *jund* military provinces. The tiniest were clustered in the Algarve (Arabic 'west') area of southern Portugal. These had minuscule military forces, though were perhaps more effective at sea. Some *taifas* had virtually no army at all while others could field small but well-equipped *qaṭā'iᶜ* (cavalry squadrons). Only the Hūdids of Saragossa, who survived until 1141, could resist both the Christian Reconquista and the African Murābiṭin who crossed the Straits of Gibraltar to save Andalusian Islam at the end of the 11th century.

STRATEGY AND TACTICS

Broad Strategy

During the 8th and 9th centuries Byzantine warfare revolved around the defence and retaking of frontier fortresses. But whether such castles were military bases or merely refuges remains unclear. Byzantium's main problem stemmed from its chronic shortage of military manpower which necessitated moving troops over huge distances, which often caused resentment. Above all the Byzantines concentrated on covering the few mountain passes through which a Muslim army could invade. If these could not be held, the invaders would be harassed and their communications attacked rather than attempting to meet them in open battle. This strategy led to what was known as *Shadow Warfare*, a guerrilla concept now brought to near perfection. As far as possible civil populations would be removed from the enemy's line of advance, along with crops and items of value in a scorched earth policy designed to starve the raiders into withdrawal.

By the 10th century, however, the Byzantine army was capable of concentrating large numbers of troops at the right place and time, particularly in the strategic passes. The 10th century also saw the Byzantine Empire take the offensive against the fortified cities where Muslim raids originated. The strategic road system and the oasis-like fertile valleys of eastern Anatolia played a vital role in such counter-attacks, the town of Malagina (now Bilecik) south-east of Constantinople being the normal assembly point for troops from the capital. Muslim frontier cities were set in fertile but oasis-like valleys surrounded by barren mountains. As a result Byzantine offensives were designed to conquer one valley at a time, necessitating self sufficient, highly mobile and above all adaptable armies. Once they had crossed the mountains the Byzantines enjoyed several strategic advantages. The open plains of northern Syria enabled them to approach their targets indirectly, rather than being confined to a small number of passes. The climate of the Fertile Crescent also permitted winter operations, which were impracticable in Anatolia. Whereas the Byzantine 'target' population was dispersed and rural, that of Syria was concentrated in cities surrounded by vulnerable, intensively cultivated oases-like 'gardens'.

In the small Christian states of northern Iberia, the pattern of early medieval western European infantry armies gradually evolving into the cavalry forces of the High Middle Ages simply does not fit. In reality Christian Spanish warfare was,

Part of a carved stone altar-screen from Tsebelda Church; Georgian, 9th–10th centuries. Although sometimes regarded as being of some centuries earlier, the turban worn by the mounted figure of St. Eustace Placidus, and above all the shape of his saddle and his use of stirrups point to a period when Christian Georgia was under Islamic rule or influence. The Guards at the Holy Sepulchre, above St. Eustace, are armed only with spears and shields. (S. N. Djanashiya State Museum, Tbilisi, Georgia)

until the 11th century, modelled on that of the Muslim Andalusians with raiding by light cavalry being the main offensive operation. As early as the 9th century a major Asturian expedition under the king or leading nobleman was called a *fonsado* or *fossato*, a smaller cavalry raid being an *algarada*, while the primary function of infantry was to defend towns, fortified *castra* and villages. The same was seen in 10th- and 11th-century León and Castile, though on a more ambitious scale. A *fonsado* would now, however, only involve cavalry it an enemy town was to be attacked or battle with a large enemy army expected. While *fonsados* could also be undertaken by individual towns, a larger-scale offensive under royal command was called a *hueste*. An *apellido* was a *levée en masse* in the face of enemy invasion; *cavalgada*, *algara*, *corredura* or *azaria* all being small raids into enemy territory. Two types of war were also recognised; *guerra* being an internal conflict between Christians, *bellum* being Holy War against the Muslims. Both Christians and Muslims fought to control passes through the mountain ranges which straddled the Iberian peninsula while the high plains of La Mancha and Extramadura in Spain were characterised by sheep ranching, raiding and rustling.

Although the great age of Arab-Islamic conquests had passed by the time the ᶜAbbāsids came to power, the armies of the Caliphate had remarkable capabilities and highly sophisticated strategy, particularly in long-range campaigning and the combining of several forces deep inside enemy territory. Small-scale raids against the Byzantines assembled in the fortified cities of the *awasim*, then strikes through one of the main passes: the Cilician Gates from Tarsus or the Darende valley pass from Adana or Malatya. Raids sometimes entered by one and left by another. Once across the Byzantine frontier larger raids split into several columns, even wintering in enemy territory though men and horses generally suffered greatly in the harsh Anatolian climate. The objectives of such raids were to capture imperial horse herds, take prisoners for ransom, seize grain stores or the valuables kept in fortresses and generally to undermine the Byzantine Empire's economic foundation. Only if serious damage were being inflicted would the shadowing Byzantine forces challenge the raiders in open battle.

Internal ᶜAbbāsid warfare was similar. During 9th-century campaigns in mountainous northern Iraq and against rebels in the southern marshes, Caliphal armies showed great concern to protect their extended lines of communications and to get detailed information about enemy dispositions. This was followed by a gradual seizure of enemy territory from bases protected by field fortifications. In such operations infantry played a more important role than the more celebrated *mamlūk* cavalry.

The successor states attempted to continue this cautious but effective strategy. The 11th-century scholar al-Mawārdi, for example, stated that the major duties of a commander were to conserve his troops' energies, ensure that horses were well looked after, discharge men who were undermining morale and to avoid favouritism between units. He should beware of unexpected enemy attacks, have plenty of scouts, ensure that the camps were defensible with adequate water supplies, guarantee sufficient food for men and animals, confer with his aides, seek the advice of experts and ensure discipline in the ranks. Above all he and his soldiers must be more enduring than their enemy. Al-Mawārdi then placed patience and endurance as the main duty of ordinary soldiers, followed by not fleeing unless outnumbered by more than two to one, distributing booty fairly, abandoning all personal friendship with non-Muslims in time of war, and immediate obedience to orders. There was no scope for the pointless heroics of some medieval western European armies.

Highly detailed information from the 10th century mentions cavalry reconnaissance units being sent several days ahead of a main body when entering and leaving enemy territory. Meanwhile the invasion of Sicily was an astonishing example of combined operations and involved the shipping of large forces from Tunisia. It was also carefully planned; three small bridgeheads being seized and consolidated before further offensives were launched in a limited and highly focused manner. But such conquests needed continued support from at least one major Muslim country. The troops who seized part of southern Italy, for example, established an autonomous Sunni state in Apulia in 866, but then, cut off from support by the rise of the Shia Fāṭimid Caliphate in North Africa, were defeated and absorbed by the local Christian population.

The main thrust of Andalusian operations was against enemy fortresses and fortified towns from which Christian forces raided southward. According to a remarkable 10th-century Andalusian book on farming and agriculture, called the Cordoba Calendar, the enlistment of volunteers for such summer campaigns began on 28 February each year.

Troop Types

Light cavalry characterised both Byzantine and Islamic armies in the 8th and 9th centuries, together with a decline in Byzantine horse-archery. Lance-armed heavy cavalry revived as Byzantium took the offensive in the 10th century, probably as an internal Byzantine development. At the same time there may also have been a revival of horse-archery under the influence of the *mamlūk* élite of neighbouring Islamic forces, though it still remained much easier for the Byzantines to raise and train lance-armed troopers. Byzantine infantry always included armoured close combat *oplitai* and larger numbers of lighter javelin-, sling- or bow-armed philoi. During the offensive of the 10th and 11th centuries élite infantry were also mounted, giving them great strategic mobility.

The basic troop types seen in Christian Iberian armies were the same as those of Muslim Andalusia to the south; light cavalry armed with javelins and infantry using long spears .

The ᶜAbbāsid army's recruitment philosophy was based on the idea that each regional group had its own particular fighting skills. Nevertheless the famous 9th-century commentator, al-Jāḥiz of Basra probably exaggerated such differences. In reality troops from Iran, the Jazira (northern Iraq, northern Syria and south-eastern Turkey) and Syria itself were similar in their military styles. According to tradition, however, the Turkish *mamlūk g͟hulām* élite was characterised by high morale, rapid manoeuvre, self sufficiency, equal skill with bow, short spear and lasso, the bow normally being used in disciplined and often static ranks rather than the dispersal tactics of his tribal Turkish counterpart. The élite *abnā* infantry, though sometimes mounted, traditionally fought with long spears, short swords and heavy armour. At the other end of the military spectrum the *ᶜurāt* urban poor of Baghdad made and rode what can only be described as pantomime horses in a desperate effort to make themselves look formidable from a distance.

Similar troops were employed by the successor states, though others also rose to prominence. The G͟haznavid cavalrymen who conquered much of northern India reportedly had two horses; one for battle and one for baggage. The fundamentalist Arabian *k͟hawāriji* led their war horses until battle began, and were noted for physical endurance, light equipment, high mobility and use of traditionally long Arab spears. The Arab light cavalry of northern Syria similarly fought with spear and sword, though were probably more like their Byzantine foes than the bedouin of Arabia. In fact a force of Banu Kilāb who deserted to the Byzantines in the late 10th century were described as wearing mail hauberks, lamellar cuirasses and brocade-covered mail coifs.

In 9th- to 11th-century Islamic armies infantry often enjoyed higher status than their counterparts in Byzantium. Elite armoured Daylamis, for example, had younger warriors as shield-bearers in battle, suggesting that such shields were large enough to be called *mantlets.* On the other hand the basically Arab armies of Syria included relatively few infantrymen, the most important being archers. The re-appearance of elephants in 10th-century eastern Islamic armies may have been part of a revival of Sassanian tradition but is more likely to have resulted from contact with Hindu India. One beast was even recorded in Muslim Kās͟hgar, north of the Karakoram mountains in Central Asia, though it was captured by the rival Buddhists of K͟hotan. The G͟haznavids used larger numbers of them, each with four spearmen or archers on its back, and towards the mid-11th century the Buwayhids brought some to the Middle East.

The importance attached to the misleading of the enemy characteristic of Islamic warfare led to the use of curious

'Apostles bribing the guards at the Garden of Gethsemane', Byzantine manuscript, 9th century. The soldiers have mail hauberks and in one case an apparently one-piece helmet with a mail aventail similar to those seen in earlier Central Asian and Transoxianan art. (Psalter, MS. no. 61, f. 89r, Monastery of the Pantocrator, Mount Athos)

ruses. In 987/8, for example, a Kurdish force gathered the local civilians on a mountainside and mounted them on mules and cows so that, from a distance, they looked impressive enough to inhibit the enemy from storming the mountain.

The main problem faced by the Fāṭimids was the unsuitability of their largely Berber North African troops when facing Turkish *mamlūk* horse-archers. Even the use of Arab cavalry did not solve the problem, though bedouin auxiliaries were highly effective in disrupting enemy supply lines. The best Fāṭimid cavalry were equipped in essentially the same manner as the Byzantines, and their best foot soldiers operated as mounted infantry on camels or horses. They included many infantry archers and it is worth noting that the Nubians who served the Fāṭimids in substantial numbers used *ḥusbān* (darts), presumably shot from *majra* (arrow-guides) as early as the 9th century.

By the early 10th century the Berbers had adopted Arab-style infantry bows and spear-armed cavalry tactics, though this only applied to the military élite. In Andalusia infantry played the leading role in the sierras while cavalry dominated on the high plateau. But as the frontier threatened to collapse under Christian pressure, small fortified, almost monastery-like *ribāṭs* came into their own. From here remarkably disciplined volunteers conducted their own small-scale counter-raids. Early Murābiṭ armies from the western Sahara and Morocco were largely infantry, including many mounted infantry whose camels caused panic among Spanish cavalry horses.

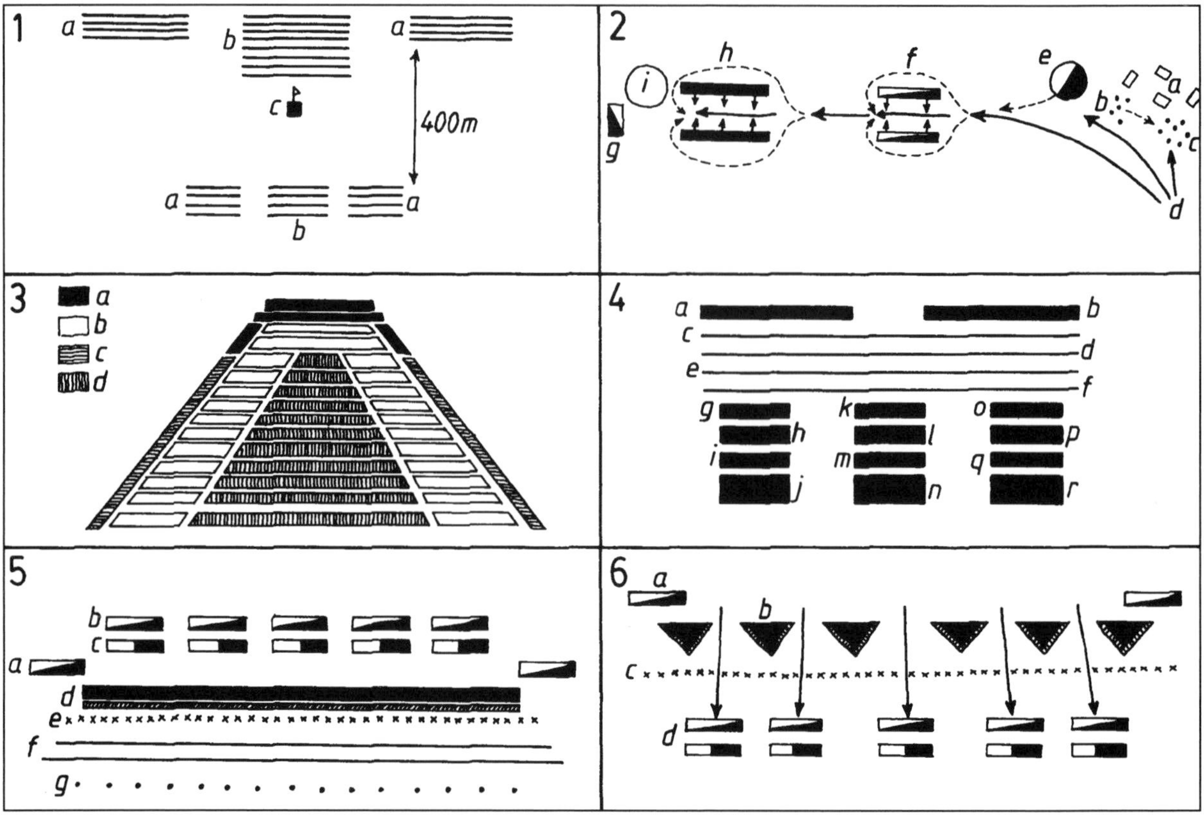

Battle Tactics

The book on skirmishing attributed to the 10th-century Byzantine warrior Emperor Nicephorus Phocas includes remarkably detailed tactics. For example infantry were to hold high ground ahead of an advancing enemy whereas cavalry would only be employed in suitable terrain. Infantry could block narrow defiles with a shield-wall backed up by javelin men while archers, slingers and rock-throwers held the mountainsides ahead of each flank. Infantry ambushes in such defiles should be backed up by cavalry while smaller enemy groups such as surveying parties looking for billets could be attacked by élite cavalry alone. Troops shadowing the enemy should be camouflaged in dull-coloured cloaks while some scouts could be disguised as farmer labourers to observe the enemy at close range, though it would be better if they had horses and thus looked like farm managers.

The sophistication of Byzantine tactics enabled them to vary their formations to meet different challenges. On the march armoured cavalry generally protected the infantry, horsemen covering the retreat of returning raiders and supporting the light infantry who guarded camps inside enemy territory. In the Balkans cavalry led the march, followed by infantry with flank guards, but against Turks or Arabs a Byzantine army kept large numbers of infantry archers around the main body to keep enemy skirmishers at bay. Axe-armed pioneers cleared roads and passes; light infantry held a pass as the main body marched through. In battle such light foot withdrew behind the shield wall of heavier infantry.

The *Tactika*, also attributed to Nicephoros, primarily dealt with large-scale offensive operations. It indicated that both cavalry as well as mixed cavalry and infantry forces could be sent into the Fertile Crescent. In the latter case cavalry operated from a defensive square of infantry; normally four foot soldiers to each horseman. Square or rectangular infantry formations had gaps through which cavalry could launch counter-charges, these being followed up by lighter cavalry skirmishers while the infantry, four ranks deep, remained on the defensive.

Armoured cavalry on armoured horses became the main striking power of Nicephoros Phocas' army and were first mentioned in 965, but they were slow and tired quickly so were only used for a final decisive charge. They advanced at a measured pace, with the ordinary cavalry close behind, in the same shock cavalry tactics characteristic of subsequent 'knightly' armies in western Europe. Unlike western armies, however, the Byzantines also used horse-archers; thus combining European and Central Asian tactics into a highly effective whole. Similar tactics had in fact been used by the ᶜAbbāsids in the 9th century and may have been developed by Chinese forces earlier still. But a blunted wedge-shaped cavalry formation is said to have been invented by Nicephorus Phocas. This had archers on armoured horses at the centre surrounded by men with swords, maces and axes, with lancers

Opposite page: The Theory of War; Archetypal Byzantine, Muslim and Indian Battle-plans

1. Late 6th–early 7th centuries Byzantine cavalry array based on descriptions in military manuals.
a cursores
b defensores
c commander and guards.

2. Ambush by separate units from the military manual, De Velitatione, written for the Byzantine Emperor Nicephoros Phocas in the mid-10th century.
a village target of Arab raiders
b 100 cavalry sent to attack enemy pillagers
c enemy pillagers
d Muslim Arab main force and reinforcements for pillagers
e support force of 200 cavalry to resist Arab counter-attack
f first ambush of Arab main force by 2,000 cavalry
g second blocking ambush by 3,000 cavalry
h infantry in support of second blocking ambush;
i strategus in command of Byzantine force. (after Dagron and Mihăescu)

3. Schematic representation of wedge-shaped offensive cavalry formation developed by or for the Byzantine Emperor Nicephoros Phocas in the mid-10th century.
a cavalry armed with sword or mace on armoured horses
b cavalry armed with sword or mace on unarmoured horses
c cavalry armed with lances on armoured horses
d horse-archers on armoured horses.

4. Battle array of the Hindus, according to a 13th-century Indo-Muslim military manual written by Fakhr-i Mudabbir-Mubārakshāh.
a left advance guard
b right advance guard
c infantry archers with large shields
d infantry shock troops
e armoured elephants supported by sword-armed infantry
f spear-armed cavalry on armoured horses
g left flank
h armoury
i flocks of animals
j priests and prisoners
k centre
l ruler's harem
m horse herds
n army bazaar
o right flank
p treasury
q hospital
r camp-followers.

5. Classical Muslim Arab offensive battle-array as developed during the ᶜAbbāsid dynasty in 8th–10th centuries and still used by the Fāṭimids in the 11th–12th centuries.
a light cavalry shujᶜān on flanks
b light cavalry shujᶜān supporting heavy cavalry; heavy cavalry abṭāl
d infantry in files headed by armoured infantry forming a shield-wall
e line of stakes or a ditch
f skirmishers consisting of infantry archers supported by infantry javelin men
g champions challenging enemy to individual combat.

6. Classical Muslim Arab defensive battle-array as developed during the ᶜAbbāsid dynasty in 8th–10th centuries and still used by the Fāṭimids in 11th–12th centuries
a light cavalry shujᶜān on flanks
b infantry drawn back into triangular formations with armoured men forming external shield wall to allow cavalry to launch counter-attacks through the gaps
c line of stakes or a ditch
d heavy cavalry abṭāl supported by light cavalry shujᶜān launching limited counter-charges through gaps in infantry wall and defensive stakes or ditch.

in the front and flanks. The little that is known of Christian Iberian tactics at this time indicates that cavalry still relied on the *turna-fuye* tactics of repeated charge and withdrawal used by late Roman horsemen and continued by Arab cavalry who knew it as *karr wa farr*.

Several Arabic military manuals, theoretical and practical, survive. Ibn Qutayba al-Dīnawarī, writing in the late 9th century, mainly focused on cavalry but included a chapter on '*Shadowing Warfare*' decades before the Byzantine work on the same subject. Most other evidence indicates that on the march the ᶜAbbāsid army still used the *khamīs* array first recorded in pre-Islamic south Arabia. The centre was led by heavy cavalry with heavy infantry and infantry archers behind. The right and left flanks, van and rear largely consisted of light cavalry with the baggage, hospital, any siege train and flocks of animals as food 'on the hoof' bringing up the rear. Each division marched in a rectangular formation with each man strictly in position, and reconnaissance parties obviously went ahead. In 838 one of several columns invading Byzantine Anatolia learned of an enemy ambush, so the Muslim commander concealed his troops during the night and sent scouts to seek a way out of the trap.

In the open, early ᶜAbbāsid armies placed armoured foot soldiers in the front rank, kneeling with their spears as pikes, infantry archers behind them with cavalry ready to launch counter-charges through spaces opened by the infantry or round their flanks. Later armies varied this tactic by placing archers in front, supported by spear-armed infantry. In 867–8 élite fire-grenade-throwers broke the shield-wall of opposing Daylami infantry, but in 933-4 another army tried similar tactics with *naft*-propelling flame-throwers, but this failed when the wind changed and blew the fire back into ᶜAbbāsid ranks. Meanwhile Arab cavalry seem to have advanced in line rather than the wedge formation invented by the Byzantine Emperor and relied on repeated attacks and withdrawals rather than one overwhelming assault.

Small variations are recorded from the successor states. For example élite *mamlūk ghulām* (cavalry) provided advance, flank and rear-guards for raiders operating out of Tarsus, such raiding forces also leaving ambushes to catch the Byzantines shadowing them. Small close-packed units of raiders would also remain on guard while the bulk of their force scattered to plunder the countryside. In open battle most Muslim forces still preferred to await the enemy's first move, Ghaznavids and Buwayhids normally placing élite cavalry in the centre with lower grade horsemen in reserve. During one battle in 957 units of Ghaznavid *mamlūks* took turns to attack enemy infantry to avoid one detachment tiring, but at the end of the day, with their arrows spent and the enemy unbroken, the *mamlūks* feared an infantry counter-attack. Only a misunderstood order which sent unreliable but fresh reserves into the attack saved the day.

Daylami infantry normally hoped to exhaust an enemy by absorbing his attacks before themselves advancing in lines or phalanxes with large shields, axes and javelins. The Muslim invaders of Sicily used similar tactics, each unit remaining passive behind its flags, then shouting its battle cry as the enemy attacked. According to one 11th-century book on military theory, each unit was assigned a different *shi*ᶜ*ār* or shout. Commanders might take position on available raised ground, or use a camel or elephant as a command post surrounded by a cavalry guard. In defence an Arab north Syrian army defeated a larger Byzantine invasion force by constantly harassing it with light cavalry units, eventually pinning the invaders into their fortified camp until, desperate with thirst, the Byzantines attempted to break out but lost cohesion, panicked and were cut to pieces.

Fāṭimid tactical concepts were supposedly based on those of the Prophet Muḥammad and the Caliph ᶜAlī, but were essentially the same as those of their rivals. Additional details, which probably applied to most professional Muslim armies, included the parading of flags to the troops before marching to ensure that every man recognised his own banner, checking thickets for ambushes while pursuing an apparently beaten foe, and describing infantry/cavalry battle-formation as a *ḥiṣn* (fortress). Here cavalry and infantry formed up behind their officers in such close ranks and files that no one could squeeze through. In battle the cavalry ranks were straightened by their officers before making a charge, and commanders had special aides who carried orders to units on the flank.

Fāṭimid forces permitted single combat of champions between opposing armies, followed by an infantry charge with cavalry on the flanks. If the enemy counter-charged, the infantry knelt behind their shields and thrust the butts of their spears into the ground as pikes, armoured men in the front supported by archers and javelin-throwers. Any hesitation on the part of the enemy would result in a limited counter-charge by a minimal number of men, a general advance being permitted only after the foe had clearly been defeated. The troops then moved off in the same formations as when they arrived on the battlefield. If the enemy broke completely he would be pursued by cavalry and light infantry archers only, in case this was a ruse. An interesting Byzantine reference to *Aethiopians* in a Muslim array probably referred to Nubian troops in an early Fāṭimid army. These infantry archers wore quilted armour and used very large simple rather than composite bows. They operated ahead of the cavalry and, like other Muslim infantry, often rode pillion behind a cavalryman to give greater strategic mobility.

Evidence from mid-11th-century North Africa indicates that an army was particularly vulnerable at the moment of *nuzūl* (halting and reforming). Similarly armies tried to strike the enemy at just such a moment. This *nuzūl* probably included the time it took for an army to establish camp and sort out its baggage. Other sources indicate that North African armies tended to march with their infantry at the centre, protected by a cavalry screen. In battle North African and Andalusian armies both relied on an infantry phalanx, while cavalry were

The baṭn al-ḥajar ('belly of stones') was a particularly desolate stretch of the Nile valley in what is now northern Sudan which served as a defence in depth between Muslim Egypt and the Christian kingdoms of Nubia to the south. Most is now flooded beneath man-made Lake Nasser, but the southern part of the baṭn al-ḥajar here at Kosha remains basically the same as it was in the Middle Ages. (Author's photograph)

expected to deliver the knockout blow once an enemy was exhausted. The early Murābiṭin who, as an essentially Saharan military force, consisted of camel-mounted infantry with very few cavalry, introduced some significant changes. Since their discipline verged on the fanatical, they would neither advance nor retreat, however strong the enemy. Instead they remained in rigid ranks with spear and shield men and standard-bearers in the front ranks, supported by soldiers carrying several javelins. They would often not pursue a beaten foe, and could accept high casualties. If their own flag fell, the troops would simply sit down. Similar tactics remained in use among Saharan tribes until the French conquest of the 19th century.

Before the arrival of the Murābiṭin, Andalusian commanders attempted to seize high ground or an eminence from which they could survey the battlefield. Otherwise élite cavalry formations, divided into recognised squadrons, raided enemy territory for booty and captives while fast-moving infantry forces attempted to seize enemy fortifications or relieve those under attack. Battle in open terrain tended to rely on repeated *karr wa farr* attacks identical with the *turna-fuye* of their Christian enemies.

Combat Styles

In the 10th century it appears that Byzantine horse-archers shot volleys of arrows by command and in static ranks. The front rank loosed first then bent forward with their shields on their necks as did infantry archers. The use of poisoned arrows was justified on the grounds that horses were so expensive in Muslim territory that fear of poisoned arrows inhibited the enemy from coming close. It was also stated that a javelin was quite powerful enough to unhorse a horseman even if he were not wounded.

On the Muslim side of the frontier an Arab, disputing military merits with al-Jāḥiz of Basra, maintained that the power of the Turk lay in his arrows but that he was weak without them, that the power of the Khurāsāni lay in his sword but that he soon tired, while the *abnā* were skilled with all weapons and better able to endure cold, wet and the weight of armour. The Khurāsāni horseman was also accused of 'wheeling aside' rather than closing with the enemy, perhaps indicating that he relied on skirmishing tactics. During Hārūn al-Rashīd's siege of Eregli on the Black Sea coast, a duel took place between an Arab and a Byzantine champion. They fought with spears until their horses tired, then started again with swords. The Muslim's weapon bounced off the Byzantine's iron reinforced shield whereas the latter's blade penetrated the Arab's shield. The Muslim pretended to flee, the Greek pursuing with sword-arm raised whereupon the Arab suddenly turned, caught his enemy with a lasso, dragged him from his horse and slew him. During this campaign the Byzantines tried to block a narrow defile with burning trees but the Caliph's fire-troops in flame-proof clothing doused the flames.

Turkish *mamlūk* horse-archers used the Persian-style finger draw with a special leather half-gauntlet, and the more tiring Central Asian or Turco-Mongol thumb-draw. At Dazimon in 838 such troops shot in disciplined ranks to drive back a Byzantine charge. This was an example of Sassanian-style high-density 'shower shooting' at a area rather than an individual foe. A fully trained man was supposedly capable of loosing a handful of five arrows in two and half seconds, then snatching another five from an open-ended quiver on his left hip, which differed considerably from the enclosed box-like Central Asian quiver. Additional details from the 10th century show that Muslim armies now excelled at night manoeuvre, like their pre-Islamic southern Arabian ancestors. An eye-witness account of a battle between two Muslim forces in northern Syria also describes how a highly skilled horseman penetrated deep within enemy ranks, striking rapid but carefully aimed sword blows against the head, shoulder and sword-hand of an opponent before being overwhelmed.

Duels between opposing champions were just as common in North Africa and al-Andalus, sometimes being resolved by a wrestling match on horseback or on the ground. A detailed study of *Mozarab* ('Arabised' Christian) illustrated manuscripts from Spain suggests that spears were thrown as javelins, could make both thrusts and lateral cuts and could be used with both hands when not carrying a shield, but only one hand if a shield were used.

Field and Camp Fortifications

Byzantine sources provide most detail about field fortifications. One 10th-century book even mentions a special corps of 'measurers' riding ahead of the army to select camp sites. The Byzantine army clearly took great care to defend its encampment, scattering spiked *calthrops* around the perimeter, these being attached by cords to a small stake so that they could be retrieved for re-use and to avoid injuring friendly troops. Strings of bells could also warn if a surreptitious enemy got past the outer sentries. ᶜAbbāsid encampments or brushwood *zarības* appear to have been similarly surrounded by ditches within which troops would erect tents on summer campaign, wooden huts in winter. *Zarības* of woven vine stems, willow osiers or brambles could also be used in open battle, some being large enough to protect fifteen to twenty archers.

WEAPONRY AND HARNESS

The professional attitude of eastern Mediterranean armies is well illustrated by a 10th-century military treatise which criticises extravagantly decorated arms and harness, recommending high-quality plain iron equipment. Nevertheless the warrior's characteristic love of display could not be suppressed, as is shown in descriptions of élite weaponry in almost all countries. It is also worth noting that, as men of Turkish origin dominated armies of the eastern and central Islamic regions, so earlier Central Asian decorative motifs spread westward despite the fact that such troops were now Muslim.

Archery and Slings

Simple bows of one-piece construction were widely used in sub-Saharan Africa but played a negligible role in Byzantium and the Muslim world where various forms of composite bow dominated. The Byzantine bow appears to have been of Hun rather than Turkish type, could be up to 1.3m long and was essentially an infantry weapon like the Arab bow. Distinctions between Arab and Persian bows are not entirely clear though the Persian was probably a shorter weapon for use on horseback. The fully developed Turkish composite bow, which combined the strength of the Arab with the size of the Persian, could be described as the ultimate cavalry weapon of the Middle Ages. It had an effective range of 250 metres, achieving good penetration up to 100 metres. The Sassanian finger-protecting leather half-glove was later called a *kustubān* or *dastaban*. Turkish-style thumb-rings for long-range flight-shooting were rarely used in warfare.

Other variations were the *bunduq* or pellet bow used only in hunting, and the far more lethal arrow-guide known as a *majra* or *nāwak*. This was a groove or tube held against the right side of a composite bow when required, and used when shooting a projectile, of a length somewhere between the normal arrow and the later crossbow-bolt. It was first recorded in the 8th century, though it may have been known earlier, and was highly effective in the hands of infantry. It was also used in Byzantium where it was known as a *solenarion*.

Crossbows may have been reintroduced to the Middle East from China in the 10th century or may have survived since Roman times. A large frame- or wall-mounted crossbow was known in late 10th-century Iran and shot arrows as large as javelins. Its Persian name of *charkh*, in Arabic *jarkh*, meant 'wheel', which suggests it was spanned by a windlass. The more elaborate Arab *qaws al-ziyār* was a ballista with two separate arms, powered by twisted skeins of horse-hair or sinew, known in later Europe as an *espringal*. It could throw containers of *nafṭ* (Greek Fire).

Smaller crossbows were used by Muslim infantry from the 10th century onwards, being known as 'foot' or 'stirrup' bows. The Byzantines knew of the large crossbow or *tzarchat* (from the Arabic *jarkh*) by the late 10th or early 11th century. Crossbows may have been known in 10th-century Andalusia, suddenly appearing in 11th-century Iberian art. Early crossbows did not oust the composite bow as an infantry weapon, perhaps because they could not be aimed beyond a range of eighty metres because raising the stock to allow for the arrow's drop obscured the target. Slings continued to be used in several areas by more primitive forces, though even the sophisticated Byzantines used ordinary and staff-slings in siege warfare.

Swords and Daggers

Most Byzantine and Islamic swords were straight during these centuries, Byzantine cavalry wielding a 1m-long double-edged *spathion* often slung from a baldric. A detailed description from Andalusia of about 975 specifies three different styles of sword: 'Frankish' western European, Berber and Arab. A shorter form of *sayf ṣārim*, may have been the early Arab infantry style. All could be decorated with gold, silver inlay or niello, though in general inscriptions on blades were more common in Europe than in the Middle East.

Central Asian curved sabres were known among the Khazar Turks by the early 9th century. Shortly afterwards Byzantine horsemen adopted single-edged swords as secondary weapons, including the *paramerion*, while the single-edged *romphaion* appeared in the early 11th century. The sabre also reached eastern Iran from Transoxiana; various 10th- and 11th-century eastern Persian and Arabic sources mention a sword known as a *qalāchūr*, *qalājūlīyā* or *qaljūri*. Its precise

identification remains a matter of debate, and the seemingly obvious link with the later Turkish *kilich* sabre has been denied by one specialist. Grave finds of the 8th century on the eastern coast of the Black Sea include a sabre, but could be Khazar or Byzantine, while a sabre from 9th- or 10th-century Iran is similar to weapons from the Altai mountains north of China. Some aspects of its hilt and grip are remarkably like those of later Japanese swords, suggesting a common Chinese influence. In addition to the straight swords found in a late 10th- or early 11th-century Islamic shipwreck in the Aegean, fragments of a possible curved sabre were also recovered. Large daggers were now more widespread, particularly in Muslim armies where they were normally known as *khanjars*.

Spears and Javelins

The Byzantine army continued to use a variety of specialised spears and javelins. The former included the *kontarion* which was 4 metres long for cavalry, the latter the *riptarion* and *berutta*. On the Islamic side earlier spears and javelins continued to be used, together with the distinctive *zūpīn* (heavy javelin) of Daylami infantry. The *zūpīn* also had a symbolic function, serving as a symbol of authority as did the mace among Turks and mamlūks.

Other Weapons

Byzantine troops used four types of axe: single-bladed, single with a spike at the back, round-bladed with a hammer at the back, and double-bladed. Two-handed axes were the favoured weapon of 11th-century *Varangian* guardsmen. Single-handed cavalry axes may have been used in Byzantium, but such weapons became more characteristic of Muslim regions where they were generally known as *ṭabarzīn* (saddle axe).

The Byzantines may have used maces but these were again more typical of their Turco-Muslim foes; animal-headed maces

Left: *Cast-bronze sword-hilt of late 10th–early 12th centuries, found in a shipwreck at Serçe Liman off the south-western coast of Anatolia. It was probably an Islamic merchant ship and the bronze of this hilt included lead mined in or near Armenia. But the bird which decorates the guard is based on Sassanian or Indian motifs. This evidence suggests that the weapon was made in Muslim-ruled Armenia or western Iran, and indicates the remarkable mix of technological and artistic influences at work in Middle Eastern military technology at this time. (Castle Museum, inv. GQ 56, Bodrum, Turkey)*
Top right: *Cast-iron sword guard found in the fortified early Islamic 'way-station' at al-Rabadhah in central Arabia; 7th–10th centuries. It is in the same tradition as earlier Roman and Romano-Byzantine swords and was clearly for a broad-bladed (up to 6 cms) but probably quite short weapon used by Muslim Arab infantry. (Department of Archaeology, King Sa'ud University, Riyadh, Saudi Arabia)*
Right: *Cast-bronze sword quillons and pommel, Egypt or Syria; 9th–10th centuries. The quillons are inscribed with Sura CXII of the Koran, which is specifically critical of the Christian concept of the Trinity, suggesting that the weapon was made for war against the Byzantines. This style of sword-hilt continued to appear in Islamic art from the Middle East for several more centuries. (Ex-Storm Rice Collection; present whereabouts unknown)*

being regarded as weapons of the élite. But a heavy infantry club does seem to have become popular among 10th-century Byzantine infantry. Maces are generally believed to have been copied by western European knights from Byzantine or Muslim troops via the Crusades, yet such weapons had been known in 10th-century Andalusia and so may have spread northwards from the Iberian peninsula.

The question of cutting rather than thrusting infantry staff weapons or pole-arms is more difficult. Ten different kinds of blade were found in the Aegean shipwreck, including two not seen in western Europe, including a massive blade in a wooden scabbard which may have been a specialised rope-cutting naval weapon. An Andalusian description of a military review of about 975 describes a special form of *ḥarba*, usually a heavy javelin or short infantry spear with a large blade 'like a Christian sword' on a brightly coloured haft. A similar object appears in Christian Iberian and Andalusian illustrations so perhaps this Andalusian *ḥarba* may be one of the earliest specialised infantry staff weapons in western Europe. The *dammāja* mentioned in the same Andalusian source may have been a form of trident as seen occasionally in Iberian art. One scholar has also tentatively attributed the origins of the widespread European *guisarm* to Andalusia. More exotic devices included the lasso, used for hunting in 10th-century Syria, but a slightly later ringed spike from the Aegean shipwreck may have been the top of a ceremonial parasol rather than a weapon.

Opposite page:
Top left: *Helmet from Yasenovo near Stara Zagorska, Bulgaria; probably Byzantine 9th–10th centuries. The dome of the helmet is of an advanced one-piece construction, with a broad lower band and reinforcing strips across the top. The rim was intended to have a mail aventail. (Historical Museum, inv. no. 200, Kazanlik, Bulgaria)*
Bottom left: *Silk-covered leather cap or hood with metal finial, from Moshchevaya Balka in the northern Caucasus; Alan, 8th–9th centuries. This type of headgear appears in Byzantine, Caucasian and Islamic art of these and earlier centuries. They sometimes appear to be worn over helmets by soldiers. (State Hermitage Museum, St. Petersburg)*
Top right: *Crocodile-skin helmet, said to be from Wadī Jarāra, east of Kalabsha in Nubia. Although undated, the use of a lamellar neck-guard suggests an early medieval date. (Antikenmuseum, inv. 30882, Berlin)*
Bottom left: *A one-piece iron helmet from Tunisia. Although this helmet has been attributed to the Hafsid period, 13–15th centuries, it could be considerably earlier and has much in common with other low-domed one-piece helmets of the early Islamic or Byzantine centuries. Unfortunately so few examples survive, and so little study has been made of them, that a more accurate dating is as yet impossible. (Musée Nationale des Arts Islamiques, Kayrawan, Tunisia)*

Shields

The normal range of large and small, wooden or leather shields was used by Byzantine and Muslim warriors from the 8th to 10th centuries, a small Byzantine leather shield being called a *dorka* from the Arabic *daraqah.* This period also saw some interesting developments such as iron plates being laced or stitched to ordinary shields; an example of just such a defence having been found in a 12th-century Transoxianan site.

In Islamic regions the large wooden *turs* and lighter leather *daraqah* were known from India to the Atlantic, also being used in Christian northern Spain. A taller 10th–11th-century infantry shield was sometimes called a *ṭāriqa,* and is the likely prototype of the kite-shaped European *targe.* Some Byzantine horsemen also adopted elongated shields in the 10th century. The most extraordinary shield, however, was the huge leather *lamṭ* which traditionally originated in southern Morocco or the western Sahara, becoming the most typical item of Berber military equipment. Those used by the Murābiṭin measured ten spans by three cubits (roughly 2 x 1.3 metres). In contrast mantlets made of reeds or rush-matting by the citizens of 9th-century Baghdad, though the same as shields used in Mesopotamia for thousands of years, now proved totally ineffectual against arrows from composite bows.

Helmets

Most changes in early medieval helmets had taken place by the 8th century, though the general spread of more advanced metallurgical techniques from east to west continued. Pointed, segmented helmets of Central Asian form replaced late Roman types in Byzantine armies, similarly shaped one-piece helmets probably appearing in the 10th century, often with a face-covering mail aventail originating in Central Asia. These *peritrachelia* were normally thickly padded, but apparently not always being of mail. The Byzantine *skaplion* was more like a *tippet* as it also covered shoulders and upper arms. A thick felt *kamelaukion* cap covering the back and sides of the head may have been worn over helmets and could account for the extraordinary shape of some helmets in Byzantine art.

Elite Muslim troops wore heavy *k̲h̲ūd̲h̲* or lighter *bayḍah* helmets, the importance of archery again leading to considerable facial protection; references to soldiers whose eyes alone were visible being common in documentary sources. In Persian an aventail, coif or gorget was called a *grībān,* in Arab areas a *mig̲h̲far.* In Andalusia there were several variations, perhaps reflecting European influence, including the larger or heavier late 10th-century *ḥāṣina.* Its precise appearance is not known, but helmets with integral rigid face-masks suddenly appeared in late 11th-century Iberian art as predecessors of the 13th-century European *great helm.* At the same time other 11th-century Iberian illustrations show an open-faced helmet extended at the back to protect the neck.

Body Armour

Mail was the most widespread form of armour throughout the early medieval period, being worn with other defences in the Middle East and Iberian peninsula. In general from the 7th to 9th centuries the weight of Byzantine armour decreased as the

imperial armies relied on light cavalry and infantry, resulting in short-hemmed, short-sleeved mail hauberks and sleeveless lamellar cuirasses. More extensive mail appeared in the 10th century, though this was regarded as a western fashion by an Italian observer writing in 968. The Byzantine *zaba* and *lorikion* were essentially the same, though the former could be lined with padding and was probably copied from the Turco-Muslim *jubbah*.

The Arabs largely adopted Iranian armour during this period, both mail and lamellar, though the *dir*^{c} mail hauberk was much the more widespread. Manuscript illustrations from 11th-century Catalonia include unexplained rectangles in the upper chests of some mail *hauberks*, as also seen in the later 11th-century Anglo-Norman *Bayeux Tapestry*. In both cases they probably represent early forms of unlaced face-protecting mail *ventails*. Other forms of mail defence were the padded *jubbah* and the padded and cloth-covered *kazāghand*. This originated in eastern Iran or Transoxiana then spread west and was eventually adopted by European knights as the *jazeran* or *jazrain hauberk*.

The Byzantine *klibanion* was a relatively light lamellar cuirass, worn alone or over a mail hauberk, and made of hardened leather, horn or metallic lamellae. The 10th-century *thorakes* was a heavier protection, possibly scale or lamellar, which tended to glint in the sun. The Islamic *jawshan* was highly effective and remained in fashion for centuries as far west as Andalusia. It could be made of iron, bronze or hardened leather lamellae laced with leather thongs. References to 'Tibetan' armours in 10th-century Tarsus probably indicate that they were made of hardened leather like the so-called 'Tibetan' shields. They may also have been larger than the ordinary *jawshan*; more like Mongol lamellar cuirasses of the 13th century. Unlike the Byzantine *klibanion*, some 10th-century *jawshans* were extremely heavy.

Soft armours were highly developed in the early medieval Middle East, some subsequently being adopted in western Europe as a result of the Crusades. The Byzantine *epilorikion* was of felt or quilted material and might have an integral coif. The felt *kabadion* was similar, though smaller and suitable for infantry. The *kremasmata* seems to have been a quilted skirt, sometimes with iron elements to protect groin and thighs.

In Islamic areas the *jubbah* could be a simple quilted armour lacking any mail, but the *kārwa* or *gārwa* used by infantry in Afghanistan, remains a bit of a mystery. It was made of cow skin stuffed with cotton, could be covered in decorative cloth and 'carried on the shoulders' to protect the wearer from head to foot.

Limb Defences

Limb protections were rare, though shoulder, arm and leg pieces were among the remarkable 8th-century Byzantine or Khazar finds from the Black Sea coast. Byzantine sources mention *cheiropsella* for the arms while a little later quilted *manikia* or *manikellia* seem to have been laced to the upper arms or shoulders of a ceremonial quilted *epilorikon*. Metal-covered leather gauntlets were issued to specialist troops such as standard-bearers, and vambrace-like protections for the lower arms were clearly used in 9th–10th-century Muslim armies. These were usually called *bāzīkand* in Persian areas or *sa*^{c}*ad* in Arab areas.

Left: *Gilded bronze shield-boss from* ^{c}*Ayn Dāra; Byzantine, 10th–11th centuries. This was probably for parade purposes since its rim is decorated with hunting-dogs chasing deer. (Archaeological Museum, nr. 1/64, Aleppo, Syria)*

Above: *'Angel slaying the Beast', in a Mozarab manuscript from 1091–1109. Mozarab manuscripts were made by a Christian community living under Muslim rule and largely Arab in culture, or in recently reconquered territory. The strange stitching in the chest of the angel's tunic may indicate that it was made of felt and was a form of soft-armour. (Beatus Commentaries on the Apocalypse, MS. Add. 11695, f.198, British Library, London)*

In 9th–10th-century Byzantium, leg defences were called *chalkotouba*, perhaps indicating that they were of splinted construction, or *podopsella*. Leg armour worn by heavily armoured rebels in the mid-11th century, and that worn by the élite *Varangian* Guards, were likely to have been of mail like western European mail *chausses*. There seem to be no references to leg armour in the 9th-century ᶜAbbāsid army, though a slightly later Byzantine source states that Muslim cavalry from Syria or Egypt wore leg protections like those of Byzantine horsemen.

Horse Harness

The Muslim Arabs' adoption of stirrups in the 8th century had no immediate influence on tactics, and even as late as the 10th century stirrups and wood-framed saddles were not used by Andalusian cavalry. A hundred years later Andalusian and Christian Iberian documents both indicate that two forms of saddle were still in use; the Arab-Andalusian and the Berber. A plate-like horseshoe which protected the whole of the horse's hoof probably originated in Arabia, then spread to Persia in the east and Portugal in the west.

Horse Armour

Horse-armour became widespread in early medieval Byzantium and the Muslim world, 8th-century Byzantine versions probably still being in an Avar style which only covered the front of the animal. By the 10th century, however, horse-armour was made of layers of glued felt, or of iron or hardened leather lamellae, sometimes covering the entire animal and hanging down almost to its feet. Even mail horse-armour may have been known by the 11th century.

Whereas horse-armour was little used until the early 10th century in North Africa and Egypt, east Iranian Khurāsāni cavalry certainly used felt or quilted horse-armours called *bargustuwān*. The Persian Shāhnāmah epic describes cavalry dropping their horses' armour as they rode so that they could flee more quickly. Farther west felt quilted horse-armour was known by the Arabic term *tijfāf*, and was used by the ᶜAbbāsid cavalry élite in the early 9th century. By 952/3 the best horsemen of northern Syria rode horses with mail or metallic lamellar armour. An eye-witness account of a military parade in Cairo in 1047 describes cavalry mounts with iron horse-armour and weapons slung from their saddles. More surprisingly, perhaps, *tijfāf* horse-armour was also used in late 10th-century Andalusia - two centuries before horse-armour was supposedly known to western Europe. There are even 10th- and 11th-century Andalusian and Christian Iberian references to a plated and sometimes gilded piece of armour called a *tashtīna, testinia* or *tishtanī*. These were probably early versions of the rigid head-piece for a horse-armour known in late 12th-century Europe as a *testeriam* and later as a *testière*.

FORTIFICATION

Within what had been the Roman Empire, Byzantine and Muslim military architects tended to re-use earlier fortifications. In the case of Byzantium several massive non-military structures were also converted to fortresses, but while there was general consistency of construction techniques within the Byzantine Empire, there was greater variation in Islamic military architecture which drew upon several separate traditions.

Christendom: The Byzantine Empire

The main cities of Byzantium were strongly fortified, though the huge land walls of Constantinople were untypical. Most Byzantine cities had citadels at their highest point with multiple walls for the most important, numerous towers and double gates enclosing a 'killing zone'. The vital military centre of Ankara also had early examples of arrow-slits in vulnerable sections of wall by the 9th century, as well as the first Byzantine example of a 'bent entrance' gate. Meanwhile the inhabited area of ancient Ephesus had shrunk by half, but was given a new wall and water cisterns replacing the vulnerable aqueducts.

The rural landscape of Anatolia was soon dotted with smaller fortified towns and castles. The long walls and relatively few towers of the former suggested passive defence, the latter were more varied in design than the old Roman *castrae*. Castles in flat terrain tended to be square with corner towers reached by wooden stairs; those in mountainous areas making greater use of topographical features and often having covered galleries within their walls. In many cases the frontier itself was hardly defended; large castles being some distance to the rear. The frontier wall reportedly erected between the Danube and hills close to the Black Sea in north-eastern Bulgaria was clearly unusual.

Construction techniques in such Byzantine fortifications ranged from rough-hewn stone over a rubble core in the 7th to 9th centuries, to layers of mortared rubble used from the 10th century. Armenia was more densely fortified than elsewhere, having seventy castles in the province of Vaspourakan alone, in addition to fortified villages, churches and monasteries. Not surprisingly 11th-century Armenian military architects were regarded as the best in the Middle East.

Christendom: The Iberian Peninsula

Fortification was not yet highly developed in Christian Iberia, but the Christian states used series of watchtowers and small forts linking larger castles, as also seen in Muslim al-Andalus. Small fortifications were in fact known by the originally Arabic terms *almenara* and *atalaya*. The use of brick construction, however, is likely to have shown Italian influence.

Islam: The Early ᶜAbbāsid Caliphate

Towers were always central to Islamic military architecture. In early days they were usually solid, merely giving a height advantage to the defenders. The Round City of Baghdad, built from 762 to 765, was by far the most ambitious fortification of the early ᶜAbbāsid Caliphate. Apart from its size, which set it apart from anything previously seen in that part of the world, its design sprang from ᶜAbbāsid architects' earlier experience in Khūrāsān and Transoxiana. The basic concept of an imperial palace set within gardens surrounded by administrative offices and barracks also had more to do with Iranian traditions of a ruler set above ordinary men than with Islamic concepts of equality before God. As a palace the Round City of Baghdad felt like a prison and the Caliph soon built a new residence outside, close to the main military parade ground. Between the outer and inner walls of the Round City of Baghdad were the offices and homes of senior functionaries; ordinary troops and merchants lived in suburbs. By 800 Baghdad had a population of half a million - more than that of some western Europe states.

The fully developed *bāshūra* bent-gates of Baghdad were another new feature for the Middle East. These were a defence against surprise attack by cavalry, and comparable structures were added to existing Roman gates in other Islamic cities such as Damascus. Some cities, like Wasit in Iraq, were divided by a large river, the two parts joined by a floating bridge. The stronger western half also had a double wall with a deep moat and a *faṣīl* or additional low third wall some distance from the main defences, an idea which had parallels in China (see Chapter V).

In most parts of the Muslim world there was little in the way of rural fortification except near strategic frontiers where *ribāṭs* probably served as watch-towers. Others were close to barely governed areas such as the Arabian peninsula. Nevertheless even these could include very advanced features such as a doubled gate with a *portcullis*, and an elongated *machicolation* incorporated into the wall.

Real frontier defences were more impressive. In Cilicia, for example, the ex-Byzantine cities were re-populated and their defences repaired. Tarsus was given a moat, double wall, eighty-seven towers and six gates in the late 8th century. Muslim strategy in the *thughūr* and *awasim* provinces was basically to link major fortified towns by chains of garrison forts with fortified military depots to the rear. The best-preserved 9th-century *thughūr* fortress is Anavarza/ᶜAin Zarba which is surrounded by a buttressed wall with numerous small towers projecting only a small distance. The *ribāṭs* of the Palestine coast were towns rather than forts, and kept watch against Byzantine naval attack. Jaffa, for example, had strong defences and a mosque whose minaret served as an observation post.

Islam: The Successor States

The successor states often built more advanced fortifications than those of the ᶜAbbāsids, though not on the same scale. By the 10th century Tarsus had a doubled wall and five gates, those in the outer wall being covered in iron, those of the inner entirely of iron, though such an all-iron gate may in reality have been a *portcullis.* The inner wall of Tarsus had no less than 18,000 *shurrāfa* (crenellations) and one hundred towers. Three of the towers had *manjanīq* (beam-sling mangonels) on top, twenty had smaller *ᶜarrāda* (stone-throwing machines), and the remainder were manned by troops armed with crossbows.

In contrast the great city of Aleppo could not withstand the Byzantine attack. Instead the citizens fled to a man-made tal or hill on the eastern side of the city, barricading it with timber while the enemy plundered the city. By the 11th century Aleppo possessed a city wall almost fifteen metres high, and most northern Syria towns had been strongly fortified by the late 11th century. Farther east, Diyarbakir had particularly massive towers and four 'iron gates'. Ahead of the main wall which incorporated a passage large enough for armed men to fight in, was a smaller wall whose watch-towers were ten cubits (approximately 5 metres) high. Damascus had been refortified in the late 10th century but its walls were still only of mud-brick.

Within the desert areas rough tribal fortifications remained adequate as shelters to protect the harvest and conserve water supplies. Within Arabia an early 11th-century Persian traveller described many large and small castles as well as some fortified towns such as Lahssa near the Gulf coast which had four walls of earth or mud-brick.

Islam: The Fāṭimids (to 1171)

The architects who designed the fortified towers of Fāṭimid Syria and Egypt showed great originality. In Egypt itself the Fāṭimid Caliphs had a fortified palace enclosure similar in concept, though not in scale, to the Round City of Baghdad. Named al-Qāhira (The Victorious) (modern Cairo), it included the ruler's palace, plus administrative offices and barracks for guard units. The city was rectangular with eight gates and a high brick wall. The famous existing Fāṭimid stone gates were built later in the 11th century and although they are often

Interior of the gate of the fortified desert palace of Ukhaidir, Iraq, c.778. Unlike the earlier Umayyad palaces in Syria and Jordan, the fortifications of this huge complex are both strong and very advanced. (Iraqi Ministry of Culture photograph)

attributed to Armenian architects, their design appears more Syrian. The main function of these magnificent structures was symbolic, the twin northern gates being used by official embassies while the Bab al-Naṣr originally had a small *muṣallah* (prayer hall) outside as a kind of religious talisman to protect the city within.

Above: *The remarkable hill-top town and caves of Uçhisar in central Anatolia served as a refuge for the local inhabitants during the centuries when this eastern part of the Byzantine Empire was regularly raided by Muslim Arab armies. (Author's photograph)*

Islam: The Far Maghrib and al-Andalus

The early Islamic period saw a considerable increase of urban fortification in North Africa. Numerous coastal *ribāṭs* were built from Tunisia to Morocco, in Sicily and Andalusia against Christian piracy and may have influenced the development of Christian Military Orders in the Iberian peninsula. A completely independent style of fine masonry fortification also developed in Morocco and Andalusia, the barely projecting towers of the 9th century being replaced by larger structures which could have counter-battery stone-throwing machines on top.

The most distinctive form of construction in the far west of the Muslim World was a form of concrete which developed in the 10th century in Andalusia and then spread to Morocco. Its closest technological predecessor was the traditional mud and straw architecture of southern Arabia which is still capable of erecting buildings many storeys high. The wet mixture was laid within wooden shuttering, additional layers being added as the first dried. But in Andalusia and Morocco a mixture of gravel, earth, lime, straw and bones called *ṭabīʿa* or 'tabby' in its European derivation, replaced the ancient mud and straw. This was not only fast to use but could be used to repair damaged stone fortification and make defences almost as strong – and almost as ugly – as 20th-century 'pill-boxes'.

Al-Andalus was strongly fortified from the start since Muslim manpower always remained dangerously low. Many Andalusian fortifications seem to have used magical or totemic number combinations in their design. At first urban defences followed the lines of existing Roman walls but the rapid growth of Andalusian cities soon necessitated expansion. As a result cities in the plains had regular plans while those in the highlands enclosed, where possible, a high-point or hill for their citadel. Next door the *qaṣr* or *qaṣabah* was a governor's fortified residence and garrison. Viking naval raids also encouraged the fortification of the deep south.

Other distinctive features of Andalusian fortification were the widespread use of *barbicans* ahead of city gates, gate towers with overhanging balconies like *machicolations* known as *buheradas* in Spanish, and separate towers linked to the main wall by bridges known in Spanish as *albarranas*. As in the Middle East, the provision of reliable water supplies was basic to the design of Andalusian fortifications, caves like St. Michael's Cave beneath the Rock of Gibraltar being used for this purpose. Elsewhere large underground cisterns called *jayb* were sealed with waterproof lime plaster. In other cases city walls were extended to reach a reliable source of water, sometimes with a bastion at the water's edge a hundred metres from the main defences.

In the 10th century the Andalusians responded to Christian thrusts southwards by building a series of extremely large fortresses in the mountainous *thughūr* border provinces to serve as regional defence centres and garrisons. Smaller isolated fortifications were also characteristic of both the Muslim and Christian parts of the Iberian peninsula, those along the main military roads of Andalusia being called *rutba* or *marṣad;* fortified hostels were known as *manzil*. Isolated circular towers, probably used as beacons, were called *ṭalᶜīya* in Arabic, which entered Spanish as *atalayas*. Other small castles with a wall and a cistern, usually on hilltops, were probably used to keep watch on the mountain passes, and high in the hills could be found small towers with remarkably large storage facilities, variously known as *qubba, burj* or *qalᶜa*.

SIEGE WARFARE

Most developments in siege engineering originated in China then spread westwards to the Muslim world and Europe. Stone-throwing machines were still of limited power and tended to be made on the spot, though metal or other key pieces were brought 'from store' with a besieging force.

Christendom: The Byzantine Empire

Most armies attempted to reduce enemy strongholds by prolonged raiding of surrounding countryside. But if a direct attack were necessary, cavalry would survey the fortifications then secure the ground outside before the infantry took up

Below: *The walls of the Castelo dos Mouros at Sintra in Portugal, basically dating from the early Islamic period though they were constantly repaired in later centuries. They take advantage of every cliff and crag in the manner typical of Andalusian military architects. (Jane Carter photograph)*

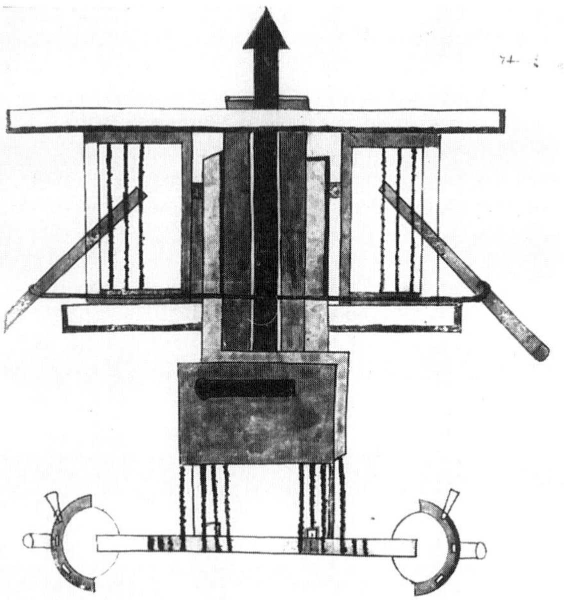

position opposite the gates. A camp was set up at least two bowshots from the wall, and units asigned to defend siege machines in case the enemy tried to destroy them. Direct assaults would aim at the weakest stretch of wall or across the shallowest moat, and involved battering-rams, 'tortoise' wheeled protective sheds, assorted *petroboli* stone-throwing machines, scaling ropes, ladders and wooden towers. An artificial hill might be erected to provide a better artillery position.

Left: *A schematic plan-view of a crossbow-like weapon known in Europe as an espringal and in the Muslim world as a qaws al-ziyar, shown here in an 11-century Byzantine military treatise. It was powered by two separate bow-arms under tension from twisted skeins of sinew or animal hair. The bow-string was pulled back by a windlass and the weapon shot a large heavy bolt. (Bibliothèque Nationale, MS. Grec. 2442, Paris)*
Below: *The city walls of Diyarbakr, dating from the 11th to early 13th centuries, are among the most extensive surviving medieval fortifications anywhere in the world, extending for 5½ kilometres around the old city. (Author's photograph)*

Byzantine sources sometimes use the term *manganikon* for a single-armed torsion-powered stone-throwing device, but the term *mangonel* and its various linguistic derivations normally referred to a beam-sling machine of Chinese origin. The Byzantine *cheirotoxobolistrai* and *toxobolistrai* of the 9th and 10th centuries seem to have been large frame-mounted crossbows; the prefix *cheiro* probably meaning that it could be operated by one man though it was usually carried by more. Byzantium was best known for *Greek Fire* and other incendiary weapons. Hand-pumped *Greek Fire* siphons appear in 11th-century manuscripts, but they had been mentioned a century earlier on the Muslim side of the frontier. Mouth-blown tubes of *Greek Fire* did not appear until the 12th century, and were used in mines.

Islam: The Early ᶜAbbāsid Caliphate

From the 8th to 11th centuries Muslim armies tended to rely on surprise attack, blockade and *naqb* (mining) to overcome fortifications, with minimal reliance on *kabsh* or *sinnawr* (battering-rams) and *manjanīq* (beam-sling siege engines). One particularly well-recorded siege was that of Wasit in the mid-8th century. At first the defenders fought outside their walls to stop the attackers establishing siege positions, sorties being made from an area between the main wall and a lower outer defence. Night fighting also continued outside, illuminated by torches on the walls. The similarity between such tactics and those of China at about the same time is remarkable and suggests mutual military influence between these two most powerful civilisations of the day. The vital role of cavalry in defence of another fortified place was also illustrated when a sortie by Muslim horsemen struck enemy assault squads in the flank as they attacked a breach in the wall. A century later, during the siege of Byzantine Amorium, each engine was operated by four men; the machines having been transported on carts. The Muslims also erected siege towers but these proved ineffective because the Caliph's men had been unable to fill the defensive ditch properly. In contrast, the siege of the sprawling city of Baghdad during a civil war degenerated into house-to-house fighting and the entrenchment of streets.

The ᶜAbbāsid army included a special corps of specialist *manjanīkīn* (siege machine operators), most of whom started their careers as ordinary soldiers. The *ᶜarrāda* (light siege and counter-siege machine), with a single beam powered by twisted rope on a fixed chassis was essentially the same as the Romano-Byzantine *onagros*. The *burj* (movable wooden siege tower) was rarer, and one source specifically accuses the 9th-century Arab bedouin of not knowing about the *dabbābah* (ram with a protective timber roof). They were similarly accused of not knowing about the *rutīla*, which was probably an early form of frame-mounted beam-sling mangonel which looked like a spider.

ᶜAbbāsid forces made considerable use of fire-weapons, one of the earliest references to oil-based *nafṭ* being in 776 though there was no mention of its being thrown. By the beginning of the 9th century the technique of winding *nafṭ*-soaked rags around rocks hurled from *mangonels* is recorded. There may already have been a distinction between ordinary *nafṭ* and *nār*, the former perhaps being more explosive than the latter. By 837 the *naffāṭ'īn* were a specialist unit under the same command as infantry archers. Other variations included javelins with containers of *nafṭ* attached. The so-called 'snakes' which were hurled into enemy strongholds may have been incendiary devices since, a few decades later, semi-explosive fire-weapons used for the same purpose in China were also known as 'snakes'.

Islam: The Successor States

The successor states used basically the siege and counter-siege techniques developed by the ᶜAbbāsids, the only real variation being in the east where the Ghaznavids learned from the Indians how to use elephants as live battering-rams. The 11th-century Fāṭimid arsenal included fire weapons known as 'Chinese arrows' which were probably incendiary devices that included the vital explosive element of saltpetre, plus *qawārīr al-nafṭ* (long-necked glass grenades), *makāḥil al-bārūd* (jars of saltpetre), and *satā'r* (screens) to conceal the movement of troops during siege warfare.

Early in the 12th century, while defending Tyre against the Crusaders, a Fāṭimid naval officer designed iron hooks to

Above: The walls and towers of the Citadel of Ankara, probably built during the reign of the Emperor Constans II, mid-7th century. The massive pointed towers are typical of the main eastern Byzantine fortifications of a period when the Empire was on the defensive against Muslim invasions. (Author's photograph)

Left: The so-called 'Cistern of St. Helena' at Ramla in Palestine is in fact an ᶜAbbāsid construction dating from about 800, and was built for the Caliph Hārūn al-Rashīd. This kind of enormous subterranean reservoir enabled Middle Eastern cities to endure prolonged sieges. (Author's photograph) deflect and destroy enemy rams operated from wooden siege towers. Another sailor invented a large T-shaped counter-balanced beam with panniers at one end for tipping refuse, faeces and burning substances on to the heads of enemy troops. It was moved by the same pulleys and ropes used aboard ship, but the extraordinary similarity between this device and one used in China suggests that the sailor may have voyaged to the Far East. The *manjanīq* (beam-sling mangonel) spread further, reaching Andalusia in the 10th century. New devices also appeared. For example the two-armed javelin-shooting machine later known in Europe as the *espringal* was known in 11th-century Byzantium and in the Muslim Middle East where it was called a *qaws al-ziyar*.

Counter-siege measures included the normal topping-up of water cisterns, the storage of weapons including *ᶜarrādas* as counter-battery engines, and the construction of flour-mills within the defences. More original were hidden pits dug by the Muslim defenders of Brindisi in southern Italy, into which counter-attacking Lombard cavalry tumbled.

NAVAL WARFARE

There was a clear distinction between official warfare and piracy, but the latter was so common that valuable cargoes were often carried aboard warships. Sea battles were a matter of grappling and boarding; artillery was more useful against stationary coastal targets. There were no slaves aboard Byzantine or Muslim ships other than a few personal servants, galley slaves being a feature of ancient and later centuries – not of the Middle Ages.

The Mediterranean and Atlantic

Geographical factors gave a clear advantage to the powers of the northern side of the Mediterranean over the south. There were more island 'stepping-stones' and good harbours in the north; the winds were generally more suitable for coastal navigation and the north had far more timber with which to build ships. Lack of suitable timber became even more of a problem for the Muslim southern coasts with the adoption of lateen sails which required huge masts and spars. By the 9th and 10th centuries Egypt was importing wood from Italy, Dalmatia and Crete which became a major centre of the timber trade. Meanwhile the need for secure sources of timber contributed to the Byzantine Empire's restoration of control over the Albanian coast. Attacking the enemy's stores, particularly of sails, also played an important part in naval warfare.

Muslim Mediterranean fleets survived the fall of the Umayyad Caliphate and Islam now enjoyed a large degree of naval domination. By the mid-8th century their galleys were defending themselves against Byzantine *Greek Fire* by using various systems of water-soaked cotton. But the Muslims' lack of timber may have stimulated a revival in the construction of very large ships; the economies of scale being at work. The change from hull-first to a more economical frame-first construction had also been completed by the 11th century (see Volume I), together with the widespread use of lateen sails attributed to the Arabs as a result of Indian Ocean influence. Stern sweep rudders were shown in 11th-century Islamic Mediterranean art, but only on small boats. A further wave of essentially Chinese maritime influence would, however, introduce the stern rudders to Islamic ships in the Indian Ocean, Gulf and Red Sea during the 11th century.

Islamic and Byzantine Mediterranean warships were much the same, with a considerable exchange of technology and terminology. The Arabic *adrumūnun* (galley) came from the Greek *dromon*, *sanadīl* similarly from *sandalion*, *s͟halandī* from *chelandion*, *akatia* perhaps from the Italian *acatenaria* which in turn may have come from the Greek *katena*. Even the general term for a ship, *safīna*, may have come from *sagini* – or vice versa. Arabic terms were soon being used for Italian cargo ships; such as *gatti* possibly from *acatia*, *barce* from *barka*, *curabii* from *g͟hurab* and *garabi* from *qārib* which may in turn have come from the Greek *karabos* or *karabion*. It has even been suggested that Dick Whittington's Cat was an Arab, in the sense that it was actually a *gatti* merchant ship of ultimately Islamic derivation!

Some war-galleys had a single bank of oars, some two; and from one to three masts. The ship-breaking ram was finally ousted by the oar-breaking and boarding *beak* in the 10th century, perhaps as a result of the increasing value of ships resulting from a shortage of timber. The Byzantine Emperor Basil I was credited with the 'invention' of a much larger fighting platform or forecastle called a *xulokastron*, and there are references to fighting castles being erected in the centre of the largest 10th-century galleys. Islamic sources differentiated between 'big galleys', 'long galleys' and 'decked galleys'. The normal type had 100 to 200 oarsmen, and a maximum of 150 marines concentrated in the forecastle. Both the *s͟hīnī* and *s͟halandī* had two banks of oars, and pictorial sources suggest that very curved stem and stern posts may have been characteristic of Muslim ships.

Some merchant ships were more like oared barges; these including the *qārib*, *g͟hurāb* and *ṭarīda* specialised horse-transports. Some 8th–9th-century Egyptian *qāribs*, however, were large, decked vessels with fighting castles, and by the late 9th–10th century the Byzantine navy was also building large ships known as *koumbaria*. Standard late 10th-century North African *ṭarīda* (horse-transports) could carry forty animals, whereas mid-11th-century Italian and Byzantine ships apparently only held about twenty.

The three-masted, two-decked sailing ships used by Muslim fleets may have been known as *qarqūra* which in turn lay behind the later medieval *caracca* or *carrack* in which Columbus and his contemporaries explored the world. One Andalusian vessel of 955 was said to be almost 100 metres long and nearly 40 metres wide, but such ships remained rare. Other merchant ships were often heavily armed, large fighting castles being added to the sterns of Islamic sailing ships though not galleys during the 11th century. Fighting forecastles, as used by the Byzantines, were less popular in the Muslim regions.

In Byzantium marines and the most vulnerable oarsmen wore lamellar cuirasses, though often only on the front of the body, while less exposed oarsmen had felt or leather armour. Oarsmen were expected to fight in Islamic fleets, and to a lesser extent in Byzantium. Both sides mainly relied on archery and javelins, plus special anti-rigging halbards or long-hafted axes and long spears to attack opposing oarsmen. Whereas Byzantine marines used *solenarion* arrow-guides, an élite unit of about 500 Egyptian Fāṭimid marines had light hand-held crossbows by the late 11th century.

Some warships had stone-throwing machines or frame-mounted crossbows and there are also references to those mysterious 'snakes' used in siege warfare. The most powerful Byzantine galleys were armed with six *ballistas* and three *Greek Fire* projectors, the latter consisting of bronze tubes in the form of wild animals' heads. The ᶜAbbāsid fleet was using comparable *nafṭ* in 842, and Egypt's pre-Islamic tradition of fire-based weapons probably accounted for the fact that, by the mid-10th century, the Fāṭimids were more advanced than their Byzantine foes in this form of warfare. Egypt, of course, was also in commercial contact with China where pyrotechnics were even more sophisticated. In 835 *ḥarrāqat* (fire-ships) were used successfully against Byzantine vessels, and in 964 other Byzantine ships were destroyed at anchor by swimmers using incendiary devices. On the other hand the Muslim use of ceramic amphorae to store drinking water may have reduced their operational range compared to Christian fleets which had already adopted wooden water barrels.

The islands of the Mediterranean served as vital stepping-stones and assembly points for raiding enemy ports, often to forestall an expected enemy raid. Efforts were also made to control potentially threatening naval bases, as when the Andalusian Umayyads briefly seized Ceuta and Melilla on the north Moroccan coast. Similarly, possession of such bases enabled a fleet to transport armies and their horses quickly to a threatened region. Several states developed sophisticated coastal observation systems. Muslim observers along the Syrian coast warned of approaching Byzantine fleets, but could not know their destination; naval commanders relied on spies in enemy territory for such information. During summer, when the 'seas were open', infantry and cavalry garrisons camped on the coast whereas in winter, when the 'seas were closed', a few soldiers manned watchtowers while the garrisons withdrew to inland towns. Ports could be very strongly protected, some reportedly having arches over the harbour mouth, though more often relying on floating chains across the entrance and stone-throwing engines on their sea walls. In the 10th century, however, Muslim navies pioneered a change from coastal raiding to attacking enemy ships at sea, this again perhaps contributing to the building of larger ships better able to defend themselves.

Contrary to popular opinion, the Muslims followed Romano-Byzantine fleets into the wilder waters of the Atlantic; stories about the terrors of this 'Sea of Darkness' coming from eastern Islamic regions, not from al-Andalus or Morocco. The Andalusians developed Atlantic bases at Alcaser do Sol, Silves, Seville and Algeciras with many coastal defence *ribāṭs* between these ports. Naval patrols sailed up the coast of Portugal, probably even into the Bay of Biscay, from the mid-9th century onwards, an Andalusian Umayyad squadron defeating the Vikings in a sea battle in 966 and again in 971. A generation later an Andalusian fleet transported the infantry of an army attacking the north-westernmost corner of the Iberian peninsula while the cavalry went overland. Trading and diplomatic links were established with the British Isles and Andalusian traders or fishermen returned with descriptions of whales being hunted off Ireland, Britain or perhaps even Iceland by the 11th century.

The extraordinary story of the 'Adventurers of Lisbon' was based on fact but has proved very difficult to interpret. These sailors made several voyages and came back with tales of islands out in the Atlantic, some inhabited by fair-skinned men with long hair, no beards; ships and cities and a king whose interpreter already spoke Arabic. These were probably the British Isles or Ireland, but Moroccan and Andalusian mariners certainly knew of the Canary Islands and claimed to have sailed sufficient degrees westward to reach Madeira, though not the Azores. Other evidence indicates that raiding and trading voyages northwards were less profitable than those to the south, and that Muslim mariners habitually reached Cap Blanc on the Saharan Atlantic coast of what is now Mauretania. They may even have reached the Cape Verde Islands, though this is debatable.

The Indian Ocean and Riverine Warfare

The Mediterranean *ṭarīda* (horse-transport galley) evolved from the simple Red Sea *ṭarāda* (cargo raft), but other Red Sea and Indian Ocean ships were far more advanced. Most technological developments travelled from east to west and the importance of links across the Indian Ocean can hardly be exaggerated. Egypt even imported shipbuilding timber from India after the Fāṭimids lost control of Crete. The canal which linked the Nile to the Red Sea, and thus by extension the Mediterranean with the Indian Ocean, had silted up by 723, but was back in service by the mid-10th century; its purpose remains unclear. There was no need for merchant ships to sail from the Red Sea to the Nile, so this medieval version of the Suez Canal was probably military, enabling squadrons based near Cairo to defend both the Mediterranean and Red Sea coasts.

Hinged stern rudders had been known in China for centuries, possibly appearing in Islamic art in the 9th and certainly by the 11th century. Whether these showed visiting Far Eastern vessels or local ships is unknown. By 942/3 *nafṭ* was also being used in the relatively infrequent naval wars of these eastern seas, Omani ships manned by 'operators with fire tubes' destroying several vessels from Basra, though the Basrans later used fire-ships to sink the Omanis.

Ḥarrāqat (fire-ships) were also used in riverine warfare in Iraq, perhaps manned by these same specialists from Basra. Another way in which the Caliph dealt with *zuṭ* rebels in southern Iraq was to blockade all outlets from these southern marshes.

III
TURKS, MONGOLS AND THE RISE OF RUSSIA (600–1400)

TURKS, MONGOLS AND THE RISE OF RUSSIA (600–1400)

Major Campaigns 94
ARMY RECRUITMENT 94
Turkish Central Asia 94
Non-Turkish Peoples 95
Russia 95
The Mongols 97
The Rise of Tīmūr-i Lank 98
ORGANISATION 98
Turkish Central Asia 99
Non-Turkish Peoples 99
Russia 100
The Mongols 101
The Rise of Tīmūr-i Lank 103
STRATEGY AND TACTICS 103
Broad Strategy 103
Troop Types 104
Battle Tactics 105
Combat Styles 108
Field and Camp Fortifications 108
WEAPONRY AND HARNESS 108
Archery and Slings 109
Swords and Daggers 109
Spears and Javelins 109
Other Weapons 109
Shields 112
Helmets 112
Body Armour 114
Limb Defences 116
Horse Harness 116
Horse Armour 117
FORTIFICATION 118
Turkish Central Asia 118
Non-Turkish Central Asian Peoples 118
Russia 118
The Mongols 120
The Rise of Tīmūr-i Lank 120
SIEGE WARFARE 120
NAVAL WARFARE 122

The military history of Russia, Central and Northern Asia during the Middle Ages was one of population movements, migrations, cultural and linguistic exchange, conquest and religious conversion. The historical evidence is less detailed than that for western Europe and the Middle East and the identity of some peoples remains unclear. In some cases it has been confused by nationalist propaganda; particularly where the origins of the Rus are concerned. They created the first Russian state and were probably a mix of Slavs, Scandinavians, Finns and others. Some of the foundations of medieval Russia had already been laid by Turkish rulers such as the Jewish Khazars, the 'White Ugri' who may have been eastern Magyars probably controlling Kiev on behalf of the Khazars before the rise of Russia in the late 9th century. Prince Vladimir's conversion to Christianity broke this eastward orientation by changing Kiev's ruler from a Slav *khān* to a Grand Prince in the Byzantine mould.

The main thrust of Russian ambition was southwards, seeking closer links with Byzantium and attempting to join Kiev with the isolated Russian principality of Tmutarakan on the Black Sea.

The Principality of Muscovy, which dominated Russia by the end of the Middle Ages, arose in a region which originally had a Finnish population, through with an increasing Slav element. Suzdalia, slightly farther east, has been described as the melting-pot of Slavs and Finns which produced the 'Great Russian' people (as opposed to the 'Little Russians' or Ukrainians and the 'White Russians' of Belarus). The assimilation of the Finns was closely connected with the spread of Christianity though some Finnish tribes were already culturally similar to their Slav neighbours. By the 12th century most of the remaining Finnish-speaking peoples survived in isolated enclaves, as their descendants do to this day. Elsewhere Slav domination was interrupted by the Mongol conquest of Russia, while some east-Finn tribes were more influenced by Turkish Bulgars and by the Mongols than by advancing Slavs.

Far to the north Novgorod was founded by several different peoples, including Slavs, Finns and Balts. Still farther north the sub-Arctic regions were inhabited by scattered Finn and Ugrian tribes, through the latter appear to have been pushed east of the Ural mountains during the Middle Ages. Many Ugrian tribes were, like the Finns, forest dwellers rather than nomads and although they were not warlike people, the Ugrians were primitive enough to terrify their Slav neighbours. In fact the Russians believed the Ugrians to be so awful that God had locked them behind the Ural Mountains until Judgement Day.

Many Mongol and Turkish tribes also lived in the Siberian forests rather than the steppes; among these being the Bashjirt of the middle Volga. They, however, also included forest-dwelling Finno-Ugrian Magyars, known as Outer Bashjirts and related to those Magyars who migrated westwards into Hungary in the late 9th century. Other Bashjirts inhabited the steppe fringe as vassals of the Muslim Turkish Bulgars of 'Great Bulgaria' on the Volga – not to be confused with the now Balkan Slav kingdom of Bulgaria.

By the 7th century the peace established by the Great Turk *Khānate* in Central Asia had led to a considerable expansion of towns and agriculture, particularly along the Silk Road, a network of caravan routes linking China with the Middle East. However, the fragmentation of this state and of its most advanced successor state, the Uighur *Khānate* in what is now Chinese Turkestan, led to a period of great instability and resulted in another wave of massive migrations westward. The 7th century also saw a sudden period of expansionism in

__Below:__ Part of a leather-covered wooden shield from the castle of Mug in Transoxiana; Sughdian early 8th century. It is decorated with a painted picture of a horseman wearing a lamellar cuirass and splinted arm defences or vambraces. He has a dagger across his waist, a long straight sword, two unstrung bows in a bow-case slung on his left hip and a quiver on his right. This is the same military equipment shown in greater detail on similarly dated wall-paintings from Transoxiana. (State Hermitage Museum, St. Petersburg)

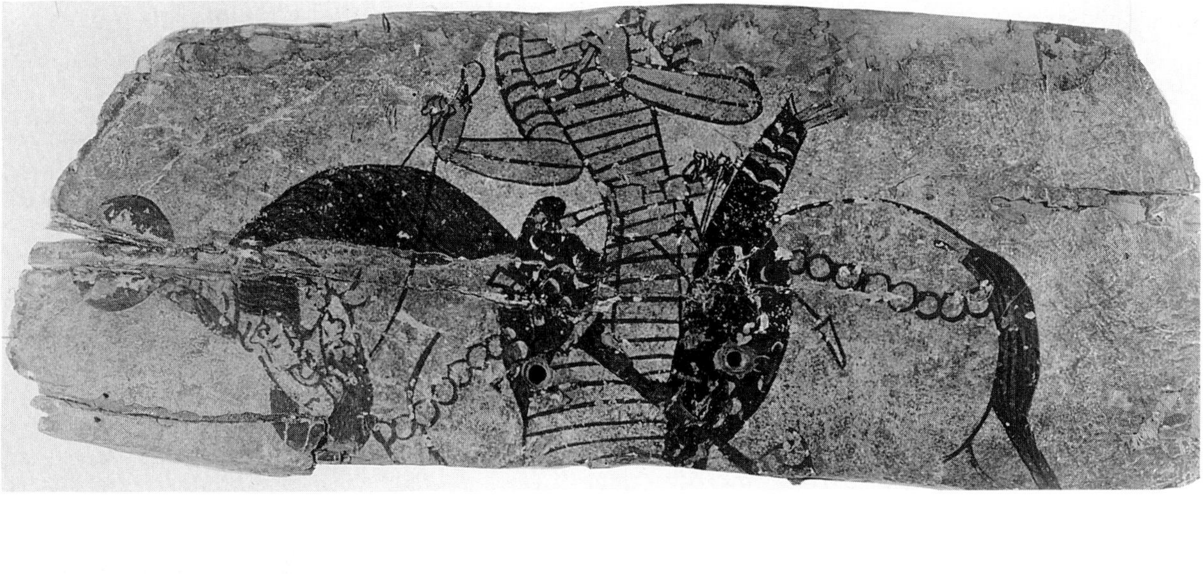

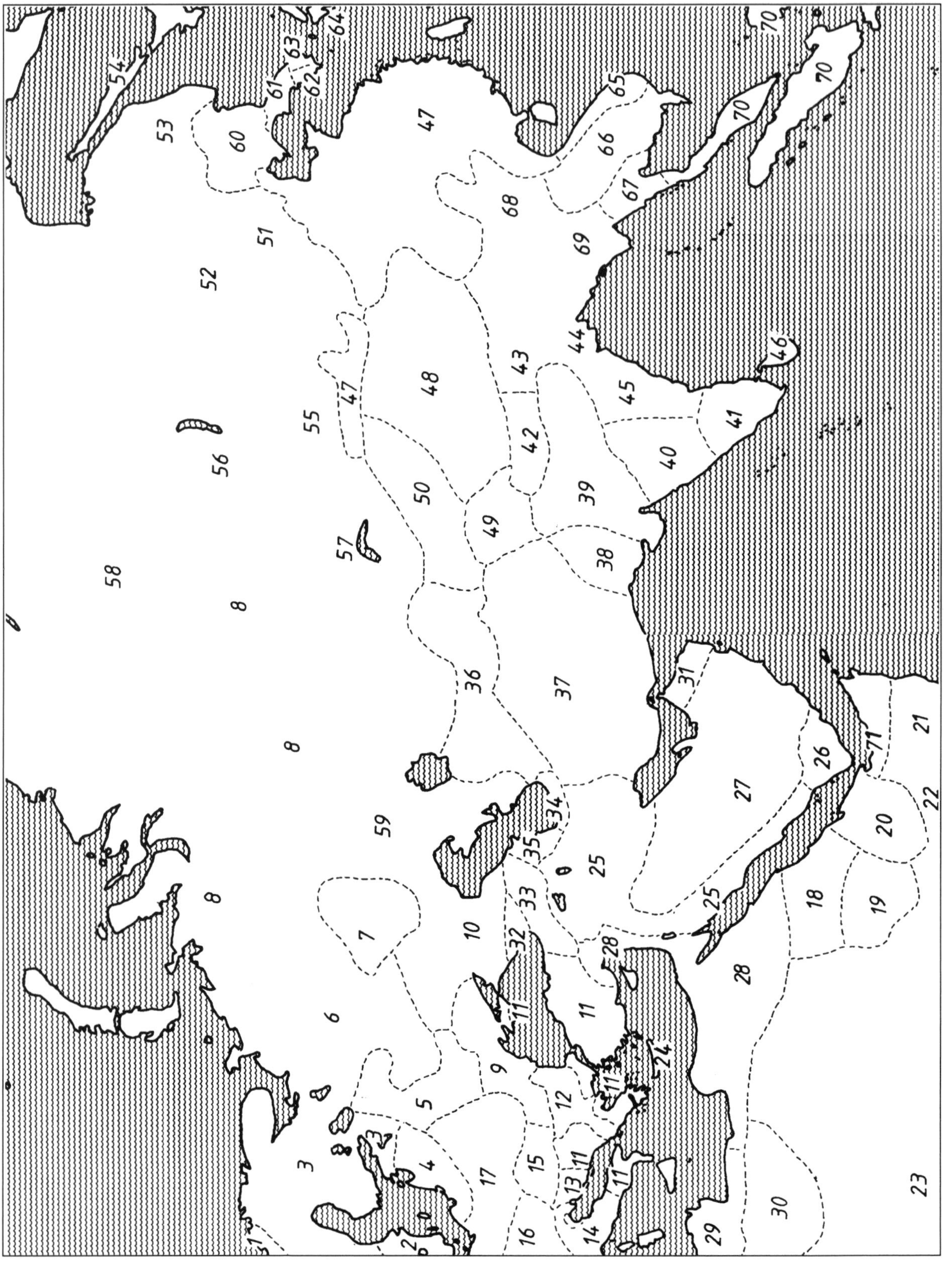

Left: Asia, eastern Europe and north-west Africa, c.900

1. *Norwegians*
2. *Swedes*
3. *Saami (Lapps) and western Finns*
4. *Balts*
5. *Kievan Russia*
6. *Eastern Finns*
7. *Volga Bulgars*
8. *Ugrians*
9. *Pechenegs*
10. *Khazars*
11. *Byzantine Empire*
12. *Bulgaria*
13. *Croatia*
14. *Kingdom of Italy*
15. *Hungary*
16. *Germany (East Frankish Kingdom)*
17. *Slavs*
18. *Makuria*
19. *Alwa*
20. *Ethiopia*
21. *Somalis (Zanj)*
22. *Galla*
23. *Kanem*
24. *Local Muslim rulers*
25. *^{c}Abbāsid Caliphate*
26. *Ziyādids*
27. *Qarmatians*
28. *Ṭūlūnids, under ^{c}Abbāsid suzerainty*
29. *Aghlabids*
30. *Fezzan*
31. *Julanda*
32. *Abasgia*
33. *Armenia*
34. *^{c}Alīds*
35. *Sajids, under ^{c}Abbāsid suzerainty*
36. *Sāmānids, under ^{c}Abbāsid suzerainty*
37. *Ṣaffārids, under ^{c}Abbāsid suzerainty*
38. *Arab rulers of Manṣura*
39. *Gurjara-Pratiharas*
40. *Rashtrakutas*
41. *Cholas*
42. *Nepal*
43. *Assam*
44. *Palas*
45. *Chalukyas*
46. *Lanka*
47. *China, fragmented under 'Five Dynasties'*
48. *Tibet*
49. *Kashmir and other small independent states*
50. *Uighurs*
51. *Khitan*
52. *Keraits*
53. *Jürchen*
54. *Ainu*
55. *Kirghiz*
56. *Kurikan*
57. *Kimāks*
58. *Samoyeds*
59. *Ghuzz*
60. *Parhae*
61. *Koryŏ*
62. *Paekche*
63. *Silla*
64. *Japan*
65. *Champa*
66. *Khmer*
67. *Dvaravati*
68. *Nan-Chao*
69. *Pyu*
70. *Srivijayan Empire*
71. *Zaila*

Tibetan history and was associated with the introduction of Buddhism. After a brief clash with the Muslim Arabs in Transoxiana, Tibetans and Muslim Arabs generally enjoyed good relations until, in the mid-9th century, Tibet's Central Asian empire suddenly collapsed, after which the Tibetans retreated into isolation.

It would be very wrong to think that the peoples of Central Asia, even the nomadic, were culturally homogeneous. Nor were they any more warlike than the peoples of medieval Europe. The Kitai, for example, inhabited the forests of north-east Mongolia and southern Manchuria rather than the steppes. The Qarluks included settled and nomadic elements, many of whom were Nestorian Christians by the 9th century. The Semirechye region south of Lake Balkash was similarly settled, and here Islam spread rapidly. The Qipchaqs' name, as well as others given to this people by enemies and neighbours, has sometimes been thought to indicate 'yellow hair' but in reality referred to the 'yellow' desert spaces from which this nomadic eastern Turkic people originated. Displaced by the Uighurs in about 744, the Qipchaqs eventually re-established stability in the steppes from the Chinese to the Hungarian frontiers.

The steppes of southern Russia and the Ukraine served as a corridor through which various nomadic peoples migrated westward, pushed by more powerful groups to the east. The most important were the Pechenegs, the Uzes (also known as Torks), the Qipchaqs and finally the Mongols who were not, of course, pushed by anyone. Some were driven across the Carpathian mountains into the Hungarian plain or into a cul-de-sac of steppe-like territory of Wallachia in Romania, while other were pushed into the forests of western Ukraine, Moldavia and the Bukovina north of the Carpathians. Although defeated by eastern rivals, these Turkish peoples often became locally dominant military élites. Others were recruited by existing states as frontier troops, sometimes ending up far to the west of the steppes.

The Mongols were no longer really nomads by the time they marched west, but had, like the Huns, become dominant predators bent on extorting tribute. Nor were the Mongols interested in conquering Europe, still less in venturing into western waters such as the Black Sea and Mediterranean. They wanted to dominate the steppes and neighbouring forest states including Russia, while their overriding priority remained the conquest of China. By the mid-13th century the Mongol élite was strongly influenced by Chinese culture and although much of Mongol army was probably Nestorian Christian, the more sophisticated aspects of Mongol warfare had a distinctly Chinese character. As the vast Mongol 'World Empire' fragmented it was succeeded by smaller local *khānates*. Those of western Asia and eastern Europe, though still bearing the name Mongol or Tatar, were overwhelmingly Turkish in speech and population though their armies clung to Mongol traditions. The most settled and civilised was the Īl-Khān state centred upon Transoxiana and Iran, but even here sedentarisation of the Turco-Mongol tribes was more common in central regions than on frontiers where nomadism and a warlike predatory mentality survived longer. By the end of the 14th century the Mongol tribes of Transoxiana had been almost entirely Turkified, the only real Mongols remaining being those farther east including Mongolia itself.

The Black Sea region was home to various less formidable peoples, including Christian Georgians and a mosaic of Muslim and semi-pagan peoples, many of them descended from passing conquerors whose remnants had been washed up against the northern slopes of the Caucasus mountains. Within the Crimean peninsula the descendants of Goths who had briefly ruled the area at the start of the Middle Ages survived at least until the Mongol invasions of the 13th century. Dotted around the Black Sea also were strongly fortified Italian trading colonies, many of which outlived the Mongol onslaught, only to be overrun by Timur-i Lenk and his Ottoman enemies in the 15th century.

Major Campaigns

607: Unification of Tibet.
665-92: Tibetan conquests northward into eastern Turkestan (modern Sinkiang).
714-44: Central Asian Great Turks defeated by T'ang Chinese
744-45: Destruction of the Eastern Turkish Khānate; creation of Uighur Turkish Empire in eastern Turkestan.
759-63: Tibetan expansion cuts Silk Route; collapse of T'ang authority in Central Asia.
840-2: Fragmentation of Tibet and collapse of Tibetan Empire.
840: Uighur Empire overthrown by Kirghiz Turks.
862: Novgorod founded by 'Rurik the Viking'.
913-15: Pecheneg Turk migration west into steppes north of Black Sea; first raids into southern Russia.
916: Establishment of Khitan state in Mongolia.
934-44: Pechenegs join Hungarian and Russian invasions of Byzantium.
965-7: Russian Kiev breaks power of Jewish-Turkic Khazar state north-east of Black Sea.
1032: Novgorod sends expedition to 'Iron Gates', probably east of river Pechora.
1036: Russian Kiev defeats Pechenegs at Kiev.
1054: Kievan Russia fragments into rival principalities; start of Qipchaq raids into Russia.
1079: Large Novgorod military expedition against Ugrians of Ob river disappears.
1091: Byzantines and Qipchaqs defeat Pechenegs.
1093: Qipchaqs sack Kiev.
Early 12 century: Novogorod trading and tribute expeditions reach north-western Siberia.
1120s: Khitans displaced by Jürchen; latter establish Chin dynasty in northern China.
1125: Unification of Qipchaq tribes in southern Russia and Ukraine.
1130s: Fragmentation of Kievan Russian state.
c.1140: Displaced Khitans establish Qara-Khitai state in Turkestan.
1204-6: Temüchin (Genghis Khān) unites Mongol tribes.
1206: Start of Mongol conquests under Genghis Khān.
1220-1: Mongols invade Transoxiana.
1222-4: Mongols invade southern Russia; defeat Qipchaqs and Russians at river Kalka.
1236-41: Mongols defeat Volga Bulgars and Qipchaqs in southern Russia and Ukraine; conquer Russia.
1238: Mongols defeat Russians at river Siti.
1240: Mongols sack Kiev; Alexander Nevski defeats Swedes at river Neva.
1241-2: Mongols invade Hungary.
1242: Alexander Nevski and Novgorod defeat Crusaders at Lake Peipus.
1268: Fragmentation of Mongol Empire.
1301-64: Moscow (Muscovy) occupies neighbouring Kolomna, Dimitrov, Galich, Vladimir, Mozhaysk, Serpukhov and other cities.
1371: Tīmūr-i Lank (Tamerlane) invades Khwārazm.
1375-6: Tīmūr-i Lank invades Jagatai Mongol territory as far as Mongolia.
1380: Muscovy defeats Golden Horde at Kulikovo Field.
1381-8: Tīmūr-i Lank invades Afghanistan and Iran.
1382: Golden Horde sacks Moscow.
1389-1425: Muscovy occupies neighbouring Volodga, Nizhniy Novgorod, Murom and Meshchera.
1391-2: Tīmūr-i Lank defeats Golden Horde at Kunduzcha.
1392-6: Tīmūr-i Lank invades Golden Horde.
1392-6: Tīmūr-i Lank invades Iran, Iraq and Georgia.
1398-9: Tīmūr-i Lank invades Muslim northern India.
1399-1404: Tīmūr-i Lank invades Anatolia, Iraq, Syria, Georgia, defeats Ottomans at Ankara, retakes Izmir from Crusaders.
1399: Golden Horde defeats Lithuania at Vorskla.

ARMY RECRUITMENT

The impact of ecology on history was of considerable importance among the nomadic peoples of the Eurasian steppes. For example, the availability of grazing imposed a limit on the number of horses a tribe could maintain, and the harshness of nomadic life meant that it was so normal for a Central Asian tribesman to be a warrior that there were no separate words for 'soldier', 'peace' or 'war' in the earliest Turkish and Mongol languages. Fighting was essential for group survival; courage, discipline and military training being basic to nomadic culture.

Turkish Central Asia

The armies of the Great Turks, Eastern and Western Turk, and Uighur *khāns* of the eastern steppes were recruited almost entirely from within the dominant tribal confederation. Only on the southern and western fringes did the existence of other peoples encourage more varied recruitment. The urbanised Semirechye region, for example, was dominated by the Turkish Karluks from the 8th century, but had become an autonomous part of the Muslim Qarākhānid state by the 11th century with its own army recruited from Muslims, Christians, Buddhists and others. Farther north the 9th-century Kimāk Turks of the western Siberian forest never became Muslim, but had close links with the Oghuz or Ghuzz from whom the strongly Islamic Saljūq Turks sprang.

The 6th-century Great Bulgar state of the western steppes was led by Turks but included Slavs and Alans. Bulgars who then migrated to the Balkans were absorbed by their Slav subjects, whereas those who migrated north to create the Volga Bulgar state in what is now east-central Russia became Muslim and fielded a powerful army which dominated, as well as recruiting from, the neighbouring Slav and Finn tribes. Their neighbours, the Bashjirt (Bashkir) may have originated in south-western Turkestan but were first recorded in the Ural foothills bordering the Volga Bulgars. They also converted to Islam and dominated the local eastern Magyar (eastern Hungarian) tribes, many later entering western (European) Hungarian service in the 12th century.

The Khazars who expelled the Bulgars from the western steppes established their state in southern Russia in the 7th century and were at first a typical Turkish tribal horde. But the

Buddhist shrine attached to the fort at Miran. It is basically built of beaten earth reinforced with layers of bamboo; probably Tibetan, late 8th–early 9th centuries. (Aurel Stein photograph)

Khazars converted to Judaism in the 8th century and recruited a sophisticated army which included Alans, eastern Magyars and Slavs, under their own commanders, while the élite remained Khazar cavalry modelled upon the heavily armoured troopers of neighbouring Islamic states, plus guard units of Muslim mercenaries from Khwārazm. Their Pecheneg successors were pushed west by the Qipchaq in 1116, many being driven northwards into Russian territory or southwards into Byzantine territory together with their rivals the Torks and Uzes.

The Qipchaqs who expelled the Pechenegs now established a remarkably sophisticated state consisting of semi-independent eastern and western halves or flanks. Like some of their predecessors the largely Turkish Qipchaqs were ruled by dynasties of perhaps Mongol origin while the trading towns under their control were inhabited by Persians, Jews, Armenians and many others, some of whom provided military support.

Non-Turkish Peoples

The role of non-Turco-Mongol peoples tended to be localised. The Tibetans, for example, recruited many foreigners since their own numbers were small; the Finn and related Ugrian tribes were regarded as fearsome fighters but rarely emerged from their forests; the substantial Jewish population of southern Russia were commercial rather than military. The armies of pre-Islamic Transoxiana on the southern side of the steppes seem to have been recruited from a local Iranian-speaking Sughdian rural *dihqān* (aristocracy), but its retainers were generally led by a Turkish ruling élite. Similarly Iranian-speaking Alan tribal nomads played a prominent role in the western part of the Khazar state and remained as a wealthy warrior élite in the Caucasus mountains throughout the Middle Ages. In the coastal mountains of the Crimean peninsula a Germanic Goth community was probably reinforced by Anglo-Saxons from the Byzantine *Varangian* Guard in the late 11th and 12th centuries, and as a result had become known as *Saxi* by the 13th century. After the Mongol conquest, however, this isolated Germanic community rapidly disappeared. To the west the Romanian-speaking Vlach nomads of Wallachia and Moldavia gave military support to the neighbouring Turkish nomad states while also raiding other neighbours on their own behalf.

Russia

An Alan élite may have dominated several Slav tribes in what is now southern Russia before the rise of the Kievan state in the 9th century. This might have been because they were horsemen, while the earliest Russian armies do not seem to have included cavalry until the 10th century, these being provided by Turkish nomad allies and auxiliaries.

Stone icon of St. George; Russian, c.1250. Whereas most medieval Russian illustrations of warrior saints portray them in highly stylised Romano-Byzantine armour, this St. George has a full-length, long-sleeved mail hauberk, lance and kite-shaped shield, closer to the military reality of the period. (State Russian Museum, St. Petersburg)

The Scandinavian merchant-warrior adventurers who contributed to the creation of the first Russian state had greater military influence in north rather than south Russia where the military élite of Kiev were of mixed origins. Nevertheless Norse mercenaries played a significant role in the army of Vladimir I, Grand Prince of Kiev, in the late 10th century. These pagan warriors may in fact have been avoiding the advance of Christianity in Scandinavia though paradoxically Vladimir went on to become Russia's first Christian ruler, earning himself the title of Saint in the process.

Kievan Russian armies of the 11th to mid-13th centuries served dynastic rulers who were almost nomadic in their lifestyle, moving from principality to principality across vast distances. Each had a *druzhina* or armed retinue, that of the Grand Prince being the strongest. Bound by oaths similar to those which cemented 10th-century Middle Eastern Muslim armies, these *druzhinas* recruited men of established and humble origins. Most were Slav, though Scandinavian *Varangians,* Ossetians (Iasy) and Kosogians (Circassians) from the Caucasus, Magyars, Turks and others were all mentioned. The majority had been Russianised by the 11th century, membership of the Orthodox Christian church meaning acceptance into the community of Rus whatever an individual's language. The flow of Scandinavian *Varangian,* or as they were known in Russia *Varjazi,* mercenaries through Russia to Byzantium continued into the 12th century, though few were now diverted into Russian service.

Druzhinas eventually formed the basis of medieval Russia's *boyar* aristocratic class, together with other land-owning, tribal and merchant élites. The *postrig* Christianised but originally pagan initiation ceremony which marked a boy's entry into the princely élite at the age of four or five may have had parallels for the *boyar* class. In the 12th and 13th centuries it involved cutting the boy's hair, putting him on a horse for the first time, and then giving a great feast. The *posadnik* 'mayors' of Kievan Russian towns were recruited from the *boyar* class and over the centuries Slav tribal levies were gradually replaced by militias from such towns. Archery was an infantry affair in Kievan Russia, archers being recruited from younger soldiers, probably from urban militias.

The ordinary *smerdi* peasants were only called upon to fight in dire emergencies. But in the 12th century the steppe frontier of Kievan Russia was garrisoned by warriors who lived in virtually autonomous farming communities comparable to the later Cossacks. Throughout this period Turkish soldiers from the steppes also played a vital role as allies, sometimes similarly settled in military colonies along the steppe frontier. The *Chernye Klobuki* 'Black Caps' (*Karakalpak* in Turkish) were different in that they were recruited from entire clans that had been driven out of the steppes by newly arrived conquerors. First recorded in the late 11th century, many were from the Berend, Pecheneg and Tork tribes. They were given land along the river Ros in the Ukraine as well as farther west, retaining their tribal organisation and serving in the armies of several Russian principalities. Qipchaqs also fought for the Russians as auxiliaries, providing vital horse-archers, but after the Mongol conquest many Qipchaqs were also absorbed into existing *Chernye Klobuki* communities. Others were recorded in Alexander Nevski's army far to the north.

The isolated Russian principality of Tmutorokan, beyond the Turkish-dominated steppes on the shore of the Black Sea, had its own *druzhina* and this, not surprisingly, was recruited from different sources, a majority perhaps being from the Caucasus. Links between Russia and the Armenian principalities may date back as far as the 9th century, but the supposed presence of Armenian mercenaries in a Russian army fighting against Poland in the mid-11th century remains doubtful. Nevertheless the commercially important Armenians of Kiev and other southern Russian towns probably contributed to local militias. Far to the north the wealthy militia of Novgorod employed warriors from the neighbouring Finn tribes against Swedish and other invaders from the Baltic in the mid-13th century.

Under Mongol Golden Horde rule Russian recruitment and organisation changed considerably. During the later 13th and early 14th centuries, for example, Russian armies still included *druzhinas,* the *dvorjane* (aristocracy who provided the *bojarskye deti* young warriors led by more experienced noblemen), plus the *gorodskoe opolchenie* (urban militias) and various mercenary units. But the Mongol tradition of demanding military service from an entire male population meant that the rural peasantry were now more involved in warfare. As the Golden Horde declined in the later 14th century, Russian princes took over this right of general conscription, resulting in armies very different from those of western or central Europe. Similarly the later medieval Cossacks, whether in Russian or Polish-Lithuanian armies, originated in steppe regions which had formed an essential part of Golden Horde territory. They were of extremely mixed ethnic and cultural origins, though they became some of the fiercest proponents of Russian Orthodox Christianity.

The Mongols

Mongol armies themselves were much larger than those of their Middle Eastern and European foes, though their size was still hugely exaggerated by their victims. Even under Ghengis Khān, conquered Turks were recruited in substantial numbers to supplement the limited supply of ethnic Mongols. These Turks included some Muslims in 1219, despite the fact that Muslim states would become the Mongols' most devastated victims. Larger and militarily more significant numbers of ex-Chinese soldiers were also enlisted as infantry and specialist siege troops. A Mongol habit of transferring part of various conquered communities to distant provinces of their 'World Empire' resulted in Orthodox Christian Alans as well as many Russians serving in eastern Mongol armies. Some Russians subsequently returned home, having presumably witnessed the advanced military ideas used by Chinese troops against whom, and alongside whom, they fought.

The bulk of the army with which Hülegü conquered much of the eastern Muslim world was no longer strictly Mongol but included many Qipchaq Turks plus Chinese siege-machine operators under the Chinese general, Kuo K'an. Among the Mongol troops who did accompany Hülegü were Oirats from a forest tribe west of Lake Baikal, some of whom eventually deserted Hülegü's descendants to serve the strictly Muslim Mamlūk rulers of Egypt. Other Oirats remained in Central Asia, taking the new name of Kalmyks to become the most dedicated Buddhist enemies of Islam.

The army of the Īl-Khānid descendants of Hülegü in Iran and Iraq continued to claim a Mongol identity, though it was largely Turkish. In late 13th-century Anatolia local Īl-Khān forces may have included Muslim *ṣūfī* (mystical religious fraternities), while on the eastern frontier of the Īl-Khān state a new group of 14th-century warriors called *qarawnas* may have been descended from Mongol fathers and Indian or Kashmiri mothers. During the 14th century the Jagatai tribe regarded itself as the guardians of Mongol identity, retaining Mongol costume, tribal organisation and a nomadic way of life, though in reality it too had been largely Turkified. The Jagatai did, however, produce the *qawtchin* (élite guard) which over the years became a sort of separate tribe in its own right.

The easternmost Mongol successor state was that of the Yüan in China (see Chapter V), while the westernmost was the Golden Horde which held sway from the Altai mountains to

'Civilian dignitary seized by soldiers', in a fragment of wall-painting from Kumtura; Uighur Turkish, 8th-9th centuries. The style betrays strong Chinese influence, but the lamellar armour for men and horses is distinctly Turkish Central Asian. (Staatliche Museum Dahlem, Berlin)

Russia. It was dominated by four or five 'ruling tribes' though membership of these was fluid, kinship bonds being nominal except among ruling families. At the end of the Golden Horde period these 'ruling tribes' were listed as the Şirin, Barın, Arğın and Qipchaq; the latter being of Turkish origin. These provided the administrative and military élite, including many of the *bashaks* who supervised non-Mongol rulers such as the princes of Russia; other *bashaks* were recruited from Muslims, Armenians and Turks.

Subordinate peoples who served in Golden Horde armies included Muslim Turkish Bashjirts from the Ural mountains and Slav Ruthenians who also raided their European Hungarian neighbours without prompting from the Golden Horde. Small numbers of western European mercenaries were recruited from the mid-13th century, most being specialists such as crossbowmen and perhaps marines. Accounts of European troops serving in Khān Mamay's army at the battle of Kulikova in 1380 were probably exaggerated. On the other hand he might have had a handful of Venetians in his guard for prestige purposes. Ossetian and Cherkess troops from the Caucasus had served the Golden Horde for many years, but the presence of Muslim militiamen from various Golden Horde towns would merely indicate that Mamay could no longer rely on support from the militarily much more significant Turco-Mongol tribes.

The Rise of Tīmūr-i Lank

Tīmūr-i Lank claimed to be a Mongol, but he and the greater part of his remarkably successful army were Turkish or at least Turkified. Forty so-called Mongol tribes formed the basis of his army, each providing an agreed contingent depending on the tribe's size. From these were drawn the ruler's élite units and larger regional forces which could, however, be summoned without reference to the regional governor. On several occasions women fought in close combat alongside the men, though it would be misleading to regard this as evidence of pre-Islamic attitudes.

Both Tīmūr and his 15th-century successors enlisted defeated enemy troops, though Tīmūr's advice to his descendants not to trust troops who had failed to fight loyally for their previous leader must have reduced the number of such recruits. Those whom he himself enlisted included *sarbadār* (urban militias) from Khurāsān and Samarkand, large numbers of other Iranian troops and even a few western Europeans who had got caught up in his lightning campaigns around the eastern Mediterranean and Black Sea. Farther to the north-east, beyond Tīmūr's ability to conquer if not to raid, the Uzbeg Turks were as yet divided into many small nomadic tribes which would be welded into a unified and powerful fighting force until the later 15th century.

Pecheneg or Qipchaq Turkish funerary statue, probably 12th century. This example is from Kerch in the Crimea, an area close or perhaps within a zone under Byzantine rule, which would account for the portrayal of pseudo-Roman elements in the armour. (State Historical Museum, Moscow)

ORGANISATION

Settled rather than nomadic regions of Central Asia would have an enormous influence on many aspects of medieval military organisation and technology; far greater than their mili-

Khazar Turkish graffito on a fragment of plaster from southern Russia, perhaps 9th century. So little pictorial evidence survives from the powerful Jewish Khazar Khānate that the appearance of its troops remains almost unknown. The horseman shown here, however, seems to include Central Asian and eastern Mediterranean elements. (Author's photograph; State Hermitage Museum, St. Petersburg)

tary potential would suggest. Turco-Iranian Khwārazm south of the Aral Sea, for example, played a leading role in the early development of armoured spear-armed cavalry and horse-armour before the Middle Ages began.

Nevertheless there are widespread misconceptions about Central Asian warfare. Unlike the bedouin nomads of the Middle East, Turco-Mongol steppe societies were basically self-sufficient with many small towns in and around the open grasslands. Most peoples engaged in agriculture to some degree, others were involved in mining and metallurgy; several steppe tribes were related to peoples of the neighbouring Siberian forests. The organisation of Central Asian nomadic tribes was on basis of 'heads' rather than land or property; hence society already resembled an army. While many tribes could retreat into the 'grass sea' of the steppes, this was only done in an emergency. The main problem for Central Asian societies was to maintain the enormous horse-herds upon which their power depended, particularly when they conquered intensively cultivated or semi-desert lands. In reality their armies were often short of horses and their military élites frequently fought on foot.

Turkish Central Asia

The Uighur *khān's* own army included an élite infantry bodyguard and was supplemented by the forces of seventeen sub-chiefs. While the nomads of the eastern steppes covered great distances, many state-building peoples of the western steppes such as the Khazars, Great Bulgars and Volga Bulgars were not true nomads, but transhumants who migrated a relatively short way up and down the rivers.

The wealth of the Khazars' state came partly from agriculture and this enabled them to maintain professional mercenary armies and fixed garrisons in the nine districts of their state. The two halves or flanks of the Pecheneg state were similarly each divided into four provinces, each of five districts. The ruling élite inhabited the three richest districts, though all were supposedly capable of supplying a thousand cavalrymen, the ruler having his own full-time professional guard which formed the nucleus of any larger army. The state as a whole was a kind of military democracy where all important issues were decided at a general council, much like that of the later medieval Cossacks, though senior ranks were hereditary. The main Pecheneg cities still largely consisted of tents.

The subsequent Qipchaq state had no supreme ruler but was similarly divided by the river Ural into two halves, each of about twelve tribes or clans having their own defined zone of migration and political centre. The numerous carved *baba* statues of warriors and ladies which dotted the western steppes are believed to have marked the sites of these largely lost tented towns.

Non-Turkish Peoples

Pre-Islamic Transoxiana consisted of many little states recognising the suzerainty of about five larger kingdoms, some of which in turn occasionally acknowledged the Sassanian or Chinese Emperors. Though loosely organised they indulged in elaborate ceremonial but, unlike a Sassanian Emperor, a Transoxianan ruler was merely 'first among equals'. Some were known as *ikhshīd* although the countryside was really dominated by an aristocracy of *dihqān* living in manors or castles. Below them in the social scale came the *kadīvar* (farmers), *khidmatgār* (servants) and *atbāi*^{c} (military followers).

Among the professional troops of Transoxiana were a groups of armed retainers called *chākarān*, described by Chinese visitors as cavalry of great valour. They were recruited by merchants as well as aristocrats, having administrative and business duties as well as acting as bodyguards. It has been suggested that these *chākarān* influenced the development of

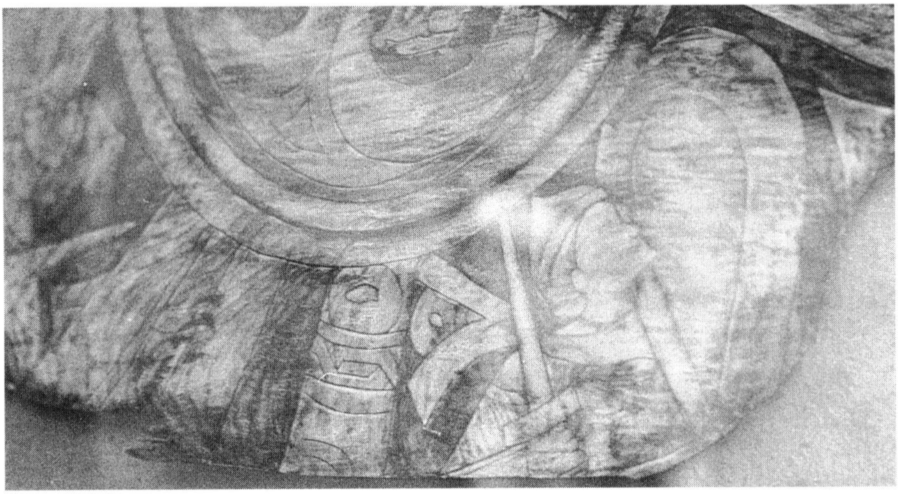

Left: *Carved 12th-century wooden plaque, probably an architectural decoration, from Novgorod, northern Russia. The soldier near the rim is virtually identical in costume and equipment with those in Scandinavia, and the carving is itself in Scandinavian style. (Author's photograph; Kremlin Museum, Novgorod)*

the *mamlūk* or *ghūlām* slave-recruited guard troops of the Islamic period.

Various Muslim dynasties dominated Transoxiana until the rise of the partially Mongol, Buddhist Qara-Khitai whose state straddled the Tien Shan mountains in the 12th and early 13th centuries. Their culture and military organisation was strongly based upon those of China; the Qara-Khitai having previously ruled northern China where they were known as Khitans. The army was divided into small, regular units which were probably paid by the ruler rather than maintained by military or tribal *fiefs.* No officer ranks were recorded above that of 'leader of one hundred men', but in other respects this army was similar to that of the subsequent Mongols. The Qara-Khitai were to some extent the reality behind distorted stories of a great eastern ruler named Prester John which reached medieval Europe in the 12th and 13th centuries.

Russia

While early medieval Russians lacked cavalry, some Slav tribes of the forest-steppe border did include horsemen. The little that is known of these eastern peoples indicates that they lived in *rod* (clans), each with its own recognised territory; the *zadruga* (extended family) being their basic social unit under a *muzhi* (tribal aristocracy). Free men fought as warriors, while the 'unfree' slaves probably did not; the role of a hazy 'half-free' class being unclear.

The *druzhina* armed retinues of the first princes of Russia were initially used for tribute gathering, developing a cavalry capability only after clashing with nomadic peoples of the steppes. The earliest *Varangian* mercenaries seem to have organised themselves into military 'corporations' comparable with those already seen in Scandinavia, often with their own pagan priests. Grand Prince Vladimir of Kiev, the first Christian ruler of Russia, retained some of the *Varangians* who had helped him to power, putting them in charge of towns or districts where they collected revenues to maintain themselves and their equipment.

For two centuries *Varangian* mercenaries, professional *druzhinas* and the *voi* or tribal levies formed the Kievan armies. By the early 13th century, however, the *Varangians* had disappeared, the *druzhinas* had become in many ways comparable with the cavalry retinues of western European princes, and the tribal *voi* had been replaced by urban militias. Considerable differences in military organisation and equipment had also developed between northern and southern Russia, with far greater steppe influence in the latter. The vast northern territory of Novgorod was unlike any other Russian state. It was under the titular rule of a bishop who was in turn dependent upon the Grand Prince of Kiev, while in reality power lay in the hands of an almost republican *veche* (town council). Nevertheless Novgorod urban militia was incapable of fending off serious foreign threats and often summoned help from the Grand Prince or a neighbouring Russian prince.

The fully developed Kievan *druzhinas* of the 12th and early 13th centuries were in two parts; a senior and a junior. The former included senior officers such as the *ognishchanin* (bailiff), *koniushi* (master of horse), *tium* (steward) and *podiezdnoi* (adjutant). The junior officers or *grid'* consisted of household cavalrymen and servants. Unlike the western European system, a *boyar* aristocrat who left his ruler's *druzhina* did not forfeit his lands.

The overall commander of a Russian army was called the *voevoda* and could be drawn from the *druzhina* or be a *tysiatski* (militia leader). This clearly shows the importance of urban forces, and in fact the ranks of *voevoda* and *tysiatski* eventually merged. A general levy was known as the *smerd,* the same name being given to individual ordinary soldiers. Like the better-armed and organised urban militias, it was led by officers given the theoretical titles of *sotski* (commander of a *sotnia* unit of 100 men) and *tysiatski* (commander of a *tysiacha* unit of 1,000 men).

The best-known and probably most effective Russian urban militia was that of Novgorod, which was organised and equipped by the city's autonomous quarters. These were also responsible for maintaining and defending their own stretch of city wall. The town-council of Novgorod selected the militia commander who also served as a police chief. In addition it selected the mayor from among the local *boyars,* though his

***Above:** The massive earth rampart of medieval Suzdal in central Russia, with a broad but now frozen swampy area and the river to the left. The kremlin of Suzdal was not given stone walls at the end of the Middle Ages, as were so many other major Russian cities. (Author's photograph)*

position normally needed to be confirmed by the Grand Prince or the bishop, as well as the keeper of the city's treasury, the governor of state lands and various other officials. Furthermore Novgorod sent mayors to all the subordinate cities, the most important of which was Pskov.

Frontiers were often far distant from the capital of the principality into which they fell. As a result military structures comparable to the *limitanei* of the Byzantine Empires existed in a rather primitive form in Russia. Such troops played a particularly important role in defending the south-eastern steppe frontier, first appearing in the 10th century when a line of frontier forts was largely manned by recruits from the north. The isolated Russian principality of Tmutorokan, centred upon the Taman peninsula, remained strategically and commercially important until the mid-12th century. But generally speaking Kievan Russia did not have enough troops to garrison its most distant conquests and lost a great deal of territory to the steppe states in the 12th century. In the far north Novgorod faced little effective opposition from the scattered tribes of what came to be known as its 'fur empire'. As a result Novgorod's tiny *pogost* trading and military outposts soon reached the Arctic Sea and the northern Ural mountains.

The most important auxiliary troops in most Russian armies were allied or resident Turco-Mongol 'Black Cap' horse-archers. Those who had arrived as refugees tended to be settled around existing fortifications close to the forest-steppe frontier and to be organised into regular military units under their own tribal leadership. Many existing southern Russian and Ukrainian villages are in fact named after these *Chernye Klobuki.*

Under Mongol Golden Horde suzerainty the armies of later 13th- and 14th-century Russia changed considerably. Russian rulers were now under the watchful eyes of Mongol *bashaks* stationed in the main cities to oversee the collection of taxes, the raising of militias, and the loyalty of Russian princes. These *bashaks* gave military advice or assistance where appropriate and may have had their own units of Mongol and Russian troops. Russian princes were in fact calling upon Mongol aid to settle their own internal squabbles as early as the 1270s.

Princely *druzhinas* took part in Mongol campaigns thousands of miles from their home territory. During the 13th–14th centuries *druzhinas* were joined on major campaigns by the military aristocracy and urban militias, though the importance of the latter was now in decline. Meanwhile a new official had replaced the old *tysiatski;* this new *okolnichi* 'quartermaster-general' possibly being modelled on the similar Mongol *bukaul.* The *druzhinas* themselves changed from the old free association of warriors into something more like a Mongol ruler's *ordu* with much stronger ties to its prince. Even the term *druzhina* eventually faded away to be replaced by a *dvor* or princely retinue. Like a Mongol *ordu,* a *dvor* was bound to its prince for life or for a fixed contractual term.

These later medieval Russian professional armies consisted almost entirely of cavalry, the inferior infantry forces largely confined to garrison duties. At the same time there was a considerable increase in horse-archery. The only real variation to this pattern was found in Novgorod whose army, though organised along the same lines, showed less immediate Mongol influence and was in many cases equipped like its western European Baltic rivals.

The Mongols

The fact that the Mongols were under strong Chinese cultural and military influence by the mid-13th century obviously had a profound impact on their military organisation. Even the typically Mongol regional *ulus* or 'four *bey*' system reflected the four gates of the ancient Han Chinese capital, the four 'horns' of the early medieval Hsuing-nu, Great Turks and other Central Asia states, and the three to five 'horn' military system of 7th–9th-century Tibet.

The Mongol *khānates* which dominated the steppes from the Pacific to the Black Sea put conquered peoples at the bottom of the social ladder, including various Turkish and Finno-Ugrian tribes. The Russians, however, were regarded as tributary states outside Mongol society. Next in status came previously dominant tribes, with the currently dominant Mongol tribes providing the *Great Khān*, with subordinate *khāns* and their military administrative élite.

The Mongol armies themselves had a more cohesive command structure than those of Europe, though not of Byzantium and the Islamic world. The legitimacy of military leaders depended on their membership of the ruling Chingizid family descended from Genghiz Khān, and on proven military success. Devotion to Mongol tradition meant that the old *yāsā* (tribal law) remained the basis of military organisation even after the Mongols in the Middle East and southern Russia converted to Islam in the 14th century.

Mongol tribal cavalry normally needed five horses per man, but in the Middle East they are said to have had up to eight, giving Mongol armies extraordinary mobility and speed. While the Mongol Yüan dynasty in China became Chinese in all but name, the Īl-Khān dynasty in the Middle East retained several features of Turco-Mongol military organisation even after becoming Muslim. For example the *amīr* of an *ulu* frontier or 'marcher' province was called a *berlerbey*, as was the commander of a full army. The Arabised version *tūmān* of the basic *tümen* (Mongol military unit) still meant 10,000 men, but also referred to the province which theoretically supported such a force. In fact the new *tūmān* was merely the old *wilāyat* renamed. At the end of the 13th century Khān Ghāzān re-introduced the earlier Islamic *iqṭā*ᶜ system of military *fiefs*. Unlike previous *iqṭā*ᶜ*s*, however, these became hereditary and mirrored the army's *hazāra* (units of 1,000) and their smaller subdivisions.

The Mongol Golden Horde which ruled the steppes and huge areas of Siberia and Russia, remained far more traditional in social and military organisation even after largely becoming Muslim. Nevertheless the Golden Horde was not a tribal state. Instead a number of 'ruling' tribes or families dominated other tribes and conquered peoples. Each 'ruling' tribe had its own virtually independent state under the general suzerainty of the Golden Horde Khān. Here the traditional 'four *bey*' system was known as the *qaraçi*, and remained in existence within the numerous lesser *khānates* which emerged, often out of the original *qaraçi*, following the fragmentation of the Golden

'Uighur Turkish chieftains offering allegiance to the Chinese general Guo Zui', on a hand-scroll by Li Gonglin; 11th–12th centuries. The Chinese artist has exaggerated the difference between the barbaric splendour of the Turkish warriors and the refined and unarmed appearance of the Chinese commander. Nevertheless the details of Uighur arms, armour, costume, horse-harness and horse-armour are essentially realistic. (National Palace Museum, no. 29 [SV.4.b], Taiwan)

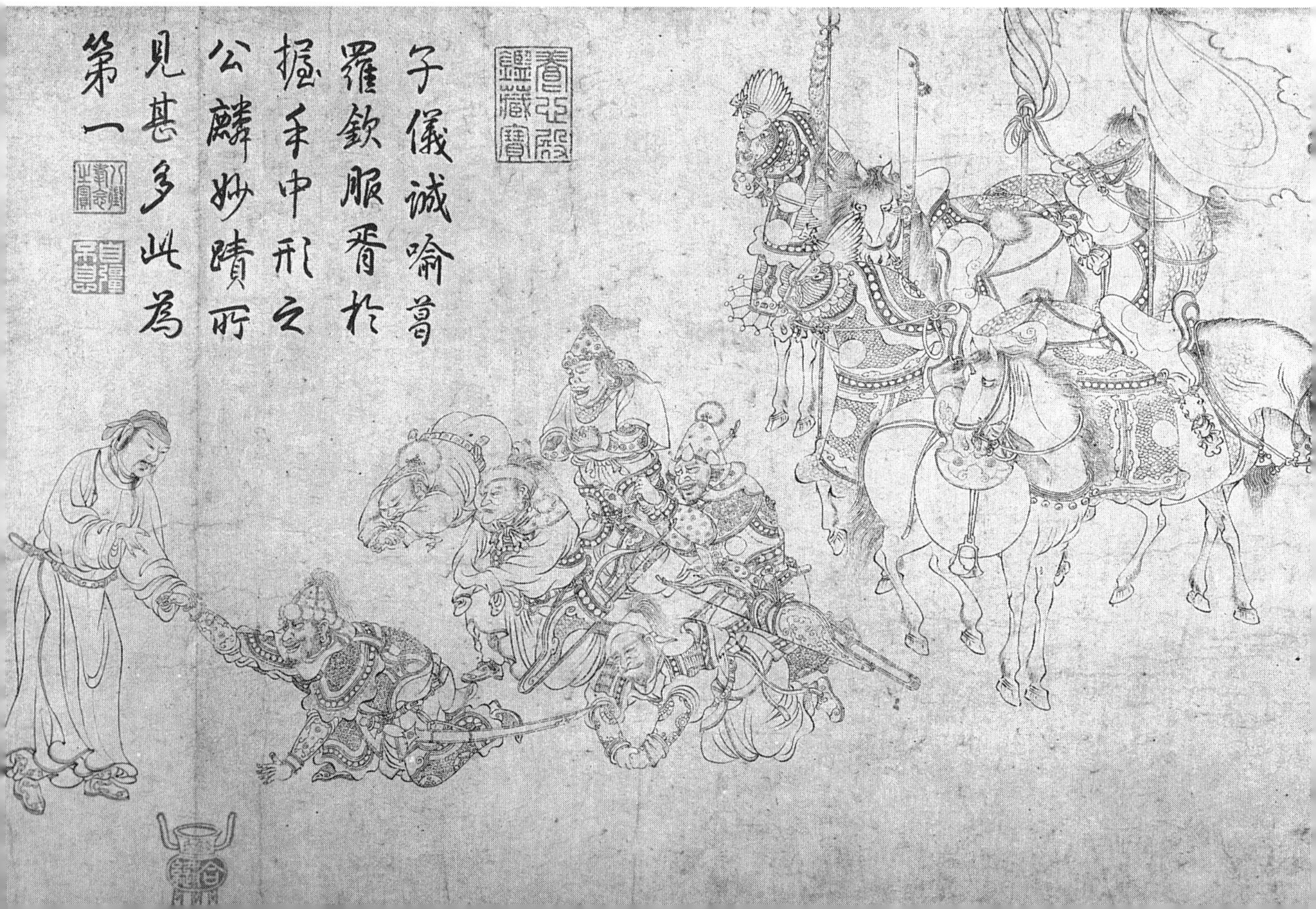

Horde. The senior *beys* of these *qaraçi* served as a council of state and controlled the army, the *beylerbeyi* (overall army commander) probably being the senior *qaraçi bey* while other *qaraçi beys* or *ulu beys* probably commanded the flanks. Other officer ranks included seventy 'commanders of 10,000' each in charge of a number of 'commanders of 1,000' responsible for specific regions or cities. These lesser officers were given Arabic, Turkish or Persian titles depending on the regions they governed. As Golden Horde power declined, the *bashaks* stationed in Russian principalities were withdrawn to be replaced by *daruga* officials who, while still having the same tasks, operated out of the main Golden Horde cities along the lower Volga.

The Rise of Tīmūr-i Lank

Tīmūr-i Lank claimed to be restoring the Mongol Empire but in reality he and his state were Turkish. The Tīmūrid government was largely in traditional Islamic mould, having four departments one of which dealt with the army. In addition Tīmūr had three *viziers* or chief ministers responsible for the north and southern frontiers, and for internal security. The state was divided into *vilayats* and *tūmān,* the former largely being found in Iran, the latter mostly in Transoxiana. Each had three officials responsible for military forces, the civil population and what was euphemistically called 'abandoned property'.

The Tīmūrid military system was based upon that of the Jagatai Mongol *khānate* of Transoxiana, most military terminology being Mongol. Like Genghiz Khān, Tīmūr imposed ferocious discipline but also introduced novel ideas. For example the hereditary *suyūrghal* (military fief) system permitted greater independence to fief-holders. The army itself was built around an élite of forty clans which claimed Mongol descent, though Tīmūr broke down the old Turco-Mongol tribal structure as a precaution against rebellion, removing its leaderships and replaced it with members of his own family or loyal followers. Some of Timur's closest associates were also put in charge of vital horse herds, but Tīmūr kept his élite forces with him at all times.

Otherwise Tīmūrid society was divided into twelve classes; those having a military role being men of government experience, purely military leaders, close friends of the ruler, and technicians who trained the troops. Theoretically the army was divided into decimal units; a complete army being called an *ordu,* a large corps a *fauj.* The officer corps was the *aymak;* its most senior members being *amīrs,* followed by *ming bashi* (commanders of 1,000), *yuz bashi* (leaders of 100), and *on bashi* (leaders of 10). Another rank was that of *sardār,* though this may only have been introduced in the 15th century. Senior officers were also given honorific titles such as *bahādur* and were distinguished by special flags or drums. Military units themselves were known as *tūmāns* of 10,000, *binliq* of 1,000, and *qoshun* or *yuzliq* of 100. The smallest units of 10 men were based on the idea that all members were jointly responsible for one another's actions, all suffering for the failings of one. Disloyal larger units would simply be disbanded or incorporated into others. Promotion, however, was not encouraged and soldiers were supposed to be adequately rewarded within their existing ranks. Although Tīmūr's army consisted mostly of cavalry, it included plenty of infantry, specialist siege engineers and mobile gendarmeries to suppress banditry. On the other hand Tīmūr declined to enlist all the Central Asian tribes under his control because this would have meant further dividing the booty won by his essentially predatory state.

STRATEGY AND TACTICS

Broad Strategy

The living style of steppe tribes inevitably led to a wide dispersal of the population, which meant that an army took considerable time to assemble. Horses were usually considered 'ready for war' by autumn which consequently became the main campaigning season. Nomad armies tended to follow watersheds between main rivers, at least when campaigning in southern Russia, rather than the river valleys which were where settled populations concentrated. Nomads also disliked campaigning in forests where they and their animals were vulnerable to ambush. Nevertheless the Mongols undertook successful operations far beyond the northern fringe of the steppes. Mountains rarely posed a problem because both Turks and Mongols made considerable use of Bactrian camels for transport; these being capable of enduring high altitude and rough terrain. When confronting Slav encroachment upon the steppes, the nomads simply destroyed the invaders' crops.

Chinese and Arab records add several additional details. For example when 8th–9th-century Central Asian Turks were preparing for a campaign, they undertook large-scale hunting expeditions for meat supplies; carcasses being dried and hung from saddles along with the Turks' normal diet of fresh mutton. Troops then assembled under recognised banners and behind regional leaders. In battle a commander occupied any available high ground and communicated with senior lieutenants through a corps of drummers.

Before the rise of Kievan Russia the eastern Slav tribes were in many ways part of a wider Central Asian world, many being under nomad domination. Only when Russian rulers turned their back on Asia did they find it necessary to erect forts along the frontier between the Russian forests and the nomad steppes. A tradition that competitors for the Russian throne must, as a matter of honour, send a formal challenge to the incumbent before undertaking military operations lasted until the late 10th century, and may have been a relic of this Central Asian heritage.

By the early 12th century the Kievan Russian élite was largely mounted, and was capable of taking the battle to a nomadic enemy, even catching encamped Qipchaqs unprepared in 1103. In the far north Russian armies often found that winter was the easiest time to undertake long-range campaigns, since they could move easily across the frozen swamps in sledges and use the frozen rivers as ready-made highways deep into enemy territory. In rarer summer campaigns the only way to transport large amounts of equipment was by boat along these rivers. Spring and autumn were literally a wash-out, being known as the seasons of *rasputitsa* (roadlessness) when the landscape sank into mud and rain.

Mongol strategy was like that of the Huns and Turks, though with greater sophistication as a result of Chinese influence. Mongol forces were notably good at maintaining communications between widely separate columns, as when four or more Mongol armies invaded eastern Europe. Nevertheless even the Mongols faced difficulty in crossing large rivers and marshes, except in winter.

In peacetime Mongol cavalrymen may have changed horses three times a day to avoid tiring the animals. Care for their enormous horse-herds was paramount, the main forces being preceded by scouts who rode some ten days' ahead, seeking not only the enemy but adequate pasture. The availability of grazing had a particularly large impact on Mongol campaigning in the hot dry Muslim world. The G̲h̲azna area of Afghanistan, for example, was capable of supporting large mounted forces and consequently served as a base-area for campaigns into northern India. Azerbaijan at the eastern end of the Caucasus and Hamad̲h̲ān in western Iran similarly served as springboards for campaigns into Iraq, Syria and Anatolia. Even so the problems faced by Mongol cavalry in Syria highlighted the basic unsuitability of their horses, and their way of feeding them, in arid zones. In 1300, for example, a Mongol army in northern Syria was accompanied by huge numbers of camels carrying fodder for the horses; nevertheless so many starved that much of the Mongol army ended up on foot.

Tīmūr-i Lank's armies successfully combined the strategic and logistical traditions of the Mongols and the Middle East. In addition Tīmūr deceived his foes by using different assembly areas for successive campaigns, and by marching his armies along often quite circuitous invasion routes.

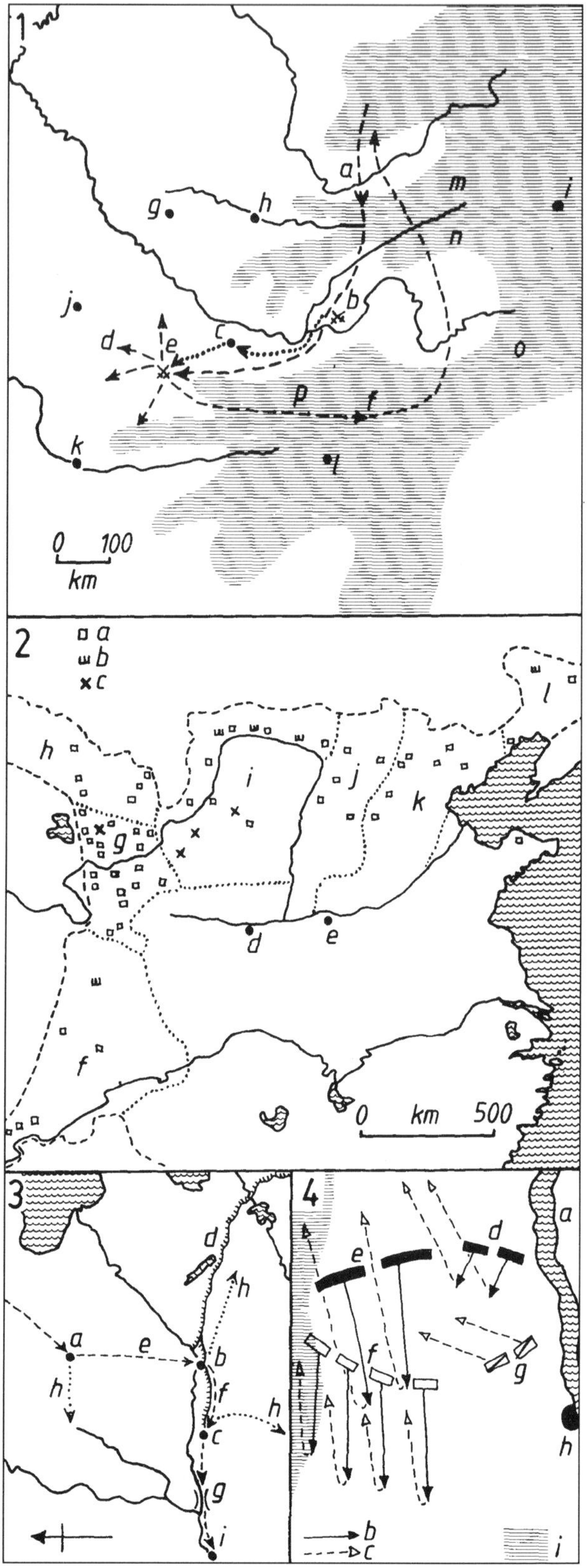

Troop Types

Written descriptions of Central Asian troops come from their enemies or neighbours. According to the Byzantines, for example, those K̲h̲azars who burst through the Caucasus frontier in 627 were lightly equipped horse-archers. According to Arab writers of a century later the K̲h̲azars included heavily armoured horsemen equipped in the same manner as later Umayyad armies. Chinese descriptions of Western Turks refer to cavalry armed with spears and bows, and mounted infantry riding two-humped Bactrian camels. Similarly the 8th-century Uig̲h̲urs of Eastern Turkestan could field large forces of armoured horse-archers using tactics of dispersal, harassment and encirclement, but also had many infantry.

Once 12th–century Qipchaq horse-archers had expended their arrows they would use light spears as javelins, then close with sabres. The number of fully armoured cavalry on armoured horses within the truly nomadic zones remains unclear. Such troops were certainly known in Turco-Iranian Transoxiana where they fought as spear-armed cavalry, but they also appear as heavily armoured horse-archers on simple rock drawings in Mongolia. These were probably made when the region was dominated by the Great Turkish or Eastern Turkish k̲h̲ānate in the 6th or 7th centuries; a supposition supported by Chinese descriptions of eastern steppe forces.

Russian armies were composed almost entirely of infantry until the 10th century; subsequently consisting of infantry archers and a small cavalry arm. At first the latter were modelled upon the nomadic and semi-nomadic cavalry of south-eastern Europe, but from the late 10th century Russian horsemen increasingly adopted central European or Byzantine heavy cavalry systems. Byzantine influence probably remained paramount until the early 13th century, Russian cavalry being equipped with straight sword, bow, mail hauberk, segmented helmet and large round shield. Archaeological evidence shows that steppe horse-harness was used in the 10th–11th centuries but was gradually supplemented by European harness in the 12th–13th centuries. On the other hand an adoption of horse-armour between the mid-12th and mid-13th centuries could reflect western or Asian influence or both. The 12th–13th century *Epic of Prince* Igor refers to Russians having 'Latin' or western European helmets, and Polish lances and shields, though these may merely have been poetic generalisations. Accounts of Alexander Nevski's victory over the Crusader Teutonic Knights on the frozen surface of Lake Peipus in 1242 already suggest strong Turco-Mongol influence in the *druzhinas* of central Russia, if not in the militias of Novgorod.

Perhaps one in six Mongol warriors wore armour, these forming the front line in battle while ordinary Mongol troops had several bows, though not always of the best quality. Camel-riding mounted infantry were included in late 13th-century Mongol armies invading Syria, while elsewhere women rode as horse-archers to increase the size of a Mongol army. It was among specialists and siege infantry that the most obvious Chinese influence could be found, especially where the use of fire weapons and early forms of gunpowder were concerned.

Similarly only the élite of Tīmūr-i Lank's army wore full armour. The elephants which played a minor role in some Tīmūrid forces were a revival of an earlier idea. Each had a *howdah* on its back carrying four or five soldiers, plus the *mahout* driver. Men got in and out of the *howdah* by ropes when the animal was kneeling down. The creature's hide could be painted bright colours and it could have large iron blades fastened to its tusks. Trained fighting elephants attacked in a series of short forward rushes, sweeping upwards with their tusks.

Battle Tactics

The White Huns or Hephthalites of eastern Iran and Afghanistan used sophisticated battlefield ruses in the mid-5th century, by which time they like the Black Huns in Europe had

Left: Campaigns and Military Organisation

1. Umayyad campaign against the Khaqān in Transoxiana, 737.

a advance of Turks under Khaqān in October

b Muslim Arab column under Asad ibn ᶜAbd Allāh surprised by Turks while encamped

c Muslim Arab force takes refuge in Balkh from October to December

d Turks scatter in search of plunder

e sudden Muslim Arab counter-attack defeats Khaqān in December

f Khaqān retreats but is surprised again in mountains 200 kilometres south-east of Balkh, probably in January 737

g Būkhāra

h Samarkand

i Kashgar

j Marw

k Harāt

l Kabul. (after Glubb)

2. The northern frontier provinces of China under the T'ang dynasty. Note a considerable concentration of forces in the north-west, at the end of a corridor of Chinese territory linking China proper with its possessions in Central Asia. This corridor also formed the usual route for Turks attacking China.

a jun army

b zhong garrisoned fortress

c pasture directorate for cavalry horses and remounts

d Changan, the western capital

e Luoyang, the eastern capital

f Chien-nan frontier province

g Lung-yu frontier province

h Hexi frontier province

i Shuofang frontier province

j Ho-tung frontier province

k Fan-yang frontier province; Pinglu frontier province. (after Ranitzsch)

3. The rebellion of An Lushan, 755.

a rebel advance and seizure of Hengzhou

b Bianzhou

c eastern capital of Luoyang

d canal

e rebel advance takes Bianzhou and cuts main canal supplying Luoyang

f rebel advance takes eastern capital of Luoyang

g Imperial loyalist army makes stand and blocks narrow Tong-guan Pass, but is ordered to counter-attack and is defeated

h unsuccessful rebel advances to west, east and south

i rebels advance and take western capital of Changan. (after Ranitzsch)

4. The battle of Babayn in 1167, where a mixed Crusader and Fāṭimid Muslim force was defeated by a Syrian-Turkish army under Shīrkūh and his nephew Ṣalāh al-Dīn (Saladin).

a river Nile

b movements of opposing forces during first phase of battle

c movements of forces during second phase

d Fāṭimid contingents, largely infantry, left behind when Crusaders attack, then defeated by Shīrkūh

e Crusader contingent under Almaric charges Muslim centre and baggage but is attacked in flank by Shīrkūh, then in other flank by Ṣalāh al-Dīn's forces who make counter-attack

f Ṣalāh al-Dīn in command of centre-left with Arab troops and baggage acting as 'bait' forced back by Crusader charge, but turn to counter-attack through sand-dunes on western flank

g Shīrkūh with élite Turkish cavalry on right flank, defeats Fāṭimid infantry and attacks Crusaders in flank

h Al-Minyā

i sand-dunes, one of very few places in Egypt where a large area of soft sand comes within eight kilometres of the Nile. (after Zaki) been largely assimilated into regions they had already conquered. In 459, for example, a Hephthalite army dug a series of camouflaged pits ahead of its static ranks. In the middle of these pits was left a gap wide enough for horsemen riding six abreast to pass through. One Hephthalite squadron made a feint attack through this gap and then withdrew. The opposing Sassanians counter-attacked and fell into the hidden pits.

Even within steppe nomadic areas a cavalry army which found its archery outclassed would attempt to close with the enemy in a massive charge. Judging by Chinese descriptions of Great Turk horsemen, they would advance in a wedge or arrow formation, making repeated attacks and withdrawals. How far such tactics were an indigenous development or showed Chinese or Iranian influence is unknown, but Sughdians from Transoxiana certainly served as military advisers to Turkish *khāns* further east.

Western Central Asian peoples continued to use the harassment, dispersal and horse-archery tactics which would characterise them throughout the Middle Ages. According to the Byzantine Strategikon the Avars appeared to draw their troops up in one continuous formation though in reality this line consisted of several large groups plus a formidable reserve ready to make flanking attacks or waiting in ambush. Like other Central Asian peoples, but unlike their Middle Eastern, the Avars sought the total destruction of an enemy. Arabic evidence confirms that Central Asian Turkish cavalry were lighter and swifter than their Muslim counterparts; Turks also employing novel tactics such as driving herds of panic-stricken sheep ahead of them as they surged down upon an Arab force in a surprise night attack.

According to a neutral Arab account, a Pecheneg army defeated a Byzantine force twice its size in 943/4. Both forces were in extended line, the Pechenegs putting most of their cavalry on the flanks. The Pecheneg right attacked the Byzantine centre with horse-archery while the Pecheneg left harassed other sectors of the enemy line. The two Pecheneg cavalry wings then swapped roles until the Byzantine cavalry counter-charged. The Pechenegs rapidly retreated and the pursuing Byzantines lost cohesion, whereupon the uncommitted Pecheneg heavy cavalry centre charged and slaughtered the confused Byzantines.

A detailed account of the 'battle plan of the Khāqān' in a 13th-century Indo-Muslim military treatise was probably based on the proto-Mongol, Buddhist and strongly Chinese-influenced Qara-Khitai of 12th-century Central Asia. Its similarity to tactics adopted by medieval Chinese forces when facing Central Asian nomad foes is remarkable. The Khāqān's army was arrayed in nine separate groups consisting of a left wing of cavalry and infantry, a centre with the commander and most of his armoured troops, a right wing of cavalry and infantry. A left flank behind the left wing consisted of cavalry and infantry to resist enemy attempts to outflank. Behind the centre were craftsmen, the ruler's harem and animal herds; to the rear right wing cavalry intended to outflank the enemy. On the left of the rearguard were cavalry and infantry guarding additional horse herds; to the rear of the centre were 'hostages' and other important persons guarded by cavalry, while behind the right flank were sick and wounded with a cavalry escort.

The oldest traditional Russian battle array was in five parts: van, centre, rear and two wings, astonishingly similar to the early Islamic *khamīs*. The high status accorded to a right flank was said to reflect pre-Christian shamanistic beliefs though in reality it reflected the fact that the right was offensive while

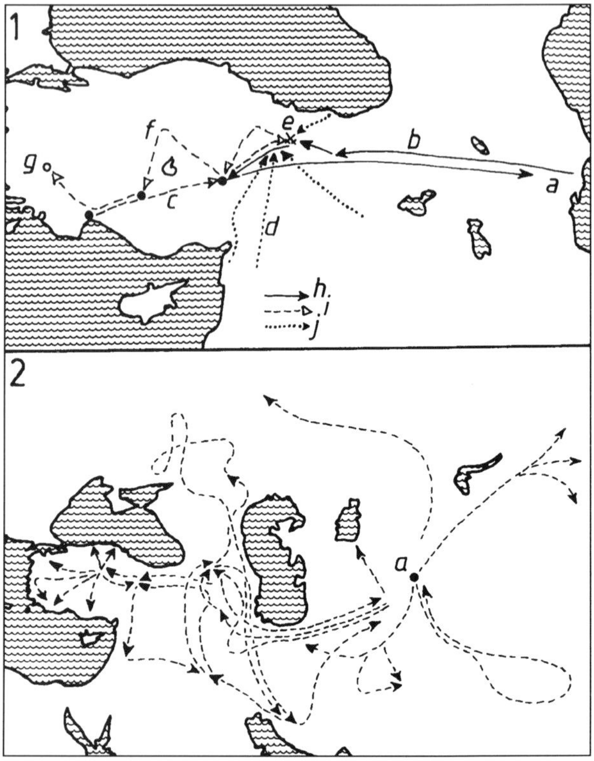

Above: Campaigns and Military Organisation

1. The Mongol defeat of the Saljūqs of Rūm in 1242–3.

- a *Mongol base-area on Mugan steppes of Azerbaijan*
- b *Mongol invasion of eastern Anatolia in winter, late 1242*
- c *Saljūq army marches from winter quarters in Antalya to assembly point at Sivas*
- d *Saljūq auxiliaries and allies assemble at Sivas*
- e *Mongols defeat Saljūq forces at Kösedağ*
- f *Saljūq sultan flees to Antalya via Ankara*
- g *Saljūq sultan probably seeks alliance with Byzantine Empire of Nicea in 1243*
- h *Mongol line of march and return*
- i *Saljūq line of march and flight*
- j *assembling of Saljūq allies. (after Matuz)*

2. The campaigns of Tīmūr-i Lank. Perhaps no other conqueror covered so much ground or undertook so many separate campaigns as Tīmūr. But the fact that he had to do so also showed that while he was able to defeat his foes he was rarely able to subdue them totally. From 1371 until his death in 1404 he fought eight separate campaigns, some of which went on for nearly five years.

- a *Samarkand.*

Above: *Carvings of horsemen on the exterior of the Cathedral of Dimitri Sobor; Russian, 1193–7. The costume and horse-harness is similar to that of central Europe, whereas the artistic style has much in common with the Orthodox Balkans and the Byzantine Empire. At this date there seems to have been virtually no Turco-Mongol influence on the military culture of central Russia. (Author's photograph; in situ, Cathedral of Dimitri Sobor, Vladimir, Russia)*

the left was defensive in almost all medieval armies. From the 11th to 13th centuries Russian forces, when facing nomad foes, placed low-grade infantry *voi* at the centre, infantry archers shooting from behind a shield-wall of perhaps higher grade infantry with cavalry protecting their flanks. Large wagons comparable to those of nomadic peoples were used to carry supplies in the open areas of southern Russia and the steppes. Meanwhile the Russian military élite followed an almost chivalric code similar to that of western Europe.

In the later 13th and 14th centuries Russian tactics changed, cavalry adopting sabres, light lamellar armour, helmets with face-covering mail aventails and small round shields. Russian infantry began using western crossbows in greater numbers, operating in disciplined ranks while light infantry skirmishers continued to use composite bows. In 1380, at the victorious battle of Kulikovo, the Russian commander still took the precaution of placing a river at his back and dense woods on each flank since he was facing a Turco-Mongol foe.

It was perhaps the iron discipline of the early Mongols which made them so formidable. This also enabled commanders to remain behind the fighting line rather than getting involved in combat, and thus retaining a wider view of what was happening. Mongol armies reputedly put their most unreliable, non-Mongol troops in the front to absorb enemy attacks, with their best men on the wings to encircle a foe. Naturally they preferred to fight with a numerical advantage but saw no shame in retreating from excessive odds. Mongols generally volleyed their arrows during repeated charges by waves of horsemen aimed at different parts of the enemy line. These probably involved single shots from close range rather than the prolonged long-range harassment preferred by Middle Eastern forces. Several units would be involved, each turning and shooting three or four times so that the result was a sustained barrage at sufficiently close range to penetrate most enemy armour. The smaller number of élite heavily armoured Mongol cavalry would protect these horse-archers from counter-attacks, and would make a final charge to complete an enemy's discomfort. A more novel feature may have been the Mongol habit of opening up a gap, once they had surrounded an enemy, seemingly to permit escape but in reality forcing him down a corridor of murderous archery.

The Mongols were also noted for their use of imaginative battlefield ruses; for example putting straw dummies on the backs of spare horses to make their army look several times larger. It is interesting to note that a similar idea had been used by Indian forces in southern Burma a few generations earlier. Mongol forces operating in Burma a little later found that their horses were terrified by Burmese war-elephants, so the Mongols dismounted and shot at the elephants with their bows. Unable to reply with their own inferior bows, the Burmese fell into confusion whereupon the Mongols remounted and overwhelmed the numerically superior enemy.

Tīmūr-i Lank made highly effective use of traditional Mongol and Islamic Middle Eastern tactics, plus some novel ideas of his own, and massacres on a scale which would have daunted even Genghis Khān. Cavalry dominated open battle, though Tīmūr's infantry still had a role to play. When facing the Golden Horde deep in the forests of what is now eastern European

'Barbarians seize Rome', in a Russian historical manuscript of c.1318–27. The defenders are dressed in Russo-Byzantine style, as are the fleeing Roman rulers on the left. The barbarians are depicted as Turkish or Mongol nomads in lamellar armour, carrying typical Central Asian banners. (Chronicle of Georgi Amartola, Lenin Library, No. 15, f.25v, Moscow)

Russia, Tīmūr divided his troops into no less than seven divisions, with the centre and wings each having their own vanguard plus a strong reserve behind the centre. This enabled him to drive off a Golden Horde force which broke through his left and then attacked it from the rear. When fighting the Delhi Sultanate in northern India, Tīmūr's army secretly scattered large *calthrops* ahead of its position. Next day his cavalry attacked through lanes left in this 'medieval minefield', then retreated in apparent flight, pursued by the enemy's elephants. These, having left the safety of their own infantry, panicked when several of their number trod on the *calthrops* and fled back into their own ranks, pursued by terrified camels carrying some form of inflammable material.

Combat Styles

Little is known about individual combat styles in Central Asia and medieval Russia because so little relevant literary material survives. Nevertheless history proves that settled or urban armies could never totally defeat Central Asian horse-archers within their own steppe homelands before the widespread adoption of firearms. Turco-Mongol horses, though smaller than European and slower than Arabian horses, were tougher and more resilient than their stall-fed rivals. They also appear to have been better at climbing, jumping and swimming and were better able to endure a cold climate.

Field and Camp Fortifications

Most nomadic peoples made considerable use of wagons for transport and occasionally as field-fortifications. The Chinese even divided the early medieval Turks into those 'with wagons' and those 'without wagons'. In the mid-11th century Pechenegs in the Balkans used wagons as a wall; drove off a Byzantine attack then pursued their defeated enemy with horse-archers. Qipchaqs retreating from Byzantine territory in the 12th century made a comparable waggenburg for the families. Here carts were put close together and covered with hides in a highly effective field fortification, possibly with a ditch dug in front. A hundred years later the Russians made considerable use of prefabricated wooden palisades called *obos* to protect their military encampments. In 1402 Tīmūr-i Lank defended his camp at the battle of Ankara with a ditch, boulders and wooden palisades, as well as poisoning wells between his position and that of his Ottoman Turkish foes.

WEAPONRY AND HARNESS

Influences in the design and construction of arms and armour generally flowed from east to west during the Middle Ages. Yet there was also an Iranian influence upon Central Asian and even Chinese weaponry during the early period. The Volga Bulgars were under strong Russian influence in the 12th–13th centuries and northern Russia remained under Scandinavian influence until the 11th century. Nevertheless the introduction of high-quality Asian arms and armour to Russia by Tork and Berend 'Black Cap' auxiliaries was a more typical trend.

Subsequent Mongol influence spread beyond Russia, medieval Western European commentators taking a particular interest in Mongol body armour which proved so much more effective against archery than their own. Within the Mongol world itself the heroes of verse-epics were kitted out as normal Mongol cavalry whereas Chinese infantry weapons were placed in the hands of assorted monsters. The idea that Russian arms and armour technology stagnated under Mongol domination is nonsense. Mongol equipment, for example, was adopted enthusiastically by the Russian principality of Galich as early as 1246. Thereafter later medieval Russian troops copied many aspects of Mongol arms and armour. But, like their predecessors, the Mongols were short of iron, most sources lying within the forest rather than the steppe zones.

Archery and Slings

Composite bows dominated warfare in the Central Asian steppes and neighbouring areas. Archery was so important to the Turco-Mongols, Finno-Ugrians and eastern Slavs that bows and arrows were thought to possess magical properties; that arrows could be redirected by sorcery. Yet there was considerable variety within these weapons, many poorer Central Asian warriors using arrowheads of bone because they were so short of iron.

The archery equipment of the richer early 13th-century Volga Bulgars was very similar to that of the Russians. A surviving bow from Novgorod was a composite of juniper and birch, lashed with sinew and covered in birch bark, about 190cm long and almost certainly an infantry weapon. The same went for slightly larger Ugrian bows from the Ob basin in northern Siberia, with a pine inner core, a beech outer part, and covered in birch-bark. Furthermore the word for quiver in some Ugrian languages had an Iranian rather than Turkish or Mongol origin. There are several references to quivers being closed or 'locked' in the Russian *Epic of Prince Igor*, indicating that they were of the fully enclosed Central Asian box type rather than the smaller open-ended Middle Eastern form. Large box-like Mongol quivers could carry as many as sixty arrows according to some 13th-century European travellers.

Crossbows were used by some Mongol infantry in siege warfare, including the large multiple-shot *charkh kamān* which, despite its Persian name, was brought from the Far East where repeater crossbows were first used by Sung armies of southern China. Otherwise crossbows were more common in northern rather than southern Russia in the 12th to 14th centuries; reflecting European rather than eastern military influence.

Swords and Daggers

Curved sabres spread across Central Asia into eastern Europe with the Avars, the earliest datable example from the western steppes probably being no earlier than the mid-8th century. It then remained largely unchanged until the 12th–13th centuries when heavier armour led to the adoption of heavier sabres by steppe peoples.

Straight double-edged swords of western European form continued to be preferred in Russia, but the Turkish Khazars were said to despise such weapons as tribute from subordinate tribes. Even in southern Russia developments in European straight swords were faithfully mirrored well into the 14th century, though a few single-edged Byzantine straight swords were also used. The Russians may in fact have been among the first to introduce the 13th-century thrusting rather than slashing sword to northern Europe. Some curved *palash* (sabres) were used in southern Russia as a result of nomad influence, but they did not predominate until after the Mongol conquest.

Remarkably little is known about daggers among steppe warriors, though such weapons were characteristic of Turco-Iranian Transoxiana to the south. In Russia an otherwise unknown form of dagger called a *zasapozhniki* was mentioned in the 11th to 13th centuries, the larger *tesek* coming into use in the 13th and 14th centuries. This was almost certainly based on the Islamic *khanjar* which in turn was adopted by the Mongols under Turco-Iranian influence.

Spears and Javelins

The paucity of references to spears in Central Asia presumably reflects the low status of this weapon. Western descriptions indicate that by the mid-13th century Mongol heavy cavalry had adopted Chinese hooked spears designed to pull an opponent from his saddle. This is confirmed by slightly later archaeological and pictorial evidence. In 11th- to 13th-century pre-Mongol Russia the heavy *rogatina* and the light *sulitsa* were both used, the latter possibly also being thrown as a javelin.

Other Weapons

The importance of infantry axes in Russia was within a European tradition whereas the use of small-bladed cavalry axes by the Mongols almost certainly reflected Islamic influence. By the 15th century these had been adopted by Russian horse-archers, this time as a result of Mongol influence.

The mace was more typical of steppes peoples where larger forms, especially those with anthropomorphic heads, had a special status among officers or élite troops. Maces were also reserved for senior figures among the Mongols, though the *kisten* (mace) and *chekan* (war-hammer) were more evenly spread among 13th–14th-century Russian cavalry. The even more widespread studded iron or bronze light mace of eastern and central Europe was of steppe origin, possibly having been introduced to Europe by the Pechenegs in the 11th century. Its names – *buzogány* in Hungarian, *buzgan* in Qipchaq, *bozdağan* or *bozṭoghan* in Turkish – stem from a Qipchaq or Saljūq-'Othmānli dialect word for 'grey falcon'.

The lasso was even more characteristic of Central Asia, having always been used by nomadic warriors and those from settled communities. Iranian Alan nomads as well as Turkic Huns used it in earlier centuries, both for hunting and pursuing defeated foes. The fact that soldiers from Moscow were

Above: *Sword with its hilt covered in bark; Russian, 11th–12th centuries. (Author's photograph; Kremlin Museum, Novgorod)*
Below: *Hilt of a sabre from the northern Caucasus, with the remains of inlaid silver decoration; Turco-Mongol Golden Horde, 13th–15th centuries. (Author's photograph; State Hermitage Museum, St. Petersburg)*

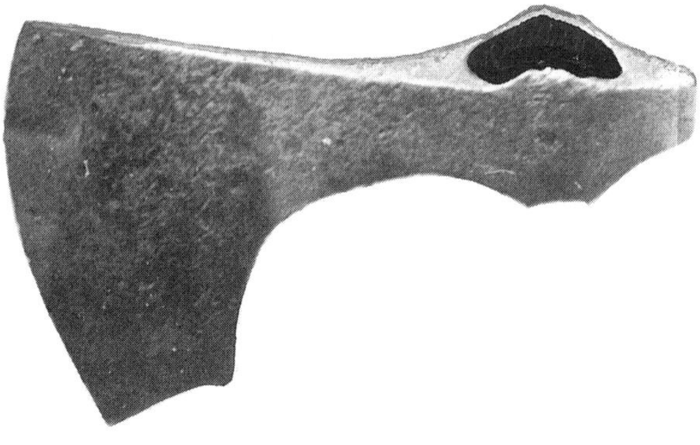

Above, left and right: *A silver-inlaid iron mace-head and a bronze mace-head; Russian, 13th–14th centuries. This type of light cavalry weapon was of steppe origin but spread across much of eastern and central Europe from Finland to the Balkans. (Author's photograph; Kremlin Museum, Novgorod)*
Right: *Russian axe-heads, 14th–15th centuries. The axe remained a widespread infantry weapon in northern Russia throughout the medieval period. (Author's photograph; Kremlin Museum, Novgorod)*

reportedly carrying lassos by 1361 is particularly stark evidence of Mongol influence.

Fire weapons were not widespread among Central Asian armies, despite other strong Chinese military influence. A specialist fire-operator in a Qipchaq army came from Muslim Khwārazm rather than further east, and the effect of his weapon suggests that it might have contained a primitive form of gunpowder. Although the first waves of Mongol conquerors had Chinese pyrotechnic specialists in their ranks, the subsequent Golden Horde does not seem to have continued

Right: *Icon of St. Demetrius of Thessaloniki; Russian, late 12th–early 13th centuries. If the dating is correct, the picture includes one of the earliest European examples of the so-called Italian Grip where a swordsman placed his forefinger over a quillon of his sword. This style of fencing probably originated in India and had been known in Sassanian Iran since the pre-Islamic period, but does not seem to have spread beyond the Byzantine Empire and the Iberian peninsula until the 13th or 14th centuries. (Tretyakov Gallery, inv. 28600, Moscow)*

this practice. Nor did they adopt firearms when these became available in western Europe, China and the Middle East. On the other hand several Central Asian cities, including Bulgar on the river Volga, did so on their own initiative. As a result the Russians' first experience of firearms was during their siege of Bulgar in 1376. Some guns were captured; the Russians being sufficiently impressed to obtain more from western Europe.

Shields

The kite-shaped Byzantine and European form of shield was used by some Russian cavalry, but Central Asian smaller round types predominated, particularly in the south. The kite-shaped shield and associated couched-lance style of fighting then seems to have been almost entirely abandoned following the Mongol conquest. Mongol influence also led to a wider adoption of spiral cane shields in the Middle East, though these had been introduced by the Turks. The armies of Tīmūr-i Lank made use of several versions with a clear distinction drawn between the large *tūreh* and the small *sipar*. In the Jagatai *khānate* the *tūreh* is specifically described as a large shield or mantlet, almost certainly for infantry.

Helmets

Helmets used in pre-Mongol steppe armies were similar to those in Russia, Byzantium and the Muslim Middle East, all of these neighbouring civilisations having adopted Central Asian types of helmet. Most were of tall, pointed and segmented construction. The Mongols, however, introduced a new and more rounded headpiece of Chinese origin. Some had peaks at the front which again was a Chinese concept, but the use of metal or leather discs over the ears was probably a Mongol invention. Such peaked Mongol helmets eventually evolved into the 15th-century Turkish and Mamluk *chichak* which in turn was the original behind the 17th–18th-century western European *zischage* – popularly known in England as the *Cromwellian Helmet*. Disc-shaped ear-pieces, again probably inspired by earlier Mongol fashions, were adopted in 15th-century western Europe.

A sub-Roman form of two-piece helmet may have remained in use in Russia until the 10th century, but in general Russia followed western steppe and Byzantine fashion until the coming of the Mongols. Tall pointed *scholom* helmets beaten from a single piece of iron, but similar in shape to segmented nomad types, may actually have been a southern Russian development. These were often called *sterzhen* 'pointed' helmets while the mail *aventail*, known far earlier than comparable *aventails* in western Europe, was known as a *barmitsa*. Comparable helmets from the immediate pre-Mongol period with life-like iron visors hinged from the brow were associated with the 'Black Hats' and Volga Bulgars rather than Russians themselves. More typically Russian were helmets with broad nasals and 'half-visors' protecting the upper part of the wearer's face. Considerable debate revolves around the early use of brimmed 'war-hat' helmets in both Russia and Byzantium, some of which seem to have more in common with Chinese brimmed helmets than those of western Europe.

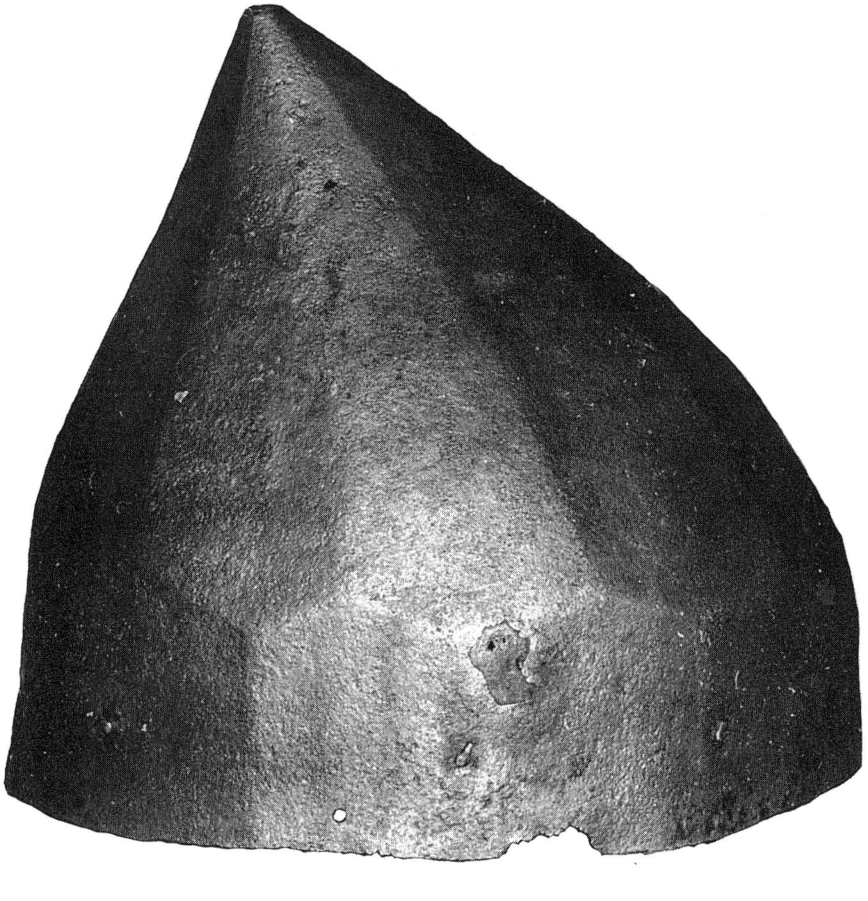

Top left: *12th-century gilded iron helmet of a Qipchaq ruler from Čingul'-Kurgan, Ukraine. This type of highly sophisticated helmet and face-covering aventail had a profound influence upon the armour of Russia and probably also the Balkans and Byzantium. (Ukrainian State Historical Museum, inv. AZS-3607, Kiev, Ukraine)*
Top right: *Qipchaq helmet of the 13th century. This fine piece of metalwork came from a nomad's grave in Hungary and was probably made either shortly before or shortly after many Qipchaq clans migrated into Central Europe to flee the Mongol onslaught. (Author's photograph; National Museum, Budapest)*
Bottom left: *A large number of these tall, fluted, one-piece helmets with highly realistic visors have been found in southern Russia. Some scholars believe that they were used by Chernye Klobuki 'Black Cap' nomads in Russian service and date from the 12th–early 13th centuries; others consider that they are from the Mongol Golden Horde and date from the late 13th–early 14th centuries. (Author's photograph; State Hermitage Museum, St. Petersburg)*
Bottom right: *Italian bascinet reduced in size for use in Russia or Byzantium, 14th century. (Author's photograph; National Historical Museum Conservation Department, inv. 4981, Moscow)*

Left: *Western European great helm, probably German 14th century, considerably reduced in size for use in Russia or the western steppes, perhaps in the late 14th–15th centuries. (Author's photograph; National Historical Museum Conservation Department, inv. 14373, Moscow)*

Right: *A 13–14th century Russian Kujak or scale cuirass. This form of armour attached to a soft leather base is extremely ancient and may have been reintroduced to eastern Europe by the Mongols. It probably lay behind the sudden development of the scale-lined coat-of-plates in western Europe. (State Historical Museum, inv. no. 14309, Moscow, Russia)*

Body Armour

Lamellar was the typical armour of these regions, a full lamellar cuirass making use of differing shaped lamellae, some of them large enough to give the name 'hand-span cuirass' to an armour used by élite Turkish cavalry in the 8th century. Lamellar armour was also used by the Tibetans, usually of hardened leather. Apparently lamellae made from slivers of bamboo were found among the 13th-century aboriginal peoples of the eastern Tibetan foothills and some Khalj Turks of the western foothills, together with bone lamellae in eastern Siberia and Alaska. Lacquered lamellar armour worn by Mongol troops reflected Chinese craftsmanship, while the best equipped 13th- and 14th-century Mongol cavalry also used plain hardened leather and iron and bronze lamellar cuirasses. The most common form was the *khuyagh* in which sheets of lamellae were buckled at the side of the wearer's body or down his back, normally being supported by shoulder-straps. Lamellar armour was used in Russia by the 13th century, probably before the arrival of the Mongols since the 'bright cuirasses' of Russian troops were noted by Baltic Crusader chroniclers in the early 13th century, though the 14th-century Russian *kuyuk* clearly came from the Mongol *khuyagh*. There were also great similarities between the shapes and lacing systems of Russian and earlier Central Asian armours. The armour produced in Islamic Iran changed slowly after the Mongol conquest. Nevertheless local armourers were making Mongol-style lamellar cuirasses by the 14th century, as well as helmets having typically Mongol lamellar aventails. A combination of Mongol and Islamic technologies would produce startling innovations in the late 14th century which would then spread farther, perhaps partly as a consequence of Tīmūr's conquests.

The even more typical Mongol *khatangku dehel* ('coat as hard as steel') was originally a coat-shaped soft armour made of felt or buff leather, worn alone or beneath a lamellar cuirass. During the late 13th and 14th centuries, however, the *khatangku dehel* was often lined with metal scale; this highly effective form of armour remained in use throughout much of eastern Asia until the 19th century. It evolved into the characteristic *coat of a thousand nails* in India and led to the equally distinctive *tegheliay* in Russia. The Mongol *khatangku dehel* may even have been the inspiration for the 13th–14th-century western European *coat-of-plates* and *brigandine* as well as a variety of later medieval Islamic armour. The small 'mirrors' shown on front and back of the *khatangku dehel* in Islamic miniatures were too small to provide much protection and may have been talismanic elements designed to ward off the 'evil eye'. On the other hand they are more likely to have been an early step in the development of the Persian *chahār āʿīnah* 'four mirrors' form of mail-and-plate which in turn was to lead to the Russian *zertzallo.* The development of mail-and-plate armour took place in the Middle East, probably in western Iran or Iraq under the Mongol Īl-Khāns or their successors. From there it spread to Egypt, India, the Ottoman Empire and Russia where it was known as the *bekhter.*

Archaeological evidence shows that the Russians of Novgorod used scale as well as mail and lamellar armour between the 11th and 14th centuries. Their scale protections on a leather or quilted base were unlike western European armour, however, and may have reflected Byzantine influence or have been an indigenous development. They may also have been the *pantsir* armours of written sources and could have had some influence on the development of later scale-lined version of the Mongol *khatangku dehel.* By the 1230s northern Russian troops were using an early form of *brigandine,* which suggests that perhaps Russia had an unrecognised influence on the appearance of the European *coat-of-plates* in Germany; perhaps via the Baltic Crusades. These Russian armours were so successful that they tended to replace mail during the 14th century.

Mail was extremely rare among the nomadic peoples but remained common in Russia from the 10th to 13th centuries; its normal name of *bron'a* indicates a German origin from *brunja.* Yet most Russian mail hauberks were of the short-sleeved Byzantine type; long-sleeved versions remaining rare even in the 13th century. The size, frequently flattened shape and linking of alternate soldered and riveted links in Russian mail also betrays strong Middle Eastern influence, as did the fashion for buckled openings at the neck of hauberks.

While the Mongol *khatangku dehel* came to include metallic scale lining, other forms of simple soft armour remained in use in the Mongol states and 13th-14th-century Russia. Here such *tegyljaj* or *teghhilay* were worn by light cavalry and horse-archers.

Limb Defences

In 13th-century Russia armour for the limbs was a remarkable mix of eastern and western traditions, sometimes consisting of a European-style mail chausses called *noznicy,* plus rigid *vambraces* for the lower arms - of obvious Asiatic origin. Comparable protections would not be known in western Europe for another hundred years. Limb protections in Mongol-ruled areas of the Middle East were, however, in a long-established Islamic tradition while virtually no information survives concerning the use of such armour in the Central Asian steppes.

Horse Harness

As might be expected in regions completely dominated by cavalry, the horse-harness of Turco-Mongol steppe peoples was highly developed and often very decorative. Early medieval Turkish harness, for example, included the *kemeldürük* (breast-strap), *koşkum* (crupper-strap) and *içlik* (thick saddle-blanket). Horsemen could in fact ride on this blanket alone. The *al* was a more decorative blanket often used as badge of rank, as were *beçkem* tassels hanging from beneath the bridle's throat-lash. One of the most notable differences between European and steppe horse-harness was the way in which the latter's stirrups were set far forward, making the saddle more of a chair. This was extremely comfortable for riding long distances but gave a less secure seat in hand-to-hand combat. Wooden stirrups, or of leather with a wooden tread, used in the northern Caucasus from the 6th to 12th centuries, had been used in eastern Central Asia during the early Middle Ages together with the all-leather loop stirrups which remained in use until the end of the medieval period. But horseshoes were not common among steppe nomad horsemen.

Generally speaking, Russian horsemen copied both their eastern and western neighbours; abundant harness from 10th–11th-century grave sites showing trade in such items from the Finns in the east, nomads in the south, Hungarians and Germans in the west. There was also a gradual move away from elaborately decorated to more functional horse-harness mirroring an increasingly widespread use of horses by the 12th century. Bridles, saddles and stirrups showed that there was now a clear distinction between the harness used by light and heavy cavalry; the former remaining essentially in the steppe style while the latter became more like the rest of Europe. For example spurs were adopted under western or Byzantine influence in the mid-11th century, whereas these were not used by the nomads. Archaeology also suggests that the *rowel spur*, with a revolving spiked wheel at the back, was known in Russia up to half a century before it appeared in western Europe and may have come from Byzantium since it too appears in Byzantine art well before western sources.

Horse Armour

Horse-armour was always reserved for a cavalry élite. Nevertheless it was used by many Central Asia steppe armies. The Turks, for example, knew it as *kedimli*. Chinese illustrations

Left: *A fragment of scale armour from Novgorod; northern Russian, 14th century. This probably formed part of a scale-lined cuirass, coat-of-plates or early style brigandine, and probably represented the technological link between the scale armours of Turco-Mongol Central Asia and those of western Europe. (Author's photograph, Kremlin Museum, Novgorod)*

Right: *Miniature painting from a manuscript probably compiled in Baghdad by Junayd al-Sultani in 1396 and depicting the type of equipment used by the élite of Tīmūr-i Lank's army. The horse has lamellar armour, probably of hardened leather; the defeated warrior is wearing a lamellar cuirass over a mail hauberk. The victorious warrior on the left seems to have an early version of a mail-and-plate cuirass. (Khwaju Kirmani's Three Romances, British Library, MS. Add. 18113, London)*

show that in the rich Turkish Uighur *khānate* some cavalry had rigid *chamfrons* to protect their horses' heads, plus full horse-armour. By the mid-13th century the horse-armour of a Mongol heavy cavalry élite also included such *chamfrons,* plus lamellar neck pieces, *peytrals,* two *flanchards* and *crupper.* Some of this lamellar was of iron, though it was normally of hardened leather.

FORTIFICATION

Turkish Central Asia

The rulers of steppe empires, though to some degree always nomadic, still built palaces and fortifications. The former were based upon the idea of having separate summer and winter residences. An *ordu* had to be close to summer pasture normally found in the mountains, close to villages where metal-workers and bow-makers lived, and preferably close to trade routes so that a ruler could reap taxes. Some elaborate *ordus* consisted of two concentric walls with fortified towers.

Winter residences could also be fortified and may have been larger, the ruler's herds having to find safety within their walls. Among the best-documented were the Ordu-Örgin or the Uighur *khāns* and the Ordu-Balik of the Western Turks. In each case an inner area was reserved for the princely family, the outer ring being for his retinue - remarkably similar in concept to Caliphal Baghdad. The Western Turks also built fortified towers in the mountains, the construction of which had, like the *ordu,* much in common with Chinese frontier defences. But, unlike the Chinese linear system, Turkish fortifications were isolated outposts. The small fortified towns known as *baliqs* similarly incorporated Chinese defence ideas. By the early 11th century some were quite imposing, including the Semiran capital of the Tarim Basin which had a triple wall and a subterranean canal linking its water supply to the river. Others incorporated flanking towers called *ükeks.* Extensive fortifications were similarly built by some rulers of the western steppes, for example, by the Khazars on the lower Don.

Within the forest zone to the north several peoples erected elaborate fortifications of wood and earth, perhaps the largest being those of the Volga Bulgars. In addition to their fortified capital city, these Bulgars had many small wooden castles which made full use of natural features such as escarpments, river junctions, hill-tops and river islands. There were even instances of artificial islands being constructed for such fortresses.

Non-Turkish Central Asian Peoples

The threat of nomad raids motivated most fortification in areas bordering the steppes. Much of the *dihqān* élite of pre-Islamic Sugd lived in *kūshk* (fortified rural villas), while far to the west the tribes of the lower Danube also erected large fortified camps against the Qipchaqs in the 12th century .

In 7th-century Tibet stone-walled towns were centred upon high-altitude oases, while deep within the forests of east-central Russia several Finn peoples developed advanced earth and timber fortifications to rival those of their Volga Bulgar and Russian neighbours.

Russia

The majority of early Russian fortifications were in the south-east, along the Dnieper. In the 10th century, having failed to conquer the neighbouring steppes, Kievan Russia erected numerous simpler earth and timber castles along the edge of the forest as bases from which to attack the nomads. Almost all were built next to rivers, but this castle-based offensive provoked a counter-attack and the forts were destroyed by the Pechenegs and Qipchaqs. In the 11th and 12th centuries

Below: *A fortified hilltop known as Truvor's Farmstead outside Izborsk, near Pskov, 8th–9th centuries. All early medieval Russian fortifications were made of earth and timber. (A. G. Naletov photograph)*

another series of larger but more defensive fortresses was constructed within Russian territory, many having fields inside their walls so that garrisons could withstand a prolonged siege.

Deeper within Russia round earth, rubble and timber forts of the common Slav type had existed since at least the 10th century. This form of construction continued, often on a massive scale, with little use of stone or brick until the 13th century. It was highly successful, particularly during the steady expansion of Russian territory eastwards at the expense of Finn peoples such as the Mordva.

The architecture of northern Russia was similar, but less elaborate than that of the south. A rich trading city like Novgorod had a defensive wall by the 11th century, though it appears to have been made in various ways depending upon the whim and wealth of the 'quarter' which it protected. Part was of stone, but another sector consisted of a timber palisade on an earthen rampart. Pskov may have had some stone fortification even in the 10th century, Old Ladoga to the north certainly having a high stone wall by the 12th century.

The idea of defending an ill-defined frontier with a series of small forts was attempted in the north-west by Alexander

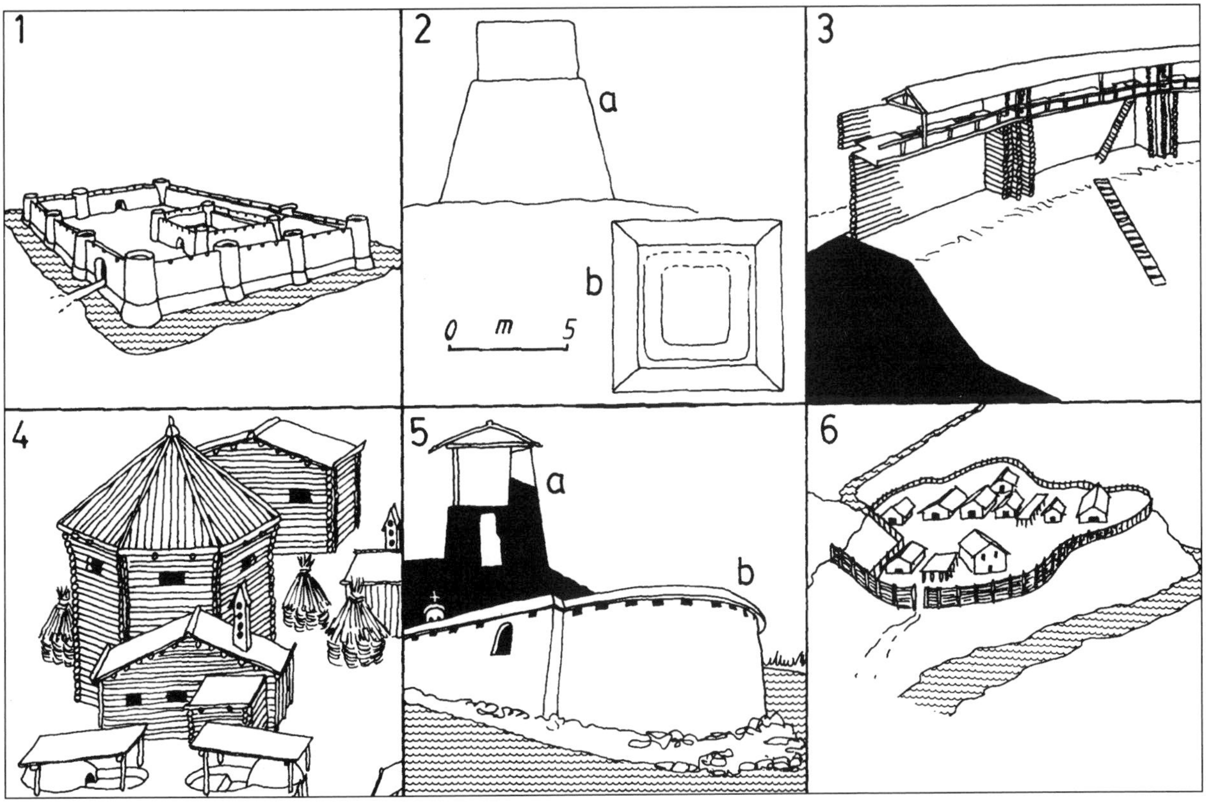

Above: *Fortification; Central Asia and Eastern Europe*
1. Reconstruction of a Uighur Turkish fortress in the Tuva region, 8th–9th centuries. The basic plan reflects Chinese influence whereas the earth-brick construction and use of an inner citadel is fully within a Turco-Mongol tradition found right across the steppes and mountains of Central Asia. (after Pletnyeva)
2. Signal-tower for smoke beacon in Khwārazm, Transoxiana, undated medieval. Although this one may have been erected before the Muslim conquest of Transoxiana, chains of comparable beacons would soon cover the Caliphate from the Atlantic coast to the Indian frontier.
a elevation;
b plan. (after Tolstov)
3. Reconstruction and section of the earth and timber defences of a typical 11th–12th-century Russian town. The timber wall has a continuous overhanging gallery and roof. (after Rappoport)
4. Reconstruction of a wooden tower and surrounding residential and agricultural structures at Yureva na Rusi, southern Russia, 12th–13th centuries. (after Orlova)
5. Reconstruction of the citadel of Old Ladoga, northern Russia, 1114.
a section through wall showing wooden roof and superstructure, and internal gallery
b northern corner of citadel overlooking junction of rivers Volkov and Ladoga. (after Arapovoi)
6. Fortified settlement of the Merya eastern Finnish tribe at Bereznyaki, 6th–10th centuries. The settlement or citadel is on a steep bluff in a curve of a small river which flows into the Volga north-east of Moscow. (after Tretyakov)

Above: *Hilltop fortress of Zamr-i Atish Parast in the Pamir mountains, close to the frontier between Chinese-ruled Sinkiang in the east and Transoxiana in the west; probably 13th–15th centuries. The style of fortification is more Iranian than Chinese, and the fact that most of these castles are attributed to the 'infidel' by the local populace suggests that they had pre-Islamic origins. (A. Stein photograph)*

Nevski as a defence against Lithuanian raiders. In fact Russia's first stone or brick castles, similar to the *donjons* of western Europe, were constructed in response to western rather than Mongol pressure in the later 13th and 14th centuries. These 'one-sided' stone fortresses relied on naturally defensible positions and generally consisted of a plain wall with a single tower on the most vulnerable side; methods of construction indicating Hungarian and Polish influence. Meanwhile the majority of Russian cities continued to rely on earth and timber, the oak walls of the Moscow *kremlin* or citadel only being replaced by stone in 1367–8.

The Mongols
The Mongols' success in siege warfare should come as no surprise, given the fact that the art of fortification was well known among the peoples of Central Asia. Nevertheless the rapid success of their initial conquests meant that for many years the Mongols had no apparent need of fortifications. On the other hand the ability, as well as the ruthless willingness, of Mongol rulers to dismantle, move and rebuild fortresses or entire towns in the later 13th and 14th centuries indicates a thorough understanding of their importance. This habit was particularly prevalent in Transoxiana, eastern Iran and Afghanistan where fortifications were made of mud-brick which lent itself to such tactics.

The Rise of Tīmūr-i Lank
Although Tīmūr came from a mixed Turkish and Mongol military heritage, his attitude towards fortification seems to have been thoroughly Iranian. He was, for example, particularly concerned to defend his north-eastern frontier against attacks from the steppes, and so built or repaired many fortifications. He then went further, erecting a series of forts beyond the river Syr Darya almost far as Mongolia, most of these being sited in low-lying areas and river valleys.

SIEGE WARFARE

The role of Central Asian peoples in the spread of medieval siege warfare techniques can hardly be over-estimated. Nevertheless they acted as transmitters rather than originators of new ideas. Even so, the Turks, having learned much from their Chinese and Sassanian neighbours, were sending technical advisers to help their Tibetan allies by the 8th century.

In the east the Indian-influenced and Iranian-speaking Khotanese attempted to defend their city wall against Mongol stone-throwing *mangonels* by hanging netting of tree

***Right:** The Golden Gate of the city of Vladimir; Russian, 1164. This was the only stone part of the city's fortifications, the remainder consisting of a high earthen rampart - seen to the left of the gate. This was originally topped by a tall timber wall. (Author's photograph)*

bark in front of them. In the western steppes the 10th-century Pechenegs subdued Russian forts by simply blockading them, but in the 12th and early 13th centuries the Qipchaqs relied on active methods, including direct assault and fire-weapons. The Russians adopted more active defence measures in the 12th century, and a century later were under strong Mongol, and thus by extension Chinese, influence in the techniques of siege and counter-siege. As a result large numbers of *mangonels* were adopted quite suddenly, proving highly effective against the Russians' western foes: Hungarians, Poles and German Baltic Crusaders. A remarkable all-iron crossbow bolt with fins, about two metres long and probably designed to carry a fire-cartridge, was discovered in the 13th–14th-century fortress of Vladimir in eastern Russia though this object might have been of Mongol origin. The widespread impression that Russian military engineering stagnated under Mongol domination is an over-simplification, but Russia did not follow the elaboration of military architecture seen in western Europe.

Although the Mongol armies which invaded central Europe were not equipped for siege warfare, this does not mean that the Mongols lacked capability in this field. Yet they did tend to rely on Chinese or Muslim specialist engineers; the latter being in advance even of the Chinese in some fields. The Mongols also made used of massed batteries of *mangonels* as well as other machines such as the Chinese-operated but Persian-named *kamān-i-gāv* ('ox-bow') which shot large bolts dipped in burning pitch to a range said to be 2,500 paces! Otherwise the Mongols employed massed infantry archers, assorted fire-weapons, the blocking or diverting of small rivers to undermine defensive walls, and of course prolonged blockade.

***Right:** The defences of the kremlin or fortified city of Novgorod in northern Russia. The existing stone walls and towers date from the 15th century, before which the rampart behind the broad moat was topped by various sorts of timber and some stone fortifications, reflecting the wealth and preference of the inhabitants of this particular quarter. (Author's photograph)*

'The Death of Abimalek', in a Russian historical manuscript, 1318–27. In this illustration the troops of both armies are wearing brimmed helmets and mail hauberks, and have kite-shaped shields, straight swords and spears. Only the pennons and flags indicate any Turco-Mongol influence. (Chronicle of Georgi Amartola, Lenin Library, No. 43, f.74r, Moscow)

All these tactics and machines were used to devastating effect by Tīmūr-i Lank at the end of the 14th century. Minor variations included blockading an otherwise inaccessible mountain fortress into surrender by building several surrounding watchtowers, though in the end it still took twelve years for this fortress to fall, and even then it was a result of treachery. At Sivas in Anatolia in 1400, Tīmūr's engineers erected a substantial man-made hill, overlooking the main gate, from which ᶜ*arrāda* (ballistas) threw blazing *naft,* and *manjanīq* (mangonels) hurled rocks into the city.

NAVAL WARFARE

It might seem strange to write of 'naval' warfare in Central Asia, but large ships had sailed the Caspian Sea at least since early medieval times. A supposedly *Varangian* fleet even raided northern Iran after having presumably sailed down the Volga. These Scandinavian *Varangians* were useful to early Russian rulers because of their naval skill. The importance of water-borne communications, if not naval warfare, in this part of the world was illustrated by the fact that the partially man-made Uzboy channel linking the Caspian Sea and Amu Darya was still operating in the 15th century; serving as a sort of 'Suez Canal' in the heart of Asia.

Various types of river craft were used by steppe nomads and forest peoples; including dug-out canoes, coracle-like skin boats comparable to the *juffas* of the Euphrates and Tigris, crude inflated animal skins, and rafts. Paradoxically perhaps, the word *caique* still used for small coastal trading vessels in the Aegean, eastern Mediterranean and Black Seas is of Turkish origin, despite the Greek naval tradition of these seas. The Turkish word *kayak* is, of course, also related to the small skin-covered seagoing canoes of the Arctic.

The huge and numerous waterways of Russia were mainly used as arteries of communication. One specific reference to Grand Prince Vladimir's campaign of 985 stated that the Russian infantry went by river while their cavalry steppe allies rode along the bank. On the other hand *ushkúynik* river pirates were a serious problem in many of the more remote areas of later medieval Russia. In response, and as a defence against nomad raiding, several Russian princes stationed military units to protect important portages between rivers, as well as building wooden slipways or roads along such portages and even clearing rocky obstacles from the rivers themselves. In the deep south of Russia, Slav fishermen inhabited the river banks while the Turkish nomads roamed the neighbouring hills. The rivers provided these Cossack-like *brodniki* communities with security and food, while the *brodniki* helped keep the rivers open for the Russian merchants and armies.

IV
CRUSADE, RECONQUISTA AND COUNTER-CRUSADE (1050–1400)

CRUSADE, RECONQUISTA AND COUNTER-CRUSADE (1050–1400)

Major Campaigns 125
ARMY RECRUITMENT 129
Christendom: The Byzantine Empire 129
Christendom: Armenian and Georgia 131
Christendom: The Crusades and Crusader States 131
Christendom: The Iberian Peninsula 133
Islam: The Eastern Lands 134
Islam: The Middle East 135
Islam: North Africa and al-Analus 140
Islam: Sub-Saharan Africa 140
MILITARY ORGANISATION 141
Christendom: The Byzantine Empire 141
Christendom: Armenia, Georgia and Christian Africa 142
Christendom: The Crusader States 143
Christendom: The Iberian Peninsula 145
Islam: The Eastern Lands 145
Islam: The Middle East and Egypt 146
Islam: North Africa and al-Andalus 149
Islam: Sub-Saharan Africa 149
STRATEGY AND TACTICS 150
Broad Strategy 150
Troop Types 153
Battle Tactics 154
Combat Styles 158
Field and Camp Fortifications 159
WEAPONRY AND HARNESS 159
Archery and Slings 159
Swords and Daggers 161
Spears and Javelins 163
Other Weapons 163
Shields 163
Helmets 163
Body Armour 165
Limb Defences 167
Horse Harness 167
Horse Armour 167
FORTIFICATION 167
Christendom: The Byzantine Empire 167
Christendom: Armenia and Christian Africa 168
Christendom: The Crusader States 168
Christendom: The Iberian Peninsula 170
Islam: The Eastern Lands 171
Islam: The Middle East and Egypt 171
Islam: North Africa and al-Analus 172
SIEGE WARFARE 173
NAVAL WARFARE 178
The Mediterranean 178
The Atlantic 182
The Indian Ocean and Red Sea 182
Riverine Warfare 182

The Muslim and Byzantine worlds both faced assaults from western Europe during the 12th to 14th centuries. There was also migration into the Balkans by waves of nomadic peoples from north of the Black Sea. This period was, in fact, characterised by the movement of various militarily significant peoples; the most obvious being the Turks. Arabs also came to dominate most of North Africa at the expense of Berbers while the 14th century saw another sudden collapse of Byzantine military power. The only Middle Eastern Crusader state to survive was Cyprus, but the eruption of Ottoman Turks into the Balkans stimulated a new series of Later Crusades. There were few changes to the military systems of the Muslim world during the 14th century, however, and most of the Muslim world was entering a period of conservatism that would last almost until modern times. On the other hand North Africa was developing military links with newly Muslim African peoples to the south of the Sahara. The Guanches people of the Canary Islands were excluded from this link and remained ignorant of iron or boat-building despite the fact that they were visited by Muslim sailors. The one major exception to such creeping conservatism was the Ottoman Empire which became a cultural and military melting-pot.

The Muslim conquest of India contrasted with the peaceful spread of Islam across much of Africa. The amount of cultural contact around the Indian Ocean was also enormous and resulted in the spread of Islam throughout many islands including what is now Indonesia. Madagascar meanwhile had already been subjected to large-scale colonisation by Indonesian peoples from the far side of the Indian Ocean and more recently by Bantu peoples from southern Africa. The spread of Islam in East Africa reached as far as southern Mozambique. Further north, in the Horn of Africa, the situation is less clear because the Somali people may have originated in southern Ethiopia and northern Kenya before migrating to their present homeland. The Muslims faced a deeply entrenched Christian civilisation in Ethiopia and much of what is now the Sudanese Republic. From the 7th century Ethiopia was largely isolated from the rest of Christendom, but its kings continued to be seen as protectors of Monophysite Christians throughout the Middle East.

To the east of Ethiopia, in what is now Sudan, Nubian Christianity probably spread much farther west than was once thought, while the long-established Bāja nomads of north-western Sudan largely remained pagan many centuries after the arrival of both Christianity and Islam. Nubia's decline in the 13th to 14th centuries remains unclear though it was Muslim Fung people from the west who finally destroyed the last Nubian state at the end of the 15th century. There had been urban civilisations in sub-Saharan West Africa since antiquity and these emerged into recorded history with the establishment of the kingdom of Ghana in the 8th century. The next large cultural changes came with the spread of Islam during the 10th to 14th centuries.

Major Campaigns

11th–12th centuries: Expansion of Christian Ethiopia under Zagwe dynasty.

1011–25: Muslim Ghaznavids break power of Hindu states in India.

c.1050–7: Arab tribes invade Libya and Tunisia.

1054: Murābiṭin raid Ghana.

1055–65: Kingdom of León-Castile reduces Andalusia to tribute.

1055: Saljūq Turks occupy Baghdad.

1056–69: Saharan Murābiṭin conquer Morocco and southern Spain.

1064: Portuguese capture Coimbra.

1067: Murābiṭin destroy kingdom of Ghana.

1071: Saljūq Turks defeat Byzantines at Manzikert.

1081: Byzantines defeated by Italo-Normans at Durrës.

1085: Castile conquers Muslim Toledo.

1086–91: Murābiṭin conquer al-Andalus except Saragossa.

1091: Balkan Pecheneg Turks defeated by Byzantines.

1094–9: El Cid seizes control of Valencia.

Carved relief of two cavalryman jousting with spears, on an ablution basin from Jativa; Andalusian, early 11th century. (Museo Archeologico, Jativa)

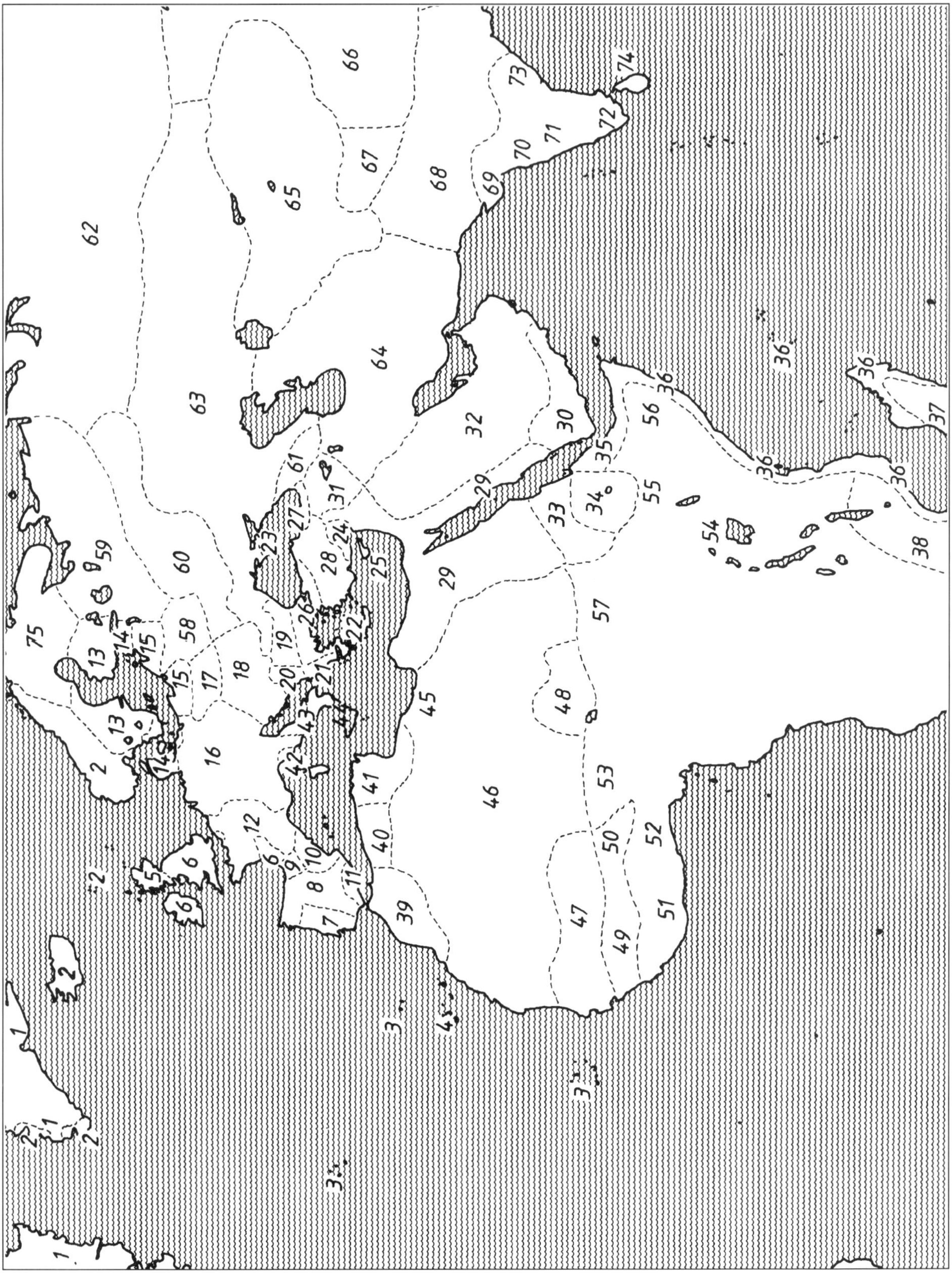
1
2
3
4
5
6
7
8
9
10
11
12
13
14
15
16
17
18
19
20
21
22
23
24
25
26
27
28
29
30
31
32
33
34
35
36
37
38
39
40
41
42
43
44
45
46
47
48
49
50
51
52
53
54
55
56
57
58
59
60
61
62
63
64
65
66
67
68
69
70
71
72
73
74
75

1096–9: First Crusade; conquest of Jerusalem.
1100–01: Un-numbered Crusade defeated by Saljūqs in Anatolia.
1108: Murābiṭin defeat Christian alliance at Ucles; Byzantines defeat Norman Bohemond of Taranto.
1110: Crusaders conquer Sidon.
1118: Aragon conquers Muslim Saragossa.

Left: Europe, Africa and western Asia, c.1300

1. *Inuit Eskimos*
2. *Norway and dependencies*
3. *Uninhabited*
4. *Guanches, possibly under Marīnid suzerainty*
5. *Scotland*
6. *England and dependencies*
7. *Portugal*
8. *Castile*
9. *Navarre*
10. *Aragon*
11. *Granada*
12. *France*
13. *Sweden*
14. *Denmark and dependencies*
15. *Teutonic Order*
16. *Western Empire (Germany)*
17. *Poland*
18. *Hungary*
19. *Bulgaria*
20. *Serbia*
21. *Despotate of Epirus*
22. *Latin Aegean possessions*
23. *Genoese Kaffa*
24. *Cilician Armenia*
25. *Kingdom of Cyprus*
26. *Byzantine Empire of Constantinople*
27. *Byzantine Empire of Trebizond*
28. *Turkish beyliks, under Īl-Khān Mongol suzerainty*
29. *Mamlūk Sultanate*
30. *Rasūlids*
31. *Atābegs, under Īl-Khān Mongol suzerainty*
32. *Arab tribes*
33. *Alwa*
34. *Ethiopia*
35. *Zaila*
36. *Arab coastal and island settlements*
37. *Hova*
38. *Kingdom of Monomatapa*
39. *Marīnids*
40. *Ziyānids*
41. *Ḥafṣids*
42. *Pisa*
43. *Papal territory*
44. *Kingdom of Sicily*
45. *Arab tribes*
46. *Berber nomads*
47. *Mali*
48. *Kanem-Bornu*
49. *Yutenga*
50. *Songhai*
51. *Ashanti*
52. *Dogomba*
53. *Hausa*
54. *Kitara*
55. *Galla*
56. *Somalis*
57. *Darfur*
58. *Lithuania*
59. *Novgorod, Mongol Golden Horde suzerainty*
60. *Russian principalities, Mongol Golden Horde suzerainty*
61. *Georgia, Mongol Īl-Khān suzerainty*
62. *Mongol Khānate of Sibir*
63. *Mongol Golden Horde Khānate*
64. *Īl-Khān Mongol Khānate*
65. *Mongol Jagatai Khānate*
66. *Mongol Empire of the Great Khān*
67. *Kashmir-Ladakh*
68. *Sultanate of Delhi*
69. *Gujarat*
70. *Yadavas*
71. *Hoysalas*
72. *Pandyas*
73. *Jajnagar*
74. *Lanka*
75. *Saami-Lapps*

1121: Andalusian revolt against Murābiṭin.
1124: Crusaders conquer Tyre.
1127: León invades Portugal.
1129: Crusaders attack Damascus.
1137: Portuguese defeat Murābiṭin at Ourique.
1141–7: Muwaḥḥidin defeat Murābiṭin, take control of Morocco.
1144: Zangī retakes Crusader-held Urfa (Edessa).
1146–9: Siculo-Normans seize Tunisian coast.
1146–7: Muwaḥḥidin conquer al-Andalus except Murcia and Balearic Islands; Portuguese and English Crusaders conquer Lisbon; German Crusade defeated in Anatolia.
1148: Second Crusade defeated outside Damascus.
c.1150: Rise of city states in southern Nigeria
1152–9: Muwaḥḥidin expel Siculo-Normans from Tunisia.
1153: Crusaders conquer Ascalon.
1163–9: Five Crusader invasions of Egypt.
c.1165: Qarākhānids of Transoxiana overthrown by Buddhist Qara-Khitai.
1174: Saladin occupies Damascus.
1175: Ghaznavids establish first Muslim Empire in northern India.
1176: Saljūq Turks defeat Byzantines at Myriocephalon.
1177: Crusaders defeat Saladin at Mont Gisard.
1183: Defeat of Crusader naval raid into Red Sea.
1186: Vlach-Bulgar revolt against Byzantium.
1187: Saladin defeats Crusaders at Ḥaṭṭīn; Muslims retake Jerusalem.
1189–91: Crusader siege of Acre.
1195: Muwaḥḥidin defeat Castile at Alarcos.
1197–8: German Crusade to Holy Land.
c.1200: Rise of Muslim Mali in West Africa; Rise of Muslim city states in northern Nigeria.
1202–04: Fourth Crusade conquers Constantinople.
1203–07: Muwaḥḥidin conquer Murābiṭ in Balearic Islands.
1212: Muwaḥḥidin defeated by Christian Spanish coalition at Las Navas de Tolosa.
1213: Catalonia loses territory north of Pyrenees.
1218–21: Fifth Crusade defeated in Egypt.
1229–33: Civil war in Cyprus.
1229–35: Catalonia-Aragon conquers Muslim Balearic Islands.
1230s: Andalusian rebellions largely expel Muwaḥḥidin.
1236–49: Christian conquest of Cordoba, Valencia, Seville and Algarve.
1244: Khwārazmian army seizes Jerusalem; Crusaders defeated at La Forbie.
1247–58: Muslim revolt against Aragonese in Valencia.
c.1250: Rise of pagan empire of Benin in West Africa forest zone; Rise of Great Zimbabwe in southern Africa.
1256–8: Civil war in Crusader Kingdom of Acre.
1259: Byzantines defeat Crusader 'Empire of Constantinople' at Pelagonia.
1261: Byzantines retake Constantinople.
1270: Crusader invasion of Tunisia defeated.
1275–85: Four Marīnid expeditions to Spain.
1275: Establishment of Islam in northern Sumatra.
1276–80: Muslim revolt in Valencia.

Left: *Carving of a soldier wearing a helmet with an integral face-mask or visor; Navarese, c.1155. This kind of protection is not seen north of the Pyrenees and probably reflected the greater importance of archery in Iberian warfare. (Author's photograph; in situ Church of Santa Maria la Real, Sangüese, Spain)*

1282–3: Aragon conquers Sicily.
1285–91: Mamlūks conquer remaining Crusader territory on Middle East mainland.
1285: War between Aragon and France.
1288–90: Mamlūk invasions of Nubia.
1295–7: Delhi Sultanate invades Malwa, Deogir and Gujarat.
1299–1306: Jagatai Mongol invasions of India.
c.1300: Kanem-Bornu Empire in central sub-Saharan region. Rise of Benin empire in southern Nigeria.
Early 14th century: Wars between Christian Ethiopia and Muslim Red Sea state of Ifat.
1301: Ottomans defeat Byzantines at Koyunhisar.
1304–11: Muslim invasion of southern India.
1306–10: Crusader Hospitallers conquer Byzantine Rhodes.
1309–10: Crusade against Muslim Granada.
c.1310: Naval expedition by ruler of Mali from Senegal, probably to Cape Verde islands.
1311–16: Crusader States in Greece defeated by Catalan Grand Company; Catalans occupy Athens and Thebes.
1316: Southern India conquered by Sultanate of Delhi.
1320–5: Sultan of Delhi conquers eastern Bengal.
1326: Ottomans capture Bursa.
1334: Crusader fleet defeats Turks in Gulf of Edremid.
1335: Collapse of Īl-Khān Mongol authority in Iran.
1340: Castilian fleet defeated by Marīnids off Algeciras; Marīnid invasion of Castile defeated at Rio Salado.
1341: Portuguese raid Canary Islands.
1343–52: Serbia conquers most of Byzantine Greece.
1344: Crusaders take Izmir.
1346: Genoese seize Chios.
1349–50: Castilian siege of Gibraltar.
1353-54: Ottomans seize Cimpe and Gelibolu, first possessions in Europe.
1360–1: Cypriots occupy Korgos and Antalya.
c.1361: Ottomans conquer Edirne.
1364: Ottomans defeat coalition of Balkan rulers at river Marica.
1365: Cypriot Crusaders raid Alexandria.
1365: Mamlūk invasion of Nubia.
1367: Civil war in Castile; French and English intervention in Castile; Cypriots raid Cilicia and Syria.
1371–6: Ottomans conquer Thrace and Macedonia.
1371: Ottomans defeat coalition of Balkan rulers at Cirmen; Tīmūr-i Lank invades Khwārazm.
1373–4: War between Cyprus and Genoa.
1379: Navarrese 'Free Company' seizes Thebes.
1385: Anglo-Portuguese defeat Castile at Aljubarrota.
1388: Civil war in Muslim northern India.
1389: Ottomans defeat Serbs at first battle of Kosova.
1390: Ottomans conquer amirates of Sarahan, Aydin, Mentese, Hamit, Germiyan, Teke and part of Karaman; unsuccessful Crusader siege of Mahdia in Tunisia.
1396: Ottomans defeat Crusaders and Hungarians at Nikopol.
1399–1403: Burgundian naval Crusade in eastern Mediterranean and Aegean.

ARMY RECRUITMENT

The later Middle Ages saw an increasing imbalance in the manpower resources of a relatively over-populated Christendom and a generally under-populated Muslim world which led to different forms of military occupation when one side conquered a region inhabited by the other. In the Iberian peninsula, for example, Spain and Portugal eventually expelled Islam altogether whereas Muslims only became a majority in a few isolated parts of the western half of the Ottoman Empire.

Christendom: The Byzantine Empire

The Byzantine Empire's loss of much of Anatolia deprived it of a major pool of military manpower. At the end of the 11th century foreign troops may for the first time have outnumbered domestic recruits and subsequent attempts by the Comnenid Emperors to rebuild a 'national' army still had to be supplemented by large numbers of mercenaries and prisoners. The majority of domestic troops now spoke Greek and included military families from the lost provinces who had fled west. By the late 12th–early 13th century the *archontes* had emerged as a provincial élite with local military authority but no legal standing. Nor were they specifically linked with the *pronoia* system of estates or fiefs which was still in an early stage of development.

Among the non-Greek Balkan subjects or vassals recruited by the Byzantine Empire were Bulgars and Serbs. The Vlach population south of the Danube appears to have been enlisted almost as Alpine troops but they tended to be unreliable, helping Qipchaq invaders from the steppes and playing a leading role in a revolt which led to the recreation of an independent Bulgaria at the beginning of the 13th century. Various Turks were recruited into the Byzantine army, including survivors of the defeated Pechenegs in the Balkans, Qipchaqs who settled in the same area in the late 12th century, and many Muslim Turks who transferred their allegiance to Byzantium following the Comnenid reconquest of western Anatolia. Most of these converted to Christianity and were employed as garrison troops known as *Myrtaïtai*. During the 12th century other non-Greek allies or vassals included Russians, Georgians and Alans, and the numbers of previously important Armenians declined steeply. Arab troops included prisoners of war and apparently professional assassins used to kill the commander of invading Russian troops in 1161. During the late 11th and 12th centuries western mercenaries included French, Danes, Germans from Saxony, Pisans and Ligurians from Italy, Frisians, Flemings, Hungarians, men from the Crusader States and Anglo-Saxon English. The first Anglo-Saxon refugees from the Norman conquest of England arrived by sea in about 1075, but most of them were sent north to the Crimea. Larger numbers appeared in the 1080s and 1090s, apparently because sons of the defeated Anglo-Saxon military élite in England saw no future under Norman rule at home. By the late 12th century the *Varangian* Guard may have been predominantly English. Normans were prominent in the late 11th- and 12th-century Byzantine army as

Right: *Wall painting of 'St. George and the youth of Mitiline'; Crusader States, mid-13th century. The style of painting and the saint's short-sleeved mail hauberk are in the Byzantine manner, but the horse's high peaked saddle is purely western European, perhaps reflecting the mix of military equipment seen in the Crusader States of the Middle East. (Erica Dodd photograph; in situ, Church of Mar Tadros, Bahdaydat, Lebanon)*

'The Death of Hector', in a manuscript compiled at Acre, Crusader Kingdom of Jerusalem, c.1287. Although the artist has exaggerated the vulnerability of a man bending down to strip off his dead enemy's armour, the fact that mail chausses did not reach the top of the wearer's leg was real enough. (Histoire Universelle, Bibliothèque Nationale, MS. Fr. 20125, f.133v, Paris)

armoured cavalry, mostly from the newly established Norman Kingdom in southern Italy and Sicily.

Following the Fourth Crusade's seizure of the Byzantine heartland, the fragmented Byzantine successor states had to rely on more limited sources of recruitment. Even so mercenaries in the Empire of Nicea included Armenians, Germans and even 'Latins' from the Crusader Empire of Constantinople as well as a *Varangian* Guard. By the mid-13th century the Nicean army also included Spanish troops as well as Sicilians. The first domestic troops included infantry archers from Bithynia, Greeks from Thrace, Vlachs and Albanians. Qipchaq Turks from the Balkans were transferred to Anatolia and converted to Christianity while the *Mourtatoi* are likely to have been converted, captured, or renegade ex-Muslim Turks from the east.

Following the Nicean reconquest of Constantinople, a renewed Byzantine Empire under Palaeolog Emperors attempted to maintain a small professional army recruited from its own subjects. Nevertheless mid-14-century Byzantine forces still included a remarkable variety of linguistic groups including many Turks. For example the largely Muslim Ghuzz fled from the Mongols into areas adjacent to the Danube Delta; converted to Christianity and survive to this day as the *Gagautzi*. Muslim Saljūq Turks fled in an almost opposite direction from the Mongol invasion of Anatolia, crossing the Black Sea to settle in the Byzantine-ruled part of the Crimean peninsula where they too became Christian. The Byzantine term *tourkapouli* (sons of Turks) was probably used to distinguish these Christianised resident Turks from other Turkish Muslim mercenaries, whereas the *Mourtatoi* were now an infantry archer guard unit of converted prisoners and renegades. Turks were not the only people to flee the Mongols into Byzantine territory and service. The Iasians, of Alan or Ossetian origin, were pagans or highly unorthodox Christians from the northern Caucasus who lived in towns in the Donets'k area of what is now eastern Ukraine. Following the Mongol invasions, these Iasians were recruited by Hungary and were probably synonymous with those Alans who suddenly appeared on Byzantium's north-western frontier at the start of the 14th century, large numbers then being recruited into the Byzantine army. Among Greek troops the best were infantry archers from Paphlagonia. Cretan and other refugees from Venetian-occupied islands were also settled in Anatolia, apparently as horse-archers. Following the final collapse of Byzantine authority in western Anatolia, several large military groups migrated to remaining European provinces such as Macedonia. The basis of the Byzantine forces defending 14th-century Constantinople were the city's non-noble *mesoi* or middle class who presumably formed a sort of urban militia. Meanwhile the last Byzantine navies were manned by troops from southern Greece, Greeks from Latin Crusader-ruled areas, plus Russian, Spanish, Catalan and Italian naval mercenaries. Despite an economic, political and military collapse the Byzantine army was still able to recruit a few western mercenaries even in the late 14th century. The *Varangian* Guard was said to still greet the Emperor in English, though it is unlikely that any of its members now came from England. Other smaller Byzantine successor states largely relied on local recruitment with a very small number of foreign mercenaries. The 'Empire of Trebizond', for example, could draw upon Greek *stradioti* who had fled areas lost to Crusaders or Turks, though the bulk of the local population were warlike Laz and Tzan tribesmen, closely related to the neighbouring Georgians who also served as allies or volunteers in Trebizond.

Christendom: Armenia and Georgia

In addition to the independent Christian states of Cilician Armenia and Georgia, young men from the Syrian Jacobite or Syriac Christian community defended local monasteries in south-eastern Anatolia in the mid-to-late 12th century. The Armenian heartland had lost its independence, but a new Armenian state emerged in the mountains facing the Cilician coastal plain, its army originally consisting of Armenians plus an élite of Norman mercenaries from the defeated Byzantine army. By the 12th century the most effective part of the Cilician Armenian army consisted of light cavalry and infantry archers, but by the mid-13th century it was also recruiting Arab tribesmen from Syria and Latins from the neighbouring Crusader States.

Little is known about the armies of 12th- to 14th-century Georgia, except that at first they had included some western mercenaries. Local Georgian troops were again noted as archers, while the rulers' élite was built around armoured cavalry known as *aghlumi* – clearly from the Muslim-Arabic term *ghūlām* meaning a soldier of slave origin.

Christendom: The Crusades and Crusader States

The forces which marched east as the First Crusade were unlike normal western European armies in their composition, though not in their organisation. Virtually all those involved were men of relative prosperity since Crusading was not a means of escape for a poor knight seeking his fortune overseas. Similarly the bulk of foot soldiers appear to have been prosperous peasants and townsmen, plus professional sergeants. Women were mostly recorded as financiers of Crusading expeditions rather than active participants. In the early 13th century the Pope also permitted monks to go on Crusade which led to temporary changes in monastic vows.

Military recruitment within the Crusader States of the Middle East differed considerably from that of Crusading expeditions which originated in Europe. Most of the nobility of these States were from modest knightly origins; the knights of the Middle East being known as *chevaliers de la terre* by friends, *poulains* (runts) by unsympathetic sources. But large-scale emigration to the Crusader States virtually stopped after the disaster at Ḥaṭṭīn in 1187, though individual families did make their way east, often as a consequence of political difficulties at home. The number of knights available in the Crusader States of Jerusalem, Tripoli and Antioch was also small, and the lack of agricultural land meant that the bulk of the 13th- and perhaps even 12th-century military aristocracy formed an urban-based knightly class similar to that of Italy. Non-knightly troops included professional infantry and cavalry sergeants paid by these towns and by the Church, largely recruited from local commoners and visiting pilgrims. In an emergency a general feudal levy or *arrière ban* produced larger numbers of infantry sergeants and urban militias, including men from the Arabic-speaking indigenous Christian community and, in the north, Armenians. The merchant class of the coastal ports also formed *confraternities* or 'brotherhoods' to defend their own walls, while during the 13th century the various separate Italian *communes* within these cities also provided infantry militias.

Mercenaries remained essential; a steady stream of these being preferred to sudden hordes of uncontrollable Crusaders. But these should not be confused with knights who were paid stipends via *money fiefs* since these were, at least in theory, still part of a feudal system of military obligation. From the mid-13th century to the fall of Acre other outside troops included southern Italian cavalry brought by Filangieri, the *bailli* or governor of Emperor Frederick during the latter's brief rule over the Crusader States, and the French Regiment originally brought east by King Louis of France. Armenian mercenaries, including siege engineers, were particularly important in Edessa (Urfa) and Antioch. During the 13th century the Principality of Antioch also enlisted the Greek community, often in competition with the better-known Armenians. Syrian and Maronite infantry archers from Lebanon were more characteristic of Tripoli and Jerusalem. However, the warlike *jabalīyūn* hill people of Lebanon were virtually independent of all outside control during the 13th century, the Maronites generally taking a pro-Crusader stance while their Muslim neighbours naturally favoured the Mamlūks. The Crusaders would not accept defeated Muslim troops into their service but there were significantly important ex-Muslim soldiers in the Crusader States. These *turcopoles* had converted to Christianity and continued to fight as light cavalry; if recaptured they were invariably executed as apostates. Subsequently the term *turcopole* applied to troops fighting in Islamic style though not necessarily of captive Muslim origin; some apparently being eastern Christians.

***Left:** 12th-century lustreware dish, probably from Egypt. Here the soldier has a tall but flat-based infantry shield known as a januwiyāh which is also decorated with the shatrang or chess-board pattern popular among Muslim warriors. It was probably copied in European heraldry where it was called checky. (Keir Collection, no. 151, London)*

By far the most important non-feudal military force in the Crusader States were the Military Orders. Some Orders such as the Teutonic Knights recruited from a limited area, but the two greatest Military Orders, the Templars and the Hospitallers, attracted men from all over western Europe. At first such recruits needed only to be free men. Later those becoming brother knights had to be of knightly origin while *sergeants* were from free artisan or peasant backgrounds but not serfs. Otherwise all recruits had to be 'spiritually clean', free of debt and not members of another Order; visiting pilgrim knights often attached themselves temporarily to one of the Military Orders while in the Holy Land.

Much of the military élite fled to Cyprus before and during the collapse of the mainland Crusader States, but here mercenaries and foreign allies played an increasingly important role since the number of Cypriot-Crusader knights was always small. From the later 13th century onwards the Italian, Catalan and Provençal merchant communities in Cypriot towns also grew in importance, as did the Military Orders. Armenian and Syrian refugee communities similarly had a military role, though the *turcopoles* of 14th-century Cyprus appear to have been of Greek origin. The Crusader States carved out of Byzantine southern Greece had largely been conquered by men from the Champagne and Burgundy regions of France, but they found little land suitable for *fiefs*. As a result many had *money fiefs* or simply remained in a greater lord's service as household knights. The lack of land, the abundance of islands and the naval orientation of Crusader Greece also meant that many knights became little more than pirates. Another peculiarity of Latin Greece was the fact that the Catalans who dominated

Right: *'Christ before Pilate,', in a Serbian wall-painting, c.1265. Some details of the soldier's armour and costume reflect the pseudo-classical element in Byzantine art, but his tall, broad-brimmed helmet was real; this style having been adopted throughout the Byzantine Empire, much of the Balkans and Russia. (Author's photograph; in situ, Sopocani Monastery, Serbia)*

much of the area in the 14th century got on very well with the Muslims of the eastern Mediterranean and made frequent alliances with various Turkish states.

The Italian élite which dominated the rest of Latin Greece by the 14th century was essentially mercantile rather than feudal, lived in coastal towns and hired mercenaries rather than doing military service themselves. In fact, in the second half of the 14th century feudal service was gradually replaced by an *adoha* (tax) with which to pay professional soldiers. Another effect of the shortage of military manpower in Crusader Greece was the gradual integration of the existing ex-Byzantine Greek *archontes*, some even being knighted. They were arrayed as cavalry alongside the squires. From the mid-14th century Greek crossbowmen were enlisted to defend the islands, and *gasmouli* of mixed Latin and Greek parentage were highly regarded as marines. A large Armenian community which existed in north-western Anatolia at the time of the Fourth Crusade's conquest of Constantinople lent support to the new rulers, Armenians long having had close military links with Latins in the Crusader States of the Middle East. Finally there were some *turcopoles* in the army of the early 13th-century Latin Empire of Constantinople, apparently serving as mounted crossbowmen.

Christendom: The Iberian Peninsula

Normans, Flemings, Burgundians, Bretons, Poitevans, Angevins and others played a notable role in early campaigns of the Reconquista, but in general the Christian states of Iberia got little help from north of the Pyrenees after the mid-12th century. In many arid regions taken from the Muslims new *communes* were established, settled by non-noble troops. Elsewhere much of the Muslim rural population remained under Christian rule, though the old Muslim élites had to be replaced by new Christian ones.

A supposedly 'typical' western European feudal structure of military obligation was never fully imposed in the Iberian peninsula. Instead a distinctive Spanish-Portuguese system evolved whereby the poorer non-noble *peones* paid taxes and fought as infantry, the richer non-noble *caballeros villanos* served as cavalry and were generally excused taxation. Similarly *peones* who became rich enough were permitted to become *caballeros villanos*. The many Muslim Andalusian troops who remained to serve in Christian armies were simply listed as non-noble *cavallers* or horsemen. Nevertheless each Christian state differed to some extent. In Aragon the unreliability of quasi-feudal forces led King James I to raise a loyal force of noblemen related to the ruling family known as *mesnaderos*. By the 13th century a *sometent* (peasant militia) was expected to maintain the peace in the countryside, an urban *sometent* or *somatent* becoming a vital source of trained infantry by the 14th century, and by the late 14th century such urban forces appear to have been recruited by the local authority *deputation*. Even in the early 14th century the garrison of the castle of Mahon in Majorca still included so-called 'Turks', these presumably being remnants of the old Muslim population. The *almogavers* (from the Arabic *al-mughāwir* 'raiders') also included Muslims; these troops being recruited from virtually autonomous non-feudal mountain pastoralists of the mainland and fighting as light cavalry and infantry. Members of the old Muslim military élite who had been evicted from the towns during the Christian conquest still clearly remained a potent military force in the mountains. Some even continued to hold castles, retaining a quasi-noble status in Aragon and Castile.

Navarre, squeezed out of the process of Reconquista at an early date, had always had very limited manpower. Even as late as the 14th century the local military élite of *mesnaderos* included Muslim soldiers from around Tudela. In Castile the Military Orders provided a permanent army to defend the steadily advancing southern frontier, though urban militias also played an increasingly vital role from the early 12th century, and captured Muslim troops were sometimes allowed an equal legal status as *mauri pacis* (pacified Moors). In 13th-century Avila these *mauri* provided a military unit of seventy cavalry and 500 infantry. Andalusian hatred of their fellow-Muslim but African rulers meant that the last independent Muslim ruler of Saragossa similarly fought for Alfonso VII after having been overthrown by the Murābiṭin, and other local Muslim leaders helped Castile conquer Muslim areas from the 13th-century Muwaḥḥidin. Of all the Christian Iberian states, Portugal was the least influenced by French military systems. Nevertheless a new military élite did emerge in the 11th and 12th centuries. At the top the *ricos-homens* were mostly of foreign origin, then came the *ingenui* (free men from old families), *infações* or *cavaleiros* (knights) and *escudeiros* (squires). By the 13th and 14th centuries richer farmers or peasants still had an obligation to serve as *cavaleiros-vilãos*. The Iberian peninsula had special significance in the origins of the Military Orders, short-term military confraternities having been seen in this area well before the development of the permanent Military Orders. Thereafter the establishment of specifically Iberian Military Orders provided a vital source of élite troops. In 1338 King Alfonso also created the Real Confradía de Santísmo y Santiago, perhaps in an attempt to satisfy non-noble *caballeros villanos* who wanted a Military Order of their own.

Islam: The Eastern Lands

Military recruitment in the Muslim world reflected earlier traditions until the coming of the Mongols in the 13th century; with a preference for mixed armies wherever possible. The élite consisted of *mamlūks* of slave origin plus their descendants, and assorted tribal contingents, the general preference being for Turks. The Saljūqs themselves were of Muslim Turkish tribal origin, but as they spread their authority over most of eastern Islam and the Middle East they turned to traditional Muslim methods of recruitment. The famous treatise on government written by the Saljūq *vizier* (prime minister) Niẓām al-Mulk in the late 11th century included a large section on military affairs, but it still reflected traditional attitudes by advocating a mixed army to avoid the threat of rebellion. Non-Saljūqs played an important role in the armies of various minor Saljūq leaders in 11th-century Syria, including other Turkish nomads – normally referred to as Turcomans since the Saljūqs themselves were no longer really nomadic – as well as Kurds and Daylamis. Armenians offered military support to the Saljūq *atābeq* (governor) of Antioch at the end of the 11th century, and the urban militias of northern Syria and the Jazīrah (northern Mesopotamia) defended their walls both for and against the Turks at a time of near anarchy. The Khwārazmshāhs who took over Transoxiana following the decline of the Saljūq again relied on troops of slave origin, though the garrison which defended Samarkand against Genghiz Khān reportedly included Turks, Ghūrids, Khurāsānis and others. Traditional military recruitment did not reappear in Mongol Īl-Khān Iran and Iraq until the 14th century (see Chapter III for the Mongols) though there is some evidence that attempts were made to recruit 'Frankish' western European crossbowmen. Traditional military values then revived under the Sarbadārs who also encouraged religious or *ṣūfī* dervish fraternities as a basis for urban militia forces.

A rather different army evolved in Muslim northern India under the Sultans of Delhi where large numbers of indigenous Hindu troops were enlisted. Even so the military élite of the Sultanate of Delhi remained largely Turkish in origin though Persian in culture. Otherwise the military élite or aristocracy also included Arabs, Afghans, Muslim Abyssinians, Egyptians, Javanese and local Indian converts. By the later 14th century the ordinary soldiers in the Sultanate of Delhi included a bodyguard from Sīstān, the professional *jāndār* or *mamlūk* élite, Turks, Ghūrids, Khurāsānis, Khaljī Turks, Persian-speaking Tajiks, *Rawats* who are believed to have been Indians, Hindus, so-called Khitai who presumably claimed Central Asian descent and possibly even Chinese. When needed the entire Muslim population of the state could also be called to arms.

Those serving as infantry auxiliaries were known as *paidah* whereas Hindu infantry auxiliaries were called *pāyaks.*

Islam: The Middle East

The most significant military development in the heartlands of Islamic civilisation was a further professionalisation of most armies. The only real exception to this trend was Arabia itself, and even in Yemen the core of the 13th–15th-century army appears to have consisted of full-time professionals. The 12th and early 13th centuries also saw a limited revival of ᶜAbbāsid military power in Iraq; the Caliph's small army including Turcomans and refugees from the defeated Khwārazmian army, and was at one time commanded by a eunuch. Similarly small armies characterised the *Atābeg* or successor states of the Fertile Crescent following the fragmentation of the Great Saljūq Sultanate. Typically such rulers could only afford a small *ᶜaskar* bodyguard of slave-recruited *ghūlāms* or *mamlūks,* forming the centre of a larger force of *ajnād* provincial or *jund* soldiers, most of whom were Turks or Kurds plus a few Arabs. In a crisis the rulers of Syrian cities such as Aleppo and Damascus could also summon 'allied' Turcoman warriors from as far away as northern Mesopotamia, clearly having some sort of agreed arrangement with the tribal leadership. A Damascus army of 1138 also included Armenians, described in the Arabic sources as sun-worshipping *ariwurikᶜ*, probably residual members of the Manichaean/Paulician heresy from eastern Anatolia. Early 12th-century Damascus was also home to refugees from coastal areas conquered by the Crusaders, including virtually the entire garrison of Tyre and Sidon who now fought for Damascus. Finally there were untrained religiously motivated volunteers, the *mutaṭawiᶜah,* who were organised on a semi-permanent basis and included a group known as the 'robbers' who specialised in operating behind Crusader lines. *Ahdath* urban militias still played a passive role, and in specifically Arab areas such as the tiny city-state of Shayzar women not only fought in defence of their homes but donned full armour when the need arose. Farther south the bedouin Arab tribes of Jordan and Palestine tended to avoid trouble with both Crusaders and Muslim rulers.

The largest *Atābeg* army was that of the Zangids who ruled Mosul and later Aleppo and Damascus. It also included infantry from Aleppo, highly regarded siege engineers from Aleppo and from Khurāsān, Armenians, professional *naffāṭun* (fire-troops) and large numbers of non-combatant local labourers. Ṣalāh al-Dīn (Saladin) started out as the Zangids' deputy in newly conquered Egypt. Here he and his Ayyūbid successors created a powerful military system founded on the Zangid and the Fāṭimid Egyptian inheritance. Although Ṣalāh al-Dīn himself was of Kurdish origin, the role of Kurds in Ayyūbid armies has been greatly exaggerated. In fact the troops were largely Turkish. The *halqa* or élite of all Ṣalāh al-Dīn's army were slave-recruited Turkish *mamlūks,* such men forming the élites of all subsequent Ayyūbid forces. Ṣalāh al-Dīn 'inherited' the military service of various Arab tribes in southern Palestine, the Sinai peninsula and Egypt from his Fāṭimid predecessors. Other Arabic-speaking troops included specialist fire-troops supplied by the Caliph in Baghdad, Muslim refugees from Crusader territory and low-grade *jund* or territorial Egyptian militia who seem to have served as spear-armed infantry. The local Muslim and Jewish population of Palestine also rose against their Crusader oppressors after Ṣalāh al-Dīn had defeated the main Crusader army. Among the

Gilded bronze elements from the sword-belt of al-Ṣālih Ismāᶜīl; Mamlūk, mid-14th cent. The vertical pieces are stiffeners; two of the circular medallions had holes through which the supporting straps for a scabbard passed. (David Salomons Charity Trust private collection)

Carved wooden panel from Qasr Ibrim depicting a mounted saint; Nubian, 12th–14th centuries. Although based on the Coptic Christian art of Egypt, this horseman wields the exceptionally large-bladed spear shown in Nubian art for many centuries. Similar weapons continued to be used by Sudanese and Saharan cavalry until the late 19th century. (Author's photograph; British Museum, EA. 71889, London)

more exotic troops in the Ayyūbid armies were ex-Fāṭimid infantry guards of African slave origin, but they were unreliable and were soon disbanded, as was the case with regiments of ex-Fāṭimid Armenian soldiers. North Africans or *Maghribis* were considered the best sailors in the Muslim world and were recruited for the navy. Various soldiers of western European origin also served the Ayyūbids, including large numbers of renegades following Ṣalāh al-Dīn's reconquest of most of the Crusader States. A number of captured French and other Crusaders also converted to Islam in the mid-13th century.

The army of Mamlūk Egypt was essentially the same as that of the preceding Ayyūbid dynasty. All that really changed was the relative status of various units and sources of recruitment; *mamlūks* of slave origin were now not only the military élite but also the ruling élite. Under the Baḥrī Mamlūk Sultans the majority were of Turkish origin. Then in the late 14th century another group of *mamlūks* took control as the Burjī Mamlūk Sultans. They and their supporters were described as being of Circassian origin from the Caucasus mountains, though they included men of Russian, Alan, Greek and even western European background. Muslim soldiers of slave origin always maintained some degree of contact with their places or families of origin, but under the Burjī Sultans this meant that *mamlūks* often invited their families to come and take up a military or administrative post in the Mamlūk state. A quite separate system of recruitment was used for the eunuchs, whose military role lay in the education of young soldiers. Most came from Greece or Ethiopia with a few Indians and West Africans.

Freeborn troops had a far lower status in the Mamlūk army than they had under the Ayyūbids. Nevertheless they still formed the *halqa* which probably remained the largest single part of the army. By the later 14th century, however, civilians could buy the status and privileges of a *halqa* soldier, the *halqa* in Egypt having largely ceased to be a real fighting force. In Mamlūk Syria, meanwhile, the *halqa* remained effective, drawing upon the abundant freeborn soldiery of the area even though it soon largely consisted of infantry rather than cavalry. Other freeborn troops in Mamlūk Syria included Turcoman and Kurdish tribal auxiliaries and Oirat Mongol tribesmen who had deserted from the Īl-Khān Mongol rulers of Iran and Iraq. Arabs, particularly the semi-nomadic *ᶜashir* of the steppes rather than deep desert, served not only as tribal auxiliaries under their own chiefs but also in the service of high-ranking Mamlūk provincial governors in Syria. Yet the status of Arab auxiliaries declined sharply within Egypt, and Mamlūk persecution of Egypt's bedouin was one reason why so many migrated south into the Sudan. During the 14th century some of the poorest in Cairo, known as the *ḥarfūsh* (ruffians), sometimes attached themselves to a leading Mamlūk officer or factional leader as bully-boys in return for food and clothing. The infantry archers of the Lebanese mountains and Biqāᶜ valley defended their own territories as virtually autonomous vassals. Infantry and cavalry could also be raised from all the villages of Palestine and Syria. A small number of Europeans also entered Mamlūk service, including some members of the knightly élite of the Crusader States who remained under Muslim suzerainty.

The Saljūqs of Rūm, who ruled the ex-Byzantine regions of central Anatolia, attempted to model their army on that of their Great Saljūq predecessors. At first their military forces consisted of Turcoman tribesmen around a small élite of slave-recruited *ghulāms*. The latter came from many backgrounds and included Russian slaves and Greek prisoners of war. But by the later 12th and early 13th centuries the bulk of the professional élite seem to have been freeborn Turkish cavalry holding *iqṭā*^{c} (*fiefs*). The assimilation of the previous Byzantine, Armenian and Georgian military élites was even more typical of the Dānishmandid Turkish rulers of eastern Anatolia. The Saljūq Sultanate of Rūm also encouraged urban *fityān* and *ikhwān* Muslim brotherhoods as a source of religiously motivated volunteers; a system which was even more important under the subsequent fragmented Turkish *beylik* principalities when they became more commonly known as *aḥi* or *runūd* fraternities and maintained law and order in towns and along major highways. At one time western European mercenaries formed one of the sultan's bodyguards and in fact the Saljūqs of Rūm made far greater use of European mercenaries than any other Middle Eastern Muslim state. This was possible because the Muslim rulers of ex-Byzantine territory in Anatolia were regarded by the Church as slightly less 'infidel' than other Muslim rulers.

The armies of the subsequent small *beylik* states relied almost entirely on tribal Turcoman warriors. Once these states broke through to the Mediterranean, Aegean and Black Sea coasts, some developed small fleets which not only raided the

'The arrest of Jesus', in an Armenian manuscript, c.1270. Armenian art was always very close to that of the Byzantine Empire, but was also under Islamic and at times Crusader influence. Here the soldiers, one of whom has a mail aventail across his face, are shown equipped with a mix of Byzantine, Islamic and even Mongol arms and armour which probably reflected the reality in Armenia in the late 13th century. (Four Gospels, Freer Gallery of Art, Ms. 32-18, f. 310, Washington)

Huntsman equipped as an infantryman, on a silver-inlaid bronze basin, probably made in Syria; Mamlūk, late 13th century. Infantry do not appear very often in Mamlūk art but they clearly played a major role in Mamlūk armies. This man is distinguished from a dismounted horseman by wearing leggings or puttees rather than riding-boots. (Author's photograph; Victoria and Albert Museum, inv. 740-1898, London)

neighbouring islands but also the Balkan mainland. Much of the Byzantine military establishment also transferred their allegiance to these *beyliks* as Byzantine authority collapsed. In late 14th-century eastern Anatolia and western Iran two Turkish states emerged known as the Aq Quyunlī and the Qara Quyunlī (White Sheep and Black Sheep) Turcomans. But as yet they were little more than confederations of nomadic Turcoman and Kurdish clans supported by Arab tribesmen and refugees from Ottoman Turkish expansion to the west.

At first the Ottomans were just one of many small Turkish *beyliks* on the frontier of a disintegrating Byzantine Empire. Like the others they attracted refugees, military and civil, from the Mongol occupation of central Anatolia, but the fact that they were the only *beylik* still to have an open frontier with the Byzantines meant that they appealed to a greater number of religiously motivated *ghāzis* (Fighters for the Faith). These earliest Ottoman armies were entirely traditional, consisting of a majority of Turcoman tribal cavalry, a tiny élite of *ghūlāms* recruited from slaves or prisoners, and a few ill-trained infantry. The *ghāzis* may have evolved into the *akinji* (raiders) and *deli* (fanatics) light cavalry of the Balkan frontier, though many of these appear to have been recent converts from the previous Slav military élites. Meanwhile some of the tribal Turcomans similarly became the nomadic Muslim *Yürüks* of the southern Balkans. Ottoman rulers then broke with tradition, or – perhaps more accurately – modified it to create the beginnings of a dramatically new form of Muslim army. The first of these were *müsellem* cavalry recruited from Muslim and Christian mercenaries and supported by *fiefs*. In about 1338 the Ottoman ruler already had a small force of slave-recruited *ghūlāms* wearing the white caps which later distinguished the *Janissary* infantry. Though they were not yet known as *Janissaries*, the latter may have grown out of this earlier formation. The first attempt to raise properly trained infantry featured the *yaya* or *payadeh* who were recruited from free Muslim and Christian peasants and served as a territorial defence force. They proved too independent for the Sultans' purposes, but such local forces remained important enough for Ottoman rulers to transfer large numbers of people from Anatolia to newly conquered parts of the Balkans. As such they would have included the *derbendci*, military families having a status between that of auxiliaries and professional soldiers and charged with the defence of key communication links. Many Byzantine *gasmouloi* marines also transferred their allegiance to the Ottoman conquerors in the mid-14th century. The most famous Ottoman military formation was the *Janissaries* or *Yeni Çeri* (new army). The earliest *Yeni Çeri* were drawn from the Sultan's one-fifth share of prisoners of war during the reign of Murat I. Like later *Yeni Çeri* recruits they are said to have been sent to work for farming families in Anatolia to learn Turkish and the basics of the Muslim faith, returning to the Sultan's court after four years. This remarkable force was within a long-established tradition of slave-recruited military élites, but differed by being predominantly recruited from 'enslaved' members of the Ottoman Sultan's own non-Muslim population. Strictly speaking this was contrary to Muslim religious law. The *devsirme* or 'tax' of a certain number of young Christians as recruits for the *Yeni Çeri* corps seems to have been initiated by Sultan Bayazit in the late 14th century but this was still only on a small scale and did not become an essential characteristic of the *Yeni Çeri* until the 15th century. Members of the *Yeni Çeri* were technically the Sultan's own *kul* or slaves, but this was not a term of abasement within Ottoman society. Rather it was a mark of dignity and status meaning that the *yoldash* or soldier in question was a member of the ruler's aristocracy of service rather than a slave in the European sense. It is also important to note that the élite of the *Yeni Çeri* corps consisted of a few of cavalry regiments though the great majority of units remained infantry.

The 14th-century Ottoman army was also characterised by its large number of Christian élite troops, in addition to those Christians who formed part of infantry militias. It was in fact

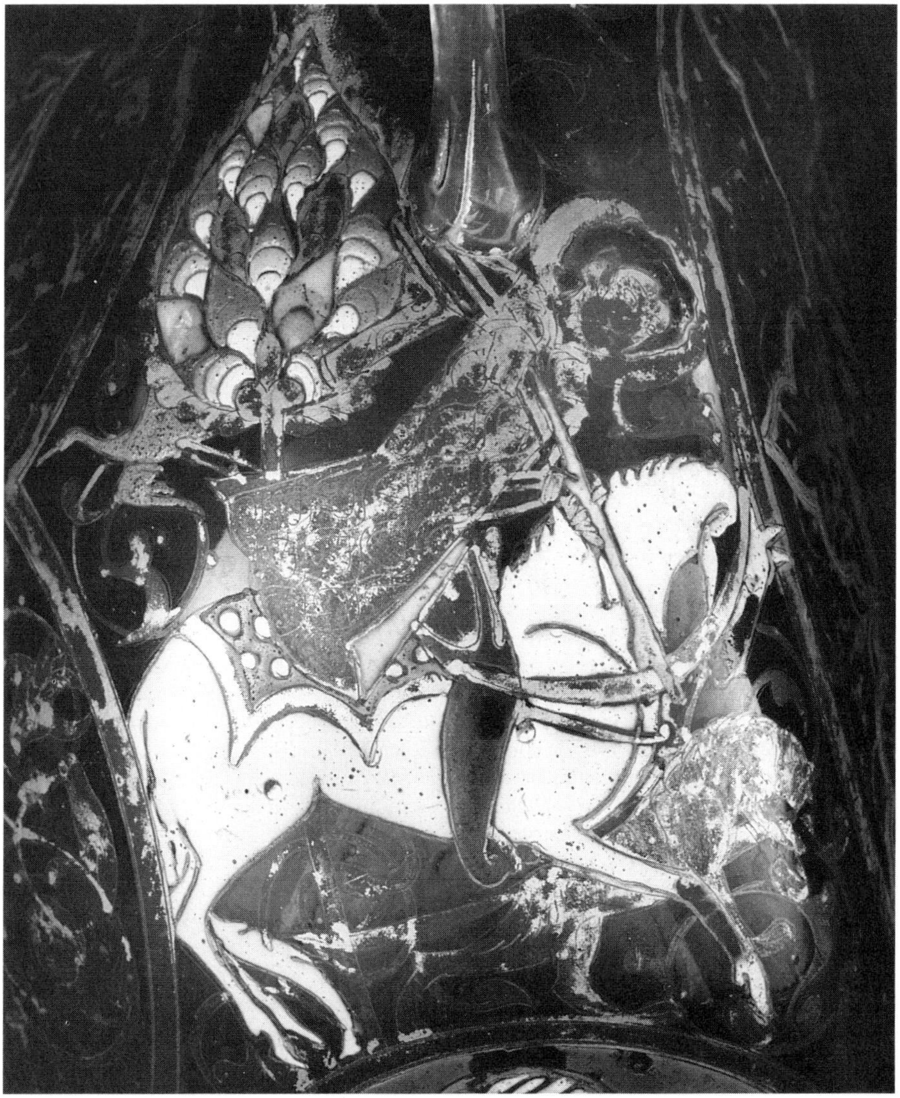

Huntsman using a crossbow from horseback; enamelled glass flask, Mamlūk Syria, 1250–60. The Mamlūks used mounted crossbowmen in war, the weapon being considered suitable for an inexperienced man. (British Museum, no. 69.1-20.3, London)

Ottoman policy to leave the existing military élites in place wherever possible. Many such military families converted to Islam after the second or third generation in order to confirm their position in the new military structure. Thus an entirely new Muslim military élite emerged in the European provinces, very different from that of the Anatolian provinces, consisting of Turkish conquerors and assimilated old aristocracies, both holding relatively small *tīmār* estates based upon the old Byzantine *pronoias* in return for military service as *sipāhi* (cavalry). At a lower rank or status were the specifically Balkan Christian *voynug, voynuk, wojnūq* and *doganci* auxiliary cavalry, and by the late 14th century Christian troops may have been the majority in several Ottoman Balkan armies. Before being finally incorporated into the Ottoman Empire, Bulgaria, Macedonia, Serbia, the remnants of the Byzantine Empire, Wallachia and Moldavia all recognised the Sultan's suzerainty and supplied military units to his army.

Islam: North Africa and al-Andalus

Military systems in the far west of the Muslim world remained old-fashioned. In the 12th century the Zayrid rulers of Tunisia could also draw upon a small number of Muslim refugees from Norman-ruled Sicily as well as recruiting mercenaries who retained their Christian religion. Farther west the army of the Murābiṭin who conquered most of North Africa and al-Andalus was largely of Saharan Berber origin but also included men from northern Morocco and Spanish, Catalan or French mercenaries who formed one of the Murābiṭ ruler's guard units. The army of the subsequent Muwaḥḥidin rulers was more of a Moroccan than Saharan tribal levy, relying primarily on men from the Lamṭa, Zanāta and Maṣmūda tribes of the high Atlas mountains. But it also included slave-recruited African soldiers, former Murābiṭin troops, an élite training unit from the sons of tribal leaders, Spanish Christian prisoners of war and a guard formation of Spanish or Catalan mercenaries. Later rulers of North Africa such as the Hafṣids of Tunisia based their armies on that of the former Muwaḥḥidin, though with additional units recruited from Arab bedouin and people from the cities enlisted individually. In addition the Hafṣid army included the usual urban militias and religious volunteers and a small number of Middle Eastern troops. A guard unit of black African slave origin known as *Gaṇāwa* or men of Guinea seems to have been largely for parade purposes, together with a bodyguard of Christian mercenaries. Militarily more significant were a large number of Christian converts to Islam, probably ex-prisoners, who fought as light cavalry. The army of 14th-century Marīnid Morocco was very similar, again including a small number of Turkish horse-archers, western European mercenaries plus a great many Andalusian infantry archers and crossbowmen. These Muslim Andalusians were also famous as siege engineers and for establishing a naval arsenal at Salā on the Atlantic coast.

Within al-Andalus Islamic civilisation was on the defensive by the 12th century but survived in the little kingdom of Granada throughout the 14th and most of the 15th centuries. There was also a second *taifa* period of small independent statelets between the collapse of Murābiṭin North African domination and the imposition of Muwaḥḥidin domination in the 12th century, characterised by remarkable alliances between Andalusian Muslims and northern Iberian Christians against North African rule. Most Andalusian troops appear to have been professional mercenaries, large parts of the countryside being in the hands of a local military élite. Further to confuse the issue, some of this Andalusian élite were in fact *Mozarab* (Arabised) Christians. The second *taifa* period in the Algarve region of southern Portugal was also notable for the rise of local town-based armies often built around *ṣūfī* (mystical religious) associations. A third *taifa* period following the collapse of Muwaḥḥidin domination was rapidly stifled by the Spanish conquest of all of Andalusia except the rump state of Granada. Nevertheless it was characterised by military systems which often had more in common with those of the Christian north than with Muslim North Africa. Local military obligations were assessed on a family basis and were inherited by succeeding generations, many local Muslim *qā'id* (urban leaders and castle-holders) then coming to terms with the Spanish or Portuguese conquerors, being known as *Mudejar* lords and supplying troops as vassals. Most emigrated to Granada or Morocco following the failure of a series of Muslim uprisings later in the 13th century.

The Naṣrid Kingdom of Granada emerged out of a native revolt against North African rule, its army consisting of the ruler's own clan and its political clients. Additional troops came as refugees fleeing Christian conquest or volunteers from Morocco; the latter mostly being from the Zanāta tribe. In the mid-13th century the ruler of Granada tried to introduce a militia system based upon these Berbers, many of whom originally came from the G͟humāra mountains and thus came to be known as *gomeres* in Spanish. Large numbers of indigenous infantry and mounted crossbowmen were also recruited in the Alpujarras mountains south of Granada. But there was considerable friction between Zanāta Berbers and local Andalusian militias and as a consequence Muḥammad V reduced the numbers of North African volunteers in the mid-14th century and recruited a bodyguard of Christian renegades called *maᶜlūghūn* plus *mamlūks* drawn from younger Christian captives.

Islam: Sub-Saharan Africa

During the 13th century the Muslim merchant communities on the Somali coast began hiring local Somali warriors as *abaan* (protectors) against banditry by nomads. Meanwhile a new Islamic civilisation developed south of the Sahara with its own distinctive military characteristics. Even as early as the 11th century Arab geographers had described the savanna grasslands 'south of Nubia' as full of warriors, many serving as mercenaries in Egypt but not using the bows which characterise most sub-Saharan tribal forces. In the late 12th century Christian Nubian forces were unexpectedly strengthened by the arrival of Armenian and other ex-Fāṭimid soldiers disbanded by Ṣalāh al-Dīn.

Far to the west the armies of pre-Islamic Ghana and Mali had a remarkably rigid social hierarchy, with lower ranks being little more than slaves. On the other hand enslaved captive enemy troops could reach high rank. Most West African warriors were infantry until conversion to Islam in the 13th and 14th centuries encouraged the rise of highly effective cavalry based on traditional Muslim patterns. The hugely rich king of 14th-century Mali also had a guard regiment of Turkish and other *mamlūks* purchased in Egypt. The bulk of his army, however, was based on tribal forces from vassal rulers or governors from the Atlantic to what is now northern Nigeria.

MILITARY ORGANISATION

Christendom: The Byzantine Empire

The Comnenid Emperors of the late 11th and 12th centuries took care to retain personal control of the army which basically consisted of two forces, one in the European and one in the Asian provinces under the overall command of the *Grand Domestic*. Infantry and cavalry were increasingly organised on the basis of ethnic origin. The army was further divided into central and provincial forces administered by a special department. There appear to have been twelve senior *patrician* or *strategos* officers, each responsible for two *turmarch* officers, in turn leading five *drungarios*, leading five or so *comites*, leading five *quintarchs* (their role not entirely clear) who in turn commanded forty troops subdivided into units of ten men under a *decurion*. How far this theory existed in reality is a matter of debate. A senior officer called a *sebaste* commanded foreign troops. Byzantine provincial forces never recovered from the disasters of the late 11th century. Some *theme* armies had survived in the Balkans and the far south-eastern coastal province of the Black Sea. Elsewhere the Comnenids tried to rebuild a *theme* structure in territory they regained from the Saljūq Turks while much of the Balkan provinces consisted of two *duchies* designed primarily for defensive purposes. Provincial forces themselves included many *stradioti* who either served in person or supplied a substitute or commuted their service for a cash payment. By the late 13th century the *pronoia* system of money-raising estates was becoming an essentially military institution designed to maintain cavalry throughout much of the Byzantine state. The *pronoia* differed from a western *fief* because it was not normally inheritable by the holder's son and was part of a wider effort by 13th–14th-century Byzantine rulers to centralise military administration.

Following the Fourth Crusade the largest surviving Byzantine state, the so-called 'Nicean Empire', had a standing force known as the *tagmata* which included household troops, a field army of foreign mercenaries and the remaining *theme* units. This was now divided into *allagion* (regiments); élite guard units being commanded by the *Primmikerios*. Otherwise the army was led by the Emperor or his *Grand Domestic* with a *Protostrator* as his deputy. Other officers included the *Megas Konostoulos* (Grand Constable) in charge of western mercenaries, and various *stratopedarchs* who commanded the local *monokaballoi* (cavalry), *tzaggratores* (crossbowmen), *mourtatoi* (ex-Turkish infantry) and *tzakones* (infantry from southern

Incised slab depicting two armoured donor figures wearing the coat of arms of the ruling Lusignan family; Cathedral of Aya Sofia, Famagusta, Crusader Kingdom of Cyprus, late 13th–early 14th centuries. It is interesting to note that both carry their sword-scabbards on baldrics slung from the shoulder rather than from a sword-belt. (Department of Antiquities of Cyprus photograph; probably now in Limassol Museum)

Left: *'Alexander's army attacking a city', in a mid-14th century Byzantine manuscript. The soldiers' mail and lamellar armour, and above all their archery equipment, include the variety of earlier Byzantine and newer Turco-Mongol elements typical of later medieval Byzantine forces. (Romance of Alexander, f. 96v, Instituto Ellenico, S. Giorgio dei Greci, Venice)*

Greece). By this time the commanders of Byzantine forts and citadels were known as *kastrophylakes* and their garrisons were under a *tzaousios* whose title came from the Turkish term *çauş*. A further unit or more properly group were the *tzouloukonai* (military servants) who only fought in an emergency. Little changed after the Palaeolog Emperors regained Constantinople, except that the *pronoias* tended to become hereditary. By this date Byzantine military titles reflected status rather than much real military function. Nevertheless the commander of the *Varangian Guard* was still called the *Akoluthos* and had a *Grand Interpreter* to assist him, suggesting that he or some of his men might still have been of English origin. By the late 14th century the *pronoia* cavalry were organised into *allagia* or larger *megalla allagia* regiments which served both as tactical and administrative formations. They in turn seem to have been subdivided into '*lances*' or squadrons along western European lines. The term *allagia* was also applied to infantry and lower-grade frontier forces. Defenders of Constantinople included an urban militia based on the city's quarters, each militia probably under that quarter's *demarchos*. Although the Byzantine Empire was shrinking fast it still had provincial forces under some degree of central command. The old title of *Doux* had given way to that of *Kephale* (head) of such provincial administration in the late 13th century; the provinces themselves including one or more *kastron* (fortified towns). The military organisation of the Byzantine Despotate of the Morea in southern Greece remains unclear, though it seems to have consisted of troops in the *Despot's* immediate entourage and those of the most senior vassals, foreign mercenaries under their own commanders, tribal Albanian and Slav auxiliaries under their own chiefs. The Qipchaq Turkish refugee community in the Balkans may also have sent a small professional force to the Emperor's court in Constantinople. The Anatolian border between Byzantium and various Turkish *beyliks* consisted of a wide no man's land with Christian *akritoi* (frontier warriors) on one side and Muslim *ghāzis* on the other. Elsewhere Greek crossbowmen formed an infantry élite and sometimes organised themselves into 'brotherhoods' similar to rival Muslim military-religious associations. Greek Orthodox monasteries also hired their own paramilitary guards - an idea later mirrored in other Orthodox Christian countries such as Russia. The Despotate of Epirus had its own little known military forces organised and administered along traditional lines under one or more *protostrator* (commander of troops). At the same time there was increasing Italian influence on the military organisation of Epirus. The army of the Comnenid Byzantine Empire of Trebizond on the Black Sea coast of Anatolia could field large cavalry forces, again subdivided into European-style '*lances*' in the 13th and 14th centuries, though the Emperor of Trebizond also had a guard of horse-archers.

Christendom: Armenia, Georgia and Christian Africa

It is not clear when Armenians began organising their own defences against the Saljūq invaders, but it was probably before the final collapse of Byzantine authority in eastern Anatolia. At the same time there was a massive migration by the Armenian military élite from eastern Anatolia into the mountains bordering Cilicia, the heartland of an emerging Cilician Armenian state. By the late 12th century the military organisation of this new kingdom is said to have incorporated sev-

Above: *Wall-painting of St. Theodore Tiro, Byzantine 1308–21. The youthful warrior saint is shown as a late Byzantine light infantryman with a triangular shield, small mail shirt beneath a sleeveless tunic, and armed with a sword of normal 14th-century western European type. (Author's photograph; in situ, Kariye Cami ex-Church of Theodore Metochites, Istanbul)*

eral western European features but this is probably an exaggeration, King Leon's attempts to 'westernise' his country proving superficial and short-lived. The army still consisted of *azat* (élite cavalry), now often called *jiavors,* a term of Turkish origin, plus an infantry peasant levy. It was headed by a *connétable,* to give him his westernised title, or *spasalar* in traditional Armenian terms, a *bayl* or *bailli,* and a *marachakhd* or *marshal.* Provincial forces were mustered behind the *avak baron* or chief baron while the few towns had their own urban militias. The great majority of troops were feudally organised; the élite being spear-armed cavalry supported by a few horse-archers. Even fewer details survive concerning the 12th to 14th century Georgian army or *djayi,* except that it was organised around the local clan or *t'hemi* (possibly from the Byzantine term *theme*) supported by an *eri* which was probably an urban contingent.

Although the Christian kingdoms of Nubia were now in political decline, they were to remain relatively secure behind the *baṭn al-ḥajar* (belly of stones), a singularly desolate stretch of the Nile valley between Akasha and the Second Cataract. The Nubians, however, had lost any control they once had over the regions between the Nile and the Red Sea. By the 14th century Ethiopia remained a Christian kingdom but now had a substantial Muslim minority and maintained reasonably good relations with the powerful Mamlūks of Egypt. Its army had no *dīwān* (government department), as in Islamic states, but was based upon a recognised *jund* territorial force whose size was checked against a system of presumably numbered 'special stones' when mustered.

Christendom: The Crusader States

Most early Crusading expeditions were organised around the most senior lords or barons taking part. On a few occasions ordinary knights or 'the poor' grouped themselves under one of their own number; for example the ferocious *Tafurs* of the First Crusade who were led by a 'poor Norman knight'. Others, especially infantry, fought and presumably also marched in 'national' groups reflecting their place of origin. The more highly organised Crusades of the 13th century suggest that each *banneret* or minor member of the aristocracy was expected to have two horses and five companions, an ordinary knight having only one horse and two followers. Meanwhile ordinary pilgrims and Crusaders still tended to travel eastward in groups known as *socii* under the leadership of a knight or lord, though others travelled alone.

The military organisation of the Crusader States was essentially that of western European armies, with local variations. As elsewhere, the king could create additional knights when needed, the knightly élite distinguishing itself from the bulk of the population by wearing brightly coloured clothes or cloth-of-gold and distinctive pieces of military equipment such as decorated spurs, sword-belts and swords. But within the Kingdom of Jerusalem the feudal élite declined in wealth during the late 12th and 13th centuries, the shrinking amount of land for *fiefs* leading to the creation of even more *fiefs de soudée* or *fiefs en besants,* money *fiefs* similar to the *iqṭā*ᶜ estates of Muslim territory. Meanwhile there was a steadily increasing

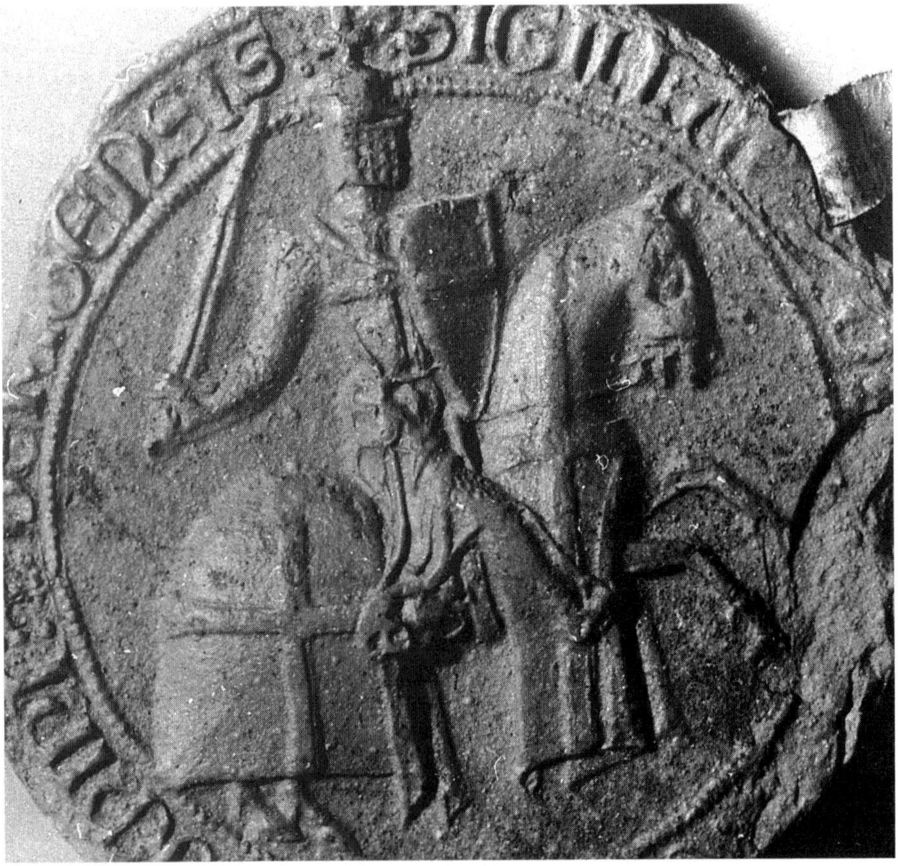

Seal of Jean II, Lord of Beirut in the Crusader States, 1261. As a very senior member of the nobility of the Kingdom of Jerusalem, Jean d'Ibelin is portrayed as a fully armoured knight, displaying his coat of arms - a red cross on a gold ground - on his shield, surcoat, saddle and horse's caparison. (Archivio di Stato, Venice)

proportion of non-noble *sergeants*, most of whom were raised and paid by the Church. Most served as infantry and may also have been responsible for local law and order. Religiously based confraternities also flourished in the 13th-century Crusader States; often serving as the basis for urban militias associated with a particular 'national' group, such as the Confraternity of St. George and Belian for indigenous Melchite Syrian Christians.

The King of Jerusalem commanded the army, though usually in consultation with leading barons and the commanders of the Military Orders. In fact the military organisation of the Crusader States remained temporary and often amateur compared to that of the opposing Muslim armies. In practice the *Connétable* led the army, sorted out the *batailles* (military formations), assigned specific duties and took overall command when the king was not present. His second in command, the *Maréchal*, recruited troops, controlled and checked their kit and organised supplies. The *restor* system of replacing knights' horses lost on campaign also enabled the *Maréchal* to ensure the army was properly mounted. Immediately under the *Maréchal* the *Grand Turcopolier* commanded *turcopole* light cavalry. The king's *Senechal* was in charge of castles and their *baillies* or commanders, except those who formed part of the Royal Household. This structure, however, was permanently damaged following the disastrous battle of Ḥaṭṭīn in 1187. The military organisation of the County of Tripoli and Principality of Antioch were almost identical with that of Jerusalem, though on a smaller scale. The only real differences seem to have been that the *Connétable* of Antioch was helped by two *maréchaux* while the Prince's own castles were held by *châtelains*. The feudal structure of the short-lived County of Edessa appears to have been more rigid and even more specifically military than those of western Europe.

The Military Orders each formed a regiment of disciplined cavalry plus *sergeants* and, in the case of the Templars and Hospitallers, *turcopoles*. Nevertheless only a small proportion of the overall Templar, Hospitaller and Teutonic Orders were actually stationed in the Crusader States, these being supported by much larger structures in western Europe. Within the Kingdom of Jerusalem the local Templar *Commander* was supported by a *drapier, sous maréchal* and *gonfanonnier*. Hospitaller organisation was similar, though by the early 14th century the Hospitaller *Commanderie* of Cyprus had eight senior officers; a *Grand Commander, Marshal, Hospitaller, Drapier, Treasurer, Admiral, Turcopolier* and *Conventual Prior*. The *Master Crossbowman* and *Master Sergeant* of the Hospitallers were not actually members of the Order, and may simply have been mercenaries. Each brother knight was supposed to have three horses and a squire - later rising to four horses, though a *turcopole* light cavalryman had from five to eight horses. While on a *caravan* or raid, a Templar force was organised by the *Marshal* then put under command of the

Gonfanonnier who also organised squires when they were foraging away from camp. Otherwise the squires and grooms appear to have been under the authority of the *Master Esquire* of each *Convent* or barracks.

Whereas the political organisation of the Crusader Kingdom of Cyprus was a mix of western and Byzantine systems, its military structure was almost entirely European. The king took the lead in war, retained control of the main towns, roads and castles. As in Jerusalem, there were more *sergeants* than knights, and urban militias only defended their own walls. Late in the 14th century the island was also restructured into twelve *chevetaine* (military districts), each under a *captain*, largely as a result of the threat of war with the Mamlūks of Egypt. The military circumstances of Crusader Greece differed from those of Crusader Syria because the previous military élite had been conquered and then gradually assimilated rather than wiped out or expelled. Generally speaking a western feudal structure was imposed on the mainland whereas a greater degree of Byzantine military administration survived in the Italian-ruled Greek islands. When Crusader Greece fell under the rule of the Angevin kings of southern Italy a *vicar* and a *bailli* were sent from Naples as civil and military governors. The Catalan Grand Company which conquered Crusader Athens organised itself and its territories rather like an autonomous military corporation, under a civil *vicar general* and a military *marshal*. When Catalan Athens subsequently accepted the suzerainty of the Aragonese Spanish rulers of Italy these two governors were imposed from outside, though the *marshal* was always selected from the ranks of the Catalan Grand Company.

Christendom: The Iberian Peninsula

Two basic facts distinguished the military of 12th and 13th century Christian Iberia from the rest of western Europe: the relatively loose command structure of most Spanish armies, and the large amount of conquered rural land handed over to Spanish Military Orders as the Christian frontier pushed southwards. The old Pyrenean heartland of Aragon had never been fully feudalised; its ancient *Cortes* parliament consisting of three sections or *Brazos*. The first represented leading noble families who owed little military service; the second represented the middle-ranking nobility and towns, the third represented clergy. The feudal concept of military service based on *vassalage* to a superior only appeared in the 13th century and by then Aragon was dominated by its cities. Many if not most soldiers were paid professionals, the largest number being urban militias. Castles were held by *bailiffs* and *castellans* of the king or his leading barons who had their own professional followers. During the near anarchy of the second half of the 13th century the towns formed their own *hermandades* (police forces) comparable to Islamic *shurṭas* to maintain local law and order. Urban forces increased in importance during the 14th century, often being based upon craft or merchant guilds. In Barcelona, and perhaps elsewhere, they were led by their own captain under the overall command of the *Coronel* of the Catalan and Aragonese army. The newly conquered south was organised along similar lines, though the rugged mountain territory inland from Valencia was divided into military zones based upon small towns and inhabited by a warlike Christian and Muslim peasantry, much of which was led by the old Muslim military élite as late as 1276.

Urban forces also played a vital role in León and Castile. The old term *apellido* still meant defensive operations while the *fonsadera* or duty of taking part in offensive operations had generally been commuted for money payment. The French term *hueste* (a major expedition) appeared in the 13th century. By the 14th century a *hueste* necessitated urban militias assembling according to their *collacita* (quarter) under a *juez* (town leader) appointed by the crown. Each *collaciea* elected its own *alcalde*, but this was an administrative rather than battlefield command function. Castile and León's sudden expansion southwards in the 13th century had led to problems. Much of the Muslim rural population remained and the Muslim kingdom of Granada was only a short distance away. As a result southern towns were given virtual autonomy when it came to defence, some coming together in *hermandad* mutual aid agreements not only against Granada and Morocco but during internal Castilian civil wars. Otherwise Castilian forces still included knights and non-noble *caballeros villanos* who paraded twice a year to have their kit checked; crossbowmen were clearly the most important infantry forces. An *almocadén* (commander of infantry) was clearly distinguished from an *adalid* (commander of cavalry). These militias also selected *talayeros* (scouts) who had the best horses and additional pay, as well as other groups with special duties such as *guardadores* who looked after prisoners and *pastores* who looked after the animals. The organisation of the Castilian frontier under the Military Orders and local forces mirrored the *thughūr* or *thagri* on the Muslim side of the border, and the most effective Castilian frontier forces were *almugaver* (mountain troops) comparable to those of Aragon. In the 13th and 14th centuries these had a well-defined ranking system, most of these titles reflecting their Arab-Islamic origin.

Until the 14th century Portugal remained traditional and militarily backward, the only consistent command position being that of *alférez môr* (army commander) who was in charge of both administration and operations. Great changes came in the wake of English and French involvement in Spanish affairs during the late 14th century. The King of Portugal first insisted that some of his leading vassals equip themselves in English and French style, and then in 1382 the entire military system was overhauled, the old *alférez môr* being replaced by a *Condestabre* and a *Marichal*. The Iberian Military Orders were created primarily because the Templars and the Hospitallers were using Spain and Portugal as a source of men and money for their Middle Eastern operations rather than giving effective help to the Reconquista. Nevertheless the Iberian Orders were structured along much the same lines as these better-known 'international' Orders.

Islam: The Eastern Lands

Traditional systems of organisation as well as of recruitment characterised Muslim armies until the Mongol invasions. For example the Ghaznawid army was still administered by a government department called the *dīwān al ᶜarḍ*, and ranks remained much the same, including *amīr, sarhang* and *sipahsālār*; the Ghaznawids' *Sarā'iyān* (palace guard) remained an élite force. The Great Saljūq Sultanate of 11th–12th-century Iran and the Middle East was divided into twenty-four military zones by the famous vizier Niẓām al-Mulk, each commanded by an officer whose title reflected the culture of the district in question. Each raised, trained and equipped a specified number of local troops who appeared at an annual military review. But this idealised traditional system proved inadequate and was followed by an extension of the *iqṭaᶜ* system of money-raising fiefs which dominated Saljūq military administration by the beginning of the 12th century. Although largely destroyed by the Mongols, this was recreated in part by the Muslim Mongol Īl-Khāns and their successors. By then, however, the military structure of the eastern Muslim world had been deeply influenced by Mongol traditions. The Sultanate of Delhi was less influenced by the Mongols. Here Persian, Turkish and Hindu Indian traditions predominated, and to some extent the old *Rajpūt* Hindu military élite had simply been replaced by Muslim volunteers and mercenaries. The main elements of the 13th–14th-century Delhi *lashkar* (army) were the largely slave-origin *jāndār* who formed the ruler's guard and were either paid a salary or held *iqṭāᶜ* (fiefs); the *wajihdar* (regulars) under the permanent control of the ruler; the *ghayr wajihdar* ('not *wajihdar*') irregulars paid directly by the treasury; the religiously motivated volunteers and the *hashm-i iqṭāᶜ* (*fief*-holding provincial forces). Provincial garrisons commanded by *kōtwāls* also played an important role in newly conquered territory. Nevertheless most of the cavalry and all the war-elephants were concentrated in the capital, together with an élite of mounted infantry. The best infantry of the Delhi Sultanate were in fact archers as was also the case in Hindu armies. The Muslim Bahmanid state of later 14th-century central India had a similar military structure, though perhaps even more influenced by Hindu traditions.

Islam: The Middle East and Egypt

The success of the Ayyūbids, Mamlūks and Ottomans in expelling the Crusaders and defeating further Crusading expeditions reflected superior organisation, logistical support, discipline, tactics and to some extent armament. But this sophistication was not seen in all Middle Eastern armies. Within the Arabian peninsula military forces remained tribally organised or were based upon town militias dominated by infantry. Other armies were too small to have more than a localised impact, including that of the revived ᶜAbbāsid Caliphate. In the late 12th and 13th centuries the Caliph did, however, try to make himself the spiritual leader of existing *futūwa* (religious-cum-militia organisations) in an attempt to win greater influence throughout the Muslim Middle East. Once again the army of 12th-century Damascus is the best documented of the many small *Atābeg* forces. It was divided into five sections. The militia sometimes took part in offensive campaigns against the Crusader States. Like the militia, the *mutaṭawwiᶜa* (religious volunteers) were paid, being more like a part-time force rather than short-term auxiliaries. Regular troops lived within the city whereas tribal forces summoned for a single campaign camped in the *Ghūṭa* (irrigated orchards) outside. There were three senior military ranks: *isfahsalār* (commander in battle) who was often the ruler himself; *ra'īs* (head of the *ahdath* militia) who was immediately superior to the *shiḥna* (head of internal security forces). The ruler's own élite units or bodyguard formed his *ᶜaskar* of regular cavalry organised into *ṭulb* (platoons). Essentially this was the military structure enlarged by the subsequent Ayyūbid dynasty, but there was another small though distinctive Muslim military force operating in the area. It was drawn from the *Ismāᶜīlīs*, the so-called 'Assassins' of mountainous northern Iran and western Syria who exerted an influence far beyond the small territories they dominated. The entire organisation of these 'Assassin' mini-states was based on religious concepts; the *Ismāᶜīlī dāᶜīs* (preachers or religious leaders) becoming political and military leaders. Next in rank came the *rafīq* (comrades), the *fidā'īs* who formed the active arm or fighters, and the *lāṣiq* (beginners).

Ayyūbid power arose in and continued to be centred upon Egypt, but this led to some specific military difficulties. Cavalry were now the dominant arm, but Egypt was always short of pasture and as a direct result the Ayyūbids relied on small numbers of exceptionally well-trained and equipped cavalry. The Ayyūbids also developed the existing Fāṭimid *dīwān al-jaysh* (war ministry) which had primary responsibility for the allocation and administration of *iqṭāᶜ* (*fiefs*). The élite of the Ayyūbid army were the *jandarīyah* who consisted largely of slave-recruited *mamlūks*. These formed part of a larger professional *halqa*, the officers of both groups apparently acting as a military staff on campaign. Another cavalry unit known as the *qarāghulām* remains something of a mystery, but were probably lower-grade *mamlūks*. *Rajjāla* (infantry) remained essential for siege warfare but mostly consisted of mercenaries and volunteer auxiliaries.

Ayyūbid tactical units were not necessarily the same as administrative formations. The term *jānib*, for example, simply meant a unit of infantry or cavalry. The *ṭulb* was a smaller cavalry platoon comparable, perhaps, to the earlier *katība*. The *jarīda* was also a small cavalry unit, perhaps one that had been designated to act independently while the *sarīya* was smaller still and tended to be used for ambushes. The *jamāᶜa* was apparently a temporary group of about three *jarīdas*. The Ayyūbid logistical support organisation was especially sophisticated, consisting of an *atlab al-mīra* (supply train) under its own *amīr* or senior officer, in addition to a recognised *sūq al-ᶜaskar* or mobile military market of civilian though specialised merchants.

The army of the Mamlūk state was a remarkable institution and was the reason for the state's very existence. Yet its structure was merely a development of that of the Ayyūbid army and consisted of three main elements. The most important were the 'royal *mamlūks*' or *mustakhdamū* including the *khāṣṣakīya*, an élite bodyguard within the '*royal mamlūks*' mostly stationed in Cairo's Citadel. Lower in status were the *mamlūkūn* or *mamlūks* of a senior *amīr* officer. Thirdly there were the *halqa* (freeborn cavalry) whose status was in steady

'The Betrayal' and 'Peter's Denial of Christ' in an Ethiopian manuscript, 14th century. This is one of very few illustrated manuscripts to survive from medieval Abyssinian civilisation. Its style is based loosely on that of Coptic Egyptian art, but has its own highly distinctive African character. The military figures have no armour, but are armed with daggers, short straight swords without quillons, and what appear to be clubs or maces. Wooden clubs were certainly used by the warriors of most medieval sub-Saharan armies and were much like the knobkerries of later centuries. (David Buxton photograph; Gospel Book, Monastery of Debra Maryan, Kohain, Eritrea, damaged since this photograph was taken)

decline and who, at least within Egypt, had virtually no military value by the end of the 14th century save as a source of infantry militiamen.

The Mamlūk army's ranking structure was equally elaborate. Until the late 13th century the most senior was the *na^{c}ib al-salṭana* (Viceroy of Egypt), after which the *atābak al-^{c}asākir* ('father-leader of soldiers') became senior. Other senior military ranks had more to do with functions at court than campaigning. Ordinary or junior *mamlūk* troops seem to have been known as *julbān*. It is also worth noting that the *awlād al-nās* (sons of slave-origin *mamlūks*) could rise to junior officer rank, but not high rank except occasionally in Syria. Ordinary officer ranks were based upon the number of soldiers the man maintained as his own retinue, rather than the number he commanded on campaign. For example an *amīr* of one hundred maintained 100 horsemen but theoretically commanded about 1,000.

The Mamlūk élite were extraordinarily reluctant to stay on their *iqṭā^{c}* (estates), preferring whenever possible to live in Cairo or at least Damascus. This attachment to the main cities even extended to ordinary *mamlūk* soldiers who disliked being stationed on the coast, while banishment to a distant garrison was a form of punishment. The *iqṭāᶜ* system of *fiefs* was even more important under the Mamlūks than under the Ayyūbids, some of the largest being in territory recently reconquered from the Crusader States and capable of supporting from forty to one hundred horsemen. Nevertheless provincial forces remained vital for the Mamlūk state; each *qirāṭ* (military district) was theoretically capable of supplying one thousand soldiers. Syria was by far the most important region outside Egypt. Here the *nā'ib al-salṭana* or Viceroy of Damascus was appointed by the Sultan and probably arrived with his own force of *mamlūks*. Another viceroy, the *nā'ib al-qalᶜa*, was in charge of the Citadel in Damascus. The commander of the army in Syria was called the *'atābak 'amīr kabīr* and was again directly responsible to the Sultan in Cairo. Other military officials in Damascus included the Citadel's Treasurer, three *nuqabā' al-jaysh* (adjutants) and a chief of police. Syria was also divided into smaller *mamlaka* districts, each with a local administration mirroring that of the state as a whole, with a *naib al-salṭana* in charge of local military forces. The *wāli* or governor of a small town similarly had a small force of *shurṭa* (police) at his disposal.

The army of the Saljūqs of Rūm differed from that of the Great Saljūqs in being clearly divided into two parts. The 'Old' or traditional army mainly consisted of Turcoman tribesmen and the ruler's *ghulāms* or *mamlūks*, a large proportion of whom were maintained by *iqṭāᶜ* (*fiefs*), plus the *ḥavāshvī* (armed retainers) of *fief*-holders and urban governors. The 'New' army was essentially a mercenary force under the ruler's more immediate control. Following the Mongol conquest the élite *ghulāms* largely disappeared to be replaced by Turcoman tribesmen who tended to be concentrated near the frontier under their own tribal *beys* or chiefs. Local militias of probably mixed origins known as *igdish* were responsible for maintaining security in the towns and subsequently rose to greater prominence during the chaos which followed the final collapse of the Saljūqs of Rūm. The small *beyliks* which then emerged necessarily had small military forces under the command of the local ruler or *bey*. Many of the *ghāzis* (Fighters for the Faith) who typified this period formed *futūwa* (religious brotherhoods linked to urban militias) characterised by a very egalitarian spirit. Some of their elaborate initiation ceremonies were similar to those seen in the Christian Military Orders. By the 1330s several Aegean islands close to the Anatolian coast also became *illik kafırleri* ('infidel frontiersmen'), paying tribute to the neighbouring Turkish *beylik* and warning it of the approach of enemy fleets. The Turkish Aq Quyunlī and Qara Quyunlī states in eastern Anatolia were very different, their armies being organised along Mongol lines and consisting of

Illustration from the Persian national epic; probably Iraq, c.1380 . The only visible protection worn by this lightly armoured horseman is his helmet with its mail aventail, though in reality his coat might have been a mail-lined kazāghand. (Shāhāmah, MS. Haz. 2152, f. 48r, Istanbul)

the ruler's own 'war-band' supported by those of his tribal vassals. These war-bands were also self-sufficient, having their own armourers and being directed by a *dīwān* (supreme council).

At the beginning of the 14th century the Ottoman ruler was only the first-among-equals, his army consisting of Turcoman forces led by their own tribal chiefs whose loyalty was based on traditional Turco-Mongol rather than Islamic concepts. Even at that date, however, Islamic tradition could be seen in the payment of such troops while Byzantine influence was more obvious in its ceremonial aspects. The conquest of the Byzantine city of Bursa first prompted the Ottoman ruler to establish a regular army and state structure. By the late 14th century the Ottoman army consisted of two parts: the freeborn *tīmārli* holders of *tīmār* (estates) who were mostly *sipāhi* (cavalry), and the *maaşli* recruited from slaves or prisoners of war who received salaries direct from the government. In reality the irregular and auxiliaries formed an 'unrecognised' third part of the Ottoman army. By the end of the 14th century military organisation was basically what it would remain for the next three centuries; an élite including *sipāhi* cavalry and *Yeni Çeri* (*janissary*) infantry being supported by larger numbers of *ṭoprāqlī* (provincial light cavalry) under their own *beys*. Ottoman élite troops were already renowned for a degree of discipline no European forces could match; this being based on prolonged training, total obedience and loyalty to officers, promotion only by merit and extreme respect for old or senior soldiers. At the very heart of the later 14th-century Ottoman army were the élite *silahdar* (guardians of ruler's weapons) who formed one of six *gureba* or Palace cavalry regiments. Quite when the two *Yeni Çeri* cavalry *ortas* (regiments) were established is unclear though another élite *Yeni Çeri* unit, the *Solak* infantry bodyguard, certainly existed from an early date. The *Sekbans* or 'dog-handlers' were another early palace regiment whose reputation for discipline would eventually cause them to be incorporated into the *Yeni Çeri* to improve the discipline of the latter. The *Yeni Çeri* themselves consisted of a single *ocak* ('hearth') commanded by the *Yeniçeri Ağasi* and subdivided into *orta* companies of between one and two hundred soldiers. The officer in charge of each *orta* was called a *Çorbaci başi* ('soup chief'), each *orta* having a *kazan* (cauldron) as its primary main symbol of group solidarity, while several junior *Yeni Çeri* ranks also had culinary names.

Ottoman provincial forces were divided into European and Asian armies, those in the Balkans consisting of three *Uc* (frontier marches) which had, in fact, existed even before the Ottomans crossed the Dardanelles into Europe. By the late 14th century the Ottoman Empire was divided into *sanjaq* (provinces), each of which was supposed to furnish a specified number of cavalrymen. Nevertheless such *tīmārli* (*fief*-holders) were still under direct government authority, being grouped into *alay* (regiments) under *alay bey* (officers) who were in turn led by the *Sanjaq bey* (provincial governor). Several *Sanjaq beys* were commanded by the *Beylerbeyi* of the wider *Eyalet* (military province).

Islam: North Africa and al-Andalus

Compared to the Ottoman army, the organisation of military forces in North Africa and al-Andalus was simple. The Hafṣid army of Tunisia, for example, was commanded by the ruler who could delegate authority to a *wazīr al-jund* or 'Minister of War'. Other officers included a *ṣāḥib al-ṭacām* in charge of equipment and supplies, several *qā'ids* in command of sections of the army such as cavalry, with *a*^c^*rīfs* and possibly *muḥarriks* (junior officers) in charge of smaller operational units. The most primitive forces in this part of the world were, of course, the technologically 'stone-age' Guanches of the Canary Islands. Here there appear to have been several rulers in each island; society being stratified into classes or groups whose names indicated their Berber-Libyan ethnic origins.

The military organisation of indigenous forces in Muslim al-Andalus had several features in common with their Christian neighbours though Andalusian society was not so differentiated along class lines as that of the Christian states. Instead it consisted of extended family networks which ran across economic categories. As a result poorer soldiers could garrison a castle held by a richer or more powerful figure who shared their clan or tribal origins. Similarly a Muslim ruler remained first-among-equals rather than seeing himself as set apart from the rest of society within a stratified system based upon Roman Law. In Granada the army was commanded by a *wālī* who was usually a member of the ruling family; the *jund* or provincial forces being administered by a *dīwān al-jay<u>sh</u>* and commanded by a *ra'īs*, this system being reorganised in the mid-14th century with fairer recruitment and pay resulting in separate Andalusian and North African Berber units under their own leaders. North African volunteers were led by the *<u>sh</u>ay<u>kh</u> al-<u>gh</u>uzāt* who was usually related to the ruler of Morocco, while local provincial units had commanders called *<u>sh</u>iyākha <u>kh</u>aṣṣā* (*<u>sh</u>ay<u>kh</u>s* of the *<u>kh</u>aṣṣā*). Theoretically an *amīr* led 5,000 men, a *qā'id* 1,000, a *naqīb* 200, an ^c^*arif* 40 and a *nāẓir* 8 men; infantry and cavalry both being divided into small squadrons. The *<u>th</u>ag<u>h</u>rī* (frontier provinces) were at first garrisoned by *murābiṭ* (religious volunteers) (not to be confused with the Murābiṭin ruling dynasty of the 12th century) but this system proved inadequate and was soon backed up by eleven major provincial military bases with their own *jund* forces.

Islam: Sub-Saharan Africa

The close and long-established links between the Horn of Africa, Arabia and Egypt led to the development of sophisticated Muslim urban centres along the Somali coast by the 12th and 13th centuries. Nevertheless these remained separate from the interior until a broader sense of Muslim Somali identity began to appear at the end of the 14th century, possibly as a result of the threat of Christian Ethiopian expansion eastwards. By then the largely Muslim state of 'Awfāt had emerged in what is now central Ethiopia. It had a large army with roughly equal proportions of cavalry and infantry led by *amīr* officers, though its military equipment was relatively primitive. In pre-Islamic West Africa kingship was a semi-divine status while ethnic, tribal and clan divisions tended to be very rigid, each with its own established hierarchy. The pre-Islamic armies of states such as Mali probably reflected this hierarchical system until the coming of Islam led to profound social changes and ruling élites which looked to North Africa and Egypt for political and military models. More is known about Mali than most others; this state including large areas under vassal rulers as well as royal governors. Each probably had local military forces which, by the mid-14th century, included cavalry led by *amīr* officers. Some of the old semi-divine status still clung to the king of Mali, despite the egalitarian spirit of Islam, and he was said to progress beneath an elaborate *jitr* (parasol) topped by a golden 'falcon'. The next Muslim Empire to emerge in sub-Saharan Africa was that of Songhay slightly farther east; its army being dispersed in strategic garrisons each under a royal prince known as a *Kurmina Fari* or a member of the provincial aristocracy called a *Dendi Fari*. In general terms these new sub-Saharan Islamic states were also approaching the level of organisation and civilisation seen in the Christian Empire of Ethiopia to the east.

STRATEGY AND TACTICS

Broad Strategy

Byzantine defensive strategy failed against the Saljūq Turks in the 11th century because these new invaders occupied the hills as well as the plains. There is also evidence that defensive guerrilla 'shadowing warfare' was not attempted until too late. After western Anatolia was regained in the early 12th century it was secured by a zone of depopulated no man's land and fortresses. The northern coastal strip was naturally protected by forested mountains where raiders could be ambushed. The first line of defence was everywhere provided with garrisons and militias supported by mobile central forces. This system worked well until the second half of the 13th century when the Crusader occupation of Constantinople seriously weakened the ability of central armies to support the frontier forces. Even after the Byzantines regained their imperial capital they were more concerned about further western European invasions, thus weakening the eastern frontier which relied on static defences to plug the valleys against Turcoman raiders. To the west the Byzantine army relied on guerrilla tactics, cutting enemy communications then isolating their forces. Its failure against the Serbians and Ottomans in the 14th century reflected the greater economic and manpower resources of those enemies.

Cilician Armenia used similar defensive tactics, the Taurus mountains serving as a refuge while the Cilician Plain was a source of revenue and provided rapid east-west communications. Since the plain was completely enclosed by mountains and sea, and allied Christian fleets dominated the latter, Muslim invaders had to come across the mountains; the coast was also very exposed and had few harbours. The Crusader States eventually adopted similar strategies, though during the 12th century the newcomers remained trapped within their traditional view of their own overwhelming military superiority long after it had ceased to be true. By the 13th century, however, the Crusader States had accepted the need for caution, and the Crusaders' greatest asset remained the dissent endemic among their enemies. Even in the mid-13th century, however, the Crusader States were still capable of making savage counter-raids, sieges and naval skirmishes also being characteristic of warfare between Crusaders and Byzantines.

Crusades launched from Europe never lost a broader strategic vision, the primary intention soon being the conquest of Egypt. Most Crusades were, nevertheless, launched in response to Muslim successes and remained reactive rather than proactive. Even King Richard on the Third Crusade sought to avoid a major battle with Ṣalāh al-Dīn, adopting the same cautious approach he had used in France. Richard's eventual decision to abandon his march on Jerusalem resulted from his inability to secure his lines of communications. Most smaller offensive operations launched by the Crusader States themselves were retaliatory; the most effective being rapid *chevauchée* raids by relatively lightly armoured forces known as *caravans*. More attention seems to have been given to maintaining cohesion on the march than on any other aspect of warfare in the Crusader States, probably because slow-moving western-style forces remained vulnerable to their more rapid and manoeuvrable eastern foes. In general a rectangular formation was adopted in open country, a column with strong flank guards in the hills, possibly with *turcopoles* in advance and further out on the flanks. Squires marched ahead of their knights and the baggage train brought up the rear, and, according to the Rule of the Templars, no one was allowed to leave his allotted place while on the march.

The precise function of Crusader castles remains a matter of debate. They clearly did not 'plug' potential invasion routes, and their role as places of refuge was limited. In the 12th century they were probably intended as bases for offensive operations, but they evolved into defensive positions in the 13th century. Some simple Crusader fortifications east of the Jordan were sited to deny water sources to an enemy, several campaigns being fought to control such springs. The successful defence of the Kingdom of Jerusalem against Ṣalāh al-Dīn in 1183 also focused on retaining control of water sources then remaining on the defensive until the thirsty Muslim army was obliged to retreat.

Comparable ecological factors played their part in strategies developed by the Christian Iberian states in the 12th to 14th centuries. Control of winter and summer pastures was economically and militarily important for both Christian and Muslim frontier communities. In November cattle and sheep would be assembled at an agreed location. In December one *esculquero* (guard) would be put in charge of each herd of cows, three guards for every flock of sheep. These *esculqueros* then elected a leader before moving south into the high plains. They and the animals returned in mid-March, the guards being disbanded and the herds driven to summer pastures of the high sierras with a smaller escort of infantry from the villages. A comparable system was used by the Muslims who came north from their winter grazing in the southern sierras.

Offensive warfare during the Iberian Reconquista consisted of small-scale raids and larger campaigns of conquest, opera-

'Story of the Miraculous Removal of a Crossbow Bolt'; Spanish manuscript illustration, late 13th–early 14th centuries. The cavalry are heavily armoured as normal western European knights, but several foot soldiers including the crossbowman wear scale cuirasses. (Miracles of the Virgin Mary, Biblioteca Nazionale Centrale, Florence)

tions usually taking place in the dry summer and autumn. The Reconquista was largely channelled by the main roads, bridges and passes. As a result major river crossings were invariably defended by castles or fortified towns. The main concern of those taking part in smaller raids was to keep their escape route open. For example a small 12th-century Castilian army on such a campaign was divided into two parts, the *azaga* which built and defended an encampment and an *algara* which did the raiding. A remarkable early 14th-century book on military affairs by Don Juan Manuel emphasises the importance of fortresses as bases for attack and as centres of resistance, but also indicates that the raiding strategy still had a major part to play. The author stresses the role of espionage to sow dissension within enemy ranks and the importance of defensive positions while moving through enemy territory, both of which stem from Islamic rather than western European military concepts. But the guerrilla tactics used by Aragonese light cavalry to defeat a French invasion in the late 13th century were closer to Byzantine '*shadowing warfare*' than normal western European warfare.

Although the Mongols were the most dramatic invaders of the eastern Muslim world, their influence on strategic thinking was short-lived. Even successor states such as the Karts of Harāt remained extremely cautious in war, avoiding excessive ruthlessness, relying on good intelligence sources and being primarily concerned to control trade centres. In Muslim northern India the Sultanate of Delhi adopted traditional Indian attitudes to warfare, with a considerable emphasis on the

The Roman theatre at Busra in southern Syria was converted to a fortress by the Ayyūbid ruler of Damascus in the early 13th century. The ancient theatre formed the inner citadel on the right, and a new wall with massive towers was built around it. (Author's photograph)

psychological impact of display. Warfare in the Muslim Middle East was more constrained by ecological factors such as summer heat, winter rains and the availability of water. In fact armies avoided deserts whenever possible. By the late 12th century the Muslims had realised that the only way to overcome the Crusader States was to reduce their castles and fortified cities one by one, Ṣalāh al-Dīn being the first to do this in a systematic manner. Here the main professional army protected siege operations or challenged the Crusaders to a major battle, while tribal and other auxiliary forces were used for frontier raiding, harassing a less manoeuvrable foe and spreading chaos inside enemy territory. The main difficulty with such campaigns was that seasonal, tribal and other volunteer forces tended to drift home if operations went on too long. Ayyūbid armies had special formations for raiding warfare, most organised on a temporary basis to meet an immediate military need. These included a *yazak* (advance guard) of selected cavalry which was also expected to carry out reconnaissance and the *jālīsh* which was a special vanguard of light cavalry carrying banners at the head of the main force and attacking enemy encampments. It could also protect technicians during siege operations. The *qufl* ('fortress') may have referred to soldiers sent to close main routes, a duty often given to Arab light cavalry. The term *ḥarāfisha* or 'rabble' referred to guerrillas operating inside enemy territory, whereas the *liṣūṣ* were light cavalry attacking enemy supplies or *caravans*.

Basically the same strategy was used by the Mamlūk and early Ottoman armies. In the latter case their raids deep into the Christian Balkans were not spontaneous but formed part of a broad strategic plan, often being followed up by the seizure of territory weakened by such raiding. The breadth of Ottoman strategic vision was seen in the tasks of their three *Uc* (frontier marches); the eastern or right-flank *Uc* aiming at the Thracian Black Sea coast to isolate Byzantine Constantinople, the centre pushing up the Maritsa valley towards Serbia and Bosnia while the western or left-flank *Uc* followed the Aegean coast towards Thessaloniki and Albania. By the late 14th century the Ottoman army had evolved its own pattern of campaigning. Mobilisation orders were sent to *sipāhi* cavalry and other provincial forces in December; the troops mustering in spring at a pre-arranged point. The campaign itself normally ran from August to October. Behind a screen of raiders and reconnaissance troops came a cavalry vanguard, then the main infantry force accompanied by specialist troops and armourers, their flanks guarded by the cavalry. Finally came the rearguard with the baggage train and supplies. Newly conquered enemy territory was often garrisoned by Christian allies or auxiliaries while the main Muslim force pressed ahead to avoid getting bogged down. A variation on this pattern appears to have been used by some later Mamlūk armies, where a baggage train accompanied the vanguard ahead of the main force which largely consisted of cavalry, the commander riding with a particularly powerful rearguard. The Mamlūks also developed a highly successful, if ruthless, form of scorched-earth strategy against Mongol forces invading northern Syria.

Similar strategies were used by Muslim armies in North Africa and al-Andalus, relying on their superior mobility compared to their Iberian Christian foe. Meanwhile the rump state of Granada had to rely on counter-raiding rather than full-scale invasions of its more powerful Christian neighbours. According to their enemies the Muslims of Granada were particularly effective in *cabalgada* (raiding) by light cavalry at night. In defence the weakened Andalusian forces reverted to guerrilla strategy, their most ambitious operations being to seize isolated mountain castles and thus threaten enemy communications.

Troop Types

The Byzantine army never regained its strength in horse-archers after the disaster at Manzikert. An early 14th-century description of Byzantine light cavalry suggests that in the Balkans they were equipped almost identically with those of Italy whereas those of Trebizond appear to have had more in common with Turkish horsemen. The cavalry of Georgia and Armenia were also increasingly influenced by neighbouring Muslim Turkish regions.

The military effectiveness of Christian African states was now in decline, the archers of Nubia no longer being able to deal with armoured cavalry from Egypt. In contrast the spread of cavalry warfare south of the Sahara meant that the Alwah region around present-day Khartoum was already famous for horses by the 10th century. According to the same sources Christian tribes of Kordofan, west of the Nile, used the same weaponry and tactics as Saharan tribes south of Morocco and it was probably this similarity which enabled major changes to spread so rapidly in the 12th to 14th centuries. There was also considerable similarity between these African peoples and those of Ethiopia where large-bladed javelins and large bows of simple construction were the most common 14th-century weapons.

The troops of the Crusader States were essentially the same as those of Mediterranean Europe, with the addition of *turcopole* light cavalry who also included horse-archers. By the second half of the 13th century military commentators were suggesting that the most effective troops against Muslim and Mongol cavalry were mounted crossbowmen, though it seems that such soldiers remained rare in the Crusader States. Instead infantry crossbowmen were vital for all the Crusader States, whether in the Middle East or Greece, and the proportion of infantry to cavalry seems to have been increasing throughout the 12th and 13th centuries. Infantry archers armed with composite bows were raised from indigenous eastern Mediterranean peoples while an early 13th-century forty-day Papal *indulgence* encouraged ordinary English Crusaders to train in the use of longbows.

While European heavy cavalry were proving ineffective in the Middle East, they were becoming temporarily more widespread in Iberia. There was then a reversal of this trend, with the majority of 14th-century Spanish cavalry generally being lighter than those of France, being trained as light cavalry *à la jineta* as opposed to heavy cavalry *à la brida*. As such they were clearly under military influence from Granada and Morocco, the term *jineta* stemming from the Berber Zanāta tribe.

As usual there was considerable variety among the troops of the eastern Muslim countries, ranging from the Ghaznawids' élite heavy cavalry armed with *nāchakh* (axes) to the Turkish horse-archers of 13th-century northern India. The best foot soldiers of northern India were already operating as mounted infantry, and war-elephants were used to a greater or less degree by all the Muslim forces of India and Afghanistan. Those of the Delhi Sultanate were clearly intended more for fighting than for show, and were probably more effective than most European historians believe.

In general the armies of the Middle East were more lightly armoured than those of invading Crusaders, but were better disciplined. *Furūsīyah* (training manuals) from the Ayyūbid and Mamlūk periods indicate that cavalry were still trained to fight as 'attackers' and 'defenders' in the old Romano-Byzantine manner and that infantry also remained true to earlier Islamic traditions. Heavy cavalry remained a minority; a relative lack of armour for arms and legs showing that Mamlūk horsemen still mainly operated as light cavalry even in the 14th century. The little available information about the Arabian peninsula reveals that cavalry remained rare in southern Arabia and military equipment was old-fashioned. During the late 12th and 13th centuries the élite of Muslim Andalusian cavalry were equipped like their Christian Iberian opponents, having two war-horses and being supported by squires. This may have been part of an attempt to meet Christian cavalry on equal terms. In the mid-14th century, however, the horsemen of Granada abandoned the western European fashions which had failed to stop the Christian Reconquista and adopted Berber-style weapons and harness. Although this light cavalry had few horse-archers, its tactics of harassment and rapid flank attacks had much in common with the Muslim Middle East. The only major difference was that Granadine armies made considerable use of crossbows on foot and on horseback. According to 14th-century Spanish sources, the small army of Granada was also exceptionally resilient, capable of riding very long distances, and surviving on minimal rations. North African and Granadine infantry were relatively more important than those of the Middle East. Some were armed with axes, spears or javelins, but the majority appear to have been archers. Infantry crossbowmen of Andalusian origin were also prominent in Morocco though there may have been a continued preference for the traditional Arab form of composite bow. In complete contrast the Guanches of the pagan Canary Islands were still armed with stone knives, small hardened wood javelins and specially sharpened 'throwing stones'; this last weapon recalling the 'hand stones' used by Berber tribal warriors in earlier Muslim centuries.

Considerable changes did take place in sub-Saharan Africa, however, as a result of contact with the north. The most dramatic was a sudden rise in the importance of cavalry. During the 13th century more sophisticated forms of bridle and saddle, as well as horses themselves, were also imported from Morocco so that by the 14th century the cavalry of Mali may even have included a number of horse-archers. Before these changes the armies of 10th-century Ethiopia had virtually no horses, and infantry archers remained by far the most numerous troops throughout the sub-Saharan grasslands and forests. Many warriors in these areas used arrows poisoned with snake venom. Other perhaps more unusual military phenomena were 10th-century Bāja who, unlike the Arab bedouin, fought on camel-back, and the war-elephants which, according to Marco Polo, were used by pagan warriors on the late 13th-century East African coast. Most commentators dismiss this as a misunderstood second- or third-hand report, though African elephants had earlier been used in warfare in Ethiopia and the Sudan .

Battle Tactics

Several sources provide minor details about tactics during this period. For example Byzantine cavalry tried to avoid charging an enemy if the sun were in their eyes. When ambushing their enemies in mountainous or close country, the Byzantines still relied on archery, supplies of arrows being delivered by mules. On another occasion a Byzantine force lit many camp fires to make their numbers appear larger, and against Crusader forces the Byzantines used heavy cavalry to hold high ground while light cavalry harassed the enemy in the valleys. Otherwise Byzantine cavalry tactics remained traditional; cavalry still using the *suntagma* (close formation) in an otherwise unclear *parataxis* formation; the ordinary *taxeis* probably being one of three divisions. A battle-line was formed of *allagia* (regiments or squadrons), divided by ethnic origin or role. One battle in 1345 stated that Byzantine cavalry, probably relatively heavy, were placed on the defensive left, with allied Turkish horse-archers on the offensive right and the best troops, infantry and cavalry in the centre. Cavalry were still clearly the dominant arm, though *pezoi* (infantry) had an important part to play. By the 14th century Byzantine armies were quite small and this would fit the Italian-educated Prince Theodore Palaeologus' assertion that if a force were caught by surprise it should not waste time trying to form divisions but should gather into one large formation. Other interesting observations made by this Byzantine prince were that obstacles such as rivers and passes should be defended from a slight distance and that some of the enemy should be permitted to cross before being attacked. The best cavalry should be in the van with a division of inferior cavalry one crossbow shot behind the first. A third division should be to the left where it would be able to hit a foe in the flank. In reality this probably reflected northern Italian as much as Byzantine theories.

The tactics soon adopted by Crusaders in the Middle East mirrored those of Byzantium. Perhaps the most immediate response was a use of smaller cavalry units which gave a commander more flexibility. On the other hand smaller formations were more vulnerable if the enemy counter-attacked, particularly as Muslim horses tended to be faster and more responsive. Greater discipline, tactical restraint and the use of reserves also came to characterise tactics in the Crusader States. Although the cavalry charge remained virtually the only offensive option available to Crusader armies, more sophisticated tactics were attempted such as hiding a reserve behind hills. But this could fail as a result of the westerners' characteristic over-enthusiasm and indiscipline. The 13th-century Rule of the Templars sheds interesting light on how knightly charges actually worked. *Brother knights* would attack in a single line of *eschielles* (squadrons), with a more densely packed formation of mounted sergeants in support. Great efforts were made to keep the horses close together and

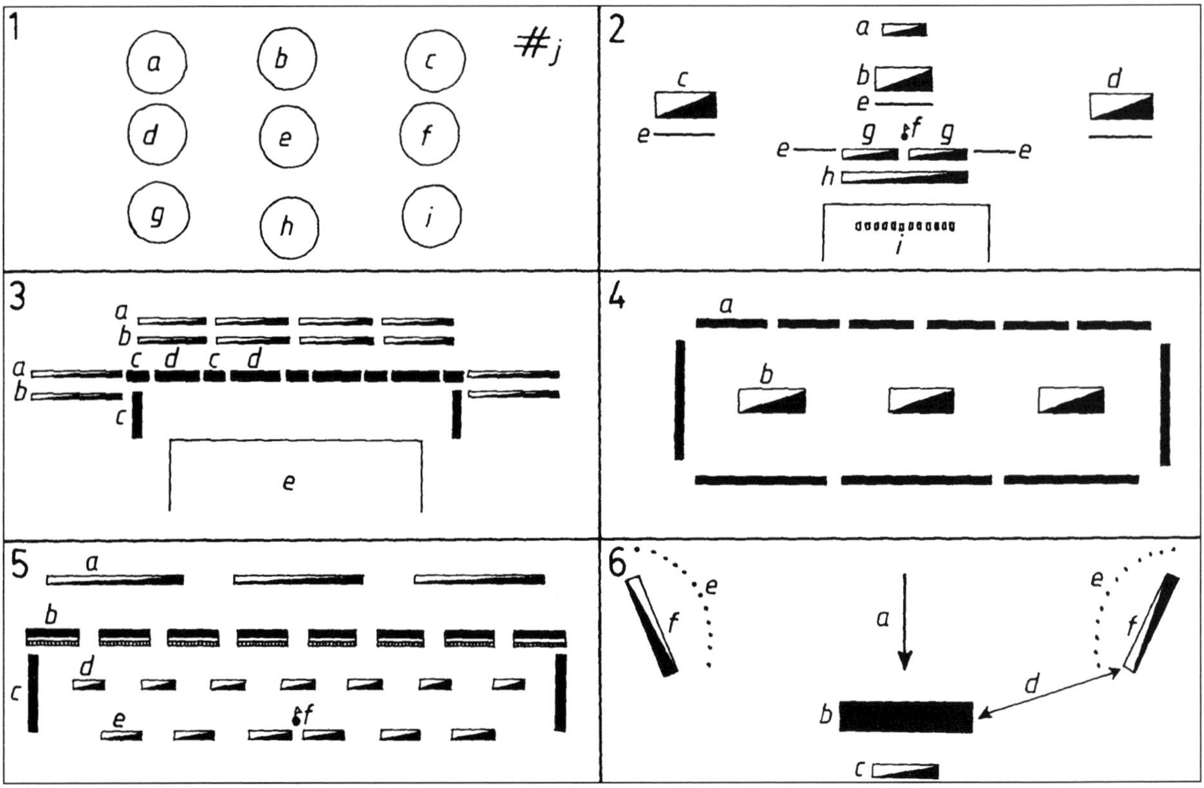

a man would be punished if he moved from his place. Unarmoured men were permitted to withdraw if injured, but armoured men had to maintain position unless specifically permitted to leave. The function of sergeants was to keep the enemy at a distance while knights reformed. Squires came behind the *sergeants* with spare horses; the *turcopoles*, though normally operating as a separate unit, could be distributed in support of the knights like the other *sergeants*.

Despite elaborate rules governing the knightly charge, it remained most effective when used against static foes. Crossbowmen and other infantry kept enemies at bay until an opportunity came to use the charge. As a result the Crusaders' single most important military capability was to endure prolonged harassment. Passive reactive tactics led to close co-operation between horse and foot, and even in the 12th century the most common battle formation saw the cavalry placed behind a defensive array of spear- and bow-armed infantry. But this reflected an existing Mediterranean tradition and had not been learned in the Middle East. A slight variation was seen during the Third Crusade's march down the Palestinian coast, with the cavalry protected by the sea on their right and a column of infantry on their left. King Richard's use of a line of infantry and dismounted knights with spears thrust into the ground as pikes while being supported by crossbowmen was not as new as his chronicler suggested; this having long been used by both Muslims and the Crusader States. Nevertheless late 13th-century European observers were aware of the limitations imposed by traditional tactics, some of them urging the Crusaders to adopt the highly disciplined formations of the Mamlūk army and the larger amounts of horse-armour of the Mongols

Slightly different tactics developed in Christian Iberia as a combination of French influences from the north and Muslim from the south. They were characterised by large numbers of light cavalry, often operating from a fortified encampment defended by crossbowmen. Cavalry also operated independently without infantry in direct support. Even so, heavier horsemen formed the front rank with lighter squires or *sergeants* in the rear. The military sections of the mid-13th-century Siete Partidas by King Alfonso el Sabio of Castile were an updating of the late-Roman author Vegetius, though their similarity with tactical advice by the 10th-century Byzantine Emperor Nicephoros Phocas suggests other influences as well, particularly when Alfonso advocates a wedge-shaped cavalry formation for attacking superior numbers. More than a century later the Spanish knight Don Juan Manuel maintained that Andalusian tactics were more pragmatic and scientific than those of Christian armies, but he still emphasised the defensive role of crossbowmen and *escuderos* (shield-bearers) to protect cavalry in case of a setback. He also listed varied cavalry formations which showed the influence of Islamic *furūsīyah* theory. They included *el haz* ('the closely packed bundle') which was defensive, *el tropel* ('the mad rush') which was offensive, and *el punta* ('the point'). Although Iberian tactics had been successful against French invaders in the 13th century they were less so in the 14th, traditional light cavalry,

Left: The Theory of War; Later Medieval Archetypal Battle-plans

1. Battle array of Turks when the Khaqān (supreme ruler) was present, according to a 13th-century Indo-Muslim military manual written by Fakhr-i Mudabbir Mubārakshāh. This probably reflects the military practice of the Qarakhitai and is virtually identical with the 'well' 9-part formation adopted by Chinese armies when campaigning against Turkish foes.

- *a left wing of cavalry and infantry*
- *b centre with commander, advisers and armoury*
- *c right wing of cavalry and infantry*
- *d left flank of defensive cavalry and infantry*
- *e artificers, harem and flocks*
- *f right flank of offensive cavalry*
- *g horse herds*
- *h hostages with cavalry escort*
- *i infirm with cavalry escort*
- *j Chinese character meaning a 'well', indicating the 9-part Chinese battle array.*

2. Mongol battle array according to Chinese sources.

- *a cavalry advance guard*
- *b cavalry vanguard*
- *c cavalry left flank*
- *d cavalry right flank*
- *e 'fire wagons', probably infantry formations*
- *f commander*
- *g horse-archers of centre*
- *h heavily armoured lance-armed cavalry of centre*
- *i bridging equipment in a fortified encampment. (after Von Pawlikowski-Cholewa)*

3. Archetypical Crusader battle array of the early period, 12 cent.

- *a knightly cavalry*
- *b squires*
- *c crossbowmen and archers*
- *d close-weapon infantry*
- *e baggage. (after Von Pawlikowski-Cholewa)*

4. Archetypical Crusader battle array of late period:

- *a infantry*
- *b cavalry. (after Von Pawlikowski-Cholewa)*

5. Traditional battle array attributed to Muwaḥḥidin of North Africa and the Iberian peninsula.

- *a volunteer cavalry*
- *b regular infantry in three ranks, with spearmen in front, then swordsmen, then archers*
- *c provincial infantry levy*
- *d fief-holding cavalry*
- *e professional cavalry*
- *f Caliph with bodyguard. (after Von Pawlikowski-Cholewa)*

6. Ambush technique as depicted in a 13th–14th-century Mamlūk military manual, based on an earlier Islamic source.

- *a direction of enemy attack*
- *b main Muslim force, probably dismounted*
- *c concealed cavalry ambush also serving as reserve*
- *d maximum distance of 2,000 metres*
- *e scouts*
- *f concealed cavalry ambushes on both flanks. (after Tantum)*

A horseman with lamellar cuirass and mail coif beneath a sharbūsh fur hat pursues a horse-archer on an armoured or at least caparisoned horse; silver inlaid bronze candlestick base, Egypt or Syria, early-mid-13th century. Horse-armour was widely used by Muslim cavalry at this time and the swordsman's horse is also caparisoned, though perhaps only decoratively. (P. Costa private collection)

Andalusian *jinetes* and relatively poorly equipped militias being unable to break the professional French and English armies which intervened in Spanish affairs.

The arrival of the Saljūq Turks in eastern Islam led to a widespread but brief dominance of Central Asian horse-archery dispersal and harassment tactics, but then the area's own tradition of concentrated shower-shooting horse-archery gradually revived. But this demanded a higher degree of professional training, an élite horse-archer supposedly being able to loose a 'handful' of five arrows in 2½ seconds. Other minor details refer to Ghūrid élite troops dismounting to attack the bellies of armoured elephants. The role of war-elephants normally seems to have been to form a living wall behind the cavalry and infantry. An Indo-Persian military theoretician writing in the 13th century described an ideal battle array which was very similar to Hindu Indian traditions. The front rank consisted of infantry with javelins, the second of armoured infantry with swords and spears, the third of infantry archers, the fourth of junior officers with swords and maces. Plenty of spaces would be left between various units so that the cavalry could launch their charges. Elephants normally remained in one position as vantage points for archers and javelin-throwers surrounded by a protective wall of infantry. Other evidence suggests that they could charge at about twenty-five kilometres an hour, one of the few defences against such an assault being buffalo firmly tethered together as a living fortification.

The Muslim Middle East was somewhat less exotic and also saw a return to traditional shower-shooting tactics in the 12th and 13th centuries. The Muslims' debt to their ancient predecessors was recognised in several training manuals; three late 13th-century battle formations being described as 'ancient' from the days of the Greeks while six were 'modern' and in current use. The latter consisted of a crescent, a broken crescent with slightly recurved wings, a reversed crescent, a diamond shape with its obtuse point towards the enemy, a triangle with its longest side to the enemy, and a doubled ring with offset entrances like a fortified encampment. Even though ancient and Hellenistic Greek military theories were included in some 14th-century training manuals, these and other early sources were used selectively and critically rather than being included to demonstrate the author's breadth of knowledge. Despite this flourishing of theoretical military writing most commanders still learned by experience, often in the company of older members of their own family or at the side of senior officers. *Furūsīyah* military literature was varied and dealt with every aspect of warfare, including the launching of raids where the link between reality and theory was particularly clear. A later 14th-century theoretician added his opinion that night raids should be made in cloudy, windy or rainy conditions to conceal their approach. The assault was also better launched just before dawn when the enemy would be sleepy and confused. One of the first things the raiders should do was to hamstring the enemy's horses so that they could neither escape nor counter-attack. A similarly strong connection can be drawn between theory and what actually happened when an army was on the march. One whole section of an early 13th-century Ayyūbid military manual was dedicated to this subject, emphasising the need of careful organisation and above all care when setting out and when re-assembling at the end of a day's march. Ambushes were, in fact, frequently launched when an enemy was ending his march, at a moment of vulnerability known as *nuzūl*. This is probably what happened at the battle of Arsūf, which began when the best archers from each of Ṣalāh al-Dīn's regiments were sent forward to harass the still disrupted Crusaders. According to the *Nihāyat al-Su'l*, one of the oldest surviving Mamlūk *furūsīyah* manuals, ambush tactics formed a major part of a military leader's knowledge. Large-scale set-piece battles feature more prominently in history books and accounts of medieval warfare than they did in reality, and this was as true of the Muslim world as of medieval Europe. Nevertheless certain features remain clear. For example the Turks, use of harassment archery techniques gave them an advantage over Arab forces in 11th-century Syria but failed against the First Crusade a few decades later. Thereafter Muslim commanders adopted a more cautious approach, usually relying on evasion and harassment. Traditional Middle Eastern shower-shooting tactics had sufficiently revived by the late 12th and 13th centuries for Ayyūbid and Mamlūk forces to face the Crusaders with greater confidence. The primary aim of all Muslim commanders seems to have been to separate the enemy's cavalry from his infantry. Once that had been achieved the enemy's horses could be shot down by arrows from long range; in close combat an opponent's horse remained a primary target – this being almost totally at variance with western European military practice. The actual formations used in such set-piece battles remained traditional, with infantry forming a defensive shield-wall supported by archers and some crossbowmen, while the cavalry were divided into offensive *shujᶜān* and defensive *abṭāl*, still based on the Romano-Byzantine *cursores* and *defensores*. It also seems that Ṣalāh al-Dīn's army still used the long-established Islamic *khamīs* formation, though now generally with his best cavalry divided into *ṭulb* (squadrons) at the front rather than in the centre. A manual written in about 1200 adds that a commander should face the enemy's best with his own best, the weakest with the weakest and so on, and should seek to launch his counter-attacks against those forces that had just attacked his own line, presumably on the assumption that they would be tired and disorganised. The evidence of battles shows that Ṣalāh al-Dīn and other Muslim leaders made use of hills and other natural features to hide their reserves and that the ability to resupply troops during the fighting could tip the balance.

A reference to 13th-century Mamlūk cavalry charging the centre of an enemy's line to overthrow his flags and shoot his signal drummers, thus depriving the commander of his means of communication, recalled similar tactics many centuries earlier. Battlefield communications were of paramount importance to such a disciplined army as that of the Mamlūks since their tactical formations were controlled and re-assembled by means of drums and trumpets. The Mamlūks of Egypt and Syria remained essentially within Islamic military tradition, though with the addition of several new ideas learned from the Mongols rather than brought from the steppes by adolescent slaves destined for the Mamlūk army. Ibn Khaldūn's famous description of basic early 14th-century Mamlūk tactics could hardly be less Central Asian. He maintained that Mamlūk forces habitually divided into three formations drawn up one behind another. The men then dismounted, emptied their quivers on the ground then shot from a kneeling or squatting position. Each rank was protected by the one ahead, which suggested that they might have been trained to move forward or backwards in battle in an alternate sequence of ranks. A somewhat 'desk-bound' Mamlūk theoretician writing at the end of the 14th century still added some interesting advice, such as having a reliable deputy in the centre of the army if the commander had to take up position on a high place which was not in the centre of his line, erecting some tall structure so that the commander could observe the battlefield even if the terrain were flat, trying to fight when the sun, wind or dust were in the enemy's eyes, and dismounting his own cavalry if they themselves were suffering from the dust because dust was a bigger problem for cavalry than infantry. At the battle of Kossovo in 1389 the Ottomans were so concerned that the dust was blowing in their direction that they delayed their attack until the following day, by which time it had rained. The role of Ottoman *Yeni Çeri* (*Janissary*) infantry has been exaggerated by most authors, since *sipāhi* cavalry remained the dominant arm; most Ottoman cavalry being placed on the flanks with regular infantry at the centre to provide a refuge in case cavalry attacks failed.

The skills demanded of troops within this overall military tradition seem to have put as much emphasis on avoiding an enemy's charge as on making one themselves. In fact the skill of Muslim cavalry and eventually of Muslim infantry in avoiding the fearsome Crusader cavalry charge rendered this latter tactic almost redundant. One of the main concerns for a Muslim commander was to ensure that the terrain immediately in front of his position was unsuitable for a cavalry charge; resulting in positions being adopted behind steep rocky slopes or patches of soft sand, and the troops themselves were trained to watch for the moment when the enemy 'put their lances in rest', in other words lowered them for a charge.

Battlefield tactics in North Africa and al-Andalus may have been simpler than those seen in the Middle East, but they still evolved in response to current conditions. On other occasions they seem remarkably old-fashioned, as when 12th-14th-century Arab nomad tribes used tented encampments erected at night, and containing herds of animals as well as families, to make a field fortification from which cavalry could launch repeated attacks and withdrawals. Such Arab tribal forces also used infantry and cavalry mixed together, unlike other armies. In fact according to European observers, some North African armies now consisted primarily of infantry, particularly in what is now Tunisia. The role of infantry and camel-riding mounted infantry had been paramount in Murābiṭin forces since the late 11th century, and this resulted in very defensive tactics where a small number of horsemen made controlled charges from behind a shield-wall of spear, javelin and bow-armed foot soldiers, the latter having been trained to open their ranks obliquely to left or right. On the other hand Murābiṭin infantry armed with very large leather shields and javelins were capable of advancing from behind their field fortifications to attack Spanish cavalry and panic their horses. The Murābiṭin's reliance on infantry was developed further by the Muwaḥḥidin who normally deployed their foot soldiers in an open rectangle rather than a solid phalanx, placing their own more abundant cavalry in the centre and again attacking through aisles opened up by the infantry. At the battle of Las Navas de Tolosa in 1212 the Muwaḥḥidin and their Andalusian vassals apparently adopted similar formation ahead of a fortified encampment. But on this occasion the Muslim horsemen, having defeated the Spanish cavalry, were themselves driven off by the Christian infantry. More than half a century later, at the battle of Ecija, a North Africa expeditionary force used precisely the same traditional tactics; on this occasion the Muslim infantry defeated the Castilian cavalry who were then scattered by Marīnid horsemen.

Although theoretical military literature was not so highly developed in the Muslim west as in the Middle East, some sources survive. According to 14th-century Spanish sources the army of Granada was characterised by a great deal of noise at the start of a battle, intended to overawe its enemies. Its light cavalry would then launch repeated attacks in an *esplonada* or 'spur' formation, also making considerable use of feigned retreats to lure an enemy into a ambush.

Combat Styles

The 12th-century Comnenid Emperors of Byzantium tried to train their own heavy cavalry along western 'knightly' lines and although this failed dismally against the Turks it was probably more effective against western invaders. On the other hand several supposedly 'old-fashioned' methods of using the cavalry lance were re-adopted by Crusader knights when fighting the Muslims in the Holy Land. Here the slow rate of shooting of a crossbow compared to a hand-held bow was less a disadvantage than might have been expected since the Muslim and even Turkish tactic of separate and limited rather than continuous cavalry attacks gave Christian infantry time to reload.

The effectiveness of Iberian light cavalry skills is well illustrated by an event in 13th-century Crusader Greece where a captured unarmoured *almogavar* was pitted against a fully equipped Angevin knight. The *almogavar* awaited the knight's charge, then at the last moment hurled his javelin into his opponent's horse, dodged the latter's lance then jumped on the unfortunate knight as he fell from his wounded horse and held a knife to his throat. At this point the duel was stopped. Less anecdotal information from the Muslim side of the frontier pointed out that a horse-archer was always vulnerable to a lancer if the latter attacked from the right and that a heavily armoured European knight, while virtually invulnerable when mounted, was almost helpless when unhorsed. This may, in fact, have contributed to the increasing use of horse-armour on both sides. On the other hand the 12th-century Arab *amīr*, Usāmah Ibn Munqidh, recommended the use of the European-style couched lance, though not to the exclusion of other methods. Isolated pieces of information can build a broader picture. For example a horse's reins were slackened before charging; a man who dismounted to retrieve a dropped spear was in great danger if his horse were restive; a horse-archer should aim at an opponent's saddle-bow so that the arrow hit the horse if it flew low or the rider if it flew high; if a cavalryman attacked with a sword it was better for an archer to wait until the man was close before shooting but that he should start shooting from a greater distance if his opponent were armed with a spear or bow, and it he were attacked by both a lancer and a swordsman he should try to shoot the lancer first. Shooting from beneath a shield was only practical with the Asiatic thumb-draw where the arrow goes to the right of the bow. This technique was still described in 12th–13th-century Muslim training manuals, and was considered suitable for siege warfare as it enabled an archer to get close to the enemy before emerging from the protection of his shield. According to a late 12th-century manual infantry archers could hold their bows horizontally when shooting from behind a wall, and horse-archers should hold three additional arrows in their left hand while shooting. By the mid-14th century the use of crossbows from horseback had been added to these skills, and a clip had been invented to hold the *bolt* or arrow in place if a restive horse made the crossbow unstable – a feature which would not be known in western Europe for at least a century. The death of one élite *mamlūk* soldier whose horse was killed during the siege of Acre, described him as having stood with his back to a rock and using his bow until his arrows were exhausted, then fighting on with his sword until overwhelmed. By the late 14th century Mamlūk training manuals summarised cavalry skills as attacking, maintaining such an attack, feigning retreat, wheeling around in battle, evading an enemy and renewing an attack. Infantry skills were more prosaic, being summarised as marching long distances, anticipating enemy attacks, taking cover, checking and chasing cavalry, scattering and startling horses. Other manuals were more specific, including chapters dealing with the use of specific weapons against opponents armed in a variety of ways, horseman against horseman, infantry against infantry and in mixed combats, each being analysed in detail. The *Khurāsāni* technique of using a cavalry spear was essentially the same as 19th-century cavalry 'tent-pegging'. The *Muwallad* style was suitable for an unarmoured man since it involved lying flat along the horse's neck to reduce his profile, and the '*Syrian attack*' was basically the couched lance by another name. Unit manoeuvres were at least as important as individual skills, each team exercise being known as a *bāb* ('gate'). These involved soldiers going through a sequence of movements individually or as a group, probably to improve unit cohesion and morale in a medieval form of 'square-bashing'.

A comparable variety of skills was expected of professional troops in North Africa and al-Andalus. Here soldiers had a more practical view of fighting than had the supposedly 'chivalrous' western knights. It was, for example, perfectly normal to hit an enemy in the back and to aim for his horse. The problem of fear was also faced in a matter of fact manner. One 14th-century Andalusian training manual advised that swords should not be drawn until the last moment because they could make the user nervous. It was also important for a horseman to beware of getting his weapons tangled in overhead branches, to avoid swinging a weapon too wildly as this could injure his own horse or even his own foot. As in Mamlūk training manuals, a mounted swordsman trained by riding past a series of reeds placed in the ground, chopping off a measured portion at each pass. He aimed his spear against a *darīᶜa* (target), first passing the blade through a suspended ring and then extracting it without snapping the weapon as the rider passed the target. When it came to crossbows the cautious Andalusian commentator warned about using them in cold weather as such weapons were liable to snap. Training with the crossbow also involved ranging shots, 'bracketing' until a bull's-eye was achieved; a sequence normally using a total of six arrows.

Field and Camp Fortifications

Field fortifications feature less prominently in written sources from the 12th to 14th centuries. Nevertheless The Rule of the Templars still included specific instructions of what brother knights and sergeants should do if an encampment were attacked; those nearest to the threat joining the defence, others assembling around the chapel tent to await instructions. Some of the most specific information comes from Muslim northern India, where army camps were fortified with a ditch and palisade, trees sometimes being felled to form a smooth *abatis*, and buffalo could be tethered outside as a defence against elephants. In the Middle East a camp was sometimes described as being a circle of tents with a ditch outside; an advance guard being stationed outside the perimeter, sometimes with a unit detached towards the enemy's expected line of approach. In Ayyūbid sources the troops were advised not to light fires unless it was very cold. In that case the fires should be put in pits around which men could sleep. Attacks on fortified encampments involved skills similar to those of street fighting, including the use of *naft* (fire-weapons) thrown by hand. Sometimes rival encampments were established close enough for the opposing troops to be able to engage one another with fire-weapons, rocks thrown by *mangonels* and oversized javelins shot from frame-mounted siege engines. On one such occasion a unit of *mamlūks* dismounted and sniped at opposing Crusaders from behind a barricade of stones.

The late 14th century saw a revival in the use of elaborate field fortifications, but the fact that ready-made *zaqāzīq* (spiked hurdles) were no longer in use was a matter of regret for at least one Mamlūk author. These seem to have been used in earlier years as an outer defence and were virtually identical with those recorded in China. A perhaps new development for Muslim Middle Eastern armies was the Ottomans' adoption of *waggenburg* field fortifications made from specially prepared carts. This seems to have been copied from the Hungarians in the Balkans and may not have been seen until the early 15th century.

WEAPONRY AND HARNESS

Whereas the arms and armour of the Crusader States, Christian Iberia and Byzantium had much in common, those of the Muslim world varied considerably and were often more similar to those of their opponents than to those of another but distant Muslim country. Meanwhile there was also an increase in the use of iron weaponry across sub-Saharan Africa. The only people who remained outside this free flow of technological developments were the Guanches of the Canary Islands who continued to rely on obsidian stone knives, *tabonas* ('cutting stones') and wooden javelins. Nor did the Guanches have any form of protective armour.

Archery and Slings

Simple bows were unusual enough for a large captured example to be shown to Ṣalāh al-Dīn during the siege of Acre, though simple bows with strings of tree fibre were the standard weapons of 11th-12th-century pre-Islamic Ghana. It also seems that the Nubians' large infantry bows were of simple acacia wood construction, as used in ancient Egypt. The 14th-century Ethiopian simple bow was a very long weapon with a short draw and a string made of cotton.

In contrast to such primitive weapons, the composite bows which dominated archery throughout the Muslim world came in a variety of sophisticated forms. One of the earliest had angled 'ears' or tips which acted as levers to produce an easy draw but which also wasted kinetic energy. This type was largely abandoned in eastern Islamic countries and the Middle East in favour of the smoothly recurved Turkish-style composite, except in some Mediterranean regions where the angled composite continued as an infantry weapon. The recurved Turkish bow was stiffer to draw and required considerable training as well as strength, but stored a greater amount of potential energy and was shorter. Meanwhile the effective range of the 13th-century crossbow was little more than half that of the Turkish composite and was difficult to aim over long distances. On the other hand it shot a shorter, aerodynamically more efficient but potentially heavier bolt than the long, lightweight Turkish arrow.

Crossbows were used by most settled rather than tribal armies in the Middle East. The Byzantines knew of this weapon before the Crusaders arrived, their word for it, *zanggra* or *tzaggra,* probably coming from the Persian-Turkish term *charkh* or *jarkh*, while crossbows incorporating bow-arms of composite construction may have been known in 13th-century Byzantine Trebizond. The impact of the crossbow on later medieval warfare has already been mentioned in Volume I, but it is still worth noting that the 11th-century Egyptian *qaws al-rijl* ('foot-bows') or early types of crossbow were mainly associated with marines. The earliest reference to a belt and hook to span more powerful forms of hand-held crossbow were found in a late 12th-century Egyptian military manual, just as a clip to keep a crossbow bolt in place when shooting from horseback or downwards from an elevated position first appears in a mid-14th-century Egyptian military manual.

The terminology of Islamic crossbows is not always clear. For example the 12th-century *jarkh* was described as less powerful than the frame-mounted *qaws ziyar* which had two separately powered arms and was, in fact, an *espringal*. This *jarkh* was spanned by means of a small *lawlab*, a word which could mean a lever or a pulley, and was more powerful than the basic *qaws al-rijl* 'foot-bow' which was spanned with a waist-belt and hook. By the 14th century, at least in the Mamlūk Sultanate, the name *jarkh* was given to a hand-held crossbow spanned by a belt hook, possibly incorporating the system of cords and pulleys shortly seen in Europe. The early 12th-century *qaws al-lawlab* had, however, been capable of shooting missiles weighing about 1½ kilograms and must have been frame-mounted. Another Arabic name for a crossbow in the 12th-century western Mediterranean was ^{c}*aqqār*. This generally referred to weapons which were spanned by a small *lawlab* or pulley, were between the *qaws al-ziyar* and *qaws al-rijl* in power, and generally incorporated a simple yew rather than a

composite bow. The western Islamic term *lashqah* also referred to a crossbow, though of what type is not known.

A remarkable variety of specialised arrowheads had already been developed in early medieval Central Asia, where the bow ruled supreme. By the 13th century these had reached northern India where Fakhr al-Dīn Mubārakshāh listed those for use against different targets. By the 13th century special armour-piercing arrowheads had similarly reached the Iberian peninsula. Fakhr al-Dīn Mubārakshāh also mentioned a special dart shot from an arrow-guide, and Indian arrows with bone heads designed to break off inside a wound and cause infection. In contrast to slightly different composite bows made in various regions, the traditional Indian simple bow was made of cane, just as bows made of reed were used by the 12th-century tribal peoples of West Africa. Among other equipment used by archers during these centuries was the pellet bow used in hunting, and the Persian *kustubān* (protective glove). The *siper* gradually superseded the tube-like *majra* (arrow-guide): It consisted of a broad plate attached to the left wrist which caused less friction and could shoot a short dart an even greater distance.

Swords and Daggers

The similarity between the straight swords of Christian and Muslim armies was often superficial. For example two 12th-century swords found in a cave in Gibraltar look European, but their all-iron hilts are unlike those found elsewhere in Europe except in Iberia where military technology had much in common with the Muslim world. The Gibraltar swords were early versions of a light straight weapon which was to evolve into the highly distinctive *jinete* swords of the later 14th and 15th centuries. Light *jinete* swords were also associated with a fencing technique of Indian or Persian origin known in Europe as the Italian Grip.

By the late 11th century the use of the *baldric* rather than sword-belt was rare, only being found in Arab tribal areas of the Middle East and among some troops in North Africa and Andalusia. In the latter regions *baldrics* and some sword-belts were made of woven material rather than of leather. The Crusader cavalry élite were, by contrast, among the first Christian warriors to copy the long-established Middle Eastern fashion of carrying two swords.

In Turkish-speaking or strongly Turkish-influenced regions the sabre was called a *qilic*, the less specific term *tīgh* probably meaning a straight sword. But curved sabres only became widespread in the Middle East in the 14th century - and not in Europe until early modern times. Sabres also spread across

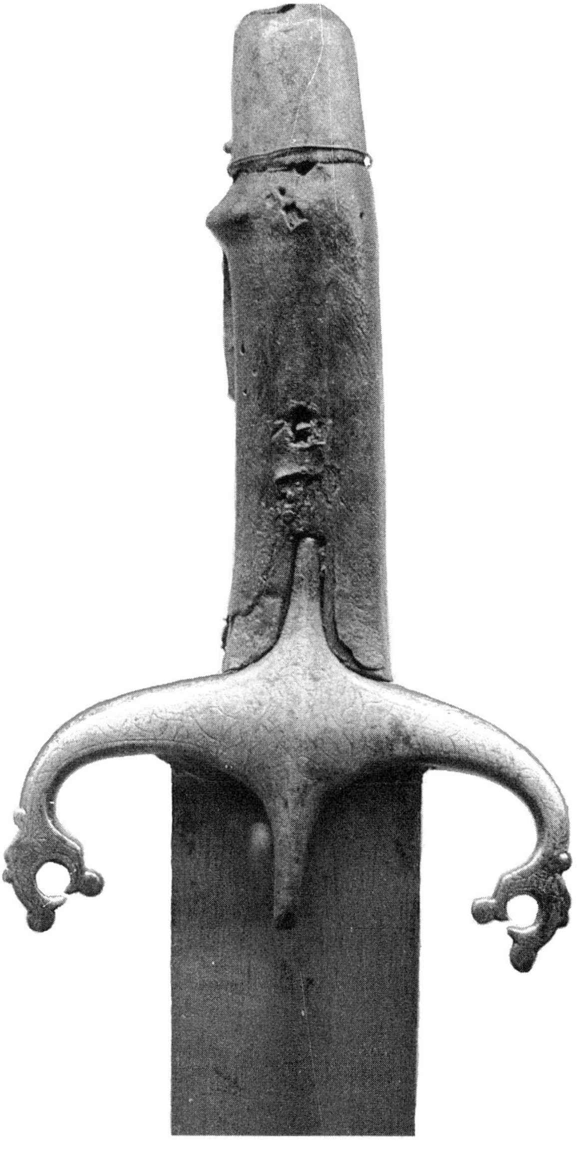

Opposite page, left: *Andalusian or North African sword from a cave in Gibraltar, mid-12th century. The entire hilt of this sword, including its quillons, iron grip and spherical pommel, is decorated with crescents made from tiny tin or silver studs. Although this straight sword looks superficially European, the details of its construction and decoration are within a long-established Islamic tradition. (Author's photograph; Royal Armouries, inv. 67.12.23.1, Tower of London)*

Opposite page, right: *Hilt of a 'Viking-style' sword found in the province of Seville. Scandinavian raiders did attack southern Spain in the early medieval period but there is no reason to suppose that this weapon must be Viking. It is more likely to have been of a type used throughout the Iberian peninsula by both Muslim and Christian troops in the 10th–12th centuries. (Museo Archeologico, Madrid)*

Left: *Hilt of a straight sword attributed to an unnamed early 13th-century ʿAbbāsid Caliph of Baghdad. Many of the swords in the Topkapi Reliquary had been given new hilts during the Mamlūk period, but this example probably dates from the 13th century. (Author's photograph; Reliquary, Topkapi Palace Museum, Istanbul)*

Far left: *Hilt of a Mamlūk or North African sword, perhaps 14th century.. A number of late medieval narrow-hilted swords of this type survive. They are clearly in an earlier Arab tradition but their exact dating and place of origin remain a mystery. (Author's photograph; Askeri Müzesi, Istanbul)*
Near left: *Hilt of a sword attributed to the ^{c}Abbāsid Caliph al-Musta^{c}ṣim, 1242–58. The quillons of this sword may date from the 13th or perhaps 14th centuries, but the pommel with its floral decoration was added in the 15th century when the weapon formed part of the Ottoman Sultan's reliquary. (Author's photograph; Reliquary, Topkapi Palace Museum, Istanbul)*

Left: *Quillons of a gilded sword-hilt; Iran, 13th–14th centuries. This highly decorated hilt is clearly within an earlier tradition dating back at least to the 9th century. It was probably for a straight-bladed weapon, and the 'sleeve' beneath the quillons would have enclosed the top of the scabbard. (Saint Louis Art Museum, acc. no. 45:1924, St. Louis)*

North Africa, most being of *Mamlūk* form, though the late medieval Moroccan version evolved into a lighter weapon reflecting *jinete* cavalry fencing styles. A different but not entirely clear weapon mentioned in mid-to late 12th-century Spain was the *faussar* and might be an early reference to a weapon known in 13th–14th-century western Europe as a *falchion.*

Spears and Javelins

For reasons which are not clear, the 12th century saw considerable variation and experimentation in cavalry spears. In Morocco those used by Muwaḥḥidin horsemen were described as notably shorter than those of their Murābiṭin enemies, while in Syria the militia of Ḥims invented a compound lance eighteen to twenty cubits (9–10 metres) long. The weight of the lance of one of Ṣalāh al-Dīn's élite soldiers caused astonishment to the Crusaders; at the other end of the scale light javelins called *ausconas* or *azconas* remained the characteristic weapons of 12th–13th-century Navarrese infantry. *Dardos* (light javelins) were used in Castile, and a javelin almost entirely of iron was used by Berbers throughout this period, that of the 14th century being called a *madas.* An even more distinctive iron javelin with a rope fastened to it was also used by the people of 12th-century West Africa to hunt hippopotami.

Other Weapons

Several of the tribal peoples of pre-Islamic 12th-century West Africa were noted for ebony war-clubs, particularly the Janāwa tribe of the deserts bordering Ghana. More sophisticated maces were popular among Muslim troops in the Middle East where Turkish maces were listed among equipment used by the Military Orders in the Crusader States. Nevertheless it was in 13th–14th-century Turkish areas that the mace had its highest prestige; the sometimes anthropomorphic-headed *gürz* being kept in a special *ṭirfil* (scabbard or holder). Among other weapons were the large *ṭabr* battle-axes used by Middle Eastern infantry and the more obscure *nīzah-i mard gīr*, a long staff weapon with a curved blade, recorded in Muslim India, which sounds like the curved bladed staff weapon used by Chinese troops. Lassos remained typical of Turcoman tribal warriors, but were also recommended in some Mamlūk training manuals.

Firearms appeared at a very early date in the Muslim world but were not adopted as enthusiastically as they were in western Europe. Byzantium's apparent lack of firearms until the 1390s may, however, have reflected its poverty rather than an unwillingness to use such weapons. Various Anatolian Turkish forces may have used very small numbers of *tüfenk* early hand guns in the mid-14th century, but the Ottomans do not seem to have made any serious use of them until they encountered such weapons in the late 14th-century Balkans (see also Chapter VIII).

Shields

There were fewer changes in the shape of shields in the Muslim world than in Christian western Europe, though there was variety within existing traditions. According to a late 12th-century Egyptian source, shields could be decorated with animal skins, leather or painted patterns. They could be made of spiral cane bound with cotton, or be a kite-shaped *ṭārīqah* as used by Crusader cavalry, or a flat-bottomed *januwiyāh* (infantry mantlet) originally imported from Genoa. This remarkable document also describes an experimental shield with a crossbow fixed inside in an attempt to refine the existing technique of 'shooting under a shield'. The Sahara, North Africa and Muslim Andalusia were noted for the large and expensive all-leather *lamṭ*. This was described as ten hand-spans across and three cubits long, though still light, pliable, white like paper and capable of protecting both a rider and his horse. Although this remained an essentially Berber form of shield, it may have been used to a limited degree in Christian Spain where it was called an *adarga de lante.*

Helmets

In contrast to the lack of development of shields, helmets saw several important changes, most clearly in Byzantium and Christian Iberia where facial protection was given added importance. A helmet worn by the Byzantine Emperor Manuel in 1150 was described as having a visor or some kind of facial covering. Anthropomorphic helmet visors were, in fact, found in association with a coin of Manuel Commenus in the Great Palace of Constantinople; these being comparable to visors found in greater numbers in grave-sites associated with the Qipchaq Turks and Volga Bulgars. Various helmets covering the wearer's face similarly appeared in 12th-century Christian Iberian art, some of them being predecessors of the western European great helm. The earliest written references to such a face protection date from the early 13th century, when it was known as a *viseria* or *visal.*

Another form of European helmet which may have reappeared in Byzantium was the brimmed *war-hat*. Comparable helmets had been seen in 11th-century northern China and may have been brought west by the Mongols or their nomad predecessors. They were also popular in the 13th-century Crusader States. The evolution of the mail *coif* is easier to chart in pictorial sources than in written ones. For example the 12th–13th-century Georgian *muzaradi* was clearly of mail, as its name implied, and may have been linked with the mid-14th-century Turkish mail coif or helmet called a *zirh külah.* Despite the fact that Spanish and Portuguese armour looked the same as that of the rest of Mediterranean Europe, much of it had names which also derived from Arabic; for example the mail *coif* was called an *almofar.* On the Muslim side of the frontier plain ungilded helmets were apparently regarded in 14th-century Granada as a Spanish fashion. Silvered or gilded helmets of the heavier *khudh* rather than *bayḍāh* type had of course been popular in the Middle East for a long time. During the 14th century a form of helmet popularly known as a *turban helmet* because of its bulbous shape appeared, first in Turkish Anatolia and then in some neighbouring Muslim countries. It was probably worn over a form of arming cap. The 12th–13th-century Georgian *chabalakhi* might have been such an arming cap and according to one 14th-century Mamlūk

Left: *Spanish, Portuguese or Andalusian helmet said to be 14th century, but probably up to two centuries earlier. It is very similar to helmets with integral visors shown in Spanish carvings and manuscript illustrations from the 12th–13th centuries. (W. Scollard Collection, Los Angeles)*

Below Left: *So-called Helmet of Orhan Ghāzi, 1326–60. The helmet does in fact have an inscription dedicated to Orhan Ghāzi around the rim, but is more likely to have belonged to a member of his élite guard. It is also the earliest known example of the 'turban helmet' style characteristic of 15th- century Ottoman, Mamlūk and other Middle Eastern Islamic cavalrymen. (Author's photograph; Askeri Müzesi, Istanbul)*

Below: *One-piece Mamlūk helmet, perhaps early 14th century. (Musée de la Porte de Hal, Brussels)*

Right: *The rear of a one-piece iron helmet from Ozana in Bulgaria, said to be Byzantine, 9th–10th centuries. It is unlikely to be that early and at first sight looks like a 14th-century western European bascinet. But the presence of a metal peak at the front and large iron rings to support some kind of aventail suggest that it was an eastern, perhaps Byzantine or even Mongol helmet, perhaps from the 13th–14th centuries. (Historical Museum, inv. no. 199, Kazanlik, Bulgaria)*

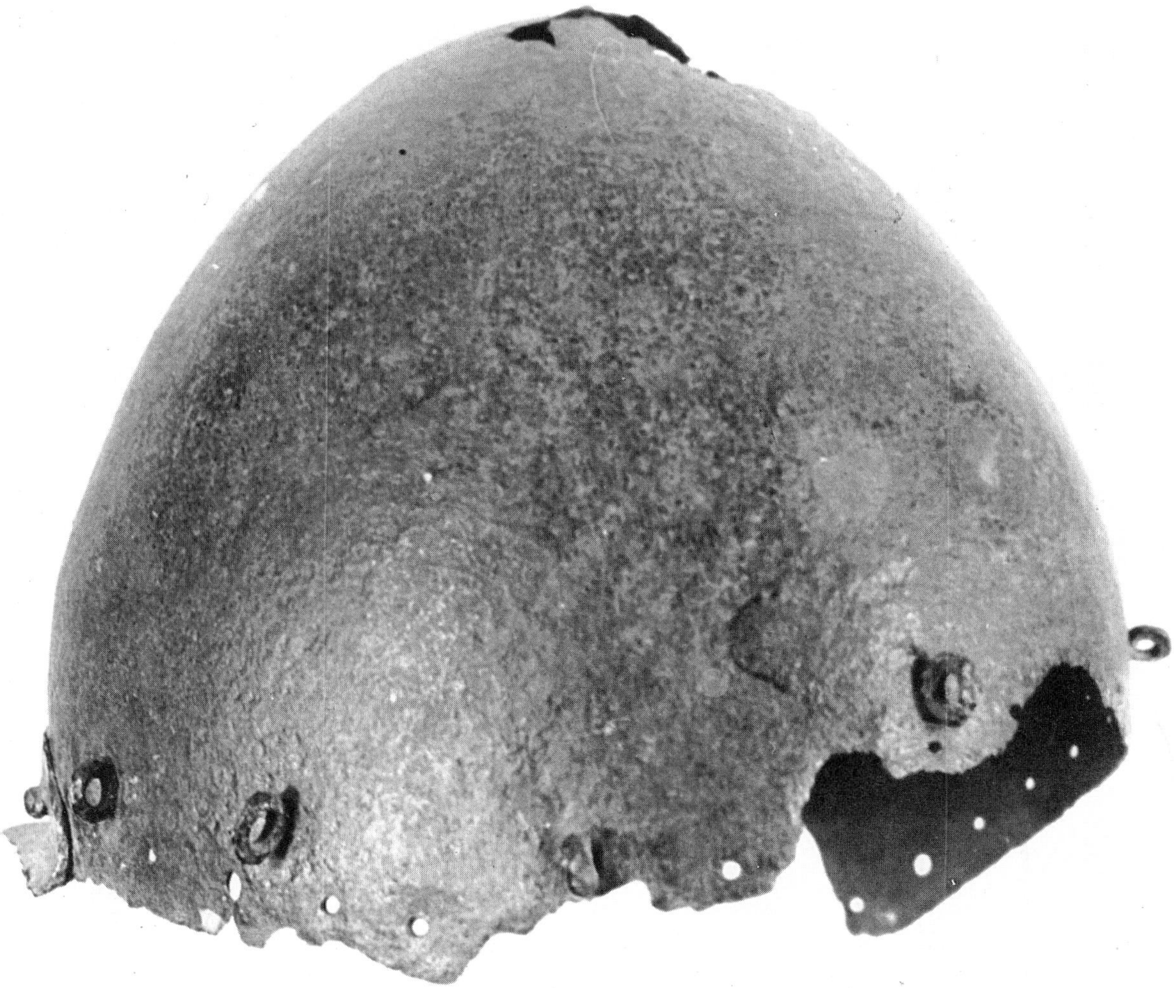

training manual helmets were worn over a skull-cap padded with fibre to which the helmet was then fastened.

One of the most distinctive pieces of Iberian armour was a tall gorget around the neck which first appeared in the late 13th century and later spread to other parts of Europe. It may have evolved out of the earlier *espalière*, a thickly quilted shoulder and neck defence which, like the padded *jupeau d'armer*, was bulky enough to require its own separate storage sack. Like most pieces of medieval European quilted armour, the *espalière* may also have had Middle Eastern or Islamic origins.

Body Armour

Mail continued to be used extensively, as in the simple Byzantine *oplon* or *hauberk*, while the Georgian *djadchvi* may have been a padded and fabric-covered defence based on the Turco-Islamic *jubbah*. Mail hauberks remained the standard form of body protection among Muslim Andalusian cavalry, as it did among their Christian Iberian opponents until the 14th century. The eastern Islamic *kazāghand* padded and cloth-covered mail armour was known in the Crusader States by the second half of the 12th century, where it was called *jaserant* mail. Documentary details from the Crusades can, however, shed light on various forms of western armour, such as the will of an Italian Crusader who died in 1219, bequeathing his '*panceriam* with one long sleeve and a coif' to the Teutonic Knights. Just such an armour with a single mitten for the right hand was illustrated in late 12th-century Italian art. In 12th-century Muslim armies the wearing of two *zardiyah* (mail *hauberks*) was considered proof against sword-blows, and the *kazāghand* could also incorporate two mail *hauberks*. Such *kazāghands* had also been popular in 12th-century Andalusia where they were known as *jaucerants*, but seem to have fallen out of favour by the 14th century. In Granada light cavalry preferred a lighter mail-lined *jubbah*, and relatively light mail *cebe*, *ğebe* and *ğebelü* armours were similarly preferred by most Anatolian Turkish soldiers. Another form of 13th–14th-century Turkish Anatolian armour was the *çuqal* which might have been a scale or lamellar coat secured by buckles, comparable to the 14th-century Mamlūk *qarqal*, itself perhaps based upon the scale-lined Mongol *khatangku dehel*. Like the Mongol armour the *qarqal* incorporated small iron scales and was similar to the western European *coat-of-plates* or even early forms of *brigandine*. An armour of scale-lined construction sewn to a fabric base or covering was also mentioned in a later 14th-century military manual from Granada, where it was called a *misruda*. The *coirasses* or *corazas* worn by Spanish infantry during this period appear to have been heavy forms of scale armour, sometimes with a coloured *xamete* (covering), and the term *foja* (girdle) was used to describe another form of early 13th-century Spanish body protection worn with an ordinary mail *hauberk*. Some of the earliest European illustrations of *coats-of-plates* also come from late 12th- or early 13th-century northern Spain though the adoption of heavier scale and lamellar armours in 13th–14th-century Christendom and Islam basically stemmed from Mongol influence.

Lamellar remained essentially an Asian and Middle Eastern form of armour, though the *jawshan* was known in 14th-century Granada. The written source from Granada stated that a *jawshan* only protected the front of the body, and a 12th-century Syrian source described how the side of the chest could be vulnerable if the buckles of a *jawshan* were not fastened properly. *Jawshans* could be made of iron, horn or hardened leather, some being laced with gut and others, rather later, with silk cords. As in earlier centuries, some *jawshans* were so heavy that only the strongest soldiers could wear them, these perhaps being known in 14th-century Turkey as a *cebe cevşen* (complete cuirass). A comparable lamellar armour in Georgia was called a *djavshan*. Whether the hardened leather armours used in 13th–14th-century Tunisia were of lamellar or scale construction is unclear, those made by the people of Kākudam south of Morocco being of the same leather as their better known *lamț* shields. The main technological advance in armour construction in the later medieval Middle East was the invention of *mail-and-plate* armour in which relatively small pieces of iron plate were linked by larger or smaller areas of mail. It probably first appeared in mid-14th-century western Iran or eastern Anatolia where it was probably known as a *zirh-i çuqal*, then spread across much of southern Asia, North Africa, Russia and parts of eastern Europe. Some late 14th-century Ottoman Turkish sources mention an obscure *bürüme* armour associated with richer fief-holding cavalry which might have been a form of *mail-and-plate*.

Various forms of soft armour had always been widespread in western Asia because of the area's climate. In late 12th–early 13th-century Byzantium the *linothorax* was made of linen, though this might merely have been an unpadded *surcoat*, and in Syria *tijfaf* (felt) was used as a soft armour beneath a mail *hauberk*. The later 12th-century *yalba*, in which a soldier could sleep before a battle, was perhaps a quilted soft armour, and the Crusader's *jupeau d'armer* was worn beneath a mail *hauberk*. The Berber troops of 14th-century Tunisia were known for quilted cloth or soft leather armour, and comparable protections were both illustrated in Iberian art and clearly used by *almogavar* (light troops). Here it was given a variety of names such as *gonella*, *cassot*,

Laced opening down the left side of a scale cuirass; Spanish, said to be 12th–13th centuries. The dating of this remarkable armour may be a century or so too early, but it still represents a form of protection not seen elsewhere in Europe and was almost certainly of Muslim-Andalusian derivation. (Author's photograph; Armeria, Museo Archeológico de Alava, Vitoria, Spain) camisa and *burdas*. Simple, quilted soft armour was even more widespread in sub-Saharan Sudan. Yet more distinctive was fireproof clothing impregnated with talc, silicate of magnesium and powdered mica, worn by specialist *naffaṭūn* (fire-troops).

Limb Defences

The reasons for a sudden revival in the use of separate limb defences are unclear, but might have been associated with the spread of the sabre or the adoption of the so-called Italian Grip fencing style. Among the first illustrations of separate *gauntlets* in medieval European art are those in late 13th-century Byzantine and Crusader States manuscripts; perhaps being the *cheroptia* of late 13th–14th-century Greek literature. *Kap'hi* lamellar arm protections are also mentioned in late 12th-early 13th-century Georgian sources, clearly stemming from the earlier Arab-Islamic *kaff* (arm defences). A rigid *vambrace* for the lower arm now came into fashion as a result of Sino-Mongol influence, this still being called a *sāʿd* in Arab areas, a *bāzūband* in Persian-speaking regions and a *qoluq* in 14th-century Turkey. Arm defences in late 12th- and 13th-century Christian Iberia developed as part of a western European tradition though these Spanish examples are among the earliest, being known as *brassonieras, braoneras, brafoneras* or *brofuneras*.

Solerets for the feet, mentioned in the late 12th–13th-century Rule of the Templars, appear to have been protective and were among the earliest references to a specific form of foot-armour. Otherwise the Georgian *sabarculli* were probably of mail, similar to the mail *chausses* of Europe, though a form of rigid *greaves* did appear in 14th- or 15th-century Georgian art. The obscure *sidera gonatia* of 14th-century Byzantine sources may also have been mail *chausses* or a form of leg harness imported from the west, and the 14th-century Turkish *budluq* was a mail or *mail-and-plate cuisse* covering the front of the thigh and knee. In the Iberian peninsula mail *chausses* were used by both Christians and Muslims.

Horse Harness

Primitive all-leather loop stirrups were still being used in 12th-century Cyprus, while on the mainland the Islamic School of horsemanship reached its peak in 12th- and 13th-century Syria and Egypt. This emphasised a firm seat and the ability to ride long distances in comfort rather than the westerners' pre-occupation with remaining in the saddle despite the most powerful of blows. It was also different to the *jinete* style of North Africa and the Iberian peninsula and the Turco-Mongol horse-archery riding style, both of which were characterised by rising in the seat like a modern jockey. Virtually nothing is known about Byzantine riding styles, except that they were under increasingly strong Turkish influence.

By the 12th or 13th century a distinctive Berber or North African saddle, harness and light cavalry riding style had developed, later known as the *jinete* style. This made early use of a rather fierce form of palate bit perhaps earlier than it appeared elsewhere in Europe. In complete contrast the late 13th century, when many Muslim Andalusian cavalrymen copied the heavy cavalry styles of the north, saw the use of a waist-strap attached to the saddle to hold the rider firmly in place, though this device was not recorded elsewhere until it appeared in 14th-century Italy.

Horse Armour

Horse-armour was now being adopted in western Europe, and some Arab sources were astonished at the size of some mail horse-armour used by 12th-century Crusaders. But this always remained rare, expensive and, according to a 13th- or 14th-century Turkish source, some Byzantine cavalry used horse-armour which only covered the front of the animal. Though this sounds like a reversion to a much earlier style used in the 7th century, it probably reflected Iberian influence via the many Catalan mercenaries in the Aegean area. Within Iberia itself horse armour was generally referred to as a *peytral*, meaning the front part of a complete *bard*, and had again been mentioned since the late 12th century.

One of the oldest surviving examples of a medieval rather than Roman iron *chamfron* for a horse's head was excavated near Khartoum in the Sudan, dating somewhere between the 8th and 14th centuries. Whatever its exact age the object was almost certainly imported from Egypt. Horse-armour, probably of mail, was used by the heavy cavalry of late 13th-century Muslim al-Andalus, lamellar horse-armour being used by élite *ghulām* horsemen in the 11th–12th-century Saljūq army and by Khwārazmian troops fighting the Qara-Khitai in early 13th-century Transoxiana, though the real spread of such defences had to await the Mongol invasions. Gilded iron elephant armours recorded in the late 14th-century Delhi Sultanate of India were probably of lamellar construction as were horse-armours of post-Mongol Iran.

FORTIFICATION

Christendom: The Byzantine Empire

The Comnenid Emperors of Byzantium put great effort into fortification after regaining part of western Anatolia, some fortresses attempting to block the valleys leading from the Turkish-held interior to the coast. Their design reflected the growing importance of crossbows and a few incorporated larger towers on which stone-throwing *mangonels* could be mounted. The policy of trying to block valleys from the interior to the more fertile Byzantine-ruled coasts was continued well into the 14th century in independent Trebizond as well as Constantinople. The Emperor Michael Palaeologus was even credited with planting new forests to impede Turkish raiders. The fortifications of Constantinople itself were also strengthened in the late 14th century when the Byzantine Empire was nearing complete collapse. Little study has been made of the smaller Byzantine *kastra* of this later period, though the characteristic isolated towers are thought to have been built by monasteries and local landowners as refuges against bandits or pirates. One interesting 13th–14th-century Turkish account states that fortified monasteries were defended by large crossbows and movable wooden palisades.

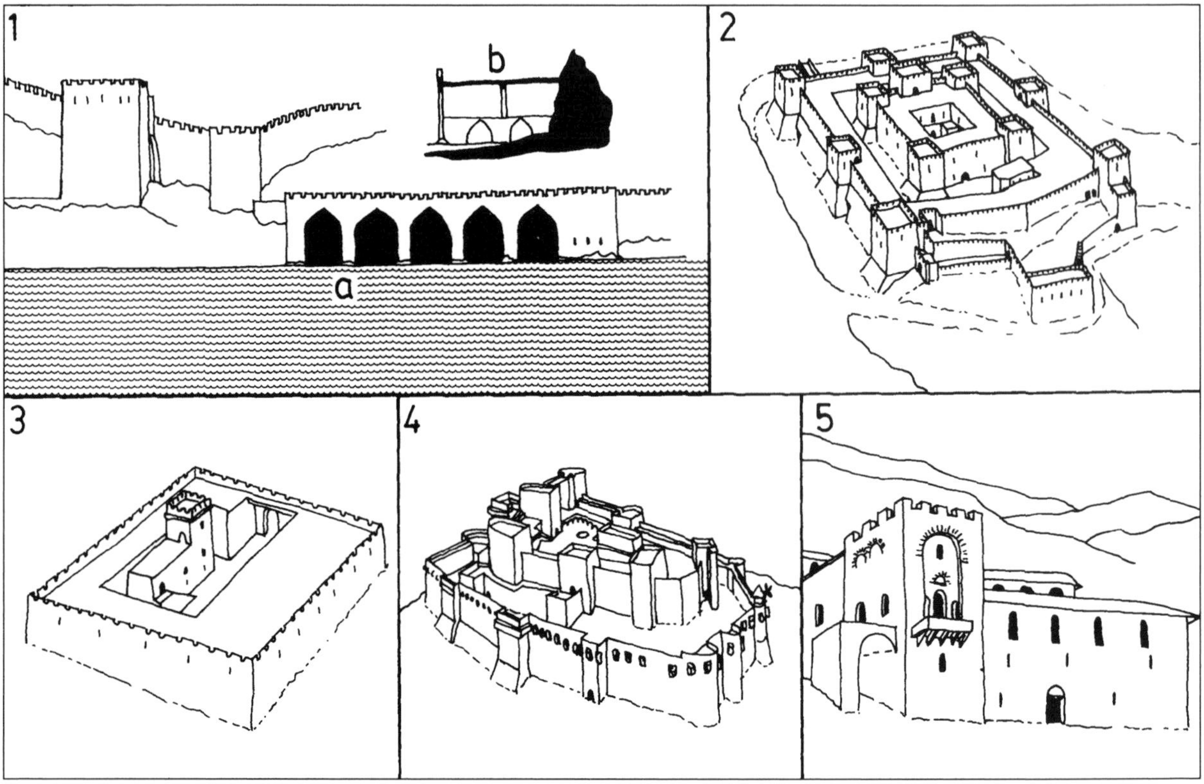

Christendom: Armenia and Christian Africa

There were three distinct types of fortification in Cilician Armenia, small watch-posts, fortified baronial manors and large garrison bases; the watch-posts apparently being able to communicate with the garrison bases via beacons. Larger coastal castles were in a different category, some having been built by the Crusading Military Orders. The situation in later medieval Nubia is less clear, fortifications dating from the 12th century being few and simple whereas the final period of Christian Nubian independence in the 14th century seems to have been characterised by much more substantial castles.

Christendom: The Crusader States

The basic question of why many Crusader castles were built remains a matter of scholarly debate. Some may have been affirmations of royal power, others were sited in vulnerable spots as defensive strong points, refuges, bases for aggression against Muslim neighbours or to overawe the local populace. In the early years Crusader castles made use of existing 'second-hand' masonry for, as a Crusader proverb had it, 'A castle destroyed is also a castle half-built.' Even in later years the impact of local architectural traditions on masonry was obvious. In general terms, however, the characteristic Crusader castle tended to combine the Muslim 'tower' tradition with the Byzantine 'curtain-wall' tradition. Crusader architects also copied the *machicolation* from the Muslims or Byzantines, replacing the wooden hoardings used for the same purpose in western Europe. In addition the Crusaders adopted the Muslims' sloping *talus* or anti-mining revetment at the base of a wall. It has also been suggested that the concentric castle plan originated in the Crusader east, the earliest example being at Belvoir in Palestine, but this was built by the Hospitallers and is likely to have been symbolic. In the 1120s a series of 'anti-castle castles' blockaded fortified ports held by the Fāṭimids while large stretches of frontier remained unfortified. Some of the easternmost castles in what is now southern Jordan were very rudimentary, but they could include churches as architectural statements that the land now belonged to Christendom. Farther north the Crusaders took the Byzantine-Muslim idea of excavating a fosse (ditch) to extraordinary lengths, no less than 170,000 tons of rock being cut away at Sahyūn in Syria. Generally speaking, however, the most massive pieces of military engineering dated from the 13th rather than the 12th century. The garrisons of such castles varied considerably; the night patrol of al-Marqab, for example, consisted of only four Hospitaller *brother-knights* and twenty-eight other soldiers while the total inhabitants of the castle numbered about 1,000. The cost of maintaining and garrisoning such places

Right: *The west postern gate, outer wall and rock-cut moat of Belvoir Castle in Palestine, overlooking the Jordan valley and built in about 1130. It is considered to be the earliest example of a concentric castle in 'western' architecture, though its design may have been largely for symbolic reasons. (Author's photograph)*

Left: Fortification; the Eastern Mediterranean

1. The Tersana or covered naval arsenal at Alanya, Turkey. Built for the Saljūk Sultan of Rūm in 1226, this is the best-preserved covered dockyard in the Mediterranean. Here fighting galleys could be built and repaired.

a seen from the sea

b section showing how the slipway has been cut into the base of the cliff. (after Lloyd and Storm-Rice)

2. Reconstruction of Belvoir Castle overlooking the Jordan valley in Palestine, Crusader mid-12th century. The concentric plan is now thought to have been symbolic rather than defensive, the inner castle serving as a monastic retreat for Hospitaller brother-knights.

3. The fortified church and courthouse at Parva Mahumeria (now al-Qubaiba). This was a Crusader settler village built in 1164 on the road between Jerusalem and Jaffa on the coast.

4. Reconstruction, considerably simplified, of the huge Crusader castle of Krak des Chevaliers (now Ḥisn al-Akrad), as it probably appeared in the early 13th century. One tower in the outer wall even has a windmill. (after Tuulse)

5. The so-called Palataki house in Mistras, Greece. The earliest and largest fortified mansion in this Byzantine town, built in about 1300, its similarity to Italian urban fortifications shows strong Italian influence. (after Orlandos)

The Bāb Wustani gate in Baghdad was built in 1123. It is a typical example of the brick fortifications of medieval lower Iraq and would originally have had a water-filled moat in front of it. (Author's photograph)

went beyond the capability of local rulers and the main castles were soon handed over to the wealthier Military Orders.

Generally speaking, the Crusaders restored existing Arab urban fortifications in the 12th and early 13th centuries. Within these walls the newcomers were grouped according to their place of origin. In some places additional internal walls had to be built because the existing Muslim defences were too extensive. The degree of available space also permitted the doubling of walls which provided an unobstructed means of communication between different sections of wall. During the second half of the 13th century the rival Italian merchant communes also erected their own urban towers, not as defences against Muslim attack but against rival Italian communes. Acre had a small tower and garrison on a rock at the harbour mouth which looked after one end of the floating chain which could seal off the harbour. Another form of Crusader fortification consisted of caves such as abandoned Byzantine *lavra* (monastic retreats) like ᶜAin Ḥabīs overlooking the river Yarmūk in northern Jordan.

There was little fortification in the Crusader Kingdom of Cyprus during the 13th century though the Castle of Forty Columns at Paphos did contain 1,500 carefully carved stone catapult or *mangonel* balls, perhaps stored ready for shipment to Crusader Syria. In contrast to the impressive castles of the Holy Land, those in Crusader Greece were of old-fashioned and sometimes shoddy construction. Another feature of 13th-century Crusader Greece was the large number of isolated towers which, like the similar towers in Byzantine-ruled areas, were probably rural refuges for people and livestock.

Christendom: The Iberian Peninsula

The Iberian peninsula had a greater number of castles than any part of Europe. This area was also a melting-pot of external influences. The remarkable walls and towers of the city of

Avila, for example, are said to have been designed by a Burgundian, though their overall appearance looks Italo-French with a strong Islamic element. A large number of Muslim Andalusian military architects must have been captured during the Reconquista which would account for the notable Andalusian influence in the design of Spanish gates, but during the 14th century a stronger French architectural influence resulted in more regular plans and less interest in the use of topographical features, while a continuing Islamic influence was seen in a preference for high *keeps*, elaborate curtain-walls and an abundant use of brick.

Islam: The Eastern Lands

As in so many aspects of military technology, the 12th to 14th centuries were a period of consolidation rather than innovation. The huge mud-brick walls of Harāt in Afghanistan now surrounded a mile-square area and topped a tall embankment. The walls themselves were almost 5 metres thick at the base, 3 at the top, plus a parapet more than 2 metres high. Harāt also had five gates projecting almost 70 metres from the wall to enclose an area like that typically enclosed by Chinese city gates (see Chapter V). Another characteristic of Afghanistan and Muslim northern India was the use of minarets and water-towers as observation posts. Mud-brick walls were not necessarily inferior to those of stone and had several advantages; being easy to raze if an area was going to be lost, quick, cheap and easy to rebuild, and able to absorb the shock of battering and earthquakes better than most stone structures.

Islam: The Middle East and Egypt

The urban fortifications of most Middle Eastern Islamic cities were less impressive than those of Harāt, though they were serviceable enough. Undefended Moṣul, for example, had a plain wall added in the late 11th century; this being given stronger ramparts and a ditch in the early 12th century, a new gate a few years later, then a doubled wall and many towers. By the end of the 12th century Mosul's walls incorporated an enclosed passageway and at least eleven gates. The Crusaders were not the only ones to erect isolated castle, Ṣubayba on the Golan Heights probably being built to defend Damascus in the early 12th century and incorporating the latest form of bent entrance. In contrast to this sophisticated fortification, the ancient Roman Temple of Artemis in Jerash was converted to a small fort by a garrison from Damascus.

The powerful Ayyūbid dynasty of late 12th- and early 13th-century Egypt and Syria inherited a variety of architectural traditions from the plain mud-brick wall which surrounded Bilbays to the stone fortresses of Syria which inspired Ṣalāh al-Dīn's massive Citadel in Cairo. Ṣalāh al-Dīn soon decided to concentrate the scattered suburbs of Cairo into one area south-west of his Citadel, and then protect the whole city from Crusader attack. This ambitious project included a fortified aqueduct from the Nile to the Citadel and was completed by his successors. The main architectural change during this period reflected the adoption of the counterweight *trebuchet*. Larger and more closely spaced towers now served as raised firing platforms for the new weapon; the best example being in the Citadel of Damascus. At the other end of the scale the 13th century also saw smaller castles and isolated watch-towers being built in southern Syria and Jordan to give warning of Crusader raids. These ideas were taken even further by the Mamlūk dynasty which demolished coastal fortifications that could be used by invading Crusaders; these normally being replaced by small *burj* (towers) as observation points against the increasing threat of piracy. Fortifications along the Nile Delta coast, however, were not destroyed because this area was close to Cairo and could be rapidly reinforced. Meanwhile inland fortifications were often strengthened, particularly in mountainous areas. Damascus and Aleppo were also given immense citadels, not against the Crusader menace but against that of the Mongols.

The wealthy Saljūq Turkish rulers of Anatolia felt little need of fortifications, their most notable defensive architecture being walled *caravanserais* ('hostels') along the main trade routes. The Ottomans also had little interest in fixed fortifications; the very little that can be attributed to them being almost entirely within an old-fashioned Byzantine tradition.

Islam: North Africa and al-Andalus

Many fortifications in Muslim al-Andalus continued to be made with *ṭabīʿa* ('tabby'), an early form of concrete made of earth, branches, straw, bones and lime, invented several centuries earlier. Pressure from the Spanish Reconquista also spurred some innovation such as the external *albarrana* (tower) (Arabic *barrānī* meaning 'exterior') linked to a main curtain-wall by a permanent or temporary bridge. Once a stable frontier had been re-established between the remaining Muslim kingdom of Granada and its Christian neighbours in the later 13th century, this was once again fortified along traditional lines. While walled towns and castles were seen along the densely populated western frontier, the eastern section ran across sparsely populated mountains and steppe inland from Almeria and had few such defences. Urban fortification often used *albarrana*, and the frontier hills were dotted with isolated observation towers called *atalaya*, from the Arabic *ṭalīʿa*. Western European influence was also seen in the use of *donjon* keeps, doubled walls and styles of masonry.

The castle of Hieron, or Anadolu Kavagi as it is now known, dates from the mid-12th century and was built in a typical Comnenid or late Byzantine style with alternating rows of stone and brick. Together with another fortress on the European side of the straits, it defended or at least overlooked the northern entrance to the Bosphorus. (Author's photograph)

The 11th and 12th centuries had seen a spread of Andalusian military architecture to Morocco and other parts of North Africa. The result was a gradual move away from simple rubble walls to ones of '*tabby*' concrete and eventually to the erection of some *albarrana*. The true bent entrance reached al-Andalus in the 12th century but was not recorded in Tunisia until the 13th century. Before Christian pirates began attacking Morocco's Atlantic coast in the 12th and 13th centuries, this area was largely unfortified; many ports being completely undefended. Tit, dating from the mid-12th century, was the oldest major Atlantic coastal fortress, but was built by a local leader rather than the central government. Christian piracy and the need to maintain a naval link with Granada also led the Marīnids to strengthen Sabta (Ceuta) on the southern side of the Straits of Gibraltar in the 14th century. These formidable fortifications eventually included a ditch right across the isthmus, new walls, towers and gates as well as a tower on tidal rocks to defend the southern harbour, linked to the mainland by a bridge.

SIEGE WARFARE

Siege technology was the field in which Byzantine and Islamic superiority over western European Crusaders was most pronounced, though the Byzantines were slipping behind as a result of their reliance on traditions which had served them well. At one end of the scale local defence forces could drive off Balkan nomad raiders in the 12th century by erecting a barricade of farm carts around a local church. At the other, the Byzantines possessed extremely advanced siege machines; the earliest illustrations of a *great crossbow* mounted on a chassis coming from 11th-century Byzantium. In the 12th century Byzantine forces used small stone-throwing *ballistas* mounted on wagons and the late 13th-century French scholar Egidio Colonna attributed the *biffa* or *trebuchet* with an adjustable counterweight to the 'Romans', by which he probably meant Byzantines.

The Crusaders arrived with a less sophisticated tradition. In attack they dug trenches to isolate the besieged from relief, formed a *testudo* of shields to enable men to force a breach and even posed as a band of lost travellers in an attempt to trick the night watchman at Shayzar castle to open his gate. While besieging Damascus in the mid-12th century a large Crusader army found itself counter-besieged in its own camp by defending forces, though a Crusader charge broke the formations of the Muslim garrison which emerged from Acre to challenge them two generations later. While this bitter siege was going on, the younger boys from both armies fought mock fights between the opposing lines.

In defence it appears that Crusader castles had a minimal impact on full-scale invasions, though it took the Muslims a great deal of time to reduce those which could not be taken by surprise. According to the *Rule of the Hospitallers*, the gates of castles near the frontier were closed after *Compline*, the last service of the day, and would not be opened until the following morning. Others sources describe how Crusader cavalry dismounted outside the gate of a 12th-century castle and used their lances as pikes to defend the entrance. On another occasion those making the sortie included men riding mules, though it is unclear if they were mounted infantry or knights who lacked proper mounts. Apart from making sorties, Crusader garrisons often defended themselves so vigorously that anyone coming within range of their walls had to wear armour.

The Crusaders also came east with a tradition of wooden siege engines which were vulnerable to the fire-based weapons of both Byzantines and Muslims. For example the First Crusade used a wooden tower on wheels during its attack on al-Bāra; this having knights on top while other armoured knights pushed it forward. The two wooden siege towers used during the attack on Tyre in the early 12th century were between 20 and 25 metres high, and contained rams with heads weighing about 10 kilograms and suspended by ropes. Both were burned by the enemy, however. The *chats châteaux* used against Dumyat in the mid-13th century combined siege-towers and protection for miners attacking the base of a fortified wall; the *chat* or 'cat' being a roofed structure for the miners with two *châteaux* towers and two 'houses' behind the towers where men could watch for Muslim counter-attacks. The troops inside wooden siege-towers were also said to have had stores of water and vinegar to douse fires. In turn Crusader archers shot fire-arrows at the bundles of straw which defenders would hang in front of their walls as buffers against stones or rams. The Crusaders never used stone-throwing *mangonels* in the same numbers

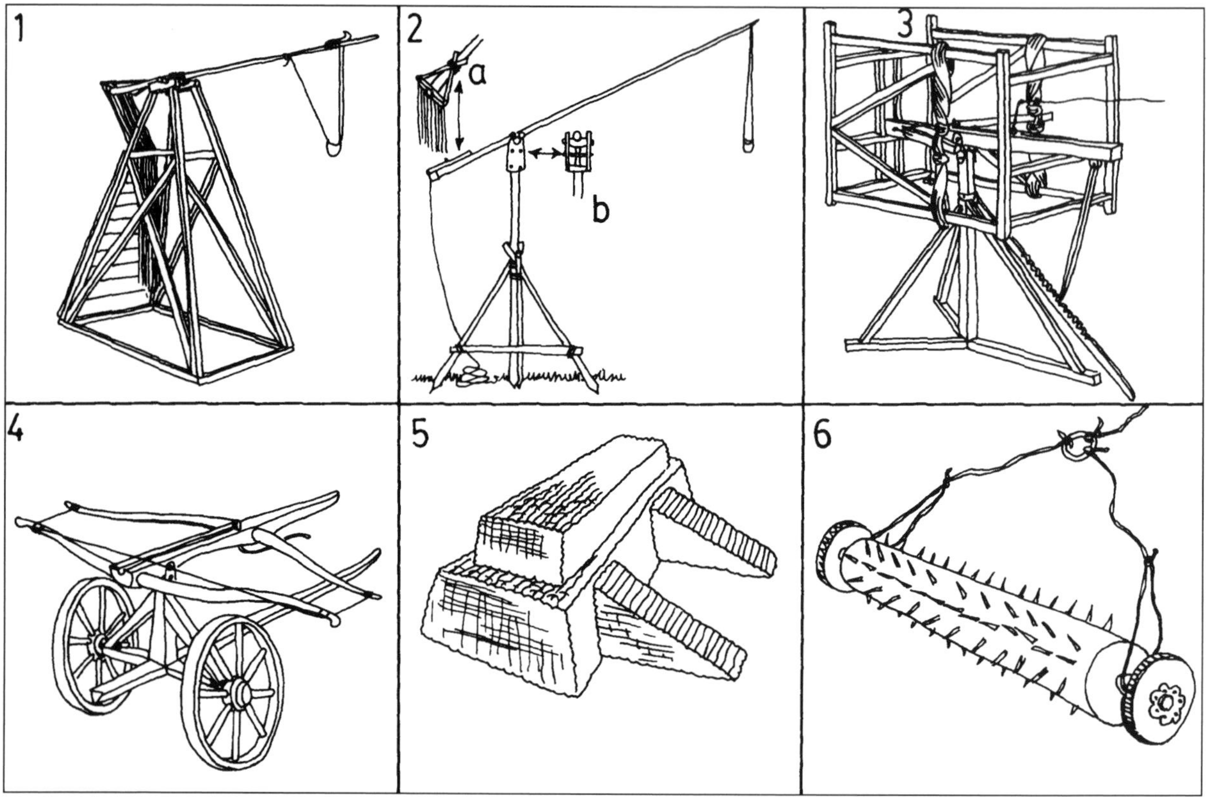

Above: Siege warfare
1. Man-powered manjanīq stone-throwing device. This was known as the Arab type in the 12th-century Muslim Middle East, being more powerful than the Turco-Persian and Frankish forms though more difficult to construct. It incorporated a protective wooden screen for its crew.
2. Light form of Russian man-powered mangonel, 12th-13th centuries. This was clearly based on Byzantine or Turco-Mongol military technology and could be turned to shoot in any direction. (after Kirpitchnikov)
3. The qaws al-ziyār or 'skein-bow' had been known in Byzantium since at least the 11th century and in Muslim territory by the 12th century, though it had probably been known in both areas much earlier. Two bow-arms were powered by twisted skeins of silk, horse-hair or other material to shoot a large crossbow-bolt. (after Leibel)
4. So-called 'double crossbows' are mentioned in several Chinese sources, and can be seen in 12th–13th-century Cambodian carvings mounted on wheeled carriages and on the backs of elephants. Various stringing systems have been suggested, but the one shown in this reconstruction is the simplest; the string from the rear bow running through notches in the arms of the front bow so that they are bent towards each other when the string is drawn back. (after Mus and Needham)
5. The pasheb was a massive mound of hundreds of sandbags enabling besiegers to reach the top of an enemy's wall or shoot down at the defenders. Such huge devices, needing an enormous work force, were characteristic of medieval Indian warfare. (after Haider)
6. The 'thunder-stick' was a large spiked roller which was sent careering down the foot of a fortified wall if an enemy attempted to attack. It was used in both China and India and came in several forms. This version included ropes so that it could be retrieved and used again. (after Needham)

Right: *The Puerto del Sol, one of the city gates of Toledo, built by the Hospitallers in Mudejar or Islamic style in the early 14th century. (Author's photograph)*

as their Muslim foes but they clearly had the latest types, including *boves* which had adjustable counterweights. Those defending Acre at the end of the 13th century could also throw a stone weighing forty-five kilograms. The *espringal* was an anti-personnel rather than a wall- or machine-breaking engine. It came in various sizes, the best being made of beech, elm or oak, and its torsion power was provided by horse or cattle hair.

The Iberian Reconquista was primarily aimed at cities, some of which were so large and so well fortified that sieges took several years. In some cases the final struggle was resolved by street fighting of almost modern savagery. Siege engineering in the Christian states of northern Iberia was also greatly influenced by that of the Muslim south, the Spanish *algarrada* itself came from the Arabic *al-^{c}arrāda* (anti-personnel ballista). The *manganell turquès* or Turkish *mangonel* mentioned in early 13th-century Aragon was probably a new form, perhaps with an adjustable counterweight.

Muslim armies themselves used various siege techniques. Light troops still went ahead of the main force to blockade a castle or city, surrounding orchards were progressively destroyed in an attempt to force surrender, and the first phase of a siege involved erecting defensive palisades and digging entrenchments. A 13th-century theoretical account of siege warfare lists the sequence of events. First the commander gathered his labourers and ordered them to assemble siege machines. Bombardment of the enemy began with the smallest engines, followed by those of increasing power to put the enemy under increasing psychological pressure. The besiegers must defend themselves with trenches as they were vulnerable to sorties, and units of cavalry should be posted an arrow-shot from each gate. The resulting camp could be like a small town. Ṣalāh al-Dīn's *t̲h̲uql* (siege train) included a variety of specialists such as *naqqābūn* (engineers), *naffāṭūn* (fire-troops), *zarrāqbūn* (fire-throwers), craftsmen and *massāḥīs* (surveyors). It is also clear that the Muslims used much more mining than did the Crusaders. The originally Chinese tactic of erecting mounds of earth as firing positions for stone-throwing *mangonels* was similarly used throughout these centuries; such machines steadily removing the battlements so that defending archers could not shoot at assault parties. The latter were commanded by the best officers and the troops carried fire-weapons and tools further to demolish the wall. Once this had been achieved the defenders were given a final chance to surrender. A further variation was to use any numerical advantage to make small attacks against different parts of the wall and thus exhaust the garrison.

In defence Muslim garrisons resorted to imaginative stratagems including psychological warfare, for example sending men with torches out of a postern gate by night, returning with their torches extinguished and then coming out again relit to make the size of the garrison appear more formidable. Local militia used their knowledge of the surrounding orchards and lanes to trap and destroy small groups of invaders to defeat a Crusader attack on Damascus in 1148. Sorties would often be made at night in an attempt to destroy the enemy's siege machines. During the Third Crusade's siege

Above: *The Gibralfaro hill-top castle of Malaga, Andalusian 14th century. It is connected to the Alcazabar fortified palace lower down the hill by the long double-walls seen here. (Author's photograph)*

Right: *The Alcazabar or fortress of Merida was one of the most important military bases in the western part of Andalusia, completed in 835 but strengthened in later centuries. The basic architectural style is Syrian, reflecting the origins of the ruling Umayyad dynasty of 9th-century Andalusia. The separate external albarrana towers, joined to the main wall by bridges, may have been added by the Muwaḥḥidin in the 13th century. (Author's photograph)*

of Acre the son of a copper-smith annoyed professional fire-troops by designing a more effective way of shooting nafṭ thereby destroying the Crusaders' siege engines. During this same siege the defenders used a long grappling hook to ensnare one of King Richard's leading men, and hauled him up the wall.

The counterweight *mangonel* or *trebuchet* had been invented in the eastern Mediterranean region in the mid-12th century or a little earlier, being first illustrated in detail together with many other sophisticated devices in a manuscript written for Ṣalāh al-Dīn. Although the author was dealing with machines which had been used by Fāṭimid armies for some time, the counterweight *trebuchet* only came into really widespread use in the 13th century. He also described other simpler man-powered *mangonels*, of which the Arab form was considered the most reliable. It consisted of a flat-topped wooden frame with a roof or wall to protect its operators. The Turco-Persian type needed less work and materials; it was mounted on a single sloping pole supported by another at an angle, the 'Frankish' or European type being supported by two crossed poles. Meanwhile the smallest *luᶜab* type had the least range, but being mounted on a single pole could be turned to aim in any direction. During the late 13th century some of the largest counterweight machines were pre-fabricated and transported to the scene of a siege where they were assembled. Elsewhere they were mounted on towers to defend a harbour entrance.

Apart from unexplained references to '*black bull-like*' *mangonels* which could shoot large bolts or arrows, the main low-trajectory bolt-shooting machines included the *great crossbow*, mounted on a rotating wooden tower and probably spanned by a winch known since at least the 12th century. The *qaws al-ziyār* or *espringal* was an even more devastating device with two separate arms powered by twisted skeins of hair, silk or sinew and was spanned by a winch having the power of twenty men. A later reference from Morocco said that it took eleven mules to carry a dismantled *qaws al-ziyār*.

Dabbāba (wooden sheds) to protect men working *kabsh* (rams) were still used by Muslim armies, but, like the *burj* (wooden siege-tower), were considered ideal targets for *nafṭ* and other forms of fire-weapon. Perhaps for this reason they largely fell out of use from the late 13th century. Other more abundant devices were screens and mantlets to protect sappers and miners. One example used during the final siege of Crusader-held Acre consisted of a large piece of felt erected on a system of pulleys. It not only hid individual men but absorbed *mangonel* balls and crossbow bolts. The *zaḥāfah* is more obscure, but seems to have been a fixed wooden tower for archers.

Fire-weapons continued to be developed and elaborated. In 12th-century Syria, for example, clay and glass grenades were designed for different purposes, some apparently being anti-personnel weapons. On the other hand the apparent decline of fire-weapons from the later 13th century may have been a result of their own success in driving suitable wooden and other suitably inflammable targets from the battlefield (see Chapter VIII).

Siege technology in the western parts of the Muslim world was virtually identical with that in the Middle East, and became particularly sophisticated under the Muwaḥḥidin in the later 12th century. Here the commander of siege forces sometimes had a *marqaba* or special observation post erected from which he could direct operations. Another notable feature of sieges in these western regions was the building of complete towns with their own stone fortifications next to the city under attack. The moral impact of such commitment must have been enormous; the walls and minaret of one such 'counter-city' survive at al-Manṣūrah outside Tilimsān in Algeria. Otherwise the usual sequence of events was followed. The defenders fought outside their walls until they became convinced that the attackers could not be driven away. In 14th-century Granada this was followed by walling-up all the city gates except those needed for sorties, while stone-throwing mangonels shot at those of the attackers. Particularly advanced semi-explosive pyrotechnics also seem to have suddenly appeared in North Africa and Andalusia in the late 13th century, some of them possibly incorporating primitive forms of gunpowder.

NAVAL WARFARE

The Mediterranean

Piracy was often seen as an acceptable form of business in the later medieval Mediterranean. The sea was also an area where Christians and Muslims felt free to make temporary individual or group alliances. There was also such similarity in ship design that Christian and Muslim vessels could only be differentiated by their flags and the fact that Christian sailors tended to be clean-shaven. During the 13th century armoured crossbowmen became a specialist marine élite; larger ships often even having armourers to maintain their crossbows. Crossbows were also used aboard Muslim ships, though to a lesser degree, while in Aragonese fleets the lightly equipped *almugavars* were largely armed with javelins.

During the 11th and 12th centuries most European galleys changed from the old *alla sensile* 'simple fashion' of having oars evenly spaced, usually at two levels, to the technique of grouping the oars on a single level supported by an outrigger. In this they were soon followed by Byzantine and Islamic fleets. On the other hand Muslim shipwrights were more advanced in building large merchant and transport ships with up to three masts. The question of northern European influence on Mediterranean ship design is less clear. Square-rigged northern-style *keels* with stern rudders and reefing points on their sails were known in mid-14th-century Barcelona, but the presence of mizzen masts with lateen sails suggests a mixture of northern and southern traditions rather than visitors from outside the Mediterranean.

Despite the Byzantine Empire's unrivalled maritime heritage, its navy was in decline from the late 11th to 14th centuries. But there is no evidence that Byzantine ships or crews were inferior to those of their rivals, and 12th-century Byzantine marines were highly regarded. Even so, efforts to rebuild

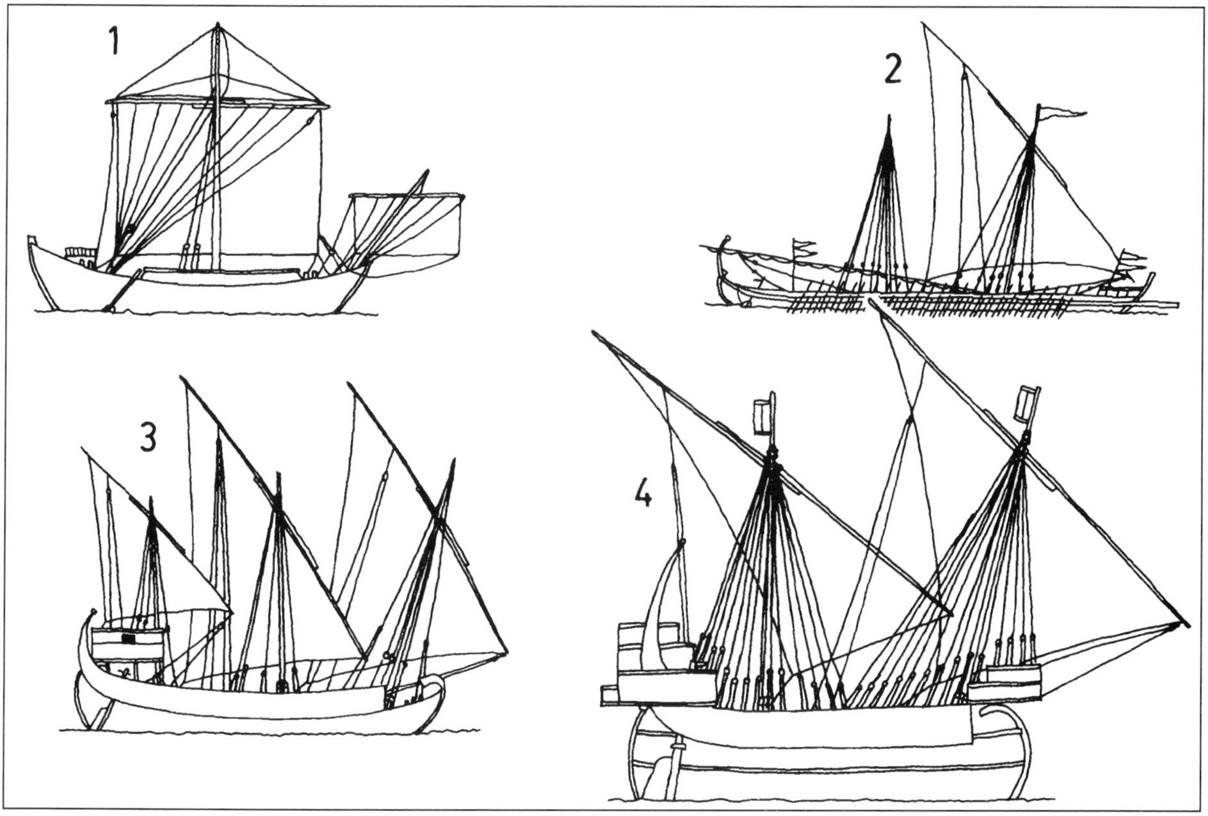

Shipping in the Mediterranean
1. Reconstruction of the Yassi Ada ship, a Byzantine wreck dating from 626. Two types of sails have been suggested by marine archaeologists, but the square-rigged version previously used by Roman vessels is seen here. Both were probably used at this time. (after Throckmorton and Parker)
2. A 12th-century war galley of the type used by Byzantine and Muslim fleets for several centuries. The only distinguishing feature between the two navies may have been the more curved stem and stern-posts of Muslim ships. This galley also has its oars evenly spaced at two levels in the early medieval style. (after Landström)
3. A large Islamic merchant vessel as used in the Mediterranean and Atlantic. Having probably disappeared in the 5th–6th centuries, three-masted ships were re-introduced by Muslim shipwrights at least two centuries before they reappeared on the northern or Christian side of the Mediterranean. This has long been known from documentary sources, but has recently been proved by pictures on ceramics made in al-Andalus or the Balearic Islands in the 10th–11th centuries.
4. A Crusader 'round ship' or transport of the early 13th century. These vessels can be reconstructed from the surviving and very accurate dimensions listed in contracts for their construction. Tests have indicated that they were extremely clumsy, but these sturdy vessels provided a vital link between the Crusader States and western Europe. (after Pryor)

Byzantine naval power in the early 12th century had to rely to a great extent on Venetian help and even the hiring of complete Italian fleets. Early in the 14th century the remnant of the Byzantine navy was disbanded, some of its crews seeking employment with the Crusader States though the majority transferred their allegiance to Turkish *beyliks* of the Aegean coast. Byzantine naval power in the Black Sea faced fewer challenges and the independent Empire of Trebizond made great efforts to stop the Anatolian Turks from reaching the coast. Once the Turks managed to do so, however, they found rich pickings on the trade route linking Trebizond with the Crimea. Nevertheless the 13th-century Trebizond navy remained a small but effective force under a *Grand Admiral of the Fleet* who had a fleet of *katerga* (galleys) well into the 15th century. At the far eastern end of the Black Sea the kingdom of Georgia also had a navy in the 13th century, again consisting of galleys known by the originally Turkish word *catargha;* Georgian merchant ships were known by the originally Latin term *navi.*

The Crusader States relied on Italian vessels, particularly for ambitious operations such as invasions of Egypt. Nevertheless the Crusader States did have some ships in the mid-12th century; the County of Tripoli raising its own small fleet after Egyptian warships broke into Tortosa harbour in 1180. An officer known as the *Commander of Ships* was probably responsible for ship-building rather than naval operations, and the Military Order of Hospitallers, like the Templars, only assembled a real navy after the fall of Acre. Crusader vessels included *chelandre* (horse-transports) (from the Greek *chelandrion*), the ability to carry cavalry mounts from Europe remaining a primary concern. These were at first specialised galleys, whereas the *salandria* of the later 13th century appear to have been similarly specialised sailing ships. Descriptions of 12th-century Mediterranean naval conflict suggest that larger galleys still had their oars at two levels; the top level being captured by boarders so that the upper and lower oars could even attempt to row against each other.

By the 13th century Crusading expeditions from Europe to the Middle East included troops and horses transported in ships which had been specifically built for that expedition. Within the Crusader States themselves there were also arsenals for the repair and building of the ships which provided a vital lifeline to Europe. Some ships were probably only used for coastal traffic and carrying passengers or goods ashore from deeper draught vessels which could not reach the beach. These may, in fact, have been the barges which served as floating *mangonel* batteries during the final siege of Acre. Shallow-draught vessels could similarly bombard the enemy on a coastal road and on one occasion Muslim pioneers countered by erecting wooded breastworks along the most vulnerable stretch of such a road. The menace of piracy meant that the Muslim authorities locked Christian merchants into their hostels at night or when the local inhabitants were at Friday prayers. Meanwhile European domination of the Eastern Mediterranean enabled Crusaders, Italian merchants and pirates alike to maintain footholds on mountainous coasts where Muslim rulers were unable to concentrate their forces. The Aegean islands were also meeting-places for pirates of varied origins, mostly preying upon Venetian merchant ships.

The navies of Christian Iberia were suitable for both the Mediterranean and the Atlantic, serving as an important link between two maritime traditions. In the Aragonese, as in the Castilian, fleet there was a clear distinction between '*great galleys*', ordinary galleys and smaller *galiotes*. Unlike most Christian Mediterranean fleets, professional crossbowmen only seem to have been used in an emergency. Instead oarsmen doubled as crossbowmen while true marines were mostly *almogavers* armed with bows, javelins and light swords, reflecting the powerful Islamic maritime heritage of Iberia. Another small but interesting detail was the Catalan-Sicilian fleet's use of trumpets as a challenge to battle in Malta harbour in 1283.

On the Muslim side the Turks were newcomers to Mediterranean naval warfare. Their first fleets were at Tarsus in Cilicia in 1085, probably in co-operation with the long-established Arab fleet at Tripoli in Lebanon, and at Izmir between 1090 and 1097 before they were driven back inland by Byzantine, Armenian and Crusader counter-offensives. It was to be more than a century before the Turks again reached the Anatolian coast, and not until the beginning of the 14th century did they challenge Christian domination. The Turks then sought alliances with Catalan freebooters and Italian colonies around the Aegean as well as sending raiding forces to the European

mainland. The fleets used in this *ghāzi* maritime warfare consisted of large numbers of small vessels; only the *beylik* of Aydin having war-galleys. Small ships were successful in transporting raiders and siege equipment, but could not face Christian galley fleets in open battle. Consequently 14th-century Turkish fleets avoided combat at sea except when they were accompanied by Christian allies. The Turkish challenge in the Black Sea came earlier than in the Aegean, the Saljūk (governor) of Sinop sending a naval squadron to ravage the Byzantine-Trebizond-ruled Crimean coast in 1220. Here the Turkish term for a transport ship capable of carrying thirty to forty men was a *qayiq* while a war-galley was called a *qadirga*. Turkish *ᶜazap* (marines) fought with crossbows and hand-held composite bows using *semberek* or *zembūrek* (arrow-guides), *tüfek* (guns) being adopted at the end of the 14th century.

The Fāṭimid fleet may have declined by the time Ṣalāh al-Dīn took over Egypt, but it still existed and the new ruler soon established a special government *dīwān* to deal with naval affairs. Muslim naval tactics, weapons and ships were very much the same as those of their Crusader and Italian opponents in the 13th-century eastern Mediterranean, though for some unknown reason the term *harrāqa* ceased to mean a fireship and was instead used for a small galley or rowing-boat. There was also an apparent increase in the use of crossbows at sea, just as there was on the Christian side. The Mamlūks' policy of demilitarising reconquered Crusader coasts resulted in fewer active harbours. Instead a series of small forts served as a coastal early warning system. The last forested areas of Egypt were also cut down for agriculture during the Mamlūk period, making Egypt even more dependent on Lebanese, Syrian and imported Anatolian timber for shipbuilding. Despite the fact that their Genoese allies provided the vital maritime link between the Mamlūk Sultanate and the southern Russian sources of slaves who replenished the Mamlūks' own ranks, the Mamlūks generally had a negative attitude towards the sea; their fleets being manned by low-grade troops. There was neither a permanent navy nor a permanent naval administration; each being recreated in response to a particular need. Yet the Mamlūks' distaste for the sea may have been exaggerated and several documents concerning naval matters seems to suggest considerable interest in naval warfare. For example marines were led by a *qā'id* or *muqaddam* while a *ra'īs al milāḥa* captained the ship and commanded the sailors. Books on naval tactics, comparable to *furūsīyah* manuals for warfare on land, dealt with the operation of small squadrons rather than large fleets. Although they included translations from earlier Byzantine naval treatises, these were practical books, updating traditional information for current conditions. A Mamlūk fleet raised for an attack on Cyprus included élite *nafāṭa* (fire-troops), and books dealing specifically with fire-weapons indicate that the Mamlūks used or at least experimented with very advanced pyrotechnics including a rocket-powered torpedo described as an 'egg which moves itself and burns'.

Painted wooden panel depicting a 'round ship' or transport being attacked by two galleys. The man in the prow of one galley appears to be cutting the merchant ship's rigging with a type of axe. The apparent chain or rope between the prow and calcar (beak or ram) of the galley also appears in 5th-century late Roman art. (Museo de Arte de Catalualley)

North Africa also continued to have effective navies. The especially large sailing vessels built in Andalusia seem to have been capable of brushing aside attacks by Christian galleys. Compared with Egypt or even Syria, North Africa had adequate supplies of timber and this enabled even relatively minor dynasties such as the Hafṣids of Tunisia to maintain a navy commanded by a *qā'id al baḥr* whose status remained high, but by the mid-14th century Muslim North Africa was no longer able to challenge European domination of the Mediterranean. Muslim sea-power lasted longer in al-Andalus; the Naṣrid kingdom of Granada perhaps being relatively stronger at sea than on land. The navy of Granada was organised in *usṭūl* (squadrons), each under a *qā'id* officer. Aboard ship a *raīs* was in charge of manoeuvre and a junior *qā'id* commanded the marines whose main strength lay in archers and crossbowmen. Almeria served as Granada's main arsenal.

The Atlantic

The survival of the Muslim kingdom of Granada depended on the maintenance of maritime communications with North Africa. In contrast the Christian states of the Iberian peninsula needed passage through the Gibraltar Straits to maintain communications between their Atlantic and Mediterranean fleets. As a result the straits saw considerable naval warfare in the 13th and 14th centuries. Some larger ships had fighting castles at the prow, stern and main mast; such vessels continuing the Muslims' existing tradition of Atlantic voyages. Not surprisingly, perhaps, the native Guanches of the Canary Islands knew all about trade and exchange when the first European explorers arrived, despite their own reported lack of any seagoing boats. Although the Christian states of Iberia's Atlantic coast inherited their predecessors' experience of sailing the Atlantic, the first 13th-century Castilian navy was built in Galicia with Italian help. By the 14th century Castilian galleys were the largest and most effective warships operating in the Atlantic. Their design was based upon that of Genoese galleys, though they were 50 per cent larger and had a significantly higher freeboard to deal with Atlantic waves. Their officers included a *comit* (quartermaster) who was also in charge of oarsmen and manoeuvre in battle, a highly paid *patrón* or master in charge of navigation and of the marines in battle, and a deputy quartermaster with the originally Arabic title of *alguazil* who transmitted the senior quartermaster's orders to the oarsmen. Ambitions to conquer Morocco had, in fact, been one reason why Castile revived Seville as a naval base shortly after 1248. Then there was the dream of getting closer to the source of gold which crossed the Sahara from West Africa. Surprisingly, perhaps, Portugal came relatively late to Atlantic navigation. Nevertheless the old maritime traditions of Lisbon and the Algarve were not broken by the Reconquista; the Algarve probably being decisive in fostering the development of long-distance Atlantic voyages. This may also have been the birthplace of the *caravo, caravela* or *caravel;* a ship which had once been a perhaps smaller Arab sailing-vessel but which evolved into the sturdy ocean-going ship which took Columbus to America. Even more significant was the store of geographical knowledge which the Portuguese inherited from their Andalusian predecessors, knowledge which included the concept of a spherical world, the fact that it was possible to sail south around Africa and that there were real islands out in the Atlantic. After the Genoese, who were the first Christian mariners known to have reached the Canary Islands in 1312, the Portuguese unsuccessfully tried to occupy them in 1341. For their part the Muslims knew of six inhabited Canary Islands and the Murābiṭin ruler ᶜAlī Ibn Yūsuf even planned a naval expedition to conquer then in the 12th century. Another voyage in the late 13th century claimed to reached ten degrees west of al-Andalus which would have included Madeira but not the Azores. Little is known about the ships used in such voyages, though a late 14th-century graffito from Malaga appears to show an advanced form of galley with several features in common with the later *xebec* in which Moroccan pirates raided as far as the British Isles. The contribution of African Muslims to Atlantic exploration has not been properly studied, except by Afro-American scholars with a political point to make. Nevertheless an expedition sent into the Atlantic by Sultan Mansa Musa's father early in the 14th century probably set sail from what is now Senegal and may have been heading for the Cape Verde Islands.

The Indian Ocean and Red Sea

The Indian Ocean continued to provide a vital link between China and the Middle East, supplementing the Silk Roads across Central Asia. These latter even had their own naval element with ships plying a coastal trade across the southern Caspian Sea. There were few naval conflicts in the Indian Ocean and warships seem to have been converted merchant vessels. Large numbers of horses were, however, carried great distances. By the 14th century, if not earlier, the specialised horse-transporting *ṭarīda* was capable of disgorging fully armoured cavalry on to a beach. Even so, oared vessels remained rare in the Indian Ocean because their crews needed larger volumes of drinking water than were normally available. Although the stern rudder might have been known since the 10th century, certainly by the 12th, side-rudders or steering oars were also still used. The crow's nest or enclosed masthead observation position was also more common in the Indian Ocean than in the Mediterranean, perhaps because ships plying the eastern seas ventured much farther from land than was normal in the west. Egypt's decline as a Mediterranean naval power was not mirrored in the Red Sea where Ṣalāh al-Dīn's fleet defeated Crusader attempts to push southwards, and maintained a vital strategic link with the Indian Ocean. Egypt's main Red Sea port also shifted southwards from Suez to ᶜAydhab, though the reasons for this are unknown.

Riverine Warfare

This had never been significant in the Middle East but it now disappeared almost entirely; the only exception being bedouin river pirates of the eastern Nile Delta who caused Ṣalāh al-Dīn' some difficulties in the 12th century. Far away in West Africa the big war-canoes and tradition of raiding along the huge river Niger pre-Islamic states were inherited by the Muslim warriors of Mali and Songhai.

V
CHINA, THE FAR EAST AND INDIA (400–1400)

CHINA, THE FAR EAST AND INDIA (400–1400)

Major Campaigns 187
ARMY RECRUITMENT 189
China 189
Korea 189
South-East Asia 189
India 190
MILITARY ORGANISATION 191
China 191
Korea and Japan 194
South-East Asia 194
India 194
STRATEGY AND TACTICS 195
Broad Strategy 195
Troop Types 195
Battle Tactics 196
Combat Styles 198
Field and Camp Fortifications 198
WEAPONRY AND HARNESS 198
Archery 199
Swords and Daggers 200
Spears and Javelins 200
Other Weapons 201
Shields 201
Helmets 201
Body Armour 201
Limb Defences 202
Horse Harness 204
Horse Armour 204
FORTIFICATION 204
SIEGE WARFARE 205
NAVAL WARFARE 208

The military history of eastern and southern Asia saw as many dramatic changes as did western Asia and Europe. China constantly refined its military and technological traditions and these were to serve as the main source of influence for peoples near and far. Pre-Islamic India saw a period of overseas colonisation in which Buddhists took a lead. Most of the Indian settlers of south-east Asia came from the Dravidian south rather than the supposedly 'Aryan' Indo-European north. Despite the military influence which China exerted across much of the world, Chinese culture retained a strong pacifist ethos. The concept of holy war was virtually unknown and military heroes were not put forward as role models for the young. In Chinese warfare primacy had been given to morale and mental attitudes since the 4th century BC when Sun-Tzu wrote his famous treatise *The Art of War*. The *wen* (civil authorities) were constantly striving to dominate the *wu* (military). This often led to a reliance on part-time militias who caused little trouble but who were less effective than professional troops.

Throughout the Middle Ages peoples of nomad origin either settled on China's frontier or succeeded in conquering part of China itself; and then being rapidly absorbed into Chinese culture. Some Chinese dynasties arose in militarised frontier regions and were uncharacteristically dominated by a military élite. In contrast, the Sung of southern China were dominated by the civilian bureaucracy. Unlike previous nomad conquerors, the Mongols also took over the south and then raided Vietnam, Burma and Indonesia. The Ming dynasty which expelled the Mongols retained the Mongols' militarism while reverting to cultural isolationism.

The Koreans were less warlike than their neighbours, but the aristocracy continued to provide a military élite. In fact the Koreans' constantly had to fight to preserve their independence from northern and western neighbours, to which a Japanese naval threat was added in the 14th century. Meanwhile China remained the strongest influence upon Korean military organisation, tactics and weaponry. In turn Korea became the main agent in spreading civilisation and statecraft to Japan. The greatest cultural changes in Japan were the arrival of Buddhism in the 7th–8th centuries, together with other aspects of Chinese and Korean civilisation. By the late 12th century Japan was dominated by warrior clans. In 1185 an almost unique form of military government was established under *shōguns* who controlled a puppet imperial court, and dominated the country via a system of feudal alliances.

South-east Asia had its own indigenous cultures but was also an arena in which Chinese and Indian civilisations competed. The third force of Islam only arrived in the late Middle

Below: *'Archery Practice', in a scroll-painting; Japan, late 13th century. Japanese horse-archers were unusual in using very large bows like those of infantry elsewhere. As a result their techniques and to some extent tactics were different from those of most other mounted archers. (National Museum, Tokyo)*

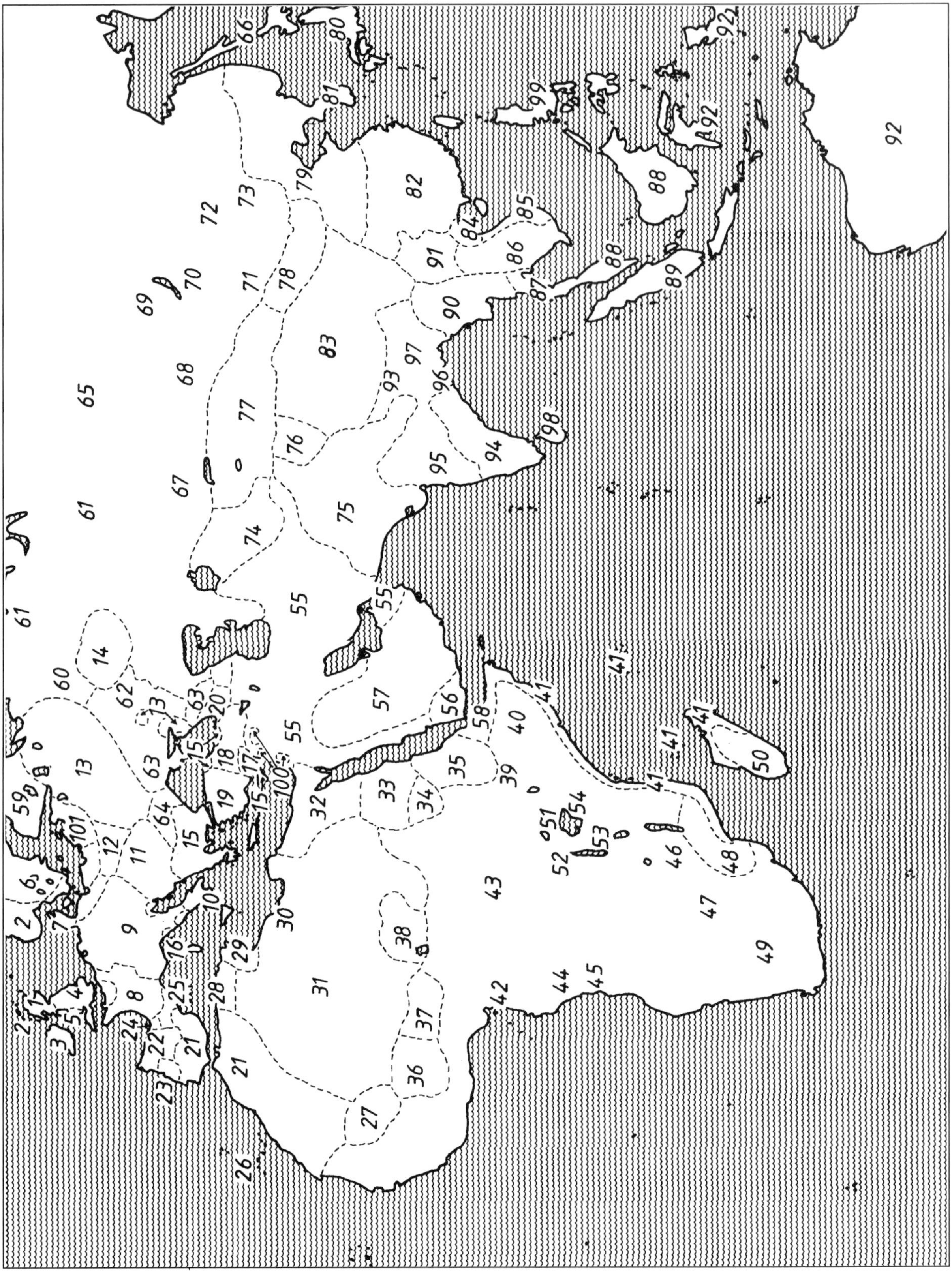

Left: Europe, Africa and Asia, c.1100

1. *Scotland*
2. *Norway*
3. *Irish kingdoms*
4. *England and Normandy*
5. *Welsh principalities*
6. *Sweden*
7. *Denmark*
8. *France*
9. *Germany*
10. *Italo-Normans*
11. *Hungary*
12. *Poland*
13. *Russian principalities*
14. *Volga Bulgars*
15. *Byzantine Empire*
16. *Pisa*
17. *Cilician Armenians*
18. *Dānishmandids*
19. *Saljūqs of Rūm*
20. *Georgia*
21. *Murābiṭin*
22. *Leén-Castile*
23. *Portugal*
24. *Navarre*
25. *Aragon*
26. *Guanches*
27. *Ghana*
28. *Ḥammādids*
29. *Zayrids*
30. *Arab tribes*
31. *Berber and Tuareg tribes*
32. *Fāṭimid Caliphate*
33. *Makuria*
34. *Alwa*
35. *Ethiopia*
36. *Mossi kingdoms*
37. *Hausa*
38. *Kanem-Bornu*
39. *Galla*
40. *Somalis*
41. *Arab coastal and island settlements*
42. *Fang*
43. *Azande*
44. *Loango*
45. *Bakongo*
46. *Baluba*
47. *Balunda*
48. *Kingdom of Mono-matapa*
49. *Khoisan peoples*
50. *Meri'na*
51. *Kitara*
52. *Nkole*
53. *Rwanda*
54. *Ganda kingdoms*
55. *Great Saljūqs*
56. *Local Yemeni states*
57. *Qarmatians*
58. *Adal*
59. *Western Finns*
60. *Eastern Finns*
61. *Ugrians*
62. *Qipchaqs*
63. *Alans*
64. *Pechenegs*
65. *Samoyeds*
66. *Ainu*
67. *Kimäks*
68. *Kirghiz*
69. *Oirats*
70. *Merkits*
71. *Keraits*
72. *Mongols*
73. *Tatars*
74. *Qarākhānids*
75. *Ghaznawids*
76. *Kashmir-Ladakh*
77. *Qara-Khitai*
78. *Tanguts*
79. *Empire of China, Jürchen*
80. *Japan*
81. *Koryŏ*
82. *Empire of China, southern Sung*
83. *Tibet*
84. *Annam*
85. *Champa*
86. *Khmer*
87. *Dvaravati*
88. *Dvipantara*
89. *Sri-Vijaya*
90. *Pagan*
91. *Nan-Chao*
92. *Aboriginal peoples*
93. *Nepal*
94. *Cholas*
95. *Chalukyas*
96. *Kalinga*
97. *Palas*
98. *Lanka*
99. *Maid*
100. *Crusader enclaves*

Ages but would prove the most successful. The main power in the Indonesian archipelago from the 8th to 12th centuries was, however, the Sailendra Empire which was Mahayana Buddhist rather than Hindu. In Cambodia small warrior states had emerged by the 12th century, that of Annam pushing against Champa in what is now Vietnam while Thai principalities appeared in Thailand. Malaya and southern Burma also had Indian coastal colonies during the early medieval period. The indigenous Kingdom of Arimaddanapura in upper Burma was, in fact, converted to Buddhism by Indo-Burmese missionaries in the late 11th–early 12th centuries, while most aspects of Malayan material culture stemmed from Indian civilisation. Sri Lanka played a small part in this spread of Buddhist civilisation, though its sudden collapse as the rich trading state in the late 13th century remains a mystery.

India had its own highly distinctive military traditions. These were firmly based upon Hindu religious principles. According to the Arthashastra, for example, a powerful state should be aggressive while a weak should be conciliatory; these ideas arising when India consisted of several states among whom there was a general balance of power. India's external relations were not covered by this religiously based system, yet India became one of the most active colonising civilisations of the early Middle Ages with a sphere of influence ranging from Vietnam in the east to Yemen and Madagascar in the west.

Within India competition for land between peasants and aboriginal forest tribes led to both being very warlike, despite the theoretical Hindu confining of warfare to an élite warrior caste. But there was no co-ordinated resistance to Muslim conquest; each linguistic or religious group fighting alone. The Muslim tide probably came to a gradual halt in southern India as a result of a general over-extension of military capabilities within Muslim northern India. The Muslim successor states in India then had the same difficulties resisting northern invasions as did their Hindu predecessors.

Major Campaigns

402–39: Toba (Tabgatch Turk, northern Wei) rulers of northern China conquer neighbouring nomad states in Central Asia.

480–4: White Huns (Hephthalites) overthrow Gupta Empire in India.

c.550: Juan-Juan (Avars) driven westwards from Mongolia by Blue Turks.

c.585: Blue Turk Khānate fragments into Eastern and Western Turkish Khānates.

589: China largely re-unified by Sui dynasty.

617–24: Sui dynasty overthrown by T'ang dynasty in China; China re-unified under T'ang.

635–48: Tibetan invasion of China and India.

668: Unification of Korea.

714–44: T'ang Chinese defeat Central Asian Turks; extend control north of Tien Shan mountains.

c.753: Establishment of Rashtrakuta state in central India; beginning of Rashtrakuta expansion.

756–63: An Lu-shan rebellion in China; collapse of T'ang

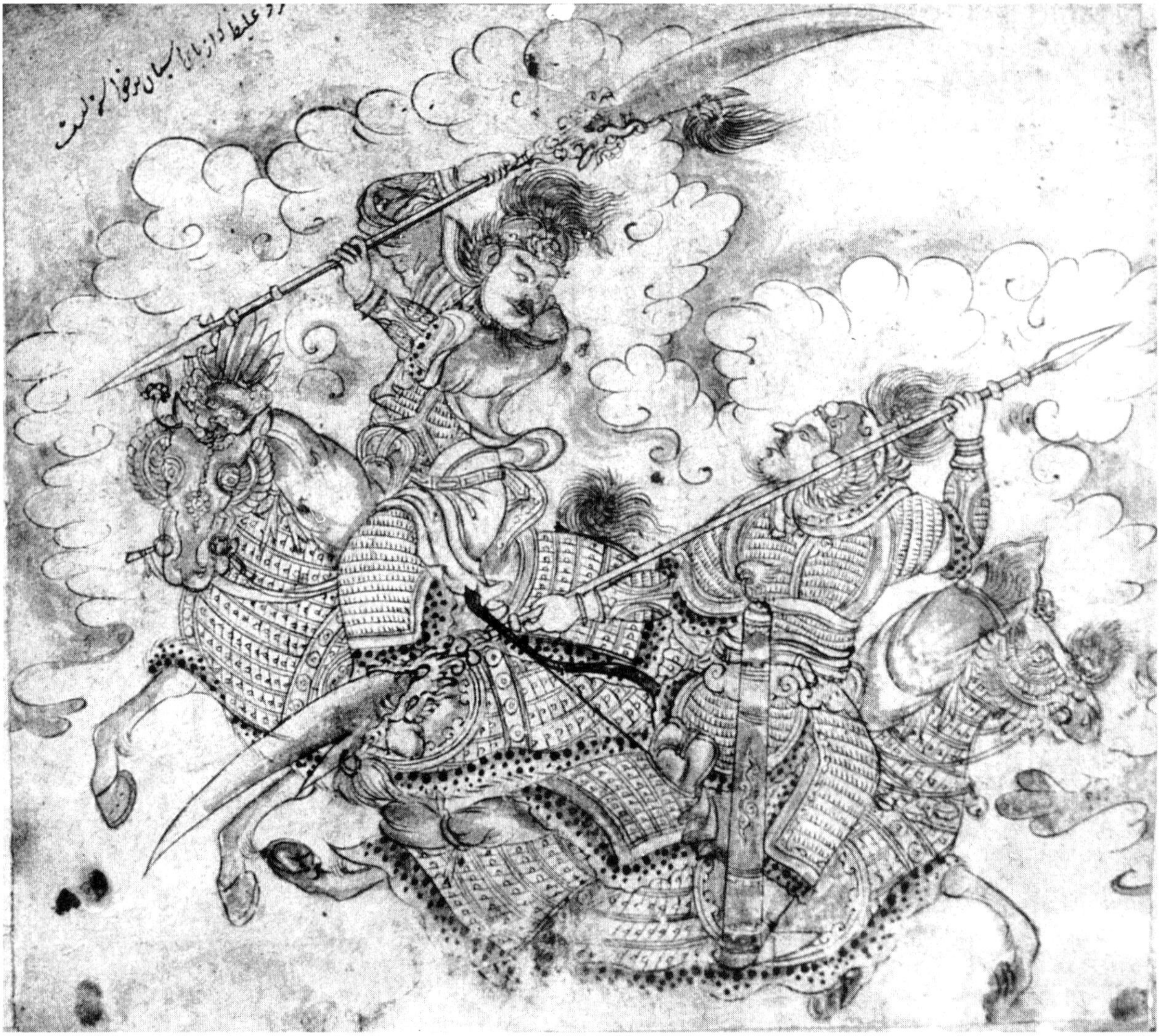

Above: *Chinese or Chinese-style Central Asian cavalrymen in combat, in a Perso-Transoxianan manuscript, late 14th–early 15th centuries. This picture was clearly made for a Persian prince, but was probably drawn by a Chinese artist. The soldiers are equipped in a Chinese manner and wield the massive double-ended staff weapons used by both cavalry and infantry in late medieval Chinese armies. (Fatih Album, MS. Haz. 2153, f.87r, Topkapi Library, Istanbul)*

authority in Central Asia.
c.900: Cholas become dominant power in southern India.
907–60: Collapse of T'ang authority; fragmentation of China.
935: Kingdom of Silla overthrown by Koryŏ, in Korea.
947: Khitans overrun northern China.
979: China largely re-united by Sung dynasty.
1018–21: Cholas conquer Sri Lanka and invade Bengal.
1044: Creation of first Burmese state at Pagan.
1125–6: Manchurian Jurchen (Chin) conquer Khitan northern China; Khitans migrate west.
c.1170: Maritime Srivijayan Empire at greatest power in East Indies.
1185: Taira and Minimoto civil war in Japan ends in Minimoto victory.
c.1200: Rise of Thai kingdom.
1211–15: Mongols invade China; capture Beijing.
1234: Mongols overthrow Jurchen dynasty in northern China.
1257–8: Mongols invade Vietnam.
1273–4: Mongol invasion of Japan.
1277: Mongols invade Burma.
1279: Mongols overthrow Sung dynasty in southern China; China re-united under Kubilai Khān.
1281–8: Mongol invasions of Japan.
1287: Mongol invasion of Burma.
1292–3: Mongol expedition to Indonesia.

1347: Rising against Muslim rule in southern India; collapse of Muslim domination.
1349: Chinese settlement of Singapore.
Mid-14th century: Majapahit Empire of Java at greatest power.
1356–70: Civil wars and uprisings in China; Mongol Yüan dynasty overthrown by Ming dynasty.
c.1370: Hindu Vijayanagar state dominates southern India.
1388: Ming offensive against Mongols.
1392: Koryŏ dynasty of Korea overthrown by Yi dynasty (lasted until 1910).
1394: Thais invade Khmer Cambodia.
1399-1402: Civil war in China.
End of 14th century: Collapse of Srivijayan Empire in Indonesia.

ARMY RECRUITMENT

China

Chinese ruling dynasties followed different recruitment policies. For example the Toba of early medieval northern China had nomadic 'late Hun' tribal origins and formed a ruling clan rather than a true dynasty. The military élite owed their primary loyalty to their own family and in an effort to avoid anti-government uprisings the Toba rulers moved the tribal leadership from frontier steppes to the centre of the state and as a consequence undermined its military effectiveness. The Toba also found it necessary to recruit large numbers of Chinese infantry. This pattern would be followed to some extent throughout medieval Chinese history.

The T'ang dynasty similarly arose on the frontiers of China, though from within the Chinese military establishment, many of its early aristocracy having been leaders of *fu-ping* (special military districts) under the previous Sui dynasty. Nevertheless even this powerful military class became increasingly dependent upon the state in the usual Chinese pattern. The first T'ang armies largely consisted of soldiers from the previous Sui dynasty, but once the T'ang came to power they established their own system of 'military wards' in which men from farming families with inherited military obligations served from the age of sixteen to fifty-eight or sixty. Legally speaking these registered soldiers were unfree bondsmen. Conscripts were drawn every three years from the fittest and most suitable members of these families. Additional soldiers could be recruited temporarily from 'civilian' families when needed. The T'ang also forced convicts to settle in military colonies and, in the 9th century, introduced a new system of *hsuin-pien tzu-ti* (frontier braves) recruited from the mountainous south-west. In contrast the guard units of the T'ang period were often of noble origin; the aristocracy providing the bulk of the officer corps since the military examinations system only existed in a rudimentary form. The higher echelons of the T'ang military élite also included Turks and Koreans. Eunuchs were often put in command of T'ang armies after the An Lu-shan rebellion of 756–63, they being thought to lack family ambitions.

The subsequent Sung dynasty is often thought to have been unmilitary, though it had enormous armies. In the early days these were recruited from previous T'ang units, surrendered rebels, volunteers, conscripts and convicts serving their sentences as soldiers. A provincial militia was also selected from registers of local families. Garrisons of frontier forts were often recruited from non-Chinese tribal allies and formed the lowest rung of this complex military structure. By the 11th century such non-Chinese frontier allies had, however, increased in importance. The Mongol Yüan rapidly established their own largely Chinese armies, though Mongols remained the military élite. The Yüan Imperial Guard also included Manchurians, Koreans, Chinese and *se-mu* (westerners) of Qipchaq, Alan and Russian origin. In typical Mongol fashion the Yüan also imposed rural conscription whenever they needed large numbers; this *Han Chun* or 'Chinese army' being largely infantry. The fourth, lowest ranking and least reliable element in Yüan forces consisted of captured ex-Sung troops called the *Hsin-fu Chun*, mostly consisting of infantry and artillerymen. Another aspect of Chinese military tradition which the Yüan inherited were military colonies, again manned by non-Mongols. Muslims of probably Arab merchant origin commanded some Yüan naval and riverine squadrons. Otherwise, it seems that sailors were recruited from fishing and trading coastal communities.

The Chinese rebels who formed the backbone of the Ming army which overthrew the Mongol Yüan largely consisted of infantry, but once they had consolidated their own power the Ming Emperors continued to enlist a great many Mongol troops as frontier allies. Nevertheless the Ming relied on the traditional system of hereditary military families.

Korea

Early medieval Korea had its own distinctive aristocratic structure based upon families of *kolp'um* or 'bone rank'. These provided military leaders for the kingdom of Silla and recruited their own soldiers in an almost feudal manner; the élite of such troops forming units of *sŏdang* ('oath bannermen') Younger members of the 'bone rank' aristocracy similarly formed the *hwarang* ('flowery princes') who became an officer corps. The northernmost Korean state of Koguryŏ is also known to have had a *kyŏngdang* military élite similar to these *hwarang*. The subsequent Koryŏ state abolished the 'bone rank' aristocratic structure and replaced it by a bureaucratic system of military promotion based upon Chinese principles. Meanwhile the *yangmin* ('good people') – peasants, artisans and merchants – of the Koryŏ state paid taxes and served as soldiers when required.

South-East Asia

Military recruitment in the various states of south-east Asia was almost entirely internal, though the army of the 13th-century Champa state in Indochina did include Muslim artillerymen. In what is now Indonesia, society was organised along Hindu caste lines, members of the indigenous military élite only needing to undergo a *brāhman* religious rite to become *kshatriya* or members of the warrior caste. This Indonesian élite also cemented its status by marrying settlers of Indian origin.

The élite *ahmudan* 'guards' units of the 12th-13th-century Buddhist Burmese state were recruited from an established aristocracy. The most loyal were men of ethnic Burmese origin from the centre of what is now Burma rather than partially Indian Talaigns from the southern coast or Arakanese from the west. Large numbers of local levies also played a major role, including captured and militarily more advanced Talaigns. King Anawrahta, founder of the Burmese kingdom in the mid-11th century, is also credited with recruiting foreign specialists including Muslim sailors. References in documentary sources to *feringhi* (European) troops in late 13th- and 14th-century Burma were later insertions, perhaps by a writer who confused 'western' Europeans with 'western' Arab sailors.

India

Within Hindu India the religiously based caste system formed the theoretical foundation of military recruitment. Before the collapse of the Gupta state in the early 6th century conscription may have been largely limited to the *kshatriya* warrior caste, but from then on the reality rarely reflected the theory. Under this caste system the *brāhman* (priests) were of the highest status, followed by the *kshatriya* (warrior and ruling

Left: *Relief carving with a warrior and two female figures from Rajastan, 10th century. In addition to his reverse-curved sword, the warrior has a dagger at his belt and rests his hand on a rectangular shield. These were typical items of equipment for early medieval Indian infantry. (Harvard University Art Museum, acc. no. 1961.134, Cambridge Mass.)*

Right: *Terracotta plaque illustrating an infantryman from Comilla, Bengal, 8th century. This warrior from Bengal in eastern India has a straight sword and what appears to be a leather shield. He also has boots of a type rarely seen elsewhere. (British Museum, inv. 1964. 10-14.1, London)*

caste), then the *vaiśya* ('commoners') - farmers and merchants - and finally the *śūdra* (serfs). This resulted in an extraordinary degree of social and ethnic segregation which had many features in common with Sassanian Iran. Armourers were considered part of the *vaiśya,* free but supposedly non-military artisan caste, but the dividing line between the *kshatriya* and *vaiśya* became blurred; both including soldiers and traders. Only in the later medieval period did the status of *vaiśya* seriously decline. Boys from the *kshatriya* were 'invested' into their caste between the ages of six and eleven but did not become full *kshatriya* until the age of twenty-two. Those who failed to reach this status lost their privileges and became outcasts.

The *Arthashāstra (Utilitarian Book),* written in the early Middle Ages, sheds light on the reality rather than the ideal of recruitment and organisation. Here an army was described as consisting of a *maula* (hereditary élite), *bhṛitaka* (mercenaries), *shreṇībala* (short-term contingents from 'guilds'), plus allies and 'non-Aryan' aboriginal auxiliaries). Women also had a designated role, bringing drinks to men in battle, tending the wounded and even serving as night-watch 'persons'. On at least one occasion a late medieval Hindu army, that of the Maratha ruler Ramchandra, was commanded by two women. By the 11th century Northern Indian armies consisted of relatively small professional élites plus large numbers of assorted vassals and auxiliaries. Here the Rajpūts formed a distinct military aristocracy or caste claiming descent from earliest *kshatriya* and existing solely for war. Meanwhile the military role of non-*kshatriya* declined in areas under Rajpūt control and the Rajpūts were themselves defeated' whereupon resistance generally collapsed. Another distinct military community were the *Jāts* or *zuṭṭ* as they were known in Arabic sources. During the 7th and 8th centuries they fought hard against Muslim invasion, then re-emerged in the 11th century as a still warlike community which now included both Hindus and Muslims. The apparent inexorability with which Muslim forces pressed southwards eventually loosened the military caste system in Hindu India, but even before this attempts by local rulers to build up their own permanent forces had enabled members of the *kshatriya* caste to find employment beyond their own immediate territory. Perhaps in desperation the rulers of central and southern India also recruited warriors from previously despised 'non-Aryan' Dravidian hill and aboriginal tribes. The Tamil people of the deep south of India had a reputation for being hard workers and hard fighters, but here the *kshatriya* warrior caste hardly existed at all.

MILITARY ORGANISATION

China

Military organisation in medieval China was very sophisticated. Military-agricultural colonies had played a major role in frontier defence since at least the 1st century BC and by the early medieval period there were several provincial armies as well as central or 'palace' forces. The T'ang army, for example, consisted of four distinct parts: *yajun* (palace army), *wei* (élite guards), *fangren* (frontier troops) and *fu-ping* who were militia based upon a nation-wide system of *Chün-fang* (military wards). None of the three big government departments which

Carved relief of dancing warriors watched by men, women and children; Java, 8th century. The Hindu art of Java and other Indonesian islands is based upon that of India, but the military equipment and costumes are slightly different. The most distinctive items seen here are the double curved swords and a large rectangular shield on one warrior's arm. (Koninklijk Instituut voor Taal-, Land- en Volkenkunde photograph; in situ, Borobudur, Indonesia)

dominated the T'ang state was solely military. Instead the *Bingbu* consisted of four sub-sections dealing with the army, the regions, military equipment and military stores in general. Every level of the administration was also scrutinised by a corps of *censors* who reported back to the central government. The T'ang palace army evolved out of a small guards élite dating from the start of the T'ang rebellion, but it was given different names at various times. Over the years the palace forces were also reorganised and strengthened several times, eventually evolving into the large *Shen-ts'e* army. Within the palace army the Imperial Guards served as an officer corps in the supreme military headquarters; other guards regiments had less clear-cut functions but formed part of the overall *San Wei* (guards officers). In some ways the Imperial Guard served as a military academy, and although its members were trained in the martial arts many used it as a stepping-stone to senior ranks in the civilian administration. In fact all state functionaries, military or civil, had a clearly defined rank consisting of two numbers representing the nine *pin* (grades) and the several *jie* (classes).

Ordinary T'ang military forces were given various names depending on the functions they were carrying out. For example a large force was called a *jun*, a smaller one a *zhouzhou*, a *cheng* (fortress) had a *zhen* (garrison). On campaign a *xingjun* (mobile army) or *daojun* (route army) was made up of units which would then be disbanded or returned to barracks when no longer required, each unit being placed under the most suitable officer. The élite *lo-tzu-chün* (mule corps) which formed part of some armies was probably a mobile unit of mounted infantry archers and close-combat troops while another élite of assault troops called the *t'u-chiang* probably consisted of heavy cavalry.

Frontier forces were organised separately. The most important were those of the vast northern frontier which was divided into three parts. Beyond this the T'ang Empire's nearest neighbours, or at least those that were friendly, formed part of a *tu-hu-fu* (protectorate) system where local chiefs submitted to the Emperor. In the 7th century there were two main protectorates: those of the Western Turks and those of the Uighurs which in turn were divided into six governorates dealing with the thirteen recognised tribes. But as T'ang power declined in the 8th century defence of the frontier relied ever more on fortresses and increasingly large *chün* (permanent frontier armies).

The *fu-ping* (militia) was, perhaps, the single most characteristic element within the T'ang military system. It consisted of units numbering between 800 and 1,500 men; ten men to each *huo* (section) which also had six horses or other pack animals, five *huo* making a *tui*, two *tui* to each *lii*, twenty *lii* to a *tu'an*, five *tu'an* making a *fu* or army. The *fu-ping* was also designed as a self-supporting organisation whose members were not paid, instead returning to their own homes at the end of each campaign or emergency and maintaining themselves by farming. The later decades of the T'ang dynasty saw a shift of military emphasis away from the traditional Central Asian threat to a new menace posed by Tibet. But the basic military structure remained the same, though with less emphasis on cavalry, and the use of smaller field armies. In contrast the size of the palace army was considerably increased after the defeat of the An Lu-shan rebellion. This became known as the *Shen-tse* army and included many refugees from lost western provinces.

Following the fall of the T'ang dynasty, the first armies of the succeeding Sung dynasty were small, professional and well paid. In later years, however, Sung armies became much larger and notably less efficient. Like those of the T'ang they initially consisted of *chin-chün* (palace armies) which included the Emperor's Guard, *hsiang-chün* (provincial armies), *hsiang-ping* (local militias) and *fan-ping* (non-Chinese allies). The Sung also seemed even more concerned to prevent rebellions than were other Chinese ruling dynasties, to the extent that no army could be mobilised unless its commander had two halves of a marked tally in his hands; one half which he always kept and the second part of which was kept in the Imperial capital. In fact Sung military administration as a whole seems to have been in two parts, dealing with internal security and frontier defence, all based upon the *shu-mi yüan* (Bureau of Military Affairs). Frontier troops were the particular responsibility of special *Circuit Military Intendants*, but these could command large forces and had a greater degree of independent action than other senior officers. Units closest to the Sung Emperor were called the *pan-chih* (Imperial Elite); the palace armies as a whole being in three sections stationed in the palace, in the surrounding Inner City and in the Outer City beyond, the latter being the largest. These palace troops also rotated between the capital and the provinces though most cavalry were based along the northern and north-western frontiers. This rotation system was thought to toughen the men, and helped the central government maintain control over more distant areas, being similar to the ᶜAbbāsid Caliphate's method of retaining control over strategically important frontier zones. It was expensive, however, and was eventually abandoned in favour of raising the status of frontier troops who remained in roughly one area. The Sung also made considerable use of military-agricultural colonies called *yng-tien*, particularly in previously abandoned land. Their garrisons largely consisted of infantry archers, but unlike the previous T'ang military colonies the officers and men were expected to do the agricultural work themselves and as a result their military effectiveness was limited.

Two waves of conquerors from Manchuria dominated parts of northern China during the Sung era; the Liao or Khitan and the Chin or Jurchen whose rule lasted until the coming of the Mongols in the 13th century. Unlike the Mongols, however, both these earlier conquerors soon lost their own traditional nomad cavalry dominance and adopted traditional Chinese military systems. The Mongol Yüan may have learned from these errors and continued to pay five times as much to maintain a cavalryman as a foot soldier. Otherwise they too adopted many traditions of Chinese warfare. The fully developed late 13th- and early 14th-century Yüan army was therefore divided into *wei* (cavalry) and infantry units; the army as a whole being in two parts, the élite Mongol troops of the Yüan Emperor and various autonomous tribal leaders, and the mass of Chinese troops. A third small élite force consisted of the *su-wei* (Imperial Guard) which was intended to be the main prop of the Mongol regime. But even the *su-wei* increased in size and declined in quality during the 14th century.

The Chinese armies which eventually expelled the Mongol Yüan and brought the Ming to power were highly disciplined and also had very effective river fleets, though they included

Small figure of an attendant on a carved statue of Surya the Sun God, central India, c.700. This figure is unlike most other warriors in medieval Hindu Indian art and probably reflects continuing Sassanian Iranian or perhaps even early Islamic military influence. This is most noticeable in the hood or hat, and the man's small kite-shaped shield. (British Museum, inv. 1962. 12-10.1, London)

few cavalry in the early days. In 1364 the Ming thoroughly reorganised their forces on highly structured Chinese lines. The result was a more unified army built up of *wei* brigades each consisting of five battalions, each of ten companies, each of theoretically 1,000 men. This time, however, the *ch'in chun wei* guard units also served as an administrative bureaucracy and as a secret police.

Korea and Japan

The military organisation of Three Kingdoms and Silla reflected the aristocratic structure of early Korean society. The army of Silla consisted of six *chŏng* (garrisons or divisions); one in each *chu* (province), each led by a member of the '*true bone*' aristocracy. On the other hand it seems that many garrison troops, or perhaps their officers, lived in the capital unless they were doing a tour of duty. The successor dynasty of Koryŏ was more militaristic than Silla. The Korean state also shrunk to what is now the Korean peninsula. Koryŏ administration consisted of three main *samsŏng* (departments) including a State Council which itself had six *cho* (boards), one of which was the *Board of War*. Meanwhile the army initially consisted of six *wi* (guard battalions) each of six regiments of 1,000 men. Following a devastating Khitan invasion from Manchuria two separate armies were set up, plus five *pu* (regional headquarters) under the *chungbang* (supreme military headquarters) and four government departments called *tobyŏngmasa*. The influence of Chinese bureaucratic traditions was unmistakable. In Korea, however, the role of military commanders and even of ordinary officers was often hereditary. Even Buddhist temples formed their monks into military units known as 'nation-protecting Buddhism'.

Korean influence may also lie behind some aspects of later medieval Japanese military organisation. Here, in the early 13th century, the *shōgunate* was taken over by a new family of regents. The result was an extraordinary system that saw a titular emperor whose functions had been usurped by an abdicated emperor who had delegated power to an hereditary military dictator who was himself little more than a puppet in the hands of his hereditary adviser. The *bakufu* (regent's headquarters) then took land from political opponents and gave it as *fiefs* to its supporters in a system of patronage. Those who received such estates were known as *jitōs* or *shugōs* whose quasi-feudal status was formalised in 1232. One result of this militarisation of Japan was its ability to defeat Mongol invasions later in the 13th century.

South-East Asia

In south-east Asia the caste system introduced from India was more of an ideal than a reality, at least in the military field. The little that is known about military organisation in what is now Indonesia is summed up in a surviving *Manual of Court Organisation*. This describes the functions of the two most senior courtiers, the *apatih* (prime minister), responsible for internal security and military affairs, and the *dhyakṣa* (senior religious figure), responsible for maintaining and enhancing the ruler's dignity. To the north even less is known about the military structure of the Hindu state of Langkasuka in what is now Malaya, though a Chinese traveller stated that its king rode on an elephant in a white *howdah*, escorted by drummers, banners and guardsmen. In the 11th-century pre-Buddhist central Burmese kingdom of Arimaddanapura the ruler had his own élite unit of guards supposedly backed up by a powerful regional aristocracy. Every town and village was graded according to its military potential in a system further refined by Anawrahta, founder of the Buddhist Kingdom of Pagan. During the 11th and 12th centuries the army of Pagan included infantry, cavalry and war elephants. The *ahmudan* (guards) formed an élite, supposedly founded by king Narapatisithu in the late 12th or early 13th centuries and consisting of two divisions. Later the *ahmudan* appears to have consisted of four *win* (regiment) under a *winhmu* (commander), each with barracks around the palace.

India

Standing armies had existed in India since at least the 3rd century BC, their organisation being based on an ideal presented in Hindu religious epics such as the Mahābhārata. The Atharvaveda, a Hindu text on government and administration written many centuries later, gives a more realistic picture. Here the *senā* (army) was commanded by the *senāpati* and traditionally consisted of four arms; infantry, cavalry, chariots and elephants, though in some areas the additional arms of a fleet and an armaments support system were also added. Foreign observers confirmed this traditional system, including the Chinese traveller Hiuen Tsang who describes the huge army of King Harsha in AD 630-45 as consisting of no less than 50,000 infantry, 20,000 cavalry, and 5,000 elephants, later increasing to 100,000 foot soldiers and 60,000 elephants. Like almost all medieval Indian armies, this included huge numbers of support services and camp-followers. Hiuen Tsang also mentions chariots, which would seem a remarkably archaic form of fighting arm by the 7th century. A *senāpati* (army commander), for example, rode in one drawn by four horses, driven by two charioteers, surrounded by a bodyguard and attended by *nāyaka* (officers). By the 13th and 14th centuries Muslim pressure led to a tightening up of military administration in central India and the raising of more cavalry, though traditional Hindu ideals of military organisation remained. Meanwhile in the deep south large areas of the kingdom were formed into *palaiyam*, literally 'military camps', in what appears to have been a clear militarisation of the state. The army of 14th-century Hindu Vijayanaga was notably large and effective. It was organised by a special department of government called the *kandāchāra* and was led by a *dandanāyaka* or *dannāyaka* (commander- in-chief). Regular soldiers received an *amaram* (income), that of officers or senior men coming from the taxes which such men could raise from towns, villages or other pieces of land given to them by local chieftains. On the other hand the army of Vijayanagar was not noted for its discipline.

Ivory chess-piece from north-western India or Afghanistan, 8th–9th centuries. This is part of a chess-set said to have been given to Charlemagne by the ʿAbbāsid Caliph of Baghdad. In addition to the ruler on his elephant, the carving includes lightly armoured horsemen using stirrups, and infantry with sword and buckler. (Bibliothèque Nationale, Cabinet des Médailles, inv. 311, Paris)

STRATEGY AND TACTICS

Broad Strategy

Given the deep-seated dislike of Chinese civilisation for warfare, it is not surprising to find that defence took precedence over offence. Even the expansionist T'ang seemed more concerned to pacify rather than to seize territory. The aim of offensive operations was normally to undermine the defenders' economic base through devastating raids. It was also quite acceptable to use trained assassins to pick off the enemy's leadership. For similar reasons frontier defence in Central Asia was based upon fertile oases with substantial garrisons backed up by local allies. Such bases were connected by almost 2,000 beacons and could be erected in only two months. The situation in the remote, mountainous and sparsely populated south-west was different, the terrain here being so difficult that invasions by Tibetan forces tended to sweep round from the north rather than aim directly down the river valleys.

Although the Sung dynasty of China made huge efforts to avoid wars in the first place, many of the most famous Chinese military treatises were compiled during this 'anti-military' period. The Mongol conquerors of China inherited this sophisticated military tradition. Yüan Mongol commanders also tried to use particular types of troops in specific tactical or climatic situations; for example relying on Chinese and Muslims for sieges and technological warfare, putting Mongols in the northern garrisons, Chinese in the south. The subsequent Ming dynasty generally reverted to traditional T'ang and Sung strategy and tactics, using their excellent logistical organisation to enable several armies to converge upon an enemy.

Their geopolitical situation surely lay behind the medieval Koreans' reputation as supreme defensive fighters who were less effective in open battle, but why the Burmese developed a reputation for complicated strategy and military leaders who changed sides at critical moments is less clear. By the late 14th century Burmese warfare still depended upon raids, ambushes and low-intensity skirmishing, with few casualties and both sides going home in the rainy season, while the effort Burmese commanders put into catching an enemy unawares was sensible given the importance of fortified stockades in this densely forested region of south-east Asia.

After the Hun invasions of the late 5th century, the Gupta armies of northern India put greater emphasis on mobility and greater use of spear-armed cavalry and even horse-archers relying on shock tactics. Following the collapse of the Gupta state in the 6th century Hindu armies reverted to ponderous tactics, positional warfare and a reliance on fortifications. In fact Hindu Indian armies remained less mobile than their northern foes, with apparently outmoded strategy, an inferior cavalry arm and a great reliance on the moral impact of elephants. The importance of elephants also resulted in a strategic need to control jungle areas where the animals lived. As in Burma, warfare was very rarely attempted in the rainy season; most Indian campaigning taking place from December to March or in May and June.

Troop Types

Chinese armies included all forms of troops, but the majority of Chinese soldiers were virtually unarmoured infantry. This remained the case throughout the medieval period, though the Mongols demonstrated their adaptability by using a small number of war-elephants in the deep south of China. These apparently carried crossbowmen as well as archers. Mongol cavalry in China also carried infantry to battle, though not of course fighting in this manner. The Koreans were regarded as

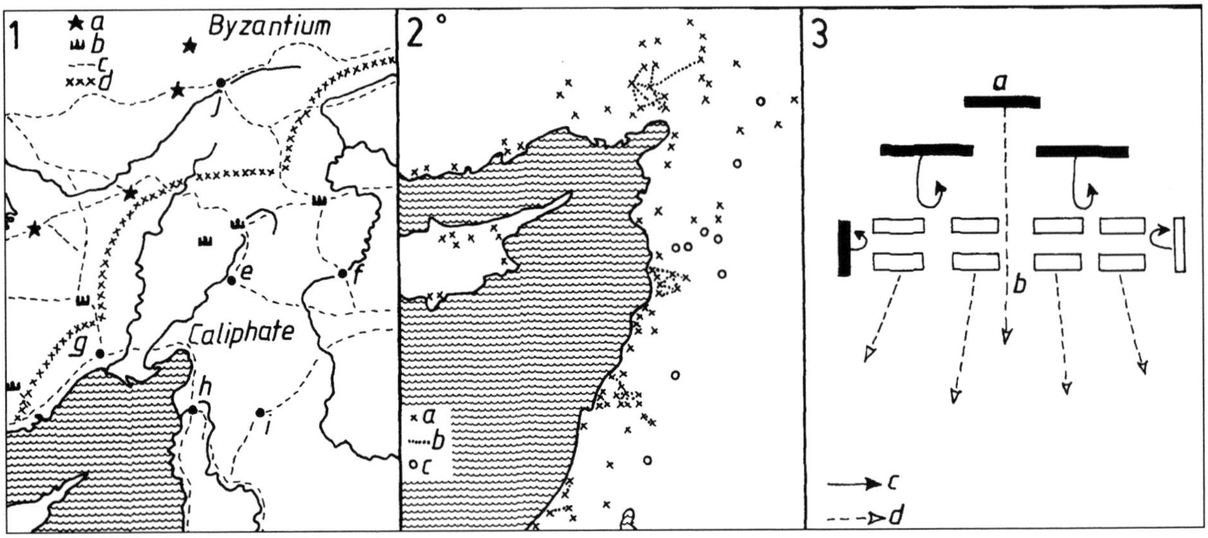

Above: Campaigns and Military Organisation

1. The defence of the Taurus mountain frontier between the Byzantine Empire and the Muslim Caliphate c.900.

- a *aplekta, Byzantine army mustering points*
- b *frontier fortresses*
- c *main roads and passes*
- d *approximate line of frontier following mountain crests*
- e *Maraş*
- f *Samsat*
- g *Tarsus*
- h *Antakya (Antioch)*
- i *Aleppo*
- j *Sivas (Sebastea).*

2. The main 12th–13th-centuries fortifications from northern Palestine to Cilicia showing the very few cases of inter-visibility between castles.

- a *Christian castles and fortified towns*
- b *lines of inter-visibility*
- c *Muslim castles and fortified cities. (after Fedden)*

3. The second battle of Tarai in 1192 between a Muslim and a Hindu army 100 kilometres north of Delhi. In the first battle of Tarai the Muslim Ghūrid Sultan Mu'izz al-Dīn had been overwhelmed by the sheer size of the opposing Hindu force. In the second battle both sides relied on their own traditional methods of warfare, but this time the Ghūrids used superior discipline and tactics to defeat a far more numerous Hindu coalition under the Rajpūt leader Prithviraja.

- a *Ghūrid force holds back its infantry and heavy cavalry while its horse-archers continuously harass enemy's front and flanks*
- b *Rajpūts adopt traditional static formation, attempting to lure Muslims into close combat*
- c *harassing attacks by horse-archers*
- d *Rajpūts withdraw under constant harassment and are broken by final Ghūrid charge. (after Sharma)*

particularly fine archers by their neighbours while some of the peoples of Indo-China used various types of crossbow included frame-mounted '*double-bows*' on the backs of war-elephants. Horse-archery was apparently unknown to the Cham people of Vietnam until this was introduced to them by a shipwrecked Chinese officer in 1172.

Climatic factors lay behind the greater importance of war-elephants than cavalry in medieval Burma. Infantry predominated in Hindu Indian warfare; cavalry forming a small élite. Archaeological evidence for some use of horse-archery in 5th century Kashmir reflects Sassanian rather than Central Asia influence. Even in the 10th and 11th centuries quivers were still attached to the rear of a saddle in a manner long abandoned in the Middle East. Chariots declined during the early medieval Gupta period though some were still used. Generally speaking, however, elephants replaced chariots as the 'heavy shock' element in Hindu armies. The camel-troops mentioned in the army of 14th-century Vijayanagar were almost certainly mounted infantry. In fact Hindu infantry included a variety of different troop types, some of whom would have been considered archaic in most other parts of Asia. Slingers, for example, were recorded as late as the 13th century. Indian bowmen, however, had been famous since ancient times and archery was so important that the most complete surviving Indian military manual was called the Dhanurveda or 'Science of Archery'.

Battle Tactics

Some traditional Chinese battle formations, as presented in military manuals, were a mix of the practical and semi-magical. Others were specifically for attack, defence or ambush; a typically Chinese element usually being the '*golden bridge*' or gap so that an enemy would not fight to the bitter end. Against internal foes and Koreans a commander was advised to harass the enemy's front, flanks and rear, but against a Central Asian foe he should adopt a defensive formation with cavalry in the

Above: *'Frontier warriors looting a Chinese house', in a 14th- century copy of a late 8th-century Chinese painted hand-scroll. The arms, armour, costume, harness and horse-armour in this highly detailed manuscript are still faithful to the T'ang original. Almost all the armour is in fact lamellar, some being of iron and some apparently of gilded hardened leather or bronze. (Eighteen Songs on a Nomad Flute, Metropolitan Museum of Art, Gift of the Dillon Fund, 1973.120.3, New York)*

centre, infantry and wagons outside, relying on infantry archery for defence and counter-charges by his own horsemen. As such these battle-tactics exactly mirrored those of the Islamic world, particularly when facing similar nomadic foes. Experience of campaigning in Central Asia also led to the development of the *jing* or 'well' formation which consisted of nine sections in a symmetrical grid, capable of facing an enemy attack from any side. It was, in fact, identical with the 'Battle Plan of the Khākhān' as illustrated in a military manual written in 13th-century Muslim India and representing the tactics used by the pre-Mongol Karakhitai in Central Asia. Infantry crossbowmen were regarded as useful against cavalry, so long as they were properly disciplined, with two ranks loading as the third shot. But a fully trained crossbowman could only loose three bolts in the time between an advancing enemy coming into range and reaching the crossbowman. Crossbowmen were still used defensively against cavalry during the Mìng period, while cavalry tried to use Mongol tactics. Other imaginative Chinese tactics were to stampede farm animals with pieces of blazing hemp tied to their tails, use dummy soldiers to make their own numbers appear greater, drag brushwood behind horsemen to raise sufficient dust for a much larger army and plant poisoned bamboo spikes in drinking places.

The tactics used by the peoples of south-eastern Asia remained rather primitive. In Burma, for example, battles consisted of a general charge against an enemy who either stood and fought or withdrew inside a wooden stockade, though the Indo-Buddhist Talaigns used a variation on the dummy troops tactic to defeat central Burmese invaders at the battle of Pyedavthagyun in 1084. Here they placed dummy war-elephants in vulnerable parts of the marshes which surrounded their stronghold. The invading Burmese attacked these dummies in the mist and half-light of dawn and then found themselves being counter-attacked by the fortress garrison.

According to the classic Atharvaveda military and administrative text, Indian archers shot from a kneeling position supported by foot soldiers armed with spears, javelin and shields. Some elephants carried three or more soldiers in addition to the *mahout* who controlled the animal; the importance of war-elephants also leading to the development of particularly large *calthrops.* Ruses and stratagems were declared superior to brute force, utilitarianism dominating idealism. In other

Painted clay statuette of an infantryman; China, c.500. Foot soldiers predominated in almost all Chinese armies, and this man originally had a spear in his hand, as well as his large mantlet style of shield. (British Museum, inv. 1925. 10-15.1, London)

words, if it worked it was right. The Chinese traveller Hieun Tsang maintains that Harsha's army in 630–45 consisted of ranks of infantry who advanced behind and within a protective screen of horsemen. But according to al-Bīrūnī Indian tactics were old-fashioned by the 10th century; this Muslim writer maintaining that the Hindus were too proud to learn from foreigners, and an Indo-Muslim military treatise of the 13th century certainly presents Hindu tactics as being very traditional. The presence of a ruler's harem on the battlefield seems to have been characteristic of Indian warfare, and would remain so even under Muslim rule. In general, however, the similarity between these traditional Hindu Indian tactics and those used in pre-Islamic southern Arabia lends support to the idea that Indian military influence spread to the western as well as eastern shores of the Indian Ocean.

Combat Styles

Widely known ancient and medieval books on the martial arts of the Far East generally present an idealised scenario. In reality it is clear that a fully armoured Chinese horse-archer was capable of keeping a large number of enemy at bay if he were riding an armoured horse, while in Burma military leaders sometimes indulged in individual duels from elephant-back. How far the men actually controlled the outcome seems doubtful since the fight tended to end when one of the elephants decided that it had enough. In India some horses were trained for combat against elephants, standing up on their hind legs so that their riders could reach their opponents on the elephant. Perhaps partially as a result, Indian horsemen valued strength rather than speed in their animals.

Field and Camp Fortifications

T'ang Chinese armies made especial use of field fortification and strongly entrenched camps when campaigning in Central Asia. These included a form of pre-fabricated barricade used each time an army halted. The small handcarts in which Chinese infantrymen carried their kit were also used as barriers around an encampment. Under the Ming dynasty a fortified outpost known as a *cha* was sometimes used even in pitched battles, probably as a command centre. Little is known in detail about field-fortification in pre-Islamic Hindu India, except that the shape and location of such encampments was decided by the senior *nāyak* (officer) in collaboration with the army's chief carpenter and chief astrologer.

WEAPONRY AND HARNESS

China was the most important, though not the only, fountainhead of military technological innovation throughout the medieval period, far surpassing western Europe in the breadth of its influence. Within China itself documentary sources list the kind of equipment a well-prepared army was supposed to have; including spare armour, armour-piercing arrowheads, long and short swords, rations and cooking implements, six donkeys for each squad of ten men or for fifty men according to the type of campaign.

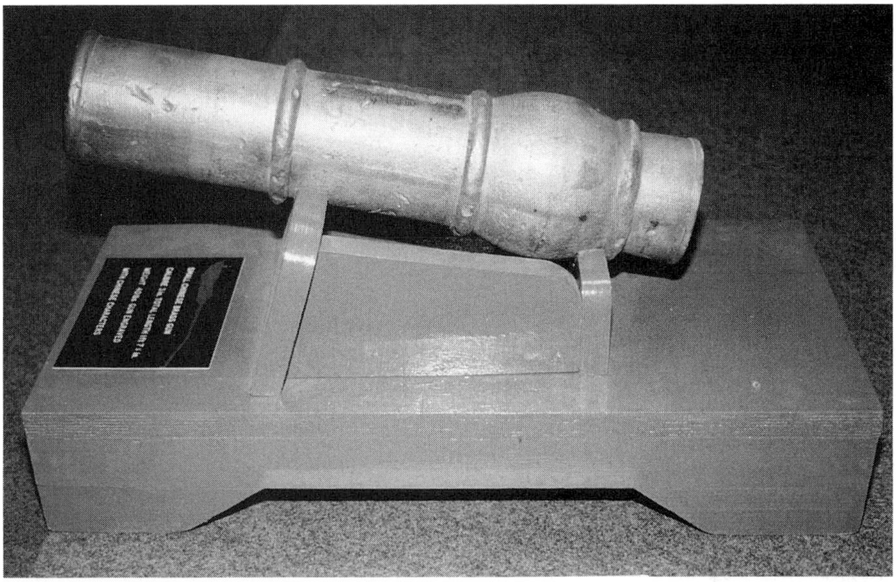

Cast iron and cast bronze cannon barrels; China, 14th–15th centuries. These guns, known as t'ungs, were made during the early Ming period and are virtually identical with the kind of guns being used in Europe and the Middle East at that time. (Museum of Artillery, inv. I/50 & III/261, London)

Archery

The simple bow survived in southern and south-eastern Asia, just as it did in most of Africa. Such weapons earned Indian infantry archers a high reputation in ancient times, but were outclassed by the composite bows used by Muslims. Simple bows were also used by the warriors of Indo-China, south-east Asia and Burma. The Korean bow was of composite construction; longer than that of the Turco-Mongols but shorter than that of the Japanese. Composite bows were known in India but were not really suited to the humid climate unless they were waterproofed with lacquer. The Indian tradition of decorating the loops of bowstrings with gold or tinsel tassels continued from much earlier times, but was considered a nuisance by more serious archers. Other items of archery equipment shed light on the relative importance of archery and the way in which it was used. For example the 10th-century Indian *bhastrā* (quiver) was hung from the shoulder in an archaic manner while many Korean quivers were virtually identical with infantry quivers shown in late 14th- or early 15th-century manuscript illustrations from Iran. Like many Muslim western Asian archers, the Koreans also used *arrow-guides* to shoot arrows midway in length between ordinary arrows and crossbow bolts.

The importance of the hand-held crossbow can hardly be over-estimated in Chinese and Korean warfare. By the 11th century it was considered the strongest weapon in China's armoury and came in several forms, sizes and methods of construction. The largest was said to have a range of 1,160 metres, the ordinary infantry type 500 metres, and the light form used from horseback 330 metres. During the Sung period a multiple-shot crossbow was also used in siege warfare, though it only had an effective range of 200 metres. Multi-bowed or multi-stringed frame-mounted crossbows appear in various pictorial sources, using an inadequately understood system to give greater power to the shot. They were probably the *kong tch'uan nou* (doubled bow), and the '*triple bow*' mentioned in Chinese sources.

Swords and Daggers

Sabres soon predominated in Central Asian warfare, but the straight sword was used more extensively in China. Within Japan the *chokuto* (straight sword) continued in use until the 10th century; early versions of this weapon incorporating hollow-ring pommels like those seen right across the Eurasian steppes as far as Europe. The single-edged Japanese proto-sabre then developed between the 6th and 9th centuries. The straight *khadga* or *asis* sword remained the favoured form in Hindu India long after the Middle Ages, while the *niṣṭriṃśa* may have been a heavier broadsword. The *khadga* and *khanda* may have been synonymous, both terms possibly applying to the distinctive 'waisted' blades which broadened rather than narrowed towards the tip, as seen in Hindu art. Later medieval *khandas* still had some features in common with such early illustrations. Straight broadswords appeared in south-east Asia, these evolving into the straight *sundang* swords of later centuries. Even the distinctive *keris* (dagger) of the Malay peninsula may have been a larger weapon in the 14th century. Another feature which appears in early medieval Chinese art was the hanging of a scabbard behind the right shoulder by foot soldiers; this habit also being seen among foot soldiers in early medieval Middle Eastern art.

The true curved sabre was rare in China, but was used in Korea and in Japan from the late 8th century where its appearance coincided with the adoption of cavalry warfare. From the 10th to mid-16th century some Japanese curved swords were also remarkably long. The most extraordinary sword seen anywhere in the Middle Ages was a reverse-curved weapon, seen in Hindu art, from India and south-east Asia. This may have been the long curved *ili* of early written sources and appears to have been more closely associated with southern rather than northern India. The remarkable lack of references to daggers in Chinese sources must surely reflect the deeply pacifist ethos of traditional Chinese society, whereas the abundance and variety of such weapons in India similarly reflected the high status of the warrior in that culture.

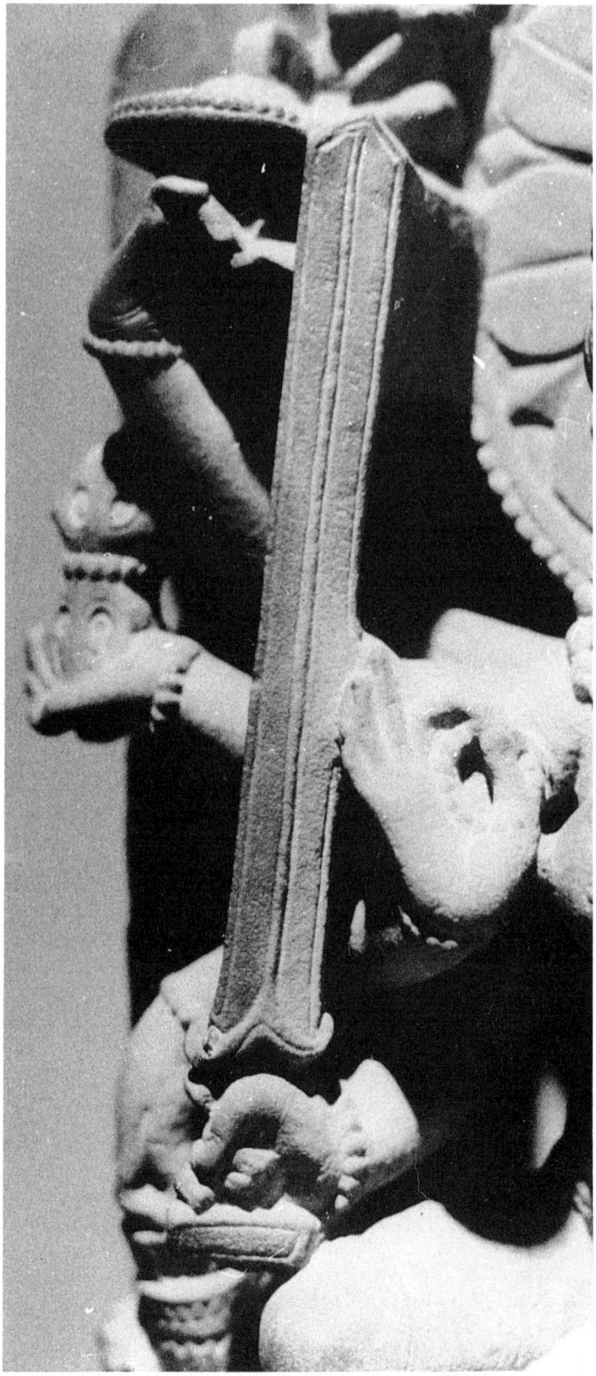

Above: *Sword of the Hindu goddess Durga, on a carving from Madhya Pradesh, India, 8th century. Most of the swords seen in Indian art have this straight but broad-bladed form. Their hilts, however, are of a highly distinctive curved form with langets tongue-like down the blade. (Author's photograph; Brooklyn Museum, inv. 79.254.2, New York)*

Spears and Javelins

Spears and javelins were used almost everywhere; in India being known as *śakti* and *śūla* respectively. In Chinese-influenced areas, however, a greater variety of spears or staff weapons appeared, often being used by horsemen in a manner not seen anywhere else. The Japanese *naginata* was a sort of halberd while in Korea such staff-weapons followed Chinese patterns and included the '*reclining moon spear*' with a curved blade and usually a hook at the back , and the '*cross spear*' with a hook on both sides. *Paraśu* (battleaxes) and *gadā* (maces) appear to have been more popular in India than elsewhere. Here, as in much of the Middle East and Central Asia, the mace had a special association, though in Hindu India this often appears to have been religious rather than concerned with political or military leadership.

Other Weapons

The continued use of a variety of other archaic and exotic weapons in India may again have indicated both the high status of violence in Hindu civilisation and its ritualised character. *Gophaṇa* (slings), for example, were still used in the early medieval centuries. In southern India *throwing-sticks* were used by aboriginal and other peoples, the *vălări kămbi* ('curved stick') being the traditional weapon of the Maravar warrior caste. Unlike the fully developed Australian boomerang, however, these Indian throwing-sticks were not intended to return to the thrower. An even more unusual Indian weapon was the *jah,* a sharpened throwing-disc; itself clearly a sophisticated development of the 'throwing-stone'. Light types of *jah* had a hole in the middle and were thrown horizontally like a quoit; heavier types were dropped vertically upon attackers. Then there was the *nalika,* a blowpipe or blowgun, though this was used in hunting rather than warfare.

Shields

According to 10th-century Muslim Arab writers, Indian leather shields were inferior to those of China, Tibet and the Sudan. Clearly leather was the preferred material for shields in most parts of southern and south-eastern Asia, though in China large wooden infantry mantlets were also used. Otherwise the general lack of shields in illustrations of armoured Chinese cavalry indicates the effectiveness of their armour.

Helmets

The making of helmets and sword-blades demonstrated the advanced metallurgy of China. Low-domed forms were probably made from a single piece of iron and may have been the earliest examples of such protections though armourers from the Middle East have a similar claim. The continued use of scale helmets in China and elsewhere did not reflect technological inferiority but meant that such shock-absorbing protections were effective as well as cheap. Comparable scale helmets appear to have been characteristic of 12th- and 13th-century Vietnamese Champa. Archaeological evidence shows the use of scale or lamellar helmets in north-western India in the pre-medieval period, and written sources hint that the Hindu *śipri* helmet may also have been of scales.

Body Armour

By the 2nd and 3rd centuries AD Chinese armour already included *hei-kuang* (black brilliant), *ming-kuang* (bright brilliant), *liang-tang* (double faced) and *liang-k'ai* (double armour).

Right: *Rear of an iron helmet with silvered decoration, northern China, early to mid-14th century. The helmet may have been made for a member of the Yüan dynasty élite guard or for a senior officer, and originally had a fabric-covered neck-protection attached to the rim. (Royal Armouries Museum, inv. XXVI A-192, Leeds)*

The black or blue-black was probably of decarbonised steel. Various forms of armour were also described as 'stitched', in other words being of scale or lamellar construction. Fabric-covered iron armour was said to have been invented in China in the second half of the 8th century, and a form of scale-lined *coat-of-plates* known as a *k'aii* was credited to Ma Sui, President of China's Board of War in the 790s. Scale-lined armours approximating to the western European *brigandine* continued to be refined and developed by Chinese armourers throughout the medieval period, whereas Chinese writers associated mail armour with Central Asian and Middle Eastern warriors. The Mongols then played a major role in spreading Chinese forms of armour-making across a large part of Asia and Europe, while in India the end of the Middle Ages saw a merging of traditional Indian and Mongol forms of armour. The most distinctive result was the '*coat of a thousand nails*' which combined Sino-Mongol and Indian scale-lined and fabric-covered or padded defences. On the other hand the quality of lamellar armour tended to decrease the farther east it was made, particularly within Chinese-dominated areas. Nevertheless lacquered hardened leather lamellar was typical of some parts of China and of Japan; the lacquering being done for decorative and weatherproofing reasons. Early Japanese armours called *tankō* had been made of iron scales laced or wired together in an almost rigid manner. Lamellar armour was then introduced from the mainland in about the 5th century, being known as *keikō*, but the Japanese only adopted the construction technique, not the shape of Chinese armour, and medieval Japanese armour remained particularly colourful. During the 10th–11th centuries the usual east Asian system of lacing *keikō* (lamellar armours) with leather or cotton thongs was replaced by the use of the more water-resistant plaited or woven silk; this was later taken westwards by the Mongols though not as a result of Japanese influence. The need to weatherproof armour in Japan's humid climate led to the production of remarkable rigid rows of lamellae in which thick lacquer was applied to the lamellae and their lacing, rather undermining the whole point of lamellar armour which had been developed to provide flexibility. Fragments of lamellar armour found in pre-medieval Kushan archaeological contexts in the north of the Hindu Indian cultural sphere show considerable similarity with Parthian armour from the Middle East, though they also provide tantalising hints that early forms of mixed *plate-and-lamellar* armour were already known in this area. Later lamellar armour was rare in northern India and virtually unknown in the south, perhaps again because of the humid local climate. India had the strongest tradition in soft-armour, again for climatic reasons. Much was made of cotton, and India may well have been the source of various forms of quilted soft-armour in the Middle East and thus by extension Europe. By the 12th century India was also manufacturing asbestos cloth, this being used in various kinds of fire-proof clothing.

Limb Defences

Where weapons for the limbs were concerned, China and Korea appear to have been under strong Central Asian influ-

Left: *Ceramic vessel in the form of a cavalryman, from Silla in southern Korea, 6th century. This is one of the earliest known representations of stirrups. (National Museum, Seoul)*
Right: *Ceramic statuette of a cavalryman; T'ang Chinese, 7th–8th centuries. This horseman is fully armoured in typical Chinese style, probably wearing fabric-covered scale armour. His horse is also fully armoured. (Author's photograph; Benaki Museum, no. 32, Athens)*

Left: *Carved slab from a funerary couch, northern China, 550-77. The horsemen seen here are still wearing Central Asian costume and clearly illustrate a ruling dynasty of recent Turco-Mongol origin. As yet they still have no stirrups. (Author's photograph; Museum of Fine Arts, inv. 12.589, Boston)*

Below: *'Scenes from the life of the Buddha', Gandhara, north-west India, 3rd-4th centuries. This carving, depicting an elephant and its mahout, may date from slightly later. (Author's photograph; Museum of Fine Arts, inv. 25.467, Boston)*

ence, though in general neither made much use of specific pieces of armour for the arms or legs, and the few references to such defences in India point to a Persian origin.

Horse Harness

Indian horse-harness was primitive compared to that of its northern and western neighbours, but, although the metallic stirrup was developed on the frontier between settled China and nomadic Central Asia, some form of leather '*toe-stirrups*' had been known in India since the 1st century BC. The appearance of the same sort of looped '*toe-stirrup*' in 8th-century Indo-Chinese art probably reflects Indian influence, at least in terms of artistic style. The first clear illustration of a wood-framed saddle appears on a Chinese carving of 637; this being similar to the framed saddles brought across Central Asia to central Europe at about the same time.

Horse Armour

Chinese chariot horses had worn armour since the 6th century BC, but the earliest Chinese illustrations of cavalry horse-armours do not appear before the 4th–5th centuries AD. The separate elements of such horse armours were the *ma-mien lien* (chamfron), *chi-hsiang* (crinet), *tang-hsiung* (peytral), *ma-shen-chia* (flanchards) and *ma-tou-hou* (crupper). In general, however, horse-armour remained more characteristic of northern than of southern China. The evidence for horse armour in India is extremely sparse, though it is possible that some was used in the early medieval Gupta period.

FORTIFICATION

The Great Wall of China did not exist as a usable piece of military architecture during the Middle Ages. The ancient wall built during the Han and Chin periods was in disrepair and was no longer required because the current Chinese frontier normally lay farther north. Some of China's most significant enemies also lay to the west and south-west - not to the north. In fact the present Great Wall of China largely dates from the 15th century. Instead the defence of the northern and western frontiers rested upon a chain of large fortresses linked by watch-towers. Those farthest from the Chinese heartland were made of layers of earth and brushwood which was easy to build. Within China fortified towns formed the basis of local defence and proved so effective that there was little change in Chinese fortification from the early centuries BC to the large-scale introduction of cannon in the late 14th century. The typical T'ang fortification consisted of an outer earthwork 2 metres high, enclosing an area where troops assembled to make a sortie. An inner citadel could also be used to regroup if the enemy broke through the main wall. During the Sung period the outermost walls were called *yang-ma-ch'eng* 'walls for sheep and horses' because animals evacuated from the surrounding countryside were kept there. In the 12th century these walls were doubled in height, perhaps because of the appearance of counterweight *trebuchets*. Paradoxically it was medieval Korea rather than China that attempted to defend its northern frontier with a '*long wall*'; the Chŏlli Castle, as it was

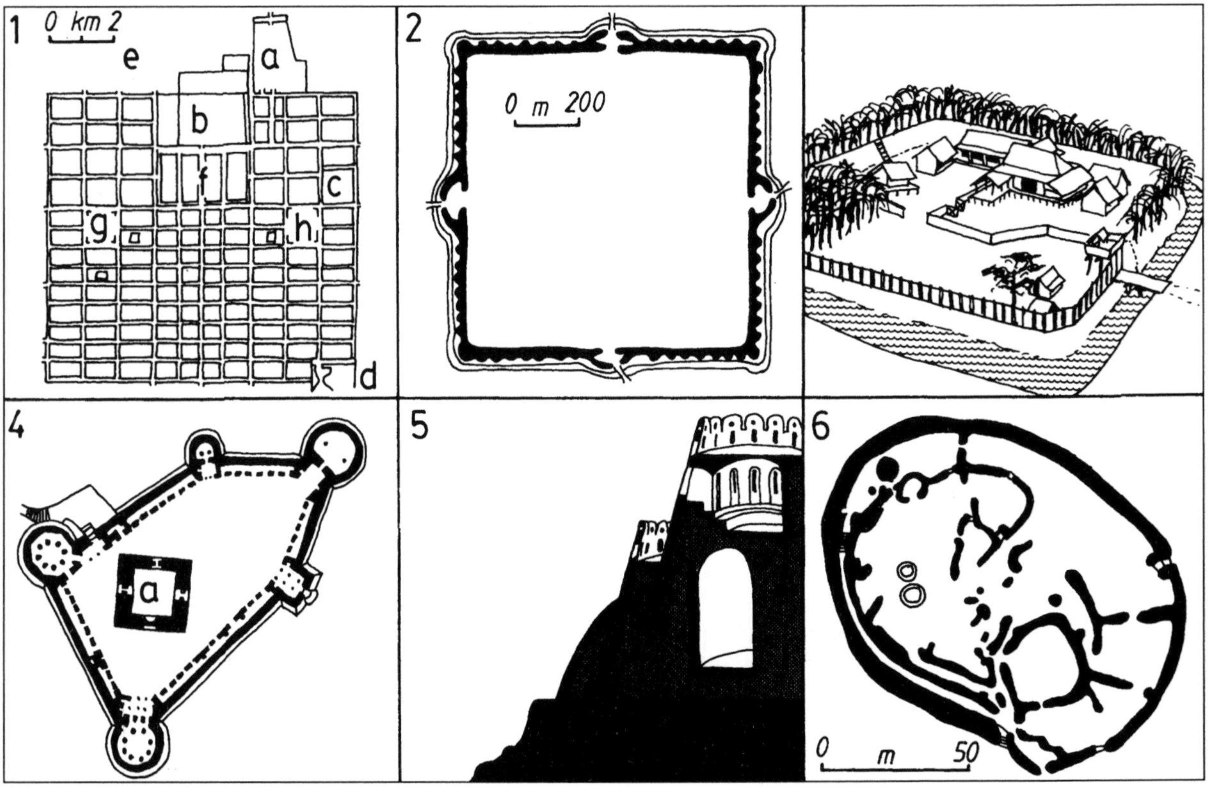

called, was built by the Koryŏ dynasty and stretched from the river Yalu to the eastern coast.

The simple fortifications in south-east Asia were largely made of wood, though a Chinese traveller stated that the yet to be discovered capital of the Malayan Hindu kingdom of Langkasuka had brick walls in the 6th century. Pre-Islamic India, however, was well fortified. Indian defences were characterised by towers which only projected a short distance from the wall, a distinct slope or *batter* on both walls and bastions, and long galleries within the main wall. The most impressive were built of dressed stone over a rubble core, but much of the Indian sub-continent lacked good stone and so brick was used in Sind, Punjab and Bengal, and wood in Kashmir. According to Hiuen Tsang, in 630-45 most Indian towns and villages had inner gates, wide walls of brick or tiles, by which he probably meant unfired and fired bricks, plus towers or additional ramparts of wood or bamboo. Differences only started to appear in Hindu and Muslim military architecture in India during the 11th century. By the late 14th century, however, both sides had begun to use that most distinctive feature of Indian defensive architecture; the ceremonial *chatris* or kiosk erected above the main gate, where a ruler could see and be seen.

SIEGE WARFARE

The Chinese term for a general assault on a fortified place was *fapi* or the '*ant attack*', which hints at the numbers of troops often involved. This, however, was only used when slower methods failed. Chinese armies made great use of wooden palisades and bamboo or thorny obstacles to defend their positions. Chinese siege forces also using multi-decked boats from which sharp-shooters could harass the defenders, or wooden platforms which could be raised or lowered to enable observers to see within enemy fortifications. Some of these elevating platforms were even mounted on carts. Other devices included the extendible '*cloud ladder*', the wheeled '*heaven bridge*', which was essentially a movable siege-tower, and the '*goose carriage*' which also incorporated an extendible platform. Chinese stone-throwing *mangonels* were in some respects less advanced than those of the Muslim world. Nevertheless they played a vital role by shattering the wooden turrets and superstructures of enemy fortifications, or by throwing blazing oil-soaked hemp or cotton and early forms of grenade.

In defence, a commander's first action was the *ch'ing* or evacuation of surrounding villages, then the foot of the defensive wall had to be cleared of all obstacles while no building within range could be as high as the fortified wall itself. Material which an enemy could use to make scaling ladders must be removed, available food supplies brought within the defended area, surrounding water sources polluted. Local manpower was recruited as a militia, and the strongest women were enlisted as a labour corps. Commanders of fortified towns were to enforce strict security within the town, taking particular care of the poor who might otherwise see potential advantage in the looting which followed the capture of a town. Male evacuees from the surrounding countryside were given identity tags and they were not permitted to leave the town without showing them, one gate being reserved for those leaving and another for those entering. Itinerant monks and those women euphemistically known as 'singing girls' were feared as potential spies, and brothels were regarded as havens for enemy agents. Once the enemy arrived he was fought outside the walls, and as a consequence Chinese military architects never developed the idea of concentric or multi-layered defences. But the T'ang and Sung dynasties did develop specialised counter-siege weapons, many of which later appeared in India and the Muslim world. Troops manning the walls

Left: Fortification; Eastern and Southern Asia
1. The city of Changan (now Xi'an), built in about 600, at a time when the Chinese Empire was being recentralised and its administration reformed. Changan was intended as a vast governmental centre with its own residential quarters.
a Ta Ming Palace
b Palace city
c Hsing-Ch'ing Palace
d Serpentine Park
e Forbidden Park
f Administrative City
g western market
h eastern market. (after Gernet)
2. The fortified town at Bali, near Zhaodong in Manchuria, north-eastern China, 10th-13th centuries. Here, on the farthest northern fringes of Chinese civilisation, the local people were under powerful Chinese cultural and military influence. The regularly planned fortresses of the area were probably built by the Chinese garrisons, however. (after Vorobevu)
3. Reconstruction of the fortified stockade and house of a Japanese samurai or professional soldier, 12th-13th centuries. The main house was made of white cedar panelled with translucent paper. (after McMullen)
4. The fortified tomb of Ghiyāth al-Dīn Tughluq, Sultan of Delhi, 1325. It formed a defensive outwork of the main city and was set in an artificial lake. The fortifications are in a mix of Islamic and Hindu traditions which would become typical of Indo-Islamic military architecture. (after Michell)
5. A section through one of the angle-bastions at Tughluqābād, built in 1321-3 by Ghiyāth al-Dīn Tughluq, Sultan of Delhi. The walls consist of a rubble core faced with roughly cut masonry and strengthened by large projecting bastions. Walls and bastions both have external and internal galleries. (after Burton-Page)
6. The huge stone walls at Great Zimbabwe, built by the Shona people in the 13th-14th centuries, were to dignify rather than defend a royal enclosure within the largest city in southern Africa. Most of the structures within this complex were ceremonial or religious. (after Davidson)

used their bows only as the enemy approached. They then dropped pots of lime and other missiles as the enemy tried to scale the wall; only men in the towers being allowed to use bows and crossbows at this stage. Urine and faeces could be collected to be dropped on the enemy. Meanwhile sharpshooters tried to pick off enemy officers. If an assault came at night, lighted bundles would be dropped outside the wall so that the enemy could be seen. During the T'ang period there are references to torches being hung part the way down the wall, just as was done in Muslim Iraq at about the same time.

Stone-throwing *mangonels* played as important a role in defence as in attack, but were placed inside the walls rather than on top of them or the towers, being directed by forward 'artillery observers' on top of the wall. Small changes in the angle of shooting could be made by the pulling-team moving its feet; changes in range by changing the numbers of people pulling the ropes. Large *mangonels* were used for counter-battery work; smaller ones for shooting at enemy personnel including leaders and coolies bringing supplies to men in the front line. The early *mangonel* powered by a team of men or women pulling on ropes was first mentioned in China in 121, and was soon mounted on a wagons when it was known as the *lei shih cchê.* By the 7th century it could shoot a ball weighing 30 kilograms to a distance of 150 metres. Later medieval sources indicate that the small types shot a 1-kilogram ball 50 metres, the largest a 45-kilogram ball to a range of 8 metres; the maximum weight of missile possible with a man-powered Chinese *mangonel* was probably 100 kilograms. The larger version or *ssu-chiao* (four-footed) type was mounted on a trestle or frame; its beam-sling arm sometimes consisting of several lengths of bamboo lashed together. In 1002 the small *shou phao* (single-handed) type was invented for throwing grenades in trench warfare. By the 12th century, though probably also earlier, Chinese *mangonels* were protected from counter-bombardment by sandbags and from fire-arrows by buckets of water. Ropes of both hemp and leather were best because they gave a uniform operation in dry or damp weather. Projectiles were either of clay or stone to uniform sizes, carefully rounded to give maximum range, though clay was better for anti-personnel missiles because it shattered on impact, causing widespread injury. The counterweight *mangonel* or *trebuchet* reached China from the Muslim world in the 12th century and this new 'far-reaching' mangonel, as it was called, soon achieved a range of no less than 350 metres. More advanced was the *hui-hui p'ao* or 'Muslim *mangonel*' which had an adjustable weight on its beamsling to make ranging easier. During the second half of the 14th century, however, all forms of *mangonel* were downgraded in favour of cannon. Walls could in turn be protected from enemy stone-throwing machines by netting made of rice-stalks hung a short distance in front of the wall. These could be raised or lowered by beam-sling devices which could also drop objects on the enemy.

Left: *A bastion on the inner wall of the moat, Dawlatabad Castle in central India, 14th century. Dawlatabad in the Deccan was originally a Hindu fortress, later strengthened by the Muslim Sultans of Delhi. The external box-like machicolations on the wall were a distinctive feature of Indian military architecture. (SOAS photograph)*
Right: *The main gateway of Dawlatabad fortress, central India, 14th century. The architectural decoration is characteristically Indian, but the elephants on each side of the gate are comparable to carvings of other 'heraldic' animals in Middle Eastern castles. (SOAS photograph)*

Right: *The ruins of a watch-tower with the remains of adjoining living quarters and stairs at the western end of the line of Chinese frontier defences across Tun-Huang. Wind-erosion has exposed the construction technique of layers of horizontal reeds and clay. Such fortifications had little in common with the famous Great Wall of China which, in fact, did not exist during the Middle Ages. (A. Stein photograph)*

Above: *Fortified magazine or arsenal on the line of Chinese frontier defences across Tun-Huang, probably from the T'ang period. This frontier zone formed a strategic corridor linking China with its western outposts and vassals in Sinkiang. (A. Stein photograph)*

Sources dating from slightly later than the period under consideration would probably also have applied to the earlier period. These state that the day was divided into three 8-hour, or two 12-hour watches. The poor were not expected to man the walls because they had to work in order to live, but militia units were allocated specific stretches of wall, though most important sections were the responsibility of professional soldiers. Each section of five battlements was defended by a *'fiver group'* under a chief; a *wall chief* being in charge of 25 battlements and so on up to garrison commander. Latrines were always placed at the base of the walls, with very strict rules on how and when they could be used. Those manning the walls also had designated mealtimes, food being cooked at the base of the wall. A rattle would sound to announce that the food was being sent up the wall by rope. Chinese counter-miners used a form of noxious choking smoke to clear enemy tunnels, and tried to protect themselves from the same threat with leather screens. Above ground the T'ang period saw the development of some extraordinary defensive devices; for example the *'thunder stick'* which was a heavy log covered in spikes to roll down upon enemy troops attempting to climb the base of a wall. By the Sung period these were made of clay rather than wood, and a wheeled version with ropes could be dragged back by a windlass and used again.

Compared with Chinese siege warfare, that seen in south-eastern Asia was extremely primitive. Burmese forces could not even deal with larger wooden stockades in the early 12th century, but in India siege, counter-siege and associated engineering were very developed. Scaling ladders were the normal means of direct assault, these being secured to mud-brick walls with iron pegs. Indian armies also used elephants with protective iron plates on the front of the head as living battering-rams against gates. Other devices included the *pāshtīb* or raised platform of sand-bags to fill a defensive ditch or the space between concentric walls, and the *gargaj* which was the Indian version of a movable wooden siege-tower. The spiked objects rolled down upon an attacker sound the same as Chinese *'thunder sticks'*, and very long spears used to defend gates from elephant 'battering-rams' were probably a local development. Indian references to the use of fire and smoke to defend fortresses sometimes sound so devastating that they recall the weapons used by gods and heroes in Hindu religious epics rather than the reality of medieval warfare. Behind such exaggeration, however, were genuinely sophisticated forms of fire, smoke and even heated iron grills, which even the most determined enemy could not open.

NAVAL WARFARE

The Indian Ocean and western part of the Pacific Ocean may have been peaceful compared to the Mediterranean, but this did not stifle technological development. Many of the most important improvements in ship design began in the Far East and then spread westward via trading links rather than naval campaigns. For example the hinged stern rudder had been known in China since at least the 1st century BC. A middle sized 13th-century ship excavated near the major medieval

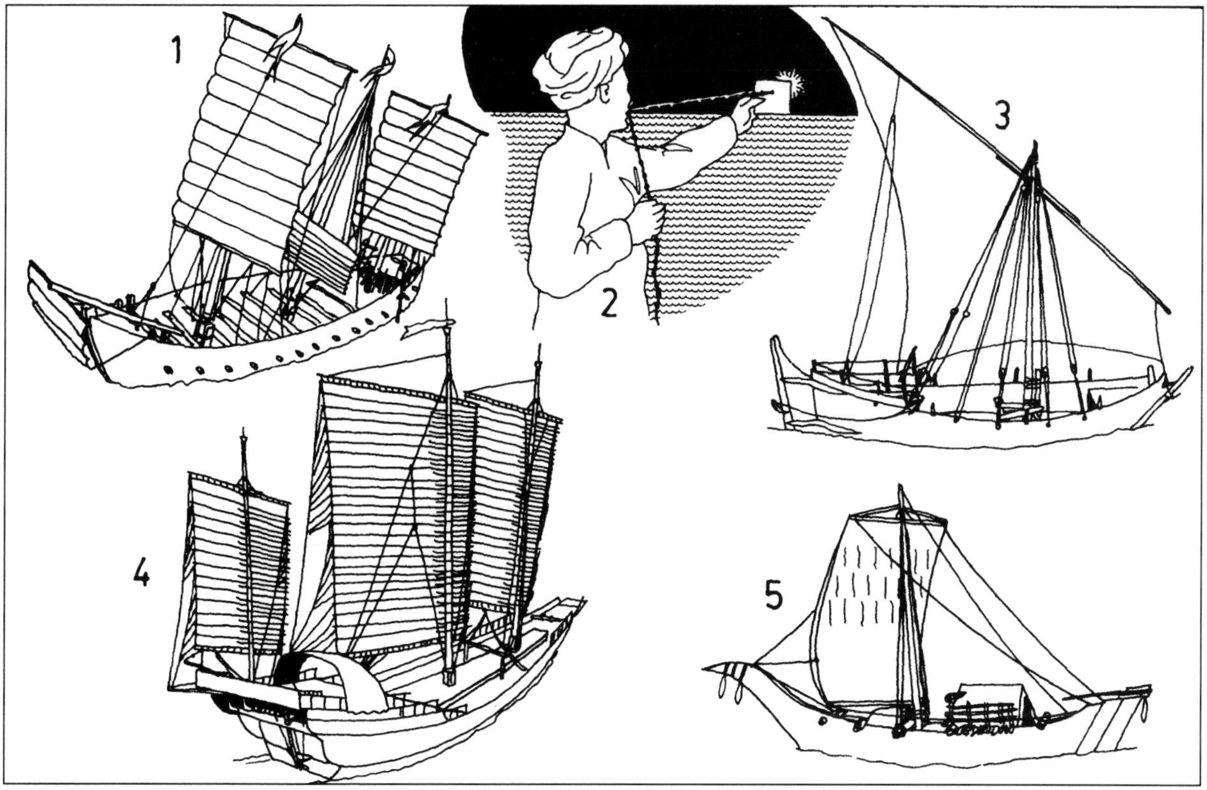

Shipping in the Eastern Seas
1. Reconstruction of a Chola ship from southern India, 6th–10th centuries. With sails of bamboo and hulls of teak sewn together with coconut fibre, these strong but flexible vessels sailed as far as Arabia in the west and Indonesia in the east. (after Bayly)
2. The kamal was an early form of sextant used by medieval Arab seamen to determine the height of the pole-star from the horizon and thus calculate their latitude. The number of knots from the square piece of wood to the man's mouth or nose gave the star's position. (after al-Hassan and Hill)
3. Reconstruction of an Omani ocean-going vessel with the hinged stern rudder adopted as a result of Chinese influence, perhaps in the 10th century, but certainly before the 13th century. Like the ships of southern India it had a sewn rather than nailed hull, but also made use of the more efficient lateen sail. (after Facey)
4. Reconstruction of a 13th-century Chinese ocean-going junk based upon a wreck excavated at Quanzou. The most sophisticated ship-builders of the eastern oceans were undoubtedly the Chinese, who invented the hinged stern rudder and hulls having several water-tight compartments. (after Green)
5. A 14th-16th-century mtepe of the east African coast. Like the culture of the coast itself, this vessel was a mix of local African and Muslim-Arab traditions. The sewn construction of its hull was like that of an Arab dhow but the square-rigged raffia sail and distinctive prow were African. (after Davidson)

port of Zaitun (now Quanzhou) in southern China, even had its hull divided into thirteen watertight compartments. Its cargo came from what is now Indonesia, which at the time was in close touch with both India and the Middle East, so the precise origin of this ship is uncertain. From the 8th century onwards the triangular lateen sail may have been introduced by Arab traders from the west, but it was equally possible that it may have come from Polynesia.

During the outward-looking T'ang period many Chinese ships had stone-throwing artillery and most marines were armed with crossbows. By the 14th century gunpowder cannon and gunpowder were being used in naval warfare. Cannon-armed Korean ships, in fact, proved particularly effective against the persistent menace of Japanese piracy. Less is known about the ships of south-east Asia, though 12th-century Chinese records state that Khmer *junk*-type vessels had the same capacity as those from China. Khmer carvings illustrate two distinct types of ship; one is an angular, ocean-going *junk*, the other seems to be a very large curved war-canoe. Sources from both east and west describe Malay sailors as far-ranging and courageous, but give no information about their ships. Malaya did, however, become a major centre of piracy in the

'Dragon Boat Race', painting on silk by Wu T'ing-huei, China, late-13th–early 14th centuries. The painting was executed at the time of the Mongol Yüan dynasty and shows the highly developed river craft which made China's many rivers and canals into a sophisticated communications network. (National Palace Museum, no. YV-113, Taiwan)

13th and 14th centuries. Meanwhile, in the 12th century the Arakanese of the western coast of Burma were regarded as superb mariners.

Riverine warfare was another area in which the Chinese were able to use their advanced technology. In 1222, for example, the Sung attempted to relieve the Mongol siege of Fanchhêng with a squadron of man-powered paddle-wheelers. Rivers were of paramount importance for communication and military transport; particularly rivers like the Huang-ho which linked the northern Chinese heartland with the northern steppe frontier. Rivers were even more important in southern China and in fact riverine warfare almost always formed part of internal Chinese conflicts. The Poyang campaign of 1363, for example, saw one river fleet trying to intercept and destroy another, culminating in a major 'sea battle' on a lake. Some of the ships used in this Poyang campaign had three decks and an average of 100 men per vessel. The upper deck had awnings for the horses being transported, and each of the oars on the lower decks was pulled by five men. Archers protected by wooden boards or palisades gave covering fire, others apparently shot from iron reinforced towers on the upper deck. During the final battle both fleets at first fought in close-packed formations, using archery, stone and incendiary materials and concluding with boarding the enemy ships. Small fire-boats rather than fire-ships were clearly filled with gunpowder as well as dummy crews made of straw.

The limited evidence from Indo-China indicates that war canoes largely fought with archery. Riverine warfare also played a major role in medieval Burma where again it was dominated by archery. By the late 14th century some fleets on the Irrawaddy consisted of hundreds of war-canoes capable of bringing enough troops to assault a major enemy stockade. In India, however, the only really large rivers were in the north, but here the surrounding open terrain lent itself to wide-ranging campaigns so there was little reason to fight on water.

VI
BIOGRAPHIES

BIOGRAPHIES

Abu'l-Ṭayyib al-Ju'fī al-Mutannabī 213
Alexander Nevski 213
Amde-Siyon I 213
Bahrām 213
Chingiz Khān 213
David IV Aghmashenebeli 215
Dhū Nuwās 215
El Cid 215
Evrenos Beg 215
Heraclius 215
Ibn Abī 'Āmir al-Manṣūr 215
James I 217
John Cantacuzenus 217
Khālid Ibn al-Walīd 217
Khaydār al-Afshīn ʿAbbāsid 217
Khusrū I 217
Li Shih-min 217
Mansa Mūsā 218
Nicephoros II Phocas 218
Rājarāja I The Great 218
Samuel Ha-Nagid 219
Tancred 219
Usāma Ibn Munqidh 219
Yūsuf Ibn Tāshufīn 220

In medieval Europe political and military leadership tended to be synonymous until the later 14th century. The same was true in Central Asia, Africa and to a large extent Hindu India. The only major exceptions were the Muslim world where political rule was theoretically identified with religious leadership, and China where direct involvement in military affairs ran counter to the ideal of the 'harmonious ruler'. Even in the Muslim world there was a tendency for military and tribal leaders to become rulers in reality whereas in China military activity remained a distasteful necessity which rulers should avoid.

Abu'l-Ṭayyib al-Ju'fī al-Mutannabī (Court poet in Aleppo 948–57, died 965)
He came from a poor family in southern Iraq, but soon showed talent as a poet. As a young man he became involved in a rebellion in northern Syria and was imprisoned. These events gave him his nickname of al-Mutannabī or 'the one who claims to be a prophet'. After his release he continued to search for a patron, got into trouble and fled into the desert before finding a secure position under the ruler of Aleppo, Sayf al-Dawla, in 948. He was also a warrior and fought at Sayf al-Dawla's side in many campaigns against the Byzantines but again made powerful enemies and had to flee. After various adventures al-Mutannabī ended up in Persia but got homesick and was killed by bandits on his way back to Iraq. Al-Mutannabī's verses express the pride that 10th-century Arabs felt in their civilisation. His writings also shed considerable light on the technical details of 10th-century warfare, describing defeat as well as victory with remarkable honesty. According to one account of a battle by a rival poet: 'Al-Mutanabbi was riding his horse and the branches of the trees were snatching at his turban. As his horse ran, his turban unravelled so that he thought the Byzantines were clutching at him. So he shouted, "I surrender!"'

Alexander Nevski (Grand Prince of Vladimir, 1252–63)
Son of Grand Prince Yaroslav of Vladimir, Alexander became Prince of Novgorod in 1236 but quarrelled with the citizens and left in 1240, the year in which he defeated the Swedes at the river Neva and won the name Nevski. His most famous victory was against the Teutonic Knights on the frozen Lake Peipus in 1242. He was a realist as well as a good military commander and realised that resistance to the Mongols was hopeless. Instead he co-operated with them and in 1252 was made Grand Prince of Vladimir as his reward. This made him the senior Prince and titular ruler of Russia under Mongol suzerainty. The tactics used at Lake Peipus suggest that he had already learned much from the Mongols. He is regarded as having saved Russia from even greater Mongol oppression. Such efforts resulted in his being canonised as a Saint of the Orthodox Russian Church.

Amde-Siyon I (King of Ethiopia, 1314–44)
As a young man Amde-Siyon had been criticised by the Church for sexual immorality, but later he developed into a fine statesman and an effective military leader. Before his reign there had been a largely peaceful military balance between Christian Ethiopia and its Muslim neighbours, but he overturned this situation and made Ethiopia the dominant regional power, which it remained until the 16th century. Amde-Siyon overran the Damot and Hadya areas in 1316–17 and then annexed the Falasha Ethiopian Jewish homeland north of Lake Tana. This expansion gave the Ethiopian ruler a huge pool of military manpower which he then used against eastern neighbours, winning control over trade routes to the Gulf of Aden and imposing Ethiopian suzerainty over several Muslim states. By the end of his reign he was ruling a vast territory, but was confronted by frequent revolts in both Muslim and Christian areas. According to a legend reported by the Arab geographer al-'Umarī: 'It is said he has ninety-nine kings under him and that he makes up the hundred.' Amde-Siyon led by example, his extraordinary personal courage being celebrated in The Chronicle of the Wars of Amde-Siyon I, a classic of Ethiopian literature.

Bahrām (*Vizier* of Egypt, 1135–7)
Bahrām or Vahram was the last in a series of Armenian Chief Ministers of the Fāṭimid dynasty of Caliphs in Egypt who had virtually ruled the country since 1074, the Caliphs themselves being mere figureheads. He was unusual in remaining Christian, previous Armenian Viziers having converted to Islam. Bahrām is said to have been an Armenian nobleman from Tall Bā<u>sh</u>ir in northern Syria and was the brother of the most senior Armenian churchman in Egypt. He commanded a powerful Armenian regiment of the Fāṭimid army which was summoned to suppress a military revolt in Cairo. In 1135 he was made *Vizier of the Sword* and given the Muslim titles of *Sayf al-Islām* (Sword of Islam) and *Tāj al-Dawla* (Crown of Religion). He pursued a peaceful policy towards his aggressive Crusader neighbours in Palestine and concentrated on restoring Egypt's shaky financial position. But this led to accusations of personal aggrandisement and to a violent anti-Armenian reaction. He died in 1140 and was buried in a monastery near Cairo, the Caliph himself joining the funeral cortège.

<u>Ch</u>ingiz <u>Kh</u>ān (Great <u>Kh</u>ān of the Mongols, 1206–27)
Temüchin, as he was originally named, became leader of an insignificant Mongol tribe but overcame all rivals to become ruler of the entire Mongol people. He adopted the name <u>Ch</u>ingiz <u>Kh</u>ān (Universal Ruler) and set out on a career of conquest which eventually covered all of Central Asia, northern China and Muslim Transoxiana. He was one of the most effective military leaders in history, imposing a previously unknown discipline on the Mongol tribes to create an army capable of continuing Mongol conquests long after its founder died. Unlike those of most previous Central Asian conquerors, his empire did not fragment with his death. He remained a Central Asian plunderer at heart, expressing his belief that: 'The greatest happiness is to defeat your enemies, to chase them before you, to rob them of their wealth, to see those dear to them bathed in tears, to clasp to your bosom their wives and daughters.'

Left: 'Genghiz Khan in old age', in a series of idealised portraits of Chinese rulers painted many decades after his death. The old warrior is still depicted in typical Mongol costume with his hair in looped plaits. (National Palace Museum, inv. N-71-a, Taiwan)

David IV Aghmashenebeli (King of Georgia, 1089–1125)
David came to the throne of the Christian kingdom of Georgia at the age of sixteen. His predecessor's reign had witnessed a series of defeats by the Saljūq Turks as well as rebellions by powerful Georgian lords. But King David threw off his Turkish allegiance in 1096 and took Muslim Tibilisi with little difficulty in 1122. Realising that Georgia remained a Christian island surrounded by powerful Turco-Muslim states, he offered an amnesty to the people of Tibilisi. According to the Arab chronicler Ibn al-Azraq: 'he soothed their hearts ... and left them alone, in all goodness'. He was an outstanding military leader, earned the title of 'The Builder' and is credited with raising a force of élite cavalry loyal only to him. He recruited many largely pagan Qipchaq Turks from the northern steppes and a smaller number of European mercenaries from the Crusader States. By the end of his reign David IV had expanded Georgia's borders to include large stretches of the Black Sea and Caspian coasts. His work was continued by Tamara, a warrior queen whose exploits entered Muslim as well as Georgian legend.

Dhū Nuwās (King of Yemen, c.523–5)
The ancient monarchy of Yemen had declined during the 4th and 5th centuries, but the country retained considerable military potential. There was also a growing Christian population, particularly in Najran. Dhū Nuwās was probably the son of the previous king Ma'dīkarib, and a Jewish mother from Iraq. He converted to Judaism, his full name being Yūsuf Ash'ar Yath'ar Dhū Nuwās. In 523 and 524 he fought several campaigns to re-establish royal control over the country. Byzantium encouraged Christian Axum in Ethiopia to attack Yemen with the help of Byzantine transport ships. Although Dhū Nuwās defeated the first Ethiopian invasion, he was himself defeated in 525 near the Yemeni coast. His story was thought to be legendary until a number of inscriptions were found recently, indicating that the struggle against the Ethiopians involved hard fighting. One of them reads: 'May God of heaven and earth assist him in vanquishing all his enemies; may this inscription be preserved from the hands of the wicked and those who devise evil by the protection of the Evil One.' His ambition may have been to establish a powerful Semitic state in western Arabia stretching from the Jewish communities of the Syrian border through the Jewish-Arab tribes of the north Hijaz to a Yemen now ruled by a Jewish king.

El Cid (Prince of Valencia, 1094–9)
Rodrigo Díaz de Bivar el Campeador was known as 'my Cid' (Arabic Sa'id; master). He earned his initial military reputation as one of those champions who traditionally fought duels between the ranks of opposing Iberian armies. Although essentially a mercenary who fought for both Christian and Muslim rulers, he became a national hero. His life is surrounded by heroic and pious legends but in practical terms his main achievement was to give the leadership of the Reconquista to Castile through his victories on behalf of King Sancho II. El Cid was apparently obsessed with the idea of a unified Spain and developed into a truly Spanish national leader when fighting for the kingdom of Aragon. His short-lived conquest of Muslim Valencia was of minor military significance, but became an example for others to follow.

Evrenos Beg (Ottoman Commander, 1362–c.1402, died 1417)
Known as Ghāzī Evrenos, he is said to have been a Byzantine Greek nobleman in the service of the Turkish *Beg* of Karāsī. He entered Ottoman service after Karāsī was taken over in 1335. He was put in command of the left or western 'march' of the Ottoman frontier in Europe, capturing Komotini in 1371, western Thrace and part of Macedonia by 1375, and sent raiding-parties as far as Albania. During the last years of his long military career he campaigned in the southern tip of Greece. His tomb at Yenitsa in northern Greece has an inscription describing him as: 'The martyr, king of the *Ghāzīs* and fighters of the *Jihād*'. He also built a variety of Islamic religious and charitable structures ranging from mosques and colleges to public baths and soup-kitchens for the poor.

Heraclius (East Roman-Byzantine Emperor, 610–41)
Heraclius came from a family of Armenian origin and seized the throne when the Romano-Byzantine Empire was in desperate straits. Much of the east was occupied by the Sassanians and the Empire's armies scattered. He then fought a six-year war against the Sassanians which was portrayed as a struggle between Christianity and Mazdaism. He also encouraged the persecution of Jews because they were suspected of being pro-Persian and he made considerable use of religion to motivate his own troops. Heraclius may even have re-invented the True Cross Legend for political purposes. At the same time he tried to develop a compromise doctine in a vain effort to bring together bitterly divided Christian sects. But by the end of his reign most of his work had been overthrown. Romano-Greek civilisation was in retreat in the Middle East where Semitic peoples were reclaiming their inheritance, Islam was a rising power and as some historians have put it: 'a thousand years of history had been undone'. Nevertheless he is credited with the military reforms that laid the foundations of the medieval Byzantine army.

Ibn Abî 'Āmir al-Manṣūr (*Vizier* of the Umayyad Caliphate of Cordoba, 978–1002)
Ḥe was a law student in Cordoba who claimed descent from one of the first Arab conquerors of Spain. He began his career as a professional letter-writer at court and became a favourite of the Caliph's mother. His subsequent political and military rise illustrates what talent plus courage and ruthlessness could achieve in the fluid social conditions of Muslim Andalu-

***Left:** 'Israelite soldiers' on a collection of silver plates illustrating the story of David and Goliath, found in Cyprus; Byzantine, 613–29. They were made for the Emperor Heraclius to celebrate his victory over the Sassanian Iranians. The soldier's armour is in an archaic Roman style which was probably only worn on ceremonial occasions. But the man in front clearly has something, probably a helmet, beneath his elaborate feathered hood. (Author's photograph; Metropolitan Museum of Art, New York)*

sia. He was appointed leader of an army despite having no military experience, yet immediately proved himself to be an effective commander, soon becoming popular both with the army and the general public. In 978 he became the military dictator of al-Andalus with the Caliph as a puppet. In 981 he adopted the title al-Manṣūr bi'llāh ('The Victorious through God'), and the fear this name aroused among the Christians was such that when he died an anonymous northern monk added the following stark sentence to his chronicle: 'In 1002 died Almanzor, and was buried in hell.'

Igor Syvatoslavich (Prince of Novgorod-Severskiy, 1178–1202) He was a Russian warrior prince and second-ranking ruler within the state of Chernigov. In 1185 he led an army consisting of the retinues of several sub-princes against the Qipchaq Turks, intending to conquer Tümän Tarqan at the mouth of the river Don which had been lost by his father some thirty years earlier. But this Russian force was defeated and Igor was captured. He escaped in 1186 and returned to continue ruling as prince, becoming the senior ruler of Chernigov in 1198. In reality Igor was not a successful military leader and was often in alliance with the Qipchaqs against Russian rivals. Nevertheless his adventures with them ensured that he became the archetypal Russian hero battling against the nomads. The Tale of the Raid of Igor described the courage of Russian troops and the huge distances they covered: 'Oh warrior, nightingale of the times of old! If you were to praise these soldiers while hopping, nightingale, over the tree of thought, flying in mind up to the clouds, weaving praises around those times, rowing the Trojan trail (the river Don), across steppes and into mountain ranges ...'

James I (King of Aragon, 1214–76)
James was born in France but came to the throne at a time when Aragonese influence in southern France had been broken. The crown of Aragon was also virtually penniless. Unlike some neighbouring monarchs, he did not have his own territorial power-base because the country was controlled by a dozen great feudal families. His conquest of the Muslim Balearic Islands was carried out by feudal and urban forces but resulted in a strengthening of the king's finances. It also earned him the name of 'James the Conqueror', enabling him to enlist volunteers from England, France, Italy and Hungary. King James renounced his French territories in 1258, ensuring that Aragonese attentions would be focused southwards during the remainder of the Spanish Reconqista. James the Conqueror is also remembered for his formulation of maritime law and for establishing a parliamentary assembly.

John Cantacuzenus (Byzantine Emperor, 1347–54)
He was a rich magnate who purchased the governorship of Thrace then took part in Byzantine civil wars of the early 14th century, rising to become commander-in-chief of the army under Emperor Andronikos III. He soon became the effective, if not yet official, ruler. He was the most astute political operator in a time of tangled intrigues. In addition he was an effective soldier but, being a military as well as a political realist, he urged the Emperor to accept a treaty in 1333 which obliged Byzantium to pay tribute to the Ottoman Sultan. He also relied on Ottoman support when he had himself crowned Emperor following another civil war, but he appeared selfless in attempting to save the Byzantine Empire, putting his own considerable fortune behind efforts to pay enormous arrears in the soldiers' salaries.

Khālid Ibn al-Walīd (Muslim Commander, 633–42)
He has been called one of the tactical geniuses of the early medieval period, yet his nickname, 'The Sword of God', implies that he was merely a weapon to be wielded by greater men. He headed an important clan in Mecca and converted to Islam in about 627, becoming the leading Muslim general before campaigning successfully in Iraq, Syria and Iran against both the Sassanian and Byzantine Empires. His epic march across virtually waterless desert from Iraq to Syria to attack the Byzantines from the rear caught the imagination of most chroniclers. His greatest victory came at Yàrmūk where he was probably the real military leader under the nominal command of others. He is credited with organising the first separate Muslim cavalry force. He may also have developed the system whereby light taxes were imposed on conquered peoples to pay an essentially full-time Muslim-Arab army. In character he was impulsive, sometimes ignoring directives from the Caliph, particularly if the latter were from a lesser Arabian clan – which suggests that Khālid still had a foot in the pre-Islamic past. He died in 642 and was buried at Ḥimṣ in central Syria.

Khaydār al-Afshīn (ᶜAbbāsid Commander-in-Chief, c.836–9)
He came from the mountains of eastern Transoxiana and was the son of the last Turkish prince of Ushrūsana. He was recruited by al-Mu'taṣim before the latter became Caliph, becoming governor of eastern Libya and crushing an Egyptian revolt in 831. When al-Mu'taṣim became Caliph, Khaydār al-Afshīn was put in command of the army that was sent on a two-year campaign to crush rebels who had long defied the ᶜAbbāsid Caliph, being selected because he was an expert in mountain warfare. He was known for restraining the enthusiasm of impatient subordinates and for success in 'turning around' defeated foes. Later he was accused of wanting to bring back the pre-Islamic Zoroastrian religion and was starved to death in prison. An inquiry had shown that many of the Caliph's new Transoxianan troops were only nominally Muslim.

Khusrū I (Sassanian Emperor, 531–79)
He was responsible for re-structuring the Sassanian army, though this had been started by his predecessors. He was also remembered as a great reformer and military leader. He had to defeat a major rebellion by those with a vested interest in the old military system, and fought many wars against the Byzantine Empire. He is also credited with bringing the game of chess from India. He studied philosophy as a young man and had the works of Plato and Aristotle translated into Persian. His reputation as a 'philosopher-warrior-king', though exaggerated in later centuries, survived throughout the Middle Ages when he was regarded as an ideal ruler by Persians, Arabs and Turks.

Li Shih-min (Emperor of China, 627–49)
He was the true founder of the T'ang dynasty. He came from a northern Chinese aristocratic family, though his grandmother was non-Chinese. As a young officer, he had gained a reputation even before his timid father, Li Yüan, became Emperor in 618 following a rebellion in which Li Shih-min himself was the driving force. Since he was not the eldest son, he was not named as heir, but he made his claim nevertheless. After a civil war he executed his brothers, forced his father to abdicate and took the throne with the Imperial name of T'ai Tsung. He was brave and energetic, and fully understood the importance of cavalry in Central Asian warfare. Under his father and during his own reign, he took the war against the Turks and Tanguses of the northern and eastern frontiers deep into enemy territory, personally refusing to have the defensive Great Wall of China rebuilt. His ability to win the loyalty of subordinates, his scholarship and his skill as an administrator were, in fact, more highly regarded in China than his success

Right: *Ceramic statuette of a soldier; T'ang China, 7th-9th centuries. The decorated helmet and armour of this figure suggests that he was an officer. (Nelson-Atkins Museum of Art, inv. 34-214/1, Kansas City)*

as a military commander. In religious terms he summed up his own tolerant attitude in an edict issued in 635, which began: 'The Way has more than one name. There is more than one Sage. Doctrines vary in different lands, but their benefits reach all mankind.'

Mansa Mūsā (King of Mali, 1312-37)
Mansa, or 'King' Mūsā was the most famous ruler of the Muslim West African Empire of Mali. In the early 14th century his immediate predecessors expanded into the Sahara and along the river Niger. Mali's control of the West African gold trade made him one of the richest rulers in the known world. In addition he made Mali's army into an amalgam of indigenous sub-Saharan and newly introduced Muslim military traditions. This enabled him to consolidate the ruler's authority then expand Mali's frontiers southward into the tropical rain forests and westward to the Atlantic coast. He was also a patron of learning and encouraged the introduction of various new technologies from the Middle East. His famous *Haj* or Pilgrimage to Mecca took him through Cairo where his thousands of followers, carrying huge amounts of gold, greatly impressed the inhabitants.

Nicephoros II Phocas (Byzantine Emperor, 963-9)
He came from a famous military family and earned his reputation as military governor of the Anatolikon frontier *theme.* He was described as cool and fearless in battle, of great physical strength, considerate to his own soldiers but living an almost monastic life dedicated to the army. His relaxation seems to have consisted of religious debate with Christian holy men. He was physically ugly and made many political enemies. One of these, Bishop Liudprand of Cremona, described him as: 'A monstrosity of a man, a dwarf with a broad flat head and tiny eyes like a mole ... disgraced by a neck scarcely an inch long ... in colour like an Ethiopian; as the poet says, you would not like to meet him in the dark'. He was credited with writing a book on tactics which laid a new emphasis on armoured cavalry. He had little political or diplomatic talent and was eventually murdered by his own nephew who had been let into the Emperor's bed-chamber by the Empress herself.

Rājarāja I The Great (King of the Cholas, 985-1014)
Originally named Arumoli, this Chola king took the ruling title of Rājarāja I. He revived Chola power in the south of India after the region had suffered devastating invasions by the neighbouring Rashtrakuta Empire of the Deccan. He defeated an alliance of Kerala, Sri Lanka and the Pandyas in addition to conquering a large part of what is now Mysore in about 1000. He and his successor were dedicated Hindus, savagely persecuting the Jain religion which also flourished in this area. He

attempted to seize control of the rich maritime trade of the Indian Ocean by occupying the Andaman and Nicobar Islands, launching a naval assault on the Maldive Islands and invading Sri Lanka. He established a stable and powerful Hindu kingdom at a time when the lesser Hindu states of the north were reeling before repeated Muslim attacks.

Samuel Ha-Nagid (Commander of the Army of Granada, 1038–1055/6)
He was the Jewish Chief Minister and army commander of the Muslim ruler of Granada. He was also a rabbi, but was best known as a poet. Born in Córdoba in 993, he believed himself to be descended from the Biblical King David. His family moved to Malaga and there Samuel opened a spice shop before being recruited as a private secretary to the *Vizier* of the King of Granada. On his death-bed the *Vizier* recommended that Samuel become the new Vizier. From then on he was known as *Nagid* or 'Prince' by his fellow Andalusian Jews. Except for two years of peace, the rest of his career was involved in wars. His greatest victory was against the rival Muslim kingdom of Seville in 1039, which he celebrated in a poem about the enemy army: 'All put on their swords in that day of anger, and stripped of their cloaks to join battle, running to the slaughter in good heart and in joy.' He is credited with introducing battle poetry into medieval Hebrew literature. He died on campaign in 1055/6.

Tancred (Prince of Galilee, 1099–1112)
Tancred probably had an understanding of Muslim peoples from his childhood in Norman southern Italy. Like other Siculo-Norman commanders, he seems to have been relatively successful in getting his troops to Syria in a fit state to fight. He subsequently conquered much of northern Palestine to become Prince of Galilee, then campaigned in other parts of Syria and southern Anatolia where he showed himself effective in command of siege operations. He could also be unscrupulous and ruthless, as when a Kurdish prisoner was partially blinded before release so that he could no long serve as a soldier. Tancred's prestige, administrative abilities and military experience made him Regent of the Principality of Antioch (1100–3) and of Edessa (1104) when their rulers were captured by the enemy. He died at the age of thirty-six, probably of typhoid though there were rumours of poison.

Usāma Ibn Munqidh (Arab soldier and scholar, died 1188)
Soldier, diplomat, poet and author of books of good advice, he is best known for an autobiography. This gives an unrivalled insight into Muslim warfare during the 12th century. His own

Right: *Panel from a carved ivory box made for ᶜAbd al-Malik al-Muẓaffar; Andalusian, 1005. The horsemen are unarmoured and probably represent cavalry training. Their use of spurs, however, betrays western European influence on Muslim Andalusian riding styles, as spurs were rarely used in the Middle East. (Cathedral Treasury, Pamplona)*

***Left:** Guards attending the Emperor Anushirvan', in a manuscript compiled by Junayd al-Sultani in 1396, probably in Baghdad. Although they represent ancient Sassanians, they are dressed and equipped in the manner of Tīmūr-i Lank's guardsmen. (Three Romances by Khwaju Kirmani, British Library, MS. Add. 18113, London)*

verses are not of the highest rank, but they reflect the attitudes of the Muslim military élite: 'When the knights of war lower their thrusting lances, the eagles swoop down with them' and 'He [the enemy] fled, ducking our random arrows and deafened by the crashing of our swords.' Usāma was born into an aristocratic Arab family, the Banū Munqidh who had ruled the little fortress city of Shayzar in central Syria since about 1025. As a youth he was involved in warfare against Crusaders and rival Muslim rulers. After quarrelling with his uncle, he served as an officer in the Fāṭimid Egyptian army as well as that of Nūr al-Dīn in Syria and Iraq. He retired to write his memoirs but was summoned back to Syria by Ṣalāh al-Dīn. The final years of his life were spent as a teacher of literary style in Damascus.

Yūsuf Ibn Tāshufīn (Murābiṭ ruler, 1087–1106)
The Murābiṭin movement was founded by ᶜAbd-Allāh Ibn Yasin, a North African religious teacher brought to the western Sahara by a Berber chief returning from pilgrimage. Yūsuf Ibn Tāshufīn took over leadership of this movement following the death of its first political leader. He had already been invited by the Muslim king of Seville to come and save al-Andalus from the Christians, and his North African army won a resounding victory at Zallāka, but Yūsuf returned to Morocco. He was invited to come back for the same reason in 1090 and this time he annexed virtually the whole of Muslim Spain, adding it to the huge Murābiṭ empire in north-western Africa. Yūsuf is credited with introducing a new military tradition to the Berber tribes of the western Sudan. This involved strict military discipline, highly structured armies and tactics, and an acceptance of high casualties. He was a small, quietly spoken man with a reputation for courage, quick thinking, great generosity and a deep dislike of worldly pleasures. He made a point of having each of his decisions publicly supported by a team of Islamic legal specialists, even when on campaign.

VII
SOURCES

SOURCES

General Works 223
Byzantine, Persians and Muslims 223
Christian-Muslim Confontration 223
Turks, Mongols and the Rise of Russia 224
Crusade, Reconquista and Counter-Crusade 225
China, South-East Asia and India 227
Fortification and Siege Warfare 227
Laws of War and Prisoners 228
Military Theory and Training 228
Morale and Motivation 229
Communications 230
Horses, Harness and Land Transport 230
Naval Warfare, Water Transport and Combined Operations 230
Flags and Heraldry 231
Arms, Armour and the Weapons Trade 231
Firearms 232
Miscellaneous 232

As in Volume I of *The Medieval Warfare Source Book*, many of the works in this list contain information dealing with several facets of medieval warfare. They have, therefore, been placed in the most relevant section or in the chronologically earliest section.

General Works

Hopkins, J. F. P., and Levtzion, N. *Corpus of Early Arabic Sources for West African History*, Cambridge, 1981.

Lewis, B. *Islam from the Prophet Muhammad to the Capture of Constantinople, vol. I:* Politics and War, New York, 1974.

Ostrogorsky, G. *History of the Byzantine State*, Oxford, 1968.

Parry, V. J. 'Warfare', in P. M. Holt, et al., (eds.). *The Cambridge History of Islam,* Cambridge, 1970, pp. 824–50.

Pasdermadjian, H. *Histoire d'Arménie,* Paris, 1964.

Pollo, S., and Puto, A. *The History of Albania from its origins to the present day*, London, 1981.

Shaban, M. A. *Islamic History. AD 600-750, a New Interpretation,* Cambridge, 1971.

Vasiliev, A. A. *Byzance et les Arabes,* vol. I, Brussels, 1934; vol. II, Brussels, 1950.

Byzantines, Persians and Muslims

Akram, A. I. *The Muslim Conquest of Persia*, Rawalpindi, 1976.

– *The Sword of Allah: Khalid bin al Waleed, his life and campaigns*, Karachi, 1970.

Altheim, F., and Stiehl, R. (eds.). *Die Araber in der Alten Welt,* 5 vols., Berlin, 1964–9.

Austin, N. J. E. *Ammianus on Warfare: An Investigation into Ammanius' Military Knowledge*, Brussels, 1979.

Baynes, N. H. 'The Military Operations of the Emperor Heraclius', in *United Services Magazine*, vols. XLVI, 1913, pp. 526–666; XLVII, 1913, pp. 30–8, 195–201, 318–24, 401–12, 532–41, 665–79.

Beeston, A. F. L. *Warfare in Ancient South Arabia (2nd-3rd centuries AD)*, London, 1976.

Butler, A. J. *The Arab Conquest of Egypt*, Oxford, 1902.

Christensen, A. *L'Empire des Sassanides: Le Peuple, L'Etat, La Cour*, Copenhagen, 1907.

– *L'Iran sous les Sassanides*, Copenhagen, 1936.

Collins, R. *The Arab Conquest of Spain, 710-797*, London, 1989.

Diehl, C. *L'Afrique Byzantine: Histoire de la Domination Byzantine (533–709)*, Paris, 1896.

Downey, G. 'The Persian Campaign in Syria in AD 540', in *Speculum*, vol. XXVIII, 1953, pp. 340–8.

Foss, C. 'The Persians in Asia Minor and the End of Antiquity', in *The English Historical Review*, vol. XC, 1975, pp. 721–47.

Frye, R. N. *The History of Ancient Iran*, Munich, 1984.

Gibb, H. A. R. *The Arab Conquests in Central Asia*, London, 1923.

Goubert, P. *Byzance avant l'Islam, vol. 1: Byzance et l'Orient*, Paris, 1951.

– *Byzance avant l'Islam, vol. 2: Byzance et l'Occident*, Paris, 1965.

Graf, D. F. 'The Saracens and the Defence of the Arabian Frontier', in *Bulletin of the American Schools of Oriental Research*, vol. CCIX, 1978, pp. 11–26.

Huart, C. *Ancient Persia and Iranian Civilization*, London, 1927.

Jandora, J. W. 'Developments in Islamic Warfare: The Early Conquests', in *Studia Islamica*, vol. LXIV, 1986, pp. 101–13.

– 'The Battle of the Yarmuk: A Reconstruction', in *Journal of Asian History*, vol. XIX, 1985, pp. 8–21.

– *The March from Medina*, Clifton, 1990.

Kaegi, W. E. *Byzantium and the Early Islamic Conquests*, Cambridge, 1992.

Kennedy, H. *The Prophet and the Age of the Caliphates: The Islamic Near East from the Sixth to the Eleventh Centuries*, London, 1986.

Kister, M. J. 'Al-Hira: Some Notes on its Relations with Arabia', in *Arabica*, vol. XV, 1968, pp. 143–69.

– 'Mecca and Tamim (Aspects of their Relations)', in *Journal of the Economic and Social History of the Orient*, vol. VIII, 1965, pp. 113–63.

Lammens, P. H. *Etudes sur le Règne du Calife Omaiyade Mo'awiya 1er*, Paris, 1908.

– *Le Califat de Yazid 1er*, 5 vols., Beirut, 1910–21.

Levi Della Vida, G. 'Pre-Islamic Arabia', in N. A. Faris (ed.). *The Arab Heritage*, Princeton, 1944, pp. 25–7.

Lings, M. *Muhammad, his life based on the earliest sources*, London, 1983.

Mayerson, P. 'The First Muslim Attacks on Southern Palestine (AD 633–4)', in *Transactions and Proceedings of the American Philological Association*, vol. XCV, 1964, pp. 155–99.

McGraw, Donner, F. *The Early Islamic Conquests*, Princeton, 1981.

Nicolle, D. C. *Sassanian Armies: The Iranian Empire early 3rd to mid-7th centuries AD*, Stockport, 1996.

Parker, S. T. 'History of the Late Roman Frontier East of the Dead Sea', in S. T. Parker, (ed.), *The Roman Frontier in Central Jordan: Interim Report of the "Limes Arabicus" Project, 1980-1985*, BAR International Series no. 340. vol. II, Oxford, 1987, pp. 793–823.

Shahid, I. *Byzantium and the Arabs in the Fifth Century*, Washington, 1989.

Smith, S. 'Events in Arabia in the 6th century AD', in *Bulletin of the School of Oriental and African Studies*, vol. XVI, 1954, pp. 425–68.

Stratos, A. N. *Byzantium in the Seventh Century (vol. I., 602-34)*, trans. M. Ogilvie-Grant, Amsterdam, 1968.

– *Byzantium in the Seventh Century (vols. II-V)*, trans. Hionides, Amsterdam, 1972–80.

Taha, Abd al Wahid Dhanun. *The Muslim Conquest and Settlement of North Africa and Spain*, London, 1989.

Whitby, M. *The Emperor Maurice and his Historian: Theophylact Simocatta on Persian and Balkan Warfare*, Oxford, 1988.

Yarshater, E. (ed.). *The Cambridge History of Iran, vol. 3/1: The Seleucid, Parthian and Sassanian Periods*, Cambridge, 1983.

Christian–Muslim Confrontation

Adams, W. Y. *Nubia, Corridor to Africa*, London, 1977.

Al Jahiz. 'Jahiz of Basra to Al-Fath ibn Khaqan on the Exploits of the Turks and the Army of the Khalifate in General',

trans. C. T. Harley-Walker, in *Journal of the Royal Asiatic Society*, October 1915, pp. 631–97.
Arvites, J. A. 'The Defence of Byzantine Anatolia during the Reign of Irene (780–802)', in S. Mitchell, (ed.) *Armies and Frontiers in Roman and Byzantine Anatolia:* BAR International Reports, no. 156, Oxford, 1983, pp. 219–37.
Beshir, B. J. 'Fatimid Military Organization', in *Der Islam*, vol. LV, 1978, pp. 37–57.
Bosworth, C. E. 'Abu 'Amr 'Uthman al-Tarsusi's Siyar al Thughur and the Last Years of Arab Rule in Tarsus (Fourth/Tenth Century)', in *Graeco-Arabica*, vol. V, 1993, pp. 183–95.
- 'Ghaznevid Military Organization', in *Der Islam*, vol, XXXVI, 1960, pp. 37–77.
- 'Military Organization under the Buyids of Persia and Iraq', in *Oriens*, vols. XVIII–XIX, 1965–6, pp. 143–67.
- 'The Armies of the Saffarids', in *Bulletin of the School of Oriental and African Studies*, vol. XXXI, 1968, pp. 534–54.
- *The Ghaznavids*, Edinburgh, 1963.
Brett, M. 'The Military Interest of the Battle of Haydaran', in V. J. Parry and M. E. Yapp, (eds.). *War, Technology and Society in the Middle East*, London, 1975, pp. 78–88.
Browning, R. *Byzantium and Bulgaria: A comparative Study across the early medieval frontier*, London, 1975.
Bury, J. B.. 'Mutasim's March through Cappadocia in A.D. 838,' *Journal of Hellenic Studies*, XXIX, 1909, 120-9.
Collins, R. *Early Medieval Spain: Unity in Diversity, 400-1000*, London, 1983.
De Moraes Farias, P. F. 'The Almoradids: Some Questions Concerning the Character of the Movement during its periods of Closest Contact with the Western Sudan', in *Bulletin de l'Institut Fondamental d'Afrique Noir*, ser. B. vol. XXIX, 1967, pp. 794–878.
Frye, R. N. *The Golden Age of Persia: The Arabs in the East*, London, 1975.
Godfrey, J. 'The Defeated Anglo-Saxons Take Service with the Eastern Emperor', in *Proceedings of the Battle Conference on Anglo-Norman Studies*, vol. I, 1978, pp. 63–74.
Hassan, Z. M. *Les Tulunids*, Paris, 1933.
Ismail, O. S. A. 'Mu'tasim and the Turks', in *Bulletin of the School of Oriental and African Studies*, vol. XXIX, 1966, pp. 12–24.
Kazhdan, A. 'Armenians in the Byzantine Ruling Class; predominantly in the ninth through twelfth centuries', in T. J. Samuelian and M. E. Stone (eds.). *Medieval Armenian Culture, University of Pennsylvania Armenian Texts and Studies 6*, Chico California, 1984, pp. 439–51.
Kennedy, H. *The Early Abbasid Caliphate: A Political History*, London, 1981.
Kirkman, J. 'The Early History of Oman in East Africa', in *Journal of Oman Studies*, vol. VI, 1983, pp. 41–58.
Lassner, J. *The Shaping of 'Abbasid Rule*, Princeton, 1980.
Lev, Y. 'Fatimid Policy towards Damascus (358/968–386/996), Military, Political and Social Aspects', in *Jerusalem Studies in Arabic and Islam*, vol. III, 1981–2, pp. 165–83.
- 'The Fatimid Army, A. H. 358–427/968–1036 C.E.: Military and Social Aspects', in *Asian and African Studies*, vol. XIV, 1980, pp. 165–92.
Lévi-Provençal, E. *L'Espagne Musulmane au Xème siècle*, Paris, 1932.
Mahdjoub, A. 'L'habillement des soldats 'abbasides', in *Bulletin des Etudes Arabes (Algiers)*, vol. VIII, 1948, pp. 3–5.
Oikonomides, N. 'L'organisation de la frontière orientale de Byzanze aux Xe–XIe siècles et le Taktikon de l'Escorial', in *Actes du XIVe Congrès Internationale des Etudes Byzantines, Bucarest 6-12 Septembre, 1971*, vol. I, Bucharest, 1974, pp. 285–302.
Sánchez-Albornoz, C. 'El Ejécito y la Guerra en al Reino Asturleonés, 718-1037', in *Ordinamenti Militari in Occidente nell'Alto Medioevo. Settimane di Studio del Centro Italiano di Studi sull'Alto Medioevo*, vol. XV, Spoleto, 1968, pp. 299–335.
Sharon, M. 'The Military Reforms of Abu Muslim, their background and consequences', in M. Sharon, (ed.) *Studies in Islamic History and Civilization in Honour of Professor David Ayalon*, Jerusalem and Leiden, 1986, pp. 105–43.
- *Black Banners from the East: The Establishment of the 'Abbasid State – Incubation of a Revolt*, Jerusalem and Leiden, 1983.
Tanasoca, N-S. 'Les Mixobarbares et les Formations Paristriennes du XIe siècles', in *Revue Roumaine d'Histoire*, vol. XII, 1973, pp. 61–82.
Terrasse, H. 'L'Espagne Musulmane et l'héritage Wisigothique', in *Etudes d'Orientalisme dédiées à la Mémoire de Levi-Provençal*, Paris, 1962, pp. 757–66.
Toynbee, A. *Constantine Porphyrogenitus and his World*, London, 1973.
Von Sievers, P. 'Military, Merchants and Nomads: The Social Evolution of the Syrian Cities and Countryside during the Classical Period 780-969/164-358', in *Der Islam*, vol. LVI, 1979, pp. 212–44.
Wasserstein, D. *The Rise and Fall of the Party-Kings*, Princeton, 1985.

Turks, Mongols and the Rise of Russia

Barthold, V. V. *Four Studies on the History of Central Asia*, trans. V. and T. Minosky, Leiden, 1962.
- *Histoire des Turcs d'Asie Centrale*, Paris, 1946.
Bouvat, L. *L'Empire des Mongols*, Paris, 1927.
Boyle, J. A. 'The Capture of Isfahan by the Mongols', in *Atti del Convegno Internazionale sul Tema: la Persia nel Medioevo*, Rome, 1971, pp. 331–6.
Dachkévytch, Y. A. 'Les Arméniens à Kiev (jusqu'en 1240)', in *Revue des Etudes Arméniennes*, vol. X, 1973–4, pp. 305–56.
Dimnik, M. *Mikhail, Prince of Chernigov and Grand Prince of Kiev 1224-1246*, Toronto, 1981.
Esin, E. 'Tabari's report on the warfare with the Türgis and the Testimony of the Eighth Century Central Asian Art', in *Central Asiatic Journal*, vol. XVII, 1973, pp. 130–49.
Fennell, J. *The Crisis of Medieval Russia 1200-1304*, London, 1983.
Grekov, B. *Kiev Rus*, Moscow, 1959.
Grousset, R. *The Empire of the Steppes, a History of Central Asia*, New Brunswick, 1970.
Gultzgoff, V. 'La Russie Kiévienne entre la Scandinavie, Con-

stantinople et le Royaume Franc de Jérusalem', in *Revue des Etudes Slaves*, vol. LV, 1983, pp. 151-61.

Halperin, C. J. *Russia and the Golden Horde*, London, 1985.

Hookham, H. *Tamburlaine the Conqueror*, London, 1962.

Kwanten, L. *Imperial Nomads: a history of Central Asia, 500-1500*, Leicester, 1979.

Lantzeff, G. V., and Pierce, R. A. *Eastward to Empire: Exploration and Conquest on the Russian Open Frontier, to 1750*, Montreal and London, 1973.

Lattimore, O. 'The Nomads and South Russia', in *Byzantine Black Sea (symposium, Birmingham University 18-20 March 1978)*, Athens, 1978, pp. 193-200.

Martin, J, 'Russian Expansion in the Far North, X to mid-XVI Century', in M. Rywkin (ed.) *Russian Colonial Expansion to 1917*, London, 1988.

Meyendorff, J. *Byzantium and the Rise of Russia*, Cambridge, 1981.

Morgan, D. O. 'The Mongol Armies in Persia', in *Der Islam*, vol. LVI, 1979, pp. 81-96.

- *The Mongols*, Oxford, 1968.

Noonan, T. S. 'Medieval Russia, the Mongols, and the West: Novgorod's relations with the Baltic, 1100-1350', in *Medieval Studies*, vol. XXXVII, 1975, pp. 316-39.

Paszkiewicz, H. *The Origins of Russia*, London, 1954.

Pritsak, O. *The Pecenegs: A Case of Social and Economic Transformation*, Lisse, 1976.

- 'The Polovcians and Rus', in *Archivum Eurasiae Medii Aevi*, vol. II, 1982, pp. 321-80.

Rady, M. 'The Mongol Invasion of Hungary', in *Medieval World*, vol. III, November-December 1991, pp. 39-46.

Richard, J. 'Les causes des victoires Mongoles d'après les historiens occidentaux du XIIIe siècle', in *Central Asiatic Journal*, vol. XXIII, 1979, pp. 104-17.

Shepard, J. 'The Russian-steppe frontier', in *Byzantine Black Sea (symposium, Birmingham University 18-20 March 1978)*, Athens, 1978, pp. 123-33.

Sinor, D. 'The Inner Asian Warriors', in *Journal of the American Oriental Society*, vol. CI/2, 1981, pp. 133-44.

Stein, A. *On Ancient Central-Asian Tracks*, London, 1933.

Thompson, M. W. *Novgorod the Great*, London, 1967.

Vernadsky, G. *A History of Russia, vol. II: Kievan Russia*, New Haven, 1948.

- *A History of Russia, vol. III: The Mongols and Russia*, New Haven, 1953.

- *The Origins of Russia*, Oxford, 1959.

Crusade, Reconquista and Counter-Crusade

Al-Tarsusi. *Contribution à l'Etude de l'Archerie Musulmane*, trans. A. Boudot-Lamotte, Damascus, 1968.

Amouroux-Mourad, M. *Le Comté d'Edesse*, Beirut, 1988.

Anastasijevic, D. and Ostrogorsky, G. 'Les Koumanes Pronoiaires', in *Annuaire de l'Institut de philologie et d'histoire Orientales et Slaves*, vol. XI, 1951, pp. 19-29.

Angold, M. A. *Byzantine Government in Exile*, Oxford, 1975.

Arbel, B., Hamilton, B., and Jacoby, D. (eds.). *Latins and Greeks in the Eastern Mediterranean after 1204*, London, 1989.

Arié, R. *L'Espagne Musulmane au Temps des Nasrides (1232-1492)*, Paris, 1973.

Atiya, A. S. *The Crusade in the Later Middle Ages*, London, 1938.

Ayalon, D. 'Preliminary Remarks on the Mamluk Military Institution in Islam', in V. J. Parry and M. E. Yapp (eds.), *War, Technology and Society in the Middle East*, London, 1975, pp. 44-58.

- 'Studies in the Structure of the Mamluk Army - I, The Army Stationed in Egypt', in *Bulletin of the School of Oriental and African Studies*, vol. XV, 1953, pp. 203-28.

- 'Studies in the Structure of the Mamluk Army - II: The Halqa', in *Bulletin of the School of Oriental and African Studies*, vol. XV, 1953, pp. 448-76.

- 'Studies in the Structure of the Mamluk Army III: Holders of Offices Connected with the Army', in *Bulletin of the School of Oriental and African Studies*, vol. XVI, 1954, pp. 57-90.

- 'The Circassians in the Mamluk Kingdom', in *Journal of the American Oriental Society*, vol. LXIX, 1949, pp. 135-47.

- 'The Muslim City and the Mamluk Military Aristocracy', in *Proceedings of the Israel Academy of Sciences and Humanities*, vol. II, 1968, pp. 311-29.

Baldwin, M. W. *Raymond III of Tripoli and the Fall of Jerusalem (1140-1187)*, Princeton, 1936.

Bartusis, M. C. *The Late Byzantine Army: Arms and Society 1204-1453*, Philadelphia, 1992.

Beldiceanu, N. 'Les Roumans à la bataille d'Ankara', in *Südost-Forschungen*, vol. XIV, 1955, pp. 441-50.

Ben-Ami, A. *Social Change in a Hostile Environment: The Crusaders' Kingdom of Jerusalem*, Princeton, 1969.

Benvenisti, M. *The Crusaders in the Holy Land*, Jerusalem, 1970.

Bishko, C. J. 'The Castilian as Plainsman: The Medieval Ranching Frontier in La Mancha and Extramadura', in A. Lewis and T. McGunn (eds.). *The New World Looks at its History*, Austin, 1963, pp. 46-69.

Blondal, S., and Beneditz, B. S. *The Varangians of Byzantium*, Cambridge, 1978.

Bombaci, A. 'The Army of the Saljuqs of Rum', in *Istituto orientale di Napoli, Annali*, n.s. vol. XXXVIII, 1978, pp. 343-69.

Bon, A. *La Morée Franque*, Paris, 1969.

Bosworth, C. E. *The Later Ghaznvids: Splendour and Decay*, Edinburgh, 1977.

Brand, C. M. *Byzantium Confronts the West*, Cambridge, Mass., 1968.

Brunschwig, R. *La Berberie Orientale sous les Hafsides des origines à la fin du XVe siècle*, Paris, 1940-7.

Cahen, S. *La Syrie du Nord au Temps des Croisades*, Paris, 1940.

Chalandon, F. *Les Comnènes - Etudes sur l'Empire Byzantin*, vol. I, Paris, 1900; vol. II, Paris, 1912.

Chehab, M. H. 'Tyr à l'époque des Croisades', in special volume, *Bulletin du Musée de Beyrouth*, vol. XXXI, 1979.

Creasy, E. S. *History of the Ottoman Turks*, London, 1858.

De Curzon, H. 'La règle de Temple', in *Société de l'Histoire de France*, vol. CCXXVIII, 1886.

De Oliveiro Marques, A. H. *History of Portugal: vol. I. From Lusitania to Empire*, New York, 1972, p. 5.

Diaconu, P. *Les Coumans au Bas-Danube aux XIe au XIIe siècles*, Bucharest, 1978.

Dodu, G. *Histoire des Institutions Monarchiques dans le Royaume Latin de Jérusalem 1099-1291*, r/p New York, 1978.

Eberhard, W. *A History of China*, London, 1948.

Edbury, P. W. *The Kingdom of Cyprus and the Crusades 1191-1374*, Cambridge, 1991.

Elbeheiry, S. *Les Institutions de l'Egype au Temps des Ayyubides*, Lille, 1972.

Elisseeff, N. *Nur al Din: un Grand Prince Musulman de Syrie au Temps des Croisades*, Damascus, 1967.

Favreau-Lilie, M.-L. 'The Military Orders and the Escape of the Christian Population from the Holy Land in 1291', in *Journal of Medieval History*, vol. XIX, 1993, pp. 201–27.

Forey, A. J. *Military Orders and Crusades*, London, 1994.

France, J. *Victory in the East: A Military History of the First Crusade*, Cambridge, 1994.

Geanakoplos, D. J. 'Greco-Latin Relations on the Eve of the Byzantine Restoration: The Battle of Pelagonia – 1259', in *Dumbarton Oaks Papers*, vol. VII, 1953, pp. 99–141.

Hendrickx, B. 'Les Arméniens d'Asie Mineure et de Thrace au début de l'Empire Latin de Constantinople', in *Revue des Etudes Armeniennes*, vol. XXII, 1991, pp. 217–23.

Holt, P. M. (ed.). *The Eastern Mediterranean Lands in the Period of the Crusades*, Warminster, 1977.

Housley, N. *The Later Crusades, 1274-1580: From Lyons to Alcazar*, Oxford, 1992.

Huici Miranda, H. *Las grandes batallas de la Reconquista durante los invasiones africanas*, Madrid, 1956.

Inalcik, H. 'Ottoman Methods of Conquest', in *Studia Islamica*, vol. II, 1954, pp. 103–29.

- *The Ottoman Empire: The Classical Age 1300-1600*, London, 1973.

Jackson, P. 'The Crusades of 1239-41 and their aftermath', in *Bulletin of the School of Oriental and African Studies*, vol. L, 1987, pp. 32–60.

Jacoby, D. *Recherches sur la Méditerranée Orientale du XIIe au XIVe Siècle*, London, 1979.

- *Studies on the Crusader States and on Venetian Expansion*, London, 1989.

Kedar, B. Z. *The Franks in the Levant, 11th to 14th Centuries*, London, 1993.

La Monte, J. L. *Feudal Monarchy in the Latin Kingdom of Jerusalem*, Cambridge, Mass., 1932.

Lilie, R-J. 'Die Schlacht von Myriokephalon, 1176', in Revue des *Etudes Byzantines*, vol. XXXV, 1977, pp. 257–77.

Little, D. P. 'The Fall of 'Akka in 690/1291', in M. Sharon (ed.), *Studies in Islamic History and Civilization in Honour of Professor David Ayalon*, Jerusalem and Leiden, 1986, pp. 159–81.

Lock, P. W. *The Franks in the Aegean*, London, 1995.

Lomax, D. W. *The Reconquest of Spain*, London, 1978.

Lyons, M. C., and Jackson, D. E. P. *Saladin, The Politics of the Holy War*, Cambridge, 1982.

Mantran, R., and de la Roncière, C. 'Africa opens up to the Old Worlds', in R. Fossier, (ed.), *The Cambridge Illustrated History of the Middle Ages, vol. III, 1250–1520*, London, 1986, pp. 356–96.

Marshall, C. J. 'The French Regiment in the Latin East, 1254-91', in *Journal of Medieval History*, vol. XV, 1989, pp. 301–7.

Mayer, H. E. *Kings and Lords in the Latin Kingdom of Jerusalem*, London, 1994.

Menéndez Pidal, R. *The Cid and his Spain*, London, 1971.

Mill, W. Trebizond: *The Last Greek Empire of the Byzantine Era 1204-1461*, r/p Chicago, 1969.

Miller, W. *The Latins in the Levant: A History of Frankish Greece (1204–1566)*, London, 1908.

Morgan, D. O. *Medieval Persia* (1040–1797), London, 1988.

Murray, A. V. 'The Origins of the Frankish Nobility of the Kingdom of Jerusalem, 1100–1118', in *Mediterranean Historical Review*, vol. IV, 1989, pp. 281–300.

Nicol, D. M. *The Despotate of Epirus 1267–1479*, Cambridge, 1984.

- *The Last Centuries of Byzantium, 1261-1453*, London, 1972.

Nicolle, D. C. 'Saljūq Arms and Armour in Art and Literature', in *The Art of the Saljuqs in Iran and Anatolia, Proceedings of a Symposium held in Edinburgh in 1982*, ed. R. Hillenbrand, Costa Mesa, California, 1994, pp. 247–56.

Oikonomides, N. *Hommes d'Affaires Grecs et Latins à Constantinople (XIIIe–XVe siècles)*, Montreal and Paris, 1979.

Pears, E. *The Destruction of the Greek Empire*, London, 1903.

Powers, J. 'The Origins and Development of Municipal Military Service in the Leonese and Castilian Reconquest, 800–1250', in *Traditio*, vol. XXVI, 1970, pp. 91-111.

- 'Two Warrior-Kings and their Municipal Militias: The Townsman-Soldier in Law and Life', in R. I. Burns, (ed.) *The World of Alfonso the Learned and James the Conqueror*, Princeton, 1985, pp. 95–129.

Prawer, J. 'The Settlement of the Latins in Jerusalem', in *Speculum*, vol. XXVII, 1952, pp. 490–503.

- *Crusader Institutions*, Oxford, 1980.
- *The Crusader's Kingdom*, New York, 1972.

Richard, J. 'An Account of the Battle of Hattin referring to the Frankish Mercenaries in Oriental Muslim States', in *Speculum*, vol. XXVII, 1952, pp. 168–77

- *'La féodalité de l'Orient latin et le movement communal: un états des questions', in Structures féodales et féodalisme dans l'Occident Mediterranean (Xe–XIIIe siècles), Collections* de l'Ecole française de Rome, vol. XLIV, 1980, pp. 651–65.
- 'Le Peuplement Latin et Syrien en Chypre au XIIIe siècle', in *Byzantinische Forschungen*, vol. VII, 1979, pp. 157–73.
- *Croisades et Etats Latins d'Orient*, London, 1992.
- *Orient et Occident au Moyen Age*, London, 1976.
- *Le Comté de Tripoli sous la Dynastie Toulousaine*, Paris, 1945.
- *The Latin Kingdom of Jerusalem*, Oxford, 1979.

Riley-Smith, J. S. C. (ed.). *The Atlas of the Crusades*, London, 1991.

Russell, P. E. *The English Intervention in Spain and Portugal in the Time of Edward III and Richard II*, Oxford, 1955.

Salih, A. H. 'Le Rôle des bédouins d'Egypte à l'époque Fatimide' in *Rivista degli Studi Orientale*, vol. LIV, 1980, pp. 51–65.

Shaw, S. *History of the Ottoman Empire and Modern Turkey, vol. I, 1280-1808*, Cambridge, 1976.

Shepard, J. 'The English and Byzantium: A Study of their Role

in the Byzantine Army in the Later Eleventh Century', in *Traditio*, vol. XXIX, 1973, pp. 53-92.

Smith, J. M. *A History of the Sarbadar Dynasty, 1336-1381 AD; and its sources*, The Hague and Paris, 1970.

Vryonis, S. Jr. 'Byzantine and Turkish Societies and their sources of manpower', in V. J. Parry and M. E. Yapp, eds., *War, Technology and Society in the Middle East*, London, 1975, pp. 125-52.

- *The Decline of Medieval Hellenism in Asia Minor and the Process of Islamization from the Eleventh through the Fifteenth Century*, Berkeley, 1971.

Wittek, P. *The Rise of the Ottoman Empire*, London, 1938.

Zachariadou, E. A. *Romania and the Turks*, London, 1985.

Zakythinos, D. A. *Le Despotat grec de Morée: Vie et institutions*, London, 1975.

- The Making of Modern Greece: From Byzantium to Independence, Oxford, 1976.

Ziadeh, N. A. *Urban Life in Syria under the Early Mamluks*, Westport, 1953.

China, South-East Asia and India

Basham, A. L. (ed.). *A Cultural History of India*, Oxford, 1075.

Biot, E. 'Mémoires sur les Colonies Militaires et Agricoles Chinois', in *Journal Asiatique*, vol. XV, 1850, pp. 338-70, 529-85.

Chandra, M. 'Indian Costumes and Textiles from the Eighth to the Twelfth Century', in *Journal of Indian Textile History*, vol. V, 1960, pp. 1-41.

Dikshitar, V. R. R. *War in Ancient India*, Madras, 1948.

Drekmeier, C. *Kingship and Community in Early India*, Stanford, 1962.

Eberhard, W. *A History of China*, London, 1949.

- *Das Toba-Reich Nordchinas*, Leiden, 1949.

Fox, J. J. (ed.). *Indonesia: The Making of a Culture*, Canberra, 1980.

Gode, P. K. 'The History of the Sling (Gophana) in India and other Countries between c.300 BC and AD 1900', in P. K. Gode, *Studies in Indian Cultural History*, Poona, 1960, pp. 82-91.

- 'The Mounted Bowman on Indian Battle-fields - From the Invasion of Alexander (326 BC) to the Battle of Panipat (AD 1761)', in P. K. Gode, *Studies in Indian Cultural History*, Poona, 1960, pp. 57-70.

Harvey, G. E. *History of Burma*, London, 1925.

Hopkins, E. W. 'The Social and Military Position of the Ruling Caste in Ancient India as represented by the Sanskrit Epic', in *Journal of the American Oriental Society*, vol. XIII, 1889, pp. 357-72.

Ki-baik Lee, *A New History of Korea*, Seoul, 1984.

Liu Mau-Tsai, *Kutscha und seine Beziehungen zu China vom 2.Jh. v. bis zum 6.Jh. n. Chr.*, Wiesbaden, 1969.

Majumdar, R. C., Raychaudhuri, H. C., and Kalikindar Datta. *An Advanced History of India*, part I, London, 1960; part II, London, 1949.

Masani, R. P. 'Caste and the Structure of Society', in G. T. Garratt (ed.) *The Legacy of India*, Oxford, 1937, pp. 124-61.

Masson-Oursel, P. *Ancient India and Indian Civilization*, London, 1934.

Nahm, A. C. *Korea: Tradition and Tranformation*, Seoul, 1989.

Needham, J. 'China's Trebuchets, Manned and Counterweighted', in B. S. Hall and D. C. West (eds.). *On Pre-Modern Technology and Science: Studies in Honor of Lynn White, jr.*, Malibu, 1976, pp. 107-45.

Peers, C. J. *Medieval Chinese Armies 1260-1520*, London, 1992.

Ranitzsch, K. H. *The Army of Tang China*, Stockport, 1995.

Rawlinson, H. G. *India: A Short Cultural History*, London, 1937.

Sharma, G. *Indian Army through the Ages*, Bombay, 1966.

Stein, B. *The New Cambridge History of India, vol. I, part 2: Vijayanagara*, Cambridge, 1989.

Winstedt, R. *Malaya and its History*, London, 1948.

Fortification and Siege Warfare

Ahrweiler, H. 'Les forteresses construites en Asie Mineure face à l'invasion seldjoucide', in *Akten des XI. Internationalen Byzantinist Kongresses*, Munich, 1960, pp. 182-9.

Ayalon, D. 'Hisar: The Mamluk Sultanate', in *Encyclopedia of Islam*, 2nd. edn., vol. III, Leiden, 1971, pp. 472-6.

Burton-Page, J. 'A Study of Fortification in the Indian Subcontinent from the Thirteenth to the Eighteenth Century AD', in *Bulletin of the School of Oriental and African Studies*, vol. XXIII, 1960, pp. 508-22.

- 'Burdj: The Tower in Islamic architecture in India', in *Encyclopedia of Islam*, 2nd. edn., vol. I, Leiden, 1960, pp. 1321-4.

- 'Hisar: India', in *Encyclopedia of Islam*, 2nd. edn., vol. III, Leiden, 1971, pp. 481-3.

Cahen, C. 'Hisar: General Remarks', in *Encyclopedia of Islam*, 2nd. edn., vol. III, Leiden, 1971, pp. 469-70.

Creswell, K. A. C. 'Fortification in Islam before AD 1250', in *Proceedings of the British Academy*, vol. XXXVIII, 1952, pp. 89-125.

Edwards, R. W. *The Fortifications of Armenian Cilicia*, Washington, 1987.

Elad, A. 'The Siege of Al Wasit (132/749)', in M. Sharon, (ed.) *Studies in Islamic History and Civilization in Honour of Professor David Ayalon*, Jerusalem and Leiden, 1986, pp. 59-90.

Eydoux, H-P. 'L'architecture militaire des Francs en Orient', in J. P. Babelon (ed.) *Le Château en France*, Paris, 1986, pp. 61-77.

Fedden, R. *Crusader Castles, a brief study in the military architecture of the Crusades*, London, 1950.

Fedden, J., and Thomson, J. *Crusader Castles*, London, 1977.

Foss, C., and Winfield, D. *Byzantine Fortifications: an introduction*, Pretoria, 1986.

Franke, H. 'Siege and Defence of Towns in Medieval China', in F. A. Kierman, Jr. and J. K. Fairbank (eds.) *Chinese Ways in Warfare*, Cambridge, Mass., 1974, pp. 151-201.

Frye, R. N. 'The Sassanian System of Walls for Defence', in *Studies in Memory of Gaston Wiet*, ed. M. Rosen-Ayalon, Jerusalem, 1977, pp. 7-15.

Kostochkin, V, *Krepostnoye Zodchestvo Drevnii Rusi (Fortress Architecture in Early Russia)*, (in Russian with English summary), Moscow, 1970.

Nicolle, D. C. 'Ain Habis - The Cave de Sueth, *Archéologie Médiévale*, vol. XVIII, 1988, pp. 113-40.

Norris, H. T. 'Caves and Strongholds from the Moorish Period around the Rock of Gibraltar', in *The Maghreb Review*, vol. IX, 1984, pp. 39-45.

Rappoport, P. 'Russian Medieval Military Architecture', in *Gladius*, vol. VIII, 1969, pp. 39-62.

Rice, D. S. 'Medieval Harran: Studies in its Topography and Monuments, I', in *Anatolian Studies*, vol. II, 1952, pp. 36-84.

Rosser, J. 'Crusader Castles of Cyprus', in *Archaeology*, vol. XXXIX/4, July-August 1986, pp. 40-7.

_ 'Excavations at Saranda Kolones, Paphos, Cyprus, 1981-1983', in *Dumbarton Oaks Papers*, vol. XXXIX, 1985, pp. 80-97.

- 'The Role of Fortifications in the Defence of Asia Minor against the Arabs from the Eighth to the Tenth Century', in *Greek Orthodox Theological Review*, vol. XXVII, 1982, pp. 135-43.

Sauvaget, J. 'Notes sur les défenses de Marine de Tripoli', in *Bulletin du Musée de Beyrouth*, vol. II, 1938, pp. 1-25.

Smail, R. C. 'Crusaders' Castles in the Twelfth Century', in *Cambridge Historical Journal*, vol. X, 1950-2, pp. 133-49.

Sourdel-Thomine, J. 'Burdj: Military Architecture in the Islamic Middle East', in *Encyclopedia of Islam*, 2nd. edn., vol. I, Leiden, 1960, pp. 1315-18.

Terrasse, H. 'Burdj: Military architecture in the Muslim West', in *Encyclopedia of Islam*, 2nd. edn., vol. I, Leiden, 1960, pp. 1318-21.

- 'Hisn: The Muslim West', in *Encyclopedia of Islam*, 2nd. edn., vol. III, Leiden, 1971, pp. 498-501.

Torres Balbás, L. 'Cáceres y su Cerca Almohade', *Andalus*, vol. XIII, 1948, pp. 446-72.

Torres Delgado, C. 'El Ejercito y las Fortificaciones del Reino Nazari di Granada', in *Gladius: Las Armas en la Historia*, Madrid, 1988, pp. 197-217.

Toy, S. *The Fortified Cities of India*, London, 1965.

Udina Martorell, F. *Ingenieria Militar en las Cronicas Catalanas*, Barcelona, 1971.

Wallacker, B. E. 'Studies in Medieval Chinese Siegecraft: The Siege of Ying-Chu'an, AD 548-9', *Journal of Asian Studies*, vol. XXX, 1971, pp. 611-22.

Zozaya, J. 'The Fortifications of al-Andalus', in J. D. Dodds (ed.) *Al-Andalus: The Art of Islamic Spain*, New York, 1992, pp. 63-73.

Laws of War and Prisoners

Ayalon, D. 'Aspects of the Mamluk Phenomenon: The Importance of the Mamluk Institution', in *Der Islam*, vol. LIII, 1976, pp. 196-225.

- *L'esclavage du Mamelouk: Oriental Notes and Studies, No. 1*, Jerusalem, 1951.

Brodman, J. W. *Ransoming Captives in Crusader Spain*, Philadelphia, 1986.

Brundage, J. A. *Medieval Canon Law and the Crusades*, Madison, 1969.

- *The Crusades, Holy War and Canon Law*, London, 1991.

Burns, R. I. 'The Muslim in the Christian Feudal Order: The Kingdom of Valencia, 1240-1280', in *Studies in Medieval Culture*, vol. V, 1976, pp. 105-26.

Cahen, C. 'Note sur l'esclavage musulman et le dervichisme Ottoman: à propos des travaux récents', in *Journal of the Economic and Social History of the Orient*, vol. XIII, 1970, pp. 211-18.

Crone, P. *Slaves on Horses*, Cambridge, 1980.

Goiten, S. D. 'Contemporary Letters on the Capture of Jerusalem by the Crusaders', in *The Journal of Jewish Studies*, vol. III-IV, 1952, pp. 162-77.

Imam Malik Ibn Anas. *Al-Muwatta of Imam Malik Ibn Anas: The First Formulation of Islamic Law*, trans. Aisha Abdurrahman Bewley, London, 1989.

Kelsay, J., and Johnson, J. T. (eds.). *Just War and Jihad*, New York, 1991.

Lambton, A. K. S. 'Islamic Mirrors for Princes', in *La Persia nel Medioevo, Atti del Convegno Internazionale Roma 1970*, Rome, 1971.

Luttrell, A. 'Slavery at Rhodes: 1306-1440', in *Bulletin de l'Institut historique belge de Rome*, vol. XLVI-XLVII, 1976-7, pp. 81-100.

Løkkegard, F. 'The Concept of War and Peace in Islam', in R. P. McGuire (ed.) *War and Peace in the Middle Ages*, Copenhagen, 1987, pp. 263-81.

Palmer, J. A. B. 'The Origins of the Janissaries', in *Bulletin of the John Rylands Library*, vol. XXXV, 1952-3, pp. 448-81.

Peters, R. *Jihad in Medieval and Modern Islam*, Leiden, 1977.

Pipes, D. *Slave Soldiers and Islam: The Genesis of a Military System*, New Haven and London, 1981.

Poliak, A. N. 'The Influence of Chingiz Khan's Yasa upon the general organization of the Mamluk State', in *Bulletin of the School of Oriental and African Studies*, vol. X, 1942, pp. 862-76.

Powell, J. M. (ed.). *Muslims under Latin Rule, 1100-1300*, Princeton, 1990.

Sánchez Prieto, A. B. *Guerra y Guerreros en España, según las fuentes canónicas de la Edad Media*, Madrid, 1990.

Verlinden, C. 'Guerre et traité comme sources de l'esclavage dans l'empire byzantine au IXème et Xème siècles', in *Graeco-Arabica*, vol. V, 1993, pp. 207-12.

Military Theory and Training

Al Ansari. *A Muslim Manual of War: being Tafrij al Kurub fi Tadbir al Hurub*, ed. and trans. G. T. Scanlon, Cairo, 1961.

Ayalon, D. 'Notes on the Furusiyya Exercises and Games in the Mamluk Sultanate', in *Scripta Hierosolymitana*, vol. IX, 1961, pp. 31-62.

Bennett, M. 'La Règle du Temple as a military manual, or how to deliver a cavalry charge', in C. Harper-Bill, et al. (eds.), *Studies in Medieval History presented to R. Allen Brown*, Woodbridge, 1989, pp. 7-19.

Castro y Calvo, J. M. *El arte de gobernar en las obras de Don Juan Manuel*, Barcelona, 1945.

Coulston, J. C. 'Roman, Parthian and Sassanid Tactical Developments', in P. Freeman and D. Kennedy (eds.), *The Defence of the Roman and Byzantine East (Proceedings of the colloquium held at the University of Sheffield in April 1986), BAR International Series no. 297*, Oxford, 1986, pp. 59-75.

Darko, E. 'La Tactique Touranienne', in *Byzantion*, vol. X, 1935, pp. 443-69; vol. XII, 1937, pp. 119-47.

De Foucault, J-A. 'Douze Chapitres inédits de la Tactique de Nicéphore Ouranos', in *Travaux et Mémoires*, vol. V, 1973, pp. 281-311.

Dennis, G. T. *Maurice's Strategikon: Handbook of Byzantine Strategy*, Philadelphia, 1984.

- *Three Byzantine Military Treatises*, Washington, 1985.

Forey, A. J. 'Novitiate and Instruction in the Military Orders during the Twelfth and Thirteenth Centuries', in *Speculum*, vol. LXI, 1986, pp. 1-17.

Hyland, A. *The Medieval Warhorse from Byzantium to the Crusades*, London, 1994.

Ibn Hudayl al Andalusi, trans. L. Mercier. *L'Ornament des Armes, Paris*, 1939.

- *La Parure des Cavaliers et l'Insigne des Preux*, Paris, 1922.

Jurji, E. J. 'The Islamic Theory of War', in *The Moslem World*, vol. XXX, 1940, pp. 332-42.

Kaegi, W. E. 'The Contribution of Archery to the Turkish Conquest of Anatolia', in *Speculum*, vol. XXXIX, 1964, pp. 96-108.

Kierman, F. A. Jr., and Fairbank, J. K. (eds.) *Chinese Ways in Warfare*, Cambridge, Mass., 1974.

Kirpitchnikov, A. N. *Voennoe delo na Rusi vXIII-XVvv (L'Art Militaire en Russie des XIII-XV Siècles)*, (in Russian with French summary), Leningrad, 1976.

Kolias, T. 'The Taktica of Leo VI the Wise and the Arabs', in *Graeco-Arabica*, vol. III, 1984, pp. 129-35.

Latham, J. D. 'Notes on Mamluk Horse-Archers', in *Bulletin of the School of Oriental and African Studies*, vol. XXXII, 1969, pp. 257-67.

Makhdoomee, M. A. 'The Art of War in Medieval India', in *Islamic Culture*, vol. XI, October 1937, pp. 460-87.

Marshall, C. J. *Warfare in the Latin East*, 1192-1291, Cambridge, 1991.

McEwen, E. 'Persian Archery Texts: Chapter Eleven of Fakhr-i Mudabbir's Adab al Harb', in *The Islamic Quarterly*, vol. XVIII, 1974, pp. 76-99.

Nicolle, D. C. 'The Impact of the European Couched Lance on Muslim Military Tradition', in *Journal of the Arms and Armour Society*, vol. X, 1980, pp. 6-40.

- 'The Reality of Mamluk Warfare: Weapons, Armour and Tactics', in *Al-Masāq*, vol. VII, Leeds, 1994, pp. 77-110.

Rabie, H. 'The Training of the Mamluk Faris', in V. J. Parry and M. E. Yapp, *War, Technology and Society in the Middle East*, London, 1975, pp. 153-63.

Rex Smith, G. *Medieval Muslim Horsemanship*, London, 1979.

Ross, D. J. A. 'l'Originalité de Turoldus: le maniement de la lance', in *Cahiers de Civilizations Médiévales*, vol. VI, 1963, pp. 127-38.

- 'The Prince Answers Back: "Les Enseignements de Théodore Paliologue"', in C. Harper-Bill and R. Harvey (eds.). T*he Ideals and Practice of Medieval Knighthood (Papers from the first and second Strawberry Hill Conferences)*, Bury St. Edmunds, 1986, pp. 165-77.

Sadeque, S. F. *Baybars I of Egypt*, Oxford, 1956.

Sarraf, S. al-, *L'archerie Mamluke (648-924/1250-1517)* Lille 1990.

Shepard, J. 'The Uses of the Franks in Eleventh-century Byzantium', in *Anglo-Norman Studies*, vol. XV, 1993, pp. 275-305.

Smail, R. C. Crusading Warfare, 1097-1193, Cambridge, 1956.

- 'The Predicament of Guy of Lusignan, 1183-87', in B. Z. Kedar (ed.). *Outremer, Studies in the Crusading kingdom of Jerusalem presented to Joshua Prawer*, Jerusalem, 1982, pp. 159-76.

Smith, J. M., Jr. 'Ayn Jalut: Mamluk Success or Mongol Failure?', in *Harvard Journal of Asiatic Studies*, vol. XLIV, 1984, pp. 307-45.

Soler del Campo, A. 'Sistemas de Combate en la Iconografia Mozarabe y Andalusi Altomedieval', *in Boletín de la Asociación Española de Orientalistastas*, vol. XXII, 1986, pp. 61-87.

Zoppoth, G. 'Muhammad Ibn Mängli: Ein ägyptischer Offizier und Schriftsteller des 14. Jahrs.', in *Wiener Zeitschrift für die Kunde des Morgenlandes*, vol. LIII, 1957, pp. 288-99.

Morale and Motivation

Alexander, S. S. 'Heraclius, Byzantine Imperial Ideology and the David Plates', in *Speculum*, vol. LII, 1977, pp. 217-37.

Barber, M. (ed.). *The Military Orders: Fighting for the Faith and Caring for the Sick*, Aldershot, 1994.

Bosworth, C. E. 'Recruitment, Muster and Review in Medieval Islamic Armies', in V. J. Parry and M. E. Yapp (eds.). *War, Technology and Society in the Middle East*, London, 1975, pp. 59-77.

Boyle, J. A. 'Turkish and Mongol Shamanism in the Middle Ages', in *Folklore*, vol. LXXXIII, 1972, pp. 177-93.

Browne, E. G. *A History of Persian Literature*, London, 1902-6.

Canard, M. 'Delhemma, Sayyid Battal et 'Omar al-No'man', in *Byzantion*, vol. XII, 1937, pp. 183-8.

Constantelos, D. J. 'The Moslem Conquests of the Near East as Revealed in the Greek Sources of the Seventh and Eighth Centuries', in *Byzantion*, vol. XLII, 1972, pp. 325-57.

Cook, R. F. 'Crusade Propaganda in the Epic Cycles of the Crusade', in B. N. Sargent-Baur, *Journeys toward God: Pilgrimage and Crusade*, Kalamazoo, 1992, pp. 157-75.

Erdmann, C. *The Origin of the Idea of Crusade*, Princeton, 1977.

Esin, E. *A History of Pre-Islamic and Early Islamic Turkish Culture*, Istanbul, 1980.

Fennell, J., and Stokes, A. *Early Russian Literature*, London, 1974.

Forey A. J. 'Recruitment to the Military Orders (Twelfth to mid-Fourteenth Centuries)', in *Viator*, vol. XVII, 1986, pp. 139-71.

- 'The Emergence of the Military Order in the Twelfth Century', in *Journal of Ecclesiastical History*, vol. XXXVI, 1985, pp. 175-97.

- 'The Militarization of the Hospital of St. John', in *Studia Monastica*, vol. XXVI, 1984, pp. 75-89.

- *The Military Orders from the Twelfth to the Early Fourteenth Century*, London, 1991.

Irwin, R. 'Factions in Medieval Egypt', in Journal of the Royal *Asiatic Society*, 1986, pp. 228-46.

Jacoby, D. 'Knightly Values and Class Consciousness in the

Crusader States of the Eastern Mediterranean', in *Mediterranean Historical Review*, vol. I, 1986, pp. 158-86.

Kaegi, W. E. *Byzantine Military Unrest 471-843: An Interpretation*, Amsterdam, 1981.

Lambton, A. K. S. 'Reflections on the Iqta', in G. Makdisi (ed.). *Arabic and Islamic Studies in Honour of Hamilton A. R. Gibb*, Leiden, 1965, pp. 358-76.

Liu, J. J. Y. *The Chinese Knight-Errant*, Chicago, 1967.

Mango, C. 'Heraclius, the Threats from the East and Iconoclasm: AD 610-843', in P. Whitting (ed.). *Byzantium: An Introduction*, Oxford. 1971, pp. 39-59.

Marmardji, M. S. 'Les Dieux du Paganisme Arabe d'après Ibn al-Kalbi', in *Revue Biblique*, vol. XXXV, 1926, pp. 397-420.

Mottahedeh, R. P. *Loyalty and Leadership in an Early Islamic Society*, Princeton, 1980.

Munro, D. C. 'The Western Attitude Towards Islam during the Crusades', in *Speculum*, vol. VI, 1931, pp. 329-43.

Norris, H. T. *Saharan Myth and Saga*, Oxford, 1972.

Poliak, A. N. *Feudalism in Egypt, Syria, Palestine and the Lebanon, 1250-1900*, London, 1939.

Powers, J. 'Townsmen and Soldiers: The Interaction of Urban and Military Organization in the Militias of Medieval Castile', in *Speculum*, vol. XLVI, 1971, pp. 641-55.

Prawer, J. 'The Nobility and the Feudal Regime in the Latin Kingdom of Jerusalem', in F. L. Cheyette. *Lordship and Community in Medieval Europe: Selected Readings*, New York, 1968, pp. 156-79.

Richard, J. *Croisés, missionaires et voyageurs*, London, 1983.

Riley-Smith, J. *The First Crusade and the Idea of Crusading*, London, 1986.

- *The Knights of St. John in Jerusalem and Cyprus, c.1050-1310*, London, 1967.

Salinger, G. 'Was the Futuwa an Oriental form of Chivalry?', in *Proceedings of the American Philosophical Society*, vol. XCIV, 1950, pp. 481-93.

Turan, O. 'World Domination among the Medieval Turks', in *Studia Islamica*, vol. IV, 1955, pp. 77-90.

Tyerman, C. 'Who went on Crusade to the Holy Land?', in B. Z. Kedar (ed.). *The Horns of Hattin*, Jerusalem and London, 1992, pp. 13-26.

Communications

Ayalon, D. 'On one of the Works of Jean Sauvaget', in *Israel Oriental Studies*, vol. I, 1971, pp. 298-302.

El 'Ad, A. 'The Coastal Cities of Palestine during the Early Muslim Period', in L. I. Levine (ed.). *The Jerusalem Cathedra: Studies in the History, Archaeology, Geography and Ethnography of the Land of Israel*, vol. II, Jerusalem and Detroit, 1982, pp. 146-67.

Gaudefroy Demombynes, M. *Syrie à l'Epoque Mameloukes d'après les Auteurs Arabes*, Paris, 1923.

Sauvaget, J. *La Poste aux Chevaux dans l'empire des Mamluks*, Paris, 1941.

Horses, Harness and Land Transport

Bivar, A. D. H. 'Cavalry Equipment and Tactics on the Euphrates Frontier', in *Dumbarton Oaks Papers*, vol. XXVI, 1972, pp. 271-91.

Bulliet, R. W. *The Camel and the Wheel*, Cambridge, Mass., 1975.

Digby, S. *War-Horse and Elephant in the Delhi Sultanate, a study of military supplies*, Oxford, 1971.

Douillet, G. 'Furusiyya', in *Encyclopedia of Islam*, 2nd, edn., vol. II, Leiden, 1965, pp. 952-4.

Gode, P. K. 'The History of the Stirrup in Indian and Foreign Horsemanship - Between 852 BC and 1948', in P. K. Gode, *Studies in Indian Cultural History*, Poona, 1960, pp. 71-81.

Hill, D. R. 'The Role of the Camel and the Horse in the Early Arab Conquests', in V. J. Parry and M. E. Yapp (eds.). War, *Technology and Society in the Middle East*, London, 1975, pp. 32-43.

Kirpitchnikov, A. N. *Snaryazhenie Vsadnika i Verkhovogo Lonya na Rusi IX-XIIIbb (Harmachement du Cavalier et de la Monture en Russie aux IX-XIII Siècles)*, (in Russian with French summary), Leningrad, 1973.

Kretschmar, M. *Pferd und Reiter im Orient*, Hildesheim and New York, 1980.

Nesbitt, J. W. 'The Rate of March of Crusading Armies in Europe: A Study and Computation', in *Traditio*, vol. XIX, 1963, pp. 167-81.

Sinor, D. 'Horse and Pasture in Inner Asian History', in *Oriens Extremus*, vol. XIX, 1972, pp. 171-84.

Naval Warfare, Water Transport and Combined Operations

Abulafia, D. S. H. *Commerce and Conquest in the Mediterranean*, Aldershot, 1993.

Ahrweiler, H. *Byzance et la Mer: La Marine de Guerre, la Politique et les Institutions Maritimes de Byzance aux VIIe-XVe siècles*, Paris, 1966.

Ayalon, D. 'The Mamluks and Naval Power: A Phase of the Struggle between Islam and Christian Europe', in *Proceedings of the Israel Academy of Sciences and Humanities*, vol. I, 1965, pp. 1-12.

Balard, M. *La Mer Noire et la Romanie Génoise (XIIIe-XVe siècles)*, London, 1989.

Barber, M. 'Supplying the Crusader States: The Role of the Templars', in B. Z. Kedar (ed.). *The Horns of Hattin*, London and Jerusalem, 1992, pp. 314-26.

Basch, L. 'Navires et bateaux coptes: état des questions en 1991', in *Graeco-Arabica*, vol. V, 1993, pp. 23-62.

Canard, M. 'Les Expeditions des Arabes contre Constantinople, dans l'histoire et dans la légende', in *Journal Asiatique*, vol. CCVIII, 1926, pp. 61-121.

Charanis, P. 'Piracy in the Aegean during the reign of Michael VIII Palaeologus', in *Annuaire de l'Institut de Philologie et d'Histoire Orientales et Slaves*, vol. X, 1950, pp. 27-136.

Christides, V. 'Milaha: in the pre-Islamic and early medieval periods' (navigation), in *Encyclopedia of Islam*, 2nd. edn., vol. VIII, Leiden, 1991, pp. 40-6.

- 'Some Remarks on the Mediterranean and Red Sea Ships in Ancient and Medieval Times II: Merchant-Passenger vs. Combat Ships', in *Tropsis*, vol. II, 1987, pp. 87-99.

Dreyer, E. L. 'The Poyang Campaign, 1363: Inland Naval Warfare in the Founding of the Ming Dynasty', in F. A. Kierman

Jr. and J. K. Fairbank (eds.). *Chinese Ways in Warfare*, Cambridge, Mass., 1974, pp. 202–43.

Ehrenkreutz, A. S. 'The Place of Saladin in the Naval History of the Mediterranean Sea in the Middle Ages', in *Journal of the American Oriental Society*, vol. LXXV, 1955, pp. 100–16.

Groslier, G. 'La Batellerie Cambodgienne du VIIIe au XIIIe siècle de notre ère', in *Revue Archéologiques*, vol. V, 1917, pp. 198–204.

Kedar, B. Z. 'The Passenger List of a Crusader Ship, 1250: towards the History of the Popular Element on the Seventh Crusade', in *Studi Medievali*, vol. XIII, 1972, pp. 267–79.

Latham, J. D. 'The Strategic Position and Defence of Ceuta in the Later Muslim Period', in *Islamic Quarterly*, vol. XV, 1971, pp. 189–204.

Lev, Y. 'The Fatimid Navy, Byzantium and the Mediterranean Sea 909-1036 C.E./2977-427 A.H.', in *Byzantion*, vol. LIV, 1984, 220–52.

Mott, L. V. 'Medieval Ship Graffito in the Palau Reial Major at Barcelona', in *The Mariner's Mirror*, 1990, (vol. not known) pp. 13–21.

Nicolle, D. C. 'Shipping in Islamic Art: Seventh through Sixteenth Century AD', in *American Neptune*, vol. XLIX, 1989, pp. 168–97.

Pryor, J. H. 'The Crusade of Emperor Frederick II: 1220–29; The Implications of the Maritime Evidence', in *American Neptune*, vol. LII, 1992, pp. 113–31.

- 'The Naval Architecture of Crusader Transport Ships and Horse-Transports Revisited', in *The Mariner's Mirror*, vol. LXXVI, 1990, pp. 255–72.

- 'The Naval Architecture of Crusader Transport Ships: a reconstruction of some archetypes for round-hulled sailing ships', in *The Mariner's Mirror*, vol. LXVIV, 1983, pp. 171–219, 275–92, 363–86.

- 'Transportation of Horses by Sea during the era of the Crusades: Eighth Century to AD 1285 (part 1 to c.1225)', in *The Mariner's Mirror*, vol. LXVIII, 1982, pp. 9–27.

Pryor, J. H., and Bellabarba, S. 'The Medieval Muslim Ships of the Pisan Bacini', in *The Mariner's Mirror*, vol. LXXIII, 1990, pp. 99–113.

Robson, J. A. 'The Catalan Fleet and Moorish Sea-Power, (1337-1344)', in *English Historical Review*, vol. LXXIV, 1959, pp. 386–408.

Schneidman, J. L. *The Rise of the Aragonese-Catalan Empire 1200–1350*, London, 1970.

Sinor, D. 'On Water-Transport in Central Asia', in *Ural-Altaische Jahrbücher*, vol. XXXIII, 1961, pp. 156–79.

Zachariadou, E. A. 'The Catalans of Athens and the Beginnings of the Turkish Expansion in the Aegean Area', in *Studi Medievali*, vol. XXI, 1980, pp. 821–38.

Flags and Heraldry

Ackermann, P. 'Standards, Banners and Badges', in A. A. Pope and P. Ackermann, *A Survey of Persian Art*, vol. VI, London, 1939, pp. 2766–82.

Allan, J. W. 'Mamluk Sultanic Heraldry and the Numismatic Evidence: A Reinterpretation', in *Journal of the Royal Asiatic Society*, 1970, pp. 99–112.

Artin Pasha, Y. *Contribution à l'étude du blason en Orient*, London, 1902.

Calmard, J. 'Alam va 'Alamat: History', in *Encyclopedia Iranica*, vol. I, London, 1985, pp. 785–90.

Canard, M. 'Le Cérémonial Fatimite et le Cérémonial Byzantin', in *Byzantion*, vol. XXI, 1951, pp. 355–420.

Dennis, G. T. 'Byzantine Battle Flags', in *Byzantinische Forschungen*, vol. VIII, 1982, pp. 51–60.

García Gómez, E. 'Armas, Banderas, Tièndas de Campaña, Monturas y Correos en los "Anales de al Ḥakam II" por 'Isà Rāzā,' Andalus, vol. XXXII, 1967, pp. 163–79.

Ibn Hudayl (Hudhayl), trans. M. J. Viguera. *Gala de Caballeros, Blason de Paladines*, Madrid, 1977.

Khan, G. M. 'The Islamic and Ghaznawide Banners', in *Nagpur University Journal*, vol. IX, 1943, pp. 106–17.

Leaf, W. 'Developments in the System of Armorial Insignia during the Ayyubid and Mamluk Periods', in *Palestine Exploration Quarterly*, vol. CXV, 1983, pp. 61–74.

Leaf, W., and Purcell, S. *Heraldic Symbols: Islamic Insignia and Western Heraldry*, London, 1986.

Mackerras, C. *The Uighur Empire, according to the T'ang Dynastic Histories, Canberra*, 1972.

Mayer, L. A. *Saracenic Heraldry*, Oxford, 1933.

Solovjev, A. 'Les emblemes heraldiques du Byzance et les Slaves', in *Seminarium Kondakovianum*, vol. VII, 1935, pp. 119–64.

Arms, Armour and the Weapons Trade

Allan, J. W. *Persian Metal Technology, 700-1300 AD*, Oxford, 1979.

Allchin, F. R. 'A piece of scale armour from Shaikhān Dherī, Chārsada (Shaikhān Dherī Studies 1)', in *Journal of the Royal Asiatic Society*, 1970, (vol. not known) pp. 113–20.

Al-Tarsusi. 'Un traité d'armurerie composé pour Saladin', ed. and trans. C. Cahen, in *Bulletin d'Etudes Orientales*, vol. XII, 1947/8, pp. 103-26.

Bahnassi, A. 'Fabrication des Epées de Damas', in *Syria*, vol. LIII, 1976, pp. 281–94.

Bivar, A. D. H. *Nigerian Panoply*, Apapa, 1964.

Boudot-Lamotte, A. 'Kaws' (bow), in *Encyclopedia of Islam*, 2nd. edn., vol. IV, Leiden, 1978, pp. 795–803.

Canard, M. 'Les Relations entre les Mérinides et les Mamelouks au XIVe siècle', in *Annales de l'Institut d'Etudes Orientales de la Faculté des Lettres d'Alger*, vol. V, 1939–41, pp. 41–81.

De Hoffmeyer, A. B. *Arms and Armour in Spain, a short survey*, vol. I, Madrid, 1972; vol. II, Madrid, 1982.

Dien, A. E. 'A Study of Early Chinese Armor', in *Artibus Asiae*, vol. XLIII, 1981/82, pp. 5–66.

Elgood, R. (ed.). *Islamic Arms and Armour*, London, 1979.

Gomez-Moreno, M. 'Album de la Alhambra', in *Cuadernos de la Alhambra*, vol. 4, Granada, 1970.

Guerrero Lovillo, J. *Las Cántigas: Estudio Arqueológico de sus Miniaturas, Alhambra'*, Madrid, 1949.

Haider, S. Z. *Islamic Arms and Armour of Muslim India*, Lahore, 1991.

Haldon, J. F. 'Some Aspects of Byzantine Military Technology from the Sixth to the Tenth Centuries', in *Byzantine and*

Modern Greek Studies, vol. I, 1975, pp. 11-47.

Holstein, P. *Contribution à l'étude des Armes Orientales. Inde et Archipel Malais*, Paris, n.d.

Kirpitchnikoff, A. N. 'Russische Helm aus dem frühen Mittelalter', in *Zeitschrift für historische Waffen- und Kostümkunde*, vol. XV, 1973, pp. 89-98.

- *Drevnerusskoye Oruzhie (Les Armes de la Russia Medievale)* (in Russian with French summary), Leningrad, 1971.
- 'Russische Körper-Schutzwaffen des 9.-16. Jahrhunderts', in *Zeitschrift für Historische Waffen- und Kostümkunde*, vol. XVIII, 1976, pp. 22-37.
- 'Russische Waffen des 9.-15. Jahrhunderts', in *Zeitschrift für Historische Waffen- und Kostümkunde*, vol. XXVIII, 1986, pp. 1-22.

Kolias, T. G. *Byzantinischen Waffen*, Vienna, 1988.

Kozhomberdiyev, I., and Khudyakov, Y. 'Reconstruction of Ancient Turkic Armour from Sary-Djon Monument', in *Bulletin no. 17: International Association for the Study of the Cultures of Central Asia (UNESCO)*, Moscow, 1990, pp. 56-62.

Laufer, B. 'Chinese Clay Figures', in *Prolegomena on the History of Defensive Armor, part 1*, Chicago, 1914.

Melikan-Chirvani, A. S. 'Notes sur la terminologie de la metallurgie et des armes dans l'Iran Musulman', in *Journal of the Economic and Social History of the Orient*, vol. XXIV, 1981, pp. 310-16.

Mus, P. 'Etudes Indiennes et Indochinoises: III - Les Balistes du Bàyon', in *Bulletin de l'Ecole Française d'Extrême-Orient*, vol. XXIX, 1929, pp. 331-41.

Needham, J. *Science and Civilization in China, Vol. 5. Chemistry and Chemical Technology, Part VI. Military Technology: Missiles and Sieges*, Cambridge, 1994.

Nicolle, D. C. 'Armes et Armures dans les épopées des croisades', in *Les épopées de la croisade (Premier colloque international, Trier University 6-11 August 1984) in Zeitschrift fur franzosische Sprache und Literatur*, vol. XI, Wiesbaden, 1986, pp. 17-34.

- 'Arms and Armor illustrated in the Art of the Latin East', in B. Z. Kedar (ed.). *The Horns of Hattin*, Jerusalem and London, 1992, 327-40.
- 'Arms Production and the Arms Trade in South-Eastern Arabia in the Early Muslim Period', in *Journal of Oman Studies*, vol. V, 1984, pp. 231-8.
- 'Byzantine and Islamic Arms and Armour; evidence for mutual influence (Papers from the Second and Third International Congress on Greek and Arabic Studies)', in *Graeco-Arabica*, vol. IV, 1991, pp. 299-325.
- *Early Medieval Islamic Arms and Armour*, Madrid, 1976.
- *Islamische Waffen*, Graz, 1981.
- *The Arms and Armour of the Crusading Era 1050-1350*, 2 vols, New York, 1988.

Nishamura, D. 'Crossbows, Arrow-Guides and the Solenarion', in *Byzantion*, vol. LVIII, 1988, pp. 422-35.

Pons, A. 'La Espada en Mallorca durante el siglo XIV', in *Hispania*, vol. XI, 1951, pp. 536--606.

Pryor, J. H. 'In Subsidium Terrae Sanctae: Exports of foodstuffs and war material from the Kingdom of Sicily to the Kingdom of Jerusalem, 1265-1284', in *Asian and African Studies*, vol. XXII, 1988, pp. 127-46.

Robinson, H. R. *A Short History of Japanese Armour*, London, 1965.

- *Oriental Armour*, London, 1967.

Rubin, B. 'Die Enstehung der Kataphraktenreiter im Lichte der Choreszmischen Ausgrabungen', in *Historia*, vol. IV, 1955, pp. 264-83.

Schreiner, P. 'Zur Ausrüstung des Kriegers in Byzanz, im Kiewer Russland und in Nordeuropa nach bildlichen und literarischen Quellen', in *Acta Universitatis Upsaliensis*, Figuera, n.s. vol. XIX, 1981, pp. 215-36.

Soler del Campo, A. 'El Armemento Medieval Hispano', in *Cuadernos de Investigacion Medieval*, vol. III/6, 1986, pp. 1-51.

Trousdale, W. *The Long Sword and Scabbard Slide in Asia*, Washington, 1975.

Welsby, D. A. 'Soba Excavations', in *Azania*, vol. XVIII, 1983, pp. 165-80.

Werner, E. T. C. *Chinese Weapons*, Shanghai, 1932.

Woolley, G. C. 'The Malay Keris: its origins and development', in *Journal of the Malay Branch of the Royal Asiatic Society*, vol. XX/2, pp. 60-103.

Firearms

Ayalon, D. *Gunpowder and Firearms in the Mamluk Kingdom*, London, 1956.

Collin, G. S. 'Barud: General and The Maghrib', in *Encyclopedia of Islam*, 2nd. edn., vol. I, Leiden, 1960, pp. 1055-8.

Goodrich, L. C., and Fêng Chia-Shêng. 'The Early Development of Firearms in China', in *Isis*, vol. XXVI, 1946, pp. 114-24.

Partington, J. R. *A History of Greek Fire and Gunpowder*, Cambridge, 1960.

Zaky, A. R. 'Gunpowder and Arab Firearms in the Middle Ages', in *Gladius*, vol. VI, 1967, pp. 45-58.

Miscellaneous

Ashtor, E. *Histoire des Prix et des salaires dans l'orient médiéval*, Paris, 1969.

Cahen, C. 'L'Administration Financière de l'armée Fatimide d'après al-Makhzumi', in *Journal of the Economic and Social History of the Orient*, vol. XV, 1972, pp. 163-82.

Canard, M. 'Djasus' (spies), in *Enclopedia of Islam*, 2nd. edn., vol. II, Leiden, 1965, pp. 486-8.

Constable, G. 'The Financing of the Crusades in the Twelfth Century', in B. Z. Kedar, et al. (eds.). *Outremer: Studies in the History of the Crusading Kingdom of Jerusalem*, Jerusalem, 1982, pp. 64-88.

Mitchell, P. D. 'Leprosy and the Case of King Baldwin IV of Jerusalem', in *International Journal of Leprosy*, vol. LXI, 1993, pp. 283-91.

Nicolle, S. C. 'Wounds, Military Surgery and the Reality of Crusading Warfare; the Evidence of Usamah's Memoirs', in *Journal of Oriental and African Studies*, vol. V, Athens, 1993, pp. 3-46.

VIII
MISCELLANEA

MISCELLANEA

LAWS OF WAR 235
Byzantium, Reconquista and Crusade 235
The Muslim World 236
Other Religions 237
VICTORS AND VANQUISHED 239
Distribution of Booty 239
Prisoners, Enslavement and the Treatment of Non-combatants 241
INTELLIGENCE AND ESPIONAGE 244
TRAINING 246
THE SINEWS OF WAR 251
Taxation and Pay 251
Feeding an Army 255
MEDICAL SERVICES 257
MORALE 258
Religion 258
Literature and Literacy 263
Music 265
Drugs and Alcohol 267
LONG-DISTANCE COMMUNICATIONS 267
TRANSPORT 268
Land Transport 268
River Transport 273
COMBINED OPERATIONS 273
Raiding 273
Horse Transports 274
Coastal Landings 275
FLAGS AND HERALDRY 277
The Orthodox World 277
Iberia and the Crusader States 278
The Muslim World 278
Non-Islamic Asia 283
UNIFORMS: THEIR DECLINE AND RISE 284
THE MEDIEVAL ARMS INDUSTRY 288
Mining, Materials and Techniques 288
Arms Manufacture 290
The Arms Trade 291
FIREARMS: ORIGINS AND DEVELOPMENT 294
Fire Weapons 294
Gunpowder 294
Grenades and Rockets 296
Cannon 296
Handguns 296

LAWS OF WAR

Byzantium, Reconquista and Crusade

The Laws of War governing western Latin Christendom have been covered in Volume I, but there were variations in the Byzantine Empire and where fighting against Muslims or other non-Christians was concerned. The Byzantines inherited the Roman concept of victory in battle as a judgement from God. This element of 'trial by combat' on a larger scale persisted at least until the 10th century. Byzantine armies also tried to maintain the Roman tradition of limiting the destructiveness of war. For example the 6th-century Strategikon described the punishments to be inflicted on undisciplined soldiers while urging commanders to set a good example by avoiding unnecessary damage to cultivated areas. Despite Byzantine influence on other aspects of warfare in the Orthodox Christian states of eastern Europe, legalistic restraint was not characteristic of warfare in medieval Russia. Instead the members of a prince's *druzhina* or armed retinue were motivated by honour for themselves and glory for their leader, like the knights of western Europe.

Both Christian and Muslim concepts of *Just War* drew heavily on their predecessors, but there was a clearer distinction between *Just War* and *Holy War* in Christian countries, 'church and state' being officially separate throughout most of western Europe. *Just War* was essentially secular; Christian *Holy War* was seen as a response to injuries inflicted upon Christendom rather than upon a state which happened to be Christian. A tendency for *Just War* and *Holy War* to fuse into one struggle called *Crusade* was first seen along Christendom's frontier with Islam, most notably in the Iberian peninsula. This merging of *Just War* and *Holy War* caused problems for later medieval *canon* (religious) lawyers, yet many of the leading legal thinkers of the age of Crusade and Reconquista were influenced by Muslim ideas where the legal framework of warfare was concerned. In the 13th century the three preconditions laid down by St. Thomas Aquinas for *Just War* had clear parallels in Islamic Law; these being due authority, just cause and good intentions. On a more basic level, in 11th- to 13th-century Spain and Portugal the *fueros* or rules governing the activities of urban militias, their sources of information, spy-

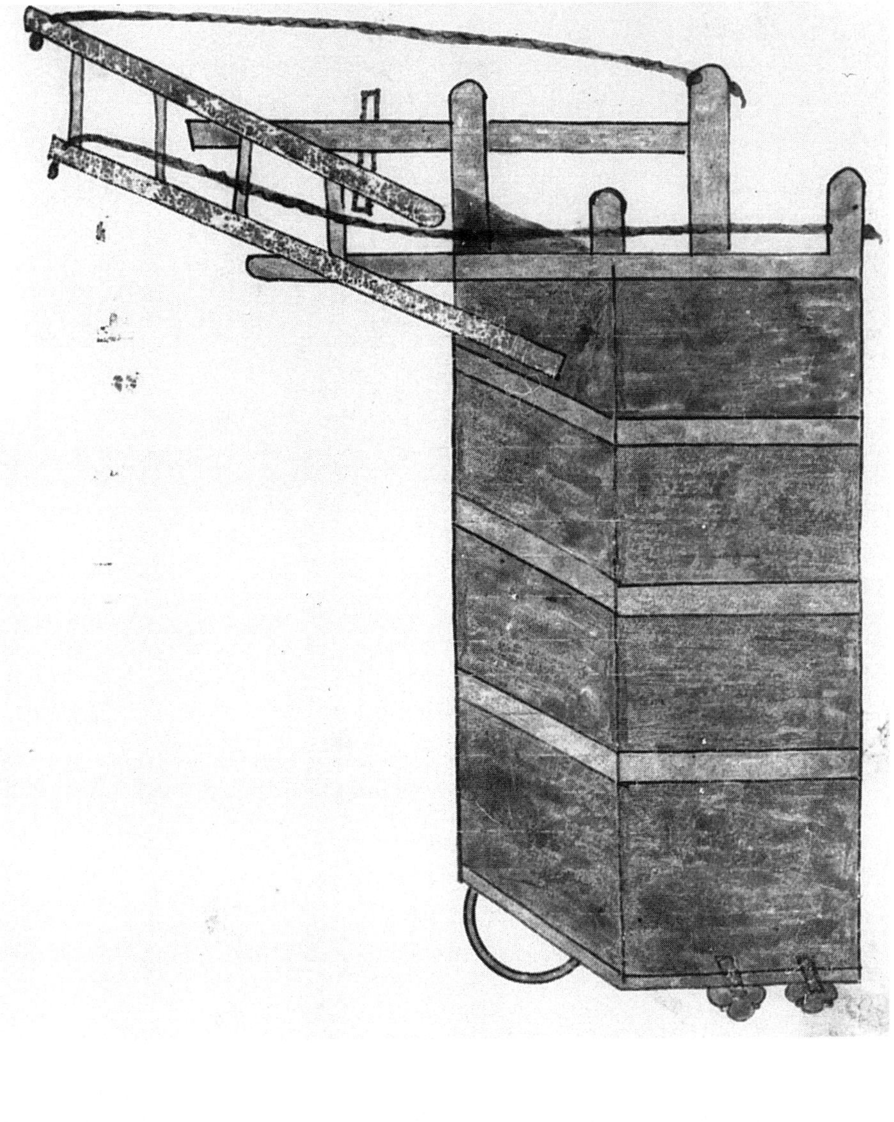

'Siege tower with an extending bridge', in an 11th-century Byzantine military treatise. Precisely the same device was described in Chinese manuals, suggesting that there was an extraordinarily free flow of military technological ideas across most of Asia during the medieval period. (Bibliothèque Nationale, MS. Grec. 2442, f.97r, Paris)

'Siege of Jerusalem', in a Catalan manuscript from Gerona, c.1100. It is worth noting that the man-powered mangonel is not mounted on one of the towers but behind the city wall. The lack of visible mail hauberks worn by any soldiers could suggest that they wore their tunics over their armour in the eastern Mediterranean or Islamic fashion. (Biblioteca Nazionale, MS. J.II.j, ff.189v-190r, Turin)

ing, counter-espionage, division of spoils, compensation for injury and exchange of prisoners were again remarkably similar to those seen across the Muslim frontier.

The Papacy, having given the *miles* or knightly class a new role in Christian society, consciously tried to divert the *miles'* warlike energy against Islam which the Church described as the 'most blameworthy nation'. Only the Church could, of course, proclaim a *Holy War* or Crusade. At the same time the *canon* lawyers of the late 11th to 13th centuries developed a legal framework for Crusading warfare, just as the civil lawyers developed 'laws of war' for ordinary political struggles, promising participants the status of heroes in this world and salvation in the next. Some thinkers, however, were soon suggesting that the repeated failure of the Crusades showed that they were at best misguided and might actually be immoral aggression. To counter such views those *canon* lawyers in favour of Crusading maintained that Islam existed merely so that Christians could gain merit by fighting it.

The Muslim World

The legal framework in which war took place was clearer in the Muslim world than in Christendom, though historians disagree on just when the legal and religious framework of Islamic society actually came into being. It existed from very early in Islamic history and Muslim 'laws of war' were firmly based upon Koranic Law. It is also clear that Muslim concepts of *Just War*, as distinct from *Holy War*, drew heavily upon the tribal traditions of pre-Islamic Arabia and were characterised by a wish to dominate politically rather than convert religiously. Conquest was a means to an end; not an end in itself.

The Koranic basis meant that 'physical' *jihād*, as opposed to the superior 'spiritual' *jihād*, was the only completely legitimate form of warfare. The *Ḥadīth* or 'Sayings' of the Prophet provided more detailed guidelines; for example stating that even sinful Muslim rulers should lead the *jihād* and that helping to equip a soldier for the *jihād* was itself a form of *jihād*. All defensive wars were in some respect a *jihād* since Islamic civilisation was theocratic and thus injury to the state was an injury to Islam and thus to God. As the centuries passed the waging of *jihād* became an increasingly important way for Muslim rulers to demonstrate their own political legitimacy, and by the 11th century it had become little more than a political tool in the hands of a ruling élite. The European Crusades then led to a revival of interest in the laws of *jihād*, the most famous legal scholar of this period being Ibn Rushd; his treatise of 1167 remaining a standard work for centuries. In this he maintained that *jihād* was essentially defensive and that the enemy could be any polytheist (believer in more than one god which, in Muslim eyes, included the Christian concept of the Holy Trinity). He went on to describe the damage which could be inflicted on the enemy; including destruction of property, injury to the person and enslavement, but he could not be attacked before being offered the chance to accept Muslim rule and pay the *jizyah* (tax) demanded of all non-Muslim subjects. More detailed 12th- and 13th-century works on *jihād* dealt with the problem of how outnumbered a

Muslim force must be before it was permitted to retreat, stating that the struggle should not be left to the military élite, soldiers also being considered as taking part in *jihād* even if they remained on garrison duty. Earlier books on *jihād* had already provided remarkably detailed regulations. For example if a man were given arms, armour and harness to take part in *jihād*, these remained his property after the campaign. A volunteer must also return home if recalled by his parents or by someone to whom he owed money. The *siyar* or regulations governing a soldier's behaviour had been codified in the mid-8th century. They prohibited the killing of women, children, the old or sick, the destruction of fruit-bearing trees, bee-hives and private houses, and the slaughter of flocks or herds except when needed for food. Soldiers should not mutilate the enemy, nor break promises or offers of safe conduct even if these had been given by gesture rather than the spoken or written word.

Laws governing peace between foes were equally detailed. Although *halakah*, or the annihilation of an enemy, existed in theory, it was restrained by the Koranic insistence on a lack of excess in human affairs. Instead wars were brought to a close through *amān*, *hudnah* or *ṣulḥ*. *Amān* was quarter or safe conduct and was intended to make warfare more humane. *Hudnah* was a truce, and as such was often regarded as an undesirable state of affairs between the *Dar al-Islam* (Land of Peace or Muslim world) and the *Dar al-Ḥarb* (Land of War or non-Muslim territory) since these two were theoretically supposed to be in a state of perpetual conflict. *Ṣulḥ* meant complete peace between equals and was a 'state of affairs' rather than a military objective. Normally it could only be between Muslim states; not with a neighbouring 'infidel' state. Warfare between Muslim states was normally known simply as *ḥarb* 'war' and had no religious sanction.

Despite this legal framework underpinning the conduct of war in Muslim civilisation, however, there was still a great contrast between theory and reality. A survival of tribal traditions in frontier areas could also lead to un-Islamic barbarism. For example the Saharan Berber Murābiṭin may have introduced head-hunting to Iberian warfare, a practice then copied by their Christian foes, though both sides apparently returned the decapitated bodies for burial. It also took some time for the Mongols, once converted to Islam, to abandon their old Central Asian military tradition of the total destruction of an enemy in favour of merely defeating them.

Other Religions

Nothing is known about the Laws of War in Sassanian Iran except that victory in battle was seen as proof of divine approval. Sassanian rulers were expected to be warlike, successful and show a ferocity towards their enemies which had much in common with Hindu India.

The ferocity characteristic of pre-Islamic Central Asian warfare had different origins, stemming from the difficulty of survival in a harsh environment. In fact the Mongols are said to have regarded their own lives as the property of their rulers, and that they slaughtered their opponents because they were

'Siege of a castle', on a silver plate from Malo-Amkovkaya in Siberia; Sughdian, probably Semirechye, 9th–10th centuries. The fortress is very similar to those seen in early 8th-century wall-paintings from Penjikent. The attackers are wearing a mix of mail and lamellar armour, and one of them is riding an armoured horse. (State Hermitage Museum, St. Petersburg)

In the early 13th century the aqueduct running from the bank of the Nile to the Citadel of Cairo also served as a fortified wall along the southern side of the city. As the channel ran uphill, there would probably have been a water-powered mill beside the river to lift water into the aqueduct, and thence a series of wind- or animal-powered mills to raise the water up a series of steps. (Author's photograph)

an enemy ruler's property. Central Asian armies' non-acceptance of 'rules of war' which were common to both Christian and Muslim societies led to widespread fear and confusion, particularly when this involved the breaking of truces, peace-agreements and promises of mercy. The basic Central Asian legal code was the *yāsa* or tribal law. Even after a Turkish or Mongol tribe became Muslim, several generations passed before their old *yāsa* gave way to Islamic law, particularly in the conduct of warfare; a mixed tribal and Muslim code called the *siyāsat* often followed in the intervening period. For example the Mamlūks, despite being the champions of Islam against Mongol aggression, remained sufficiently close to their Eurasian steppe origins to regard their enemies' Great *Yāsa* of Ghengiz Khān as a kind of legal model. In return Central Asian laws of war were gradually influenced by those of Islam after most of the peoples of the steppes themselves became Muslim – but never completely so.

The deeply anti-military character of medieval Chinese society led to warfare being seen in terms of profit and loss. Not only was damage to one's own side to be avoided, but it was thought better to inflict the least possible damage on the enemy so that there would be greater profit once he was subdued. There was also a persistent clash between the Confucian emphasis on morale and 'virtue' as aids in warfare, and an equally Chinese emphasis on good weaponry, good fortification and good training. The Korean *hwarangdo* or code of the *Hwarang* ('flowery youth') military élite probably lay behind the later Japanese *bushidō* code of the *bushi* or *samurai* élite. It consisted of 'five secular injunctions' set out by the Buddhist monk Wŏn'gwang early in the 7th century. These were: loyalty to the king, loyalty to parents, loyalty to friends, never retreating in battle and refraining from unnecessary killing.

In medieval India the code of the warrior and the laws of war were based upon Hindu scripture. The duties of the *kshatriya* warrior caste had, for example, traditionally been laid down in the ancient Vedic Laws of Manu which had probably been formulated in the 4th to 6th centuries. As in Sassanian Iran, victory in battle decided which side was right and which wrong. Might was right and military success was essential to maintain a ruler's legitimacy. A Hindu soldier captured in battle became the servant or slave of his captor, though only as long as it took to pay off his own ransom. He could then hope to be freed and 'born again' as a member of the *kshatriya* caste. In the Hindu states of what is now Indonesia the ruler's need of military strength was accepted as overriding other moral considerations, though the killing of the *brahmin* or priestly caste was regarded as a last resort.

VICTORS AND VANQUISHED

Distribution of Booty

The élite cavalry unit raised by the Sassanian Emperor Shāpūr II was forbidden to stop and collect the spoils of victory, which suggests that ordinary soldiers were prone to turn aside to do just that. Otherwise one may assume that some of the regulations in medieval Persian armies had been inherited from Sassanian times. In addition to the other benefits enjoyed by Byzantine professional soldiers, the troops had a right to a share of booty but the proportions were not fixed in law. The same ambiguity is seen in medieval Russia where only the Turkish *Cherniye Klobuki* 'Black Hats' had their rights legally defined, perhaps as part of the treaty whereby they offered their services to a Russian prince.

The generally greater consistency in the sharing of booty in Christian Iberia than in other parts of Europe was probably another example of Islamic influences. From the 11th to 16th

'Andalusian and Berber troops returning from a raid laden with booty', in a Castilian Spanish manuscript of the late 13th century. (Escorial Library, Cantigas of Alfonso X,Cod. T.I.1, Madrid)

Fragment of a carved ivory plaque from a Lombardic grave at Nocera Umbra near Perugia; Byzantine, probably 7th century. The cavalryman appears to be wearing the cloth hood or cap over his helmet, though this still has the plume associated with previous centuries. (Museo dell'Alto Medio Evo, inv. 528, Rome)

centuries it was normal for a Spanish ruler to take one-fifth of the total, the rest going to his army, and in 12th-13th-century Castile the soldiers elected an officer, known as the *quadrillo*, to supervise the division of spoils. The earliest Crusaders followed accepted western European practice, and here huge losses of horses and problems with even basic supplies meant that battlefield booty became an obsession. The Crusader States' continuing shortage of money probably also accounted for the fact that the King of Jerusalem took half the loot; more than was normal in western Europe.

Once again the legalistic and soon bureaucratic character of Islamic states led to clearly defined regulations concerning the division of the profits of war. *Fay'* had covered officially recognised booty since the early days and this was supposed to be distributed communally, one-fifth being reserved for government expenses. *Ghanīmah* was any other form of booty and was used as an incentive for unpaid volunteers. Early regulations provide interesting detail; for example one captured camel equalled ten sheep, and if a non-combatant labourer were present on the field of battle he got the same share as a fighting soldier. A hundred years later troops involved in *jihād* along the Byzantine frontier received one of three forms of reward or payment: a full share of the booty but no salary, wages but no booty, or small 'gifts' known as *raḍkh*. The booty from such border warfare was so important that military units had to be rotated so that every one got his fair chance of reward. This did not, of course, always improve military efficiency. Some Andalusian troops raiding Byzantine-held Sardinia in the early 8th century threw away the blades of their swords so that they could stuff more gold coins into their scabbards and so avoid having to add this to the common pool. Basically the same rules lasted throughout the Middle Ages, as when a cavalryman got twice or three times as much as a foot soldier, depending on which School of Law was being followed, because the cost of maintaining his horse was the equivalent of that for one or two men.

Prisoners, Enslavement and the Treatment of Non-combatants

The behaviour of different cultures towards the victims of war varied considerably. The Sassanian Empire almost had a culture of terror in which the Sassanian Emperor was expected to show no mercy. Those taken prisoner by the Sassanians were normally sold as slaves or used as military colonists. The élite cavalry unit raised by Shāpūr II, however, were forbidden to give quarter to an enemy or take captives; Shāpūr II himself being known as the 'shoulders man' because he dislocated the shoulders of all captured Arabs of military age to render them incapable of military service.

The pre-Islamic Arabs also cultivated a reputation for ferocity. The Lakhmid rulers of al-Hira mutilated some prisoners, whereas the mutilation of the body of a slain Muslim by his pagan enemies outraged the pagans' bedouin allies. In fact the pre-Islamic Arabs' ferocity appears to have been a carefully cultivated myth to inspire fear among non-Arab enemies. This was almost certainly the case when an Arab warrior in Byzantine service 'drank the blood' of a Germanic Goth he had just slain, terrifying the unfortunate German's comrades who retreated in dismay.

In many ways the Byzantine Empire was as ruthless as its Sassanian rival, though such ferocity was never given religious sanction. Nevertheless public cruelty played an important part in maintaining the status of the Emperor. The torture and dismemberment of captured enemy messengers in full view of their comrades was more characteristic of earlier rather than later centuries, but Emperor Basil II became known as the Bulgar Slayer when he blinded all his Bulgarian prisoners of war, except for a few who lost only one eye so that they could lead their fellow captives home. Prisoners who survived intact were, according to late 10th-century Byzantine law, the property of

'Army of Holofernes', in a manuscript from Acre in the Crusader Kingdom of Jerusalem, late 13th century. Despite being made in the Crusader States, the arms and armour seen in this manuscript are specifically Byzantine and probably give one of the clearest impressions of 13th century Byzantine cavalry. (Arsenal Bible, MS. Ars. 5211, Paris)

those who captured them. Enslaved prisoners worked in mines and bakeries, but prisoners of senior rank were probably kept in the *Great Praetorium* in the Byzantine capital. Such large numbers of Muslim men, women and children fell into Byzantine hands during the reconquests of the 10th century that the government had to buy large numbers of slaves from private owners to be returned home as part of various peace treaties. Muslim prisoners of war were, in fact, normally released and exchanged once peace was made. On the other hand Arab Muslim captives were regarded as such good military material that they were offered very generous terms if they converted to Christianity. This practice continued into the 12th century when large numbers of Qipchaq Turkish captives were settled, with their families, in various strategically located military colonies.

Slave-trading and the holding of prisoners for ransom became a major source of income for piratical fleets in the 14th-century Aegean, by which time the slave-raids had led to widespread depopulation throughout the south-eastern Balkans. Byzantine rather than western European or Central Asian influence probably lay behind the 10th-11th-century Russian habit of using large numbers of captives as agricultural labour, though the ransoming of more senior prisoners also became an important source of income for the aristocratic *boyar* class.

In the Iberian peninsula warfare appears to have been more ruthless along the frontier in the 9th and 10th centuries; military prisoners were rarely taken, but there were large-scale seizures of civilian populations for ransom. The French Crusaders' massacre of women and children at Barbastro in 1064 caused shock-waves throughout al-Andalus, as did the Crusaders' sending of several thousand female prisoners to the Byzantine Emperor. Thereafter the Christian armies of the *Reconquista* made a policy of slaughtering the Muslim religious élite, destroying mosques and burning books. They also tended to massacre military prisoners of African origin. Otherwise it was normal for both sides to hold prisoners for ransom, the only difference being the prospect of a new military career in Muslim territory if the captive were young enough and prepared to convert.

Sophisticated systems of prisoner-exchange developed along several Christian-Muslim frontiers, together with accepted ways of treating at least those captives of rank. In early 10th-century Byzantium, for example, Muslim prisoners of war were permitted to watch races in the *Hippodrome* and could attend the ceremonial Easter banquet wearing white tunics without belts. On at least one occasion they were entrusted with weapons so that they could help defend Constantinople against invading Bulgars. During prisoner-exchanges each released Muslim man was interrogated by a *Master of the Frontier Post* on the Muslim side to weed out spies, each telling his story which was then written down.

In Iberia the Church and the Military Orders played a primary role in prisoner-exchange in the 11th and 12th centuries, the Order of Mary of Mercy being established in early 13th-century Barcelona specifically to ransom captives. During that century officials known as *alfaquequas* sought out and arranged the ransoming of captives; the *alfaquequas* themselves being immune from capture even in time of war. The *mudejar* or remaining Muslim population of conquered territories also played a leading role in paying and delivering the required ransoms; the prisoners themselves then being given into the custody of *mudejar* mosques. Generally speaking families were expected to pay the cost of such ransoms, though a town might also help if a son or daughter offered themselves as surety. Town councils had their own officials called *exeas* who carried the ransom to the enemy, bringing back the freed prisoner and then keeping one-fifth of the proceeds as profit. Christian raids on the North African coast in the late 14th century in turn prompted new religious charities designed specifically to ransom Muslim prisoners; some of these subsequently evolving into military brotherhoods dedicated to the *jihād*.

Taking prisoners was not a characteristic of the First Crusade, though Christian sources made more of the massacres and mass rapes than did Muslim and Jewish sources, which suggests that these stories were exaggerated by their perpetrators rather than by their victims. An interesting letter written by a Jewish merchant stated that some Jews survived the First Crusade's conquest of Jerusalem, and were forced to wash the bodies of dead Crusaders before burial. Even the rape of Jewish women by Lotharingian and Flemish Crusaders may have been symbolic humiliation rather than true rape. Forced conversion of Muslims was rare and there does not appear to have been much compulsion even when Christian priests offered conversion to dying Muslims on the field of battle. On the other hand there were cases of prisoners being mutilated before release; as when Tancred I of Antioch destroyed the right eye of a Muslim captive so that he could no longer look around his shield. Captured Muslim men and women were normally sold in the slave-markets of Acre where, however, any sale would be declared void if the captive proved to be a leper. By the mid-12th century there were so many Muslim slaves in the Crusader states that these could be released in batches to buy off a threatened Muslim attack. One interesting letter sent to a mid-13th-century Pope complained that Italian ships were taking captured Greeks, Bulgarians, Vlachs and even Ruthenians from Central Europe to the west, pretending that they were Muslim captives from the Crusader states. Meanwhile the Hospitallers on the island of Rhodes habitually killed all their Muslim prisoners, and used Greek prisoners as galley-slaves. Similarly the Catalans who ravaged early 14th-century Anatolia killed all Muslim males over ten.

Compared with the brutality seen in so many Christian countries, the treatment of captives in the Muslim world was generally more humane, this being rooted in religious belief. Several *ḥadīths* or Sayings of the Prophet Muḥammad extolled the ransoming of prisoners as a pious act, and Muslim religious law banned the mutilation of prisoners of war. Enemy civilians who behaved as neutrals had to be treated as non-combatants. Slaves were similarly regarded as non-combatants because they were not free to decide their own actions. Rural civilians were generally left in peace, and urban civilians fared almost as well because the Muslims wanted to take such lands intact – including their wealth-producing populace. As

Wall-painting from Qasr al-Hayr al-Gharbi; Umayyad, c.728/9. This is one of the few illustrations of a horse-archer in specifically Arab-Islamic costume. Nevertheless his bow, quiver, bowcase on the far side of his saddle, and his use of stirrups indicate strong Turkish Central Asian influence even at this early date. (Author's photograph; National Museum, Damascus)

such Muslim military philosophy was closer to that of China than western Europe. Forced marriage or domestic enslavement was also contrary to Muslim law; one notable exception being in 8th-century southern France, where the Muslim conquerors were probably far from any available Muslim women. It is also interesting to note that rape of captured women had been a feature of pre-Islamic Arab tribal warfare and continued into the early Muslim centuries, though in both periods this involved a symbolic act of communal humiliation rather than sexual penetration. During this early expansionist period relatively few Muslim soldiers were captured by the Byzantines and not until the reign of the Caliph Hārūn al-Rashīd did Muslims feel it necessary to replace the old system of ransoming captives with something more organised. A number of locations were then designated as prisoner-exchange points. By the mid-9th century such exchanges would be supervised by a squad of 100 selected soldiers representing the main elements of the Caliph's army, presumably so that each group felt that its own men were given proper consideration. Most is known about Tarsus in Cilicia, where a specified proportion of the local wheat harvest was set aside to feed prisoners of war, probably meaning those awaiting ransom. By this time there was clearly a strong sense of shared interest among the military élites of the Middle East which in turn led to less savagery in battle and better treatment of prisoners. By the 10th and 11th centuries the ordinary soldiers preferred to show mercy to their opposite numbers and thus avoid unnecessary slaughter to avoid blood-feuds, in hope of winning over the enemy and because they might all be serving in the same ranks within a few years. This was particularly true of the officer class who could rarely be sure who their next ruler or commander might be at a time of acute political fragmentation. Nevertheless there were instances of savagery, particularly in the parading of the heads of slain enemy leaders on spear points.

When the Muslims reconquered Edessa (Urfa) from the Crusaders in the 12th century they massacred the city's Armenian infantry, perhaps because they were regarded as traitors. The Muslims also killed captive *Turcopoles* from the Crusader armies because they had once been Muslim and as apostates were subject to the ultimate penalty. Occasional massacres of captured Crusader crossbowmen reflected fear of such troops, and was contrary to Muslim law, though attempts were made to justify the slaughter of captured members of the Military Orders on the grounds that they were impossible to convert and were, of course, fanatical foes. On other occasions the garrisons of captured Crusader castles were permitted to go free, though they had to leave their weapons and horses behind. Refugees from Jerusalem, following its recapture in 1187, reported being better treated in Alexandria than in the fellow Crusader cities of Tripoli or Antioch. Nevertheless such large numbers of prisoners fell into Muslim hands from the later 12th century onwards that many of the 'soldiers' markets' attached to larger armies included a section where soldiers could sell captives for ready cash. Many captives abandoned hope of ransom and entered the service of various Muslim leaders. On other occasions prisoners found themselves released when one Muslim army conquered a citadel held by another, then sometimes fighting for their liberators before returning home.

An increase in battlefield savagery during the 13th and 14th centuries reflected not only the bitterness of the struggle against invading Crusaders but also the domination of most Muslim armies by Turks and Mongols. In Mamlūk armies, for example, it was quite common for the heads of slain enemies to be hung on the saddles of captured horses during a victory parade. Elsewhere some early 14th-century Ottoman Turkish leaders are said to have been buried with the corpses of dead foes in a pale survival of the ancient Central Asian Turkish practice of human sacrifice. Tīmūr-i Lank behaved more like a Central Asian pagan than a Turco-Persian Muslim ruler, using prisoners as front-line sappers, hurling an entire garrison over a cliff, building live captives into mud-brick walls and erecting towers of mud and skulls as a warning to those who might oppose his power.

The practice of capturing young men as military recruits, *mamlūks* or *ghulāms*, became a feature of Muslim armies from the 9th or 10th centuries until the end of the Middle Ages. It had no foundation in Islamic law but would provide many Muslim states with élite troops. The largest number came from the Central Asian steppes via Transoxiana and later by sea from what is now southern Russia and the Ukraine. This system of military slaves reached its final and most remarkable form in the 13th to early 16th-century Mamlūk Sultanate, a state run by and for *mamlūks*. In this fully developed system the first 'master' of such a slave was the merchant who bought him at or near the frontier. This man assessed his potential and was the first link in a chain of owners or masters as the recruit made his way to a *ṭabaqa* (training school) near one of the main barracks of the Mamlūk state. There he would be purchased by the state or by an individual and begin a military career which could culminate on the Sultan's throne. To some extent the Ottoman Empire adopted many aspects of the fully developed Mamlūk system. With the development of the *devsirme* system, however, the Ottomans diverged from previous practice by recruiting military 'slaves' from within their own frontiers which was clearly against Muslim law, though Ottoman scholars invented a variety of ingenious arguments in an attempt to justify it.

The treatment of captives in other parts of Asia varied according to the culture, time and place. A Turkish *khān's* slaves, servants and perhaps wives cut the long hair worn by both men and women, sometimes even trimming part of their ears, and placing these relics in the dead ruler's tomb. In Korea, and to some extent in China, defeated soldiers were liable to be enslaved, but as there was little use for slaves in nomadic society Central Asian Turks and Mongols often slaughtered prisoners out of hand. In fact the huge massacres carried out by the Mongols of the 13th century were normal in tribal warfare, though now done on a massive scale. An ancient Mongol belief that the soul resided in the thumb reflected the importance of archery among such people and also accounted for the occasional mutilation of the thumbs of defeated enemies.

The situation in India differed again. Here Hindu and Buddhist doctrines of *dharma* or highly visible 'correct conduct' led to more humane warfare, particularly when *kshatriya* (warrior-caste) was fighting fellow *kshatriya*. The Hindu moral and religious code also tried to forbid the use of weapons against non-combatants, those fleeing a battle, or wounded, or disarmed, or pleading for mercy. According to the 7th-century Chinese traveller Hiuen Tsang, however, a general was ill-advised to return home defeated since he was liable to be given women's clothing and driven out to seek his own death. On the other hand enslaved prisoners were better treated in Hindu India than in ancient Greece or Rome. Buddhist cultural influence from India also accounted for the fact that a 14th- century Burma ruler who ate a meal off the chest of a dead enemy was regarded as demonstrating his barbaric family origins.

INTELLIGENCE AND ESPIONAGE

Official missions or embassies played a vital role as sources of information and for planting false information between the Romano-Byzantine and Sassanian Empires. A number of Sassanian works were subsequently preserved in early Arab Muslim books and one of these stated that rulers would test the loyalty of proposed ambassadors by first sending them on less important missions within the state where their actions were observed by the Sassanian government's informers. Embassies were also designed to impress potential rivals with Sassanian power and wealth, though such ostentatious displays could backfire. For example before the battle of Qādisīyah the Sassanian commander received a Muslim envoy on a tall gilded throne, wearing a jewelled uniform and surrounded by splendidly dressed officials standing on fine carpets. For his part the Muslim envoy arrived dressed in coarse cloth, his sword wrapped in cloth rather than a scabbard, and riding a small shaggy horse. Both were, in different ways, making a political point.

The Byzantine Empire had a sophisticated espionage system and a tradition of using bribes to win over poorer neighbours. The Byzantine authorities in early 7th-century Syria clearly tried to subvert the leaders of the first Arab Muslim attacks, as they had done with previous Arab raiders but this time they failed because these new invaders had different motives. Once a new frontier was established across eastern Anatolia the Byzantines tried to make it a clear ideological barrier between Christendom and Islam. Embassies and merchants still crossed this ideological frontier and, like those supervising the exchange of prisoners, played a vital role in intelligence-gathering. In return envoys from foreign courts had a special status and function in the Imperial Court where they were termed *filoi* or 'friends'; being provided with guards to protect them and, more importantly, to stop them making unofficial contacts within Byzantine territory. Byzantine envoys were similarly called *filoi* when sent abroad but there was also a system of 'hidden friends', these being unofficial sources of information such as merchants, pilgrims and spies. The use of itinerant monks as sources of information was again seen in Orthodox Christian Russia where, in the 12th century, some leading soldiers are known to have retired as monks and to have travelled far abroad on behalf of their princes.

Western Christian states did not have highly developed intelligence-gathering systems, though the emphasis which a 14th-century Spanish book on war and government put upon spies and false rumours to undermine enemy morale was remarkably similar to the views expressed in both Byzantine and Islamic manuals. Once they had established themselves in the Holy Land the Crusaders also learned fast; the notorious Reynald of Châtillon developing such an effective spy network among the bedouin tribes of southern Jordan and the northern Hijaz that Ṣalāh al-Dīn had to mount a special campaign to bring these tribes back into line. But by far the most effective western intelligence networks were those of Genoa and Venice. Although their primary interests were commercial rather than military, Genoese merchants regularly traded with China and brought back extremely accurate information about affairs throughout western and Central Asia.

The Muslim states inherited the intelligence-gathering apparatus of several sophisticated states, though various imaginative cases of intimidation seen to reflect the Arabs' own military heritage. For example, the Muslim army at the battle of Qādisīyah put long swaying palm-branches on some of their camels to make them look monstrous and thus frighten the Sassanian army's elephants. Then there was the case of a Mus-

'Man assassinated while playing backgammon', in a manuscript compiled in the Crusader Kingdom of Acre or in France, late 13th–early 14th centuries. The Crusader States were a channel not only for advanced military technology from Asia to Europe, but also other aspects of the knightly way of life including music and various games. (Histoire Universelle of William of Tyre, MS. Fr. 9081, f. 160r, Bibliothèque Nationale, Paris)

lim commander who bent over a brazier to make his eyes bloodshot before negotiations with the *khātūn* or 'queen' of Bukhara, so frightening the poor woman that he won a better deal. A few decades later an Umayyad commander had false information from supposed spies shot into the enemy camp, and Ṭāriq, leader of the first Muslim raid into Spain, burned his own ships and had his men pretend they were cannibals as part of a wider propaganda campaign to frighten the Visigoths. This cannibalism ruse was used by Umur, the 14th-century Turkish ruler of Aydin, to terrify some Vlach Romanian prisoners; he then released them to spread panic far and wide. Prolonged military march-pasts to impress foreign envoys, lasting from dawn to midday, was part of the same tradition of psychological warfare.

Observation of enemy movements was, of course, a primary responsibility of frontier forces; coastal towns in Syria and Palestine monitoring the movements of Byzantine fleets. At the same time foreign merchants in such ports were confined to specified lodgings for fear they might be Byzantine spies. Although Muslim states had similar intelligence systems, their interests differed. In Andalusia merchants were used to gather information about Christian countries to the north, and both sides used professional guides known as *dalil* in Arabic, *adalides* in Spanish. Many of the latter were, in fact, renegade Muslims. But throughout the rest of the Muslim world there was a massive lack of interest in western Europe. In fact the educated élite of medieval Muslim countries regarded western males as brave and strong but also ignorant, dirty and promiscuous, while western women were of no use at all. In comparison Byzantine men and women were regarded as more honest and more intelligent.

Despite religious reservations about using spies within Muslim states, as opposed to sending them into 'infidel' territory, state espionage and intelligence systems played an increasingly important role in both external warfare and internal security. Since the mid-8th century these involved the *jāsūs*, or spy operating in enemy territory, and the *ᶜayn* ('eye') who was either a counter-espionage agent within his own country or served as an 'observer' for a Muslim army. By the 10th century a dynasty such as that of the Sāmānids in Transoxiana had a special department, the *diwan al-mushrif*, which dealt with agents and assessed their information. A book on government, written by an 11th-century chief minister, stated that such spies could be disguised as merchants, travellers, dervishes, medicine sellers or beggars. The Mamlūk state brought this intelligence system to a fine art; Sultan Baybars being renowned for his preoccupation with military secrecy and keeping a close eye on his own commanders. The destination of a Mamlūk raiding force was often kept secret even from its own commander, who opened his sealed orders one by one as the march progressed. The continuing importance of this intelligence structure is shown by the fact that a late 14th-century Mamlūk treatise on warfare devoted no less than three chapters to the subject of keeping spies loyal, controlling them and specifying the qualifications they needed. A ruler should be friendly towards his own spies, pay them well before and after missions, look after their families and not blame them for failure.

On the other side of the frontier the Mongol Īl-Khāns also had a highly developed espionage system with 'secret police agents' known as *kourtch* based upon Turco-Persian and Chinese models. These, however, were noted more for their concern with internal security, and for the imposition of harsh penalties for disaffection, than with external information-gathering. China itself had an exceptionally highly structured intelligence service, often using Buddhist pilgrims as sources of information about foreign lands. Under the Sung dynasty a new *Bureau of Military Affairs* took over these duties, though the old *Board of War* continued to make and store military maps. These in turn were of a standard of accuracy and detail not seen anywhere else in the medieval period. In 1012 Chinese military maps were said to cover China and foreign lands, concentrating on tactically significant features such as hills, streams, routes in and out of Chinese territory, 'inner' and 'outer' defences, secure and insecure areas. Copies were made for those who needed them.

TRAINING

Military training in the professional armies of the Middle East and eastern Asia involved structured programmes and exercises, many of which evolved over centuries. Although the drill training of the Roman army had declined by the 5th century, the following years saw the development of different military skills often focusing on archery. For example an anonymous mid-6th-century Byzantine military treatise stated that an archer's skills emphasised accuracy and power rather than speed of shooting. Although many Byzantine towns had their own cavalry training grounds, called a *campus martius* in Latin or a *pedion* in Greek, larger-formation manoeuvres and mock battles appear to have required additional training before the start of a specific operation. The basic elements of Byzantine military training persisted throughout the early medieval period. The military élite of the 9th and 10th centuries trained in the use of weapons, shields and the wearing of armour, riding, archery and tactics. By the late 11th century this also included horse-archery, and infantry archers were trained to shoot in disciplined ranks, often at a diagonal angle in order to get around the opposition's shields. Despite the low opinion of later medieval Byzantine soldiers held by their western contemporaries, structured training programmes remained central to Byzantine military administration. The sons of aristocratic families still tended to study at military schools from the age of sixteen onwards; youngsters destined for higher military careers were trained at court. Others, destined for ordinary officer ranks, served in court or guard regiments where raw recruits were trained by veterans. During the 12th century there was a slight shift towards western European skills such as the use of the *couched lance*, but new recruits still played the eastern cavalry training game of *tzykanion* (polo). A western-style *tournament* was held in Byzantine territory in 1332, but most 14th- and early 15th- century cavalry

'Huntsman', in a mosaic from Antioch; Syrian-Byzantine, 6th–early 7th centuries. Hunting provided essential training for almost all medieval armies. On this mosaic floor infantry and cavalry are fighting, struggling against assorted wild animals. (Author's photograph; Art Museum, Worcester, USA)

training appeared increasingly Turkish or Islamic in style. Warlike 'games' involving teams of equal size armed with maces sound exactly like those in the late medieval Armenian epic of David of Sassoun, and virtually identical with Mamlūk *furūsīyah* exercises, as did 'games' involving lances or horse-archery.

The little evidence from 12th to 14th-century Armenia also indicate Muslim-style rather than western European cavalry training. The situation in Russia was slightly different. Here the ritual combats characteristic of pre-Christian Russia continued until the 12th century, and huge and prolonged hunting expeditions had much in common with those of Central Asian nomads. *Tournaments* as knightly entertainment and cavalry training do not appear to have been recorded in Christian Spain until the 13th century and not in Portugal until the late 14th. On the other hand early forms of *tournament* were held in Crusader Antioch in the mid-12th century but not in the Kingdom of Jerusalem until the late 13th century, though such variations probably reflect inadequate written records. Detailed Rules of various Military Orders shed interesting light on training in the Crusader states. The Rule of the Templars, basically dating from the mid-12th century, shows that training was essentially tactical rather than theoretical, and information about the Hospitallers shows that military exercises were mostly performed in the afternoon, three times a week, and featured 'drill' and the use of weapons including the crossbow.

The Muslim-Arab conquerors of the Middle East inherited not only training grounds but also their predecessors' professional attitudes towards training. This included a deep interest in strategy and tactics. As a result both theoretical and practical military 'advice' and manuals survive from a remarkably early date. A greater number of works are known only by name, including original works as well as translations of Latin, Greek, Persian and Indian military treatises. The oldest surviving source is included in a collection of 'letters of good advice'

Horseman playing polo, on a ceramic bowl from Nīshāpūr, eastern Iran, 10th century. Polo played a central role in cavalry training from Korea and China through India and Central Asia to the Muslim Middle East and Byzantium. (Museum für Kunst und Gewerbe, inv. 1956, 153, Hamburg)

sent by the Arab scholar ᶜAbd al Ḥamīd ibn Yayḥī to the last Umayyad ruler in 747, at a time of considerable change in the organisation and tactics of Muslim armies. A wide-ranging military treatise was then written by one of the commanders of the Caliph al-Ma'mūn which survives in an 11th-century Fāṭimid abbreviation, though such books were written for senior rather than junior officers. An idealised training schedule attributed to the élite guards regiments of the 10th-century Sāmānid rulers envisaged one year as a foot soldier, two years' basic horsemanship, a fourth year using mace and bow on horseback, and subsequent years of gradual promotion. Large reviews also gave a senior commander a chance to practice the drawing up and movement of large bodies of men as units, as well as testing battlefield communications, discipline and responsiveness. Medieval Muslim cavalry took part in various exercises including polo which the Arabs learned from the Sassanians. The earliest Arabic references to a cavalry exercise called *kurra* might have referred to javelin-throwing comparable either to earlier Roman cavalry exercises or to the Turkish horsemen's javelin game of *jirid* or *cirid*. Cavalry javelin-throwing exercises, including variations on ordinary hunting skills with the bow, continued to be used until Tīmūrid and Ottoman times.

Practice to improve individual skills also featured prominently, and by the late 9th century cavalrymen were tilting with spears against metal rings mounted on top of columns to improve their dexterity. The Caliph Hārūn al-Ras̲h̲īd is credited with introducing archery against the *burjās* into established military exercises; this included horse-archery but probably was also used with the spear. Turkish influence lay behind the adoption of the *qig̲h̲aj* or *qīqaj* exercise in which a horseman shot at a ground-level target while on the move at very close range. This had more of a military application than the *qabaq*, a target mounted high on a pole which was used to improve a horse-archer's dexterity when shooting at difficult angles. A style of horsemanship known as the Arab or Islamic School reached its peak of development in Egypt, Syria and al-Andalus in the 12th and 13th centuries, involving initial training bareback. Such constant honing of professional military skills rendered the old citizen armies of the early Islamic period out of date by the 9th or 10th century; yet infantry skills were still in demand and could involve some unusual training devices such as the 10th-century Syrian ᶜ*ajala*, an archery target in the form of a stuffed animal mounted on a four-wheeled cart which was rolled downhill. At about the same time young *g̲h̲ulām* (recruits) in the frontier city of Tarsus were formed into units under the guidance of an elder shaykh who educated and trained the youngsters. Each age group was given weapons appropriate to their size and strength, including Arab infantry and Persian cavalry bows, crossbows and swords. On coming of age they were attached to a regular infantry unit and took part in border raids, but only joined a cavalry regiment as 'mature adults'. This was much the same as the *ḥujra* (training barracks) system recorded in 10th- to 12th-century Ikhshīdid and Fāṭimid Egypt. It proved so successful that it was greatly expanded in the 12th century to face the new Crusader threat, its recruits being trained in riding and the use of spear, heavier lance, bow, sword, and other military skills.

'Icon of St. Sergius', probably painted in the Crusader States, late 13th century. The warrior saint is here equipped as a horse-archer and probably reflects the appearance of the turcopoles who formed a vital part of the armies of all Middle Eastern Christian states. (Monastery of St. Catherine, Mount Sinai, Egypt)

Fragment of a plate from Madinat al-Zahra; Andalusian 10th century. This broken piece of pottery provides virtually the only illustration of a fully armoured Muslim-Andalusian cavalryman from the Caliphate of Cordoba's period of greatest power. He has a helmet possibly of two-piece construction with a very broad nasal, a full mail hauberk and coif, and what appears to be a kite-shaped shield. The plate may have been part of an architectural decoration. (Madinat al-Zahra Museum, inv. MA/VM-96, Cordoba)

Under the Ayyūbids most senior military positions went to members of the ruling family rather than to specially trained officers. But the Fāṭimid *ḥujarīya* system continued with several modifications throughout the Ayyūbid and Mamlūk periods. No less than twelve *ṭibāq* (training schools), as they were now known, existed in Cairo's Citadel under the Mamlūks, each selecting youngsters of a specific ethnic origin. Some of the manuals written during this period would have been used in these schools, at least by the instructors, as they were no longer merely theoretical works of strategy and organisation but dealt with the smallest details of the use and repair of military equipment. Those slave-origin recruits who passed through these training barracks were freed on completion of their courses, though they proudly retained the name of *mamlūks* ('slaves').

Each Muslim city had one or more *maydān* (parade or military training grounds) comparable to the old Roman *campus martius*. Some included a covered kiosk where the ruler could watch his men train. In time of military emergency troops also trained in the courtyards of their own houses and it may be that individual weapons training was normally carried out in such privacy while the *maydān* was reserved for training in battlefield manoeuvres. Full-scale military reviews were no mere game; sometimes being held in full armour in the heat of summer as a test of endurance. Other *maydān* were designed for long-range 'flight shooting' with a line of ranging markers.

Although surviving training manuals include quotations from much earlier sources, including ancient Greek works, these anachronistic insertions generally deal with tactics and theory rather than training exercises. A few books on *furūsīyah* seem more concerned with 'gentlemanly conduct' and the knowledge which might prove useful in company rather than in the tumult of battle. Nevertheless one of the most prolific writers of works on magic, on foretelling the future, on being a courtier and a ruler, on military training, archery, battlefield tactics, naval warfare and grand strategy, had himself been a senior army officer. In fact the Mamlūks, like the traditional British military élite, had a profound belief in 'square-bashing' as a way of producing good soldiers with the habit of immediate obedience. The skills involved in *furūsīyah* exercises were above all use of the lance, polo, two or more forms of archery, crossbow shooting, swordplay, the mace, wrestling, various displays associated with public processions, hunting and horse-racing. The final phase of a Mamlūk horse-archer's training, after he had achieved an adequate standard in the *maydān*, took place in the open countryside and probably involved manoeuvres much more akin to battlefield conditions. Training with the spear still involved the *birjas*, this now being described as seven pieces of wood piled on one another with a ring on top, the horseman attempting to lift off the ring without knocking over the wooden blocks. A mid-14th-century Mamlūk training manual included a cavalry exercise called 'playing the Frank [western European]' and was clearly based upon jousting, but there were 129 other ways of handling the lance, plus twenty-one disengagement exercises or parries and thirteen unit manoeuvres. Practice with the sword was almost as complicated, various sword-strokes being made against from five to 100 layers of wet felt placed on a heap of wet clay. A few exercises even involved two swords, as was featured in some Far Eastern 'martial arts'. Basically the same training was continued by Ottoman armies in the 14th century and later. Now, however, the *Yeni Çeri* corps had its own distinctive programme suited to its role as an infantry force. Training of *devsirme* recruits took from five to seven years, the best being selected for higher promotion; even ordinary trainees were instructed in mathematics and some degree of literacy.

Much the same forms of military training schedules developed in North Africa and Andalusia. In the 12th and 13th century the Muwaḥḥidin trained specially selected youths, called *ḥuffāẓ*, to ride, shoot, swim and row; the latter not being recorded in the military training schedules of any other Muslim dynasty. Later in the 14th century the Andalusian scholar Ibn Hudhayl described the sort of training expected of a soldier from Granada during his day. This was similar to that seen in Mamlūk Egypt except for the major role given to the use of the crossbow on foot and from horseback. Ibn Hudhayl also stated that a cavalryman stood in his stirrups to strike with the sword, *à la jinete*, as it was known on the Christian side of the border.

Compared with such an abundance of information, little is known about Mongol military training. Large-scale and prolonged hunting expeditions played a major role, though they were largely used to develop a commander's ability to coordinate widespread forces. The only other forms of 'exercise' were little-known riding ceremonies which took place at the accession or death of a ruler. The lack of information about Chinese military training is more surprising. During the T'ang period the *fu-ping* (militia) are known to have been reviewed every month, but carried out their training in winter so as not to interfere with agricultural work. Such training involved archery and was carried out as military units, as were basic manoeuvres, responding to commands by bell and gong, and polo for the cavalry. The long-established Chinese tradition of examinations in both tactical theory, real combat skills, horse-riding and leadership still existed for the selection of officers, and the manuals used in such training were considered so sensitive that great efforts were made to avoid their falling into enemy hands. Under the following Sung dynasty, Chinese professional soldiers trained daily but this routine later declined, together with the men's military skill, when they were used in forced labour. The high-ranking *Military Intendants* of the Sung period could, however, only be selected from men who had reached a certain level of military-academic qualifications, such as '*auxiliary academician*' or '*academician in waiting*'. Polo was also played by the military élite of Korea, being known as *kyŏkku*. In 12th-century India the cavalry of Karnataka similarly played polo, but medieval India was better known for another contribution to the science of military training – chess. In its earliest form it was known as *chaturanga* and was played by two pairs of allied teams. The ancient *kshatriya* (warrior caste) was expected to 'indulge in pleasure' when not actually involved in warfare, though they presumably also trained, and by the medieval period the Hindu warrior élites were supposed to be fully trained infantry archers by the age of sixteen.

THE SINEWS OF WAR

Taxation and Pay

Reforms to the tax system of the Sassanian Empire in the 6th century provided the financial basis for subsequent reforms to the Sassanian army. This restructured tax system was then inherited by the Muslim conquerors who continued to use many aspects of it, alongside their own religiously based form of Islamic taxation. As a result of a series of financial crises in the 5th and 6th centuries, Romano-Byzantine troops often did not get their pay, and although soldiers could expect additional rewards if their unit took the first honours in battle, this was hardly a reliable source of income. In 588/9 there was an attempted overhaul of the pay system and by the end of the 6th century soldiers received a yearly cash allowance with which to kit, clothe and feed themselves. The importance of financial administration in early Byzantine armies was such that an officer with the rank of *Sakellarios* (treasurer) was sometimes put in command of a whole army, probably to reassure the men that they would get paid. A much smaller *roga* (allowance) was paid to some Arab bedouin tribes to patrol the desert frontier and guard the official frontier entry points. In the 7th century a gradual trend began whereby frontier troops were allocated land on which to support themselves. This did not, of course, mean that the soldiers in question became farmers; rather they lived off the rents of such estates. *Theme* armies of the 9th and 10th centuries continued to be paid three times a year, but since they also earned money from their estates, these tri-annual cash payments were probably to cover the additional expense of maintaining horses, armour and harness. Troops based in far-flung provinces also raised money directly from the local populations. Only the *tagmata* troops based around the capital were paid solely in cash. Young recruits received very little, but their pay increased

significantly once they were fully trained. There were also enormous differences in the pay rates of various officer ranks. Nevertheless ordinary Byzantine soldiers received less than their Muslim opponents.

The later Byzantine Empire and its fragmented parts tried to keep this system going but often could not afford it. Even so the mercenaries of the 13th and 14th centuries appear to have been paid monthly, this sometimes being advanced by independent merchants and bankers because the government itself lacked sufficient cash. Special taxes could also be raised for specific military emergencies. Byzantine influence probably also lay behind the system of paying full-time professional soldiers in early Christian Russia where the Varangians demanded fixed sums even in peacetime, plus additional bonuses for long-distance campaigns. Russian princes partially solved this problem by settling such troops in provincial towns where the soldiers could live off local tribute.

Military payment was one of the areas in which Islamic influence was most obvious in Christian Iberia, the pay of ordinary soldiers being highest in regions most recently conquered from the Muslims. Pay also varied according to military role and the expenses involved; cavalry on armoured horses receiving twice that of men on unarmoured horses, while a mounted crossbowman could be paid twice an infantry crossbowman. The idea that men went on Crusade in hope of carving out a rich new life for themselves in the fabled East was rarely true; Crusading being very expensive as well as dangerous. In reality the rich supported the poor and men were generally financed by their lords. Once the Crusader States had been established in Syria and Palestine, direct taxation was used to pay for mercenaries. The size and value of *fiefs* varied considerably; *money fiefs* for a knight normally being twice the value of those for a squire or *turcopole*. It is also interesting to note that by the 14th century a mercenary recruited abroad was paid one-third more than a man recruited locally in Crusader Greece. The increasing cost of being a fully equipped knight also meant that an early 14th-century Crusading knight should receive four times the pay of an infantry crossbowman.

The earliest information about pay in the Muslim armies shows that this varied according to when the tribe to which a man belonged joined the Muslim cause, but even so the differences were relatively small. This was in the form of a salary known as an *ᶜaṭā* given to all Muslim Arab soldiers, though perhaps only during prolonged expeditions. As the century of Umayyad rule progressed the Caliphs' élite Syrian troops received four times the pay of an ordinary soldier. The Umayyad army was, in fact, an expensive as well as effective fighting force. Otherwise the main source of revenue for the early Islamic conquerors was the *fayᶜ* or booty demanded from the local populace. The ruling Umayyad family also owned large estates in Syria, which were another source of revenue with which to pay élite guards units. Khālid Ibn al-Walīd is said to have been the first to impose the *jizya* tax upon a conquered non-Muslim population during the first wave of Arab-Islamic expansion; this being justified on the grounds that 'protected' non-Muslims should thus pay for the Muslim troops who defended them. This *jizya* maintained not only the local *jund* garrison but also its families. The families of men killed in action also received a state pension. By the end of the Umayyad period the army was divided into *ᶜirāfa* (pay-units) of about ten to fifteen men. As in most armies of the period, cavalry received twice as much as infantrymen and by the 10th century senior officers received ten times as much as their men; the rewards given to military commanders were huge. Quite staggering sums were given to successful commanders by the 9th century and even an ordinary late 8th-century ᶜAbbāsid soldier received about forty times the pay of an unskilled labourer. The old *ᶜaṭā'* pay system soon declined under the ᶜAbbāsids, being replaced by various other forms of pay such as the *juᶜl* which was given directly to individual soldiers, unlike the *ᶜaṭā'* which had been distributed via tribal or other units. By the 9th and 10th centuries payment was only made four or six times a year, reflecting the cash crisis faced by the ᶜAbbāsid Caliphate, one of these payments being made during the annual *ᶜarḍ* or review.

Basically the same systems of pay and assessment continued under the successor dynasties which took control of most of the Muslim world following the fragmentation of the ᶜAbbāsid Caliphate. The Buwayhids of western Persia were among the first to hand over responsibility for the collection of some taxes to the army. But rather than paying themselves directly from such revenues, the forces involved still sent the money to the government which then returned a certain proportion to the soldiers. This period also saw the first appearance of the *iqṭāᶜ* system of government-allocated estates or *fiefs*. In later medieval India the distinctive figure of the *kōtwāl* appeared, whose duties included acting as quartermaster responsible for ensuring that there were adequate supplies in the area where an army intended to establish an overnight or more permanent camp. The *kōtwāl* may have been an officer 'inherited' from the previous Hindu armies of India. Since several of the successor states of the Middle East were small they tended to rely on tribal troops. Nevertheless some money still had to be raised for the small number of *ghulāms* which such rulers maintained, often in the form of *ḥimāya* tribute from areas ruled by the dynasty in question. In fact raising cash for their élite forces became the central pre-occupation of most post-ᶜAbbāsid successor states, this being the main reason why variations on the *iqṭāᶜ* system appeared. The Fāṭimid Caliphate in Egypt took this a step further by dividing the *Diwān al-Jaysh* Army Ministry into two, or perhaps by adding two sub-departments; the *Diwān al-Rawātib* dealing with military salaries and the *Diwan al-Iqṭāᶜ* with government *fiefs*. Elite palace troops were treated separately from the bulk of the

***Left:** The Bayt al-Māl or communal treasury in the Great Mosque of Hama in Syria, since destroyed, was one of very few which had survived from Umayyad times. These stone 'safes' mounted on antique columns and entered by a ladder also served as weapons stores during very early Islamic times. (Author's photograph)* army, as were distant provincial garrisons. Ordinary soldiers were paid three to six times a year, largely in cash; senior officers were increasingly given *iqṭā^cs* with which to maintain themselves and their immediate followers. Once an officer retired or was incapacitated, but not if he were expelled from the army in disgrace, he had to return his *iqṭā*ᶜ which was then replaced by a state pension; a system which continued under the Ayyūbids and Mamlūks. The Turkish domination of the entire Muslim Middle East with the exception of Fāṭimid Egypt led to several other variations. Under the Saljūqs the *iqṭā*ᶜ system, which had previously included fiefs for civilian administrators, was almost entirely militarised; this remaining the case under the Ayyūbids and Mamlūks. Under the first Ayyūbid ruler, Ṣalāh al-Dīn, a form of *sub-enfeudisation* appeared in which the holder of a large *iqṭā*ᶜ could confer smaller *iqṭā*ᶜ*s* on his own subordinates. Military salaries also increased relative to the income of ordinary citizens. During the Mamlūk period payment was made in five separate ways:

Left: *Carved stone relief of a light cavalryman, from the Monastery of Poblet near Tarragona; Spanish, late 13th–early 14th century. Relatively lightly armoured horsemen of this kind were a feature of Iberian warfare, but proved quite capable of coping with invaders from north of the Pyrenees. (Author's photograph; Metropolitan Museum of Art store, New York)*

Right: *The walled Moroccan city of Fez el Bali (Fās al-Balī) is one of the few Islamic cities to retain its medieval appearance within its medieval walls, which largely date from the 14th century. (Author's photograph)* a regular monthly allowance, a daily meat ration, a twice-weekly allocation of fodder for a cavalryman's horse or at least money to buy such fodder, an additional annual grant to cover the cost of clothing and kit, and special *nafafqa* (gifts) on the accession of a new ruler or the start of a campaign. The Ottoman *timar* system of government-allocated *fiefs* was virtually identical with that of the Mamlūk *iqṭāᶜs*, though it also owed much to the similar Byzantine system of *pronoias*. Here the Ottoman *sanjak-beys* or provincial military commanders were also responsible for paying various irregular Balkan frontier troops. The higher payment given to professional soldiers in Muslim armies compared to their Christian rivals was also seen in the Iberian peninsula. The same went for Christian mercenaries in Andalusian or North African service; knights being paid twice as much as squires.

The conquering Mongol armies of the 13th century were largely tribal, but their professional élite still received regular pay and could look forward to a structured pension scheme, though this fully developed financial system dated from after the Mongol 'World Empire' had been established. Even so it soon broke down. The regular payment of military salaries for Mongol troops in Īl-Khān Iran was gradually replaced by a revival of the previous Islamic system of *iqṭāᶜ* fiefs. Not surprisingly the money economy and efficient administrative structure of China permitted Chinese dynasties to pay their professional troops in cash, this being done on a monthly basis in the Sung period and probably under most other rulers as well. Much the same was true in Hindu India where, during the Gupta period, a tax of one-sixth the value of all produce was taken for government expenditure including the army. According to the Chinese pilgrim Hiuen Tsang, the army of the great ruler Harsha in about 630–45 received regular salaries, and the widows of men killed in battle received a pension.

Feeding an Army

The story of the Persian baker who was captured by Muslim-Arab troops at the battle of Qādisīyah, together with a mule loaded with honey and date-cakes for the Sassanian commander, represents one extreme when it came to feeding the troops. At the other there is the simple fact that Sassanian cavalry fed their horses from forage gathered in one place whereas their Byzantine opponents turned their horses loose to graze. On a rather larger scale the loss of Egyptian grain supplies to the Muslims, supplies which had previously been shipped to the great city of Constantinople to feed the Byzantine army, led to significant changes in the government's attitude towards farmers in what was left of the Empire. These were now offered greater freedom and were encouraged to grow and sell their own produce to the army. The Crusaders appear to have adopted various ideas from their Byzantine neighbours; yet the Crusader States never became self-sufficient and by the later 13th century had to import live meat as well as cereals and other food from Sicily, southern Italy and southern France. Other western European or Crusader outposts, particularly those around the Aegean and Black Sea, supplemented their incomes by manufacturing ships' biscuits, figs and wine which they sold to passing fleets.

'The ger of a Central Asian tribal leader within its screened enclosure', in a 14th-century copy of a late 8th-century Chinese painted hand-scroll. These tents, popularly known as yurts in Europe, were also preferred by some Chinese rulers of recent Turco-Mongol origin. The screened enclosure protected the inhabitants from the wind as well as providing privacy. (Eighteen Songs on a Nomad Flute, Metropolitan Museum of Art, Gift of the Dillon Fund, 1973.120.3, New York)

The Muslim states faced special problems in feeding their armies since their fertile areas were relatively small, agriculture often only being possible with the aid of elaborate irrigation systems. This posed particular problems when it came to feeding horses, and one reason why the ᶜAbbāsid Caliph Muᶜtaṣim moved his capital from Baghdad to Samarra was the availability of large areas where fodder could be grown. This was in turn extended by the building of an irrigation channel called the *Abū'l-Jund* or 'Father of the Army'. On the other hand, the Muslim forces which invaded Sicily from North Africa in 827 outstripped the capabilities of their commissariat and were reduced to eating their own horses while besieging Syracuse. Muslim armies were also a valuable market for the merchants, some of whom specialised in serving such customers. This did not mean that the troops lived in excessive comfort, however; the infantrymen of 10th-century northern Iran, for example, earning a reputation for bad breath because they habitually lived on garlic, onions and bread. Many centuries later European observers were reluctantly impressed by the sober and frugal behaviour of Ottoman Turkish troops on campaign.

Nomadic Central Asian Turkish and Mongol warriors would have lived on an even more basic diet, but it was the habit of grazing their horses rather than using fodder which proved a serious weakness once they ventured beyond their own steppes. It has been estimated that if a moderately large Mongol army had, for example, tried to feed its 350,000 horses with grain in stalls they would have consumed the same amount as 1.3 million people. Not surprisingly, the armies of the main 'nomad empires' always needed skilful quartermasters to organise the feeding of their huge horse-herds. It is equally easy to see why an early 13th-century Caliph of Baghdad sent his troops to plough up the land ahead of an invading army since destroying the grass was a more effective method of driving off the enemy than meeting them in battle with inferior forces. Similarly the Mongol army which invaded Syria in 1260 had to withdraw, not because it was beaten in battle but because all the grass was used up. For their part the defending Mamlūks burned off the dried grass of summer ahead of such invaders. Even after nomad conquerors took control of cultivated areas, the lack of adequate open pasture gradually undermined the strength of the cavalry which had enabled them to conquer in the first place. Some Turco-Mongol conquerors obliterated agriculture across large areas as a short-term solution, but this undermined the wealth which had first attracted them. This insoluble riddle accounted for the speed with which each wave of nomad conquerors was absorbed by China in the east and the Muslim world in the west.

MEDICAL SERVICES

Medical services were an aspect of military administration where the medieval civilisations of western, southern and eastern Asia were clearly in advance of anything western Europe could offer. Even the Sassanian army is known to have had such a medical support system as well as a veterinary service headed by the *Stōr-bezhask*, or chief veterinarian. The Byzantine army inherited the medical services of the old Roman world and, as the celebrated late 6th-century Strategikon made clear, was aware that proper attention for the wounded, and prompt burial for the dead were vital for morale. The *Strategikon* also described special horses to carry the wounded, with two sets of stirrups so that a medical orderly could ride behind and steady the injured man. Another Byzantine military treatise written four centuries later referred to an officer known as the *Monoprosopon* who, in addition to being in charge of munitions while an army was on the march, commanded those tending the wounded. The Christian states of the Iberian peninsula could draw upon a much stronger medical heritage than the rest of western Europe except Italy. Both sides in the wars of the Reconquista employed Jewish, Muslim and Christian doctors, and there were hospitals in towns on both sides of the frontier. Laws and charters certainly emphasise the importance of *cirujanos* or surgeons, while large 14th-century Spanish war-galleys had their own doctor or at least a *barber-surgeon*.

The medical practices in 12th-century Crusader States may have been mocked by their more advanced Muslim neighbours, but there is evidence that they were better than those back in Europe. Nor was this solely a result of Muslim or Byzantine influence, for the effective use of lead oxide as an antiseptic for superficial wounds was not seen on the Muslim side. The aristocracy of the Crusader States also employed Jewish and Muslim doctors, despite Church efforts to ban this practice, and one famous Christian Syrian physician worked in both Crusader Jerusalem and Muslim Damascus. Jerusalem may even have been developing into an important medical centre before Ṣalāh al-Dīn retook it in 1187. The Military Orders also provided an honourable asylum for knights who contracted leprosy, members of the Order of St. Lazarus providing military service to the Kingdom so long as their strength lasted, and there was once a sub-section of the Order of Templars for lepers. Here it is worth noting that the medieval term 'leper' included those suffering from various forms of tuberculosis, elephantiasis, endemic syphilis and true leprosy.

The fame of Muslim physicians was enough for it to be echoed in 12th–13th-century French *chansons de geste*; even the most wicked Saracens had greater medical skill and a

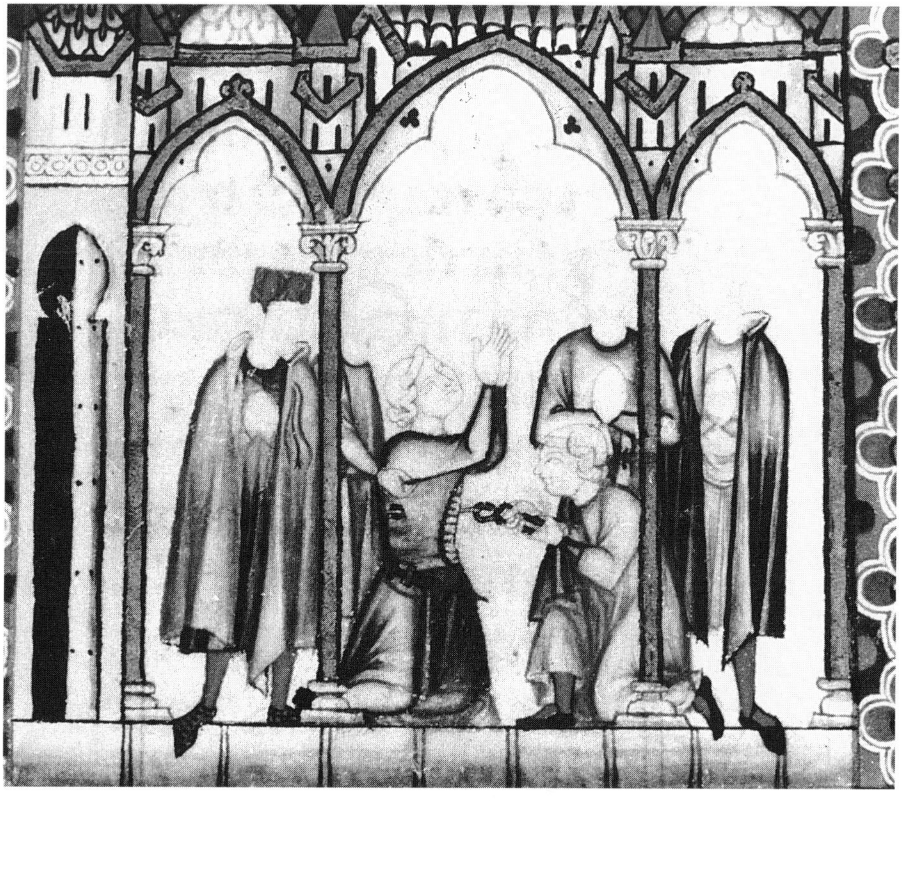

'Story of the Miraculous Removal of a Crossbow Bolt', Spanish manuscript illustration, late 13th–early 14th centuries. The unfortunate victim is being operated on with a pair of pliers. (Miracles of the Virgin Mary, Biblioteca Nazionale Centrale, Florence)

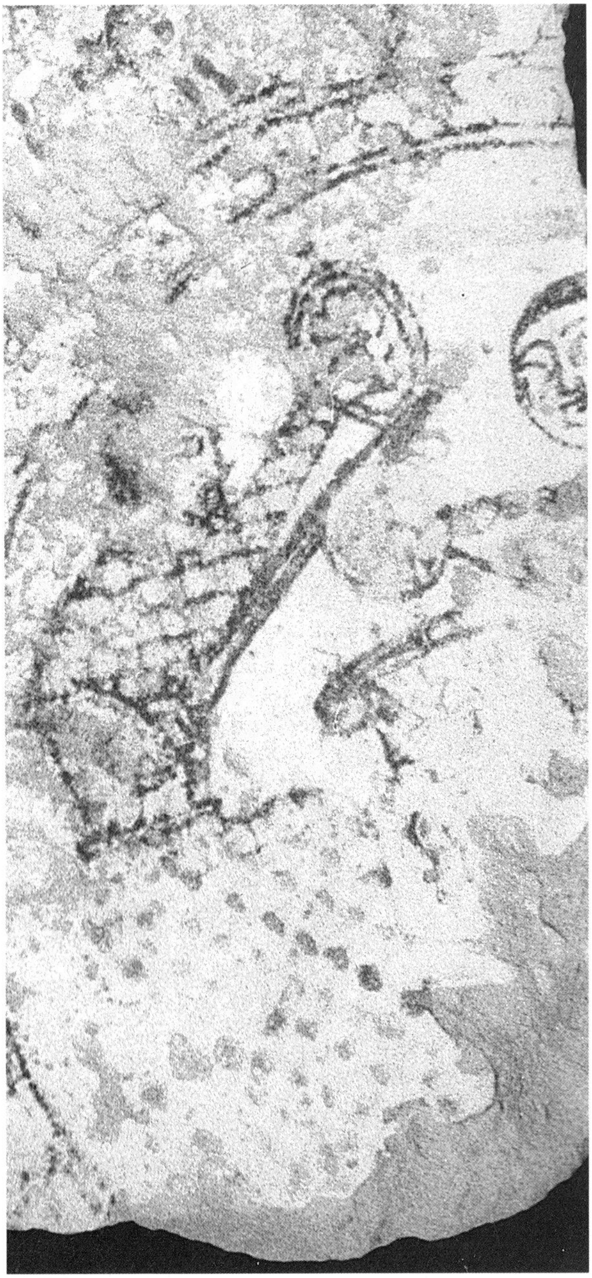

Part of a ceramic wall decoration from the Palace of Sabra in Tunisia, 10th–mid-11th-centuries. The artist has drawn a clear distinction between the bearded infantryman, who may be wearing a form of quilted soft-armour, and the 'moon-faced' – perhaps Turkish – horseman on the right. This distinction was also seen in Fāṭimid art from Cairo. (Musée Nationale du Bardo, Tunis)

greater concern for their wounded than their Christian foes. In Arab tribal society women took on this responsibility; Fāṭima, daughter of the Prophet Muḥammad, who tended the wounded at the battle of Uhud, was taken as the ideal of Muslim womanhood. Another story about the monks who looked after Muslim wounded outside Damascus during the original Arab-Islamic conquest of Syria in the 7th century may reflect the fact that Muslims first learned from those they ruled. By the 8th to 10th century, however, the ᶜAbbāsid army had its own highly developed field hospital, apparently with camel-litters for the wounded. These might have been similar to the *cacolets* used by all sides during the First World War in the Middle East. Ṣalāh al-Dīn's army similarly included a mobile hospital in its supply train. This would be set up near the army but not in the main camp for reasons of hygiene and fear of infection. Under Ṣalāh al-Dīn's rule there was also a doctor, described as 'skilled in dissecting limbs', based in Aleppo's Citadel and receiving a fixed salary.

A very different attitude towards military injuries existed in medieval China, perhaps because of the primacy of the family in Chinese civilisation. Instead of wounded soldiers being treated in hospitals, they were sent to their barracks or homes, apparently to be treated by family or friends, though officers maintained morale with gifts and wine. Such treatment would, however, apparently be done under the supervision of a recognised doctor; there being one for every 500 men in the T'ang army. Medical support services in medieval India are little known, but the medicines used are likely to have been advanced since so much Muslim medieval knowledge was based upon Hindu medical science. Otherwise the Atharvaveda, the classic Indian treatise on government and administration, refers to an extensive veterinary service for the army's horses.

MORALE

Religion

Religion was fundamental to military morale in all the societies under consideration. During the 5th and 6th centuries, for example, the Byzantine Empire built monasteries in reconquered provinces as an affirmation of Imperial control and as a way of drawing the local population into Byzantine civilisation. It was only reluctantly, and because of the vital role played by German troops, that the Byzantine army tolerated the Arian heresy within its ranks, and even after this disappeared there were continuing tensions between Greek and Armenian troops stemming from minor variations in ritual. Several of Byzantium's most bitter wars were seen in an overtly Christian light. At the beginning of the 7th century the Emperor Hereclius portrayed himself as a warlike 'new David', his war with the Sassanians being presented in ferocious Old Testament terms. During this period icons or religious paintings played a major role as morale boosters and supernatural protectors of an army, but their catastrophic failure to bring victory during the subsequent Arab-Islamic conquests contributed to a religious backlash known as the *iconoclastic* or 'icon-breaking' movement. During the early years of Arab-Islamic expansion Byzantine writers often seemed unable to distinguish Muslims from previous Zoroastrians, or regarded them as merely another Judeo-Christian heresy. By about 670, however, the Byzantines realised that they were up against something completely new, and attributed their defeats to a form of Divine Punishment. From the late 8th to early 10th centuries there was a distinct militarisation not only of Byzantine society but of Orthodox Christianity itself, with the rise of a 'holy war' ideal which foreshadowed the western Crusades of later years. Even the image of certain Saints was 'militarised', including St. Demetrius of Thessaloniki who changed from an unarmoured nobleman to a fully armoured cavalryman. Thereafter Orthodox Christianity maintained Byzantine military morale until the final fall of the Empire. Other Christian communities in the Middle East and Africa emphasised their religious affiliation as a means of affirming their separate identity, particularly in areas otherwise dominated by Islam. Abraha, the 6th-century Abyssinian governor of Yemen, built a shrine in Sana'a to proclaim Christian Ethiopian rule, just as the Byzantines built churches and monasteries to confirm their own conquests. Coptic Christianity continued to provide medieval Abyssinia with a distinct identity against the pagans of the south. Abyssinia also came to be seen as the patron and diplomatic, if not military, protector of the various Monophysite Christian communities of Egypt and other parts of the Middle East. The 9th to 12th centuries was the Golden Age of Christian civilisation in Nubia.

Before the coming of Islam, the people of the Arabian peninsula, Syria and Iraq were largely at the mercy of religious forces from outside. Meanwhile the fact that many Arab tribes chose the Monophysite or Syrian rather than the Orthodox Church may have been an unconscious gesture of defiance to religious pressure. Large-scale conversions may even have made Christians a majority in what is now Iraq by the start of the 7th century, posing a mortal threat to the Sassanian Empire though Zoroastrian remained the state religion. The conversion of Russia to Orthodox Christianity was a huge success for the Byzantine Empire and thereafter the Russian princes used conversion to Orthodox Christianity, often forcibly, as a method of confirming control over pagan Finno-Ugrian neighbours to the north and east. Even so Orthodox Russia only began to diverge politically and culturally from western Europe following the Great Schism of 1054. Thereafter Russia's increasing separation from her Catholic neighbours was encouraged by the Russian Orthodox hierarchy; so much so that the religious toleration of Mongol rule was seen as preferable to domination by, or even alliance with, 'Latins' to the west.

Not surprisingly religion played a central role during the Spanish *Reconquista*. It was in this context that Christian theologians wrestled with the contradiction between organised violence and the pacifist ethos embedded in Christianity. The result was a philosophy which had many features in common with the Muslim concept of physical rather than spiritual *jihād*, but at the same time Christian Iberia developed a degree of religious toleration rarely seen in any other part of medieval Europe. In mid-13th- century Valencia there were even cases of Christian conquerors converted to the religion of the conquered, and fifty years later the writer of a Spanish military treatise said that the Muslims were such good soldiers that their defeat could only be ascribed to Divine Intervention.

Having achieved their initial objective of 'recovering the Holy Places' during the First Crusade, those who went on the next expeditions developed the ideology of destroying Islam. At the same time Muslim soldiers were presented as cowards who fought from a distance and feared close combat because of a lack of blood in their veins; itself attributed to the hot climate. When a series of humiliating defeats showed that this objective was impossible, the Crusades focused on the more limited objective of defending the Holy Places. Recognisable relics also played their part in military motivation, a fragment of what was believed to be the True Cross being taken into battle on at least eighteen occasions during the 12th century. There was also increasing hostility towards Orthodox Christians of the Byzantine world. Those who went on Crusade to receive an *indulgence* which wiped away their sins took great care to fulfil their vows before entering battle. As a result priests and friars who accompanied Crusader armies heard confessions and offered absolution before the first arrow flew. The idea that those Crusaders who died were automatically martyrs does not seem to have been accepted during the First Crusade but came into being in the 12th century, and became central to the self-sacrificing ethos of the Military Orders, particularly of the Hospitallers. Meanwhile similarities between the 'cult of martyrdom' seen in the Military Orders and that of various militarised *ṣūfī* or mystical Islamic brotherhoods at the time of the Crusades remains a source of embarrassment to the historians of both sides.

The degree to which religious *jihād* and desire for booty motivated the first wave of Arab-Islamic conquests remains a matter of scholarly dispute. But by the later 7th century the Muslim army, and above all its élite Syrian-Arab units, was bound by strong bonds of traditional loyalty to the ruling Umayyad dynasty of Caliphs. Under the subsequent ᶜAbbāsid dynasty the army's loyalty to the Caliphal family was cemented by an almost mystical conviction which led to problems when the ᶜAbbāsid family was itself torn by dissent. The appeal of frontier life was also so strong that *g͟hāzi* (volunteers) would move from a pacified area back to the continuously war-torn Anatolian frontier. Scholars responded to this mood by writing many treatises about the benefits of the *g͟hāzi* life. In complete contrast the Iraqi Arab scholar al-Jāḥiz's analysis of the qualities required of a commander and an ordinary soldier show a remarkably rational attitude. He insisted that religious commitment was rarely enough on its own, and had to be supplemented by anger, revenge, alcohol, stupidity, inexperience of the reality of war, natural bloodthirstiness, hatred of foreigners, personal ambition or fear of punishment.

Various distinctive and unorthodox practices also appeared in the eastern Muslim lands as ways of promoting military morale. These ranged from a ruler's leading prayers for the souls of fallen soldiers to the apparent planting of 'paradise gardens' in the courtyards of Ismāᶜīli or '*Assassin*' castles in northern Iran. These are said, by the *Assassins*' opponents, to have been part of a system of indoctrination whereby 'suicide squads' were given a taste of Heaven so that they would face death more willingly. For many years such stories were treated with great scepticism, though a series of holes dug into the rocky summit of the main Ismā῾īli castle could have been for soil where the trees, shrubs and terraces of such a Paradise Garden were planted. Similar almost heretical practices also appeared in the Muslim heartland of the Middle East where the slave-recruited black African guard units of the Fāṭimids are said to have virtually worshipped their Caliph in an un-Islamic way which reflected the semi-divine status of kingship in sub-Saharan Africa. Belief in charms and talismans was more widespread, particularly among uneducated soldiers. In fact the whole question of belief in magic in medieval and Islamic armies remains a neglected area. More attention has been given to the ancient Turco-Mongol belief that the peoples of Central Asia were destined to rule the world; this becoming part of the Mongol state ideology after the initial success of Genghis K͟hān's astonishing conquests. It was revived by the Ottoman Turks who also followed the *Kızıl Elma* or Red Apple, a military goal which always remained unattainable - originally located in the Caucasus mountains then in Constantinople and finally Vienna or Rome. A sense of military destiny was not the only thing the Turks brought to Muslim armies. They also brought several beliefs rooted in pre-Islamic *shamanistic* and Buddhist beliefs; most obviously in the major role played by *ṣūfīs* and *darwīs͟h* 'dervishes' who were thought to have a specially close link with God. The Ottoman *Yeni Çeri* (Janissary) infantry had a specially close connection with the *Baktashi* dervish sect which had itself evolved out of the *Huruffi* movement, which had in turn been regarded as subversive, heretical and dangerously 'communistic' by 14th-century Muslim rulers. The *Baktashis* had taken over many folk-beliefs from the previous Byzantine Christians, including various warrior saints who were identified with existing Islamic saints or angels. For example the warrior Saints George and Theodore became one and the same as the immortal 'servant of God' K͟hidr Ilias. Some *Yeni Çeri* soldiers even carried extracts from the Gospel of St. John as talismanic good luck charms. There was a comparable increase in the role played by unorthodox, mystical or 'folk' beliefs in the later medieval western parts of the Muslim world. Some of the tiny *taifa* states of mid-12th century al-Andalus were, for example, led by warriors who also became known as *ṣūfīs* or mystics, particularly in the Algarve southern region of what is now Portugal.

The educated and religious élite of Syria and Egypt had already focused on the need of a Muslim 'moral rearmament' to face the Crusaders. Many tombs or shrines associated with the heroes of the first Muslim conquest of Palestine and Syria in the 7th century were given greater attention, and in some cases 'rediscovered' as part of a process of raising the importance of these areas in the eyes of religiously motivated military recruits. Rulers like Ṣalāh al-Dīn, who was open to criticism for being a 'usurper', were particularly concerned to retain the support of religious leaders. This was why his reconquest of southern Palestine in 1171, itself a minor military operation, was given symbolic importance as it 'liberated the *Haj* road' which enabled pilgrims from Egypt and North Africa to travel to Mecca and Medina without having to cross 'infidel' Crusader territory. In some cases this presentation of military campaigns as an extension of orthodox Muslim *jihād* became a state ideology which was projected back into history as a kind of national myth, particularly where the Ottoman Empire was concerned.

While Christian, Buddhist and even '*shamanistic*' beliefs influenced the 'folk Islam' of ordinary Middle Eastern soldiers, the pre-Islamic Zoroastrian religion of the Sassanian Empire had remarkably little impact; perhaps because the Sassanians incorporated Hellenist Greek ideas like the cult of the ruling dynasty's divine ancestry which ran counter to the egalitarian spirit of Islam. Zoroastrian had, of course, been used to motivate the troops. Priests delivered sermons before a battle, urging men to fight the unbelievers. They would also consecrate a nearby water-source, then summon the enemy to submit to the *S͟hāhans͟hāh* and accept the Zoroastrian religion. Chinese travellers in pre-Islamic Farg͟hāna mentioned gladiatorial combats - not necessarily to the death - which marked the probably Zoroastrian New Year celebrations in this part of Transoxiana, and early Muslim observers described horse-archery contests held during religious celebrations in pre-Islamic Samarkand, perhaps again Zoroastrian. It is even possible that the Pecheneg Turks who dominated southern Russia and invaded the Byzantine Balkans were largely Zoroastrian until a large part of the Pecheneg tribes converted to Islam in the late 10th century. Meanwhile Central Asia was a mosaic of different religious affiliations in the early Middle Ages. The Turkish Uighur rulers tried to impose the dualist Manichaean faith as a state religion, and the ruler of the Qara-K͟hitai may have been a Manichaean or a Nestorian Christian. In additional to the K͟hazar Turks' well-known conversion to Judaism, part of the Turkish Qipchaq tribe also converted to Judaism in the mid-12th century. Some of these religious identities were clearly adopted as a way of distinguishing people from threatening neighbours; Buddhism, for example, being taken as a 'national religion' by the Turks of Transoxiana and Afghanistan in the 6th century to distinguish themselves from Zoroastrian Iranians and Confucian Chinese. Much the same was probably the case with the conversion of Tibet to Buddhism in the 7th century; this coinciding with a period of expansionism, while the fragmented Buddhist states of what is now Afghanistan put up a more prolonged resistance to Arab expansion than other regions on Islam's eastern frontier. Medieval Buddhism was, in fact, an outward-looking religion which had influence far beyond those countries where it dominated. Even the early T'ang rulers of China tried to use Buddhism and Taoism to consolidate their own rule by portraying themselves as defenders of an ancient religious-cultural tradition. Buddhism was seen as suitable for their soldiers because Confucian traditions worked against warlike enthusiasm, since burial far from home was seen as a disaster because the family could not pray over the gravec. Confucian Chinese hated to die violently as one was thought to retain the appearance at the moment

A battle between horsemen and infantry armed in Chinese style, in a manuscript compiled for a Persian-speaking patron, late 14th–early 15th centuries. A great variety of weapons is illustrated, including double- and triple-pointed spears, though all the visible armour appears to be lamellar. This probably reflects the appearance of soldiers in many of the most Chinese-influenced parts of Turco-Mongol Central Asia. (Topkapi Library, MS. Haz. 2153, f. 77r, Istanbul)

of death through the after-life, whereas Buddhism introduced the concept of the disembodied soul. Many of these ideas spread to Korea together with other aspects of Chinese culture, and were closely associated with the *hwarang* 'flowery youth' military élite even before Korea converted to Buddhism in the 6th century.

The essence of medieval Hinduism was to obey the rules concerning one's own caste. The military caste of *kshatriyas* were, however, already members of a social élite. Hindu religious scriptures and later treatises on government and warfare made it clear that religion played a major role in motivation. The classic Atharvaveda, for example, indicated that idols were carried into the fighting line. Before a battle the king would speak to his men, promising rewards for bravery while astrologers predicted the inevitable victory. Members of the *kshatriya* warrior caste were also expected to study the Veda religious texts, though not as intensively as did the *brāhmin* priestly caste. Since it was the duty of a *kshatriya* to die in battle, it hardly mattered whether he killed or was killed – only the fact of fighting was important since the soul of *kshatriya* slain in battle went straight to heaven. Victory for an individual was, in fact, to die bravely while cowardice was a sin. Not to kill the foe was also a sin, as was begging for mercy or fleeing in disgrace. There were slight variations on this basic pattern in the Hindu states of south-east Asia. In part of what is now Indonesia a ruler was regarded as the 'pivot of the ordered universe'. Any breakdown in this system was evidence that the *Era of Kali* had arrived; this in turn preceding the pralaya 'final destruction of the world' which marked the end of the *Era of Kali*.

Since the role of religion in 'pagan' societies was almost invariably described by their enemies, it rarely appears in a sympathetic light. The paganism of pre-Islamic Arabia, for example, is only known via later Muslim writers. Nevertheless the Quraysh tribe who dominated Mecca, and from whom the Prophet Muḥammad himself stemmed, worshipped the god al-Uzza before all others, but also held processions for the gods al-Lāt and Manat as a sort of 'trinity' called the 'sons of God'. The pagan rulers of pre-Buddhist north and central Burma similarly relied on *ari* priests to maintain their warriors' morale. These *ari* walked among the troops reciting incantations, inscribing magical signs of the sun and moon on elephants, horses, weapons and shields.

The small castle of Javier is a fine example of a 14th-century Spanish fortress. It was also the birthplace of St. Francis Xavier, and a church dedicated to the saint was built next door to the castle in the 16th century. (Author's photograph)

The role of the priest-warrior-king had been established in Berber North Africa and the Sahara since ancient times, while farther south kingship often involved a semi-divine status in medieval sub-Saharan states like Ghana and pre-Islamic Mali. To some extent the special religious status of rulers even survived the introduction of Islam in the 13th and 14th centuries. The most senior rulers or *Khagans* of Central Asia were also seen as semi-divine links between their people and heaven. Warfare itself sometimes had religious overtones in Central Asia and it certainly involved a great deal of religious symbolism. Many Turkish tribes also made use of magical '*rain stones*' which were believed to have influence over the weather for military purposes; the Mongols then learning this art of *Yat* or *Jada* from the Turks. Their use also survived well into the Muslim period in Transoxiana. Notable warriors could also earn a sort of immortality; élite 'champions' forming special associations of up to twenty members distinguished by distinctive sword-belts. The sacrifice of horses on the tombs of dead leaders lasted well into the later Middle Ages in the steppes and mountains of Central Asia, and among the Ugrian forest peoples of Siberia to the north. Elements of an even more ancient human sacrifice could be seen in the funeral ceremonies for Genghiz Khān and even for Hülegü in Iran. There were many similarities between the paganism of the steppes and that of the pre-Christian peoples of Russia. The notably warlike Finnish Mordvins of the 12th and 13th centuries carried enemy skulls as totems ahead of their armies, and even used them as drinking cups. The pagan Slav tribes who eventually amalgamated to become the Russian, White Russian and Ukrainian peoples were hardly less ferocious. There were

also many similarities between the pagan pantheons of Russia and Viking Scandinavia; the senior god in each being a god of thunder and lightning – Perun in Russia, Thor in Scandinavia. The ancient Russians also worshipped a Sun God, or Svarog the God of White Light, who may also have been connected with the semi-magical techniques of weapons making.

Literature and Literacy

Literature played a prominent role in the self-identity and motivation of military personnel in widely literate societies such as those of the medieval Middle East. The epic figure of Dikenas Akritas, for example, was the idealised warrior of 9th-10th-century Byzantine frontier society. The oldest surviving version of this tale was probably written by a monk who lived near the Syrian border in the mid-11th century; the story evolving from a mixture of Greek, eastern Anatolian, Armenian, Arabic and Persian tales, the hero himself being of mixed Greek and Arab parentage. The neighbouring Armenians had a comparable hero, David of Sassoun, whose adventures became the Armenian 'national epic', though existing versions of David of Sassoun date from about the time of the Ottoman occupation of Armenia and include many Turkish and Arabic elements, particularly in military matters. This and other Armenian and Greek tales influenced Anatolian Turkish epic. The Georgian 'national epic' of The Man in the Panther's Skin, written in its final form during the 12th or early 13th centuries, is extremely close in plot, attitudes and military details to the adventures of Rustam in the better-known Persian Shāhnāmah, probably having a common origin in the Sassanian period.

The role of epic and verse in medieval Spain and in the Crusader States was the same as that seen in most of western Europe. During the 11th to 13th centuries the most important patrons of the Spanish *juglar* poets were members of a knightly élite who insisted upon authentic descriptions of warfare. On the other hand many other Iberian epic verses were written for public recitation to an illiterate peasant class which, nevertheless, also played a significant military role. Despite being increasingly urbanised, the knightly élite of the Crusader States were keen to keep up with the latest ideas from France, the fountainhead of chivalry, though during the 13th century there was also a rising tide of Italian cultural influence. One of the most effective vehicles for transmitting the latest fashions was literature. Numerous itinerant poets travelled around the Latin enclaves of the eastern Mediterranean. The artists who made wall-paintings which decorated palaces and castles also played an important role in transmitting chivalric ideas, costume and heraldry.

Many of the poets of pre-Islamic Arabia had been famous warriors as well as literary figures, their tradition of heroic verse continuing among the Arabs throughout the Middle Ages. The ᶜAntar Romance, for example, is a collection of Arabic epic poetry which evolved between the 7th and 14th centuries, reaching its final version in early Mamlūk Syria or Egypt. Another distinctive feature of Arabic military literature was the prominent role played by female heroes. In fact Dhū al-Himma (Woman of Great Heartedness) and mother of the noblest Muslim champions, was the main figure in the greatest Arabic epic which took its final form at the time of the Crusades. War poetry, as opposed to verses about the exploits of individual heroes, only became an accepted part of Arabic literature in the 10th century when some of the finest of these poems were written at the Ḥamdānid court in Syria. The late 10th and early 11th centuries were also the high-point of warrior poetry in Arab-Islamic Andalusia where, however, the attitudes displayed in such verses were remarkably similar to those seen a century later in the *chansons de geste* of French chivalry.

Persian military literature was very different. The most famous example is the Shāhnāmah of Firdawsī, written in about 1000 at a time of revived Persian cultural confidence. Its basic theme was the struggle between the Iranians and the Turanians or Turks in what is Transoxiana and Afghanistan. Other warlike Persian epics included the story of Warqa wa Gulshāh which, however, was a simple story of love and war

Above: *An exceptionally rare Nubian manuscript illustration of St. Menas, dating from the 9th–10th centuries, depicting him as a typical Nubian tribal horse-warrior. It even includes a massive spearhead comparable to the examples found at Ballana and dating from several centuries earlier. (British Library, MS. Or. 6805, f. 10, London)*

apparently written for the Turkish warrior élite of Azerbaijan or eastern Anatolia. Many of the Turkish and Mongol rulers who dominated Iran throughout the rest of the Middle Ages were themselves patrons of Persian literature, and in return Persian poets wrote verses in praise of these often bloodthirsty rulers.

Medieval Turkish literature has not been given the prestige allowed to Arabic and Persian, but it included fascinating warrior tales. These range from the Book of Dede Korkut which, though it was written in the 13th or early 14th century, was basically a collection of pre-Islamic heroic stories. The Dānishmandnāmah was first written down in mid-13th-century Anatolia and tells of the Turkish conquest of the eastern part of the Byzantine Empire, again with realistic and detailed descriptions of warfare. In a completely different vein the *Baktashi* dervish sect, though intimately connected with the élite Ottoman *Yeni Çeri* infantry corps, produced lyrical and mystical verse, but nothing military.

Some of the warrior attitudes found in this Turkish literature reflects what little is known about the epics of pre-Islamic Transoxiana. Here, for example, the Arab conquerors recorded how poetic imagery and tradition of military 'self praise' was used in diplomatic correspondence. This tradition also seems to have been influenced by Zoroastrian Avesta religious texts, especially in terms of claims to superhuman bowmanship. Farther east, in the steppes and mountains of Turkestan and Mongolia, traditional epics flourished throughout the Middle Ages. These stories have distinctive characteristics; for example their ritualised combats between heroes, usually two who fight until they have proved each other's worth, then becoming friends before riding off in search of further adventures. Such stories would influence Russian folklore where the *skomorokhi* itinerant minstrel was as characteristic of medieval Russia as the *troubadour* was of France. But they enjoyed far less prestige and were, in fact, said to be descended from the pagan priests of pre-Christian Russia. Eventually these *skomorokhi* merged, to some extent, with the more respectable *gusliari* minstrels.

Despite the anti-military streak deeply embedded in medieval Chinese civilisation, stories about military heroes remained popular with the ordinary people of China. Tales of the *Yu-hsia* (wandering warriors or knights errant) were also favourites. Although these have been compared to the chivalrous epics of medieval Europe, the exploits of the *Yu-hsia* lacked a chivalrous element. Their heroes helped the poor and oppressed but paid little attention to the law and did not belong to military élite like western hero-knights. Instead the men involved came from varied backgrounds and did not rely on their adventures as a means of livelihood. They carried on peaceful lives when not fighting for justice and, in fact, these *Yu-hsia* tended to be renowned more for their altruism than for their military prowess. Their behaviour was also contrary to the Confucian spirit by taking their opposition to injustice to extremes, refusing to yield or to forgive, and acting against existing laws. This revolutionary element also distinguished the *Yu-hsia* from the western European 'knights errant' who, despite their spirit of individual heroism, fought for the maintenance or re-establishment of a conservative 'right order' represented by a rightful king or a rightful heir deposed by a usurper.

Stories about heroes from the *hwarang* military élite remained very popular in Korean literature; in fact the war-torn mid-12th to late 14th centuries saw one of the finest flowerings of Korean literature. Meanwhile in India minstrels played a role among the *Rajpūt* élite of the Hindu *kshatriya* caste comparable to that of the *troubadours* in western Europe. Their status was such that they served as official messengers between opposing armies, traditionally immune from injury by both sides.

Music

Sassanian armies used trumpets to signal the start of battle and to maintain morale, but only a senior Sassanian *spādbadh* commander of a frontier province was permitted to enter a military camp to the sound of such trumpets. In contrast a 6th-century Byzantine military manual maintained that too many trumpets could cause confusion in battle and that silence could be more impressive; an attitude echoed by some Arab forces when facing Turks and Persians in the 10th century. The later medieval Digenes Akritas Byzantine epic described military bands with trumpets, large horns, drums, *organa* (which may have been portable organs like those used in western Europe), and singers who played cymbals. The similarity between this military band and the *mehter* of the late medieval - early modern Ottoman army is striking. Other late 11th-century Byzantine sources mention camps roused by drums, and armies marching to the sound of flutes. Trumpets were the main musical instrument used for signalling in Crusader armies, though the Order of Templars used bells to summon the troops and draw attention if their camp was attacked. Crusader fleets, like those of most European Mediterranean countries, had specialist trumpeters and drummers to transmit messages from ship to ship. The aristocratic élites of the Crusader States were strongly influenced by their Arab neighbours which resulted in their adoption of the *lute* from the Arabic *al-ūd*.

Music and dancing clearly played a prominent and indeed sexually explicit role in maintaining military morale among the pre-Islamic Arabs; most notably among the bedouin where young women danced for the warriors before and even during battle, supposedly promising favours to the bravest if later legends are to be believed. The armies of the medieval Muslim world developed sophisticated traditions of military music based upon those of earlier states. In the Delhi Sultanate of 13th- and 14th-century northern India, for example, the singular importance of musical display on the march was inherited from Hindu practice. Trumpets were also used

Below: *Terracotta plaque from Chal Tarkhan Ishkabad; late Sassanian or early Islamic Iran, 7th century. The importance of music to the military élites of the Middle East dates back far into ancient times, and was inherited by the first Arab-Islamic armies. The lady is playing a harp. The horse-archer appears to be riding his camel with the aid of stirrups. (Museum of Fine Arts, acc. no. 39.485, Boston)*

to keep order on the march when a small force of horsemen crossed Crusader-held territory in the mid-12th century; this presumably being standard practice. Half a century later an Ayyūbid military manual emphasised the importance of bands to maintain morale and intimidate the enemy, though their limitations against a determined foe were also recognised. Ayyūbid commanders also had a musical code to transmit messages using *kūssāt* (large cymbals) for 'top secret' messages, *būq* (trumpets) as well as *jāwūsh* and *munādī* ('criers'). The *ṭablkhānah* (corps of drummers) became even more important under the Mamlūks and reached a peak under the Ottomans where it eventually formed part of their *mehterhane* or military music department. Different in size and function were small drums in leather containers attached to the saddles of late Mamlūk and Ottoman cavalrymen which helped horsemen re-assemble if they became scattered after a reversal.

The same sorts of musical instrument were used in North Africa and Muslim Andalusia. Here, however, strong African influence lay behind the even greater importance given to drums which formed part of royal insignia. These instruments were such important symbols of leadership in North Africa that Berber tribes such as the Ṣanhāja were divided into rival '*drum groups*' which also served as military units, as they did under the Murābiṭin of the 11th century. The first Murābiṭ ruler had disapproved of such drums on the grounds that they were a relic of African paganism, but they soon re-appeared in large numbers, terrifying the men and horses of Christian enemies in Iberia. The subsequent Muwaḥḥid dynasty continued to use massed war-drums, some of which were supported on green and gold wooden frames.

Turco-Mongol Central Asia had a remarkable tradition of military music. A senior *Khagan* or ruler had his own orchestra of eighty or so musicians playing cymbals, horns, drums, bells and other instruments. These men could also be mounted and in battle their function was to help direct the movements of forces, experienced elderly warriors beating the largest drums to mark the start of an attack. Other forms of audio-signals used by the peoples of the Eurasian steppes included the large horns with ox-headed mouths of the Pechenegs and the whistling arrows of the Mongols. Drums were similarly important in China, Chinese armies employing drummers to signal an advance, men with gongs signalling a retreat. According to the Harascarita of Bana, describing a 7th-century Hindu Indian army, drums woke the soldiers in camp then signalled the distance to be marched that day, while the blowing of a conch shell announced that the king was going to inspect his troops.

__Below:__ A Byzantine silver-gilt bowl decorated with a dancing girl, a musician, a cavalry lancer and a horse-archer, 11th–13th centuries. The latter two may reflect Greeks and Turks in Byzantine Imperial service. The deer and dogs running around the upper rim of the bowl are virtually identical with those decorating a 10th-century Byzantine shield-boss from northern Syria. (State Hermitage Museum, St. Petersburg)

Drugs and Alcohol

Apart from the fact that the soldiers of most nations and cultures have had a reputation for excessive drinking - not always justified - Indian warfare was different in its occasionally official use of both alcohol and even drugs to motivate élite troops. According to the 7th-century Chinese observer Hieun Tsang, the army of Mahārāshtra in west-central India included champions who were encouraged to get drunk before a battle so that they might take on overwhelming odds, and even gave alcohol to war-elephants to make them charge more enthusiastically. Stories that the *fidā'īs* whom the Ismācīli leader known as 'The Old Man of the Mountain' sent out to assassinate his enemies were drugged before their suicidal missions to give them a 'foretaste of Paradise' are usually dismissed as propaganda. On the other hand the use of *ḥashīsh* and other 'soft drugs' such as *banj* (soporific henbane) was so widespread in many parts of the Muslim world, India and China that such stories cannot be entirely dismissed.

LONG-DISTANCE COMMUNICATIONS

The postal systems of several Middle Eastern and Asian states were some of the most remarkable organisations in medieval history. That of the Sassanian Empire was known as the *parvanak* and consisted of a system of roads, relay stations, couriers and administrative officials. The Byzantine Empire may have had a similar system though this should not be confused with the Byzantine network of *vigilatores* who kept watch over routes along which an enemy might invade and were backed up by a system of runners in the mountains, horsemen on the plains. This in turn was separate from the Byzantine Empire's system of warning beacons.

Sassanian and to some extent Byzantine communication networks were then taken over by the Muslim-Arabs who clearly continued the Byzantine *beredarioi* organisation of official government messengers in Egypt. This was known in Arabic as the *barīd* and was manned by armed but low-status Christian soldiers. The first Umayyad Caliph, Mucāwiya, is credited with extending the *barīd* from Damascus to Medina in Arabia, and by the late 8th-9th century the *barīd* had become an extensive system of official communications which sent regular reports about local conditions to the central government. Fresh horses were constantly available at way-stations along the main routes, ranging from the nineteen stages between Baghdad and Hamadhān to the sixty-six stages between Baghdad and the main eastern military base of Marw. Stages were normally between 24 and 36 kilometres apart - a normal day's journey though official *najjab* (couriers) went much faster. One hundred and fifty kilometres a day was

Below: *The fortified peninsula or islet of Skopa in the bay of Kotrones in southern Greece also served as a vital port of call on the long coastal voyage from Italy to Constantinople. The Crusader settlers in Greece could only maintain their hold on such places through their command of the seas. (A. Bon photograph)*

Right: *The remains of a small fort which formed part of the way-station or caravanserai at al-Rabadhah in central Arabia, 8th–9th centuries. It was one of a chain of stopping-places on the Darb al-Zubaydah pilgrim road from Baghdad to Mecca, attributed to the wife of the Caliph Hārūn al-Rashīd. (King Sa'ud University photograph, Riyadh, Saudi Arabia)*

achieved on several occasions, and in one instance supposedly reaching 400 kilometres a day, though this must surely have involved the use of carrier-pigeons. The Zangid rulers introduced camels on desert routes while the Ayyūbids used pigeons as well as *najjabūn* couriers. By the 14th century the *barīd* formed the nervous system of the Mamlūk state; its main axis running through Syria, across Sinai to Cairo. It consisted of an estimated sixty named stations along various roads, some twenty-nine of which have been identified by archaeologists. Records show that a properly mounted courier was expected to ride an average of 120 kilometres per day, so it is hardly surprising that the Mamlūks were very careful when it came to selecting such men and their horses, the best animals being obtained as a form of tribute from bedouin Arab tribes. In fact the *barīd* and its associated road-network and bridges were second only to the army and navy in Mamlūk state expenditure. Far to the west another *barīd* had long connected the political centres of Muslim Andalusia with frontier castles and coastal observation points.

The military and state postal networks of China either owed much to those of Central Asia or the latter resulted from a mix of Chinese and Sassanian influences. The powerful T'ang dynasty inherited earlier structures and extended them to include no less than 1,600 'mail stations' at 15-kilometre intervals. Whereas a horseman was supposed to cover six stations per day, a chariot could only cover four, while members of the Imperial family travelled at an even more leisurely pace. The Chinese postal system probably provided the model for that set up across Korea by the Koryŏ dynasty during the 10th to 14th centuries; this consisting of twenty-two routes, 500 courier stations backed up by a chain of fire-beacons between the main regional military headquarters and the capital. The little that is known about Indian courier systems merely states that these used chariots well into the medieval period.

As already mentioned, beacons signalling by fire at night and smoke by day played a vital role in long-distance communications. Although these could only send simple pre-arranged messages, they were much faster than couriers and were used by the early Byzantines as a frontier warning system. This system was closed down by the Emperor Michael III in the mid-9th century as the danger was thought to have declined, but the skills were passed on to the Crusader States which probably used beacons or pigeon-post to link their main castles in Syria and the Aegean.

By the 10th century the system of *mawāqīd* (coastal beacons) which the Caliph Mu^{c}āwiya had set up along the Syrian coast to warn of Byzantine naval raids had evolved into several chains of beacons connecting coastal *ribāṭs* with the main inland garrisons. A far more extensive chain of beacons also ran the length of North Africa from Alexandria to Sabta on the southern side of the Straits of Gibraltar and was supposedly capable of transmitting a warning from Morocco to Egypt in one night. Fire-beacons not surprisingly played their part in resisting the Crusades during the 12th and 13th centuries. Once the Muslims regained part of the Lebanese coast, a chain of beacons from Beirut to Damascus could warn of the approach of Crusader fleets within hours. More detailed information from the Mamlūk period indicates that such beacons were mounted on hills or tall buildings. The settled Turks of Central Asia also made use of fixed beacons known as *qargu* during the 8th century, while the Chinese chains of warning beacons were, of course, far more sophisticated. On the other hand neighbouring Turks learned to note when beacons were not fully manned and chose these moments to raid.

The third such form of rapid long-range communication was the pigeon-post. A book of instruction in the art of government written by an 11th-century Persian ruler explained how such a system should be set up, what types of pigeon to use and how they were bred. The weakness of such communications was, however, illustrated early in the 12th century when a carrier pigeon flying between Nisibin and Mardin was intercepted by Zangi's troops who changed the message and released the bird to mislead their enemy. Other evidence suggests that pigeons formed a back-up system in case couriers were intercepted or the chain of beacons was cut. Furthermore the Mamlūks are credited with using perfumed birds to carry especially good news such as significant military victories.

TRANSPORT

Land Transport

Transport by land and sea was painfully slow in medieval times. The difficulty of carrying large volumes of any sort of goods by land also meant that river or seaborne carriage was generally preferred. Although it was normally easier to have armies march to their destinations, even in the 7th century Byzantine Empire it took several months for even an élite force to assemble in Constantinople then travel to Syria; the troops marching from 25 to 30 kilometres per day with plenty of rests for men and horses. The old Roman road system was in decay, but the movement of armies and the location of major engagements were all governed by roads and choke points such as passes through hills or mountains. The often praised capability of early Muslim-Arab armies to navigate the desert like seas was largely a myth because all sides were governed by rugged natural terrain and the availability of water. Never-

Right: *The 13th-century Malabadi Bridge over the Batman Su near Silvan in east-central Anatolia. The importance of commercial as well as military communications led many of the Turkish rulers of Anatolia to build fine bridges over the main rivers in their territory. (Author's photograph)*

MALABADİ KÖPRÜSÜ

theless Arabs and Turkish forces were invariably regarded as being capable of travelling much faster than their Byzantine foes.

Russian armies were in an even more difficult situation because the central and northern parts of the country lacked roads worthy of the name, being deep into mud and mists every spring and autumn. In complete contrast, the steppes of what are now southern Russia and the Ukraine have been described as resembling 'land seas' in which towns and cities served as ports, caravans as convoys. Nomadic tribes dominated not only the steppes but also most of these urban 'ports'. The First Crusade may have faced similar transport problems as the Byzantine Empire. For example, of the eighty-nine days it took Geoffrey de Bouillon's contingent to reach Constantinople, only fifty-nine were spent on the march averaging 25 kilometres per day which was quite a respectable marching rate. Other smaller and perhaps better-mounted contingents achieved 30 to 40 kilometres a day for short periods, but all maintained a better rate within western Europe than through the mountainous Balkan provinces of the Byzantine Empire. Some larger Crusader armies had a line-of-march three days' long – no fewer than 75 kilometres of soldiers, animals, baggage carts and camp-followers. Islamic civilisation was highly urbanised with a dense network of roads or rather well-worn tracks provided with abundant bridges, well-maintained wells and protected stopping points. Although primarily designed for merchants or pilgrims, it was also useful for armies. The effectiveness of this network of roads was clearly illustrated by the fact that during an emergency in 785 an ᶜAbbāsid prince with a small military entourage was able to cover 1,500 kilometres in twenty days – an average of 75 kilometres per day.

The raising of horses was of vital importance for almost all medieval armies, particularly those of the Middle East, Central Asia and to a lesser extent China and India. The three most important 'élite' breeds of the early days were the North African Barb, the Arabian, and the Turcoman or 'Golden Horse', while the tough but smaller Central Asian horse was vital in terms of numbers. The Barb was an ancient breed but the Arabian had emerged more recently, probably in the immediate pre-Islamic centuries in northern Arabia and the Syrian desert. While the ancient and early medieval Arabs were involved in producing what is generally recognised as the most intelligent animal ever bred by man, the Byzantines were more concerned with quantity, and by the 10th century the Empire had a huge and highly organised system of imperial studs, though mainly raising pack animals rather than cavalry mounts. The steppes north of the Black Sea and the Caucasus

Below: *Problems with an unruly baggage donkey, in a 6th-century mosaic from the Byzantine Great Palace in Constantinople. The Byzantines relied heavily on donkeys when campaigning in the more mountainous eastern parts of their Empire. (Author's photograph; Mosaics Museum, Istanbul)*

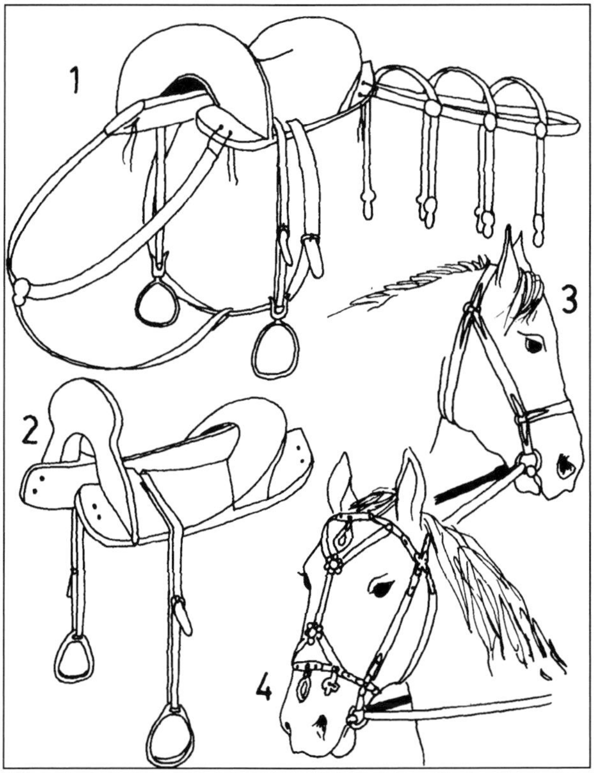

Left: Horse-harness
1. Reconstruction of a wood-framed saddle excavated at Pérechtchépina; Avar, 7th–8th centuries, simplified and with its decoration removed. This is the type of early medieval saddle which strongly influenced Byzantine harness and thus by extension the rest of Europe. (after Laszlo)
2. Wood-framed saddle with its leather seating removed, excavated at Zelenki near Kiev, 12th–13th centuries. This form of comfortable saddle was used by all peoples of the Eurasian steppes and formed the basis of saddles throughout Russia, the Middle East and China for most of the medieval period. (State Hermitage Museum, St. Petersburg)
3. Reconstruction of a bridle and bit using 'trefoil' linkages; Russian, 11th–12th centuries. A sturdy but simple form of bridle used in southern Russia. (after Kirpichnikov)
4. Simplified reconstruction of a more elaborate bridle and bit found south of Voronezh; 11th century, possibly Pecheneg Turkish. (after Kirpichnikov)

may also have been an important source for the Byzantines, as it was for medieval Russia. In fact the large horse herds maintained by the main Russian princes for their *druzhina* cavalry retinues were often tended by specialists recruited from the nomadic Turkish peoples. The problem of inadequate and unreliable sources of horses was particularly acute for the Crusader States of the Middle East. A few could be raised locally, but animals imported by sea from Mediterranean Europe remained essential. The widespread impression that the horses ridden by Crusader knights were inevitably larger and heavier than those of the Muslim foe was probably another myth, at least during the 12th century and when compared to the horses ridden by professional Muslim soldiers rather than Turkish tribal warriors.

Arab soldiers fought on mares as well as stallions and this meant that a larger proportion of available animals could be used as cavalry mounts. The art of selective breeding was already highly developed in the Middle East in pre-Islamic times and this soon became a science, the first recorded Arabic book on the subject dating from 785. By the 9th century the Arabian breed was already known in southern Europe and had already contributed to the emergence of the Andalusian which was regarded as the best riding-horse, though not necessarily the best war-horse, in Europe. The Arabian had also contributed genes to the magnificent Turkestani, 'Golden' or 'Celestial' Horse, which was admired in India and China. By the later Middle Ages the ideal *jawād* (war-horse) of Middle Eastern armies was part Turkestani part Arabian, and it was much bigger than those ridden by Mongol warriors. In general it seems that a professional cavalryman in most eastern and central Islamic armies normally had two horses, one for use in battle and one for ordinary riding or to carry baggage, plus one or more other baggage animals such as a mule or camel. The fascination fine-bred horses had for the military élite of al-Andalus was still seen in Ibn Hudhayl's military treatises. In one he devoted no less than fourteen chapters to horses, leaving only six for arms, armour and warfare in general. The importance of government stables and their associated horse-breeding establishment has already been noted, particularly in the choice of Samarra as the ᶜAbbāsid Caliphate's new military capital in 9th-century Iraq. The *iṣṭabl* or stabling establishment was, in fact, a vital part of most Islamic state or government structures and had its own veterinarians as well as grooms and administrative officials. The word *iṣṭabl*, however, like the concept of a state-organised stabling and breeding establishment, was of Roman Latin origin and probably entered Arabic via Greek having first been recorded among the Ghassānid *phylarchs* of the Syrian frontier. Of course not all horse breeding came under state control, and the bedouin tribes remained the most prestigious sources of the finest animals. Only in those countries where good quality cavalry mounts were extremely rare, for example 14th-century West Africa, did rulers impose a state monopoly on the horse trade.

The horse-breeding traditions of Turco-Mongol Central Asia were very different from those of the Byzantine and Islamic Middle East. Here there was always a precarious balance between the great horse herds which gave the nomads their military power and the need to disperse such herds in search of grazing. This in turn meant that they interbred with wild ponies, retaining their native vigour but also remaining small. The importance of raising huge numbers of horses may have accounted for the fact that the marshy, mosquito-ridden and often frozen Ob basin in north-western Siberia appears to have been an important horse-breeding centre until, for some unexplained reasons, it declined in the

'Joseph is sold into Egypt', Byzantine ivory panel, c.550. The Midianite traders in the Bible story are here shown as pre-Islamic Arab tribesmen. They are distinguished by their long hair, loose izar cloaks or wrappers, and large infantry bows. (Author's photograph; Throne of Archbishop Maximian, Cathedral Museum, Ravenna)

later Middle Ages. The relationship between the Turco-Mongol warrior and his tough little horse was extremely close, and was treated as being a virtually mystical bond in both Turkish and Mongol epic literature. The main qualities which Central Asian warriors looked for also differed from the requirements of western European knights; being a flat back for ease and comfort in riding long distances, a long neck for jumping and rapid changes of direction. The importance of Central Asian steppe grasslands as a source of cavalry horses for China can hardly be exaggerated. Good relations with the Turkish Uighurs were, for example, vital for the Chinese who paid for Uighur horses with crates of tea. Less is known about the breeding of horses in medieval India, except that the climate was often unsuitable and as a result good quality war-horses had to be imported from outside, even overseas from Arabia.

Humble beasts of burden, asses, mules and camels, were also essential to any medieval army. In the mountains of late 6th-century Anatolia Byzantine armies relied on mules, horses and camels as baggage animals. Far to the west in the Iberian peninsula the old Roman road system had fallen apart under Germanic Visigothic rule, but this may not have been a symptom of neglect. Rather it may have been associated with the large-scale use of mule-trains which were economically more efficient than the bullock carts of the Roman era. Whereas camels were more suitable in dry but generally flat terrain, mules and donkeys were more suited to rough terrain and mountains; this being why the armies of southern Arabia made much greater use of donkeys than did their neighbours in central Arabia. Many of those First Crusaders whose war-horses died during the appalling march across Anatolia were reduced to riding mules by the time they reached northern Syria. The better organised Umayyad Muslim army which had crossed Anatolia in the opposite direction in 718/9 set off with equal numbers of baggage mules and camels, the former carrying food for the men and camels, the camels themselves carrying the army's siege equipment. Later Fāṭimid armies were again described as using both mules and *bukhtī* (crossbred Arabian and Khurāsāni camels) in their supply train. The invention of the wooden-framed camel saddle had already had a great impact on the military relationship between the northern Arabs and their settled neighbours, not because it enabled men to fight but because it made the camel a far more efficient riding animal and beast of burden. The strategic superiority, greater mobility and speed of Muslim-Arab armies resulted from their greater use of the camel, particularly in semi-desert areas. Once they reached the higher lands of central Iran and Anatolia, however, these Muslim-Arab armies probably had to rely on two-humped Bactrian camels rather than their own single-humped dromedaries. This was better able to endure cold and rough terrain but was notably slower than the fleet-footed Arabian dromedary. In the later medieval period each élite *mamlūk* soldier in the Mamlūk army of Egypt and Syria is said to have been issued with one or two baggage camels, whereas the non-élite *halqa* had only three camels for every two men. Bactrian camels certainly played a major role as baggage animals and for mounted infantry in pre-Islamic Turkish Central Asia, donkeys and mules being rare – perhaps because of the ferocious climate. The late Gupta armies of northern India are also credited with having some kind of 'camel corps', perhaps of mounted infantry, though camels do not appear to have come into widespread use until the 7th or 8th centuries.

Elephants, of course, were the most distinctive baggage animals in medieval Indian armies, mostly being captured and trained within the forest areas. By the 14th century the Turco-Muslim Sultanate of Delhi was, like its Hindu rivals, using large numbers of elephants as baggage animals, together with buffalo, camels and ponies according to the terrain in which the campaign was fought.

Despite a general decline in the importance of wheeled transport during the Middle Ages, carts were still used when they proved suitable. A Byzantine army campaigning against the Sassanians within Iraq early in the 7th century certainly included many waggoners. More surprisingly, perhaps, the Muslim conquerors of Iberia in the early 8th century still relied upon wheeled carts rather than caravans to transport their booty back to Syria. One area where carts continued to play a particularly important military and economic role was the steppes. Medieval Russian armies used them to transport weapons, food supplies and heavier equipment, and the indigenous nomadic peoples used them to carry their entire families. By the late 14th century, in fact, huge wagon trains comparable to those which opened up America's West were crossing the east European steppes on behalf of soldiers, merchants and nomadic princes. Despite the popular image of the Mongols consisting of hordes of lightly armoured warriors on ponies, they in fact used large carts to transport heavy pieces of military equipment across their vast 'World Empire'. At the other extreme Chinese armies used large numbers of small handcarts in which infantrymen transported their kit. In India bullock carts served as the main form of transporting military gear and plunder in the Deccan regions.

The Sassanians had a high reputation when it came to getting their armies across major rivers, often carrying bridging equipment on campaign. These skills were then inherited by the Muslims. In fact the Arabs had long been renowned for their ability to cross rivers using inflated leather skins, rafts supported by such skins, or small leather boats. According to Roman sources, the early Arabs also built floating bridges in much the same way. Although the Byzantine Empire was less renowned in this aspect of military engineering, one 10th-century Byzantine military treatise laid particular stress on the role of pioneers to clear roads and passes though wooded areas. During the First Crusade the contingent led by Geoffrey de Bouillon was similarly preceded by men with axes, broadening the road through the Balkans. Other sources mention minor details dealing with an army on the march, such as portable leather water-troughs for Muᶜtaṣim's cavalry when he invaded Byzantine Anatolia in the mid-9th century, or the fact that the Fāṭimid army when crossing desert areas sent pioneers ahead of the main column to clean the wells.

River Transport

Rivers were more a means of communication than a barrier in the Byzantine Empire, particularly in the Balkans. This was even more true of medieval Russia where navigable rivers and strategic portages between them or around rapids played a major military role. The rivers of the Middle East were inevitably less important; yet in the 11th century the vital Shaṭṭ al-ᶜArab waterway connecting the Arabian Gulf with the Tigris and Euphrates through the marshes of southern Iraq was marked by a series of beacons or 'light-houses' on tall wooden frames called *k̲hashāb*. The great rivers which crossed the steppes of Central Asia, particularly those flowing north through Siberia towards the Arctic Ocean, were probably barriers rather than means of communication for the nomadic Turco-Mongol tribes. Nevertheless some of these peoples had a reputation as boatmen with a variety of usually simple craft.

The Chinese system of river navigation was far more sophisticated and elaborate than anything seen elsewhere. Here river transport maintained the defences of northern China under the Toba dynasty of the 5th century, the ships and their supporting administration largely being manned by the indigenous Chinese gentry rather than the Toba's own military élite. The far more powerful and long-lasting T'ang dynasty similarly relied on rivers and canals as arteries for transporting heavy equipment and large volumes of food for their armies.

COMBINED OPERATIONS

Naval warfare and communications were more advanced in the Mediterranean and the Indian Ocean than in the northern seas, with correspondingly more ambitious attempts at combined military operations. However, medieval conditions were different from those seen in later centuries. For example, Malta was not much used as a naval base in the Middle Ages because it lacked timber. The same went for many other smaller Mediterranean islands which would only come to naval prominence in later centuries.

Raiding

During the early Middle Ages naval warfare aimed at targets either on shore or moored close inshore rather than trying to engage an enemy on the high seas. Documentary sources provide a number of interesting details, as when the first Muslim raiders from Morocco landed on a rocky part of the Iberian coast at night, the men clambering ashore using their oars as boarding planks and catching the Visigothic defenders by surprise. Two generations earlier a more ambitious Muslim-Arab raid captured the Byzantine island of Rhodes, took up residence, seized local flocks and planted crops for food for a year, then used Rhodes as a base from which to attack passing shipping. This initial Muslim occupation of Rhodes was so successful that the Umayyad Caliphate re-supplied the occupiers by sea until the Caliph Yazīd withdrew the force more than eight years later. The Muslim capability of transporting substantial raiding forces and of resupplying them across long distances increased over the next centuries. One of their most remarkable expeditions was launched by the Aghlabid rulers of Tunisia against Rome in 846. Seventy-three ships assembled off the Tiber estuary then landed 11,000 soldiers and 500 horses near Ostia. This army then devastated a large swathe of central Italy. The Byzantine navy also launched annual *koursa* (raids) against Muslim coasts. Defenders were always at a disadvantage, however, because they normally had to rely on rumours or inaccurate intelligence about forthcoming raids.

Horse Transports

The ability to transport horses by sea was an essential part of large-scale raiding and combined operations. The techniques developed in Roman times having declined, the Muslim states of the Mediterranean and those bordering the Indian Ocean revived and further refined them, transporting large numbers of horses over considerable distances using the *tarīda*, a specialised galley. From the 8th to 11th centuries the Mediterranean Arabs clearly posed greater capability in this field than their Byzantine and Italian rivals. The first Fāṭimid attempt to conquer Egypt involved a dual invasion, the main force marching overland along the North African coast but reinforced by a fleet sailing alongside. The Fāṭimids were able to retake rebel-held Susa some years later; the infantry coming by sea and linking up with cavalry which marched overland from Egypt. The Byzantines used a specialised horse-transporting galley called a *chelandrion,* though it was the Venetians who were credited with being the first to carry cavalry horses directly from western Europe to the newly established Crusader States in 1123. In 1174 the Norman-Sicilians attacked Alexandria with a fleet which included thirty-six *taridas.* On the other hand not all the cavalry landed at once to seize a bridgehead; other vessels which lacked the *taridas'* ability to manoeuvre stern-first directly on to a beach, probably stood off and sent their cargoes, passengers and horses ashore in smaller craft. Deeper draught vessels such as *uissiers* certainly did this, and were reportedly capable of carrying 7,000 troops in only five ships during the Fourth Crusade. Other evidence from the 13th century indicates that horses were taken into some Crusader transport ships through doors near the stern of the vessel, these then being sealed for the duration of the voyage. Although the Indian Ocean was peaceful compared with the war-torn Mediterranean, the Muslim invasion of north-western India in 775/6 involved a substantial fleet bringing infantry and cavalry

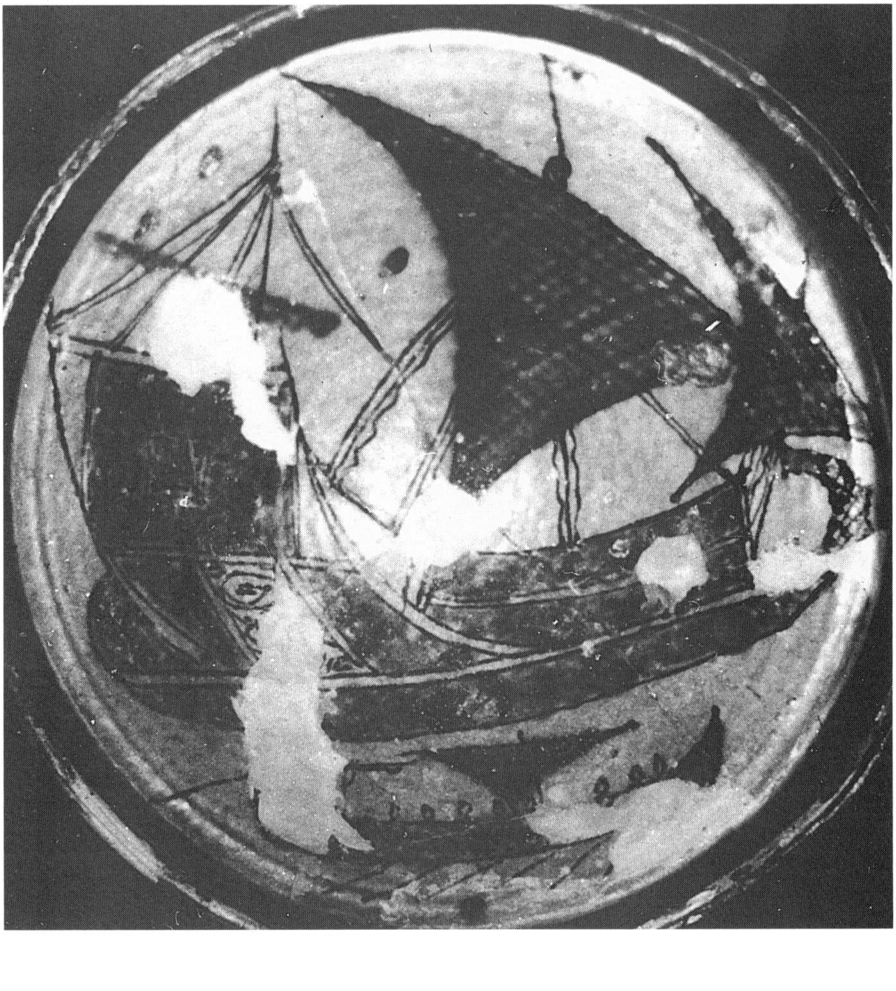

Left: *Ceramic plate showing a three-masted merchant ship; western Islamic, probably from the Balearic Islands, early 11th century. The Muslims were using large three-masted merchant ships and military transports several centuries before these appeared on the Christian northern side of the Mediterranean. (Museo Nazionale di San Matteo, Pisa)*

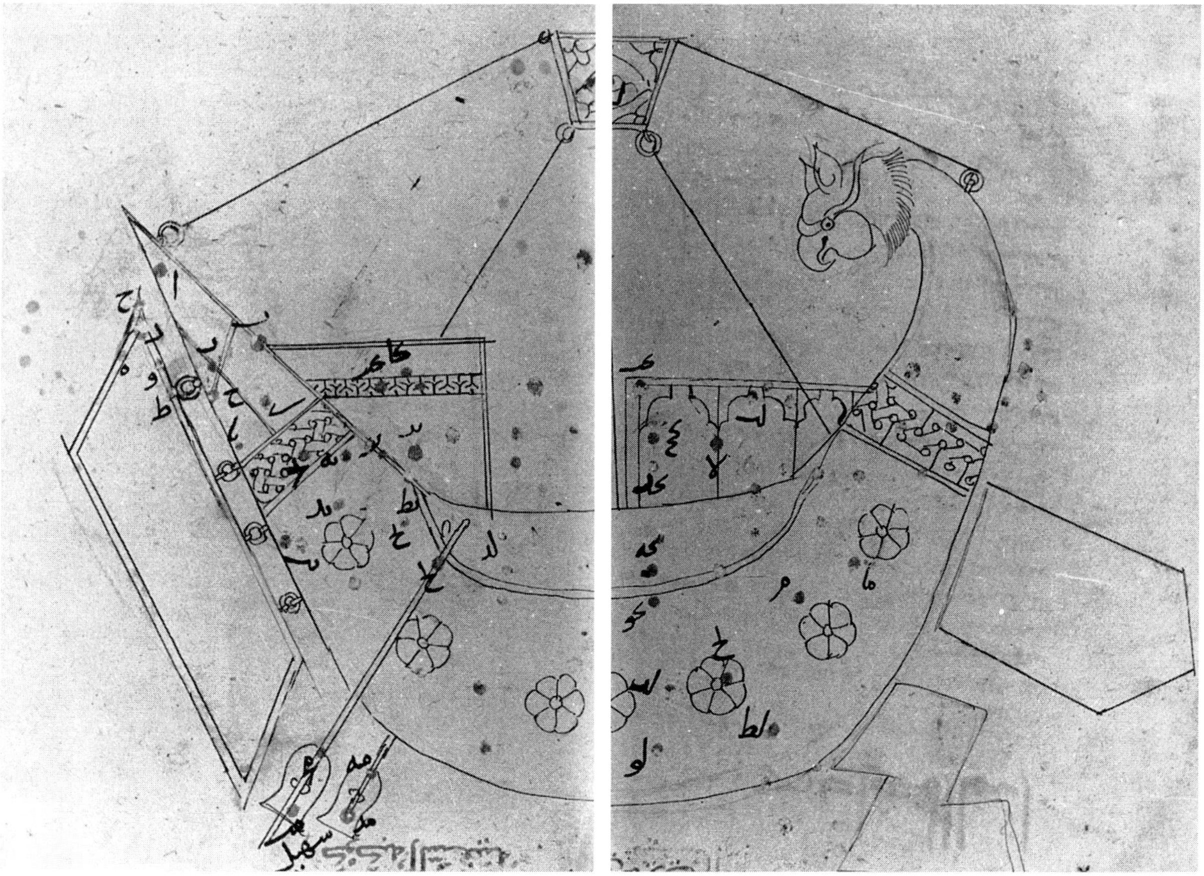

***Above:** 'Argo', in an Islamic astrological manuscript, probably from Egypt, compiled in 1130/1. There are several possible earlier illustrations of ships with stern rudders in Middle Eastern manuscripts and even on decorated ceramics, but this is one of the first to show the hinges clearly. Nevertheless this rudder looks so impracticable that it is likely that the artist was inspired by a verbal description rather than having seen such a thing himself. Chinese sailing ships in the Pacific and Indian Oceans had used hinged stern rudders for centuries and the idea had probably reached the Arabian Gulf and Red Sea by the 12th century. (Suwar al-Kawakib, Topkapi Library, MS. Ahmad III. 3493, Istanbul)*

from the Arabian Gulf. By the 14th century there were also references to stone-throwing machines aboard ships during wars around India's coasts. Even so the ability to transport cavalry horses remained militarily much more important.

Coastal Landings

The difference between a coastal invasion and a raid was merely one of size where naval technology was concerned. For example during their siege of Constantinople early in the 7th century, the Sassanian Persians seized whatever vessels they could find and then unsuccessfully attempted to transport three to four thousand cavalry and infantry across the Bosphorus to help their Avar allies on the European shore. A short while later Slav tribesmen tried to attack Constantinople's sea-walls by tying many small boats together to form platforms from which they could assault the walls. Over the next centuries such naval threats had become more serious. The sudden appearance of a Turco-Muslim fleet based at Izmir on the Aegean at the end of the 11th century even threatened to cut the Byzantine Empire in half when it forged an alliance with pagan Pechěneg Turks who had invaded the Balkans.

Naval power had, in fact, become a central part of Muslim military effectiveness since the mid-7th century. Ships from Egypt may even have conquered the Italian island of Pantelleria during the reign of the first Umayyad Caliph Muʿāwiya. Control of the western Mediterranean also enabled the Muslims to retain Narbonne long after the rest of southern France had been reconquered by the Carolingian Franks. The great Muslim-Arab siege of Constantinople which lasted from 715 to 717 was undertaken by both land and sea; the main force marching across Anatolia being preceded by two smaller forces, one of which came by sea, to initiate the siege of the Byzantine capital. But this unsuccessful project

Bronze lamp in the form of a galley; Coptic-Byzantine, 4th–5th centuries. This object provides a virtually unique three-dimensional impression of a late Roman or early medieval Mediterranean ship with its two raised stern 'wings'. Later Mediterranean horse-transporting galleys probably had a stern entry-port for the animals. (Staatliche Museum, inv. 4228, Berlin; probably lost during the Second World War)

also demonstrated the weakness of medieval combined operations, the Muslim fleet having to return to its base in Cilicia during the winter - leaving the army largely cut off deep in enemy territory. Other later references to combined operations show both the ingenuity of those involved and the limitations imposed by available technology. In 904, for example, a Muslim naval attack directly upon the great port of Thessaloniki involved tying the ships together in pairs as stable fighting platforms, making raised firing positions on the ends of the long yardarms of their lateen sails and on their main-masts, using planks and oars. In 1170 there was the famous occasion when Ṣalāh al-Dīn retook the Crusader-held castle of Qal^{c}at Fara'ūn on a small island in the Gulf of Aqaba; the assault being carried out by small prefabricated boats brought across Sinai. But the question remains; why did the Muslims need to carry these vessels overland in the first place? Probably the Crusaders who held Aqaba already posed a threat to Muslim control of the Red Sea well before Reynald of Châtillon's disastrous raiding cruise down towards the Indian Ocean in 1182–3. The initial Crusader seizure of the coastal towns of Syria, Lebanon and Palestine had largely depended on help from Italian fleets. It is also worth noting that the Christian conquest of Murābiṭin-held Almeria in 1146–7 also required naval help from Genoa, Pisa and Barcelona. Most such operations involved the use of barge-like coastal vessels to transfer men and goods ashore from the larger ships. There were cases when knights emerged fully armed on to the beach, but it is unclear whether they rode their horses out of *tarida*-type 'landing-craft' or had to lead the animals and then get into the saddle once they were on dry land. In 1220–9, during preparations for his proposed invasion of Egypt, the Emperor Frederick of Germany and Italy ordered the construction of specialised shallow-draught ships capable of operating and making amphibious landings in the confined waters of the Nile Delta.

When faced with such seaborne threats, defenders used a variety of different techniques. The mid-11th-century harbour of Acre was protected by an iron chain which could be lowered to allow friendly ships through. It was also common for ships to attack the walls of a port directly. During the Crusader siege of Acre in 1190 the Pisans built tall wooden towers on some of their vessels so that they reached the top of the sea-walls. The towers were covered with wet hides as protection against Greek Fire. The Venetians used the same against the sea-walls of Constantinople in 1204. Against Dumyat in 1223 and 1249 Crusader ships had *mangonels* with which they bombarded Muslim ships on the Nile. During Ṣalāh al-Dīn's siege of the Crusader castle of Marqab in 1188 the defenders were supported by ships lying off-shore, manned by crossbowmen who shot at Muslim troops close to the beach. The latter erected a continuous line of wooden palisades so that their archers and crossbowmen could reply. During their final defence of Acre in 1291 one Crusader ship had a large stone-throwing *mangonel* on board, though this was destroyed in a storm. For their part the Muslims attacked a Crusader fleet with fire-ships outside Dumyat in 1169, and in 1220–1 the Egyptians sank some block-ships in the Nile estuaries. During a mid-14th-century Castilian naval attack upon Barcelona, the defending fleet's larger ships lined up alongside a sandbar from where their crossbowmen and stone-throwing machines could shoot at the attacking vessels while the defending fleet's smaller ships were drawn up on the beach with 'their keels outwards', apparently to form a barricade. On the other hand attempts to resist a landing on the beach itself were rare, perhaps because armoured cavalry emerging from 'landing-craft' were virtually unstoppable. During the Crusader assault upon Izmir in 1344 the defending cavalry rode into the sea to fight the Crusaders as they emerged from their ships, but were overwhelmed by the superior numbers of the latter. Comparable efforts are recorded in the eastern oceans. The Mongols are said to have had stone-throwing machines aboard their ships when they attempted to invade Japan in the mid-13th century. The Champa of Vietnam, defending their capital against an invading Mongol fleet in 1282, are said to have shot at the enemy's ships with no less than one hundred stone-throwing machines.

FLAGS AND HERALDRY

The Orthodox World

The armed forces of Orthodox Christian Europe did not use the same system of heraldry as did the west. The Byzantine Empire, and through it several other medieval states, were more direct heirs to the Roman imperial system of flags, banners and shield motifs. The shield motifs illustrated in surviving post-medieval copies of the Notitia Dignitatum manuscript probably bore little relation to those really used by Roman armies of the late 4th and 5th centuries, though several motifs are close to shields in some late Roman carvings and as described in early Byzantine written sources. Furthermore the symbolic importance of early Byzantine military flags is indicated by the fact that the Sassanians kept some 300 captured examples in their capital of Ctesiphon. The so-called *'dragon'* form of wind-sock banner came into widespread use in 4th-century Roman armies. It was closely associated with archery, as it had been among the people of the steppes, and was used as late as the 12th century. Eagle-shaped finials or standards also remained in use well into the 7th and perhaps even 8th century. By the 10th century, however, Christian crosses were almost universal on top of flag-poles, at least according to the evidence of stylised Byzantine art, perhaps in a conscious effort to replace the spear-blades which had been used as an emblem of sovereignty in late Roman times and which continued in use in Muslim armies.

Late Roman and early Romano-Byzantine armies had used the *vexillum* form of banner which hung vertically, though this was gradually replaced by the *bandon* hung horizontally and may have reflected Germanic or Avar military influence. Meanwhile the words *signum* indicated a large flag and *flammula* meant a small pennon or tapering streamer; the latter being criticised by some military manuals as a hindrance in battle. Other evidence points to elaborate 9th-century banners being made of brocade, and the main battle-standards of one 11th-century Byzantine army were mounted on poles decorated with silver studs. The Byzantine army and navy both used a regularised system of flags whose shape, size and colour indicated something specific. Each *meros* (unit) seems to have had flags of the same colour; each *moira* (sub-unit) perhaps having different streamers on such flags. Each regiment also had its own shield colour or motif, at least during the early medieval period. One 9th-century Byzantine soldier was described as having a picture of St. John on his shield, but during the 9th century Byzantine troops also started using *'pseudo-Kufic'* patterns based on the stylised *Kūfic* form of Arabic script used in so much early Islamic decoration. Surprisingly, perhaps, the double-headed eagle, which became the most important late Byzantine imperial device, was of ancient oriental origin rather than having much connection with the ancient Roman imperial eagle. It rose in popularity in Comnenid-ruled parts of an increasingly fragmented Byzantine Empire, a single-headed eagle appearing as the distinctive emblem of the rulers of 13th-14th-century Trebizond. With such a sophisticat-

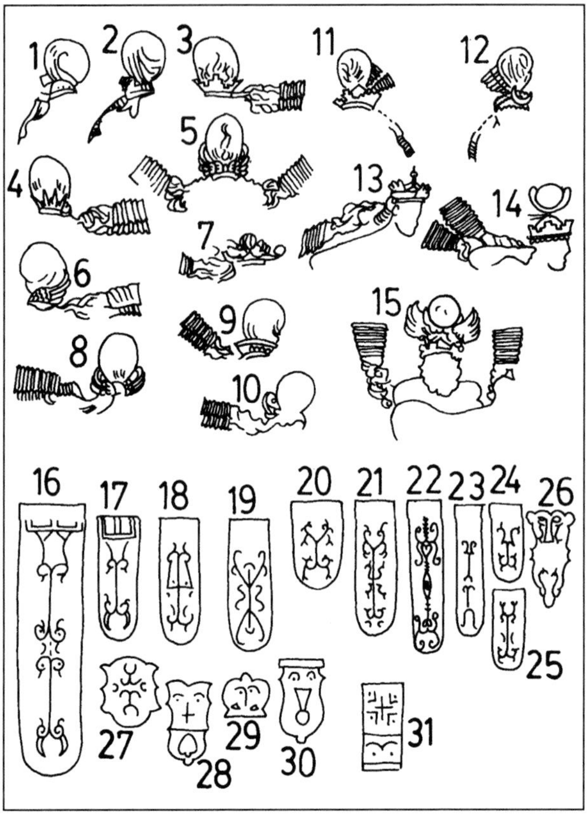

Above: Military and Tribal Symbolism
1–15. Ceremonial head-dress worn by Sassanian rulers, each slightly different and used to identify the ruler.
1–2. Ardashir I
3. Shāpūr I
4. Varahran I
5–8. Varahran II
9. Narseh
10. Hormizd II
11. Shāpūr II
12. Shāpūr III
13. Yazdagird I
14. Khusrau I
15. Khusrau II
16–31. Tamgas or tribal marks of Central Asian and north Eurasian forest peoples, mostly on metal belt or strap-ends.
16–19. Avar, from Kiskörös-Városalatt
20–27. Avar, from Martinovka
28–29. Finno-Ugrian, early medieval
30. unattributed from Caucasus, early medieval
31. unattributed early medieval from Martinovka.

ed system of flags and banners it is not surprising that Byzantine commanders used them in a variety of ways. Late 6th-century *tagma* units were advised to carry two banners to make their numbers appear more formidable, and in the early 14th century the Byzantine prince Theodore Palaeologus still advised each unit to carry reserve banners since the loss of a flag could seriously demoralise the troops.

Turco-Mongol tribal *tamga* emblems would have a strong influence on later medieval Balkan and Polish heraldry but not in Byzantium or Armenia where other influences were at work. The carved figure of a seated ruler over the entrance to a 13th-century Cilician Armenian castle reflects the talismanic use of such motifs in neighbouring Saljūq Turkish states and may have been added as a mark of loyalty to the Mongol conquerors. During the late 13th century, however, the rulers of Cilician Armenia adopted aspects of western European heraldry via the Crusader States of Syria and Cyprus. Western heraldic influence did not reach Christian Georgia, where basically Byzantine forms of flag and shield patterns were also amalgamated with powerful Islamic and Persian influence. For example the late 12th–early 13th-century Georgian *alami* was a large red-and-black royal banner, and the *drosha* was a long streamer-like flag sometimes used aboard ship. Byzantine, western European, native Slav and various steppe fashions contributed to the flags, banners and heraldic motifs of medieval Russia. Here the first pagan rulers are believed to have used tribal emblems comparable to the *tamgas* of the steppe nomads, though the use of a shield as a symbol of peace may have been introduced from Scandinavia. On the other hand an emphasis on scarlet shields, banners and flagpoles in the 12th–13th-century Prince Igor epic may have come from Romano-Byzantine tradition.

Iberia and the Crusader States

Iberian heraldry was within the western European tradition, but, like that of Italy, was also under Islamic influence. This was most apparent in the popularity of inscriptions as a motif. Islamic influence was not seen to any great degree in the heraldry of the eastern Mediterranean Crusader States, though *pseudo-Kufic* inscriptions did become a popular form of decoration in manuscripts. On the other hand the use of painted, carved or real shields to decorate the gates of a castle or town in the 13th century was similar to the symbolic or talismanic gate-decoration seen in Fāṭimid and Ayyūbid Egypt.

The Muslim World

The Prophet Muḥammad had several banners, including a black *rāya* said to have been made from his wife Aisha's head-dress. A famous champion in the Umayyad army used his wife's veil as a spear pennon; a romantic notion later adopted in Europe where such personal mementoes were called *druries*. It is also possible that the Prophet's *ᶜalam* or standard known as *al-ᶜuqāb* 'the eagle' was a late Roman-style eagle mounted on top of a pole. The ᶜAbbāsid Caliphs certainly continued to use a *ḥarbah* (javelin) or *ᶜanaza* (short spear) as a form of ruling insignia. This continuation of the old Roman use of spears as marks of sovereignty had probably been introduced into Arabia via the Arab *phylarchs* of the Syrian frontier. Furthermore it has been suggested that the *Hand of Fāṭima*, which would become one of the most popular forms of Muslim symbolism, may originally have been a tribal or military standard in pre-Islamic Arabia. The Rāshidūn Caliphs who immediately succeeded Muḥammad are said to have disapproved of the carrying of military banners other than those used by the

Right: *Heraldic carving of a cross over a crescent on the entrance tower of the castle of Hieron, or Anadolu Kavagi, overlooking the Bosphorus, dating from the mid-12th century. Whether this was meant to symbolise the triumph of Christianity over Islam is not known. (Author's photograph)*

Right: *The Pendón de Baeza or Banner of San Isidoro, Spanish, 13th century, a very rare surviving medieval banner. (Museo Lázaro Galdiano, Madrid)*

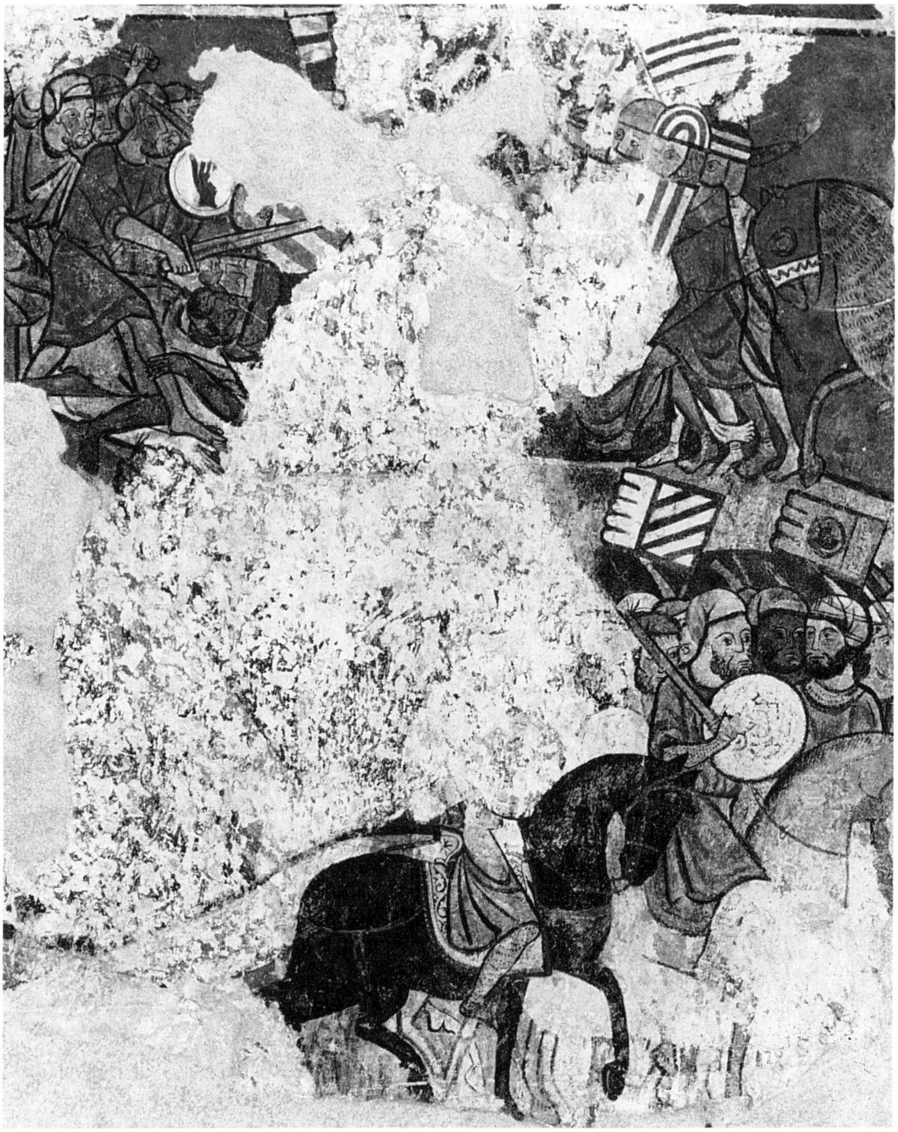

'Conquest of Majorca by James I of Aragon'; wall-painting, Spanish late 13th century. The Christian warriors have the typical mail armour and small round helmets of this period. Most of the Muslims are virtually unarmoured, but the horsemen at the bottom of the picture have the same mail armour as their Aragonese foes, though worn beneath their ordinary clothes. (Museo de Artes de Cataluese foes, tho)

Prophet himself, but this proved impracticable from a military point of view and flags came back strongly under the Umāyyads. By the 13th century manuscript illustrations showed various types, including a slender form possibly resulting from Turkish or Chinese influence, whereas more traditional triangular and rectangular flags dominated in western Islamic armies.

The crescent and star which later became a widespread Muslim symbol was at first mostly seen in areas where pre-Islamic and Sassanian tradition survived. For a long time the crescent continued to have non-Islamic associations, though it appears to have become popular in Turkish-Muslim areas during the 12th and 13th centuries. A detailed inventory of the ceremonial garments worn by an Ottoman ruler, written in 1348, specifies a red coat decorated with crescents, and a red banner though this had no crescent or star. Far to the west the Muwaḥḥidin rulers of North Africa and al-Andulus included many small crescents in their military banners, though some scholars have suggested that these represented the hoof-prints of the first conquering Muslim armies. The double-bladed *Sword of ᶜAlī*, which became a *Shī'ite* symbol, may have been based upon references to a sword with two grooves down its blade, but later developed into a talisman which could 'put out the eyes of the Devil'.

The first ᶜAbbāsid Caliphs may have introduced the idea of putting large inscriptions on military flags, justifying their rebellion against the previous Umayyads. Thereafter the Muslim declaration of faith soon became the most widespread phrase on such banners, though other Koranic quotations were used. Detailed descriptions of banners used by Fāṭimid armies mention three rows of embroidered inscriptions, and they continued to appear in great numbers in 13th-century

Middle Eastern and Iberian art. Surviving 13th- and 14th-century banners captured during the Reconquista have densely woven decoration, deep colours and a mass of separate inscriptions within bordered cartouches.

The colours used in Islamic flags eventually reflected religious or political affiliation. Black was associated with *Mahdist* movements and with ᶜAbbāsids; green with the *ᶜAlids* and thus later with *Shia* Islam in general; white the Umayyads and later the Fāṭimids; red with martyrdom and the puritanical *Kharaji* movement; it became a Sunni colour in India and the Ottoman Empire. Within Muslim Iran there was a revival of the old Sassanian colours and banners in the 10th century; this continuing to influence the non-Persian Middle East from the 11th century onwards. The *checky* or *chequerboard* pattern was associated with Muslim warriors in 12th-13th-century European *chansons de geste*, together with the basic *paly, bary* and *fleury* heraldic patterns. This may well have reflected the reality of shield devices in Arab armies during these and earlier centuries. For example in 971 one Andalusian army was described as setting off on campaign behind a banner with a *shaṭranj* or 'chessboard' design; and the *fleur-de-lys* had been a popular decorative motif in early Islamic architecture.

Andalusia was the only Muslim country where western heraldry was used, albeit to a limited degree. This had been adopted as part of a wider copying of Christian Iberian military styles in the 12th and 13th centuries. The Naṣrid kingdom of Granada was even granted a *coat of arms* by its theoretical feudal suzerain, the Christian Kingdom of Castile, after the battle of Najera in 1367. This shield with an Islamic inscription on a diagonal band was used as architectural decoration, but was not used on flags or shields. Another more dubious example of western heraldic influence might be found in the sudden popularity of the *fleur-de-lys*, and the lion and eagle in Mamlūk heraldry - perhaps stemming from their use by the Mamlūks' most powerful Crusading foes - France, England and the German Empire. Despite Islam's supposed prohibition of the portrayal of living creatures, animals, mythical beasts and human beings appeared in some forms of identifying symbol. Aḥmad Ibn Ṭūlūn, governor of Egypt, had lions carved on the gates of his palace in the later 9th century, and lions and leopards are also mentioned as banner devices in late 10th-century Persian literature. Carvings of hunting dogs and birds have been found on the excavated 10th-11th-century gate of the northern Syrian city of Harran; these being replaced by lions when the gate was rebuilt at a later date. The double-headed eagle had been a popular pattern on Islamic fabrics since the 10th century and was adopted as an identifying motif by the Turkish rulers of Anatolia and the Middle East from the late 11th century onwards. Chinese-looking dragons were introduced to the Middle East by the Turks. On the other hand the supposed human forms seen on Muslim banners by various 12th-century Crusaders might have been misunderstood Turkish tribal *tamghas*, and the so-called 'trousers'-shaped banner of Ṣalāh al-Dīn's nephew Taqī al-Dīn might have been a windsock banner as used by archers of recent Central Asian origin.

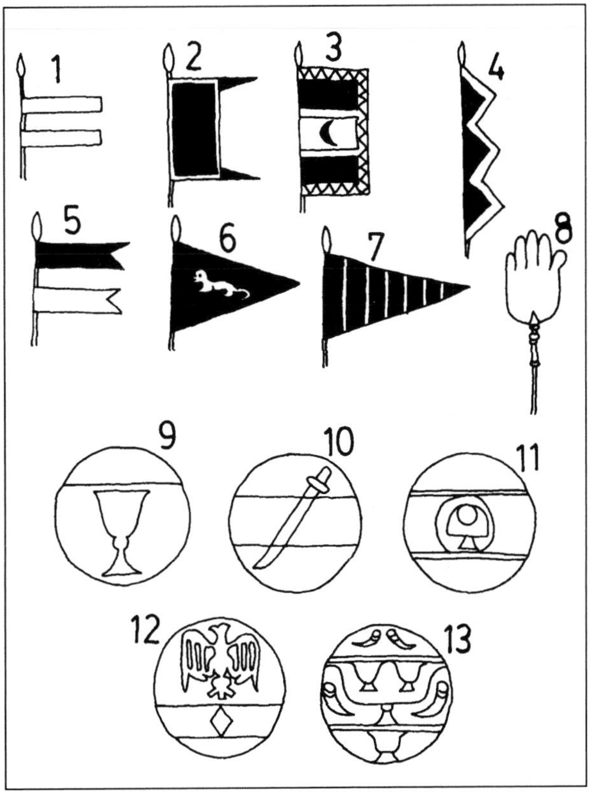

Right: Islamic Heraldry
1. The rāya or tribal flag of the Prophet Muḥammad, both streamers white. (after Hinds)
2. The līwa or battle-flag of the Prophet Muḥammad, black and white. (after Hinds)
3. Rāya or tribal flag of the Ash'arayin, red and white, mid-7th century. (after Hinds)
4. Rāya or tribal flag of the Nakha, yellow and white, mid-7th century. (after Hinds)
5. The līwa or battle-flag of the Caliph Muᶜāwiya, red and white, mid-7th century. (after Haider)
6. Corps flag of the mamlūk bodyguard of Sultan Maḥmūd of Ghazna, yellow lion on black ground, early 11th century. (after Haider)
7. Divisional flag for the right wing of the army of the Sultanate of Delhi, black and yellow, mid-14th century. (after Haider)
8. The so-called 'Hand of Fatima', a metallic standard used by various Muslim forces from the late 14th century onwards.
9-13. Mamlūk insignia, known as rank from the Persian term rang meaning 'colour', though the colours of Mamlūk insignia are mostly unknown since they only survive in carvings, inlaid metalwork and such monochrome sources.
9. late 13th century
10. early 14th century
11. mid-14th century
12. early 14th century
13. late 14th century. (after Meinecke)

Lustre-ware bowl from Iraq, 10th century. The camel in the foreground clearly has a banner attached to its saddle or harness. The rider on the second animal has a pointed hat which might be a style of qalansūwa. (Saint Louis Art Museum, inv. 16:1937, St. Louis, USA)

The system of heraldry used by the 13th- to early 16th-century Mamlūk military élite of the Middle East was different from what had been seen before. Although it was closer to the European concept of heraldry, it was not used on shields or flags but was simply a method of identifying property. Even here, however, the symbolism of military officers and rulers soon diverged; the former continuing to use a complex system of devices reflecting the duties carried out by the holder earlier in his career, while rulers used inscribed cartouches in line with long-established Islamic symbolism. Individual *mamlūks* were proud of their humble origins and of their ascent through a rigorously competitive system; this being why they used the uniquely Mamlūk system of 'first duty' symbolism. Since this was a purely individual matter it was not inherited by a second generation, and only in the later Mamlūk period did some related amirs occasionally adopt similar motifs. The most commonly used symbols were the cup of someone whose first role had been that of a cup-bearer, the napkin of a master-of-the-robes, the sword or dagger of an armour-bearer, the crossed polo-sticks of a polo master, the bow of a bow-master, and, in the later civilianised period, the penbox of a chief secretary. The system became increasingly complex after the middle of the 14th century and there were eventually some forty-five devices, often on a heraldic 'ground' divided into three horizontal bands.

A completely different tradition was represented by the Central Asian *tuq* or yak-tailed pennant which entered the Middle East with various waves of Turkish nomads and soldiers. The number of tails indicated rank, and although this device had pagan origins it continued to be used by many Turco-Muslim armies such as that of the Ottoman Empire where the yak-tailed standard was called a *tūgh*. Here six tails were reserved for the Sultan, lesser numbers being used by senior officers. Variations on the *tūgh* were seen in post-Mongol Iran where it was sometimes combined with an ordinary flag, and also among various Anatolian dervish brotherhoods where very simple forms of *tūgh* had tufts of wool instead of animals' tails. Other forms of standard or finial included a remarkable array used by the Fāṭimid Caliphs in Cairo: crescent-shaped, gilded spheres, lion-shaped windsock banners with open mouths, enormous fans to cool the ruler, and even a special crown-shaped turban with a *ḥāfir* or pin shaped like a model horse on top. But perhaps the most important symbol of rulership in the Fāṭimid Caliphate was an elaborate parasol.

The importance that all sorts of flags, standards and symbolic regalia had in medieval Islamic states was reflected in the fact that many governments had a special department dealing with them. Subordinate rulers would receive official recognition from the centre by being sent a banner suited to their rank. Under the Fāṭimid Caliphs such flags had almost mystical powers and could be sent in the hands of secret agents to try and win new allies or subvert enemy leaders. Within most medieval Muslim armies each unit had its own recognised flag.

To the west, in Andalusia, military flags were handed to their units during a ceremony in the main mosque the day before the start of a campaign. The ceremony itself involved bringing the banners from store and fastening them to their poles; this still being done by the Muwaḥḥidin in the 12th century.

Non-Islamic Asia

Of all the ancient civilisations which influenced subsequent Middle Eastern 'heraldry', the Sassanian Empire was the most important. Here the terms used for military units and their associated banners was often the same; for example the large *drafsh* or *dirafsh* unit and its flag, and the small *vasht* unit and flag. Ordinary flags were shaped like streamers or *banderoles* whereas the great state banner of the Sassanian Empire was entirely different. This *Drafsh-i Kāvyān* 'Banner of Kāvagh' was, in fact, the symbol of ruling legitimacy with its own mythical history as well as its own élite guard. It was said to have been made by the legendary smith Kāvē when the ancient 'Aryans' supposedly rose up against their Semitic or Dravidian oppressors. Basically the banner consisted of a decorated leather sheet, seven metres long and five across, encrusted with precious stones, yellow, red and purple brocade, surmounted by a golden sphere or crescent and festooned with streamers. Other heraldic motifs were used by the clans which formed the Sassanian aristocracy and, like western European heraldry but unlike the subsequent Islamic period, these could be handed down from one generation to the next. In addition to eagles, dragons, sun and moon, there were various geometric or apparently abstract shapes which had much in common with Central Asian tribal *tamghas* and were worn on the caps, costume and horse-covering caparisons of the military élite. The little that is known about such details in pre-Islamic Arabia indicates that each tribe had its own flag and that these were often carried by the tribal chief himself.

Greater detail is known about flags and other such symbolism in Turco-Mongol Central Asia. Here, the *tug* (horse-tail banner) also used yak and big-cat tails; five, seven or nine being reserved for a ruler or subordinate *khān* during the pre-Islamic period. Smaller *tugs* were also attached to war-drums. In addition to their famous horse-tail standards, the Turks used *tös* (totemic ensigns) and *batraq* or *beyraq* (individual flags or pennons). The latter was originally attached to a spear shaft and would later be known in Othmanli (Ottoman) Turkish as a *sanjaq*. The colour symbolism of the pre-Islamic Turks reflected Buddhist rather than Sassanian traditions, particularly in its association with the four points of the compass. It was also linked to the colours of various types of horse ridden by élite units, or with armies responsible for the defence of certain frontiers. The most senior 'colour' within this Central Asian tradition was gold which was used for the tents of senior rulers in the Turco-Mongol steppes and in Tibet. White was another deeply symbolic colour, representing purity among the Manichaeans. It was also adopted by rebels fighting the Uighurs *khāns* and others fighting the Muslim Umayyads in eastern Iran in the 8th century; perhaps hinting that these rebels were under Manichaean influence. The 'white raiment' rebels led by al-Muqannaᶜ against ᶜAbbāsid rule in Khurasan and Transoxiana in 778/9 also seem to have been a mixture of Manichaeans, followers of the old Persian Mazdaist religion and early manifestations of Muslim *Shiism*.

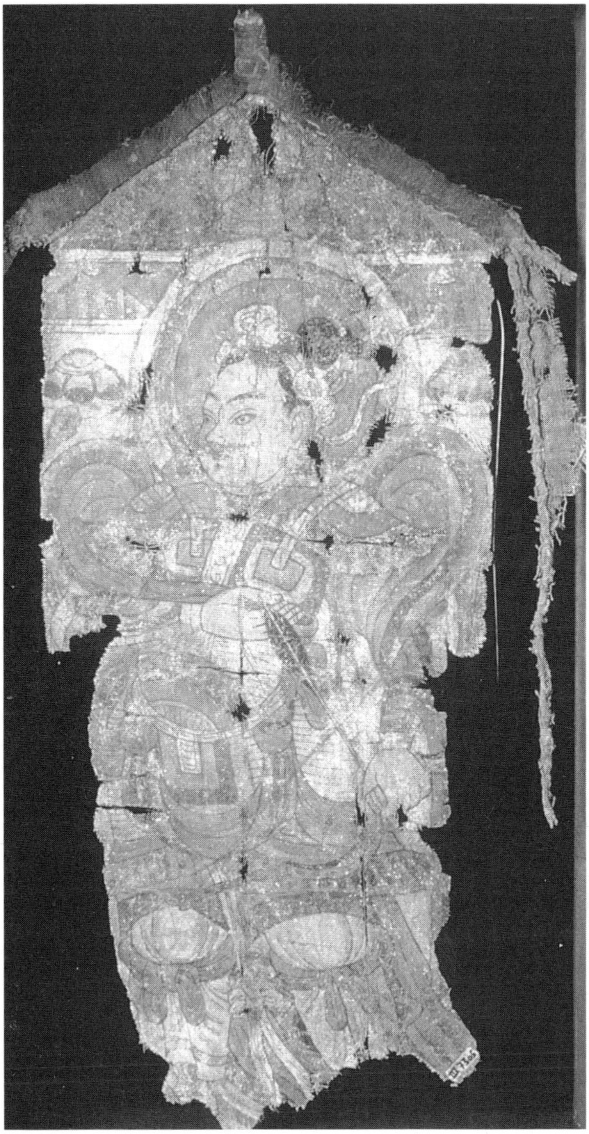

Painted temple banner from Toyuk, Uighur Turkish, 9th century. It is decorated with a Buddhist lokapala or protective spirit armed with a bow and wearing lamellar armour. (Staatliche Museum, Berlin)

The complex system of Turkish tribal *tamghas* included animals, tridents and various other symbols, though it is possible that the trident itself was a very simplified bow and arrow. It certainly became a military symbol among the Mongols in the 13th and 14th centuries. Animals and birds were equally important warrior motifs in earlier centuries, often appearing on helmets in Central Asian wall-paintings; gilded wolf's head-shaped standards were reserved for the supreme *khagan* or *khān* of *khāns*. Genghis Khān used a bird's head emblem, and Hülegü is said to have had an 'eagle banner'. There are also references to human as well as animal-shaped helmet crests in Mongol epics.

The highly structured armies of China had an array of flags for various purposes. These included the two banners carried by a T'ang army on campaign, the *jing* (flag) and the *jie* (standard) which consisted of wooden discs with red tufts as a signalling device. At the other extreme were coloured flags to identify stacks of weapons in the dust and smoke of a siege. Archaic chariots may still have been used to carry military banners in some early medieval Hindu Indian armies, but very little else appears to be known. The Tamil rulers of southern India are said to have had symbolic parasols made from peacock feathers.

UNIFORMS: THEIR DECLINE AND RISE

During the medieval period, the term 'uniform' could include the way in which sections of society such as the military élite were distinguished from the rest of the population by their clothing; particularly when this distinction was reinforced by *sumptuary laws*. These were a feature of many medieval cultures. In the Sassanian Empire, for example, all classes were defined by the quality and patterns of what they wore, especially the aristocracy. On the other hand real uniforms were very rare even in a Byzantine Empire consciously proud of its Roman heritage. The old Roman military uniform did survive into the 6th century when Byzantine recruits were given a long-sleeved white tunic, belt, trousers and cloak made in state factories. The belt continued to be the clearest mark of military service, though a new style of Central Asian origin with decorated pendants was adopted in the 6th and 7th centuries. White cloaks then remained the 'uniform' of imperial guards long after other items had been abandoned. Otherwise the colours said to have been worn by four élite *tagmata* regiments on ceremonial occasions seem to have derived from those of the old Hippodrome 'supporters' clubs'; these being blue, red, green and white. Otherwise even the élite *tagmata* now only wore white tunics or cloaks. Other fashions were also copied from the Byzantine Empire's foes, including an Avar-style cloak for 6th–7th-century cavalry because it was better when riding, and shorter Germanic tunics for the infantry. The officer's *scaramangion* was basically the Sassanian horseman's *kaftan*, a distinctive style of coat also adopted by the Muslim military élite. The Byzantine *maniakion*, a richly embroidered cape or cloak worn by senior commanders, was also of Persian origin and continued in use until the end of the Byzantine Empire in the 15th century. The coloured 'shoulder tufts' mentioned in a 10th-century Byzantine military manual are more of a problem, though they might have been later versions of the Graeco-Roman *pteruges*, consisting of strips of leather or fabric forming a decorative fringe of an arming-coak worn beneath others types of armour. The only thing approaching a uniform in medieval Russia was the ceremonial attire worn by rulers and perhaps their immediate retinue; this again being based on Byzantine court fashions.

The use of the Crusader's Cross has been described as the first form of symbolic 'uniform' in western Europe since the fall of the Roman Empire. This is an exaggeration, but costume was considered very important during the Crusades. Some expeditions drew up regulations concerning what should be worn in an attempt to remove unsuitable and perhaps sinful extravagance during an 'armed pilgrimage'. Although the wearing of 'the other side's' costume was strongly discouraged, there was a striking similarity between the symbolic colours worn by the Templars on the Christian side and the *Ismāʿīlīs* on the Muslim; most notably in shared white costume with red finishings. Meanwhile the distinctive belts and white *jupeaux d'armes* of brother knights of the Temple and the black *jupeaux d'armes* with red Crosses on front and back of Templar brother sergeants clearly constituted a uniform. The uniform of the rival Hospitallers was a cloak like that worn by ordinary monks, but this hampered their use of weapons and in 1259 they were at last given permission to wear a loose black cloak over a red *jupon* or *surcoat* with a white Cross. No distinctive provision was made for Hospitaller sergeants and this appears to have had a bad effect on morale, so in 1278 black cloaks and red *surcoats* were reserved for brother knights.

During the early years of Islam there was no attempt to distinguish the ruling Muslims from their Christian or Jewish subjects, and even after this distinction appeared there was no military uniform during the Umayyad Caliphate. Nevertheless the basic costume of soldiers differed from that worn by the civilian élite, being based upon that of men who led an active outdoor rather than sedentary life and including the head-cloth later associated with lawyers and judges. Being given this distinctive head cloth was part of being accepted as a member of the Umayyad dynasty's élite Syrian units and by the mid-8th century élite troops were popularly known as *ʿamāmah shāmīyah* or 'Syrian turbans'. The *ṭirāz* (embroidered band) worn on the sleeves may originally have been reserved for the ruler and his family, but it was later connected with the holding of an *iqṭāʿ (fief)*. Soon after the ʿAbbāsid revolution the Caliph al-Saffāḥ ordered his guard units to wear black, which had become accepted as the ʿAbbāsid colour in contrast to the Umayyads' white. He also tried to standardise the costume of those closest to the throne, but this still concerned colour rather than shape. Black remained the official colour of ʿAbbāsid guards regiments although it only appeared on ceremonial occasions – soldiers and administrators wearing white on ordinary days. The use of black was also a way of demonstrating loyalty to the ʿAbbāsid Caliphate by autonomous or effectively independent rulers. By the 9th century the basic costume of professional soldiers consisted of a *qabāʿ* (tunic) and *qalansuwa shāshīyah* (hood or cap), in a style which originated in the Transoxianan region of Shāsh. Other items of clothing and military equipment were associated with particular troops or those recruited from a specific cultural background. A parade by élite ʿAbbāsid guards to impress a

'Joseph greets his brother', Byzantine ivory panel, c.550. Joseph's guardsmen wear early Byzantine military uniforms which were white with coloured bands around the neck, down the upper sleeves, around the hem of the tunic and down the front of the trousers. (Author's photograph; Throne of Archbishop Maximian, Cathedral Museum, Ravenna)

visiting Byzantine embassy in 917/8 had all the men wearing close-fitting caps beneath pointed satin hoods, this being regarded as 'full dress'. Senior officers who had particularly distinguished themselves in the Caliph's service were given a golden *torque* or necklace; a fashion inherited from the Byzantine or Sassanian past. In contrast the Caliph Mutawakkil's order that ordinary soldiers wear light brown cloaks in the mid-9th century is more likely to have been comparable to the 10th-century Byzantine issue of 'camouflaged' grey cloaks to frontier soldiers 'shadowing' enemy raiders.

By the 10th century, as part of a gradual spread of Persian and then Turkish styles of clothing among Muslim military élites, the old Arab *durrāᶜa* (coat) gave way to the Turco-Persian *kaftan*, and the *durrāᶜa* came to be seen as the 'uniform' of high civilian officials. By the 11th century costume and textiles formed part of a complex social code in most Muslim societies. Nevertheless Islamic civilisation remained essentially egalitarian in which social classes were in a constant flux. As a result the middle classes consistently imitated those who felt themselves superior, while the latter constantly re-distinguished itself by adopting new fashions or more extreme versions of old ones.

Uniforms and special items of clothing or equipment for élite units also changed. In the early 11th century, for example, some of the Ghaznawid Sultan's guards wore a special 'two-horned' head-dress or method of winding their turbans while other guardsmen had two or four feathers in their Turkish-style caps, perhaps associated with the pre-Islamic Turkish use of helmet-feathers to distinguish an élite marksman. A century or so later one Ghūrid ruler of northern India wore a red tunic in battle, so that if he should be wounded, the sight of blood would not demoralise his men. As had already happened in the Byzantine army, highly decorative belts became the single most obvious badge of military status. These belts with their characteristic pendants, known as *minṭaqah* in Arabic, might have been of Turkish origin but they were also adopted by many Persians and Arabs. In Egypt the most senior Fāṭimid army officers wore turbans wound in the earliest recorded Arabian style known as *muḥannak* with a loose loop of cloth hanging below the chin. *Amirs of the First Class* wore jewelled collars or necklaces, those of the second rank carried a silver cane or staff. Following the fall of the Fāṭimid Caliphate and the establishment of Ayyūbid rule in Egypt, Turkish military costume finally came to dominate this country, and continued to do so under the subsequent

Carved ivory panel from Egypt, 10th–11th centuries. It shows two of the Fāṭimid Caliph's guards in full ceremonial costume with elaborate turbans, embroidered dedicatory bands around their sleeves and armed with sword or mace. (Musée du Louvre, inv. 6701 B, Paris)

Mamlūks. Under the Ayyūbids, however, the military élite were also distinguished by a fur-lined hat called a *tarbūsh* or *sharbūsh* which had an upturned brim and a piece of gilded leather at the front. It was, in fact, the one item of dress which opposing Crusaders most emphatically refused to wear. The Mamlūk era then saw newly qualified *mamlūks* being given proper uniforms as well as weapons on completion of their military training. Towards the end of the 14th century the ruling caste of Mamlūks adopted a new form of small red fluffy woollen cap called a *zamt* as their distinctive badge, and thereafter made strenuous efforts to ensure that nobody else was permitted to wear it. This later Mamlūk era was also characterised by some extraordinarily elaborately wound and large turbans, though these were reserved for the senior officers and functionaries.

To some extent these elaborate Mamlūk military fashions were copied by the Ottoman Empire, though here a long coat with slit 'false-sleeves' was even more characteristic; probably inherited from the Byzantines. Not only did the sumptuary laws of the Ottoman Empire become some of the most rigidly enforced seen anywhere in Islamic civilisation, but the Ottoman army was the first to re-introduce a widespread use of uniforms in the true sense of the term. Even in the 14th century, for example, the *Yeni Çeri (Janissaries)* wore *aq börk* (white caps), while the older but less prestigious *azab* volunteers wore red. It is also notable that the Ottoman ruler's *silahdar* (élite cavalry guard), an older unit than the *Yeni Çeri*, wore the same shaped hats as the *Yeni Çeri* but these were again red instead of white. The entire *Yeni Çeri* uniform, as it ultimately developed, was very similar to the costume worn by dervish religious brotherhoods, particularly their tall white felt caps.

A very different but equally distinctive tradition of military headgear appeared in Muslim North Africa; this being the *lithām* or face veil, long worn as a mark of élite political, social or military status among the Saharan Sanhāja Berber nomads. Despite its pre-Islamic origins and direct contravention of Islamic conventions of dress, this was retained. In fact the face veil became so closely associated with the military élite that lesser military units also tried to adopt it. It largely died out under the subsequent Muwaḥḥidin dynasty but was revived to a limited extent under the Marīnids. Otherwise the 14th-century Marīnid army wore loose Arabian turbans now considered old-fashioned in the Middle East, and the Sultan alone was permitted to wear a white cloak. Muslim Andalusian styles of military costume were basically the same as those worn in the Middle East, though they were usually old-fashioned because it took time for new styles to reach this westernmost outpost of medieval Islam. During the 12th and 13th centuries there may have been some short-lived adoption of Christian Spanish military costume. Otherwise the influence of Spanish costume in Granada had to await the 15th century.

The Turco-Mongol cultures of Central Asia, whence so many aspects of military costume stemmed, had many highly distinctive styles of dress. This included the long hair of the warrior élite; its *saç* or style of plaiting indicating rank and tribe. Sleeve decorations similar to the Islamic *ṭirāz* appear in early medieval wall-paintings in Turkestan, and this kind of 'insignia' may well have originated in the area. Military belts with decorative pendants were known as *qur* in old Turkish, their élite wearers being called *qurqapïn* or 'possessors of a belt'. Doubled belts with gilded decoration were a mark of the nobility or a military champion among the 6th-century Gök Turks, and a silver belt would be the mark of a senior vassal among the Qara-Khitai. Minor details known about warrior costume among the 13th-century Mongols include a reference to a champion who refused to wear red or to ride a strawberry roan because these would obscure blood-stains which were considered the mark of a hero. The Īl-Khān Mongol rulers of Iran subsequently had large quantities of clothing made to a designated government specification for use by their army; this being as close to a uniform as a Mongol army would achieve.

In early medieval Korea the robes worn by senior officers were in three designated colours; purple for the most senior, then down through scarlet, blue and yellow - a system probably modelled on that of China. The *kshatriya* warrior caste of Hindu India were also said to be distinguished by costume as well as armour. Some of these items were clearly ancient religious symbols, such as a hemp thread or girdle made of *munja* grass which is originally believed to have been a spare bowstring. Other ceremonial garments, which may not actually have been worn in reality, were the 'warrior-hunter's' deerskin garment which contrasted with the goatskin theoretically worn by non-warrior castes, linen or later cotton undergarments and the red madder-dyed cloaks of warriors. In fact red was so closely associated with the *kshatriya* that they were said to have lived in reddish-coloured houses and wore only red ornaments. There was clearly some truth in these traditional colours for, as the Chinese traveller Hiuen Tsang wrote of the army of King Harsha in 630-45, the *kshatriya* caste stained their teeth red, bound up their hair and

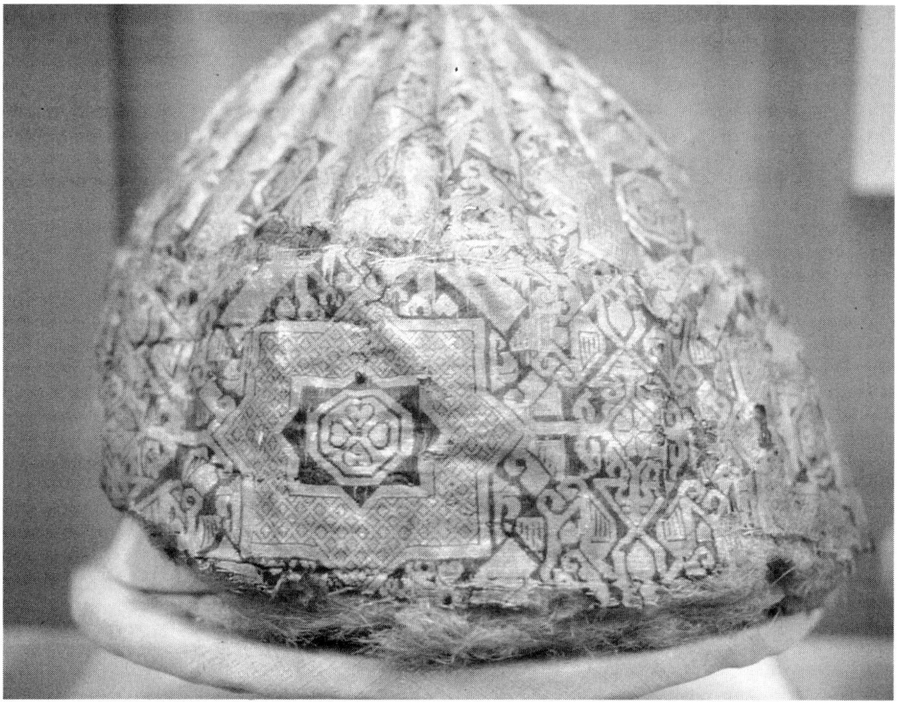

A quilted cap from Egypt, Mamlūk, late 14th–15th centuries. The basic shape and structure of this qalansūwa is the same as that seen on the small stucco statuettes of soldiers from the early Islamic palace at Khirbat al-Mafjir in Palestine, indicating a remarkable degree of continuity in costume. (Victoria and Albert Museum, London)

pierced their ears. Other sources agree that Hindu warriors bound up their long hair as a prelude to battle. Later sources mention the distinctive costumes and turbans worn by the army of the early 12th-century army of the Chālukya realm of Karnataka. Here officers wore patterned silk and the cavalry wore a yellow tunic; there were even references to green clothes and head cloths worn as a form of camouflage while hunting in the jungle.

THE MEDIEVAL ARMS INDUSTRY

Mining, Materials and Techniques

Iron resources and the fuel needed to smelt and forge iron were unevenly spread in the medieval world. The Sassanian Empire was not only rich in iron but controlled major trade routes, which made it rich in money. In contrast the Byzantine Empire was acutely short of iron resources, most of which were in frontier areas like Azarbayjan, Armenia and other parts of the Caucasus. By the 12th century Byzantine armies were seriously short of arms and armour, largely because the Empire now controlled no major mines. The Caliphate and its smaller successors faced different problems. Most of Islam's iron resources were again in frontier provinces, and the iron mines of the Middle East had largely been exhausted because this region had been civilised for so long. Consequently internal sources had to be supplemented by long-distance trade which, however, the Caliphate could usually afford because it was a rich urbanised civilisation with a money economy. But it was the lack of timber for fuel which posed the greatest problem. Despite these limitations, however, there was a considerable increase in the utilisation of available iron ore both within the Muslim world and those areas which traded with Islamic civilisation such as the Caucasus, Ural and Altai mountains, India, east Africa and parts of southern Europe. In other cases control of mines, even small ones, became a matter of immediate military concern such as the Spanish sierras during the *Reconquista,* in Lebanon and northern Jordan during the Crusades. But Egypt, for example, remained almost completely dependent on outside sources for metals and timber, which made the country vulnerable to European naval blockades or embargoes.

Most of the important iron-working areas which traded with the Muslim world also produced weaponry for more localised use. For example the Smolensk area made swords for the rest of Russia, and the Altai, Tien Shan and other Central Asian mountains probably made arms and armour for the Turks and Mongols as well as sending large volumes of iron ingots to the Muslim iron-working centres in Transoxiana and K͟hūrāsān. As a result Central Asian steppe society was largely self sufficient in weaponry as well as horses, all of which contributed to its military effectiveness. East Africa had imported weapons and tools from the Mediterranean at the time of the Roman Empire, but close technological and trading links with medieval Islamic civilisation turned East Africa into a major iron exporting region as well as one capable of making steel by the late Middle Ages.

Right: The Medieval Iron Trade.
Iron was mined and worked extensively, and traded over vast distances during the Middle Ages. Western Europe formed a vital part of this huge network, though it is unlikely that even the most well-informed Italian merchants knew quite how big the business was that they were involved in. Middle Eastern middle-men had a clearer idea, as shown in Muslim Arab geographical studies dating from the 10th to 14 centuries.
a main zones of metallurgical development
b major iron mines
c main trade routes for iron ore, iron objects and weaponry. (after Lombard)

Other materials were also required for military equipment. Leather, for example, was very important; being used to make shields, helmets, scale and lamellar armour, scabbards, straps and horse-harness. Wood was similarly needed for weapon shafts, bows, shields, saddle frames and, of course, ships. Here a warrior's requirements could be very specific, as when 7th-century Arab warriors considered that the best wood for spear shafts came from India, but that the weapons were best made or assembled on the southern shore of the Arabian Gulf. Some 13th-century crossbowmen preferred their weapons to be made of cornel or dogwood from the Trabzon area of northern Anatolia, and Ibn Hud͟hayl, writing in 14th-century Granada, went into extraordinary detail when listing the materials needed for a crossbow: five cultivated woods (bitter orange, the unknown *nismān,* apple, pomegranate and quince) and five wild (lime, wild olive, elm or ash, privet and cork oak). These also had to be taken from a particular side of the tree and cut at a particular season for the best quality. The purchasing of horn for making composite bows seems to have been equally specific; a surviving Arab agricultural calendar from 10th-century Cordoba stating that June was the month when government officials purchased goat and wild cattle horn for this purpose. Three hundred years later an Armenian armourer of one of the Crusader Kings of Jerusalem would cross the frontier into Muslim Damascus to buy horn and glue for crossbows.

Most advances in medieval metallurgy took place in China or India and then spread westward, first to the Islamic world and then to Europe. Cast iron had been known in China since the 2nd century BC, then reaching India and the Middle East but not being widely used in Europe until the 15th century. In the 5th century steel was being made in China by heating cast and wrought iron together, and by the 11th and 12th centuries this method was considered almost as good as decarbonised steel. It was passed to the Arabs in the 11th century, though again did not reach western Europe for another five hundred years. Chinese metallurgical influence also spread in other directions, Chinese and Korean sword-smiths probably settling in Japan in the 3rd century. A spread of Chinese technology might also have stimulated the development in India of machines which could blow air into shaft-furnaces; this in turn leading to a considerable advance in the manufacture of cast iron which in turn led to India's superiority in various

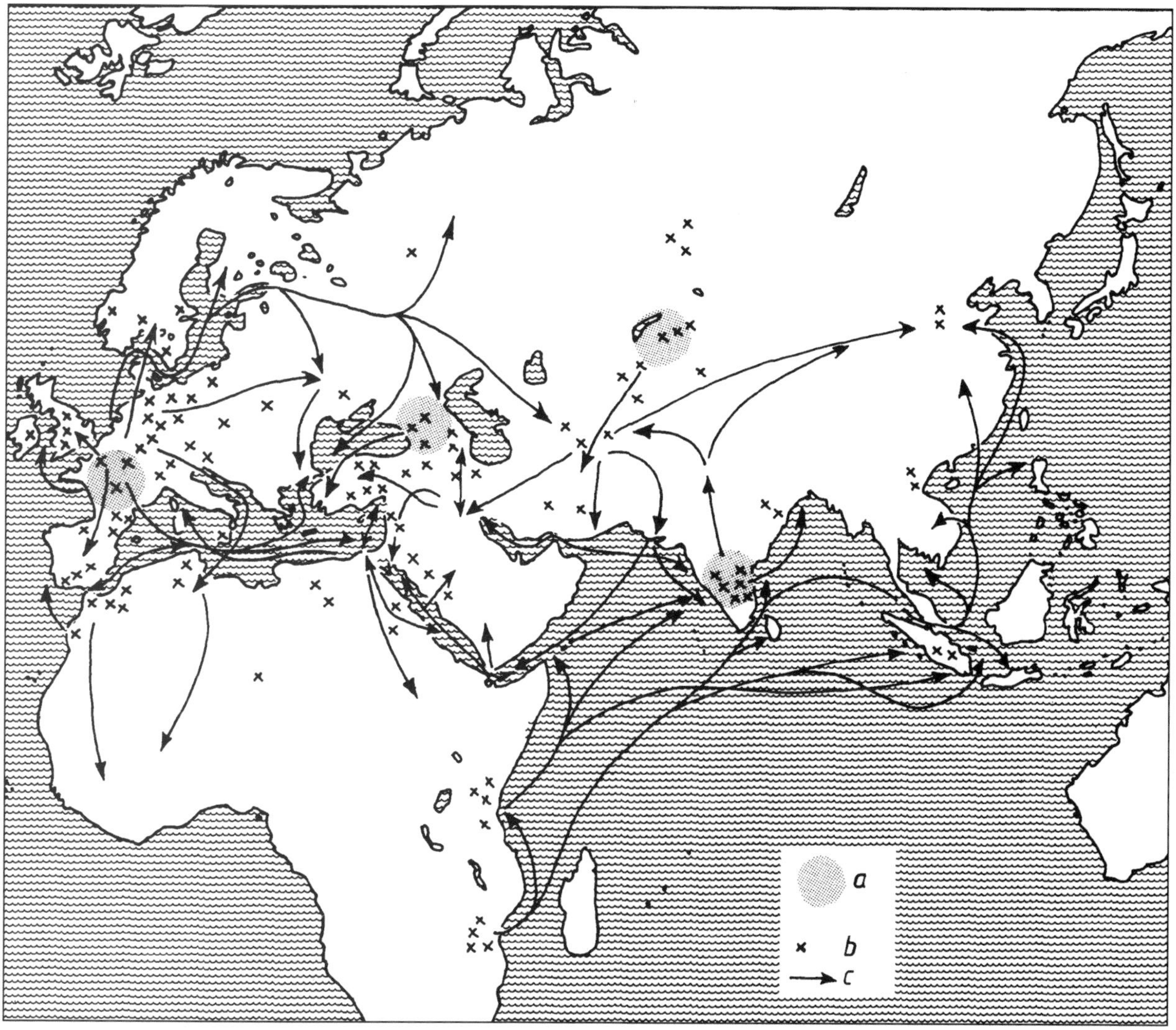

aspects of early medieval metallurgy. During the first centuries AD smiths in the southern Deccan may have been the first to cast molten steel blades. In subsequent centuries ingots of Indian steel were exported as far as Damascus and Toledo for shaping into sword-blades. Much of the ore for this Indian industry came from East Africa in Muslim Arab merchant ships, leading to a pattern of long-distance trade which had no real parallel until early modern times. The technological link between East Africa and Malaysia and Indonesia was also associated with the colonisation of Madagascar by peoples from the East Indies during this period. As a consequence of this and other technological influence from North Africa and the Middle East, there was a notable increase in iron-working throughout much of sub-Saharan Africa from the 10th century onwards.

Where Islamic civilisation itself was concerned, the highly practical Muslim attitude towards knowledge encouraged the absorption of new technologies, a rational classification of all sorts of information and a desire for military or other artefacts from distant civilisations. On the other hand the bulk of military equipment was probably made in an almost 'production-line' technique hinted at when al-Jāḥiẓ of Basra's contrasted this with the Turk's ability to make all his own equipment. Among Muslim armourers, he claimed, it took at least nine different craftsmen to make a sword, scabbard and belt. Whether the relatively sudden appearance of iron helmets wrought from a single piece of metal in early Muslim armies was an internal development, or reflected technological contact with China, remains unclear. Of all the metallurgical techniques associated with the medieval Middle East, none is more distinctive than that known as *damascening.* The earliest written reference to a *damascene* blade dates from about 540, though the technique may have been known earlier. True *damascene* and its associated surface patterning resulted from the elongation of a 'cake' or ingot of high-carbon steel. The process also enabled the smith to place the hardest metal on the outside and especially along the cutting edge while softer material in the core of a *damascene* blade provided flexibility.

The density of the surface pattern, known as *firind* in Arabic and '*watering*' in Europe, was also an indication of quality and the resulting blade could be bent but was almost unbreakable. Meanwhile other techniques were also being used in the Muslim world and by its neighbours. Al-Kindī and al-Bīrūnī agree that early medieval Byzantine, Russian and other Slav smiths used 'soft iron' whereas western Europeans made a mixture of 'hard' and 'soft' iron – in other words piling or pattern-welding – when making sword-blades; the Middle East importing blades from these areas as well as from India.

Techniques of leather-working were less sophisticated and very varied. The famous *lamṭ* shields of the Sahara and North Africa were made of several layers of hide glued together. A highly detailed late 12th-century manuscript from Egypt not only states that a *jawshan* (cuirass) could be made of horn or hardened leather as well as iron, but provides a recipe for making segments of armour or helmets. This involved rawhide clippings soaked in water then ground up fine, mixed with other substances including metal filings, then shaped in moulds to dry. Another simpler method used camel's hide soaked in milk and cut into shapes which were decorated when dry.

Arms Manufacture

The arms manufacturing business and associated trade patterns were advanced and complex in the medieval Mediterranean, Asia and parts of Africa. Indian and Yemeni swords were highly regarded in pre-Islamic Arabia, others were distributed via southern Jordan. In contrast Medina, or Yathrib as it was then called, was noted for making arrows whereas the only armourer mentioned in Mecca was an arrow-sharpener.

Where military technology was concerned, the early medieval Byzantines, like their Muslim-Arab rivals, were very keen to copy and to learn. During the first centuries, provincial craftsmen had needed government permission to make weaponry, but control over armourers and arms merchants was relaxed during the 6th to 8th centuries because of the Empire's acute shortage of military equipment. There may even have been a conscious move towards the 'privatisation' of manufacture and distribution. Nevertheless, despite its lack of iron resources, the early Byzantine Empire still had Imperial *armamenton* (arms factories) descended from the late Roman *fabricae*, mostly concentrated in the capital. The evidence of one major mid-10th century expedition indicates that the chief official of the Imperial *armamenton* passed orders for the making of the required equipment to the *katepan* of the *arma*, and various other items were ordered from the provinces. The Imperial *vestiarion* similarly made fire-weapons for the army and navy, as well as siege engines. By the 11th century many Byzantine towns had their own salaried armourers, a system which continued into the 13th century. During the 12th century there had been references to an armour-making *zabareion* in Byzantium's second city of Thessaloniki, and others may have existed elsewhere. By the 14th century bows and other simple weapons were also made locally in what remained of the Byzantine Empire's Balkan provinces.

Most information about arms manufacture in medieval Russia comes from outside observers. The Antes of the south had been notable armourers during the Roman era; the 9th–10th-century Polianians of the Kiev area maintaining this tradition while specialised metal-working quarters appeared in Kiev in the 12th century and in Novgorod in the 13th century. In contrast many parts of the Christian Iberian peninsula developed into major arms manufacturing and exporting centres, but whereas Catalonia became one of western Europe's main arms centres in the 14th century, Portugal's suddenly acquired small-scale industry, of the same date, was mostly in the hands of smiths of Jewish or Muslim origin in the south of the country. The Crusader States were more dependent on outside supplies for their military equipment than any other parts of Christendom. A tiny metal-working industry in Beirut relied on iron-ore from Mount Lebanon, but does not seem to have made weaponry, and the difficulty of supplying Latin Greece led to the establishment of an armoury in Clarence Castle in 1281.

There may have been a sudden influx of military equipment into Arabia in the immediate pre-Islamic period, possibly as a result of efforts by the Byzantine and Sassanian Empires to win support during their final war. Nevertheless the first Muslim-Arab armies remained less well equipped than these neighbouring empires. Booty and tribute were a vital way of increasing weapons stocks, as when the Prophet demanded thirty armours a year from Najrān in northern Yemen. These in turn are likely to have been of hardened leather, since this area was famous for leather production. The continuing importance of Arabia and Yemen is reflected in the fact that it was still listed, together with Iran, the Caucasus, Afghanistan and the western steppes, as a source of weapons and military raw materials for 9th-century Iraq. Meanwhile early Muslim historians credited the early 8th-century Umayyad Caliph Hishām with 'perfecting the production of weapons and armour in the Islamic state'. Information for the intervening centuries is less specific, but a late 13th-century Mamlūk military manual stated that properly trained troops were responsible for running repairs to their own kit. A similarly dated Egyptian chronicle also pointed out that the cost of raw materials, military equipment and the wages of skilled craftsmen such as sword-smiths, armourers and polishers all shot up when a major campaign was imminent. Much the same could be seen in all parts of the medieval Muslim world, though some regions also became famous for one or more specific pieces of equipment or harness. Khwārazm, for example, was renowned for both cavalry armour and horse-armour in the 8th to 10th centuries. Other eastern provinces produced armour and harness, though the most important was the mountainous Ghūr province of Afghanistan; Shāsh in Transoxiana was noted for archery equipment. Daghestan in the Caucasus had been famous as an arms manufacturing centre since the late Sassanian era and remained so in the 13th and 14th centuries; the earliest unambiguous references to *mail-and-plate* armours stemming from this region during the early 15th century. In the 10th century the frontier town of Tarsus had resident armourers and workshops, and nearby Antioch similarly made arms and horse-harness for campaigns against the Byzantines. Of course military equipment had been made in Syria since ancient times, but Damascus, having long been a major arms distribution centre, appears to have become a manufacturing centre by the 10th century. On the far side of the desert Baghdad had a similar quarter called the Archway of the Armourers in the 11th-12th century. A 10th-century Arabic geographer shed further light on the little-known arms industry of Arabia by stating that Byzantine armours were generally lighter than those made in Iraq, the southern coast of the Arabian Gulf and Oman; each of which still produced a large number of *dirᶜ* (hauberks) each year to send with a comparable supply of swords to Baghdad as tribute. By the 11th century there were even references to western European armourers working in Cairo. Farther west, Tunisia exported leather cuirasses, probably of lamellar construction, in the late 14th century, and armourers were congregated around the main mosque in what was known as the New Quarter of 10th-century Palermo. The arms of Muslim Iberia, above all its swords, were much more famous; Toledo, Almeria, Murcia, Cordoba and Seville all being major manufacturing centres at various times.

In Central Asia some tribes had a higher reputation as armourers than others. The Uighurs were rich in iron and were said to have many smiths, and the Qipchaqs were also noted metalworkers. Among non-Turkish peoples the Tibetans were more noted for leather than for iron in the 7th and 8th centuries; exporting leather shields as far as the Mediterranean. China of course had some of the finest craftsmen in the world; this being recognised throughout Asia and beyond. But the Chinese arms industry was largely under government control. During the T'ang dynasty it was divided into sections producing specific items: the *Crossbow Office* making spears, lances, bows, arrows, shields and crossbows; the *Armour Office*, armour and helmets. Major metal-working factories were sited well away from the frontier, in an attempt to stop advanced Chinese technology spreading to potential enemies. T'ang armourers were divided into grades like military ranks; four years' study being needed before an individual became a 'fine armourer', two for a smith, one for an arrow-maker. All products were marked with their date and place of manufacture. A bowyer normally learned his craft from childhood. The making of a composite bow was a long, complex and highly skilled job. The bow itself needed at least a year to make, and the setting or maturation of the glue could take from three to ten years depending on quality and condition. The Nepalese were accorded high status as sword-smiths in Mongol literature, and a 13th-century Chinese source mentions copper armour being used in Borneo. Armour of brass was still being used by the people of the southern Philippines in the 16th century.

The Arms Trade

The medieval arms trade formed one part of a trading network which brought together most of Europe and Asia as well as much of Africa. Where Asia was concerned there were two primary networks. The Silk Road or Roads across Central Asia linked China and the Middle East, and assorted maritime routes criss-crossed the Indian Ocean to connect the Middle East, East Africa, India, south-east Asia and, by extension, China. From the 7th century onwards most of the ships were Arab, but Persian vessels had been involved as had Indian, and the Chinese sometimes reached as far as Yemen. Iron ore, or more probably ingots, were shipped in very large quantities to India from the African coast and from Sumatra and Java, and completed weapons blades may have been brought from these areas directly to Arab countries.

Within individual countries such trade patterns differed considerably. In pre-Islamic Arabia swords imported from Syria, Yemen and those of Indian iron or steel exchanged hands at various annual fairs, that at ᶜUkāz being particularly important for the distribution of captured weapons. Tribes that formed part of the Byzantine Empire's *phylarch* or frontier defence system received weaponry directly from the Byzantines.

Most Byzantine soldiers received their arms and armour from the state. In the case of 8th- to 10th-century *tagmata* troops these came from government stores, though some external recruits from 'warlike peoples' brought their own weaponry with them. This seems to have been distributed to the men at the start of a campaign rather than remaining in their possession – a system still recorded in 12th-century Byzantine armies. Otherwise the weaponry of provincial troops formed part of their 'estate', to be passed from generation to generation. As far as the Byzantine army as a whole was concerned, the bulk of its kit came from Byzantine armourers, but there was a steady flow of material from outside, either as official government imports, booty, tribute, or diplomatic gifts. A large volume of southern Italian weaponry was captured from the invading Angevins in Albania in the late 13th century, but by then the Byzantine Empire's shrinking resources meant that the government offered tax exemptions and other inducements to encourage the peaceful import of western European military equipment via places like Dubrovnik and Durrës on the west Balkan coast. Mid-13th-century Nicea seems to have relied primarily on Genoa for both weaponry and horses, and during the 14th century Constantinople purchased iron and completed weaponry from Dubrovnik, Genoa and Venice.

Early medieval Russians, or perhaps the Scandinavian military élite of 'Rus', sold war-axes, knives and long-bladed 'Frankish' western European swords in the lands of the Volga Bulgars in the 10th century. Thereafter a great deal of Russia's own military equipment came from Scandinavia or western Europe. The 12th- or 13th-century Epic of Prince Igor often mentions western arms and armour but also speaks of Avar equipment, by which it might have meant Hungarian or Turkish. There was a substantial trade in arms and harness from north-central Europe through southern Poland and Moldavia to the Black Sea ports in the 15th century and this may have existed earlier. Weapons also wandered far afield among the Finno-Ugrian forest peoples to the east of medieval Russia; a remarkable decorated 12th–13th-century Armenian sabre being found in the sub-Arctic region north of the Ural mountains.

Left: *A late Sassanian or possibly early Islamic iron and bronze helmet of the 'Parthian Cap' type of construction, from Nineveh in northern Iraq, 6th–7th centuries. (British Museum, no. 22497, London)*

The movement of military equipment within Christian Iberia was essentially the same as that in other parts of western Europe. Sometimes it was in the form of tribute, as when Catalonia sent armour and swords to Córdoba in the 10th century, or formed part of the system of feudal obligation. In 12th-century León, for example, the holders of some non-noble and 'semi-hereditary' benefices could inherit their father's arms if he had died in the service of his king, but otherwise had to return them. Perhaps because of their near total dependence on weaponry imported from Europe, the rulers of the Middle Eastern Crusader States were often forced to hand over such equipment to their Muslim enemies as part of a peace agreement. This clearly happened in the mid-12th century when the Count of Edessa bought off a threatened Turkish attack by offering tribute and a number of horse-armours. Booty was also an importance source of supply, despite differences between the military equipment and tactics used in the Crusader States and most of their neighbours. Some historians have estimated that the loot from Constantinople following the Fourth Crusade included no less than 10,000 armours as well as other matériel – though this may be an exaggeration. Otherwise western European Crusaders sometimes left some arms and armour to the Military Orders in their wills, this then being shipped to the Crusader States. The Rule of the Hospitallers even specified that brother knights travelling east must bring a supply of arms with them, and that the lending of weaponry to other people was strictly forbidden. The Angevin rulers of southern Italy similarly sent large quantities of money, food and perhaps weaponry to the Crusader States of Greece in the 1270s to 1290s.

Since virtually every corner of the medieval Muslim world was incorporated into the most sophisticated trading network seen in the Middle Ages, weaponry from distant lands often changed hands in most Muslim armies. This was particularly true of sword-blades. Money and weapons were also given to freed prisoners as a gesture of reconciliation, and booty could flow back to the side which originally lost it. For example a famous inscribed sword dating from the time of the Prophet was retaken from the Byzantines following the Muslim conquest of Sicily two hundred years later. Sometimes the sheer volume of such booty could lead to a sharp, if temporary, drop in prices in the arms bazaars, as happened after the Saljūq Turkish defeat of the Byzantine Emperor at Manzikert in 1071. In earlier centuries the first Muslim-Arab armies overcame their initial shortages of matériel with such booty; to such an extent that there were cases when captured arms and armour were not distributed to the men but kept intact so that a new army could be equipped at a later date. Other evidence states that while it was normal for most 7th–9th-century Muslim sol-

Right: *A late Sassanian or probably early Islamic iron helmet of the spangenhelm type from Nineveh in northern Iraq, 6th–7th centuries. This was a more advanced style of the Parthian cap and was of ultimately Central Asian derivation. Both forms almost certainly existed alongside each other for several centuries. (British Museum, no. 22495, London)*

diers to equip themselves, poorer troops received help from richer men or from their ruler, in which case they were considered to be under an obligation to remain with the army until the end of a campaign.

Even after the Caliphate fragmented in the 10th century, these patterns of trade and tribute persisted. Trade between Khwārazm and the Slavs covered armour as well as weapons, probably even including mail *hauberks* made in the Rhineland and then sold on to Sāmānid armies. Russian merchants were said to be selling European swords in Baghdad in the 10th and 11th centuries. The Volga Bulgars also grew rich from transit trade between eastern Europe and the Muslim world. Diplomatic exchanges of gifts similarly played an important role, though not in terms of volume. Sometimes these gifts resulted from ambitious diplomatic manoeuvring. For example a European queen sent an embassy to Caliph al-Muktafī at the beginning of the 10th century, bringing gifts of spears, swords and shields. Perhaps more significantly Ṣalāh al-Dīn and the Byzantine Emperor exchanged large shipments of weaponry in mutual congratulation for defeating the Crusaders in Palestine and invading Italo-Normans in the Balkans. Medieval Muslim governments took a primary role in this arms trade, particularly when it involved imports from Europe. Most came from Italy, some of the earliest references specifying Venice in the 10th century. In 1173, at the height of the Crusader occupation of the Holy Land, Pisa reached an agreement with Ṣalāh al-Dīn to supply strategic raw materials for his army and navy despite a supposed Papal ban. The Popes tried even harder to ban this trade following the fall of the last Crusader outposts to the Mamlūks. Trade and the shipment of strategic goods within Muslim territory sometimes already formed the target of specific campaigns, as when a Byzantine fleet attacked Dumyat in the mid-9th century and succeeded in destroying stockpiles of arms ready to be sent from Egypt to the Muslim outpost in Crete.

The distribution of weaponry within Muslim armies was very similar to that seen in the Byzantine Empire; professional soldiers getting their arms and armour from government arsenals at the start of a campaign. They would then have the cost of such equipment deducted from their pay if it were lost – unless the soldier in question had a good excuse such as being wounded or defeated in battle. Ṣalāh al-Dīn's full-time troops clearly collected their kit from the *zardkhāna* (arsenal), along with their pay, at the start of such campaigns, and even in politically chaotic areas such as 12th-century Yemen rulers tried to have all weapons other than what might be called 'side-arms' kept in a communal arsenal under government control. Meanwhile the Muslims, like their Crusader foes, re-used captured military equipment that suited their style of warfare.

A similar situation developed in North Africa and al-Andalus. By the 9th century North Africa was importing swords from western Europe, and Genoa was probably still selling military equipment through the Moroccan port of Sabta in the 12th century. Within the Sahara 12th–13th-century nomads purchased virtually all their weaponry from settled neighbours, including their famous *lamṭ* shields, and in the 14th century the new Muslim rulers of Mali south of the desert imposed a state monopoly on trade in iron, weapons and horses because of their military importance. North Africa had imported arms, armour and harness from Andalusia since at least the 10th century, while at the same time Muslim al-Andalus itself imported harness from Iraq, armour and bows from Khurāsān or via this area from Transoxiana, leather helmets and other weapons from India and even farther east, while exporting its own sword-blades to eastern Islam and India.

References to Tibetan leather shields and leather lamellar cuirasses being used in the 8th-century Middle East may be based on reality, given the trading activities of this period. But Central Asia itself was generally an exporter of raw materials rather then finished equipment, and even here it could face problems. The Mongols would send officers to buy up all the available arms and armour in recently conquered territories before setting off on new conquests, and when they took over a rich industrialised area such as Iran, they established their own arsenals rather than rely on equipment sent from the far poorer heartlands of Mongolia. On the other hand eastern Central Asia's relative poverty in military equipment should not be exaggerated. In the 4th century the Chinese captured sufficient quantities from their Turkish neighbours to warrant having it repaired and overhauled for their own use. Throughout the Middle Ages it remained normal for the Chinese authorities to keep weaponry safely under the immediate control of its own *Armour Board*. Thereafter China's highly efficient distribution network enabled supplies to be sent to even the most distant frontier as and when required. Archaeologists have, in fact, found boxes of crossbow bolts, neatly wrapped and ready for return to store because they appear to have been unsatisfactory for one reason or another. At the same time the Chinese made great efforts to avoid weaponry leaving their control and falling into the hands of warlike neighbours.

FIREARMS: ORIGINS AND DEVELOPMENT

Fire Weapons

Fire-weapons had been used in Asia and the Middle East since ancient times and had, of course, also been known in the Romans. These refined into the *Greek Fire* of the Byzantines and the *nafṭ* of the Arab-Muslim world. Whether the sophisticated fire-weapons used in medieval India were an indigenous development or were influenced by *nafṭ* which Arab-Muslim invaders first used on Indian territory in 711 is unknown. One reason why *Greek Fire* and its Islamic derivative were so effective was the existence of bitumen and crude mineral oil in the Middle East; this also enabling the chemists of these civilisations to refine and improve the basic weapon. Furthermore distillation techniques reached a high level of efficiency in precisely these regions, not only because this helped in the manufacture of more effective *nafṭ*, but because it was central to the growing trade in perfumes and other distilled substances. This technology produced a terrifying petroleum-based weapon to which sulphur was soon added, making the substance even more combustible, eventually evolving into the '*white nafṭ*' which the ruler of Mosul sent to Ṣalāh al-Dīn during his struggle against the Crusaders. Al-Tarsusi, writing for Ṣalāh al-Dīn in the late 12th century, stated that *nafṭ* could be thrown on land or at sea, could be put inside blown egg-shells as a form of grenade and could even be used from horseback to terrify enemy cavalry. Perhaps the most dramatic way of using such a weapon was to propel it in a burning stream from a siphon or syringe. In Byzantium these were clearly made of copper and a reference from Mesopotamia in 927/8 states that such a siphon could engulf twelve men. A generation or so later an Iraq judge named al-Tanūkhī specified that the *zarrāqat al-nafṭ* had a handle that was pushed or pulled to expel the liquid fire. The fact that use of *nafṭ* had declined in land warfare by the late 13th century can be attributed to its success, particularly in sieges where suitable wooden targets had been virtually driven from the scene. At sea, however, *Greek Fire* and *nafṭ* certainly remained effective.

Gunpowder

Arguments about who invented gunpowder have now virtually ceased; it was first known in China during the early 11th century; the first recorded Chinese recipe being in a military manual dating from 1044. Saltpetre, the vital ingredient which made the invention of gunpowder possible, was probably discovered in China rather than the Muslim world as sometimes thought. It may be mentioned as an additional element for *nafṭ* in an Arabic book on warfare written in the late 12th century, was clearly described by an Andalusian long resident in Egypt in the early 13th century, and was generally known in Arabic as 'Chinese snow' or 'Chinese salt'. Early explosive or semi-explosive fire arrows carrying cartridges of *nafṭ* or a primitive form of gunpowder were called *sihām khiṭā'iyya* 'Chinese arrows', and saltpetre itself seems to have been known as *barūd* in 13th-century North Africa, a word which would soon mean gunpowder itself.

The situation was clearer in China where early forms of gunpowder were placed in bamboo canes to be thrown by hand. There were also larger containers thrown by *mangonels*. Furthermore these early explosive weapons could contain fragments of pottery or metal. The early 12th century also saw Chinese references to smoke and fire mixtures which burned on the surface of water. In about 1132 a new weapon called a *p'ao ch'e* consisted of a large length of bamboo filled with an explosive substance and carried by two men. This might have been a very early gun or perhaps something comparable to a Bangalore Torpedo for use against field fortifications since it could throw stone fragments two hundred paces. A gunpowder-filled flame-thrower with a range of more than three metres is described in a Chinese source of 1213, but the gunpowder weapons used by the late 13th-century Mongols seem to have been large or small grenades or bombs.

Despite China's undeniable claim to the invention of gunpowder, there is still debate about who first used it to expel a missile from a tube – in other words first fired a gun. The *sabṭāna* (blowpipe) had been used for hunting in the Muslim Middle East since at least the 10th century, and a blowpipe was used to propel a small quantity of *Greek Fire* in Byzantium in 1107/8. There is inconclusive evidence that primitive gunpowder might have been used to propel pellets or bullets from a similar device in the Muslim Middle East in the 12th century. This idea might have been taken back to China by the Mongols in the mid-13th century; the Mongol Īl-Khān ruler Hülegü establishing a chemical laboratory in his Persian capital, staffed with both Chinese and Persian scholars. Things become marginally clearer in the military writings of the Mamlūk *furūsīyah* expert Ḥasan al-Rammah in about 1270. He is very clear as to how to purify saltpetre for an explosive 'black powder' mixture which modern experiments have shown to be effective, but which he still calls *nafṭ*. It could also be used in a *midfa*ᶜ, a term used for an early form of gun a gen-

Military training manual; Mamlūk, late 15th–early 16th-century copy of a mid-14th-century original. This page deals with pyrotechnics and gunpowder. The men with fireworks attached to their fireproofed clothing at the top of the picture would take part in military displays or tattoos. The two men at the bottom of the page have large arrows with incendiary devices attached to be shot from siege engines. One of them also has a primitive hand-cannon of a type also seen in 14th-century Europe. (Keir Collection, London)

eration or so later, but, unlike al-Tarsusi's military manuscript written for Ṣalāh al-Dīn, Ḥasan al-Rammah's works only survive in later copies. Clearly *nafṭ* no longer meant *Greek Fire*, and the sudden revival in the use of this term after a lapse of many years was in entirely new circumstances. Meanwhile the explosive grenades known earlier were now almost invariably known as *qawārīr*, a sexual image possibly indicating that the grenade looked like the top of a gourd, or *qudūr* meaning a narrow-necked bottle.

Grenades and Rockets

Grenades were known before guns, a new weapon known as a *huo-chien* being mentioned in China at the beginning of the 11th century. Mid-11th-century references confirm that this was a grenade. The earliest forms of *p'i-li huo-ch'iu* seem to have been lengths of bamboo filled with explosives and assorted fragments. They were also used against river ships though in the latter case the weapon was described as bursting into a fog which affected the eyes. Another 12th-century device used by both the Sung and the Jurchen was called a *p'ao ch'e* which could throw stone fragments two hundred paces. Counterweight *trebuchets*, known to the Chinese as 'Muslim-style mangonels', were particularly useful for throwing these devices, presumably because of their greater power. In 1221 there was a clear reference to such a shell or bomb having an iron shell with a small fuse hole. Meanwhile the numerous heavy ceramic objects found in 13th- and 14th-century Muslim contexts from Turkestan and the Arabian Gulf to Egypt were almost certainly expended grenades. The discovery of virtually identical grenades in Burma is, however, unexplained.

Rockets have been popularly associated with Chinese warfare for a long time, but in fact they did not become a common weapon until the late 14th century. They were then mounted on wheeled launchers and were fired in a spread fashion like oversized arrows. In stark contrast the rockets describe by Ḥasan al-Rammah in late 13th-century Mamlūk Egypt seem to have included explosive warheads. They included a form of torpedo which skimmed across the surface of the water enclosed in a metal container and guided by two sticks.

Cannon

A Chinese reference in 1259 to something made of bamboo which could hurl one or more pellets may be the earliest reference to a gun; it was probably developed from a previous gunpowder-filled flame-thrower. A reference to a metal version of this Chinese device in 1271 is less clear and seems to be confused with the *hui-hui p'ao*, an advanced counterweight trebuchet introduced to China from the Middle East. Other evidence indicates that the Chinese did not use metallic gun-barrels any earlier than did Europe, though such weapons were common in Ming China from the mid-14th century. The earliest surviving Chinese cannon are, in fact, dated 1372 and 1379, one of iron and the other of bronze, by which time comparable firearms were in use in Europe and the Middle East. In the 1370s firearms spread from China to Korea, the Korean government establishing a '*Bureau of Armaments*' responsible for making cannon, other firearms and ships to deal with Japanese piracy. The first such Korean cannon could also fire stubby wooden arrows with fins and iron points, identical with the earliest cannon-projectiles illustrated in 14th-century western European art. The oldest realistic references to Indian explosives date from the mid-13th century, but these are particularly difficult to interpret and could indicate an explosive mine, a simple mortar or a grenade. By the end of the 13th century, however, some kind of stone projectiles were being shot by gunpowder against the walls of fortresses, and these sound remarkably similar to a weapon used in Morocco a decade or so earlier. The first references to the possible use of mortars or primitive cannon in Morocco are so early and so unclear that they are generally dismissed. Yet some kind of explosive device which expelled iron fragments or 'grape-shot' was almost certainly being used by the Marīnids against the fortified oasis town of Sijilmasa in 1274. Granada's use of a cannon shooting a red-hot iron projectile during its army's siege of Huesca in 1324 is much less controversial. The cannon which defended Algeciras against Christian forces in 1343 shot iron balls and large darts or arrows. The Crusaders who attacked Mahdia in Tunisia in 1390 also used cannon, which the defenders lacked, but the gunpowder used in cannon defending Būna in Algeria nine years later was smuggled from Spain. Perhaps surprisingly, given the fact that Aragon clearly had iron and bronze guns in the 14th century, neighbouring Castile may not have acquired these until the following century.

The adoption of firearms in the Middle East was influenced by military and cultural prejudices. For example the very conservative Mamlūks of Egypt and Syria had been among the first states in the world to use gunpowder but thereafter proved reluctant to adopt guns. Their first probable reference to cannon was during the siege of Karak in 1342 where two possible types of gun, the *mukḥula al-nafṭ* and the *midfaᶜ al-nafṭ*, are mentioned. It is possible, however, that the *mukḥula* was a flame-thrower. Between 1366 and 1368 cannon were clearly used to defend Alexandria against Crusader pirates. The Ottomans were even slower to adopt firearms, though they or their Christian vassals may have had them at the battle of Kosovo in 1389. The first clear reference to the use of cannon in Russia was in defence of Moscow against the Tatars in 1382. Although it was called a *tyuphak*, from the Turco-Persian word for a small hand-held gun, the weapon itself seems to have been a larger bombard brought from western Europe.

Handguns

References to the use of hand-held guns are even less clear than references to cannon and appear considerably later – as they did in Europe. A mid-14th-century Turkish Anatolian epic poem states that the Byzantine enemy used *tüfenk* hand-held guns, though this may have been a later insertion into the text. Meanwhile a 'hand-cannon' mounted on a wooden pole, comparable to heavier forms of hand-gun used in 14th-century western Europe, is illustrated in some 15th-century copies of Mamlūk military manuals written in the first half of the 14th century, being specifically identified as a *midfaᶜ*.

IX
GLOSSARY

Where possible terms included in the Glossary to Volume I have not been included here. Also note that the Arabic letter ᶜ (Ayn) has been inserted after the letter 'C' in this Glossary.

a la brida: Iberian heavy cavalry riding and combat style.
a la jineta: Iberian light cavalry riding and combat style.
abaan: Somali troops or guards.
abatis: smooth facing on the near-side of a defensive ditch.
abnā': garrisons of Persian origin in pre-Islamic Yemen; infantry of Arab-Khurāsāni origin in 9th–10th- century Baghdad (Arabic, lit. 'sons').
abṭāl: defensive cavalry units, Arabic.
adalid: commander of militia cavalry in Christian Iberia.
adalide: professional guide, Spanish.
adarga de lante: large leather shield, based on Berber *lamṭ*, Christian Iberia.
admiral: commander of ships in Military Orders.
adnoumia: Byzantine muster or review.
adoha: tax paid in lieu of feudal military service, Crusader States.
adrumūnun: fighting galley, Arabic.
aghlumi: Georgian élite cavalry, perhaps of slave origin (see also *ghūlām*).
aḥābīsh: mercenaries of Ethiopian origin in 6th-century Yemen; or confederacy of small clans in Arabia.
ahdath: urban militia, Arabic.
aḥi: Muslim fraternity also employed as a militia.
ahl al-khūrāsān: élite forces of first ᶜAbbāsid army.
ahl al-shām: élite Syrian troops of the Umayyad Caliphate.
ahmudan: aristocratic guard troops of Burma.
ajnād: provincial troops, Arabic (see also *jund*).
akatia: possibly a transport galley, Arabic.
akinji: Ottoman light cavalry 'raiders'.
akoluthos: commander of late Byzantine Varangian Guard.
akrites: Byzantine frontier warriors.
al: decorative horse blanket, Turkish.
alami: large flag, Georgian.
alay: regiment of Ottoman provincial cavalry.
alay bey: commander of an Ottoman cavalry regiment.
albarrana: external tower linked to main wall by a bridge (Arabic *barrānī*, 'exterior'), Christian Iberia.
alcalde: administrative leader of an urban militia, Christian Iberia.
alfaquequas: officials who sought out and arranged the ransoming of captives, Christian Iberia.
alférez môr: army commander, Portugal.
algara, algarada: small raid or raiding force, Christian Iberia.
algarrada: stone-throwing ballista, Christian Iberia (from Arabic *al-ᶜarrādah*).
alguazil: deputy quartermaster of Spanish galley.
allagion: late Byzantine regiment.
alla sensile: arrangement of galley oars in 'simple fashion', evenly spaced.
almenara: small isolated fortification in Christian Iberia.
almocadén: commander of militia infantry in Christian Iberia.
almofar: mail coif, Spanish.
almogaver: lightly equipped troops recruited from autonomous non-feudal mountain pastoral communities, Christian Iberia (from Arabic *al-mughāwir*, 'raiders').
amān: safe conduct, Arabic.
amaram: income of regular soldiers in Hindu Vijayanaga.
ambāragh: Sassanian barracks.
amir: Islamic officer or frontier governor.
amṣār: early Islamic military cantonments and garrison.
amīr: senior officer, Arabic.
amīr al-juyūsh: commander-in-chief, senior general, Arabic.
amīr al-umarā': commander-in-chief of ᶜAbbāsid army, 'leader of leaders'.
anbār: Sassanian fortified barracks.
apatih: senior minister in Hindu Indonesia.
apellido: defensive operations in Christian Iberia, or *levée en masse.*
archontes: late Byzantine provincial élite.
archontes foideraton: early Byzantine senior officer.
ari: pagan priest of pre-Buddhist Burma.
ariwurikᶜ: Armenian troops of heretical or Manichaean sect, Arabic.
armamenton: Byzantine imperial arms factory.
arrière ban: general levy, Crusader States and Western Europe.
arsenal: shipyard, Crusader States.
artīshtārānsālār: late Sassanian 'chief of the soldiers', perhaps an administrative rank or war-chief.
asāwira: Persian cavalry recruited in early Islamic armies (see also asvārān).
ashrāf: tribal aristocracy in pre-Islamic Yemen.
asis: broad-sword, India.
asvārān: élite Sassanian cavalry.
asvārān-sardār: late Sassanian commander of cavalry.
atābak al-ᶜasākir: 'father-leader of soldiers', senior officer in later Mamlūk Sultanate.
atābak amīr kabīr: commander of the army in Syria in the Mamlūk state.
atābeg: regent or local governor, lit. 'father-leader'; later an autonomous or independent ruler (Arabo-Turkish).
atalaya: small isolated fortification in Christian Iberia.
atbāiᶜ: military followers of a ruler in pre-Islamic Transoxiana.
athanatoi: 'Immortals', Byzantine guard unit of Emperor John Tzimiskes.
atlab al-mīra: supply train in Ayylūbid army.
auscona, azcona: Navarrese infantry javelin.
avak baron: 'chief baron', commander of Cilician Armenian provincial forces.
awlād al-nās: freeborn sons of slave-origin *mamlūk* soldiers.
aymak: Tīmūrid officer corps.
āzādayān: short-term volunteers, Arabic.
azaga: section of Castilian army which built and defended an encampment.
azaria: small raid, Christian Iberia.
azat, azatani: Armenian minor aristocracy and élite cavalry.
āzātān: Sassanian minor aristocracy.
azatk': Armenian military forces.

bāb: term for a single cavalry training exercise, lit. 'a gate', Arabic.
baba: isolated statue found in the western steppes, Turkish.
badū: Arab nomads of the deep desert.
bahādur: Tīmūrid honorific military title.
bailli: governor or representative sent to Crusader State by outside ruler;

military governor of Crusader Greece under Angevins.
baillie: commander of a castle and garrison, Crusader States.
baktashi: Muslim dervish sect.
bakufu: headquarters of the regent in later medieval Japan.
baliq: fortified town, Turkish Central Asia.
bandon: flag hung horizontally, Romano-Byzantine; Byzantine company, usually cavalry.
banj: soporific henbane, Arabic.
banneret: member of the minor aristocracy, western Europe and Crusader States.
bargustuwān: horse-armour, Persian.
barīd: government postal or courier system, Arabic.
barmitsa: mail aventail, Russian.
bary: heraldic pattern.
bashak: Mongol officer sent to supervise conquered non-Mongol rulers.
bāshūra: bent-gate, Arabic.
bataille: military formation in Crusader army.
batraq: individual's flag or pennon, Turkish (see also *beyraq*).
bayḍah: light helmet, Arabic.
bayl: Cilician Armenian bailli or king's representative.
bayt al-māl: early Islamic communal treasury and weapons store.
bazabanag: Sassanian arm protection.
bāzīkand, bāzūband: vambrace, Persian.
beçkem: tassels on horse's bridle, Turkish.
beg: Turco-Mongol senior commander (see also *bey*).
bekhter: mail-and-plate cuirass, Russia.
bellum: war against Muslims in Iberia.
benefice: fief.
beredarioi: official government messenger system, Byzantium.
berutta: Byzantine javelin.
bey: Turco-Mongol senior commander (see also *beg*).
beylerbey: Turco-Mongol frontier governor, also commander of a full army; governor of an Ottoman *eyalet* large military province.
beylik: small independent or autonomous Turkish state.
beyraq: individual's flag or pennon, Turkish (see also *batraq*).
bhastrā: quiver, India.
bhṛitaka: mercenary troops in Hindu India.
bingbu: T'ang Chinese government department dealing with military affairs.
binliq: Tīmūrid unit of 1,000 men.
birjas: cavalry training exercise with the spear, Arabic (see also burjās).
bojarskye deti: aristocratic young warriors in later medieval Russia.
'bone rank': system of hereditory aristocracy, Silla period, Korea.
boyar: Russian aristocrat.
bozdağan, bozṭoghan: mace, Ottoman Turkish.
brafoneras, braoneras, brassonieras, brofuneras: vambrace, Christian Iberia.
brāhman: religious caste in Hindu states.
brazos: sections or 'arms' of the Aragonese Cortes or parliament.
brodniki: military community living along southern Russian rivers.
bron'a: mail hauberk, Russia.
brother knight: member of a Military Order of knightly rank.
bucellarii: Byzantine private military followers or guards.
budluq: mail or mail-and-plate cuisse for front of thigh, Turkish.
buherada: overhanging balcony or machicolation, Spanish.
bukaul: senior Mongol administrative officer.
bukhtī: crossbred Arabian and Khurāsani baggage camel.
bunduq: pellet or pellet bow, Arabic.
būq: trumpet, Arabic.
burdas: quilted soft armour, Christian Iberia.
burj: movable wooden siege-tower; small fort or castle, Arabic.
burjās: cavalry training exercise, Arabic (see also *birjas*).
bürüme: probably mail-and-plate cuirass, Turkish.
burūz: military parade before a major military expedition, Arabic.
bushi: military élite of Japan.
bushidō: code of behaviour of Japanese military élite.
buzgan: mace, Qipchaq Turkish.
buzogány: mace, Hungarian.

cabalgada: raiding by light cavalry, Christian Iberia.
caballería: urban and non-noble cavalry militia in medieval Christian Iberian states.
caballeros hidalgos: élite cavalry in early Christian states of Iberia.
caballeros villanos: non-noble cavalry in Christian Iberia.
camisa: quilted soft armour, Christian Iberia.
campus martius: Romano-Byzantine military training ground, Latin.
candidati: Romano-Byzantine guard unit.
canon law: Christian ecclesiastical law.
captain: commander of a military district in Cyprus; militia commander, Christian Iberia.
caravan: raid in Crusader States.
caravanserai: fortified 'hostels' on main trade routes.
caravo, caravela, caravel: late medieval Iberian sailing-ship.
cassot: quilted soft armour, Christian Iberia.
castellae: small Romano-Byzantine frontier castles.
castellan: commander of a castle, Christian Iberia.
castron: small fortified Byzantine outpost.
catargha: galley, Turkish (see also *katerga*).
cavaleiros: Portuguese knights.
cavaleiros-vilãos: non-noble cavalry, Portugal.
cavalgada: small raid, Christian Iberia.
cavallers: non-noble cavalry including Muslims in Christian Iberia.
cebe: mail hauberk, Turkish (see also *ğebe, ğebelü*).
cha: small fortified outpost in Ming China.
chabalakh: possibly an arming cap, Turkish.
chahār ācīnah: mail-and-plate cuirass, lit. 'four mirrors', Indo-Persian.
chākarān: professional soldiers or retainers in pre-Islamic Transoxiana.
chalkotouba: Byzantine leg defences.
charkh: large crossbow, Persian.
charkh kamān: large multiple-shot crossbow, Persian.
chartoularios: commander of part of Byzantine provincial scholae (guard unit).
châtelain: commander of a castle, Crusader States.
chatris: kiosk over main gate of a fortification, India.
chats châteaux: combined siege-towers and protective roof for miners, Cru-

sader States.
chaturanga: chess, India (see also *shaṭranj*).
checky: heraldic chequerboard pattern.
cheiropsella: Byzantine arm defences.
cheirotoxobolistron: Byzantine frame-mounted crossbow.
chekan: war-hammer, Russian.
chelandre: horse-transport galley in Crusader States.
chelandrion: specialised horse-transport galley, Byzantine.
cheng: fortress, Chinese.
chernye klobuki: 'Black Caps', Turkish allies and auxiliaries in Kievan Russia (see also *karakalpak*).
cheroptia: gauntlets, later medieval Byzantine.
chevaliers de la terre: resident knightly class of the Crusader States.
chevauchée: raid by lightly armoured forces, Crusader States.
chevetaine: military district in 14th-century Cyprus.
chi-hsiang: horse-armour crinet, China.
chichak: helmet with peak and neck protection, Turkish.
chin-chün: palace armies of Sung China.
ch'in chun wei: guard units in Ming Chinese armies.
ch'ing: evacuation of surrounding villages as first stage in defence of a town, China.
cho: sub-section of a department in government of Koryŏ Korea.
chokuto: Japanese straight sword.
chŏng: major division of the army of Silla in Korea.
chosarion: Byzantine term for hussar-style light cavalry.
chu: province of Silla Kingdom in Korea.
chün: permanent frontier army in T'ang China.
chün-fang: military wards or districts in T'ang China.
chungbang: supreme military headquarters in later Koryŏ Korea.
cirid: cavalry game or exercise with javelins, Turkish (see also jirid).
cirujanos: surgeons, Christian Iberia.
clibanarii: Romano-Byzantine close-quarters cavalry.
coat of a thousand nails: scale-lined cuirass, India.
cohort: Romano-Byzantine infantry unit.
coirasses: scale armour or coat-of-plates, Spanish (see also corazas).
collación: urban quarter raising a militia unit, Christian Iberia.
comes: a count in early Christian states of Iberia.
comit: quartermaster in charge of oarsmen and battle manoeuvres in a Spanish galley.
comitatensis: early Byzantine provincial garrison.
comitatus: Romano-Byzantine personal following.
commander: officer in command of a local commanderie or district of the Military Orders.
commander of ships: senior naval commander in Military Order of Hospitallers.
commanderie: administrative province of the Military Orders.
commune: self-governing community, usually of merchants, within Crusader States.
condestabre: constable, army commander, later medieval Portugal.
condomae: soldiers of slave origin defending isolated Byzantine outposts.
confraternity: Christian religious brotherhood.
connétable: commander or leader of army, Crusader States.
convent: Military Orders' barracks; equivalent of a monastery in non-military orders.
conventual prior: senior administrative officer in Military Orders.
corazas: scale armour or coat-of-plates, Spanish (see also coirasses).
çorbaci başi: commander of a *Yeni Çeri* company, Turkish lit. 'soup chief'.
coronel: commander of the Catalan and Aragonese army.
corredura: small raid, Christian Iberia.
cortes: parliament, Spanish.
count: Senior Byzantine command rank.
count of the walls: officer responsible for the defence of Constantinople.
çuqal: perhaps a scale, lamellar or mail-and-plate cuirass, Turkish.
cursores: Byzantine offensive cavalry.

^{c}abīd: slaves, military or otherwise, Arabic.
^{c}ajala: moving target used in infantry archery training, Arabic.
^{c}alam: metallic standard or finial on a flag-pole, Arabic.
^{c}amāmah: turban, Arabic.
^{c}aqqār: crossbow, Arabic.
^{c}arḍ: military review, Arabic.
^{c}arīf: junior officer, Arabic.
^{c}arrāda: torsion-powered stone-throwing siege-machine, Arabic.
^{c}arūs: 'bridegroom', stone-throwing machine, probably a single-armed torsion-powered device, Arabic.
^{c}aṣabīah: Arab tribal solidarity; military morale.
^{c}aṣā: baton, symbol of command in early Islamic armies.
^{c}ashṣīra: early Islamic tribal unit.
^{c}askar: élite troops or bodyguard, Arabic.
^{c}aṭā: military pay, early Islamic period.
^{c}awd: living field fortification of kneeling baggage animals, Arabic.
^{c}ayn: lit. 'eye', either a counter espionage agent or an observer for an army, Arabic.
^{c}azap: naval marine, Turkish.
^{c}azzāb: 'bachelors', part-time frontier soldiers, Arabic.
^{c}irāfa: early Islamic pay unit or squad.
^{c}urāt: 'mob' of urban poor, Arabic.

dabbābah: ram beneath protective timber roof, Arabic.
dalil: professional guide, Arabic.
damascene: surface pattern produced when elongating an ingot of high-carbon steel (see also firind).
dammāja: possibly a trident, Muslim Andalusia.
dandanāyaka, dannāyaka: commander-in-chief of army of Hindu Vijayanaga.
daojun: army on the march, Chinese.
dār al-ḥarb: 'Land of War', or non-Muslim territory.
dār: house set aside for troops; barracks, Arabic.
dār al-islam: 'Land of Peace', or Muslim world.
daraqah: leather shield, Arabic (see also *dorka*).
dari^{c}a: cavalry spear training exercise, Arabic.
daruga: Mongol Golden Horde official supervising Russian principalities.
darwīsh: dervish, Arabic.
dastaban: archer's leather half-glove, Persian.
decurion: Byzantine officer in command of ten men.
defensores: Byzantine defensive cavalry.

deli: Ottoman frontier cavalry, lit. 'fanatics'.
demarchos: governor of an urban quarter and probably commander of its militia, late Byzantine.
dendi fari: military leader from aristocracy, Muslim African kingdom of Mali.
deputation: urban authority responsible for recruiting militia, late medieval Christian Iberia.
derbendci: Ottoman military families responsible for the defence of key communications.
devsirme: enforced recruitment of youngsters for the Ottoman Yeni Çeri corps.
dharma: correct conduct for élites, Hindu and Buddhist states.
dhī: Sassanian village chief.
dhyakṣa: senior religious figure in Hindu Indonesia.
dihqān: Sassanian and early Persian-Islamic minor military gentry.
dir^{c}*:* mail hauberk, Arabic.
dīwān: Islamic government department or ministry.
dīwān al-^{c}*arḍ:* war ministry, Arabic.
dīwān al-barid: government ministry responsible for communications or postal service, Arabic.
dīwān al-iqṭā^{c}*:* government department dealing with government fiefs, Arabic.
dīwān al-jaysh: war ministry, Arabic.
dīwān al-mushrif: government department dealing with intelligence-gathering and assessment, Arabic.
dīwān al-rawātib: government department dealing with military salaries, Arabic.
djadchvi: perhaps a padded or fabric-covered armour, Georgian.
djavshan: lamellar cuirass, Georgian.
djayi: army, Georgian.
doganci: Balkan Christian auxiliary cavalry in Ottoman army.
domestic: Byzantine military commander or general.
dorka: Byzantine small leather shield (see also *daraqah*).
drafsh, dirafsh: large Sassanian military unit and its flag.
drafsh-i kāvyān: 'Banner of *Kāvagh*', Sassanian imperial banner.
drapier: senior officer in Military Orders.
dromon: fighting galley, Byzantine.
drosha: long streamer or flag, Georgian.
droungos: Byzantine mobile field reserve or battalion.
druzhina: armed retinue of a Russian prince.
dubbāba: movable wooden shed-like structure used in siege warfare, Arabic.
duchy: Byzantine frontier province.
durrā^{c}*a:* coat opening part-way down front, Arabic.
dux: Romano-Byzantine frontier governor.
dvor, dvorjane: later medieval Russian princely retinue.

eflokion: Byzantine sailing-ship (see also *fulk*).
ēḥzāb: early Ethiopian irregular troops.
el haz: Christian Iberian cavalry formation, lit. 'the closely packed bundle'.
el punta: Christian Iberian cavalry formation, lit. 'the point'.
el tropel: Christian Iberian cavalry formation, lit. 'the mad rush'.
epilorikion: Byzantine felt or quilted soft armour.
eri: probably Georgian urban militia.
eschielle: cavalry squadron in Crusader States.
escudeiros: squires, Portugal.
escuderos: squires, Spain.
esculquero: guard for animal herds during annual migrations, Christian Iberia.
esplonada: light cavalry formation in Iberia, lit. 'a spur'.
exarch: early Byzantine senior provincial commander.
excubitores: Romano-Byzantine guard unit.
exeas: urban official who carried ransom to the enemy, Christian Iberia.
eyalet: largest Ottoman military province.

fangren: frontier troops of T'ang China.
fan-ping: non Chinese allies of Sung China.
fapi: general assault on a fortified place, lit. 'ant attack', China.
faṣīl: low third wall some distance from the main defences, Arabic.
fauj: Tīmūrid corps.
faussó: possibly an early falchion, Christian Iberia.
fay': tribute or booty distributed communally, Arabic.
fidā'īs: active arm or fighter in the 'Assassin' military structure.
fief de soudée: money fief.
fief en besants: money fief.
filoi: ambassadors, lit. 'friends', Byzantium.
firind: watered pattern on surface of a sword-blade (see also damascene).
fityān: members of a Muslim religious brotherhood.
flammula: small pennon or streamer, Romano-Byzantine.
fleury: heraldic pattern.
foederati: Romano-Byzantine allies or auxiliaries.
foja: perhaps pair-of-plates, lit. a 'girdle', Spanish.
fonsadera, fonsado, fossato: offensive operations in Christian Iberia.
fosse: ditch around a castle.
fu: Chinese militia army.
fueros: rules governing the activities of urban militias, Spain.
fulk: sailing-ship, Arabic (see also *eflokion*).
fu-ping: provincial militia of T'ang China; special military districts under the Chinese Sui dynasty.
furūsīyah: cavalry training and skills, Arabic.
futūwa: Muslim religious brotherhood.

gadā: mace, India.
galiote: small galley, Iberia.
ganāwa: troops of black African origin, specifically from Guinea, Arabic.
ganz: Sassanian arsenal.
gargaj: movable wooden siege-tower, India.
gārwa: probably quilted soft armour, Persian (see also kārwa).
gasmouli, gasmouloi: soldiers and sailors of mixed Latin and Greek parentage.
ğebe, ğebelü: mail hauberk, Turkish (see also cebe).
gentiles: locally recruited Romano-Byzantine forces.
ghanīmah: booty allowed to individual troops, Arabic.
ghayr wajihdar: irregular troops in Delhi Sultanate.
ghāzīs: troops dedicated to frontier warfare, Arabic.
ghazw: Arab raiding warfare.
ghūlām: professional Islamic soldier of slave-origin.
ghurab: possibly a cargo-barge, Arabic.

gladius: Roman short sword.

gomeres: Spanish term for Berber troops from G̲h̲umāra mountains in Morocco.

gonella: quilted soft armour, Christian Iberia.

gonfanonnier: senior officer in the Military Orders.

gonuklaria: Byzantine greaves or chausses.

gophaṇa: sling, India.

gorodskoe opolchenie: Russian urban militia.

gothograeci: Byzantine cavalry élite unit, perhaps descended from Goth soldiers.

grand commander: senior officer in Military Orders.

grand turcopolier: commander of *turcopoles* in Crusader States.

great galley: large fighting or merchant galley.

Greek Fire: petroleum- or bitumen-based incendiary weapon.

grībān: mail coif, Persian (see also grīvpān).

grid': junior part of a Russian druzhina military retinue.

grīvpān: Sassanian neck and shoulder protection.

guardadores: guardians for prisoners, Christian Iberia.

guerra: internal conflict between Christians in Iberia.

gund: largest Sassanian unit or corps.

gundsālār: commander of a Sassanian corps.

gureba: Ottoman cavalry regiments based in the Sultan's palace.

gusliari: high-grade itinerant minstrels in medieval Russia.

ḥadīt̲h̲: Sayings or Traditions of the Prophet, secondary source of Muslim Law.

ḥāfir: crest or pin in or on a turban, Arabic.

haj: Muslim pilgrimage to Mecca.

halakah: annihilation of an enemy, Arabic.

halqa: freeborn élite of all Ayyūbid armies; later non-élite troops of Mamlūk army.

ḥamra: ex-Sassanian infantry recruited into early Islamic armies.

han chun: rural levy, or 'Chinese army' in Mongol China.

Hand of Fāṭima: popular Islamic symbol shaped like a hand.

ḥara: security forces, Arabic.

ḥarāfis̲h̲a: guerrilla raiders inside enemy territory, Arabic (see also ḥarfūs̲h̲).

ḥarb: war, Arabic.

ḥarba: heavy javelin or short infantry spear, Arabic.

ḥarbīah: ᶜAbbāsid heavy infantry.

ḥarfūs̲h̲: 'ruffians' attached to a senior personage as political and military supporters (see also ḥarāfis̲h̲a).

ḥarrāqat: fire-ships, Arabic.

ḥas̲h̲am: cavalry guard, North Africa and al-Andalus.

has̲h̲m-i iqṭāᶜ: fief-holding provincial forces in Delhi Sultanate.

ḥas̲h̲īs̲h̲: cannabis, Arabic.

ḥāṣina: heavy helmet, Muslim Iberia.

ḥavās̲h̲ī: armed retainers; Turco-Arabic.

hazāra: Perso-Mongol military units of 1,000 men.

hei-kuang: 'black brilliant' armour, China.

hermandad: mutual aid agreements between Iberian towns.

hermandades: urban police forces, Christian Iberia.

hetaireia: Byzantine palace guard unit.

ḥezb: early Ethiopian army.

ḥimāya: tribute, Arabic.

ḥīra: pre-Islamic Arab tribal encampment or capital.

ḥiṣn: fortress; also infantry battlefield formation, Arabic.

household knight: knight maintained in a lord's household, not usually holding a fief.

hsiang-chün: provincial armies of Sung China.

hsiang-ping: local militia forces of Sung China.

hsin-fu chun: ex-Sung troops in Mongol Chinese army.

hsuin-pien tzu-ti: lit. 'frontier braves' under Chinese T'ang dynasty.

hudnah: truce, Arabic.

hueste: major expedition in Christian Iberia.

ḥuffāẓ: young men selected for special military training, Morocco.

hui-hui p'ao: counterweight trebuchet with adjustable weight on the beam-sling, lit. 'Muslim mangonel'.

hujarīya: training barracks, Arabic.

huo: smallest section of a Chinese militia force.

huo-chien: grenade, Chinese.

huruffi: Muslim sect or movement, widely considered heretical.

ḥusbān: small darts shot from an arrow-guide, Arabic.

hwarang: young aristocracy or officer corps in early medieval Korea.

hwarangdo: code of behaviour of Korean military élite.

hypostrategus: early Byzantine commander or general.

içlik: thick saddle-blanket, Turkish.

icon: religious painting in the Christian Orthodox Church.

iconoclasm: 'Icon breaking.' movement, Byzantium.

igdis̲h̲: local militias of probably mixed origins, Turkish Anatolia.

ikhs̲h̲īd: minor ruler in pre-Islamic Transoxiana.

ikhwān: Muslim religious brotherhood.

ilarch: Byzantine infantry squad leader.

ili: probably long curved sword, India.

illik kafırleri: 'infidel frontiersmen'; non-Muslim ruler owing suzerainty to a Turkish ruler.

indigenae: early Byzantine local troops.

indulgence: remission of sins offered to Crusaders and others by the Catholic Church.

infações: Portuguese knights.

infanzones: lesser aristocracy of early medieval Spain.

ingenui: Portuguese aristocracy and free families.

intervallum: open space around the outer part of a field fortification.

iqlīm: territorial districts with their own forces, Arabic.

iqṭāᶜ: non-inheritable revenue-providing estate, Arabic.

irān-ambārag̲h̲badh: senior Sassanian officer in charge of arsenals.

irān-spādbadh: Sassanian minister of war.

isfahsalār: commander of army in battle, Perso-Arabic.

ishkhan: Armenian higher military aristocracy.

isṭabl: stabling organisation, Arabic.

isṭināᶜ: mutual loyalty between troops, Arabic.

istirᶜāḍ: military review, Arabic.

jabalīyūn: autonomous hill communities, Arabic.

jaᶜā'il: mercenaries in Umayyad army.

jada: magic employed to change the weather with the aid of 'rain- stones', Turco-Mongol (see also *yat*).
jah: sharpened throwing disc, India.
jālīsh: light cavalry vanguard, Arabic.
*jamā*ʿ*a:* temporary operational unit in Ayylūbid army.
jān-avspār: 'self-sacrificers', Sassanian guard unit.
jāndār: professional military élite of Muslim India.
jandarīyah: slave-recruited Mamlūk élite of Ayylūbid army.
jānib: unit of infantry or cavalry in Ayylūbid army.
janissary: Ottoman infantry élite (see also *Yeni Çeri*).
januwiyāh: flat-bottomed infantry mantlet, Arabic.
jarīda: small cavalry unit in Ayylūbid army.
jarkh: large crossbow, Arabic.
jarrār: pre-Islamic Arab army commander, 'commander of one thousand'.
jaserant mail: padded and cloth-covered mail hauberk, Crusader States.
jāsūs: spy operating in enemy territory, Arabic.
jaucerant: padded and cloth-covered mail hauberk, Spain.
jawshan: lamellar cuirass, Arabic and Persian.
jāwūsh: message crier, Arabic (see also *munadi*).
jayb: underground cistern in a fortress, Arabic.
jaysh: structured army, Arabic.
jiavors: élite cavalry of Cilician Armenia.
jie: class within T'ang Chinese ranking system; also a standard or signalling device, China.
jihād: spiritual struggle, or fighting in defence of Islam.
jing: formation used by Chinese armies facing Central Asian nomad forces; also a military flag, China.
jirid: cavalry game or exercise with javelins, Arabic (see also cirid).
jitōs: fief-holder in later medieval Japan.
jitr: ruler's ceremonial parasol, Arabic.
jizyah: tax demanded of all non-Muslim inhabitants in a Muslim state.
jubbah: padded and sometimes mail lined armour, Arabic.
judicatures: local administrative and military unit in Sardinia.
juez: military leader of a town and its militia, Christian Iberia.
juffa: leather coracle used on the rivers Euphrates and Tigris.
juglar: minstrel or poet in medieval Spain.
*ju*ʿ*l:* payment made directly to individual soldiers, Arabic.
julbān: ordinary mamlūk soldier in Mamlūk Sultanate.
jun: large T'ang Chinese army.
jund: early Islamic military province and territorial army.
jund al-ḥadra: guard unit of ʿAbbāsid Caliphs.
jupeaux d'armes: surcoat, sometimes also quilted soft armour.
jupon: surcoat.

kabadion: Byzantine soft armour of felt.
kabsh: battering-ram, Arabic.
kadīvar: free farmer class in pre-Islamic Transoxiana.
kaff: arm defences, Arabic.
kaftan: coat worn by Sassanian and Muslim military élites.
k'aii: coat-of-plates cuirass, China.
kamān-i-gāv: frame-mounted siege crossbow, Persian lit. 'ox-bow'.
kamelaukion: thick felt hood or cap, Byzantine.
kanārangs: Sassanian senior officer.
kandāchāra: military department of government of Hindu Vijayanaga.
kap'hi: lamellar or splinted arm protections, Georgia.
karabos, karabion: possibly a cargo vessel, Byzantine.
karadis: small Islamic cavalry squadron.
karakalpak: 'Black Caps', Turkish allies and auxiliaries in Kievan Russia (see also *chernye klobuki*).
karr wa farr: Arab cavalry tactic of repeated attack and withdrawal (see also *turna-fuye*).
kārwa: probably quilted soft armour, Persian (see also *gārwa*).
kastron: late Byzantine fortified town.
kastrophylax: commander of late Byzantine fortified place.
katena: possibly a transport ship, Byzantine.
katepan of the arma: chief of the Byzantine armamenton (arms factories).
katerga: war-galley of late Byzantine Trebizond (see also catargha).
katība: Arab Islamic operational cavalry unit.
kayak: ship or canoe, Turkish.
kazāghand: cloth-covered and padded mail armour, Persian and Arabic.
kazan: cauldron serving as main symbol and loyalty focus of an Ottaman Yeni Çeri unit.
kedimli: horse-armour, Turkish.
keikō: Japanese lamellar armour.
keiromanika: Byzantine gauntlets.
kemeldürük: breast-strap of horse-harness, Turkish.
kephale: late Byzantine provincial governor.
keris: small sword or large dagger, Malaya.
khadga, khanda: broad-sword, India.
khagan: senior ruler in Central Asia, Turco-Mongol.
khamīs: ruler's élite force in pre-Islamic Yemen; early Islamic battle formation, theoretically in five divisions.
khān: Turco-Mongol ruler.
khanjars: small sword or large dagger, Arabic.
khānqāh: house or barracks set aside for troops or volunteers.
khashāb: wooden lighthouse for river navigation, Arabic.
khāṣṣa: ruler's attendant, middle-ranking officer, Arabic.
khāṣṣakīya: ruler's élite bodyguard in Mamlūk Sultanate.
khatangku dehel: Mongol soft armour, lit. 'coat as hard as steel', later with scale lining.
khātūn: queen, Turkish Transoxiana.
khawārijis: 'fundamentalist' rebels, Arabic.
khidmatgār: military and other servants in pre-Islamic Transoxiana.
khūdh: heavy helmet, Arabic.
khuyagh: lamellar cuirass, Mongol (see also *kuyuk*).
kilich: sabre, Turkish (see also *qilic*).
kisten: mace, Russian.
kizil elma: lit. 'Red Apple', a military goal which always remained unattainable, Turkish.
kleisourai: Byzantine commander of mountain passes.
klibanion: Byzantine light lamellar cuirass.
kolp'um: early Korean aristocracy of 'bone rank'.
kong tch'uan nou: doubled bow, siege weapon probably incorporating two bows, China.
koniushi: Russian master of horse.

kontarion: Byzantine cavalry spear.
koşkum: crupper-strap of horse-harness, Turkish.
kōtwāl: commander of provincial garrison in Delhi Sultanate; also quartermaster.
koumbaria: large ship, Byzantine.
koursa: naval raid, Byzantine.
kouttch: secret police, Mongol Īl-Khān, Persia.
kremasmata: soft armour for lower part of body, Byzantine.
kremlin: citadel, Russian.
kshatriya: warrior caste in Hindu states.
kūfic: angular form of Arabic script.
kuklos: 'living field fortification' of kneeling baggage animals, Greek.
kul: slave or servant of the Sultan, Ottoman Turkish.
kura: small Sassanian administrative district.
kūra mujannada: military province, Arabic.
kurmina fari: military leader from ruling family; Muslim African kingdom of Mali.
kurra: early Islamic cavalry training exercise, possibly with the javelin.
kūshk: Transoxianan villages sometimes fortified.
kūssāt: large cymbals, Arabic.
kustubān: archer's leather half-glove, Persian.
kuyuk: Russian cuirass (see also *khuyagh*).
kyŏkku: polo, Korea.
kyŏngdang: military élite of Koguryŏ state in Korea.

lamṭ: large leather shield of Berber North Africa.
lashkar: army, Indo-Persian.
lashqah: crossbow, North Africa and Andalusia.
lāṣiq: not fully initiated member of the 'Assassin' military structure.
lavra: Byzantine monastic retreat, often fortified.
lawlab: lever or pulley, to span a crossbow.
lei shih cchê: mangonel mounted on a wagon, China.
liang-k'ai: unclear form of 'double armour', China.
liang-tang: 'double faced' cuirass, China.
lii: middle-sized section of a Chinese militia army.
limitanei: Romano-Byzantine frontier troops.
linothorax: Byzantine quilted soft-armour or surcoat.
liṣūṣ: light cavalry used to attack enemy supplies, Arabic.
lithām: face veil worn by élite of Saharan Berber tribes.
lo-tzu-chün: mule corps, perhaps élite mounted infantry of T'ang China.
lorikion, louriken: mail hauberk, Byzantine.
luᶜab: smallest type of mangonel, Arabic.

maaşli: professional troops recruited from slaves or prisoners of war, Turkish.
madas: Berber javelin.
mahout: driver or controller of an elephant.
majordomi, majorini: senior military figure in early Christian states of Iberia.
majra: arrow-guide used when shooting short darts, Arabic.
makāḥil al-bārūd: grenades whose content included saltpetre, Arabic.
maᶜlūghūn: troops of Christian renegade origin in late medieval Granada, Arabic.
ma-mien lien: horse-armour chamfron (bridle), China.
mamlaka: small administrative and military district in the Mamlūk state.
mamlūk: professional Islamic soldier of slave-origin.
mamlūkūn: *mamlūks* of senior officer in Mamlūk Sultanate.
manganell turquès: probably trebuchet with adjustable counterweight, Spain.
manganikon: Byzantine single-armed torsion-powered stone-throwing device; later a beam-sling mangonel.
manglavitai: Byzantine palace security police.
mangonel: beam-sling stone-throwing machine (see also *manjanīq*).
maniakion: richly embroidered cape, Byzantine.
manikia, manikellia: Byzantine upper arm defences.
manjanīqīn: stone-throwing machine operators, Arabic.
manjanīq: beam-sling stone-throwing machine, Arabic (see also *mangonel*).
manzil: isolated fortified tower, Arabic.
marachakhd: deputy commander of Cilician Armenian army.
mard-u-mard: Sassanian 'man-to-man' duelling between champions.
maréchal: second in command of army in Crusader States.
marichal: marshal, deputy commander of army, later medieval Portugal.
marqab: raised observation post.
marṣad: fortified hostel, Arabic.
marzbān: Sassanian senior officer.
maṣānic: pre-Islamic Ghassānid military base.
ma-shen-chia: horse-armour flank defences, China.
masnada: military retinue in early medieval Christian states of Iberia.
massāḥīs: military surveyors, Arabic.
master crossbowman: commander of crossbowmen in Military Orders.
master esquire: commander of squires in Military Orders.
master sergeant: commander of non-noble troops in Military Orders.
ma-tou-hou: horse-armour crupper, China.
maula: hereditary military élite in early medieval India.
maᶜūna: urban auxiliaries, Arabic.
mauri pacis: lit. 'pacified Moors', also recruited into Christian Iberian militias.
mawāli: honorary member of an Arab tribe.
mawāqīd: coastal beacons, Arabic.
maydān: parade or military training ground, Arabic.
maymanah: Arab Islamic right wing.
maysarah: Arab Islamic left wing.
megalla allagion: late Byzantine 'large regiment'.
megas konostoulos: late Byzantine Grand Constable in command of western mercenaries.
mehter, mehterhane: military band of late medieval Ottoman army.
meros: Byzantine regiment.
mesnaderos: noble retinue of Christian Iberian ruler.
mesoi: late Byzantine urban middle class and probable militia.
midfaᶜ: early form of gun, Arabic.
mighfar: mail coif, Arabic.
military order: military-monastic order such as Templars and Hospitallers.
milites: élite troops of early Christian kingdoms of Iberia, probably mounted.

ming bashi: Tīmūrid commanders of one thousand.
ming-kuang: 'bright brilliant' armour, China.
minṭaqah: military belt, Arabic.
miqnab: smaller operational cavalry unit, Arab Islamic.
misruda: scale-lined cuirass or coat-of-plates, Muslim Granada.
miṭrād: Arabic short or light spear, Persian-Turkish origin.
moera: intermediate-sized Byzantine military formation.
money fief: revenue-raising fief, not involving the holding of land.
mourtatoi, myrtaïtai: Byzantine troops recruited from Turkish prisoners converted to Christianity.
mozarab: Arabised Christians in Muslim Iberia.
mubārizūn: early Islamic 'champions' who duelled between the ranks of opposing armies.
mudejar: Muslim under Christian Iberian rule.
muḥannak: form of turban having loose loop of cloth beneath chin, Arabic.
muḥarrik: junior officer in charge of small operational unit, Arabic.
mukḥula al-nafṭ: probably a flame-thrower using primitive form of gunpowder, Arabic.
munādī: message crier, Arabic (see also *jāwūsh*).
muqaddam: commander of marines, Arabic.
muqaddamah: Arab Islamic advance guard.
muqātila: local militia in early Muslim armies.
murābiṭ: religious volunteer guarding Muslim frontiers; also a North African ruling dynasty.
murtāziqah: ᶜAbbāsid regular troops.
muṣallah: prayer hall, sometimes incorporated into fortifications, Arabic.
müsellem: early Ottoman professional cavalry.
mustaᶜa'riba: 'Arabised' non-Arab troops of early Caliphate.
mustakhdamū: ruler's mamlūks in Mamlūk Sultanate.
muta'ahhilīn: full-time frontier soldier, Arabic.
muṭṭawi'a, mutaṭawiᶜah: religiously motivated volunteers, Arabic.
muzaradi: Georgian helmet, wholly or partly of mail.
muzhi: tribal aristocracy in early medieval Russia.
myrtaïtai: (see *mourtatoi*).

nāchakh: war-axes, Perso-Arabic.
nacharark: Armenian military aristocrat (see also nakharar).
nafaqa: military payment made on accession of new ruler or at beginning of campaign, Arabic.
naffāṭūn: fire-troops, Arabic.
nafṭ: incendiary liquid, Greek Fire, Arabic.
nagid: prince, medieval Hebrew.
naginata: Japanese infantry staff weapon or halberd.
nā'ib al-qalᶜa: commander of the Citadel in Damascus in Mamlūk State.
nā'ib al-salṭana: Viceroy of Egypt, senior officer in early Mamlūk Sultanate.
najjab: courier, Arabic.
nakharar: Armenian lower military aristocracy (see also *nacharark*).
nalika: blowpipe or blowgun, India.
naqb: siege mining techniques, Arabic.
naqīb: junior officer, Arabic.
naqqābūn: military engineers, Arabic.
nār: unspecified form of fire-weapon, Arabic.
nāwak: arrow-guide used when shooting short darts (see also majra).
nāyak: officer in Hindu Indian army.
naẓīr: early Islamic reserve forces.
nāẓir: junior officer, Arabic.
nipīk: Sassanian government list of military families.
niṣṭriṃśa: heavy sword, India.
nīzah-i mard gīr: long staff weapon with curved blade, Persian.
noznicy: mail chausses, Russia.
nuqabā' al-jaysh: adjutant in Mamlūk army.
nuzūl: halting and re-assembling; or an army on the march, Arabic.

obos: prefabricated wooden palisade, Russian.
obsequium: corps of smaller Byzantine palace regiments.
ocak: Ottoman *Yeni Çeri* corps as a whole, lit. 'hearth'.
ognishchanin: Russian bailiff.
okolnichi: later medieval Russia quartermaster-general.
on bashi: Tīmūrid leader of ten.
oplitai: Byzantine regular infantry.
opsikion: main Byzantine provincial army based around the capital.
optimates: early Byzantine heavy cavalry élite.
ordu: fortified tribal capital, Turco-Mongol Central Asia; Mongol ruler's armed retinue; Turco-Mongol army.
organa: probably portable musical organs, Byzantium.
orta: company of *Yeni Çeri* infantry.

pādhghūspān: late Sassanian army commander.
paidah: infantry of Muslim origin, Muslim India.
pāighān: Sassanian infantry.
palaiyam: military province of southern India, lit. 'military camp'.
palash: Russian sabre.
palatine: early Byzantine palace guard regiments.
paly: heraldic pattern.
pan-chih: imperial élite in palace armies of Sung China.
pantheotai: possibly Byzantine guards officers.
pantsir: scale cuirass or perhaps mail hauberk, Russia.
p'ao ch'e: fire-weapon made of bamboo, either large grenade or primitive gun, China.
paramerion: Byzantine single-edged sword.
paraportia: gates in Byzantine field fortifications.
paraśu: battleaxe, India.
parataxis: Byzantine operational formation.
parembole: Byzantine term for pre-Islamic Arab tribal capital.
parvanak: government postal service of Sassanian Empire.
pāshtīb: raised platform of sand-bags to fill a defensive ditch, India.
pastores: guards for animals in Spanish armies.
patrón: master in charge of navigation in Spanish galley.
payadeh: early Ottoman infantry.
pāyak: infantry of Hindu origin, Muslim India.
pāyghānsālār: commander of Sassanian infantry unit.
pedion: Romano-Byzantine military training ground, Greek.
pedones, peones, peonía: infantry in early Christian states of Iberia.
peões: infantry militia of medieval Portugal.
peones: (see *pedones*).

peonía: (see *pedones*).
periknemides: Byzantine infantry vambrace.
peritrachelia: thickly padded head and neck protection, sometimes of mail, Byzantine.
petroboli: general term for Byzantine stone-throwing machines.
pezoi: late Byzantine infantry.
pharganoi: Byzantine Turkish archer-guard from Farghāna in Transoxiana.
phylarch: chief of a tribe defending the Romano-Byzantine frontier.
p'i-li huo-ch'iu: bamboo tube filled with explosives and metal fragments, Chinese.
pin: grade within T'ang Chinese ranking system.
podiezdnoi: Russian adjutant.
podopsella: Byzantine leg defences.
pogost: Russian trading and military outpost.
posadnik: mayor of a Russian town.
postrig: initiation ceremony for young member of Russian aristocracy.
poulain: insulting term for resident knight of the Crusader States.
praefectus: Romano-Byzantine title sometimes given to frontier tribal chiefs.
pralaya: final destruction of the world in Hinduism.
prestamo: fief for early Iberian military élite.
primmikerios: commander of late Byzantine élite guard units.
pronoia: Byzantine fief or money-raising estate.
protospatharios: Byzantine honorific title.
protostrator: deputy commander of late Byzantine army.
pseudo-Kufic: form of decoration based on Arabic script, Byzantium and western Europe.
pu: regional headquarters in later Koryŏ Korea.
pushtīghbānsālār: commander of Sassanian guard units.

*qabā*ᶜ*:* tunic, Arabic.
qabaq: horse-archery exercise at target mounted high on a pole.
qabīla: early Islamic tribal military unit created from those outside the existing tribal structure.
qadirga: war-galley, Turkish.
qā'id: middle-ranking officer, Arabic.
qā'id al-baḥr: admiral or naval commander, Arabic.
*qal*ᶜ*a:* fort or castle, Arabic.
qalāchūr, qalājūlīyā, qaljūri: probably early form of single-edged sword or sabre, Arabic.
qalansuwah: hat or cap, Arabic.
qalb: Arab Islamic centre or battle array.
qanāh: long spear, Arabic.
qaraçi: Turco-Mongol frontier divisions.
qaraçi bey: Turco-Mongol frontier commander.
qarāghulām: probably lower-grade mamlūk in Ayylūbid army.
qarawnas: probably troops of mixed Mongol and Indian or Kashmiri parentage.
qargu: fire-beacons, Turkish Central Asia.
qārib: possibly a cargo ship or barge; later a large vessel with fighting castles, Arabic.
qarqal: probably a scale, lamellar or mail-and-plate cuirass, Arabic.
qarqūra: large three-masted merchant vessel, Arabic; origin of caracca or carrack.
qaṣabah, qaṣr: governor's fortified residence and garrison, Arabic.
*qaṭā'i*ᶜ*:* cavalry squadrons, Arabic.
qawārīr al-nafṭ: long-necked glass grenades, Arabic.
qaws al-lawlab: frame-mounted siege crossbow, Arabic.
qaws al-rijl: early form of crossbow, Arabic.
qaws al-ziyār: ballista with two arms, powered by twisted skeins of horse-hair or sinew, Arabic.
qawtchin: Mongol élite guard.
qayiq: merchant ship, Turkish.
qayl: tribal or territorial leader in pre-Islamic Yemen.
qighaj, qīqaj: horse-archery exercise at ground-level target, Arabic.
qilic: sabre, Turkish (see also *kilich*).
qirāṭ: military district in the Mamṣlūk State.
qoluq: vambrace, Turkish.
qoshun: Tīmūrid unit of 100 men.
quadrillo: officer responsible for division of spoils in Castile.
qubba: small fort, Arabic.
qudūr: narrow-necked bottle or fire-grenade, Arabic.
qufl: probably troops in close-combat formation, lit. 'fortress'.
quintarch: Byzantine officer in command of forty troops.
qur: military belt, Turkish.
qurqapïn: military champions, 'possessors of a belt', Turco-Mongol.
quwwād: (plural of *qā'id*).

raḍkh: lit. 'gifts' as irregular payment for non-professional troops, Arabic.
rafīq: fully initiated member of the 'Assassin' military structure.
ra'īs: head of urban ahdath militia, or village leader, Arabic.
ra'īs al-milāḥa: captain of a ship, Arabic.
rajjāla: infantry of Ayylūbid army.
rajpūt: Hindu military élite.
rajul al-musāfiyah: guard unit of ᶜAbbāsid Caliphs.
rāmīah: ᶜAbbāsid infantry archers.
rasputitsa: the mud of spring and autumn in Russia, making roads impassable.
*ra*ᶜ*w:* semi-nomadic Arabs.
rāya: flag, Arabic.
razzīa: Arab raiding warfare.
restor: system of replacing knights' horses lost on campaign in Crusader States.
rhos: Russian troops in Byzantine service.
ribāṭ: early Islamic garrison or garrison duty; later a fortified frontier or coastal outpost.
ricos hombres: aristocracy of early medieval Christian-Iberian states.
ricos-homens: Portuguese upper nobility.
riptarion: Byzantine javelin.
rod: early medieval Russian clan.
roga: pay or 'allowance' for frontier auxiliaries, Byzantine.
rogatina: Russian spear.
romphaion: Byzantine single-edged sword.
runūd: Muslim fraternity, also employed as a militia.
rustaq: smallest Sassanian territorial division.
rutba: fortified hostel, Arabic.
rutīla: probably an early form of frame-mounted beam-sling mangonel, lit. 'spider-like', Arabic.

*ṣa*ᶜ*ālīk:* adventurers grouped around a local military leader, Arabic.
*sa*ᶜ*ad, sā*ᶜ*d:* vambrace for lower arm, Arabic.

sabarculli: probably mail chausses, Georgia.
sabṭāna: Persian blowpipe.
saç: style of plaiting hair to indicate rank or tribe, Turkish.
sacellarius: Byzantine financial rather than operational officer.
ṣaff: Arab Islamic close-order infantry formation.
safīna: general term for ship, Arabic.
sagini: ship, Byzantine.
ṣāḥib al-madānah: city governor, Arabic.
ṣāḥib al-shurṭa: head of police, Arabic.
ṣāḥib al-thughūr: governor of a frontier province, Arabic.
ṣāḥib al-ṭa^{c}ām: officer in charge of equipment and supplies, Arabic.
sa'id: master, Arabic.
śakti: spear, India.
salandria: horse-transporting sailing-ship.
samsŏng: government department in Koryŏ Korea.
samurai: military élite of Japan.
sanadīl: possibly cargo-galley or transport ship, Arabic.
sandalion: possibly cargo-galley or transport ship, Byzantine.
sanjaq: military province and its banner, Ottoman Turkish.
sanjaq bey: Ottoman provincial governor.
san wei: guards officers of T'ang China.
sāqa: Arab Islamic rearguard.
ṣaqāliba: slaves, military or otherwise, of 'Slav' or western European origin.
sarā'iyān: Ghaznawid palace guard.
sarāwīt: early Ethiopian regular troops.
sarbadār: urban militias from Khurāsān and Transoxiana in later Middle Ages.
sardār: Tīmūrid military rank.
sarhang: officer rank, Persian.
sarīya: small cavalry unit in Ayylūbid army.
satā'r: screens to conceal movements of besieging troops, Arabic.
sayf: sword, Arabic.
sayf ṣārim: Arab sword, probably for infantry.
scaramangion: Byzantine officers' coat.
scholae: Romano-Byzantine guard unit.
scholom: helmet, Russian.
sebaste: Byzantine officer in command of foreign troops.
sekban: Ottoman infantry unit, lit. 'dog-handlers'.
semberek: arrow-guide used when shooting short darts, Turkish (see also *zembūrek*).
semispatha: Romano-Byzantine sword.
se-mu: Yüan Chinese Imperial Guard troops of western origin.
senā: army in Hindu India.
senāpati: army commander in Hindu India.
seneschal: senior officer in command of castles in Crusader States.
sépouh: Armenian freemen.
sergeant: professional non-noble soldier, Crusader States, etc.
shahr: Sassanian military district.
shahristān: Sassanian and Transoxianan town with a citadel.
shahrīgh: governor of a Sassanian military district.
shalandī: possibly cargo-galley, Arabic.
sharbūsh: fur-lined hat of military élite, Turco-Arabic (see also *tarbūsh*).
shaṭranj: chess, also chessboard pattern, Arab-Persian (see also chaturanga).
shaykh: tribal leader; spiritual adviser; respected elderly man, Arabic.
shaykh al-ghuzāt: commander of Berber volunteer forces in Granada.
shen-ts'e: large central or palace army of later T'ang China.
shi^{c}ār: battle-cry or shout, Arabic.
shiḥna: head of internal security forces, Arabic.
shīnī: war-galley, Arabic.
shiyākha khaṣṣā: officers in command of provincial forces in Granada.
shōguns: military 'dictators' of later medieval Japan.
shou phao: smallest form of mangonel, China.
shower-shooting: archery technique of saturation fire on a designated target zone.
shreṇībala: military units provided by 'guilds' in Hindu India.
shuj^{c}ān: offensive cavalry units, Arabic.
shugōs: fief-holder in later medieval Japan.
shu-mi yüan: Bureau of Military Affairs in Sung China.
shurrāfa: crenellations, Arabic.
shurṭa: early Islamic internal security troop; later police.
sidera gonatia: late Byzantine mail chausses or leg armour.
signum: large flag, Romano-Byzantine.
sihām khiṭā^{c}iyya: fire-arrows, probably using primitive form of gunpowder, lit. 'Chinese arrows', Arabic.
silahdar: Ottoman cavalry guard, lit. 'guardians of ruler's weapons'.
sinf: system of mutual loyalty in Muslim armies.
sinnawr: battering-ram, Arabic.
sipāhi: Ottoman cavalry élite.
sipahsālār: officer rank, Persian.
sipar: small shield, Persian.
siper: broad plate attached to the left wrist, enabling short darts to be shot from a bow, Turkish.
śipri: helmet, possibly of scales, India.
sirinapan: Sassanian leg defence.
siyar: regulations governing a soldier's behaviour in Islamic law.
siyāsat: mixed Muslim and Turco-Mongol legal code or method of government.
skaplion: Byzantine mail protection for neck and shoulders.
skomorokhi: low-grade itinerant minstrels in medieval Russia.
smerd: Russian rural levy, peasant militia or individual soldier.
socii: group of pilgrims or Crusaders.
solak: Ottoman infantry guard unit.
solenarion: Byzantine arrow-guide used when shooting small darts.
solerets: armoured shoes, Crusader States.
sometent, somatent: peasant and urban militia in Christian Iberia.
sotnia: Russian unit of 100 men.
sotski: Russian officer of a *sotnia.*
sous maréchal: senior officer in Military Orders.
sŏdang: non-noble troops in early medieval Korea.
spādbadh: Sassanian regional commander.
spasalar: commander of Cilician Armenian army.
spathion: Byzantine cavalry sword.
ssu-chiao: large type of mangonel, China.
sterzhen: pointed helmet, Russian.
stōr-bezhask: head of Sassanian army veterinary service.
stradioti: Byzantine local garrison or frontier troops.
strategos, strategus: commander of a Byzantine theme army.
strategos parembolon nomadon: Byzantine term for senior pre-Islamic tribal leader.
stratopedarch: officer of locally

recruited *monokaballoi* cavalry, late Byzantine.
stroggulion: Byzantine neck and shoulder protection.
śūdra: serf caste of Hindu states.
ṣūfī: member of a Muslim religious brotherhood; 'mystic'.
śūla: javelin, India.
ṣulḥ: complete peace between equals, Arabic.
sulitsa: light spear or javelin, Russian.
sumptuary law: law restricting certain forms of clothing to certain persons or social classes.
sunbūk: sailing-ship, Arabic.
sundang: straight sword, Malaya and Indonesia.
suntagma: Byzantine close formation.
sūq al-ᶜaskar: mobile market attached to Ayylūbid army.
su-wei: Imperial Guard of Yüan Mongol Chinese army.
suyūrghal: Tīmūrid military fief.
swāyiḥ: Arab nomads of the semi-desert.
sword of ᶜAlī: popular Islamic symbol of sword with double-blade.

ṭabaqa (plural *ṭibāq*): training school for mamlūk recruits, Arabic.
ṭabarzīn: cavalry axe, Arabic.
ṭabīᶜa: concrete, used in fortifications, Arabic.
taᶜbiya: Arab Islamic small, closely packed cavalry formation.
tabᶜīyya: ordinary soldier in the ᶜAbbāsid army.
ṭablkhānah: corps of drummers, Arabic.
tabonas: 'cutting-stones', weapons of Guanches people of Canary Islands.
ṭabr: battle-axe, Persian.
tafurs: association of 'poor knights' on First Crusade.
tagma: Byzantine small tactical and administrative unit.
tagmata: Byzantine palace regiments based around Constantinople.
taifa: fragmented small kingdoms in Muslim Iberia.
talayeros: scouts, Christian Iberia.
ṭalᶜīya: isolated tower or beacon, Arabic.
talus: anti-mining revetment or slope at the base of a fortified wall.
tamgha: Turkish tribal motif.
tang-hsiung: horse-armour chest protection China.
tankō: early Japanese scale armour.
tanūrigh: heavy armour of heavy Sassanian cavalry, lit. 'baking oven'.
ṭarāda: Red Sea cargo raft.
tarbūsh: fur-lined hat of military élite, Turco-Arabic (see also *sharbūsh*).
ṭarīda: specialised horse-transport galley, Arabic.
taride: specialized horse-transport galley, Crusader States.
ṭārīqah: kite-shaped shield, Arabic.
tashtīna, tishtanī: probably a rigid chamfron, armour for horse's head.
tasug: smallest Sassanian territorial division.
taxeis: Byzantine military formation, probably one of three divisions.
tegheliay, tegyljaj, teghhilay: quilted soft armour, Russia.
tesek: large Russian dagger.
testinia: probably a rigid chamfron, armour for horse's head.
theme: Byzantine field army; later a territorial province with attached forces.
t'hemi: Georgian clan or provincial administration.
thorakes: Byzantine heavy armour, possibly scale or lamellar.
thorax: Romano-Byzantine cuirass.
thughūr: Islamic military frontier-province.
thuql: siege train, Arabic.
tīgh: probably a straight sword, Turco-Persion.
tijfāf: felt bard or horse-armour, also soft armour for man, Arabic.
tīmār: Ottoman fief or estate for sipāhi cavalry.
ṭirāz: embroidered panel, usually on sleeves, Arabic.
tīrbadh: officer of Sassanian infantry archer unit.
ṭirfīl: scabbard or holder for mace.
tium: Russian steward.
tobyŏngmasa: government department in later Koryŏ Korea.
topoteretes: commander of part of Byzantine provincial scholae.
ṭoprāqlī: provincial cavalry, Turkish.
tös: totemic ensigns, Turkish.
tourkapouli: Byzantine troops of Turkish origin (see also *turcopoles*).
toxobolistron: Byzantine frame-mounted crossbow.
trapezitai: Byzantine light cavalry.
trebuchet: counterweight beam-sling stone-throwing machine.
tribune: early Byzantine middle ranking officer.
tu'an: large section of a Chinese militia army.
t'u-chiang: probably heavy cavalry of T'ang Chinese army.
tüfenk: early hand gun, Turkish.
tug, tūgh, tuq: yak-tailed pennant or standard, Turco-Mongol.
tu-hu-fu: frontier protectorate of T'ang China.
tui: middle-sized section of a Chinese militia army.
ṭulb: platoon, Arabic.
tūmān: Arabised version of Mongol *tümen*, Tīmūrid unit of 10,000 men.
tümen: Mongol military unit of 10,000 men.
turcopole: light cavalry fighting in Middle Eastern style, originally of captive Muslim origin (see also *tourkapouli*).
tūreh: large shield, Perso-Mongol.
turma: Byzantine brigade.
turmach: commander of a Byzantine turma.
turna-fuye: tactics of repeated charge and withdrawal in Christian Iberia (see also *karr wa farr*).
turs: shield, usually wooden, Arabic.
tysiacha: Russian unit of 1,000 men.
tysiatski: Russian militia leader, or commander of *tysiacha*.
tyuphak: gun or cannon, Russian.
tzaggra: Byzantine crossbow (see also *zanggra*).
tzaggratores: Byzantine crossbowmen.
tzakones: late Byzantine infantry from southern Greece.
tzaousios: officer in command of late Byzantine garrison.
tzarchat: Byzantine large crossbow.
tzouloukonai: late Byzantine military servants.
tzykanion: Polo, Byzantine.

uc: frontier province or march of Ottoman state.
ūd: Arab original of lute.
uissier: large transport ship, Crusader States.
ükek: fortified flanking tower, Turkish Central Asia.
ulu: Mongol military region, usually on frontier.
ulu bey: Turco-Mongol frontier commander.
ushkúynik: river pirates, Russia.
usṭūl: naval squadrons, Arabic.
uṭum: Arabic oasis communal tower fort.

vaiśya: commoner caste of Hindu states.
vălări kămbi: boomerang of Maravar warrior caste, southern India.
Varangians: Byzantine guard regiment of Scandinavian and Anglo-Saxon origin (see also *varjazi*).
varhranīghān-khvadhāy: Sassanian guard unit, 'Immortals'.
varjazi: mercenaries of Scandinavian origin in Russia (see also *Varangians*).
vasht: Sassanian battalion or regiment and its flag.
veche: Russian town council.
vedas: Hindu religious texts.
vestiarion: Byzantine state factory producing fire-weapons and siege engines.
vexillum: Banner hanging vertically, late Roman.
vicar: civilian governor of Crusader Greece under Angevins.
vicar general: civilian governor of Crusader Greece under Catalan and Aragonese rule.
viglatores: network of observers covering main invasion routes, Byzantium.
vilayat: province, Persian.
viseria, visal: helmet with face protection, Spanish.
vizier: chief minister, Arabic.
voevoda: overall commander of a Russian army.
voi: tribal levy and later rural infantry levy, Russia.
voynug, voynuk: Balkan Christian auxiliary cavalry in Ottoman army (see also *wojnūq*).
vuzurg-framādhār: Sassanian Chief Minister; also army commander in early centuries.
waggenburg: wagons arranged to provide field fortifications, originally German.
wajihdar: regular troops in Delhi Sultanate.
wālī: Islamic provincial governor.
wei: élite guards of T'ang China; cavalry of Yüan Mongol Chinese army; brigade of Ming Chinese army.
wen: civil authorities in China.
wi: guard battalion in army of Koryŏ Korea.
wilāyat: province, Arabic.
win: regiment of guard troops in later medieval Burma.
winhmu: commander of regiment of guard troops in later medieval Burma.
wojnūq: Balkan Christian auxiliary cavalry in Ottoman army (see also *voynug, voynuk*).
wu: military authorities in China.
wūsfana: black slave troops, 11th-century al-Andalus.

xamete: cloth covering of armour, later medieval Spain.
xingjun: mobile army, Chinese.
xulokastron: ship's fighting forecastle, Byzantine.

yalba: possibly padded leather soft-armour, Arabic.
yang-ma-ch'eng: lower outer wall of Chinese fortifications.
yangmin: free class, also providing non-noble troops in Koryŏ, Korea.
yāsā: Turco-Mongol tribal law.
yat: magic employed to change the weather with the aid of 'rain-stones', Turco-Mongol (see also *jada*).
yaya: early Ottoman infantry.
yazak: advance guard of selected cavalry, Arabic.
Yeni Çeri: Ottoman infantry élite, recruited from converted Christian population.
yeniçeri ağasi: commander of *Yeni Çeri* corps.
yng-tien: military-agricultural colonies of Sung China.
yoldash: ordinary soldier, members of *Yeni Çeri* corps.
yu-hsia: wandering warriors or knights errant in Chinese literature.
yürüks: Turkish Muslim nomads of the southern Balkans.
yuz bashi: Tīmūrid leader of 100 men.
yuzliq: Tīmūrid unit of 100 men.

zaba: mail hauberk, Byzantine.
zabareion: arms factory, Byzantine.
zadruga: extended family in early medieval Russia.
zaḥāfah: probably a fixed wooden tower for archers, Arabic.
zamt: small red cap of later Mamlūk military élite.
zanggra: Byzantine crossbow (see also *tzaggra*).
zaqāzīq: spiked hurdles used as field fortification, Arabic.
zardiyah: mail hauberk, Arabic.
zardkhāna: arsenal, Arabic.
zarība: obstacle of woven vine stems, willow osiers or brambles as field fortification.
zarrāqat al-nafṭ: siphon for propelling Greek Fire, Arabic.
zarrāqbūn: fire-throwers, Arabic.
zasapozhniki: Russian dagger.
zāwiya: house designated for troops or volunteers; barracks, Arabic.
zembūrek: arrow-guide used when shooting short darts, Turco-Persian (see also *semberek*).
zertzallo: mail-and-plate cuirass, Russia.
zhen: garrison, Chinese.
zhouzhou: small T'ang Chinese army.
zirh: mail hauberk, Persian.
zirh-i çuqal: probably mail-and-plate cuirass, Turkish.
zirh külah: mail coif or mail-and-plate helmet, Turkish.
zūpīn: heavy javelin of Daylami infantry.
zuṭṭ: warlike community in medieval India, later known as *jāts*.

INDEX

a la brida: 153
abaan: 140
Abkhazians: 15
abnā: 16, 55, 56, 68, 73
aboriginal peoples: 187, 191, 201
abṭāl: 71, 157
Abū'l-Jund canal: 256
Abyssinia, Abyssinians (see Ethiopia, Ethiopians)
academy, military: 192
acatenaria: 87
acatia: 87
Acre: 47, 131, 158-8, 170, 173, 178, 180, 242, 277
adalid: 145, 246
adarga de lante: 163
adnoumia: 59
adoha: 133
adrumunun: 87
Aegean islands: 148, 180; Aegean sea: 137, 152, 167, 179, 242, 255, 268, 275
Aethiopians (see also Ethiopians): 29, 72
Afghanistan, Afghans: 11, 14, 17, 29, 38, 78, 104-5, 120, 134, 153, 171, 195, 260, 263, 290
Africa, Africans: 16, 18, 125, 136, 140, 163, 199, 205, 209, 213, 220, 242, 259, 271, 291; "African drill": 32; east: 288-9; possibility of sailing around: 182; slave troops, near worship of Caliph: 260; sub-Saharan: 57-8, 73, 153, 159, 218, 289; west: 125, 136, 149, 161, 163, 182, 218
Aghlabids: 58, 274
aghlumi: 131
aḥābīsh: 15
ahdath: 57-8, 65-6, 135, 146
aḥi: 137
ahl al-khūrāsān: 62
ahl al-shām: 17, 24, 44, 55
Aḥmad Ibn Ṭūlūn: 281
ahmudan: 190, 194
Aisha: 278
akatia: 87
akinji: 138
Akoluthos: 142
akrites, akritoi: 60, 63, 142
al: 116
alami: 278
Alans: 13, 15, 76, 94-97, 109, 129-30, 136, 189: "Alan drill": 32
alay: 149
alay bey: 149
Albania, Albanians: 41, 54, 60, 87, 130, 142, 152, 215, 291
albarrana: 83, 172-3, 176
alcalde: 145
Alcazabar: 176
alcohol: 267
Aleppo: 41, 57, 65, 81, 135, 171, 213
Alexander Nevski: 96, 105, 119, 213
Alexander's Wall: 43
Alexandria: 33, 41, 47, 244, 268, 274, 296
alfaquequas: 242
alferez mor: 145
Alfonso el Sabio, king: 155; Alfonso VII: 134
algara: 67, 151
algarada: 67
algarrada: 176
Algarve: 66, 140, 182, 260
Algeciras: 88, 296
Algeria: 15, 178, 296
alguazil: 182
all sensile, spacing of oars: 178
allagion: 141-2, 154
Almanzor: 216
almenara: 80
Almeria: 172, 182, 277, 291
almocaden: 145
almofar: 163
almogavar: 134, 145, 158, 166, 178, 180
Altai mountains: 75, 97, 288
Alwah: 24, 153
amīn: 237
Amīr: 62, 65, 102-3, 146-50, 158; amīr al-juyūsh: 65; amīr al-umarā': 62, 65; Amīr of the First Class: 285; Amīr of the Second Class: 285
amṣār: 24
amaram: 194
ambāragh: 21
ambush tactics: 72, 157
Amde-Siyon I: 213
Amlash: 16
Amman: 44, 48
Amorium: 85
Amu Darya: 122
An Lu-Shan: 105, 189, 192
Anadolu Kavagi: 172, 279
Anatolia: 13, 67, 26, 51, 60-2, 80, 104, 130-3, 137-8, 142, 148-50, 163-7, 171, 181, 219, 242, 245, 259, 263-4, 268, 272, 275, 282, 288, 296
Anatolikon: 218
Anavarza/ᶜAin Zarba: 80
Anawrahta, king: 190, 194
anbār: 42
andaghān: 16
Andalus, Andalusians: 25, 67, 76, 82, 134, 140, 149, 156, 157-159, 161, 163-5, 173, 178, 182, 215-6, 239-40, 246, 251, 263, 266, 271, 280-1, 287, 294
Andaman islands: 219
Andronikos III, Byzantine Emperor: 217
Angevins: 133, 145, 158, 291-2
Anglo-Saxons: 24, 59, 95, 129
Ankara: 41, 80, 86; battle of: 108
Annam: 187
Antes: 290
anti-rigging weapons: 88
Anti-Taurus mountains: 25
Antioch: 13, 41, 131, 134, 219, 242, 244, 247, 290
antiseptic: 257
Anushirvan: 220
apatih: 194
apellido: 67, 145
Aphrodisias: 35
aplekta: 195
Apulia: 68
aq börk: 286; Aq Quyunlī: 138, 148
Aqaba, Gulf of: 19, 47, 276
aquaduct: 80, 238; fortified: 171
Arğin: 98
Arabia: 11, 15, 19, 23, 29, 37, 43, 58, 62, 68, 79-80, 135, 146, 149, 153, 209, 259, 267-8, 272, 290-1; Arabian Gulf: 47, 81, 87, 273, 275, 288, 291, 296; pre-Islamic: 236, 243, 261, 265, 272, 278, 290-1; southern (see Yemen)
Arabs: 14-6, 24, 32, 38-9, 44, 46, 51, 53, 55-9, 62, 66, 72, 93, 129, 131, 134-6, 138, 152-3, 157-8, 161-2, 170, 180, 189-90, 213, 215, 217, 241, 245, 251, 258, 264-5, 267-8, 270-1, 273-4, 281, 285, 288-9, 291; Arab-Khurāsān is: 55; literature: 263
Aragon, Aragonese: 60, 66, 134, 145, 151, 215, 217, 296; fleet: 178, 180
Arakanese: 190, 210
Aramaeans: 14
archery: 246; accuracy of: 246; belief that soul resided in thumb: 244; by volleys: 73; draw techniques: 34; finger draw, Persian: 73; flight shooting: 74, 250; archer's hand protection: 36, 73-4; horse archery: 18, 29, 31, 34, 57-8, 62, 68-73, 96, 101, 104-6, 109, 116, 140, 142, 146, 153, 158, 185, 195, 198, 243, 248-9, 260; horse, contests: 260; horse, dispersal tactics: 68, 104, 156; horse, harrassment tactics: 104; horse, static ranks: 68; Indian: 197; infantry: 16, 29-32, 51, 60, 68-72, 96, 131, 136, 140, 146, 155-8, 193, 197, 246; infantry, mounted: 192; naval: 88; archer, on elephants: 195; shooting beneath shield: 28, 158, 163; shower shooting: 33, 156; sniping: 159, 205; speed of: 31, 73, 156; squatting: 157; styles of: 34; superhuman: 264; target bracketing: 159; thumb draw: 34, 73, 158; thumb ring: 74; training: 28, 251
architects: Muslim: 171; talismanic architecture: 82
archontes: 129, 133; archontes foideraton: 19
Arctic Sea: 91, 101, 122, 273; sub-Arctic: 291
Ardashir I: 278
ari: 261
Arianism: 13, 258
Arimaddanapura: 187, 194
ariwurikᶜ: 135
armament support organization: 194
Armenia: 13-4, 17, 19, 38, 46, 51, 53-4, 57-8, 60, 64, 80-1, 95-6, 98, 129-37, 140, 142, 153, 180, 213, 215, 244, 247, 263, 278, 288, 291
arming coat: 284
armour; armour bearer: 282; Armour Board, Office: 291, 294; beneath clothes: 236; brass: 291; copper: 291; decorated: 218; fabric covered: 202; leather: 291; pseudo-Roman: 98; talismanic elements: 116; waterproofing: 202: armourers: 149, 191; armourers, aboard ship: 178; arms bazaars: 292; arms, price of: 292
army, mixed: 134
arriere ban: 131
arrow; arrow making (see also bowyer): 290-1; armour-piercing 198: arrow-guide: 36, 74, 199; bone arrowheads: 109, 161; fired from cannon: 296; Indian: 161; magical properties: 109; poisoned: 73, 153; sharpening: 290; slits, fortification: 80; specialized arrowheads: 161; whistling: 266
Arsūf: 157
arsenal: 20-1, 24, 294; naval: 140, 169, 180
artīshtārānsālār: 21, 23
Arthashastra: 187, 191
artillery; observers: 206; naval: 87
Arumoli: 218
Aryans: 185, 283
asāwira: 16-7
Asad Ibn ᶜAbd Allāh: 105
asbestos cloth: 202
Ash'arayin: 281
ashrāf: 24
asis: 200
assassination: 129, 195, 267
Assassins (see also Ismᶜīlīs): 146, 259
astrologers: 261
Asturias: 54, 60, 67
asvārān: 15-6, 21, 23; asvārān-sardār: 23
Aswan: 48, 65
atābeg: 135, 146; atābak al-ᶜ asākir: 147; atābak amīr kabīr: 148
atalaya: 80, 83, 172
atbāiᶜ: 99
athanatoi: 59
Atharvaveda: 194, 197, 258, 261
atillerymen, Muslim: 189
atlab al-mīra: 146
Atlantic: 51, 58, 66, 140-1, 173, 180, 182, 218
Atshān: 41
attack & withdrawal, repeated (see also karr wa farr): 106
ausconas: 163
avak baron: 143
Avars: 20, 34, 36-7, 79, 106, 271, 275, 277-8, 284,
aventail: 36-8, 76, 148, 164; face covering: 76, 107, 113; mail: 112
Avesta: 264
Avila: 134, 171
awasim: 62-3, 67, 80
'Awfāt: 149
awlād al-nās: 147
axe: 37, 70, 72, 75, 153; anti-rigging: 181; at sea: 88; cavalry: 75, 109; infantry: 109
Axum: 15, 24, 41, 215
Aydin: 181, 246
aymak: 103
Ayyūbids: 135, 146, 152-3, 157, 159, 171, 250, 253, 266, 268, 278, 285-6
azab: 286
azaga: 151
azap: 181
Azarbayjan: 21, 104, 264, 288
azaria: 67
azat: 143
azatani: 13
azatk': 60
azconas: 163
Azores: 88, 182
āzādayān: 57
āzātān: 13

bāb: 159; Bāb al-Abwāb: 42; Bāb al-Naṣr: 82; Bāb Wustani: 170

Babayn, battle of: 105
bad breath, of soldiers: 256
Badr al-Jamālī: 58
baggage train: 150
Baghdad: 41, 55, 62-3, 68, 85, 117-8, 135, 161, 169, 220, 256, 267-8, 291, 293; Round City: 62, 80
bahādur: 103
Bahmanids: 146
Bahrām: 213
Baḥrī Mamlūks: 136
bailli, baillie: 143-5; bailiff: 145
bakeries: 242
Baktashi: 260, 264
bakufu: 194
baldric: 20, 25, 33, 141, 161
Balearic islands: 179, 217, 274
Bali: 205
baliq: 118
Balkans: 13, 53-4, 70, 110, 125, 130, 138, 140-2, 149, 152-3, 159, 163, 173, 242, 255, 260, 270, 273, 278, 290-1, 293
Balkh: 105
ballista: 74, 173
Baltic: 96, 101
banda, bandon: 60, 277; banderoles: 283
bands, military: 266; mounted: 266
banj: 267
banneret: 143
banners: 152, 194
Bantu: 125
Banū Ḥanīfah: 23; Banū Kilāb: 57, 68; Banū Munqidh: 220; Banu ʿUqayl: 57
Bāra, al-: 173
Barbastro: 242
barbican: 83
barce: 87
Barcelona: 145, 178, 242, 277
bard: 167
barge, as floating mangonel battery: 180; coastal: 180, 277; oared: 87
Barghawata: 51, 58
bargustuwān: 79
barīd: 267-8
Barın: 98
barka: 87
barmitsa: 112
Barqīya: 58
barracks: 21, 64, 145, 244
barricade, of upturned ships: 277
barricades, pre-fabricated: 198
bārūd: 294
bary, heraldic motif: 281
bashak: 98, 101, 103
bashi: 103
Bashjirt, Bashkir: 91, 94, 98; Outer Bashjirt: 91
bāshūra: 80
Basil I, Emperor: 87
Basra: 88,
batailles: 144
Bāṭilis: 58
baṭn al-ḥajar: 72, 143,
batraq: 283
battering rams: 84-5
battle cry: 72
battle, as form of divine judgement: 235; Battle of the Masts: 47
Bay of Biscay: 88
Bayazit I, Ottoman: 139
Baybars: 246
bayḍah: 76, 163
bayl: 143
bayt al-māl: 24, 253
bazabanag: 38; bāzī kand, bāzū band: 38, 78, 167
beacon: 83, 168, 195, 267-8
beak, naval weapon: 87
beam-sling device to drop projectiles: 206
bedouin, 11, 15-6, 21, 26-7, 32, 41, 58, 65, 68-9, 99, 135-6, 140, 153, 183, 245, 251, 265, 268, 271
beg: 216
Beirut: 144, 268, 290
Beja: 15, 31, 37, 48, 125, 153
Belarus: 91, 262
bells: 265-6; as perimeter warning device: 73
bellum: 67
belt & hook, crossbow spanning: 160; decorative pendants: 62; mark of rank or status: 285; military: 287; silver: 287
Belvoir, 168-9
Bengal: 191, 205
bent entrance, gate: 41, 173
Berbers: 11, 13, 15-7, 20, 28, 30, 32, 37-8, 43, 46, 51, 56-9, 62, 66, 69, 76, 125, 140, 149, 153, 163, 166-7, 220, 237, 239, 262, 266, 287
beredarioi: 267
Berends: 96, 109
Bereznyaki: 119
berutta: 75
bey: 103, 148-9; beylerbey: 102-3, 159; beylik: 137-8, 142, 148, 179, 181
beyraq: 283
bhastrā: 199
bhṛitaka: 191
biffa: 173
Biīa: 55
Bilbays: 171
bingbu: 192
binliq: 103
Biqāʿ: 136
birds, heraldic: 281
birjas: 251
Bīrūnī, al-: 198, 290
bit: 271; palate: 167
Bithynia: 20, 130
bitumen: 294
Black Sea: 38, 47, 73, 78, 80, 93, 98, 125, 130, 137, 152, 179, 181, 215, 255, 270, 291
Blemye: 15, 24, 48
blockade: 47, 85; blockship: 277
blood-feud: 243
blowgun, blowpipe: 201
Board of War: 194, 202, 246
boarding, naval: 47, 87
boats, multidecked: 205; prefabicated: 276
Bogomils: 53
bojarskye deti: 97
bomb, iron: 296
bombard, cannon: 296
bone rank: 189
Book of Dede Korkut: 264
books; on naval tactics: 181; burning of: 242
boomerang: 201
booty, division of: 103, 236, 239
Borneo: 291
Borobudur: 192
Bosnia: 152
Bosphorus: 172, 275, 279
boves: 176
bow; bowcase: 36, 38; making: 118, 290-1; master: 282; Arab: 36, 64, 74, 153, 249; Avar: 36; composite: 29, 36, 72-4, 153, 159, 181, 199; infantry: 272; pellet: 161; Persian: 74, 249; simple: 29, 36, 72-3, 153, 159, 199; simple cane: 161; simple longbow: 152; Turkish: 74, 159; Ugrian: 109; bow, waterproofed: 199; wooden composite: 109
bowstring, cotton: 159; grass: 287
boyar: 96, 100, 242
bozdağan, bozṭoghan: 109
brafoneras, braoneras, brassonieras, brofuneras: 167
brahman, brahmins: 189-90, 239, 261
brazos: 145
bribery: 245
bridge: 151; floating: 80, 273; bridging equipment: 273
Bridisi: 87
bridle: 153, 271; bozal: 38
brigandine: 116, 166, 202
British Isles: 88, 182
brodniki: 122
bron'a: 116
bronze: 75; lamellar armour: 78
brothels: 205
brother knight: 132, 144, 154, 159, 168, 284, 292,
brother sergeant: 284
brotherhoods, Greek Christian: 142
brunja: 116
bucellarii: 19, 20
Buddhism, Buddhists: 11, 51, 53, 68, 93-4, 97, 100, 106, 185, 187, 190, 197, 203, 238, 244, 246, 260-1, 283; Mahayana: 187; monks: 194; temples, militarized: 194
budluq: 167
buffalo: 156, 159, 273
buheradas: 83
bukaul: 101
Bukhara: 17, 56, 246
Bulgar, city of: 112
Bulgaria, Bulgarians; of Balkans: 91, 140, 164, 242; Great: 94, 99; Volga Bulgars: 91, 94, 99, 108-9, 112, 118, 129, 242, 291, 293
Būna: 296
bunduq: 74
burdas: 167
Bureau; of Armaments: 296; of Military Affairs: 193, 246
Burgundy, Burgundians: 132-3, 171
burial of dead: 257
burj: 46, 83, 85, 171, 178,
burjās (see also birjas): 248
Burjī Mamlūks: 136
Burma, Burmese: 107, 185, 187, 190, 195-9, 208, 210, 261, 296
Bursa: 149
bürüme: 166
burūz: 66
bushi: 238; bushidō: 238
Busra: 152
Buwayhids: 56-7, 65, 68, 253
buzgan, buzogány: 109
Byzantine Empire, Byzantines: 11, 16, 58, 75-6, 98, 102, 106, 108, 112, 116, 125, 137-40, 145, 149-54, 157-70, 172-3, 178, 180, 213, 215, 217-8, 239-45, 248, 253-9, 263-4, 268-78, 284-6, 288, 290-4; fleet: 131, 246; law: 241; literature: 265; fashion influence: 284

cabalgada: 152
caballeria: 54, 60; caballeros hidalgos: 60; caballeros villanos: 54, 60, 134, 145
cacolets: 258
caique: 122
Cairo: 62, 65, 81, 88, 136, 147, 213, 218, 238, 268, 282, 291; Citadel: 146, 171, 250
calcar: 181
Caliph, Caliphate: 216, 288
calthrops: 33, 35, 73, 108, 197
Cambodia: 174, 187
camel: 24, 28-31, 153, 158, 240, 245, 265, 268, 271-3; as command post: 72; Bactrian: 103-4, 272-3; bukhti: 272; carrying banner: 282; carrying burning material: 108; carrying fodder: 104; corps: 273; hide: 290; hobbled as field fortification: 35; litters: 258; saddle, wood-framed: 29
camisa: 167
camouflage clothing: 70, 285, 288
camp-fires: 154, 159
campus martius: 246, 250
canal, from Caspian Sea to Amu Darya: 122; from Nile to Red Sea: 48, 88; opening of: 65; transport: 273
Canary islands: 88, 125, 149, 153, 159, 182
candidati: 18
cannibalism: 246
cannon: 296; bronze: 199; hand-: 295-6; iron: 199
canoes, war: 182
canon law: 235-6
cantonments: 24
Cap Blanc: 88
cap, quilted: 287; white: 138
caparison: 144, 283
Cape Chelidonia: 47
Cape Verde Islands: 88, 182
Cappadocia: 26
captives, as agricultural labour: 242
caracca: 87
caravan, merchant: 27; caravan (raid): 144, 150; caravanserai: 171
caravel, caravela, caravo: 182
Carpathian mountains: 93
carrack: 87
Carthage: 20, 29, 47
cartouche: 282
carts, as barricade: 173; bullock: 272-3
Caspian aea: 15, 42-3, 122, 182, 215; coast: 57
cassot: 167
caste system: 189-91
castellae: 41
castellan: 145
Castile, Castilians: 54, 60, 66-7, 134, 145, 151, 155, 163, 215, 240, 277, 281, 296; fleet: 180, 182
Castles; Castle of Forty Columns: 170; Crusader: 150; intervisibility between: 196
castra, castrae, castron: 41, 67, 80
Catalans, Catalonia: 60, 66, 131-2, 140, 167, 180, 236, 242, 290, 292; Catalan Grand Company: 145
catargha: 179
Caucasus mountains: 14-5, 38, 42, 57, 76, 93, 95-8, 104, 117, 130, 136, 260, 271, 278, 288, 290
caus: 142
cavaleiros: 134; vilaos: 54, 134
cavalgada: 67
cavallers: 134
cavalry; close combat: 29; formations: 29; heavy: 68, 105-7, 117, 153-4; light: 68, 117, 131, 134, 140, 149-55, 158, 254; reassembling of: 266; rise in importance of: 60; shock tactics: 70; spear, use of: 158-9
Çavuşin: 54
cebe: 165; cebe cevşen: 166
censors: 192
Central Asia: 45, 156, 161, 237-8, 244, 248, 261, 266, 271, 273, 283, 287, 291; influence of: 31, 73, 203
Ceuta: 88, 173
ch'in chun wei: 194
ch'ing: 205
cha: 198
chabalakhi: 163
chahārāʿīnah: 116
chain, floating harbour defences: 88, 170; iron harbour defence: 277
Chal Tarkhan Ishkabad: 265
chalkotouba: 79
Chalukya: 288
chamfron: 80, 118, 167
Champa: 187, 189, 201, 277
Champagne: 132
champions, military: 32, 34, 72, 215
Changan: 205
chansons de geste: 257, 263, 281
chapel-tent: 159
chākarān: 99
charge, cavalry: 154, 155, 157; repeated: 107
chariot: 29, 194, 196, 284; horses, armoured: 204
charkh: 74, 160; charkh kamān: 109
Charlemagne: 195
chartoularios: 60
chatelains: 144
chatris: 205
chats chateaux: 174
chaturanga: 251
chausses: 167; mail: 79
checky, heraldic motif: 132, 281
cheiropsella: 78
cheirotoxobolistrai: 85
chekan: 109
chelandre, chelandrion: 87, 180, 274
cheng: 192
Cherkess: 98
Chernigov: 216
Cherniye Klobuki: 96,

101, 113, 109, 112, 239
cheroptia: 167
chess: 217, 251
chevaliers de la terre: 131
chevauchee: 150
chevetaine: 145
chi-hsiang: 204
chichak: 112
chief astrologer: 198; chief carpenter: 198; chief of police: 148; chief secretary: 282
children, immunity of: 236
chin-chun: 193
Chin: 193, 204
China, Chinese: 37-8, 45, 55, 70, 74-5, 80, 83, 85, 87, 91, 97, 99-100, 102, 105, 108, 112, 114, 120, 134, 155, 159, 163, 167, 171, 174, 176, 182, 184, 188-91, 195-203, 209, 213, 217-8, 235, 238, 243-8, 251, 255, 258, 260, 264-75, 284, 287-8, 291, 294-6; "Chinese Arrow," incendiary weapon: 85; influence of: 93, 101, 104-5, 111, 194, 196, 198; maritime technology: 87; navy: 189; "Chinese Salt": 294; "Chinese Snow": 294; Turkestan: 65
Chinghiz Khan (see Genghis Khān); Chingizid family: 102
Chionites: 14
chivalric ideals: 263
cho: 194
chokuto: 200
Cholas: 209, 218
Cholli Castle: 204
chong: 194
chosarion: 51
Christian Church; Coptic: 259; Latin Catholic: 242, 259; Melkite Syrian: 144; Monophysite: 13, 125, 259; Nestorian: 51, 93, 260; Orthodox: 96-7, 142, 213, 235, 259; Syriac: 131; Syrian Jacobite: 131
Christianity, Christians: 13-6, 23-4, 48, 57, 63, 82, 94, 130, 140, 213, 215, 218, 242, 259, 267, 284; Arab: 17, 131; Iberian: 59; conversion to Islam: 259; doctors: 257; scribes: 65; troops, in Ottoman service: 139
Chronicle of the Wars of Amde-Siyon I: 213
chun: 192; chun-fang: 191
chung-bang: 194
churches, built as political statement: 168; fortified: 80
Cilicia: 29, 44, 47, 80, 142, 180, 243, 276; Cilician Armenia: 131, 150, 168, 278; Cilician Gates: 67; Cilician plain: 150
Circassians: 96, 136
Circuit Military Intendants: 193
cirid: 248
cirujanos: 257
cistern: 80, 83, 86; Cistern of St Helena: 86
civilians, military use of: 69
Clarence castle: 290
clay projectiles: 206
clibinarii: 18
climatic factors: 29, 196; impact on armaments: 202
cloth-of-gold: 143
clothing, flame-proof: 73
"cloud ladder": 205
club (weapon): 76, 147
coast; demilitarization: 181; bombardment: 87, 180; observation system: 88, 181
coat of a thousand nails: 116, 202; coat of arms: 144, 281; coat of plates: 114, 116, 166, 202
coif: 76, 78; mail: 57
coirasses: 166
collacita: 145
colonies, military: 241-2
colonization, Indian: 185, 187
colour symbolism: 283
combat, ritual: 264
combined operations (land & sea): 68
comes: 60
Comilla: 191
comit, comitatus: 19; comites: 141, 182
command structure: 145
commander, treatment of defeated: 244; qualities needed: 259; Commander of Ships: 180
Commanderie of Cyprus: 144
communal treasury: 24
communes: 133; Italian merchant: 170; peasant: 54
communications: 104, 139, 157; battlefield: 34; long-distance: 28; riverine: 210
commutation: 145
Comnenids: 129, 141, 158, 167, 172, 277
compensation for injury: 236
conch shell trumpet: 266
concrete, 172-3
Condestabre: 145
condomae: 15
confraternity: 131, 144; military: 134; of Sts George and Belian: 144
Confucianism: 238, 260, 264
connetable: 143-4
conscription, rural: 189
Constable: 141
Constans II, Byzantine Emperor: 86
Constantine IX, Emperor: 54
Constantinople (Istanbul): 13, 19-20, 29, 41, 44-8, 59-60, 62, 66, 130-1, 142, 150, 152, 163, 167, 242, 255, 260, 267-70, 275, 277, 291-2
continuity, technological: 31
Convent: 145; Conventual Prior: 144
conversion, of mortally wounded: 242
convicts, conscription of: 189
Copts: 17, 20
corazas: 166
çorbaci başi: 149
cord & pulley, to span crossbow: 160
Cordoba: 58, 66, 215, 219, 250, 288, 291-2; Cordoba Calendar: 68
coronel: 145
corpses, washing of: 242
corredura: 67
Corsica: 61
Cossacks: 96-9, 122
cotton; armour: 202; soaked as defence against fire weapons: 87
couched lance: 112, 158-9, 246
Count of the Walls: 60
counter-city, as siege base: 178; counter-mining: 208; counter espionage: 236, 246; counter raiding: 150, 152
County of Edessa: 144; County of Tripoli: 144, 180
coups, fear of: 59
cow's nest: 182
cows, ridden: 69
Cremona: 218
crescent, heradic: 282; & star, heraldic: 280
Crete: 87-8, 131, 293
criers: 266
Crimea: 22, 93, 95, 98, 129-30, 179, 181
"cross spear": 201
crossbow: 74, 81, 88, 107, 151, 153, 159-61, 167, 196, 199, 206, 249, 253, 288, 291; aiming of: 159; bolt, all-iron: 121; bolts, boxed: 294; clip: 158, 160; Crossbow Office: 291; crossbow, "doubled": 174, 196; "foot bow": 74; frame mounted: 200; infantry: 153, 197; inside shield: 163; large, on wheels: 173; limitations on aiming: 74; multi-shot, 200; naval: 178, 180-2; on elephant: 174, 195-6; on horseback: 133, 138, 140, 153, 160, 200, 251, 253; on wheeled carriage: 174; rate of shooting: 158, 197; training: 251; "triple": 200; woods needed to make: 288
crossbowmen: 98, 140, 142, 145, 153, 155, 244, 277; western European: 134
Crusade, Crusaders: 58, 78, 85, 105, 131, 143, 146, 150, 155, 158-9, 163, 170, 173, 178-80, 182, 220, 240, 242, 244-5, 253, 255, 259-60, 266-8, 276, 284, 286, 288, 293-4; First: 58, 131, 143, 157, 242, 259, 270, 272-3; Third: 150, 155, 176; Fourth: 130, 274, 292; Baltic: 114, 121; Crusader Cross: 284; fleets: 265; Cyprus Crusader state: 132, 145; Greece: 130, 132-3, 145, 158, 170, 253, 290, 292; States: 129, 131, 136, 143, 146, 148, 150, 153, 159, 163, 165-8, 179-80, 215, 241, 247, 257, 263, 265, 268, 271, 274, 278, 290, 292; States, settlement in: 131; States, shortage of food: 255; failure of: 236
Ctesiphon: 277
Cuenca: 64
cuisse: 167
cultivated areas, damage to: 235, 237
cuneos, cuneus: 30, 34
cup-bearer: 282
çuqal: 165
curabii: 87
cursores: 29, 33, 71, 157
customary rules (military): 28
cymbals: 265-6
Cyprus: 13, 53, 125, 132, 141, 167, 170, 181, 216, 278
Cyrenaica: 41

ᶜ-f-l-k: 48
ᶜ-s-d-q: 48
ᶜaṣā : 25
ᶜaṭā: 253
ᶜaṣ abīah: 25,
ᶜabīd: 59
ᶜAbbāsid Caliphate, ᶜAbbāsids: 18, 25, 34, 44, 51, 54, 70, 79, 85, 88, 135, 146, 161, 162, 193, 195, 253, 256, 258-9, 270-1, 278, 280-4
ᶜAbd al-ḥamīd Ibn Yaḥyā: 248
ᶜAbd al-Malik al-Muẓaffar: 219
ᶜAbd al-Malik, Caliph: 25
ᶜAbd Allāh Ibn Yasin: 220
ᶜAin Ḥabīs: 170
ᶜAin Ḥabīs: 41
ᶜajala: 248
ᶜalam: 278
ᶜAlī, Caliph: 72
ᶜAlī Ibn Yūsuf: 182
ᶜAlids: 281
ᶜamāmah shāmīyah: 284
ᶜanaza: 278
ᶜAntar Romance: 263
ᶜaqqār: 160
ᶜarḍ: 62, 66, 253
ᶜarīf: 62, 66, 149
ᶜarūs: 47
ᶜarrāda: 47, 81, 85, 87, 122, 176
ᶜashir: 136
ᶜashīra: 25,
ᶜAsir: 43
ᶜaskar: 135, 146
ᶜawd: 31
ᶜayn: 246
ᶜAzīz, al-: 58
ᶜazzāb: 64
ᶜi-t: 24
ᶜirāfa: 24, 65, 253
ᶜUkāz: 291,
ᶜUmar, Caliph: 24
ᶜuqā b, al: 278
ᶜurāt: 68

dabbābah: 85, 178
dagger: 37, 75, 109
Daghestan: 290
dāᶜīs: 146
dalil: 246
Dalmatia: 87
Damascus: 24-5, 48, 58, 65, 80-1, 135, 146-7, 152, 173, 176, 220, 257-8, 267-8, 288-9, 291; Damascus Citadel: 148, 171
dammāja: 76
Damot: 213
damascening: 289
dancing, sexually explicit: 265
dandanāyaka, dannāyaka: 194
Danes: 129
Dānishmandids: 137; Dānishmandidnāmah: 264
Danube: 13, 80, 118; Danube Delta: 130
daojun: 192
dār: 64; dar al-ḥarb: 237; dar al-Islam: 237
daraqah: 76
Darb al-Zubaydah: 268
Darband: 42
Dardanelles: 149
dardos: 163
Darende: 67
dariᶜa: 159
daruga: 103
dastaban: 74
David IV, of Georgia: 215
David of Sassoun: 147, 263
David, Biblical king: 219
Daylamis: 15-6, 43, 56-8, 65, 68, 71-2, 75, 134
Dazimon: 73
De Velitatione: 70-1
Deccan: 207, 218, 273, 289
decoration, of arms & harness: 73
decurion: 141
defensores: 29, 33, 71, 157
defile, blocking of: 73
Delhi: 196, 205; Sultanate: 108, 134, 143, 151, 153, 167, 207, 265, 273, 281
deli: 138
demarchos: 142
Dendi Fari: 150
derbendci: 139
dervish: 134, 246, 260, 264, 282, 287
desert palaces: 44
destructiveness of war: 235, 237
devsirme: 139, 244, 251
Dhanurveda: 196
dharma: 244
dhī: 21
Dhu al-Himma: 263
Dhu Nuwās: 15, 48, 215
dhyakṣa: 194
Digenes Akritas: 263, 265
dihqān: 14, 21, 43, 55, 57, 65, 95, 99, 118
dirᶜ: 37, 78, 291
discipline: 73, 149, 153-4, 157, 213, 220, 235
disguise, for scouts: 70
dismemberment: 241
dispersal tactics: 106
display, psychological effect: 152
distillation technology: 294
ditches, fortified: 42
divine ancestry, of rulers: 260; Divine Intervention: 259; Divine Punishment: 259
dīwān: 24, 25-6, 143, 149, 181; al-ᶜarḍ: 146; al-barid: 65; al-iqṭaᶜ: 253; al-jaysh: 17, 62, 65, 146, 149, 253; al-mushrif: 65, 246; al-rawātib: 253
Diyarbakr: 56, 81, 84
djadchvi: 165
djavshan: 166
djayi: 143
Dnieper river: 118
doganci: 140
dogs, heraldic: 281
Domestic: 20, 60
Don Juan Manuel: 151, 155
Don river: 118, 216-7
donjon: 172
donkey: 198, 270, 272-3
dorka: 76
Douro river: 60
doux: 142
drafsh: 21, 283; Drafsh-i Kāvyān: 283
dragon, heraldic: 281; dragon banner: 277
drapier: 144
Dravidians: 13, 185, 191, 283
drill, parade: 247

drinking water, aboard ship: 182
dromon: 87
drosha: 278
droungoi: 60
drugs: 267
drum: 65, 103, 265-6, 283; drummers: 103, 194; groups: 266; master: 34; signal: 157; small attached to saddle: 266
drungarios: 141
drury: 278
druzhina: 96-7, 100-1, 235, 271
dubbāba: 46
Dubrovnik: 291
duchy: 141
duels, individual combat: 34, 72-3; on elephant back: 198
dummy; crews of river boats: 210; elephants: 197; troops: 197; troops, on horseback: 107
Dumyat: 174, 277, 293
Durga: 200
durrāʿa: 285
Durrës: 291,
dust; military impact of: 157; raised artificially: 197
dux (duces): 18, 20, 60
dvor: 101; dvorjane: 97

eagle, double headed: 277, 281; heraldic: 281; Roman: 278
ear protections, leather: 112
Ebro, river: 60
Ecija: 158
ecology, impact of: 28, 94, 152
economic warfare: 67, 195
Edessa: 131, 219, 244; County of: 292
education: 136
eflokion: 48
Egidio Colonna: 173
Egypt, Egyptians: 13, 15-7, 20, 25, 41, 47-8, 55, 57-60, 79-81, 87, 88, 97, 116, 134-5, 140, 143, 145-50, 160, 163, 167, 171, 179-82, 213, 217, 220, 249, 251, 253, 259-60, 263, 267-8, 272-8, 281, 285-8, 290, 296; ancient: 24, 159; grain: 255; lack of timber: 181
ehzab: 24
Elburz mountains: 43
El Cid (see Rodrigo Diaz de Bivar el Campeador)
elderly, immunity of: 236
elephant: 146, 159, 194-6, 245, 261, 273; in war: 29-31, 33, 37, 56, 68, 105, 108, 153-4, 194-5, 203; armour: 29, 39, 71, 156, 167; as command post: 72; as battering ram: 85, 208; given alcohol: 267; North African forest (extinct): 29; parade: 65
elephantiasis: 257
el haz: 155
el punta: 155
el tropel: 155
Emperor Frederick: 131
Empire of Trebizond: 131
enemies, enlisting of defeated: 98
England, English: 24, 129, 131, 142, 145, 153, 156, 217, 281
enslavement, of prisoners: 242
entrenchment: 85
Epic of Prince Igor: 105, 109, 217, 278, 291
epilorikion, epilorikon: 78
Epirus, Despotate of: 142
Eregli: 73
eri: 143
Eritrea: 29, 48, 58
eschielles: 154
escuderos, escudeiros: 134, 155
esculquero: 150
espaliere: 165
espionage: 151
esplonada: 158
espringal: 74, 84, 87, 160, 176, 178
Ethiopia, Ethiopians: 15, 23-4, 28-31, 37, 41, 48, 51, 58, 125, 134, 136, 143, 147, 149-50, 153-4, 159, 213, 215, 218, 259
ethnic segregation: 191
eunuchs: 135-6, 189
Euphrates: 16, 19, 122, 273
Europe, Europeans, eastern: 55; southern: 288; western: 58, 136, 168, 290; western heraldic influence: 281; armourers, in Egypt: 291
evacuation of villages: 205
Evrenos Beg: 215
examination system, military: 189, 251
exarch: 20
excubitores: 18
exeas: 242
explosives: 85, 294
extendable ladder: 205
Extramadura: 67
Eyalet: 149

fabricae: 290
facial protection: 76
factories, state: 284
faeces, as weapon: 206
fairs, annual: 291
Fakhr al-Dī n Mubārakshāh, Fakhr-i Mudabbir Mubārakshāh: 71, 155, 161
Falasha: 213
falchion: 163
false sleeves: 286
fan-ping: 193
fan: 282
Fanchheng: 210
fangren: 191
fapi: 205
Far East, influence in ship design: 208
Farghana: 53, 260
Fars-Susiana: 21
faṣīl: 80
Fāṭima: 258
Fāṭimids: 58, 62, 66, 68-9, 72, 81, 85, 88, 135-6, 140, 146, 168, 178, 181, 213, 220, 248-54, 260, 272-4, 274, 280-6,
fauj: 103
faussar: 163
fay': 240, 253
fear: 159
feathers, in hat or helmet: 285
feigned retreat: 30, 33, 47, 158
felt; armour: 39, 789, 88; screen, to protect troops: 178
fencing; styles: 73; "Classical Grip": 34; "Italian Grip": 34, 111, 161, 167; on horseback: 159; thrusting: 109; training: 251
feringhi (Europeans): 190
Fertile Crescent: 66, 70; concentration of cities: 66
feudalism: 134, 145
Fez el Bali: 254
fidāʾīs: 146, 267
fief: 60, 65, 100, 103, 138, 143, 146, 148, 253; de soudee: 143; en besant: 143
fighting castle, on warships: 87
Filangiere: 131
filoi: 245
finial, cross form: 277; eagle shaped: 277-8
Finland, Finns: 91, 94-6, 102, 110, 117, 119, 259, 262, 291; Finno-Ugrians (see also Ugrians): 278
Firdawsi, al-: 263
fire; arrows: 206; beacons (see also beacons): 268; boats, fire ships: 88, 210, 277; grenade: 71; troops: 56, 58, 62, 73, 178; weapons: 37, 85, 105, 111, 178, 294; fireproofed clothing, 167, 202
firearms: 108, 112, 163
firind: 290
fityān: 63, 137
fixed positions, military philosophy of: 27
flag: 64, 72-3, 103, 108, 157; poles, decorated: 277
flame-thrower: 71, 295
flammula: 277
Flanders, Flemings: 129, 133, 242,
flank attacks: 153
fleuri, heldic motif: 281
fleus-de-lys: 281
flour-mill, within fortification: 87
flute: 265
fodder, for horses: 255-6
foederati: 15, 19-20, 30
foja: 166
fonsado, fonsadera: 67, 145
food, supplies in siege: 205; importantion of: 255; production for ships: 255
forest, forest zone: 28, 99, 103, 118, 150, 153, 181
formal challenge, to war: 103
fortification, bamboo: 205; brick: 80, 119, 170-1, 205; concrete: 82, 172; earth & timber or brushwood: 81, 118, 119, 204; moving of: 120; mudbrick, 44, 81, 120, 171; of non-military structures: 41, 80; reeds & clay: 207; re-use of old: 80; stone (passim); symbolic: 168-9; totemic, talismanic number combinations, etc: 82; tribal: 81; wooden: 205; governor's residence: 82; "fortress," military formation: 65; fortresses, chain of: 204; forts, frontier: 103
fossato: 67
fosse: 168
four bey system: 102
France, French: 17, 29, 53, 60, 73, 129, 132, 136, 140, 145, 150-1, 155-6, 173, 217, 242-3, 255, 263-4, 275, 281; Franks: 275; French influence: 134, 171; French Regiment: 131
fraternities, Muslim: 134
Frederick, Emperor: 277
friars: 259
Frisia: 129
frontier provinces: 24
frugality, of Ottomans: 256
fu: 192; fu-ping: 189, 191-2, 251
fueros: 235
fulk: 48
Fung: 125
"fur empire": 101
furūsīyah: 153, 155-7, 181, 247, 250-1, 295
futūwa: 63, 66, 146, 148

g-y-s: 24
g-z-w-y: 24
gadā: 201
Gagautzi: 130
Galich: 109
Galicia: 60, 182
Galilee: 219
galiotes: 180
galley: 47, 87, 179, 276; great galley: 180; horse-transport: 276; slaves: 87, 242
Ganawa: 140
Gandhara: 203
ganz: 21
garabi: 87
gargaj: 208
garrison duty: 24, 237
gārwa: 78
gasmouli, gasmouloi: 133, 139
gate, bent entrance: 80; doubled: 80; iron covered: 81; symbolic: 82
gatti: 87
gauntlets: 78
ğebe, ğebelü: 165
gendarmeries: 103
Genghis Khān: 97, 102-3, 107, 134, 213, 215,260, 262, 284
Genoa: 163, 181-2, 245, 291, 294
gentiles: 15
Geoffrey de Bouillon: 270, 273
Georgia, Georgians: 38, 51, 60, 63, 67, 93, 129, 131, 143, 153, 163, 165, 167, 179, 215, 278
ger: 256
Germany, Germans: 11, 12, 15, 17, 20, 51, 95, 116-7, 121, 129-30, 241, 258, 272, 277, 281, 284
Gerona: 236
Ghana: 125, 140, 159, 163, 262
ghanīmah: 240
Ghassānids: 13, 19, 24, 41, 43-6, 271,
ghayr wajihdar: 146
Ghāzī Evrenos: 215
ghāzī : 57, 64, 142, 138, 148, 181, 215, 259
Ghazna, Ghaznavids: 68, 71, 72, 85, 104, 145-6, 153, 285
ghazw: 28,
Ghiyāth al-Dīn Tughluq: 205
ghūlām: 55-6, 63, 68, 71, 100, 131, 135-8, 148, 167, 244, 248, 253
Ghumāra: 140
Ghūr, Ghūrids: 134, 156, 196, 285, 290
ghurab: 87
Ghūṭa: 146
Ghuzz: 55, 94, 130
Gibraltar: 83, 161; Straits: 66, 173, 182, 268
Gilāni: 57
girdle, hemp, of Hindus: 287
gladiatorial combat: 260
Golan plateau: 24, 171
gold: 218; sources of: 182, 218; "golden bridge": 196
Golden Horde: 97-8, 101-3, 108, 110-3, 270
gomeres: 140
gonella: 167
gonfanonnier: 144-5
gongs: 266
gonuklaria: 38
"goose carriage", siege tower with extending platform: 205
gophaṇa: 201
gorget: 76, 165
gorodskoe opolchenei: 97
Goths: 13, 20, 22, 93, 95, 241; gothograeci: 20, 51
Granada: 59, 140, 145, 152-3, 163, 165-6, 172, 173, 178, 182, 219, 251, 281, 287-8, 296
Grand Admiral: 179; Grand Commander: 144; Grand Domestic: 141; Grand Interpreter: 142; Grand prince of Kiev: 96, 100-1; Grand Turcopolier: 144
graneries, fortified: 41
grape shot: 296
grappling hook: 178
grasslands, grazing areas: 18, 27-8, 94, 99, 140, 153, 271-2; burning of: 256; of horses: 255-6
Great Khan, Mongol: 102; Great Palace: 163; Great Praetorium: 242; Great Schism: 259; Great Wall of China: 204, 207, 217; Great Yāsā of Genghis Khān: 238; Great Zimbabwe: 205
greaves: 167
Greece, Greeks: 55, 58, 130-2, 136-7, 142, 153, 156, 215, 242, 244, 258, 263, 266-7; crossbowmen: 133; Hellenistic: 156, 260; islands: 133, 145; language: 19, 247, 250; medieval literature: 60
Greek Fire: 45, 74, 85, 87, 277, 294, 296; projectors: 88; blown down tubes: 85
grenade: 178, 205-6, 296; from egg-shell: 294,
grībān: 76
grid': 100
grīvpān: 37
groom: 145
Guanches: 125, 149, 153, 159, 182
guard regiments: 59
guardadores: 145
guerra: 67
guerrilla warfare: 66, 150-2, 153
Guinea: 140
guisarm: 76
gun: 294-5; gunpowder: 105, 111, 178, 294
gundsālār: 21

Guo Zui: 102
Guptas: 190, 196, 255, 195, 273
gureba: 149
Gurgān: 43
gürz: 163
gusliari: 264

h-y-f: 24
Hadhramawt: 24
ḥadīth: 236, 242
Hadya: 213
ḥāfir: 282
Hafṣids: 76, 140, 149, 182
hair, cutting of: 244; length: 287
hajj: 218, 260
halakah: 237
halberd: 201
halqa: 135-6, 146, 273
Hama: 253
Hamadhā n: 104, 267
ḥamdānids: 57, 263
hamstringing of horses: 157
ḥamra, al- : 16
Han: 101, 204; Han Chun: 189
Hand of Fatima: 278, 281
handcarts: 198, 273
ḥaras: 62,
Harascarita of Bana: 266
harassment tactics: 106-7, 153, 156
Harāt: 151, 171
ḥarb: 237
ḥarba: 76, 278
ḥarbīah: 62
harbours, fortified: 88; location of: 87
ḥarfūsh: 136, 152
harp: 265
ḥarrāqat: 88, 181
harrassment tactics: 157
Harsha, King: 194, 255, 287
Hārūn al-Rashīd: 55, 73, 86, 243, 248, 268
Ḥasan al-Rammah: 295-6
ḥasham: 58-9; hashm-i iqṭāᶜ: 146
hashish: 267
ḥāṣina: 76
Ḥaṭṭī n: 131, 144
ḥavāshvī: 148
hazāra: 102
head-cloth, Arab: 36
head-hunting: 237, 243-4
"heaven bridge": 205
Hebrew literature: 219
hei-kuang: 201
Heiron: 172
helmet; crests: 284; bascinet: 164; brimmed war-hat: 112, 122, 133, 142, 163; crocodile-skin: 37, 76; European reshaped in east: 113-4; great helm: 76, 114, 163; lamellar: 201; leather: 37, 294; one-piece bronze: 37; one-piece iron: 37, 76, 201; Parthian Cap form: 16, 292; peaked: 112; rivetted: 34; sallet: 33; scale: 201; segmented: 112; silvered decoration: 201; spangenhelm: 37, 293; turban helmet: 163-4; two piece: 37, 112; with integral face-mask: 76
Hephthalites: 105-6
Heraclius, Emperor: 20, 215-6, 258
heraldry: 16, 132, 263; European: 282; Mamluk: 282; heraldic animals: 207; heraldic symbolism, of duties: 282
herds, as food "on the hoof": 71
heresies: 51, 53, 63, 258-9
hermandades: 145
Herodian dynasty: 14
heroism & physical courage: 62, 68
Herules: 13
hetaireia: 59
hezb: 24
"hidden friends": 245
Hieun Tsang: 198, 267
Hijaz: 16, 43-4, 48, 215, 245
hill, man-made firing position: 122
ḥimāya: 253
ḥims: 24, 163, 217
Hinduism, Hindus: 13, 134, 146, 156, 187-96, 261, 200, 205, 207, 218, 237, 244, 253, 264, 266, 284, 288; art: 200; influence: 146; military pride of: 198; religious texts: 194, 208
Hippodrome: 242, 284
hippopotamus: 163
ḥīra: 24
Ḥīra, al-: 15, 23, 43, 241
Hishām, Caliph: 290
ḥiṣn (fortress), battle formation: 72
Hiuen Tsang: 194, 205, 244, 255, 287
hoarding, wooden: 168
holy war: 67, 185, 235-6
hood, over helmet: 240
Hormizd II: 278
horn: 36, 288; armour: 78, 290; (musical instrument): 265-6; ox-headed: 266
Horn of Africa: 29, 125, 149
horse: 251, 270; Andalusian: 271; Arabian: 270; Barb: 270; breeding, manuals of: 271; breeding, selective: 271; Central Asian: 270; changing of: 104; Golden or Celestial: 271; feeding of: 256; herds: 103, 271; herds, dispersal of: 271; herds, Imperial (see also stables, government): 67; herds, maintainance of: 99; horsemanship: 248; Indian: 198; importation of: 272; jumping: 272; number needed: 102, 153; racing: 251; riding, bareback: 38; riding, long distance: 272; riding styles: 167; sacrifice: 262; sizes of: 271; transportation: 87, 180, 271, 274; transportion by riverboat: 210; Turcoman: 270; Turco-Mongol: 108, 272; Turkestani: 271; war-, leading of: 68; wild: 271;
horse armour: 29, 36, 38, 70-1, 79, 99, 102, 104, 117, 156, 158, 167, 197-8, 202, 204, 237, 253, 290, 292; iron lamellar: 79, 80; leather lamellar: 79, 118; lamellar: 97, 167; mail: 79, 80, 167; quilted: 79
horseshoe: 79, 117
hospital: 258; military field-: 258
Hospitallers: 132, 144-5, 168, 180, 242, 247, 259, 284
house-to-house fighting: 85
hsiang-chun: 193; hsiang-ping: 193
Hsin-fu Chun: 189
hsuin-pien tzu-ti: 189
Hsuing-nu: 101
Huang-ho: 210
Hūdids: 66
hudnah: 237
Huesca: 296
hueste: 67, 145
ḥuffāẓ : 251
hui-hui p'ao: 206, 296
hujra, hujarīya: 65, 249-50
Hülegü: 97, 262, 284, 295
hull construction, ship: 47; nailed: 209; sewn: 209; watertight compartments: 209
Ḥulubān (battle of): 28
human sacrifice: 244, 262
humid climate, effect on arms: 199, 202
Hungary, Hungarains: 94, 98, 117, 120-1, 129-30, 159, 217, 291; Hungarian Plain: 93
Huns: 13, 23, 29-30, 34, 73, 93, 104, 189, 195; Black: 105; White: 105
hunting: 247, 251; large scale: 103
huo: 192
huo-chien: 296
huruffi: 260
ḥusbān: 69
hussars: 51
Huwwārah: 58
hwarang: 189, 238, 261, 264; hwarangdo: 238
hypostrategus: 20
Iasians: 130
Iasy: 96
Iberia, Iberians: 161, 163, 167, 180, 235, 237-9, 242, 253, 257, 266, 273, 278, 281, 291-2; peninsular: 17, 47
Ibn al-Azraq: 215; Ibn Hudhayl: 251, 271, 288; Ibn Khaldūn: 157; Ibn Qutaybah al-Dīnawarī: 71; Ibn Rushd: 236
Iceland: 88
içlik: 116
icons: 258; iconoclasm: 258
identity tags: 205
ideological barrier: 245
idols: 261
igdish: 148
Igor Syvatoslavich: 216
ikhshīd: 99
Ikhshīdids: 58, 249
ikhwān: 137
Īl-Khāns: 93, 97, 102, 116, 134, 136, 146, 246, 255, 287, 295
ilarch: 29
ili: 200
illik kafırleri: 148
illumination of night fighting: 206
Illyria: 13
Imperial armamenton: 290; Imperial Guards: 192
incendiary; materials: 205; material attached to animals: 197; troops: 71; weapons: 45-6, 48, 121; weapons, on river craft: 210
incense trade: 48
India, Indians: 11, 13, 15, 37, 57, 68, 71, 88, 97, 104, 107-8, 116, 125, 134, 136, 153, 161, 163, 174, 185, 187, 193-5, 200-1, 204-5, 208, 213, 218, 237-8, 244, 247-8, 251, 253, 255, 258, 264-5, 265-7, 270-5, 284, 287-91, 294, 296; fleet: 194; high status of warrior in: 200; military influence: 198; Muslims: 135; Indian Ocean: 125, 182, 208, 219, 274-6, 291; southern: 200-1; tactics, old fashioned: 198; violence in: 201
indigenae: 13,
individual combat (see also duels): 30
Indo-Europeans: 185
Indochina: 189, 199, 204, 210
Indonesia: 125, 185, 187, 189, 192, 209, 261, 289
indulgance, Papal: 153, 259
infacoes: 134
infantry: 138, 189; formations: 29, 70; tactics: 30 (& passim); camel mounted: 15, 24, 69, 73, 105; javelin-armed: 29; light: 63, 70, 72; mounted: 15, 104, 146, 153, 158, 173, 273; status of: 68; unarmoured: 195
infanzones: 54
infection; fear of: 258; of wound: 161
infirm, immunity of: 236
inflated animal skins: 122
influence, military, normal flow east to west: 108
ingeni: 134
inscriptions; heraldic: 278; on flags: 280
inspection of troops (see also review): 266
internal security: 246
iqlīm: 65
iqṭāᶜ: 62, 65-6, 102, 137, 143, 146-8, 253-5, 284
irān-ambāraghbadh: 21; irān-spādbadh: 21
Iran, Iranians: 14, 16-7, 24, 29, 51, 56, 68, 78, 93, 97, 103-4, 120, 134, 136, 138, 146, 162, 166, 191, 217, 237, 255-6, 259, 263, 272, 281, 287, 290; military tradition: 18
Iraq, Iraqis: 16, 21, 23, 41-2, 57, 62, 80, 97, 104, 135-6, 206, 213, 215, 217, 220, 259, 271, 273, 282, 290-4; southern marshes: 88
Ireland: 88
iron: 288; grills & doors, heated: 208; ingots: 291; ore: 291; pegs, to secure scaling ladders: 208; cast: 288; lamellar armour: 78; Mongol shortage of: 109; sources in forest zone: 109; state monopoly on: 294; supplies of: 47
Irrawaddy: 210
irrigation: 256
Isauria: 13
isfahsalār: 146,
ishkhan: 19
Islam, Muslims: 51, 93, 97, 102, 125, 139-40, 150, 185, 187, 215, 220, 235-6, 262; brotherhoods: 259; Christian converts: 140; egalitarianism: 260, 285; folk Islamic practices: 260; in Africa: 141, 182; influence: 193; Law: 139, 236; legal authority: 220
islands, artificial: 118,
Ismāᶜīlī: 146, 259-60, 267, 284
iṣṭabl: 62, 271,
iṣṭināᶜ: 62, 65
istirᶜrāḍ: 62
Italy, Italians: 13, 43, 51, 54, 60, 68, 80, 87, 129-33, 145, 153, 165, 179, 181, 217, 219, 255, 257, 274, 277-8, 292-3; influence: 142, 154, 169, 171, 263; "Italian drill": 32; naval support from: 182; Italy, southern: 291; trading colonies: 93
izar: 272
Izborsk: 118
Izmir: 180, 275, 277

Jāḥiz of Basra, al-: 62, 68, 73, 279, 289
jaᶜā'il: 17
jabalīyūn: 131
jada: 262
Jaffa: 80, 169
Jagatai: 97, 103, 112,
jah: 201
jālīsh: 152
jamāᶜa: 146
James I of Aragon: 134, 217, 280
jān-avspār: 21
jāndār: 134, 146; jandarīyah: 146
jānib: 146
Janissaries (see Yeni Çeri)
januwiyāh: 132, 163
Japan, Japanese: 55, 75, 185, 194, 199-202, 205, 209, 238, 277, 288, 296
Jar'īa: 55
jarīda: 146
jarkh: 74, 160
jarrār: 24
jaserant: 165
jāsūs: 246
Jats: 191
jaucerant: 165
Java, Javanese: 134, 192, 291
javelin: 31, 56, 68, 70, 72-5, 85, 104, 153, 156-9, 178, 248; all-wood: 159; at sea: 88; infantry: 51, 60, 71-2
jawād: 271
jawshan: 38, 78, 166, 290
jāwūsh: 266
jayb: 83
jaysh: 24
jazeran hauberk: 78
Jazīrah: 57, 68, 134-5; Jazīrat al-Fara'ūn: 47-8
jazrain hauberk: 78
Jāzūla: 58
Jean II of Beirut: 144
Jerash: 171
Jerusalem: 131, 145, 150, 169, 240-4, 247, 257, 288; Kingdom of: 143-4, 150
Jews, Judaism: 13-7, 51, 57-9, 63, 91, 95, 99, 135, 213, 215, 219, 242, 260, 284, 290; doctors: 257; Jewish Arabs: 48; Jewish Berbers: 51; Jewish Turks: 91
jiavors: 143
jie: 192, 284

jihād: 63-4, 215, 236, 240, 242, 259-60
jineta: 153, 161, 163, 251
jing: 197, 284
jirid: 248,
jitō: 194
jitr: 150
jizyah: 236, 253
John Cantacuzenus, Emperor: 217; John Tzimiskes, Emperor: 59
joint responsibility of soldiers in unit: 103
Jordan: 18, 41-4, 46, 135, 168, 170, 245, 288, 290; Jordan river, valley: 23, 150
jousting: 251
juᶜl: 253
jubbah: 78, 165
judicatures: 62
juez: 145
juglar: 263
Julanda: 23
julbān: 147
jun: 192
jund: 24-5, 58-9, 62, 65-6 135, 143, 149, 253; jund al-ḥadra: 62
junk, ship: 209
jupeau d'armer: 165-6, 284
jupon: 284
Jurash: 43
Jurchen: 193, 296
Just War: 235-6
Justianian, Emperor: 13, 15, 18, 20, 45

kabadion: 78
kabsh: 85, 178
kadivar: 99
kaff: 167
kaftan: 284-5
k'aii: 202
Kākudam: 166
Kalmyks: 97
kamān-i-gāv: 121
kamelaukion: 76
kanārang: 21
kandāchāra: 194
kap'hi: 167
karabion, karabos: 87
karadis: 34
Karakalpak: 96
Karakhitai (see Qara-Khitai)
Karakorum mountains: 68
Karāsī: 215
Karluks: 94
Karnataka: 251, 288
karr wa farr: 33, 71, 73,
Karts: 151
kārwa: 78
Kashgar: 68
Kashmir, Kashmiris: 97, 196, 215
kastra: 167; kastron: 142; kastrophylakes: 142
katena: 87
katepan of the arma: 290
katerga: 179
katība: 33, 146
kayak: 122
kazāghand: 78, 148, 165
kazan: 149
keel, form of ship: 178
keiko: 202
keiromanika: 38
kemeldürük: 116
Kenya: 125
Kephale: 142
Kerala: 218
Kerch: 98
keris: 200
khadga: 200
khagan: 262, 266, 284; khākān, khākhān: 105-6, 155, 197
Khālid Ibn al-Walīd: 217, 253
Khaljis: 134,
khamīs: 24, 33-4, 71, 106, 157
khān, khānate: 91, 93, 102, 244, 283
Khān Ghāzān: 102; Khān Mamay: 98
khanda: 200,
khanjar: 75, 109
khānqāh: 64
khārajis, khawārijis: 68, 57, 281
Khartoum: 29, 153, 167
khashāb: 273
khāṣṣa: 65; khāṣṣakīya: 146
khatangku dehel: 116, 166,
khātūn: 246
Khaydār al-Afshīn: 217
Khazar: 15, 37, 51, 74, 75, 78, 91, 94-5, 99, 104, 109, 118, 260
Khazlay: 55
khidmatgār: 99
Khirbat al-Mafjir: 28, 287; Khirbat al-Baidah: 45
Khitai: 134,
Khitan: 193-4, 100,
Khmer: 209
Khotan, Khotanese: 68, 120
khūdh: 163, 76
Khurāsān, Khurāsān is: 15, 21, 35, 55-8, 73, 79-80, 98, 134-5, 283, 288, 294
Khusrau I: 14, 21, 23, 217, 278; Khusrau II: 38, 278
khuyagh: 114
Khūzistān: 14
Khwārazm, Khwārazmians: 56, 95, 99, 111, 119, 135, 167, 290, 293; Khwārazmshāhs: 134
Kiev, 91, 96, 100, 271, 290; Kievan state: 95
kilich: 74
Kimāk: 55, 94
Kindī, al-: 290
Kinda: 28, 41, 43
kingship, semi-divine status: 150, 260
kisten: 109
Kitai (see also Khitai): 93
kızıl elma: 260
kleisourai: 60
klibanion: 78
knights: 236; errant: 264; urban: 131
knobkerry: 147
Koguryŏ: 189
kolp'um: 189
Komotini: 215
kong tch'uan nou: 200
koniushi: 100
kontarion: 75
Koran: 75, 237; inscriptions: 280; Law (see Islamic Law)
Kordofan: 153
Korea, Koneans: 36, 55, 185, 189, 195-6, 199-202, 204, 209, 238, 244, 248, 251, 261, 268, 287-8, 296; literature: 264
Koryŏ: 189, 194, 205, 268
Kosedağ, battle of: 106
koşkum: 116
Kosogians: 96
Kosovo, battle of: 157, 296
Kotrones: 267
kōtwāl: 146, 253
koumbaria: 87
koursa: 274
kourtch: 246
Krak des Chevaliers: 169
kremasmata: 78
kremlin: 100, 120
kshatriya: 15, 189-91, 238, 244, 251, 261, 264, 287
Kūfa: 24
kujak: 114
kuklos: 31
kul: 139
Kulikova, battle of: 98, 107
Kuo K'an: 97
kūra: 21; kū ra mujannada: 66
Kurds: 53, 56-8, 69, 134-6, 138, 219
Kurmina Fari: 150
kurra: 248
Kushan: 14, 29, 202
kūshk: 43, 118
kūssāt: 266
kustubān: 74, 161
Kutāma: 58
kuyuk: 114
kyŏkku: 251
kyŏngdang: 189

La Mancha: 67
labourers, non-combatant: 135, 240
Ladoga river: 119
Lahssa: 81
Lake Baikal: 97; Lake Balkash: 93; Lake Peipus, battle of: 105, 213; Lake Tana: 214; Lake Van: 57
Lakhmids: 15, 18, 23, 43-4, 241
lamellar armour: 17, 33, 36, 38, 56-7, 68, 78, 87, 91, 97, 107, 108, 114, 116, 142, 156, 165-6, 197, 202, 237, 261, 288, 290-1; bamboo: 114; bone: 114; bronze: 197; gilded leather: 197; horn: 166; iron: 166; laquered: 114, 202; leather: 78, 114, 117, 166; mixed iron and bronze: 38; neck guard: 76
laminated limb defences: 38, 57
lamṭ: 76, 163, 166, 290, 294
Lamṭa: 58, 140,
lance, use of: 158, 251
land-holding, link with military obligation: 66
landing craft: 277
Langkasuka: 194, 205
Las Navas de Tolosa, battle of: 158
lashkar: 146,
lashqah: 161
lāṣiq: 146
lasso: 68, 73, 76, 109, 163
Lāt, al-: 261
lateen sail: 47, 87, 178
Latin language: 19, 179, 247, 271
Latins of Constantinople (see Crusader Greece)
latrines: 208
lavra: 170; fortified: 41
law, maritime: 217; Laws of Manu: 238; lawyers (see also canon law): 284
lawlab: 160
Laz, 131
lead oxide, as antiseptic: 257
leather: 288; armour: 20, 54, 88; armour, Tibetan: 78; boats, rafts, skins: 273; screens, against smoke, gases: 208; working: 290; hardened: 290
Lebanon: 47, 131, 136, 180-1, 268, 277, 288
legitimacy, political: 236, 238
lei-shih-cche: 206
Leon, King of Armenia: 143
Leon (kingdom & city): 54, 60, 66-7, 145, 292
leopard, heraldic: 281; "leopard armour": 38
leper, leprosy: 242, 257
Levantine archery traditions: 31
Li Shih-min: 217
Li Yuan: 217
liang-k'ai: 201; liang-tang: 201
Liao: 193
Libya: 20, 41, 46, 58, 217
light house: 273
Liguria: 129
lii: 192
limb defences: 36, 153 167, 202
lime pots: 206
limes: 25
limitanei: 13, 15, 18, 26, 101
limited diet, of soldiers: 256
line of communications, protection of: 68; line of march, length of: 270
linothorax: 166
lion, heraldic: 281; "lion armour": 38
Lisbon: 182
lişūş : 152
literacy: 65, 251
lithām: 287
Lithuania: 120
Little Russia (see Ukraine, Ukrainians)
lo-tzu-chun: 192
logistical support: 195
Lombards: 13, 87
long walls, fortified: 42-4, 204
Lord of Horses: 29
lorikion: 78
Lotharingians: 242
Louis, King: 131
louriken: 38
loyalty: 56, 65
luᶜab: 178
Lusignans: 141
lute: 265

m-h-r-m: 24
m-q-d-m-t: 24
m-s-r: 24
Ma Sui: 202
maᶜlūghūn: 140
Ma'mūn', al-: 56, 248
maᶜūna: 57, 62
ma-mien lien: 204; ma-shen-chia: 204; ma-tou-hou: 204
maaşli: 149
mace: 37, 70, 75-6, 109, 147, 156, 163, 201, 247-8; training: 251; animal headed: 75; anthropomorphic: 109
Macedonia: 13, 131, 140, 215
machicolation: 41, 46, 80, 83, 168, 207
Madagascar: 125, 187, 289
madas: 163
Madeira: 88, 182
Madhya Pradesh: 200
Madinat al-Zahra: 250
Maghribis (see also North Africa): 136
magic: 109, 196, 250, 260, 262; belief in: 109; in design of fortifications: 82
Magyars: 91, 94, 96; eastern: 91, 95
Mahabharata: 194
Maharashtra: 267
Mahdia: 296
Mahdism: 281
Maḥmūd of Ghazna: 281
Mahon: 134
mahout: 105, 197, 203
mail armour: 14, 18, 33, 36-8, 56, 62, 64, 68-9, 76, 78-9, 96, 105, 116-7, 122, 129, 165-7, 202, 237, 250, 293; aventail: 69; aventail, face covering: 137; chausses: 130; coif: 34, 38, 156, 163, 250; coif, brocade covered: 68; forms of construction: 116; mail & plate armour: 116-7, 166-7, 290
Majorca: 134, 280
majordomi, majorini: 60
majra: 69, 74, 161
makāḥil al-bārūd: 85
Makuria: 24
Malaga: 176, 182, 219
Malagina: 66
Malatya: 53, 67
Malays, Malaysia: 187, 194, 200, 205, 209, 289
Maldive islands: 219
Mali: 140-1, 150, 182, 218, 262, 294
Malta: 180, 273
mamlaka: 148
mamlūk: 55-9, 63, 66, 69, 71-3, 75, 100, 134-6, 141, 146-8, 155, 158-9, 244, 250, 272, 282; elite, self perpetuating: 56; freeing of: 250; Mamlūk state: 97, 131, 136, 138, 143-8, 152-3, 157-60, 162-5, 181, 238, 244, 246-7, 250-1, 254-6, 263, 266, 268, 272, 281-2, 286-7, 290, 293, 295-6; mamlūkūn: 146
Manṣūr, Ibn Abī 'Amīr al-: 58, 215
Man in the Panther's Skin: 263
Manat, al-: 261
Manchuria, Manchurians: 93, 189, 193-4, 205
mangonel (see also manjanīq): 44, 46, 81, 85, 120-1, 158, 167, 174-6, 178, 205-6, 277, 294; balls: 170; manganell turques: 176; man-powered: 236; manganikon: 85; manglavitai: 59; mounted on waggon: 206; on harbour entrance towers: 178; prefabricated: 178; splay-legged: 47
maniakion: 284
Manichaeans: 13, 135, 260, 283
manikellia: 78
manikia: 78
manjanīq: 46-7, 81, 85, 87, 122; Arab type: 174, 178; black-bull type: 178; Frankish (European) type: 178; manjanīqīn: 85; Turco-Persian type: 174, 178
manpower, Muslim Andalusian shortage of: 82
Mansa: 218; Mansa Musa: 182, 218
Manṣūrah: 178
mantlet: 29, 198, 201; of reed: 76
Manual of Court Organization: 194
Manuel Comnenus,

Emperor: 163
Manzikert, battle of: 153, 292
manzil: 83
maps, military: 246
marachakhd: 143
Maraş: 29
Maratha: 191
Maravar: 201
marching, rate & distance: 158
Mardin: 268
Marechal: 144; Marichal: 145
mares (see also stallions): 271
marines: 16, 58, 87-8, 98, 133, 178, 180-2
Marīnids: 140, 158, 173, 287, 296
Maritsa, river: 152
market, attached to army: 244; fortified: 43
marksman, distinctive costume: 285
Maronites: 131
Marqab, al-: 168, 277
marqaba: 178
marṣad: 83
marsh, crossing of: 104
marshal: 143-5
martial arts: 192, 198 251
Marw: 43, 267
Marwān II, Caliph: 34; Marwānids: 57
marzbān: 21, 23,
maṣāni^c: 43
Maṣmūda: 58, 140
masnada: 54
massacre: 107, 242, 244
massāḥī : 176
Master Crossbowman: 144; Master Esquire: 145; Master of the Frontier Post: 242; master of the robes: 282; Master Sergeant: 144
mathematics: 251
maula: 191
Mauretania: 88
mauri pacis: 134
Maurice, Emperor: 32
Mawārdi, al-: 68
mawāli: 15-7, 25, 58
mawāqīd: 268
maydān: 250-1
maymanah: 33
maysarah: 33
Mazdaism: 215, 283
M'dīkarib: 215
Mecca: 15, 28-9, 217-8, 260-1, 268, 290
medical services: 257; medicine sellers: 246
Medina: 44, 46, 48, 260, 267, 290
Medinacelli: 66
Mediterranean: 66, 93, 98, 137, 178, 180, 288, 290
megalla allagia: 142
Megas Konostoulos: 141
mehter: 265; mehterhane: 266
Melilla: 88
mental attitudes in warfare: 185
mercenaries: 14, 17, 58, 63, 99, 129-32, 138, 144, 146, 215, 253; European: 98, 131, 137, 141; Muslim: 95
merchants: 180, 245, 270, 273
Merida: 176
Meroe: 24
meros (meroi): 19, 277
Merya: 119
mesnaderos: 134
mesoi: 131
metallurgy: 289; metallurgical technology, spread of: 76; metalworking: 118
Michael III, Emperor: 268; Michael Palaeologus, Emperor: 167
Middle East, shortage of iron: 288
midfa^c: 295-6; midfa^c al-nafṭ: 296
mighfar: 76
miles: 236
militarization, of society: 19, 62, 259
military; brotherhoods: 242; command, learning by experience: 156; command, qualities required: 62; corporations: 100; coups: 57; equipment, repair of: 250; influence, spread of: 85; Intendants: 251; lists: 65; literature, theoretical: 158; manpower, Byzantine shortage of: 51, 66; military-agricultural colonies: 193; Orders: 82, 132, 134, 144, 163, 168, 170, 242, 244, 247, 257, 259, 292; Orders, Iberian: 145; roads: 83; technology, Chinese: 198; training: 286; units, continuity of: 64; wards: 189
milites: 54, 60
militia: 13, 62, 65, 145, 150, 156, 185, 176; territorial, provincial: 135, 189; urban: 54, 58, 97, 100, 131, 134-5, 140, 142-6, 235
mills: 238
minaret, as observation post: 81, 171
mine, explosive: 296
Ming: 185, 189, 193-5, 197, 296
ming bashi: 103
ming-kuang: 201
mining, for metals: 99; siege: 45-6, 85, 176, 242
minṭaqah: 285
miqnab: 33
Miran: 95
Mirdāsids: 57
misleading of enemy: 68-9
misruda: 166
Mistras: 169
miṭrād: 37
mobility, tactical: 30
moera, moira: 19, 277
Moldavia: 93, 95, 140, 291
monasteries (see also lavra): 142, 258; fortified: 41, 80, 167; Buddhist fortified: 63
money, shortage of: 240
Mongols: 78, 91, 93, 95, 97-8, 100-3, 106-8, 114, 116, 121, 130, 134, 136, 138, 145-8, 151-3, 155, 157, 163-4, 166-7, 171, 174, 185, 193-5, 202, 210, 213, 237-8, 244, 246, 251, 255-6, 259-61, 264, 266, 272-3, 277-8, 283, 287-8, 294-5; influence: 109, 111; language: 94; "World Empire": 93, 97, 255
Mongolia: 38, 93, 104, 120, 264
monks: 131, 245, 258, 284
monokaballoi: 141
Monoprosopon: 257
morale: 185, 257
Mordva, Mordvins: 119, 262
Morea, Despotate of: 142
Morocco: 15, 41, 51, 58, 65, 69, 76, 82, 88, 140, 145, 149, 153, 163, 166, 173, 178, 182, 220, 268, 273, 294, 296
mortar, cannon: 296
Moscow: 109, 119-20, 296
mosques; destruction of: 242; in banner ceremony: 283; prisoners in custody of: 242
Mosul: 44, 135, 171, 294
mounds of earth, as firing platforms: 176
Mount Lebanon: 290
mountains: 29; passes: 62, 66, 151, 268; warfare: 217
Mourtatoi: 130, 141
Mozambique: 125
Mozarab: 59, 73, 79, 140
mtepe, ship: 209
Mu^ctaṣim, al-: 56, 62, 217, 256
Mu^cāwiya: 16, 24, 47, 267-8, 275, 281
Mu^cizz al-Dīn: 196
mubarizun (see also champions): 32
mudejar: 140, 174, 242
Muḥammad, Prophet: 46, 72, 236, 242, 258, 261, 278, 280-1, 290, 292; Muḥammad V, king: 140
muḥannak: 285
muḥarrik: 149
mukhula al-nafṭ: 296
mule: 69, 154, 173, 271-3; corps: 192; train: 272
munādī : 266
munja grass: 287
muqaddamah: 33
Muqanna^c: 283
muqātila: 17
Muqtafī, al-: 293
Murābiṭin: 58, 66, 69, 73, 76, 134, 149, 163, 182, 220, 237, 266, 277; murābiṭ: 149,
Murat I, Ottoman: 139
Murcia: 291
murtāziqah: 62
muṣallah: 82
Muscovy: 91
müsellem: 138
Muslims (see also Islam): 94, 98, 102, 112, 121, 130, 134-5, 145, 189, 191, 194-5, 199, 205-7, 213, 217, 219, 242, 245, 253, 258, 273, 275, 288, 290; Andalusian: 59; attitude towards technology: 289; doctors; 257; lack of interest in western Europe: 246; opinion of Byzantines: 246; opinion of western Europeans: 246; religious elite, slaughter of: 242; religious law (Islamic law); sailors: 190
Musta'ṣim, Caliph al-: 162
musta^ca'riba: 17
mustakhdamū: 146
muta'ahhilī n: 64
Mutannabī, al-: 213
Mu^ctaṣim, Caliph al-: 273
mutaṭawi^cah, muṭṭawi'a: 57, 62, 135, 146
Mutawakkil, Caliph al-: 285
mutilation: 237, 241-2,
Muwaḥḥidin: 134, 140, 155, 158, 163, 176, 178, 251, 280, 283, 287; muwaḥḥid: 266
muzaradi: 163
muzhi: 100
Myrtaitai: 129
Mysore: 218

n-s-r: 24
Nabataeans: 17
nāchakh: 153
nachararks: 60
nafaqa: 255
nafṭ: 71, 74, 84-5, 88, 122, 159, 178, 294, 296; on horseback: 294; white: 294; nafāṭa: 181; naffāṭūn: 58, 62, 85, 135, 167, 176
nagid: 219
naginata: 200
nā'ib al-qal^ca: 148; nā'ib al-salṭana: 147-8
Najera: 281
najjab: 267-8
Najran: 215, 290
Nakha: 281
nakharar: 19
nalika: 201
Naples: 145
naqb: 46, 85; naqqābūn: 176
naqīb: 62, 149
nār: 85
Narapatisithu: 194
Narbonne: 275
Narseh: 278
nasal, broad: 250
Naṣrid: 140, 182, 281
naval; attack on coasts: 80; battle, on lake: 210; blockade: 288; officers: 85; raids: 82; technology, used in siege warfare: 87; troops (see marines); warfare, theory of: 250
Navarre: 60, 66, 134, 163
navi: 179
nāwak: 74
Nawrū z: 65
nāyak: 194, 198
naẓīr: 25; nāẓir: 149
Nepalese: 291
netting, to protect walls: 206
Neva, river: 213
Nicea: 291; Empire: 130, 141
Nicephoros II Phocas, Emperor: 70-1, 155, 218
Nicobar islands: 219
Niger river: 182, 218
Nigeria: 141
night fighting: 28, 34, 73, 85, 152
Nihāyat al-Su'l: 157
Nile: 143, 153, 171, 238, 277; Delta: 171, 182, 277
Nineveh: 292-3
nipīk: 21
Nīshāpūr: 56, 248
nistrimsa: 200
nīzah-i mard gīr: 163
Niẓām al-Mulk: 134, 146
Nobatia: 24, 29
nomads, nomadism: 15, 62, 99
Normans (see also Italy, southern Italy, Sicily): 54, 60, 125, 129-33, 136, 140, 143, 219, 274, 293
North Africa, North Africans: 15, 17, 20, 26, 28, 41, 47, 56-8, 62, 65, 68, 79, 82, 125, 136, 140, 149-50, 152, 157, 159, 161-3, 167, 173, 178, 182, 220, 251, 256, 260, 262, 266, 274, 280, 287, 289-90, 294
Notitia Dignitatum: 18, 277
Novgorod: 91, 96, 100-1, 105, 109, 116-9, 290; Novgorod-Seversky: 216
noxious smoke: 208
Nubia, Nubians: 11, 15-6, 24, 28-9, 31-2, 36-7, 39, 48, 51, 58, 62, 65, 69, 72, 76, 125, 136, 140, 143, 153, 159, 168, 259, 264
nuqabā' al-jaysh: 148
Nūr al-Dīn: 220
nuzūl: 72, 157

oars, of galley at two levels: 180; oarsmen: 47, 87-8
oasis character of Middle Eastern cities: 66
oath-taking ceremonies: 65; oaths, chains of: 65
Ob river: 109, 271
obo: 108
obsequium: 20
ocak: 149
Oghuz (see also Ghuzz): 94
ognishchanin: 100
oil, crude: 294
Oirats: 97, 136
okolnichi: 101
Old Ladoga: 119
Old Man of the Mountain: 267
Oman: 23-6, 42, 47, 88, 209, 291
onagros: 85
oplitai: 60, 68
oplon: 165
opsikion: 20, 26, 51, 60
optimates: 19, 51
orchards & gardens, destruction of: 46, 176
orchestra (see also music): 27, 266
Order of Mary of Mercy: 242; Order of St Lazarus: 257
orders, sealed: 246
ordu: 101, 103, 118; Ordu-Balik: 118; Ordu- Örgin: 118
organa: 265
Orhān Ghāzi, Ottoman: 164
orta: 149
Ossetians: 96, 98, 130
Ostia: 274
Ostrogoths: 13
Ottoman Turks: 93, 108, 116, 125, 129, 138, 146, 149, 150, 152, 162, 164, 166, 171, 215, 217, 244, 248, 251, 255, 260, 263-6, 280-3, 286, 296; Othmanli Turkish language: 283
overpopulation, Europe: 129

Pacific Ocean: 275
pacifism; Christian: 259; in China: 185
padded armour: 202
pādhghūspān: 23
Pagan: 194
paganism, pagans: 96, 126, 215, 259, 261, 266; gods: 263; priests: 264
paidah: 135,
paighan: 13
palace enclosure, fortified (see also Baghdad, Round City): 81; palace forces: 19, 24, 191
Palaeolog Emperors:

130, 142
palaiyam: 194
palash: 109
Palermo: 291
Palestine: 14-5, 17, 41, 47, 58, 135, 155, 168-9, 219, 253, 260, 277, 287, 293
pallisade; coastal defence: 180, 277; thorn: 205; wooden: 205
paly, heldic motif: 281
Pamir mountains: 120
pan-chih: 193
panceriam: 165
Pandyas: 218
panjgā n: 31
Panteleria: 275
pantheotai: 59
"panther armour": 38
pantsir: 116
p'ao ch'e: 296
Papacy, Popes: 131, 236, 242, 293; ban on strategic trade with Muslims: 293
Paphlagonia: 53, 131
parade ground (see also maydan): 80
paramerion: 74
paraportia: 35
parasol, ceremonial: 76, 282, 284
paraśu: 201
parataxis: 60, 154
parembole: 24
Parthians: 29, 38, 202
parvanak: 267
pāshtīb: 173, 208
pastores: 145
pasture, need, lack of: 104, 146, 150
patricians: 141
patron: 182
Paulicians: 53, 135
pay, military: 62, 65, 131, 149, 253; units: 24
payadeh: 138
pāyak: 135
pāyghānsālār: 21
Pechenegs: 53, 93, 95-6, 98-9, 106, 108-9, 121, 260, 266, 271, 275
pedion: 246
pedones: 60
pellet bow: 36, 74
pension, for widows of soldiers: 255; state: 253-5
peones, peonia: 54, 60, 134; peoes: 54
Pergamum: 13
periknemides: 38
peritrachelia: 76
Persia, Persians: 17, 53, 62, 95, 213, 217, 247, 253, 285, 291; culture: 134; influence: 146, 204; language: 217; literature: 263-4, 268, 281; military literature: 263; military tradition, revival: 65; naval influence: 47
Perun: 263
petroboli: 84
peytral: 167
pezoi: 154
Pharganoi: 53
Philippines: 291
phylarch: 15-6, 18-9, 24, 26, 43, 271, 278, 291
pigeon post: 268; breeding birds: 268; interception: 268; perfumed birds: 268
pike: 34, 71-2, 173
pilgrimage, pilgrims: 131, 143, 218, 245-6, 270; pilgrim knights: 132
p'i-li huo-ch'iu: 296
pillion, infantry riding: 72
pin: 192
pioneers, military: 70, 273
piracy: 82, 167, 171, 173, 178, 180, 209, 242, 296; river: 182
Pisa, Pisans: 129, 277, 293
pits, hidden as traps: 87, 106
plate & lamellar armour: 202
platform; elevatable for snipers: 205; raisable on cart: 205; raised as command or observation post: 157
p'oa ch'e: 294
podiezdnoi: 100
podopsella: 79
poet: 213, 263
pogost: 101
Poland: 96, 120-1, 278, 291; Poland-Lithuania: 97
Polianians: 290
police: secret: 194
polo: 246, 248, 251; polo master: 282
pommel, hollow ring: 200
pony (see also horse): 273
poor; role in siege: 208; source of risk during siege: 205
population; dispersal: 103; movement: 91; transfer: 51, 97
portage, between rivers: 122, 273
portcullis: 80-1
porters: 206
Portugal: 25, 54, 60, 66, 79, 88, 129, 134, 140, 145, 163-4, 182, 235, 247, 260, 290
posadnik: 96
postrig: 96
poulains: 131
Poyang: 210
praefectus: 20
prestamo: 60
Prester John: 100
priests: 259; priest-kings: 23
Primmikerios: 141
prisoners; exchange: 236, 243, 245; feeding of: 243; recruitment of: 58-9, 129, 137, 138, 149; ruler's share of: 139; slaughter of: 242
Prithviraja: 196
production line manufacturing technique: 289
promotion: 103, 248; structure: 62; within caste: 191
pronoia: 129, 140-2, 255
protective sheds, mobile: 84
protospatharios: 60
protostrator: 141-2
pseudo-Kufic script: 277-8
Pskov: 101, 119
psychological warfare: 176, 245-6
pteruges: 284
pu: 194
Punjab: 205
pushtīghbānsālār: 21
Pyedavthagyun, battle of: 197
pyrotechnics, explosive: 178

q-d-m: 24
q-r-n: 24
q-s-d: 15
qā'id: 25, 62, 65-6, 140, 149, 181-2; qā'id al-baḥr: 182
qabā^c: 284
qabaq: 248
qabīla: 25
qadirga: 181
Qādisīyah (battle of): 27, 2445, 255
qalāchūr, qalājūlīyā, qaljūri: 74
qalansuwa: 33, 282, 287; shāshī yah: 284
qalb: 33
qal^ca: 83; Qal^cat al-Far'ūn: 276
qanāh: 37
Qarā Khitai: 100, 106, 155, 167, 197, 260, 287; Qarā Qoyunlī: 138, 148
qaraçı: 102-3; qaraçı bey: 103
qarāghulām: 146; Qarā khānid: 65, 94
qarawnas: 97
qargu: 268
qārib: 87
Qarluks: 93
qarqal: 165-6
qarqūra: 87
Qaryāt al-Faw: 41, 43
qaṣabah: 82
qaṣr: 82; Qaṣr al-Hayr al-Gharbi: 243; Qaṣr al-Kharāhana: 43; Qaṣr al-Khusrau: 42; Qaṣr Ibrim: 136
qawārīr: 296; qawārīr al-nafṭ: 85
qaws al-lawlab: 160; qaws al-rijl: 160; qaws al-ziyār: 74, 84, 87, 160, 174, 178
qawtchin: 97
qayiq: 181
qayl: 15, 24
qighaj, qī qaj: 248
qilic: 161
Qipchaqs: 93, 95-99, 103-4, 111, 113, 118, 121, 129-30, 142, 163, 189, 215-7, 242, 260, 291; language: 109
qirāṭ: 148
qoluq: 167
qoshun: 103
Qsar al-Saghīr: 41
quadrillo: 240
Quanzou: 209
quartermasters: 256
Qubaiba, al-: 169
qubba: 83
qudūr: 296
qufl: 152
quilted armour: 20, 39, 72, 78, 116, 165-6, 258
quintarch: 141
quiver: 31, 36, 38, 73, 109, 199; attached to saddle: 196; box type: 109; open ended type: 109
Qulzum: 48
quoit: 201
Quraysh: 261
qurqapīn: 287

Rabadhah, al-: 268
radkh: 240
rafīq: 146
raft; river: 122; seagoing: 48, 88
raiding tactics: 28, 83, 151
rain, military impact: 195; rain stones: 262
ra'ī's: 146, 149, 182; al-milāḥa: 181
raising on shield, ceremony of: 59
Rajaraja I, king: 218
Rajastan: 190
rajjāla: 143
Rajputs: 146, 191, 196, 264
rajul al-musāfiyah: 62
ram, naval weapon: 87
Ramchandra, king: 191
rāmīah: 62
Ramla: 86
rank (Mamluk heraldry): 281
ransom: 238, 242
rape: 242-3
Rāshidū n Caliphs: 16, 278
Rashtrakuta: 218
rasputitsa: 103
rattle, for messages: 208
ra^cw: 15
Rawats: 134
rawhide: 290
rāya: 278, 281
razzīa: 28
Real Confradia de Santisimo y Santiago: 134
"reclining moon spear": 201
reconnaissance: 68
Reconquista: 60, 66, 133-4, 145, 151, 153, 171-2, 176, 182, 215-7, 235, 242, 257-9, 281, 288; importance of roads: 151
Red Sea: 24, 47-8, 87, 182, 275
"Red Snake": 43
refugees, from Crusader States: 135
refuse, as missile: 87
relics, religion: 259
religion, as military motivation: 215
renegades: 136, 246
reserves, use of: 154
restor: 144
retired soldiers: 57
review, military: 23, 59, 62, 65-6, 253
Reynald of Chatillon: 245, 276
Rhodes: 47, 242, 273
Rhos: 53
ribāṭ: 24, 63-4, 69, 89, 82, 88, 268
Richard I, king: 150, 155, 178
ricos hombres, ricos-homens: 54, 134
Ridda wars: 15-6
riptarion: 75
river; communications: 210; craft: 122, 210; crossing capability: 48, 104; diversion of: 46, 121; fleets: 189, 194; warfare: 210
roads: 66, 270; Roman: 268, 272
rock-throwers: 70
rockets: 296
rod: 100
Rodrigo Diaz de Bivar el Campeador: 54, 215
roga: 251
rogatina: 109
Rome, Romans: 25, 29, 146, 235, 244, 260, 272, 274, 276-7, 284, 288; art: 181; Law: 149; walls, reuse of: 82; continuing influence: 61
Romania, Romanians: 93, 95
romphaion: 74
rope-cutting weapon, naval: 76
Ros river: 96
rotation, of troops: 65, 240
rowing: 251
Royal Household: 144
rudder; side: 182; stern hinged: 88, 182, 208-9, 275; stern sweep: 87
Rule of the Hospitallers: 173, 292; Rule of the Templars: 150, 154, 159, 167, 247
rūmīs: 58
runaway peasants: 57
runūd: 137
runners: 267
rural volunteers: 58
Rus (see also Rhos): 96
Russia, Russians: 53, 58-9, 93-8, 100, 102, 104, 109-16, 129, 131, 136-7, 142, 166, 181, 189, 213, 217, 235, 239, 242, 244-5, 247, 253, 260, 262-3, 270-1, 273, 278, 284, 288, 290-1, 293, 296; folklore: 264; Great Russians: 91; Kievan state: 103; Little Russians (See Ukraine): White Russians (see Belarus)
Rustam: 263
rustaq: 21; Rustaq (Oman): 26, 42
rustling, of sheep & cattle: 67
rutba: 83
Ruthenians: 98, 242
rutīla: 85

s-r-h-t: 24
sabarculli: 167
sabre: 74-5, 107, 109, 161, 167, 200, 291
Sabta: 173, 268, 294
sabṭāna: 295
saç: 287
sa^cad: 78, 167
ṣa^cālīk: 56-7
sacellarius: 20
saddle: 67, 129, 153, 167, 271; padded: 38; wood framed: 38, 79, 204; wood framed camel: 272
safe conduct: 237
Saffāḥ, Caliph al-: 284
ṣaff: 33
ṣaffārids: 65
safīna: 87
sagini: 87
Sahara: 23, 28-9, 58, 69, 73, 76, 125, 136, 140, 147, 150, 153, 163, 167, 182, 218, 220, 237, 262, 287, 290, 294
ṣāḥib al-madānah: 66; ṣāḥib al-shurṭa: 66; ṣāḥib al-ṭa^cām: 149; ṣāḥib al-thughūr: 66
Sahyūn: 168
sail; bamboo: 209; lateen: 47, 209, 276
Sailendra Empire: 187
sailors: 47, 58, 136
Sakas: 14
Sakellarios: 251
śakti: 200
Salā : 140
Ṣalāḥ al-Dīn: 105, 135, 140, 150-2, 157, 159, 171, 176, 178, 181-2, 220, 245, 254, 257-8, 260, 276-7, 281, 293-4, 296
salandria: 180
ṣālih Ismā^cil, al-: 135
Saljūq Turks: 60, 94, 130, 134-5, 137, 141-2, 146-8, 150, 156, 167, 171, 181, 215, 254, 278, 292; of Rum: 106, 137, 169; Saljūq-Othmanli Turkish language: 109
saltpetre: 85, 294
Sāmānids: 57, 65, 246, 248, 293
Samarkand: 55, 98, 134, 260
Samarra: 62-3, 256, 271
samsŏng: 194
Samuel Ha-Nagid: 59, 219
samurai: 205, 238

San Wei: 192
Sana'a: 259
sanadī l: 87
Sancho II, of Castile: 215
sand, military impact of: 105, 157; sandbags: 35, 174, 206, 208
sandalion: 87
ṣanhāja: 58, 266, 287
sanjaq: 149, 283; sanjaq bey:149, 255
sāqah: 33
ṣaqāliba: 58-9
Saracens: 15, 257
Saragossa: 66, 134
Sarā'iyān: 145
sarakenoi: 15
sarāwīt: 24
sarbadār: 98; Sarbadārs: 134
sardār: 103
Sardinia: 61, 240-1
sarhang: 65, 146
sarīya: 146
Sassanian Empire, Sassanians: 11, 13-6, 20, 38, 47, 51, 99, 106, 120, 191, 215-7, 220, 237-9, 241, 244, 251, 255, 257-9, 263, 265, 267-8, 273, 275, 277-85, 288, 290-3; influence: 193, 196
satā'r: 85
Saxi: 95
sayā bijah: 16
sayf: 37; Sayf al-Dawla: 213; Sayf al-Islā m: 213; sayf ṣārim: 74
scabbard: 241; behind shoulder: 200
scale; armour: 14, 57, 116, 151, 165, 202; lined armour: 166
scaling ladders, ropes: 84, 205, 208
Scandinavia, Scandianians: 53, 59, 91, 96, 100, 109, 161, 263, 278, 291
scaramangion: 284
scholae: 18, 60
scholom: 112
"Scythian ambush": 32; "Scythian drill": 32
Science of Archery: 196
scorched earth tactics: 66, 152, 256
se-wu: 189
sebaste: 141
secret police: 246
Sekban: 149
semberek: 181
Semiran: 118
Semirechye: 93-4, 237
semispatha: 37
Semites: 13,215, 283
senā: 194; senāpati: 194
senechal: 144
Senegal: 182
sépouh: 13
Serbia, Serbians: 129, 140, 150, 152
sergeant: 131, 144-5, 154-5, 159, 284
Seville: 66, 88, 161, 182, 219-20, 291
sextant: 209
sexual imagery, for weapons: 47
shadow warfare: 66, 71, 150-1, 285
shaft-furnace: 288
Shāhanshāh, Sassanian: 21, 27, 260
Shāhnāmah: 79, 148, 263
shahr: 21; shahrīgh: 21; shahristān: 43
shalandi, shalandī : 87
shamanism (see also paganism): 51, 260
Shāpūr I: 278; Shāpūr II: 239, 241, 278; Shāpūr III: 278; Shāpūr's moat: 42
sharbūsh: 156, 286
Shāsh: 284, 290
shatrang, shaṭranj: 132, 281
Shaṭṭ al-ʿArab: 273
shaykh, religious guide: 64, 249; shaykh al-ghuzāt: 149
Shayzar: 135, 173, 220
sheep herds, as "weapon": 106
Shen-ts'e: 192
shiʿār: 72
Shia Islam: 57-8, 65, 68, 280-1, 283
shield; as symbol of peace: 278; bearers: 68; boss: 78, 266; kite shaped: 76, 96, 112, 193, 250; leather: 37 (& passim); spiral cane: 112, 163; Tibetan: 78; triangular: 143; wall: 70, 157; with iron plates: 76
shiḥna: 146
shīnī: 47, 87
ship; hull, construction techniques: 87; man-powered paddle-wheeler: 210; river: 296; "round ship": 179, 181; shipwrights: 47, 178; three masted: 179, 274; transport: 215; tied together: 276
Shīrkūh: 105
shiyākha khaṣṣā: 149
shock tactics: 195
shogunate, shogun: 185, 194
Shona: 205
shou phao: 206
shoulder tufts: 284
shreṇībala: 191
shu-mi yuan: 193
shugo: 194
shujʿān: 71, 157
shurrāfa: 81
shurṭa: 24, 57-8, 62, 145, 148
Siberia: 53, 91, 94, 99, 102, 109, 114, 262, 271, 273
Sicily, Sicilians: 58, 60, 65, 68, 72, 82, 130, 140, 255-6, 274, 292
sidera gonatia: 167
Sidon: 135
siege engines: 295; engineers: 131, 135, 140; engines, vulnerability to fire: 173; beam-sling: 44; counterweight: 45; prefabricated metal parts: 83; to drop objects on enemy: 45; torsion powered: 44, 46; tower, mobile: 46, 85, 205; tower, with extending platform: 235; tower, on ships: 277
siege train: 71, 176
Siete Partidas: 155
signum: 277
sihām al-nafṭ: 294
Sijilmasa: 296
Sijistān: 14, 17
silahdar: 149, 286
Silk Road: 91, 182, 291
Silla: 189, 194, 202
silver staff, cane: 285
Silves: 88
Sinai: 15, 48, 268, 276
Sind: 56, 205
sinf: 56
singers: 265; singing girls, as security risk: 205
Sinkiang: 120, 208
sinnawr: 85
Sinop: 181
sipāhi: 140, 149, 152, 157
sipahsālār: 146
sipar: 112
siper: 161
siphon, for Greek Fire: 45, 85, 294
śipri: 201
Ṣirin: 98
sirinapan: 38
Sīstān: 134
Sīvas: 122
siyar: 237; siyāsat: 238
skaplion: 76
Skirmishing, military manual on (De Velitatione): 70-71
skomorokhi: 264
skulls; as totems: 262; towers of: 244
skull-cap: 165
slave, slavery: 47, 27-8, 55, 100, 238, 241; markets: 242; merchants: 244; troops, African: 136; freeing of: 55; lack of aboard warships: 87; non-combattant: 242
Slavs: 13, 53, 59, 91, 94-5, 98, 100, 103, 142, 275, 278, 290, 293; converts to Islam: 138,
sledge: 103
sling: 29, 31-2, 36, 68, 74, 196,
slipways, wooden: 122
smerd: 100; smerdi: 96
smith: 290-1
smoke; as weapon: 208; signals: 268
Smolensk: 288
"snake," siege & naval weapon: 85, 88
socii: 143
sodang: 189
soft armour: 166, 78-9, 202
solak: 149
solenarion: 36, 74
solerets: 167
Somalia, Somalis: 29, 36, 58, 125, 140, 149
sometent, sometant: 134
Songhay: 182, 150
soporific henbane: 267
sotnia: 100; sotski: 100
sous marechal: 144
south Arabia (see also Yemen): 46-8, 71, 82; South Arabian script: 15
spādbadh: 21, 23, 265
Spain, Spanish: 11, 16, 25, 41, 58, 60, 129-31, 140, 145, 155, 163-4, 235, 240, 245-7, 263, 296; sierras: 288; influence: 287
spasalar: 143
spathion: 74
spear; blade, as standard: 277-8; double & triple pointed: 261; extra long: 88, 208; hooked: 109; training: 248; wrist-strap: 37
spies: 88, 242, 245
splinted armour: 79; limb defences: 38, 91
spurs: 117, 143, 219; rowel: 117
square bashing (see also drill): 159, 251
squire: 133, 144, 145, 150, 153, 155
Sri Lanka: 187, 218-9
ssu-chiao: 206
St Catherine's Monastery: 15; St Demetrius of Thessaloniki: 111, 259; St George: 96, 129, 260; St John, painted on shield: 277; St Michael's Cave: 83; St Sergius: 249; St Theodore: 260; St Thomas Aquinas: 235
stables: 62; government: 66, 271
staff-sling: 74
staff weapon; double-ended: 188; infantry: 76
stallions: 271
standard-bearer: 73, 78
steel: 288; blades, casting: 289; decorbonized: 202
steppes: 28, 99, 273; influence from: 100; style of life: 103
sterzhen: 112
stirrup: 38, 67, 79, 195, 202, 204, 243, 257, 265; leather: 116, 167, 204; wood: 116; lack of: 38, 203
stockade, wooden: 195, 197, 208
stone; hand thrown: 153; knives: 159; throwing machines: 43, 84; throwing machines, aboard ship: 47, 275; throwing machines, on river boats: 210; throwing machines, counter-battery: 82; throwing machines, waggon mounted: 33; weapons: 153
stōr-bezhask: 257
stradioti: 20, 60, 131, 141
Strategikon: 32-3, 35-6, 38, 106, 235, 257
strategos, strategus: 60, 71, 141; strategos parembolon nomadon: 24
stratopedarch: 141
straw bundles, to pad walls: 174
street fighting: 159, 176
stroggulion: 37
studs, imperial (stables): 270
su-wei: 193
Subayba: 171
Sudan, Sudanese: 11, 24, 29, 31, 36, 48, 72, 125, 136, 154, 167, 201
śūdra: 191
Suez: 48, 182
ṣū fī : 97, 134, 140, 259-60
Sughd, Sughdians: 15, 17, 91, 95, 106, 237
Sui: 189
śūla: 200
ṣulḥ: 237
sulitsa: 109
sulphur: 294
Sumatra: 291
Sun-Tzu: 185
sunbūk: 48
sundang: 200
Sung dynasty: 109, 185, 189, 192-3, 195, 200, 204-5, 208, 210, 246, 251, 255, 296
Sunni Islam: 57, 281
suntagma: 154
supply train: 272
sūq al-ʿaskar: 146
surcoat: 284
surgeons: 257
surveyors, "measurers": 73
Susa: 274
suyūrghal: 103
Suzdal: 91, 100
Svarog: 263
swāyiḥ: 15
Sweden, Swedes: 96, 213
swimming, in naval warfare: 88, 251
sword; belt: 135, 143; belt, as indication of status: 262; belt, fabric: 161; blade: 292; blade, pattern welded: 290; blade, piled: 290; blade, waisted: 200; carrying or use of two: 161, 251; double edged: 109; hilt, bronze: 75; Japanese: 75; long cavalry: 35, 37; pommel, ring type: 55; reverse curved: 190, 200; short infantry: 23, 31, 37; single-edged straight: 54; smiths: 290; straight: 161; symbolic: 37; Sword of ʿAlī : 280
syphilis: 257
Syr Dayra river: 120
Syria, Syrians: 13, 15-9, 22, 24, 41, 44, 47, 55, 57-8, 62, 65, 68, 72, 81-2, 104-5, 121, 131-4, 136, 146-8, 152, 157, 166-8, 171, 181, 213, 215, 217, 219-20, 246, 248, 253, 256, 258-60, 263, 266, 268, 271-3, 277-8, 284, 291; desert: 17, 41

t-m-h-r-t: 24
ṭabaqa, ṭibāq: 244, 250
ṭabaristān: 57
ṭabarzīn: 75
ṭabīʿa: 82, 172
taʿbiya: tabʿīyya: 33, 62
"tabby" concrete: 82, 172-3
ṭablkhānah: 266
tabonas: 159
ṭabr: 163
Tactika: 70
Tafurs: 143
tagma (tagmata): 19-20, 51, 59, 141, 251, 278, 284, 291
Tāif: 43
taifa: 59, 65-6, 140, 260
T'ai Tsung: 217
Tāj al-Dawla: 213
Tajiks: 57, 134
ṭalʿīya: 83, 172
Talaigns: 190, 197
talayeros: 145
Tale of the Raid of Igor (see Epic of Prince Igor)
talisman, talismanic motif: 16, 260, 278
Taman peninsula: 101
Tamara, queen: 215
tamghas: 283
Tamils: 191, 284
Tanūkhī, al-: 294
Tancred, Prince: 219, 242
T'ang: 38, 189, 191-2, 195, 197-8, 202, 204-8, 217-8, 251, 258, 260, 268, 273, 284, 291
tang-hsiung: 204
Tanguses: 217
tankō: 202
tanū righ: 38
Taoism: 260
ṭāq-i Bustān: 27
Taqīal-Dīn: 281
tar, supplies of: 47
ṭarāda: 88
Tarai, battle of: 196
tarbūsh: 286
targe: 76
ṭarīda, tarida: 87, 88, 182, 274, 277
Tarim Basin: 118
ṭāriq: 246
ṭarīqah: 76, 163
Tarragona: 254
Tarsus: 56, 64, 67, 71, 78, 80, 81, 180, 243, 249, 290

Tarsusi, al-: 294, 296
tashtīna: 80
tasug: 21
Tatar: 93, 296
Taurus mountains: 25, 150, 196
tax farming: 62, 65; tax privilages: 60; tax systems: 251
taxeis: 154
team exercises: 159
technology; mixture of: 75; spread of: 235
tegheliay, teghhilay, tegyljaj: 116
Templars: 132, 144, 145, 159, 180, 257, 265, 284
Temüchin: 213
tents, as field fortif: 35, 158
Tershana: 169
tesek: 109
testeriam, testiere, testinia: 80
testudo: 173
Teutonic Knights: 105, 132, 144, 165, 213
Thailand, Thais: 187
theme: 20, 51, 54, 59-60, 141, 143, 218, 251
t'hemi: 143
Theodore Palaeologus: 154, 278
Thessaloniki: 41, 54, 152, 276, 290
Thor: 263
thorakes, thorax: 38, 78
Thrace: 13, 130, 152, 215, 217
Three Kingdoms: 194
throwing stick: 201
throwing stone: 201
thughūr: 24-5, 62-3 66, 80, 83, 145, 149
thunder stick: 174, 208
thuql: 176
Tibet, Tibetans: 37, 93, 95, 101, 114, 118, 120, 192, 195, 201, 283, 291, 294
Tibilisi: 215
t'i-chiang: 192
Tien Shan mountains: 65, 100, 288
tīgh: 161
Tigris: 122, 273
tijfāf: 79-80, 166
Tilimsān: 178
tīmār, tīmārli: 140, 149, 255
timber; long distance trade in: 88; North African supplies: 182; shortage of: 47, 87, 288
Tīmūr-i Lank: 93, 98, 103, 105-8, 112, 114, 117, 120, 122, 220, 244; Tī mū rids: 248
tippet: 57, 76
ṭirāz: 284, 287
tīrbadh: 21
ṭirfil: 163
tishtanī : 80
tium: 100
Tmutarakan: 91, 96, 101
Toba: 189, 273
tobyŏngmasa: 194
Toledo: 174, 289, 291
topoteretes: 60
ṭoprāqlī: 149
torches, to illuminate night fighting: 85
Torks: 93-6, 109
torpedo: 296; rocket-propelled: 181
torque: 285
tortoise, siege machine: 45, 84
Tortosa: 180
torture, of prisoners: 241
tös: 283
tourkapouli (see also turcopoles): 130
tournament: 246-7
tower: 80, 171; fortified: 168; mobile: 84; wooden: 173; urban: 170
toxobolistrai: 85
trade centres, control of: 151
training; military: 238; structure: 65
Transoxiana: 11, 15-6, 29, 37-8, 43, 46, 48, 56, 63, 65, 78, 80, 91-5, 99, 103-4, 106, 120, 134, 167, 213, 217, 244, 246, 260, 263-4, 283-4, 288, 290, 294
trapezitai, 51,
Treasurer: 144, 148
Trebizond: 153, 160, 167, 179, 277, 288; Empire: 142, 179
trebuchet: 171, 173, 178, 204, 206, 296; with adjustable counterweight: 206
trial by combat: 235
tribes, artificial: 25; forces: 189, 253; peoples, armies: 60; structure, Arab: 25
tribune: 19
tribute: 268; weapons as: 292
Tripoli: 131, 180, 244
troubadour: 264-5
truce, breaking: 238
True Cross: 215, 259
trumpets: 157, 180, 265
t'sungs: 199
tu'an: 192
tu-hu-fu: 192
tuberculosis: 257
Tudela: 134
tüfenk: 163, 181, 296
tug, tūgh, tuq: 282-3
tui: 192
ṭulb: 146, 157
Ṭūlūnid: 58, 65
Tümän Tarqan: 216
tūmān, tümen: 102-3
Tun-Huang: 207-8
Tunisia: 47, 58, 68, 82, 140, 149, 158, 166, 173, 182, 258, 274, 291, 296
Turanians: 263
turban: 287; crown-shaped: 282
Turcomans: 134-5, 137-8, 148-50, 163
turcopole: 131, 133, 144, 150, 153, 155, 244, 249, 253; Turcopolier: 144
tūreh: 112
Turkestan: 264, 287, 296
Turks: 11, 13, 15, 17, 37-8, 44, 51, 53, 55-8, 60, 62, 65, 68, 73, 75, 91, 96, 98, 102-4, 108, 114, 117, 120, 125, 129-37, 140-2, 153-6, 158, 163, 165, 167, 180, 189, 215, 217, 238-9, 242, 244, 247-8, 254, 256, 260, 262-4, 266, 268, 270-2, 275, 278, 280-5, 288-92; believe destined to rule world: 260; Eastern: 94, 104; Gök: 287; Great: 91, 94, 101, 104, 106; influence: 146; language: 94, 139, 143; literature: 264; Western: 94, 104, 118, 192
turma: 60; turmarch: 60, 141
turna-fuye: 71, 73
turs: 76
Tuva: 119
typhoid: 219
Tyre: 47, 85, 135, 173
tysiacha: 100; tysiatsky: 100-1
tyuphak: 296
tzaggra: 159; tzaggratores: 141
tzakones: 141
Tzan: 131
tzaousios: 142
tzarchat: 74
tzykanion: 246

uc: 149, 152
ūd, al-: 265
Ugrians: 91, 95, 102, 259, 262, 291; White Ugri: 91
Uhud, battle of: 258
Uighurs: 91, 93-4, 97, 99, 102, 118-9, 192, 260, 272, 283, 291
uissiers: 274
ükek: 118
Ukraine, Ukrainians: 91, 93, 96, 101, 113, 130, 244, 262
ulu: 101-2; ulu bey: 103
'Umarī, al-: 213
Umayyad Caliphate: 24-5, 28, 33, 43-4, 48, 55-8, 63, 87, 105, 246, 248, 253, 259, 267, 272-3, 275, 278, 280-1, 283-4; fleet: 16; of Cordoba: 58, 66, 196, 215
Umm al-Jamal: 46
Umur Pasha: 246
Ural mountains: 91, 94, 101, 288, 291
Urfa: 131, 244
urine, as weapon: 206
Usāmah Ibn Munqidh: 158, 219
ushkúynik: 122
Ushrū sana: 217
usṭūl: 182
uṭum: 43
Uzbegs: 98
Üzboy channel: 122
Uzes: 93, 95
Uzza, al-: 261

vaiśya: 191
vālārikāmbi: 201
Valencia: 145, 215
vambrace: 78, 91
Vandals: 15, 20
Varahran I: 278; Varahran II: 278
Varangian Guard: 59-60, 75, 79, 95-6, 100, 122, 129-131, 142, 253
varhranīghān-khvadhāy: 21
varjazi: 96
vasht: 21, 283
Vaspourakan: 80
veche: 100
Vedas, Vedic texts: 238, 261
Vegetius: 155
Venice, Venetians: 58, 98, 131, 179, 245, 274, 277, 291, 293
ventail: 78
vestiarion: 290
veterinary service, veterinarians: 257-8, 271
vexillum: 277
vicar: 145; vicar general: 145
Viceroy of Damascus: 148
Vienna: 260
Vietnam, Vietnamese: 185, 187, 196, 201, 277
viglatores: 267
Vijayanagar: 194, 196
Vikings: 66, 82, 88, 263
vilayat (see also wilayat): 103
villages, fortified: 80
vinager, to douse fire: 174
visal, viseria: 163
Visigoths: 11, 16-7, 36, 54, 60, 66, 246, 272-3
visor: 163; hinged iron: 112; integral: 128, 164
vizier: 57-8, 103, 134, 146, 213, 215, 219; of the Sword: 213
Vlachs: 54, 95, 130, 242, 246
Vladimir I, Grand Prince: 91, 96, 100, 122; Vladimir, city of: 107, 121, 213
voevoda: 100
voi: 100, 107,
Volga river: 91, 103, 112, 122
volunteers: 63, 68, 237; religious: 58
voynug, voynuk: 140
vuzurg-framādhār: 21

Wādī al-Qurā: 44
waggon: 107-8, 159, 197; to transport siege engines: 85; as field fortification: 35, 108, 159
wajihdar: 146
wālī: 25, 66, 148-9
wall; chief of: 208; doubled: 80; enclosing galleries: 205; internal galleries: 80-1, 171; long: 80; mounted device to drop objects on enemy: 87; multiple: 80; painting: 263
Wallachia: 93, 95, 140
war-canoe: 209-10
war-clubs: 163
Warqa wa Gulshāh: 263
warships, tied together: 47
Wasit: 80, 85
watch-tower: 80-1, 122, 171; chain of: 204; coastal: 88
water sources: 150, 152; consecration of: 260; availability: 27, 268; poisoning of: 197, 205; supplies, security of: 83; water tower, as observation post: 171; water troughs, portable leather: 273
wazīr al-jund: 149
weapons; making: 263; distribution of captured: 291
wei: 191, 193-4
wells, cleaning of: 273
wen: 185
wheeled ladder: 205; wheeled transport: 273
White Russians (see Belarus)
wi: 194
wilāyat: 102
win: 194
wind-sock banner: 266, 281
windlass, to span crossbow or siege weapon: 74, 84
winhmu: 194
winter; campaigning: 103; rain: 152
wojnūq: 140
women; in combat: 98, 105; immunity of: 236; in military command: 191, 215; labour corps: 205; military role: 135, 191; Muslim ideal of: 258; operating siege machines: 206; prisoners: 242; role in Crusades: 131; role in epic literature: 263
Won'gwang: 238
wood, supplies of: 47
wounded, sick &: 106; wounds: 31-2, 155, 258
wrestling: 251
Wu T'ing huei: 210
wu: 185
wūsfana: 59

xamete: 166
Xi'an: 205
xingjun: 192
xulokastron: 87
xyphos: 37
yajun: 191
yak tailed banner: 282-3
yalba: 166
Yalu river: 205
Yamāmah: 23, 28
yang-ma-ch'eng: 204
yangmin: 189
Yarmūk, river: 170; battle of: 26, 217
Yaroslav, prince: 213
yāsā: 102, 238
yat: 262
Yathrib: 290
yaya: 138
yazak: 152
Yazdajird I: 278; Yazdajird II, 42
Yazīd, Caliph: 24, 273
Yemen, Yemenis: 11, 15-6, 19, 23-4, 28-9, 37, 39, 43, 47-8, 135, 153, 187, 198, 215, 259, 272, 290-1, 293
Yeni Çeri: 138-9, 149, 157, 251, 260, 264, 286; cavalry: 139; ağ asi: 149
Yentisa: 215
ymg-tien: 193
yoldash: 139
'ys: 24
Yu-hsia: 264
Yüan: 97, 102, 189, 193, 195, 201, 210
yurt: 256
Yürük: 138
Yūsuf Ibn Tāshufīn: 220
yuz bashi: 103; yuzliq: 103

zaba: 38, 78
zabareion: 290
zadruga: 100
ẓafār: 37, 39
Zagros mountains: 56
zaḥāfah: 178
Zallaka, battle of: 220
zamt: 286
Zanāta: 58, 140, 153
zanggra: 159
Zangī: 268; Zangīds: 135, 268
Zanj: 58
zaqāzīq: 159
zardiyah: 165
zardkhāna: 293
zarība: 73
zarrāqat al-nafṭ: 294; zarrāqbū n: 176
zasapozhniki: 109
Zawīla: 58
zāwiya: 64
Zayrids: 140
zembūrek: 181
zertzallo: 116
Zhaodong: 205
zhen: 192
zhouzhou: 192
zirh: 37-8; zirh külah: 163; zirh-i çuqal: 166
Zoroastrianism: 53, 65, 217, 259-60, 264
zorovar: 60
zūpīn: 75
zuṭ, zuṭṭ: 16, 88, 191